COLLINS COBUILD

COLLINS Birmingham University International Language Database

English Course

Jane & Dave Willis

Teacher's Book

3

Contents

		PAGE

Foreword

The *Collins COBUILD English Course* is a new departure in English language teaching materials. It is a lively and varied course, using plenty of natural English examples. And it is founded on the very latest evidence of English structure from the COBUILD files.

The authors set themselves a very demanding task. A good course is a remarkable balancing act, and also a miracle of compression. Course materials today attain very high standards of presentation, variety of activity and stimulation to learning. As this final Level goes to press, I am happy to note that the liveliness has been sustained, the range of activity steadily increased and the texts cover a host of interesting and useful topics.

The COBUILD research project has built up a mass of information from the careful examination of many millions of words, and it offers a new style and balance to a syllabus. Because of lack of evidence in the past, important usages have been missed, some trivial and misleading material has been prominently taught, sequencing has been fairly arbitrary and there has been a lack of respect for the natural patterns of the language. Now it is possible, with a little trouble, to offer the learner plenty of texts in quite natural English, and this Course opens up new experiences in that area.

The ordering of the Course follows a new and carefully designed methodology which has been developed by the authors. The earlier Levels of the COBUILD Course introduced spontaneous conversation to methodical English teaching, which has been welcomed by teachers and students alike. Level 3 maintains this feature, and includes recorded interviews and monologue, where native speakers talk about their life and work.

The learner is presented with tasks which expect a subtle and sensitive response to ordinary English. An increased attention to the written word and exam-related material prepares students for further study. Patterns of text organisation are featured, and the exercise of personal judgement is stressed; understanding of the attitudes of the writers and speakers is encouraged. The acquisition of reference skills is continued, and an interesting innovation is the selection from the *Collins COBUILD Essential English Dictionary* at the end of the book, which is systematically worked in to the unit material, to give the learner more independence.

The most precious resource in language teaching is classroom time. Hence it is very important that the choice of what is taught is made very carefully. Using the evidence available from COBUILD, this Course has been able to identify the most useful words and patterns, and give the learner an excellent grounding in the English of today.

Professor John Sinclair

Introduction

Who is this Course for?

Level Three of the *Collins COBUILD English Course* is the third and final part of a general English course for adult students. It is designed for intermediate students who wish to consolidate their English and extend their vocabulary and communication skills.

After completing Level Three, students should find themselves within easy reach of the Cambridge First Certificate in English examination. With this in mind, specific examination practice is included in the Practice Book.

Level Three encourages greater learner independence, and helps students to handle a wide range of more challenging texts, tasks and recordings. The range of texts includes many of the kind they will meet in real life, such as newspaper items, various kinds of correspondence, literature and radio programmes.

The Course is Complete

Like Levels One and Two, Level Three offers a complete package comprising a Student's Book in full colour, with a separate transcript booklet inserted in its back cover, a Practice Book for use in or out of class, a set of cassettes and an interleaved Teacher's Book. The Teacher's Book is designed for easy access by busy teachers, and contains clear and detailed guidance on how the course can be taught, offering a flexible approach to the materials and methodology. There is an additional Student's cassette containing songs, poems and the complete serial story for use both in and out of class.

There are of course many other ways of exploiting the materials in this book, and teachers are obviously free to adapt and use their own ideas, as best suits their students.

Basic Principles

In devising the methodology for the Course, the authors have adhered to a number of basic principles, which have been at the heart of good language teaching practice for some years. These are:

1 People learn a language most effectively by using the language to do things – to find out information, to solve problems, to talk about personal expeiences, and so on.

2 A focus on accuracy is vital. Learners need time to think about the language they are using.

3 A rich input of real language helps learners to extend their understanding of how English works, and to acquire new expressions for themselves. Exposure to a wide variety of spoken and written English is essential if learners are to gain mastery of English, and to cope with unexpected situations.

4 Grammar is learned rather than taught. Coursebooks and teachers provide useful guidelines on the language, but learners should additionally be encouraged to think and deduce for themselves.

5 Learners need strategies for organising what they have learned – they need rules, patterns, and categories.

The *Collins COBUILD English Course* realises these well-established principles through a new language syllabus – a lexical syllabus – that has been drawn from the COBUILD language research project.

The COBUILD Project

COBUILD is the Collins-Birmingham University International Language Database. Using large-scale computer facilities, an editorial team at Birmingham University has worked for seven years, analysing and recording the patterns of use in millions of words of current English text. The Database holds extensive information about how English is really used, and is an authoritative resource that has proved invaluable in the development of this Course.

The Lexical Syllabus

Level One takes 700 of the commonest words in today's English, covering their most important meanings and uses as identified by the COBUILD Project. Level Two reviews these words and goes on to cover 850 new words. Level Three recycles and extends earlier lexis, and introduces a further 950 common words, bringing the total to 2,500 words. In addition to these, students gain exposure to other less common words that occur in the chosen texts, thus acquiring a sizeable receptive vocabulary.

Unlike traditional syllabuses, the lexical syllabus starts from a description of real language. In taking words and their meanings as the core items, the syllabus offers genuine coverage of the most central and typical patterns of English, going on to look at the structure of stretches of discourse beyond the sentence level. It also provides a focus for language analysis, which allows students to develop and refine their awareness of the actual grammar of the language, and of typical patterns in both spoken and written discourse.

In the teachers' notes which follow, the lexical aims for each unit are clearly listed, with examples, opposite the last page of each unit, which includes a Review section. Additionally, words to focus on during each activity are listed in the Lexis Box for that section.

There is an index of the words covered in Level Three on pages 110T–112T of this book.

The Methodology of the Course

The methodology in Level Three follows closely the cycle that has proved successful in Levels One and Two. It is a task-based approach to learning which takes full account of the need for accuracy. It contains the following components:

1 Input
The Course provides a rich input of *real* language, both written and spoken, which is extensively recycled throughout the Course. This language is carefully selected both to provide a contextualised presentation of the target words for Level Three and to confront learners with the kind of communication problems they are likely to meet when they use the language outside the classroom.

2 Task
Each unit contains several tasks involving both spoken and written language, usually done in pairs or groups. In doing a task learners are primarily concerned with fluency – using whatever language they have to solve a problem, exchange relevant information and so on. The teacher's role is to help them complete the task in English, rather than to make corrections at this stage.

3 Planning and Report
After performing the task each group is asked to present its findings to the class in a spoken or written report. In preparing this report with the help of the teacher, and in presenting it to the class there is a clear focus on accuracy.

4 Focused Listening
Students are also given the opportunity to listen to recordings of native speakers performing the same tasks. This provides important language input and also gives useful hints as to how to go about the task.

5 Language Analysis

Students are engaged in a detailed analysis of aspects of the written and spoken texts to which they have been exposed. This enables them to gain valuable insights into the grammatical and lexical system of English and its basic discourse patterns.

6 Controlled Practice

Controlled repetition of various kinds involves students in practising useful and very frequent combinations of words in English in order to build up their confidence and their ability to produce groups of sounds and intonation patterns accurately and spontaneously.

This methodology ensures that a good deal of responsibility lies with the learners. The teacher's role is to encourage them and offer precise guidance as their students' knowledge of the language develops. It also ensures constant recycling of language material within and across units. The use of real written texts and real recordings means that the common colloquial forms of English, which have a high communicative value, occur again and again. This tendency is reinforced by a careful selection of material based on the COBUILD Database findings.

Unit Organisation

Level Three contains twenty four units, each with a different theme, organised in four blocks of six units each. The sixth unit is a revision and consolidation unit. Each unit will take up to four hours to complete, depending on the amount of writing set in class.

In Level Three, recordings and texts have been chosen from an extensive number of authentic sources from different regions and countries, including USA, Africa, Australia and the Far East, in order to broaden students' experience of English in use, and help them to cope with the international English-speaking world outside the classroom. The topics are extremely varied, and students are exposed to a wide range of accents, styles of writing, and types of text. Thus the meanings and uses of the targets words for their third level are well illustrated in memorable contexts.

There are several 'guest' personalities who recount their experiences, or give advice, for example Bob Jobbins, a BBC foreign correspondent, Suzanne Juta, an artist who teaches children, and The Yetties, a well-known travelling folk group.

Students build up their confidence in spoken English by undertaking a variety of communication tasks involving narrative, explanation, sharing feelings and opinions, and talking about texts that they have read, as well as discussing features of language. There is a gradual progression towards reading and listening to longer and more complex texts and coping with a greater proportion of unknown words.

The writing tasks include biography, narrative, description, explanation, creative writing, letters of various types, summaries and reports: these increase in complexity through the book.

Level Three follows from Levels One and Two in encouraging students to think and find out about language for themselves. There is a variety of language-focused exercises designed to develop students' reference skills and learning strategies and, together with the Practice Book, help students prepare for examinations in English.

- Grammar

Each unit has at least one, sometimes two, grammar sections, which revise major grammatical features from Levels One and Two, and extend to give thorough coverage of noun phrases and verb groups, clause and sentence structure. The Practice Book has a well exemplified Grammar Book reference section, which students can fill in themselves, using familiar examples from the Course.

- Language Study

These sections extend students' awareness of other features of English text, such as style and register, intonation and stress. In Level Three more emphasis is placed upon information structure, and common patterns in discourse, for example, the pattern Situation – Problem – Solution – Evaluation.

- Word Study

The pink Word Study boxes often appear after a reading text or a recording. Their purpose is to help students work out and remember the meanings and uses of target words in their contexts.

- Dictionary Extracts

The Blue section at the back of the Student's Book contains actual dictionary entries, or relevant parts of entries, for around 130 of the target words, including suffixes, prefixes and other grammatical information. These entries have been taken from the *Collins COBUILD Essential English Dictionary*, an ideal monolingual dictionary at this intermediate level. The entries included have been carefully selected to provide a representative range of entry types. These are used in conjunction with the Dictionary Skills sections, to give students systematic training in efficient dictionary use.

- Dictionary Skills

One or two reference skills are practised in the Dictionary Skills section in most units. These range from 'decoding' skills, for example, looking up a phrase, or finding out more about the metaphorical meanings of common words, to 'encoding' skills, where students can use a dictionary to check the typical grammatical environment of a word, to help them use new words and phrases accurately for themselves.

The lead-in and summary material in each unit is slightly shorter than for levels One and Two since Level Three units are themselves shorter and more specific in theme.

- Lead-in Activity

The first one or two activities in each unit introduce the main topic of the unit, often through visual stimuli, and promote informal discussion, during which appropriate target words can be introduced.

- Review

The last page of each unit (apart from the Review Units) includes a Short Review section, revising and sometimes extending the uses of target words and phrases for that unit.

The Cassettes

The three cassettes in Level Three contain the essential recorded material in the order in which it occurs during the Course. In addition, there is a Student's cassette, containing more songs by the Yetties, the poems, and the complete serial story. The black symbol ▭ denotes material found on one of the main cassettes. A pink symbol denotes material that is only on the Student's cassette.
Full tapescripts are given at the back of this book.

The unscripted recordings illustrate a variety of types of spoken language, dialogue, monologue, group discussion, radio, and form an integral part of the Course. They give students a suitably rich input of natural language. Students find they rapidly become accustomed to working with natural language, and can always refer to the transcript booklet in the back of the Student's Book if necessary.

Students with time for home study may like to have their own set of cassettes in addition to the Student's cassette, so they can listen again to the native-speaker recordings.

The Practice Book

This book can be used in or out of class and consolidates and extends the Student's Book material. In addition, at Level Three, there is an increased emphasis on study skills, and each unit contains a new reading text. Taken from a variety of authentic sources, they practise a range of reading skills. Many of the exercises are designed to give specific practice in FCE examination techniques.

● The Grammar Book section

Even intermediate students can make mistakes with the common words of English. For this reason we have included a Grammar Book reference section at the back of the Practice Book. It is similar in format to the Grammar Book at the back of Student's Book One, but with lines provided for students to write in their own examples. Students study one Grammar Word after completing each unit. After reading the examples given, students search in the text or transcript indicated for similar examples of the same word, and select the best one to write in. Thus students build up their own grammar reference section, improve their reading speed, and consolidate their language experience by re-reading familiar texts.

● Key

There is an answer key for selected exercises (those which do not have alternative answers) at the back of the Practice Book. There is also a key to the Grammar Book section, where a clue word from the appropriate sentence is given, to guide students towards the correct example. The complete sentences from which each clue word is taken are given in the Grammar Book Key on page 146T of this book.

Map of Level 3

Unit	TASKS AND TOPICS	TEXTS AND FEATURES	READING AND REFERENCING SKILLS	WRITING	VERBS/TENSES CLAUSE PATTERNS	NOUN PHRASES PRONOUNS ADJECTIVES PREPOSITIONS ADVERBIAL PHRASES	WRITTEN AND SPOKEN DISCOURSE
Unit 1 — Come stranger, come friend	Meeting new people. Families. Family photographs. Travel experiences past and future.	Use of gestures. Personal details. Photographs in various settings. Song: 'Come stranger come friend.'	Tables. Dictionary: headword, explanation, examples. Nouns from verbs. Phonetics: /ə/, /aʊ/, /ʌ/, /s/, /z/, /t/, /l/, /r/.	Informal personal information. Designing a table. Describing people and places; photographs. Statements about countries.	Questions. Evaluative comments. Sentences with *looks as though*, *reminds me of*, *should think*.	Uses of a/an. Adjectives and descriptive phrases. Some uses of *to*. Adverbs in *-ly*.	Discourse pattern: Situation – Comment. Intonation of comments. Fronting information for emphasis.
Unit 2 — The Yetties	Experiences of singing. Tastes in music. Describing people. An interest or hobby that developed gradually.	The Yetties folk group. Concert programme: biographical notes. History of folk singing. Song: 'The gypsy rover.'	Guessing words from context. Cohesion in text. Dictionary: meaning, pronunciation, stress. Phonetics: /uː/, /ʌ/, /ɜː/, /əʊ/, /k/, /g/, /fi/, /m/, /jl/.	Short formal biographies. Note-taking from an interview. Captions. Summary of a paragraph.	Past habit with *used to*, *would* and past simple form. Uses of common verbs: **do, go, put, take**.	Expressions of time and place. Phrases with/Uses of **thing**.	Marking stages in a conversation. Recognising sequence of information in a historical text.
Unit 3 — Into business	Evaluating job application letters. Comparing advice. Job interviews. Early job experiences. Retirement.	Golden rules for a letter of application. Success in job interviews. The business side of folk singing.	Finding relevant items in a letter. Dictionary: (N COUNT panel), grammatical notation. Phonetics: /ɛ/, /ɛɪ/, /ɒ/, /ɔː/, /u/, /ŋ/, /w/, /ʃ/, /dʒ/.	Redrafting a letter. An ideal letter of application. Report on a candidate.	Do for emphasis. Do used with nouns. Imperative forms used when listing advice. Verbs used in comments.	Nouns: countable, uncountable, mass. Comments with that. Noun phrases to do with business.	Organisation of a letter of application. Questions to structure a radio interview. Initial stages of a job interview.
Unit 4 — Survivors	Things you are afraid of; childhood fears. Working out a story about a suicide attempt. Survival after a night 'on ice'.	Poem about the dark. Frightening experiences. News report on suicide attempt. News reports on boy's survival.	Summarising facts. Using questions to predict content. Comparing two versions of a story. Dictionary: checking useful phrases.	Two versions of a news story: first with bare facts only, second with added description. Summary of a news item.	Descriptive clauses. Verbs both transitive and intransitive eg grow. Uses of *-ing* forms. Past perfect tense. The passive. Some phrasal verbs.	Nouns which have the same form as verbs.	Comparisons. Descriptive clauses in news reports. Agreeing, using words of similar meaning, eg *'Were you afraid?' 'Yes, terrified!'* Disagreeing.
Unit 5 — Self-expression	Early memories. Painting and drawing. Art: teaching and as a career. Children's writing. Dreams and nightmares. Taboo subjects. Good investments.	Suzanne Juta, artist. Child's story: 'My Wings'. Extract from novel 'Grimble'. Funds for art. Things children say.	Listing information. Use of punctuation. Dialogue in a story. Dictionary: metaphorical meanings. Phonetics: /aeɪ/, /əʊ/, /iː/, /uː/, /ɜː/, /pl/, /b/, /tʃ/.	Describing early memories. Notes about a career. Summarising attitudes. Redrafting a story.	Past participles describing reactions, eg embarrassed.	Noun + noun. Adjectives in: **What a ___ thing!** Qualifying adverbs. Prepositions after adjectives describing feelings.	Recognising examples. Going off the point. Discourse pattern: General – Specific. Stopping mid-sentence.
Unit 6 — Revision Unit	A favourite object. Personality. Embarrassing situations. Personality and position in the family.	Personality tests: self-confidence; tact; optimist or pessimist? Poem: 'Arithmetic'.	Using a key to check test results. Dictionary: special entry: Time.	Writing about people from notes. Describing an object. Items for personality test. Different reports on the same child.	Clauses with **wh-** words. Present tense, past tense and **would** for hypothesis.	**Whereas.** Prefix: **non-**. Telling the time.	Recognising comments which evaluate. Expressing hypotheses. Expressing agreement and contrast. Offering alternatives.

	TASKS AND TOPICS	TEXTS AND FEATURES	READING AND REFERENCING SKILLS	WRITING	VERBS/TENSES CLAUSE PATTERNS	NOUNS PHRASES PRONOUNS ADJECTIVES PREPOSITIONS ADVERBIAL PHRASES	WRITTEN AND SPOKEN DISCOURSE
Unit 7 Drivers	Good and bad drivers. Driving tests. A flat tyre. Speculation about a news report.	Men and women drivers. Instructions: starting the car. News report on handcuffed driver. 'Joyriding at 80'.	Concrete and abstract meanings. Metaphor. Dictionary: using it to help with writing. Phonetics: /i/, /aɪ/, /eɪ/, /ɔɪ/.	Comparing men and women drivers. Narrative: a driving test. Advice for taking test. Instructions: Changing a wheel. Definitions.	Forms used to give instructions. It + be + adjective + to. When, after, on + -ing; having + past participle. Verbs with nouns eg pass on a message	Names of vehicles. Adjectives meaning: good/bad; easy/difficult; wise/foolish. Nouns in -ist for people.	Use of The [main] thing is … Anecdotes. Explanatory language. Structure of a news report.
Unit 8 Problems and solutions	Products in adverts. Sounds. A pollution problem. Traditional sayings. Coping with problems.	Adverts from mail order catalogues. Seagulls causing water pollution. Story: peanut butter. Safety device for motorbikes.	Identifying relevant details. Predicting content. Dictionary: looking up phrases.	Notes: main points in adverts. Summaries of articles. Outline: report on experiment, with relevant queries.	Clauses with past/present participles in complex sentences. Clauses with that and to.	Signals for discourse pattern: Problem – Solution. Related words, eg inflation/inflatable.	Discourse pattern: Situation – Problem – Solution – Evaluation. Complex sentences: in news reports; intonation.
Unit 9 Reptiles	Keeping reptiles. Reptile and crocodile anecdotes. Debate: preservation of species dangerous to man?	From the local press: a reptile lover. Crocodile quiz. Crocodiles – enemies of man.	Checking hypotheses. Reading at speed. Dictionary: checking structures: broad negative adverbs. Phonetics: /ɑː/, /ɔː/, /eə/, /h/, /v/, /tʃ/, /θ/, /ð/.	The story of John Cheetham. Correcting false statements. Captions for photos. Recommendations about conservation.	Tense structure in story and anecdotes: past simple, present perfect, present simple. Clauses with whose, where, which.	It: referring back, and for emphasis. The more . . . the more . . . Word order with broad negative adverbs.	Intonation expressing surprise. Distinguishing past and present facts. Discourse pattern: Topic – Illustration.
Unit 10 Wish we hadn't . . .	Airline routes. What went wrong? A day of misfortunes. Sharing personal regrets.	Yetties' tour of Far East and official report. Problems with Gas Board. Instructions on envelopes, memos etc.	Summarising and predicting a story. Dictionary: prefixes mis-, un-, non-.	Detailed captions. Summary: Yetties' trip to Nepal. Factual account: a mishap. Summary: personal regrets.	Verbs: prefix mis-. Would/might/could have for hypothetical outcomes. Wish + had/would have. Despite, although etc.	Imprecise phrases eg you know who, . . . and things. Prepositional phrases with out, up.	Paraphrasing and defining (spoken). Expressing hypothesis: if, or, that's why, but, otherwise.
Unit 11 Maneater	Game parks in Africa. Dangerous animals. Escaping danger. Reactions under stress.	Leopard incident: official and personal letters.	Relating facts from correspondence to a personal interview. Dictionary: skimming longer entries, phrasal verbs. Phonetics: /ɪ/, /iː/.	Requesting clarification. Precise note-taking. Chronological file on leopard; final report. A personal account. Recommendations.	Would to state precautions. Had, would have for alternative outcomes. Uses of hit, beat, hold (on, up etc.).	Words with base form nation. Uses of indeed.	Giving reasons. Discourse pattern: Hypothesis – Evidence – Conclusion.
Unit 12 Revision Unit	Films from books. Extremes of weather. Feelings.	A Hollywood director. Children's writing: the seasons. Song: 'The life of a man?'	Appreciating creative writing. American English: spellings and words.	Summary of a story. Experience of storms. Survey report. Opinions compared. A poem or description. A job reference.	Clauses with to and that. Conditional clauses. Past participles. Words in -ing. Question tags. Do and have.	The bigger . . . the better . . . Adjectives in -ing.	Discourse patterns: General – Specific; Hypothesis – Evidence – Conclusion.

	TASKS AND TOPICS	TEXTS AND FEATURES	READING AND REFERENCING SKILLS	WRITING	VERBS/TENSES CLAUSE PATTERNS	NOUNS PHRASES PRONOUNS ADJECTIVES PREPOSITIONS ADVERBIAL PHRASES	WRITTEN AND SPOKEN DISCOURSE
Unit 13 Plans for a tour	Cultural appropriacy of concert programmes. Language problems. A trip to Germany.	The Yetties' tour to the Far East. Correspondence planning the tour.	Skimming letters for specific details. Dictionary: grammatical notation to show structure. Phonetics: /aɪə/, /ɪə/, /aʊə/.	Summary: an anecdote. Conventional phrases in formal letters. Letter of complaint. A memo. Account of a trip.	Verb patterns. Referring to future time. Present continuous. Present perfect.	Phrases expressing a writer's attitude. Relative clauses starting/ ending in prepositions.	Verbal report of contents of letters. Coherence and cohesion in a sequence of correspondence. Referring back.
Unit 14 BBC Foreign correspondent	Journalism as a career. What is news? Pictures for a story. How to produce a good news broadcast.	The BBC External Services. Notes for a news broadcast. Collecting the news. Song: 'Lillibulero'.	Identifying points that need expanding. Distinguishing main points and examples. Dictionary: looking up and explaining words.	Short notes. Explanations of noun phrases. Summary: main points. Notes from which to tell a story.	Of + verb in -ing; eg **way of doing it**. Past tenses in narrative.	Relationships in noun phrases, eg **ice cube** v. **ice tray**. Common noun phrases.	Attitude markers and intonation: spontaneous speech; writing. Understanding old-fashioned English.
Unit 15 Newspapers	Newspapers and their audiences. Predicting a news story from headlines. Interpreting charts, diagrams, graphs.	Names of newspapers. Various news items. Reasons for buying a newspaper. News in brief.	Predicting content from first sentence. Reading for specific points. Dictionary: headline words.	News item based on a headline. Explanations of figures in a chart. Survey report. Composing headlines.	Reporting verbs, eg **It is said/claimed** ... **wh-** + **to** + verb.	Reporting nouns, eg **announcement, rumours.** Complex noun phrases in news reports.	Comments showing attitude. Anecdote telling. Ways of reporting news: concealing the source etc.
Unit 16 What style radio news?	Making a news story. A current affairs programme. News in Brief. Making a news programme.	Broadcasting services. Styles of different radio stations.	Recognising sources of news. Understanding complex information. Dictionary: classifying new words.	Paragraphs which classify. Opening sentences. A News in Brief item. Explanatory captions. Scripting a news programme.	Past and present participles in descriptive clauses. Reporting verbs, eg **imply, deny, announce.**	Noun phrases in fronted information. Nouns replacing verbs in reports, eg **action.** Reporting nouns, eg **statement.**	Structure of news/current affairs items. Styles of news. Intonations: rising/falling tones. Contrast and classification.
Unit 17 All for the love of ...	Family Relationships: who influences who? The popular press. Justifying alternative courses of action.	Couples you know. Research report: effects of marriage on intelligence. Human interest stories.	Recognising the tone of an article. Dictionary: informal uses of common words; which word to look up in prepositional phrases.	Rewriting an informal report in a formal style. Chronological summary. Rewriting from another point of view.	**Would/should have** in hypothetical past. **Had** ... with inversion in past conditions. Past participle at start of sentence.	Adjectives expressing degrees of intelligence. Expressions of comparison and change.	Informal and formal reports/news stories. Logical relations between paragraphs.
Unit 18 Revision unit	Interesting news stories classified. Selecting songs and stories for entertainment. 'Detective' work.	A popular non-violent revolution. News and comment programmes: political background, further developments.	The metaphor 'argument is war' eg you can **attack** people's views. Other words used in a metaphorical way.	Letter: recent news. Drafting a programme. Recommendations. A news bulletin. Headlines. Letters: plans for trip.	Structure of complex sentences. Useful conventions for correspondence. Future reference.	Prepositions of time, place, and with verbs. Phrases describing places. Adjectives and adverbs.	Identifying key words in a broadcast. Rough translations of L1 songs, stories. Structure and content of news commentaries; styles of news compared.

Unit	TASKS AND TOPICS	TEXTS AND FEATURES	READING AND REFERENCING SKILLS	WRITING	VERBS/TENSES CLAUSE PATTERNS	NOUNS PHRASES PRONOUNS ADJECTIVES PREPOSITIONS ADVERBIAL PHRASES	WRITTEN AND SPOKEN DISCOURSE
Unit 19 Spot the hoax	News stories that stretch belief. Reincarnation. Hypnotism. Hoaxes.	Rescue story. Children who have lived before. Photography – a recent find.	Longer texts with many unknown words. Reading critically. Dictionary: deciding when to look up.	Chronological account. Describing personal impressions. News in Brief.	Complex sentences. Habitual states and actions in past and present time.	Lexical reference: ways of referring to the same person. Expressing degrees of disbelief.	Lexical reference and topic coherence. Expressing doubt, belief, disbelief and backing opinion with evidence. Contrastive stress.
Unit 20 Off to sea!	Travelling by sea. Difficulties of travel, sea-sickness. Explaining words of songs. Buying at an auction.	Types of ships. Songs about the sea. Chapters 1 and 2 of story 'Dip in the Pool' by Roald Dahl. Weather forecast.	Speculating on meanings. Inferring meaning from context. Dictionary: finding appropriate meanings.	Informal account of a day on board ship. Script/notes for a conversation. Weather forecast. Advice about buying something.	Verbs in **-ing** setting the scene. Expressions of movements.	Phrases describing reactions. Adverbs modifying verbs and adjectives. Compound words with **sea-**.	Development of a narrative text; scene-setting etc. Anecdote telling. Key words in a weather forecast. Set of instructions.
Unit 21 Family relationships – past and present	Ancestors and grandparents. Comparing the old days with life now. Effects of absences. Changing currency.	Story: Father and son, in the old days. 'Dip in the Pool' Chapters 3 and 4.	Inferring meaning from context. Recognising unmarked logical relationships.	Impressions of an old person. Describing the effects of absence. Writing about grandparents.	**Would** etc. to express future in the past. Conjunctions expressing addition, contrast, time, cause, result, condition.	Words with two possible opposites, eg **relaxed: stiff/tense.**	Following a narrative: distinguishing dialogue and thought from action and description.
Unit 22 If you had three wishes . . .	Future of the environment. Three wishes . . . . Solving a problem.	Teenagers' views on pollution and conservation. 'Dip in the Pool' Chapters 5 and 6.	Following narrative, and predicting continuation. Dictionary: looking up suffixes, checking spellings.	Comparing people's worries for future. Poster: conservation. Summary: procedures for ship's auction. Summary of wishes. Continuation of story.	Relative clauses in explanatory sentences. Meanings of **would**. Modals and adverbs of probability.	Noun + noun. Compound nouns with **life-**. Adjectival phrases expressing degree.	Dramatisation of story (in present) compared with original version set in the past.
Unit 23 Hopes and plans	Insecurity and stress. Physical appearance and personality. Someone else's future plans.	Future business developments: the Yetties diversify. 'Dip in the Pool' Chapters 7 and 8.	Inferring meaning from context. Narrative coherence. Dictionary: checking forms of opposites with **in-, un-, im-.**	Table of facts. Making notes at an interview. Continuation of story.	Verbs from adjectives, eg **deepen.** Adverbs which modify the whole sentence, eg **presumably.**	Predictive function of words like **thought, reason, difference.**	Radio interviews: controlling topics. Distinguishing narrative and thoughts in a text.
Unit 24 Revision Unit	The background to a picture. Recalling events. Keeping up a foreign language.	Broadcasting styles: news summary, current affairs, news and comment. Annual competition. 'Dip in the Pool' Chapter 9.	Reacting to story ending. Assessing book reviews.	Notes for a talk. Notes in tabular form. Summary of narrative. Description of two women. A news despatch. Applying for a grant. Letter to a language school.	Past perfect in narrative. Reporting thoughts, opinions, speech etc. with clauses with **that, to, of.**	Nouns in reporting that precede **of, that,** and **to.**	Discourse patterns: Situation – Comment; sequential; General – Specific; Situation – Problem – Solution – Evaluation; Topic – Illustration; Hypothesis – Evidence – Conclusion.

Come stranger, come friend

*This unit gives students plenty of opportunities to get to know each other if they haven't met before, and if they have met before, to renew acquaintances. For students new to the Collins COBUILD English Course, it will also serve as an introduction to the **task–planning–report** cycle in the methodology. The familiar topics of family, background, work, and travel are introduced to give students a chance to find out how much English they can remember and use. Other new topics – gestures and photographs – have been chosen to stimulate class discussion, and to help break the ice.*

OBJECTIVES

Lexical objectives are in TB12

Discussion topics

a Gestures and their meanings. (1)
b Travelling abroad. (10)

Social skills

a Greeting people. (1)
b Getting to know someone:
   Talking about yourself. (1,6)
   Asking other people about themselves. (3)
   Taking an interest in what is said. (5)
   Finding things in common. (1,2)
c Expressing evaluative comments using tone of voice to show feelings. (5)
d Written description of a person. (3)
e Description of a photograph and reactions to it. (6)

Communication skills

a Tabulating information. (4)
b Reacting to a statement with a brief evaluation. (4,5)
c Written report of a survey on travel. (10)

Grammar and discourse

a Tenses in biographical description: past, present perfect, present. (2,3,4)
b Identifying similarities and contrasts. (3)
c Evaluating situations: *Very nice./I'm quite lucky.* (5)
d Uses of the indefinite article. (7)
e˙ Verb phrases with **to**. (11)
f Words ending in **-ly**. (12)
g Practice Book Grammar Word: **a/an**.

Dictionary skills

a Scanning to identify the relevant entry.
b Distinguishing parts of an entry: definition, examples, other information.
c The abbreviations N and v.
d Pronunciation: vowels: /ə/ (weak vowel) as in **allowance**, /aʊ/ **allow**, /ɪ/ **district**, consonants: /s/, /z/, /t/, /l/, /r/.

For section 4 students will need to bring to class photographs of their families or friends. Bring some of your family, too, in case any students forget theirs.

Unit 1
Come stranger, come friend

1 Something in common?

a **Either** – find two people whose home and family circumstances are similar to yours (for example, someone who has the same number of brothers and sisters or children as you).
Or – find two people who have the same reasons for wanting to learn English as you do.

Find what other things you have in common. Plan what to say, then introduce your group to the class.

How would you introduce the person next to you in a formal meeting?

b In Britain, people shake hands only when they meet for the first time. Is it the same in your country?
What could the gestures in these pictures mean?
Which of these phrases are illustrated?

> *He shrugged his shoulders.*
> *She made a gesture towards an empty chair.*
> *He called them over.*
> *His daughter bowed and left.*
> *He shook his head.*

Are the same gestures often used in your country?
Think of three gestures a stranger to your country might need to know.

> Demonstrate and explain what they mean to the class.

2 We haven't met before

Chris Bates

Edmund Lee

Chris Bates

I'm from south-east London, from Forest Hill. I come from quite a small family. I have one sister who lives quite close, and then there's my mother who also lives in the same district. I work part-time for a charity as an administrator, in central London, Hatton Garden.

Edmund Lee

I was born in Kensington, in central London. After studying at Oxford I went back to London, to Brockley. I'm married now and we're expecting our first child.
I'm a professional musician so I work mostly at home, practising five days a week. I do a few concerts and competitions, but I'm still at the beginning of my career. It's very hard work getting established as a musician.

When Chris and Edmund met for the first time what do you think they talked about? Make two suggestions.

2 Find out what they did talk about. What do they have in common?

Read the information in the table. There are some mistakes.

	Lives?	Family?	Work?	Comments
Chris	South-West London – Forest Hill	mother sister	charity, administration	walks to work to get fit
Edmund	Brockley	wife - expecting first child	violinist teaches music	hopes to become famous

Listen again, copy the table correcting the mistakes, and add any further details that interest you.

> Write either about Chris or Edmund.

3 Find someone who ...

Find two people in the class whose work or fields of study or interests are the most similar to your own.

> Write about one of these people without mentioning the person by name.

1 | Something in common?

> **Aims:** 1 To build up students' confidence in using English.
> 2 To revise areas of lexis (home and family) with which all students should be familiar.
>
> **Lexis: gestures**
> Revision: **circumstances** (and other common words as needed)

This first activity should give students a chance to get to know each other, so they should be encouraged to talk freely. Since the main aim at this stage is to build up students' confidence in speaking English, encourage them to try to use English even if they are making a lot of mistakes. Don't correct the mistakes at this point, unless there is a complete breakdown.

Course lead-in – books closed

1 On entering the class, introduce yourself, and say a little about yourself – or ask if anyone already knows something about you.

2 Make sure students know the names of students sitting close to them. If this is the first time they are all together, get them to introduce themselves to their neighbour, who can then introduce them simply to other students nearby: e.g. This is _____, from _____, in _____.

Task SB1a PB1

Get students to read the instructions for themselves, and then ask them to explain to you what they have to do, to check they understand. The rubrics form useful reading material.

3 After choosing what they are most interested in talking about – family or reasons for learning English – students should stand up and wander round to talk to people. They will need a notebook and a pencil with them. Give support to shyer students and encourage them to use English. Help out by supplying words if students ask you.

Planning SB1a

4 Ask them to sit down in their groups of three, and to discuss how they could introduce themselves as a group to the whole class.

Because they will be talking to the whole class, their class introductions should be accurate and appropriate in style, as befits 'public' speaking.

5 Go round to see if any groups need your help. Rephrase or correct as required.

Sample report: In our group we all come from fairly large families. Both X and Y have three brothers and sisters. I have four. None of us are married. X comes from a small village called _____ in _____ while Y and I are both from _____.

Report SB1a

6 If all or some students in the class are new to each other (and/or you), ask them to introduce their group to the whole class. If they are not confident enough, each group could introduce themselves to the group nearest to them. If most students know each other well, get them to write out their reports without mentioning any names, and display them or pass them round for other groups to identify.

Class discussion SB1b

7 Students can stay in the same groups to talk about and demonstrate the gestures commonly used in their country/ies. Ask them to think about and explain to each other when they shake hands.

In Britain, handshaking is only used by newly introduced people in fairly formal situations, e.g. a head teacher meeting a student's parent for the first time, or at a business meeting. Occasionally it is also used when such people say goodbye.

8 Give some examples of other differences. For example in Britain, 'no' is indicated by a slight shake of the head, from side to side. In Greece to say 'no' you tip your head up and back. This looks to an English person like a nod, which means 'yes'.

9 Ask students to suggest what the people in the pictures could be expressing, e.g. *The man on the right doing this* (gesture by shrugging shoulders) *probably means he doesn't know/has no idea.*

Key:
The pictures from left to right probably mean:
Hello/How do you do?
Hello/A kiss!
He shrugged his shoulders/I don't know.
She made a gesture towards an empty chair./Please sit down.
He called them over./come here.
His daughter bowed and left./Goodbye.

Task SB1b

10 Ask students to talk in groups about the gestures they use in their country for *Yes / No / Come here / This way / After you / Goodbye.*

11 They could also compare gestures they might use if they had to express certain ideas without speaking, e.g. *I don't understand / No smoking in here / Three Cokes please.*

Planning and report SB1b

12 Students decide on three gestures that would be useful for a stranger. Help them work out how to explain their use. Ask one or two students from each group to demonstrate a gesture to the class, and explain what it means.

Unit 1
Come stranger, come friend

1 Something in common?

a **Either** – find two people whose home and family circumstances are similar to yours (for example, someone who has the same number of brothers and sisters or children as you).
Or – find two people who have the same reasons for wanting to learn English as you do.

> Find what other things you have in common. Plan what to say, then introduce your group to the class.

> How would you introduce the person next to you in a formal meeting?

b In Britain, people shake hands only when they meet for the first time. Is it the same in your country?
What could the gestures in these pictures mean?
Which of these phrases are illustrated?

> *He shrugged his shoulders.*
> *She made a gesture towards an empty chair.*
> *He called them over.*
> *His daughter bowed and left.*
> *He shook his head.*

Are the same gestures often used in your country? Think of three gestures a stranger to your country might need to know.

> Demonstrate and explain what they mean to the class.

2 We haven't met before

Chris Bates

Edmund Lee

Chris Bates

I'm from south-east London, from Forest Hill. I come from quite a small family. I have one sister who lives quite close, and then there's my mother who also lives in the same district. I work part-time for a charity as an administrator, in central London, Hatton Garden.

Edmund Lee

I was born in Kensington, in central London. After studying at Oxford I went back to London, to Brockley. I'm married now and we're expecting our first child.
I'm a professional musician so I work mostly at home, practising five days a week. I do a few concerts and competitions, but I'm still at the beginning of my career. It's very hard work getting established as a musician.

When Chris and Edmund met for the first time what do you think they talked about? Make two suggestions.

2 Find out what they did talk about. What do they have in common?

Read the information in the table. There are some mistakes.

	Lives?	Family?	Work?	Comments
Chris	South-west London – Forest Hill	mother sister	charity, adminic-stration	walks to work to get fit
Edmund	Brockley	wife expecting first child	violinist teaches music	hopes to become famous

Listen again, copy the table correcting the mistakes, and add any further details that interest you.

> Write either about Chris or Edmund.

3 Find someone who...

Find two people in the class whose work or fields of study or interests are the most similar to your own.

> Write about one of these people without mentioning the person by name.

5

2 We haven't met before

Aims: 1 To introduce two of the people students will be hearing on tape throughout the course.
2 Understanding and writing a brief autobiographical description.
3 Understanding a conversation where two English people meet for the first time.
4 Checking and tabulating information from two sources.

Lexis: administrator, administration, district, getting established as ..., concentrating on ..., piano, pianist
Revision: **actually, professional musician, mostly, really, tend to ...**

Reading and class discussion   SB2

1 Students read about Chris and Edmund, and then speculate briefly about what they talked about. Encourage all ideas at this stage, e.g. *Perhaps they talked about their work.*

Listening   SB2   2

If you have students who have not followed Levels 1 and 2 of this course, you will need to warn them that since this is natural speech at normal speed they must not expect to understand every word. They only need to try and recognise the main topics talked about.

2 Plan the recording once through asking students to identify topics of conversation and anything they find Chris and Edmund have in common.

Charing Cross is a British Rail mainline station in Central London where trains from the south-east of England terminate.

Key: Topics: where they live/used to live; where they work and what they do; the journey in to work; Edmund's career as a pianist.
In common: both know the Forest Hill district well.
Corrections to table: Edmund no longer lives in Brockley: 'I used to live near there.'
Edmund doesn't teach music at the moment. (He says nothing directly, but implies he'd like to become a successful pianist.)

3 Give students time to look at the information in the table before they listen again. Play the recording again, this time asking them to check and add to the information already in the table. To do this they will need to copy the table out.

4 Students read out any additional information they have written. Why did they choose those things to add? Ask them to compare what they chose to add with others in the class.

Writing   SB2

5 Students can work from the information they now have in their tables. (They can check this again in the transcript.) This could be set for homework.

3 Find someone who ...

Aim: To give students a second chance to walk around and talk to other students. This time the topic they must find out about is work, but the process is similar and they should be able to do this with more confidence now that they have heard Edmund and Chris doing the same.

Task   SB3 PB3

1 Make sure students understand the instructions. They will have to get up and walk around and talk to several people to find two people who are similar to themselves. Then they can make some quick notes about them.

Planning   SB3

2 Each student chooses one of the two people to write about. Help with the writing. It must be as accurate as possible, since other people will be reading it. Remind students not to include the name of the person.

Report   SB3

3 Take in the written work. Mix it up. Read out what some students have written (correct any bad mistakes as you read). Ask students to say who each piece is about. After they have guessed, comment yourself, as one would in natural conversation.

Unit 1
Come stranger, come friend

1 Something in common?

a **Either** – find two people whose home and family circumstances are similar to yours (for example, someone who has the same number of brothers and sisters or children as you).
Or – find two people who have the same reasons for wanting to learn English as you do.

▷ Find what other things you have in common. Plan what to say, then introduce your group to the class. ◁

How would you introduce the person next to you in a formal meeting?

b In Britain, people shake hands only when they meet for the first time. Is it the same in your country?
What could the gestures in these pictures mean? Which of these phrases are illustrated?

> He shrugged his shoulders.
> She made a gesture towards an empty chair.
> He called them over.
> His daughter bowed and left.
> He shook his head.

Are the same gestures often used in your country? Think of three gestures a stranger to your country might need to know.

▷ Demonstrate and explain what they mean to the class. ◁

2 We haven't met before

Chris Bates   Edmund Lee

Chris Bates

> I'm from south-east London, from Forest Hill. I come from quite a small family. I have one sister who lives quite close, and then there's my mother who also lives in the same district. I work part-time for a charity as an administrator, in central London, Hatton Garden.

Edmund Lee

> I was born in Kensington, in central London. After studying at Oxford I went back to London, to Brockley. I'm married now and we're expecting our first child.
> I'm a professional musician so I work mostly at home, practising five days a week. I do a few concerts and competitions, but I'm still at the beginning of my career. It's very hard work getting established as a musician.

When Chris and Edmund met for the first time what do you think they talked about? Make two suggestions.

▷ 2 Find out what they did talk about. What do they have in common?

Read the information in the table. There are some mistakes.

	Lives?	Family?	Work?	Comments
Chris	South-west London – Forest Hill	mother sister	charity administration	walks to work to get fit
Edmund	Brockley	wife expecting first child	violinist teaches music	hopes to become famous

Listen again, copy the table correcting the mistakes, and add any further details that interest you.

▷ Write either about Chris or Edmund. ◁

3 Find someone who...

Find two people in the class whose work or fields of study or interests are the most similar to your own.

▷ Write about one of these people without mentioning the person by name. ◁

5

4 Family photographs

a Read about Rachel and Bruce.

Rachel Sandon

I was born in the south-east of England, in Kent and I've lived in London for the last ten years. I come from a large family – five sisters and one brother. That's not counting two step-sisters and a step-brother. I don't actually have a job at the moment. I'm working on the Enterprise Allowance Scheme. I suppose I'm a music teacher really. I run music workshops and I play the violin and sing. It's jazz violin and it's very exciting.

Bruce Boynes

I come from the north of England, from a town called Barrow on the north-west coast. I've lived there all my life. I used to be a school-teacher, but I'm retired now. My wife still goes out to work so I stay at home and look after the house and do the cooking. I really enjoy being retired and staying at home.

b While they were still getting to know each other, Bruce and Rachel showed each other some photographs of their families. Before you listen, work with a partner and write down:

Five questions that you think might be answered at some point during their conversation. For example:

Who does the house belong to?

Five comments they could make about each other's photos or family. For example:

That's a nice yellow plant.
She looks really sweet.

▶ Tell the class two of the questions and comments you thought of.

6

4c **c** Listen to Rachel talking to Bruce and see if your questions are answered. Did they make similar comments to yours?

▶ With a partner, design a table to summarise the information you have already about Rachel and Bruce. Fill it in (in note form) and then show it to another pair.

d Choose any two people from the photographs, and tell your partner how you feel about them. For example:

He looks as though . . . She reminds me of . . . I should think she's . . .

5 Language study

Situation – comment
When someone gives some information, it is often followed by a comment. Look at the two examples in the table.

SITUATION	COMMENT
What are the facts? What is the situation?	What do you think of them? What opinion is expressed about it?
RS: I play jazz violin.	It's quite exciting.
CB: Where did you live? EL: Brockley . . .	CB: Not far away. EL: No. Very near. I really enjoyed it there actually.

Now discuss the following examples. Say which part is situation, and which part is a comment.

EL: I'm just concentrating on playing . . . six hours a day, that kind of thing . . . But getting yourself established is pretty difficult.

EL: I'm quite lucky. I work at home.

BB: That's me obviously, and my wife, standing in front of our semi-detached box. As you can see it's fairly conventional stuff . . .

BB: . . . garden in the front, garden at the back . . . double glazing. You know, what more could you want?

BB: As you can see, it's quite a decent-sized bush now.
RS: Very nice photo.

BB: You can't really tell from that, but he's about six foot five.
RS: Really?
BB: Yeah, enormous. He really is. It's frightening.

BB: This is up in the north-west . . . Barrow, which is on the edge of the Lake District.
RS: Oh lovely.

BB: On the coast. So it's quite a nice area.

Practise saying the comments out loud. Now find two more examples of the pattern **situation – comment**; one in what Edmund wrote in section 2 and one in what Bruce wrote in section 4.

4   Family photographs

Aims: 1 To introduce two more people that students will be hearing on tape, Rachel and Bruce.
2 More exposure to brief autobiographical writing.
3 To give students initial exposure to the type of evaluative comments that are commonly made when two people are chatting and showing an interest in what is said, e.g. *That's nice.*
4 Practice in forming specific questions.
5 Speculating about personality.

Lexis: enterprise, allowance, retired (retirement), conventional, flowers, decent(-sized), bush, inches, series, indeed, lake, district, affected
Revision: **run** (workshops), **obviously, stuff, slightly, fairly**
Phrases: **In fact what I meant was . . . , this has not improved matters . . .**
Note: **Po-faced** is an informal expression for very serious and stiff.

The Lake District is an area of lakes and mountains in the north-west of England very popular with walkers and climbers.
Sellafield is a large nuclear power station, near where Bruce lives. People are worried about the effects of nuclear pollution, especially in the sea.

Reading   SB4a   PB4

1 Students read (silently) about Bruce and Rachel and see whether they can identify them in the photographs. If you have a map of Britain, ask students to show you where Rachel and Bruce come from. Tell students about the Lake District and Sellafield, since Bruce mentions them later in the recording. Discuss briefly what Bruce and Rachel do.

2 Write the target lexis on the board. Make sure students understand all the words in the aims box. If students know a particular word or phrase ask them to explain it – in English – to those who don't. Make sure students can pronounce the words as part of a phrase.

SB4b

3 Help students in pairs to think of questions and comments to write down. (This helps students predict what they might hear in the conversation on cassette.) Ask them to read some out to the class.

Listening   SB4c   4

4 Plan the recording in three parts, stopping after each photograph. Ask students as they listen to point to the part of the photo that Bruce and Rachel are referring to in their conversation. You may need to replay each section once.

5 Make sure students can identify the questions and comments.

Planning and report   SB4c

6 Students can adapt the table in section 2, adding headings they feel more suitable. They can also read the transcript of the recording if they wish to check on factual details, spelling etc. Help them to phrase notes concisely.

7 Students exchange tables, and comment on each other's.

SB4d

8 Those who finish early can talk about how they feel about people in the photographs, or describe one person (without revealing which) for their partner to identify.

9 Ask students to bring in some photos of their family or friends, as they will be doing the same activity in section 6. (Also bring some of your own family.)

10 Optional discussion points:
Do your students know any men who stay at home and do the housework and/or look after the children, while their wives go out to work?
What could Bruce mean by 'semi-detached box' and 'pretty conventional stuff'? (Many streets in the UK are full of semi-detached or terraced houses, with small gardens, all much the same.)
The Enterprise Allowance Scheme is a Government scheme to fund unemployed people who want to begin some sort of business enterprise. Rachel runs music workshops for members of the public. She is not paid by the people who attend, but gets a weekly allowance from the state while she continues to run them.

5   Language study

Aims: 1 To show students how people often use evaluative comments to show how they feel about the particular situation, thing, or person that has just been mentioned.
2 Sometimes it is the speaker that evaluates, and sometimes the listener evaluates in response.
Note: This pattern almost certainly occurs in the students' own language (ask them!), but students often lack the confidence to comment in a foreign language – a tendency which gives a slightly stilted flow to a conversation.

SB5   PB5

1 Study the examples in the table with students. Point out it can be either the speaker (as in Rachel's case – in the first example) or the listener (or both) who add comments.

2 Students do the exercise singly or in pairs. Then discuss the exercise as a class.

Key: The comments are the second sentence/s in each case, except for 'I'm quite lucky' which comes first.
To get across the idea of the evaluative nature of comments, you could ask students which ones:
are very positive (lucky, very nice photo, Oh lovely)
sound fairly neutral (Bruce's first two)
express surprise (Rachel's 'Really?')
sound a bit negative (Edmund's '. . . pretty difficult'.)
What about 'It's frightening'? Does Bruce really mean it? Or is he being a typical father, proud of his son's height?

SB5

3 Students find two more written examples.

Key: Edmund: It's very hard work getting established . . .
Bruce: I really enjoy being retired and staying at home.

6 Bring your own photos

Aims: 1 Practice in eliciting information from someone else, and expressing suitable reactions.
2 Planning and writing a short piece to give background information about a photograph.

Task SB6

1 Pair students up differently, so they are with someone they don't know very well. If anyone has not brought a photo, you could put them with another pair, and they will simply have to ask about the others' photos rather than talking about their own. Alternatively they could interview you about your photos, and write about yours.

2 Explain they are to do the same as Bruce and Rachel did in section 4, but in addition they are to write about one of the other people's photos, so they will have to find out as much as they can and check their facts.

3 Stand back and let students talk privately. Only interrupt if you are invited to, or if students really get stuck.

Planning and report SB6

4 Help students express what they want to write. Rephrase and correct where necessary.

5 Take in the pieces of writing, and display these, jumbled, alongside the photographs, preferably on a surface which allows them to be moved around. Can students match them all up? (In some cases this will be easy; in others more difficult.)

7 Grammar

Aims: 1 To revise some common uses of **a/an**.
2 To practise one way of highlighting the subject of a sentence, using **it is/was ... who/that ...**

SB7a

1 Students can do these individually or in pairs. Then go through them with the class.

    Key: a 1,7,8
          b 2,9,10
          c 3,4,5
          d 6,11,12

Barrow is quite **a** small town in the north of England. Bruce used to work there as **a** teacher and he still lives there. He has been retired for **a** few years now, but his wife is still **a** teacher.
Peter comes from quite **a** large family. He works as **a** teacher at the local school and lectures at the university two evenings **a** week.

SB7b

2 Help students with the example, then ask them to do the quiz.

    Key: It was Columbus who discovered America.
    It was Shakespeare who wrote Hamlet.
    It was Don Quixote who fought with windmills.

Make it clear to students that this device is used for emphasis, often in contradiction or contrast. For example:
A: Sancho Panza fought with windmills.
B: No. It was Don Quixote who fought with windmills.

3 Ask students to write some similar sentences. They could be about people in their class. You could lead into this by making untrue statements about some of the students – mixing up people and jobs – for students to correct, for instance:
T: Juan works for the National Bank.
S: No. It's Cristina who works in a bank.

Bring your own photos

Find a new partner. Show each other your photos.

Write about your partner's photo. Write some facts about the people in it and the place the photo was taken. Include some comments to show what you think or feel about it.

Grammar

a   a/an

Read these phrases with the word **a** or **an** in them. Can you find:

   a   Three phrases with **quite**?
   b   Three phrases for a job or profession?
   c   Three time phrases?
   d   Three phrases that answer the question **How much ...?** or **How many ...?**

1   *I come from quite a large family.* (2)
2   *I work as an administrator ...* (2)
3   *... two evenings a week.* (2)
4   *... practising five days a week.* (2)
5   *... six hours a day ...* (2)
6   *I do a few concerts ...* (2)
7   *It's quite a long way in from Forest Hill?* (2)
8   *It's quite a journey into Central London.* (2)
9   *I'm a music teacher really.* (4)
10 *I used to be a schoolteacher, but I'm retired now.* (4)
11 *... a couple of years back ...* (4)
12 *... my younger brother. Although he looks a little older ...* (4)

Where does the word **a/an** go in these paragraphs?

> Barrow is quite small town in the north of England. Bruce used to work there as teacher and he still lives there. He has been retired for few years now, but his wife is still teacher.
> Peter comes from quite large family. He works as teacher at the local school and lectures at the University two evenings week.

b   It is/was ... who/that ...

Bruce says:
It was a German friend of my wife who took it.
We often begin with **It is/was ... that/who ...** when we want to emphasise the subject.

Here is a short quiz.
   Who was it who:
         ... discovered America?
         ... wrote Hamlet?
         ... fought with windmills?

Write three more sentences like these for your partner to complete.
      It's _____ who lives in Barrow.
      It's _____ that wants to be a professional musician.

Dictionary skills

Find the meanings

a   Guess what the coloured words mean.
   I don't actually have a job at the moment. I'm working on the Enterprise Allowance Scheme. (4)
   Barrow ... on the edge of the Lake District. (4)
   ... my mother, who also lives in the same district. (2)
   ... this is about the fourth in a series of several photos ... (4)
   That's me obviously, and my wife, standing in front of our semi-detached box. As you can see it's fairly conventional stuff, garden in the front, garden at the back ... (4)
b   Find the dictionary explanation for each word and see which meaning it has here.
c   Why are there two different types of print?
d   Which word is used mostly in informal English? Which word can make a rude expression?

[   ] is both the singular and the plural form.
1 A [   ] of things or events is a number of them that come one after the other. EG *He was arrested in connection with a [   ] of armed bank robberies... ...a [   ] of lectures on American politics.*

A [   ] is 1 an area of a town or country. EG *...doctors in country [   ]... ...a working class [   ] of Paris.*

[   ] refer to a substance, a thing, or a group of things as lot of [   ] EG *What's that [   ] in the bucket?... Quite a lot of [   ] had been stolen... She was reading the travel [   ] in the colour supplement.*

1 An [   ] is money that is given regularly to someone, in order to help them pay for the things that they need. EG *...a maternity [   ].*

e   Practise pronouncing the words below. Which word is which? What is the extra word?

/stʌf/   /ʃəʊ/   /dɪstrɪkt/   /əlaʊəns/   /stɔːrɪz/

Song

How many in your class were total strangers at the beginning of this course? How many of you have ever travelled somewhere on your own?

9   Here is a song about making friends, sung by the Yetties, a popular British folk group.

COME STRANGER, COME FRIEND

Come stranger, come friend, come if you've time to spend
And we'll share a good bottle and laughter
If your hearts can belong for a while to my song
We'll have something to share ever after.

Come traveller draw near, there's a safe harbour here
And your journey won't tire you for long.
You can sit where you are and still travel afar
There's a thousand new worlds in a song.

Come stranger etc.

There are folks who may frown on us, try to look down on us
Still we'll not worry or care
There are none that could be as contented as we
With a song and a bottle to share.

Come stranger etc.

8 Dictionary skills

Aims: 1 Introduction to the Dictionary extracts appendix in the Student's Book.
2 Scanning to identify the relevant entry.
3 Distinguishing the different parts of an entry: the explanation, the examples, and other information.
4 To show how both the explanations and the examples for each category exemplify the common collocations and patterns associated with the word. They can thus help the learner to use the word in their own speech or writing, not just simply to understand the word.
5 The abbreviations N = noun and V = verb, as found in the extra column.
6 Pronunciation: vowels: /ə/ (weak vowel) as in **allow<u>a</u>nce**, /aʊ/ **allow**, /ɪ/ **d<u>i</u>str<u>i</u>ct**, consonants: /s/, /z/, /t/, /l/, /r/.

Lexis: informal

SB8

1 Explain to students that the Dictionary Skills sections appear in each unit and are to help them to become quick and efficient dictionary users, a skill which is most valuable outside the classroom, especially when reading, studying and writing on their own.
The entries and part-entries in the Dictionary Extracts appendix to the Student's Book have been taken from *Collins COBUILD Essential English Dictionary* and have been carefully selected to help students build up specific dictionary reference skills.

2 Get students to attempt to explain to you or each other what each coloured word in *a* means. (Ask them: How might the dictionary explain this word?) Accept all explanations. Don't evaluate their attempts. They will do that themselves later when reading the dictionary entries.

3 Students work through *b–e* in pairs. Discuss their findings as a class. Ask which are nouns and which verbs (N and V in the extra column). For now, there is no need to explain more than very briefly the terms COUNT and UNCOUNT (i.e. words like **information** that cannot take an **s** to make them plural are UNCOUNT). This is covered in Unit 3 section 26.

Key:
b series, district, stuff, allowance
c Bold print for the headwords; ordinary print for explanations; italics for examples, introduced by e.g.
d **Stuff**. Explain how the entry helps students know when and how to use or not to use a word!
e The extra word is **allow**.

4 Go through the target phonetic symbols, paying particular attention to the weak vowel /ə/. Ask students to practise saying the words, but point out that when used in a phrase, they may sound different.

5 Get students to see how quickly they can find the complete entries for these in the Student's Book Dictionary Extracts appendix.

9 Song

A recording of the song is available on the Student's Cassette only.

Lexis: stranger
Revision: **belong**, **share**, **draw near** (= come nearer)
Phrases: **time to spend**, **for a while**, **ever after**, **for long**, **nothing to fear**, **pressing** (= times are hard)

This song is sung by the Yetties, a folk group who feature in several units running through Level 3. Point out the pictures of the Yetties in section 13.

SB9 9

1 After initial discussion, ask students to listen to the song and read the words. Ask students where the singer probably is (in a cafe or bar).

2 Go through any new lexis that will be useful for students.

3 Play again. Students can join in if they enjoy singing.

6 Bring your own photos

Find a new partner. Show each other your photos.

Write about your partner's photo. Write some facts about the people in it and the place the photo was taken. Include some comments to show what you think or feel about it.

7 *Grammar*

a   a/an
Read these phrases with the word **a** or **an** in them. Can you find:
  a Three phrases with **quite**?
  b Three phrases for a job or profession?
  c Three time phrases?
  d Three phrases that answer the question **How much . . . ?** or **How many . . . ?**

1 *I come from quite a large family.* (2)
2 *I work as an administrator . . .* (2)
3 *. . . two evenings a week.* (2)
4 *. . . practising five days a week.* (2)
5 *. . . six hours a day . . .* (2)
6 *I do a few concerts . . .* (2)
7 *It's quite a long way in from Forest Hill?* (2)
8 *It's quite a journey into Central London.* (2)
9 *I'm a music teacher really.* (4)
10 *I used to be a schoolteacher, but I'm retired now.* (4)
11 *. . . a couple of years back . . .* (4)
12 *. . . my younger brother. Although he looks a little older . . .* (4)

Where does the word **a/an** go in these paragraphs?

> Barrow is quite small town in the north of England. Bruce used to work there as teacher and he still lives there. He has been retired for few years now, but his wife is still teacher.
> Peter comes from quite large family. He works as teacher at the local school and lectures at the university two evenings week.

b   It is/was . . . who/that . . .
Bruce says:
It was a German friend of my wife who took it.
We often begin with **It is/was . . . that/who . . .** when we want to emphasise the subject.

Here is a short quiz.
    Who was it who:
        . . . discovered America?
        . . . wrote Hamlet?
        . . . fought with windmills?

Write three more sentences like these for your partner to complete.
    It's ＿＿＿ who lives in Barrow.
    It's ＿＿＿ that wants to be a professional musician.

8 *Dictionary skills*

Find the meanings
a Guess what the coloured words mean.
   I don't actually have a job at the moment. I'm working on the Enterprise Allowance Scheme. (4)
   Barrow . . . on the edge of the Lake District. (4)
   . . . my mother, who also lives in the same district. (2)
   . . . this is about the fourth in a series of several photos . . . (4)
   That's me obviously, and my wife, standing in front of our semi-detached box. As you can see it's fairly conventional stuff, garden in the front, garden at the back . . . (4)
b Find the dictionary explanation for each word and see which meaning it has here.
c Why are there two different types of print?
d Which word is used mostly in informal English? Which word can make a rude expression?

[   ] is both the singular and the plural form.
1 A [   ] of things or events is a number of them that come one after the other. EG *He was arrested in connection with a [   ] of armed bank robberies... a [   ] of lectures on American politics.*

A [   ] is **1** an area of a town or country. EG *...doctors in country [   ]... ...a working class [   ] of Paris.*

[   ] **1** You can refer to a substance, a thing, or a group of things as [   ]. EG *What's that [   ] in the bucket?... Quite a lot of [   ] had been stolen... She was reading the travel [   ] in the colour supplement.*

1 An [   ] is money that is given regularly to someone, in order to help them pay for the things that they need. EG *...a maternity [   ].*

e Practise pronouncing the words below. Which word is which? What is the extra word?

/stʌf/   /əlaʊ/   /dɪstrɪkt/   /əlaʊəns/   /stəriːz/

9 Song

How many in your class were total strangers at the beginning of this course? How many of you have ever travelled somewhere on your own?

`9`   Here is a song about making friends, sung by the Yetties, a popular British folk group.

COME STRANGER, COME FRIEND

Come stranger, come friend, come if you've time to spend
And we'll share a good bottle and laughter
If your hearts can belong for a while to my song
We'll have something to share ever after.

Come traveller draw near, there's a safe harbour here
And your journey won't tire you for long.
You can sit where you are and still travel afar
There's a thousand new worlds in a song.

Come stranger etc.

There are folks who may frown on us, try to look down on us
Still we'll not worry or care
There are none that could be as contented as we
With a song and a bottle to share.

Come stranger etc.

10 Travels past and future

a Write three statements about a different country. For example:
This country is in south Europe.
Its flag is red, white and green.
If you look at it on a map the country is shaped like a boot.
Can students guess which country it is?

b We asked Bruce and Rachel to do this:

> Tell each other what other places or countries you've been to, and how/why you were there.

10b Which countries have Bruce and Rachel been to, and which might they be going to? What are their impressions of each place? Why did they go?

Take notes. Compare yours with other people's.

c Do the same as Rachel and Bruce, talking to someone you don't know so well. Find out what places they have been to, or would like to go to, and why.

In groups of four plan a short report to give the class about your travels.

Listen to find which countries are popular, and why.

Write a brief review of the findings.

11 *Language study*

10b a Listen for these phrases. What exactly are they talking about? Try to explain.

. . . and you grow to like a place when you do that.
No. I haven't. I'd love to.
It is the place to walk around, I think, isn't it, really.

I used to spend hours, I must admit, . . .
. . . I found it more interesting to walk about.

10b b What word do all the examples above have in common? Listen and note down other phrases which contain the same word. Can you find seven?

12 REVIEW

UNIT 1

a Odd word out – find and replace
Find the odd word out, and say why it does not fit. Think of a better word to go in its place.

a sister family aunt cousin wife
b flower plant tree garden bush
c coast lake forest sea sky
d area place district Iron Curtain
e retirement friend schoolteacher stranger
f text section title library passage
g iron stuff plastic wood metal

Now arrange all the words from sets d–g in alphabetical order.

b Nouns from other words
Write the correct noun in the gaps. Use the Dictionary extracts. The first one is done for you.

Can you explain this word?
Find a dictionary explanation *for this word.*

NEW WORDS IN UNIT 1

administration	informal
allowance D	introduction
bush	iron
concentration	lake
conventional	library
curtain	passage
decent	piano
district D	plant
enterprise	retired
flower	retirement
gesture	series D
inch	stranger
indeed	title

26 new words
D denotes words for which dictionary entries appear in the Dictionary extracts (page 101).

Edmund has to concentrate on his playing.
He needs good powers of _____.

Chris is an administrator.
She helps with the _____.

About this time, iron was introduced in factories...
After the _____ of iron in the factories...

Dear Sir, I wish to inform you that...
Could you please give me the following _____?

c Words ending in –ly
Which words could possibly fit in each sentence?

actually	fairly	largely	mostly
partly	really	slightly	obviously

a . . . *I work _____ at home.*
b . . . *Brockley . . . I _____ enjoyed it there _____.*
c *That's me _____, and my wife . . .*
d . . . *It's _____ conventional stuff.*
e *He looks _____ tall there.*
f . . . *makes everybody look _____ reddish . . .*
g *British Museum . . . I should have recognised that _____ . . .*
h *That _____ looks like you . . .*
i . . . *a couple of years, _____ at university and _____ teaching . . .*
j . . . *German and I speak French so we manage _____ well.*
. . . *Africa . . . Whereas I've stuck very _____ to Europe.*

Check on the meanings of any words you don't know in these examples.

d To
Which sentences refer to the past?

a *Oh yeah. I used to live near there.* (2)
b . . . *and I tend to walk from there . . .* (2)
c *I used to be a school teacher . . .* (4)
d . . . *maybe that had something to do with it.* (4)
e *We decided to have the photo out there . . .* (4)
f *It's quite a nice area to be.* (4)
g . . . *if you've time to spend . . .* (9)

Unit 2
The Yetties

From left to right: Bonny Sartin, Roger Trim, Mac McCulloch, Pete Shutler.

13 The Yetties

a Read these statements about the Yetties. Then read the passage below and see if they are true or false.

1 *They called themselves the Yetties because they come from Yetminster.*
2 *Their full time career in entertainment began around the mid sixties.*
3 *They now live abroad.*
4 *They have appeared on television.*
5 *They sing mainly about country life.*

> **THE YETTIES**
> The Yetties first entered the world of professional entertaining when they took a three-month break from their day jobs in 1967 to concentrate on the many singing engagements which they had in the villages around Yetminster. Since then their success has taken them beyond Dorset as far as Greece, Cyprus, Malta and Romania as well as all over the United Kingdom, and has included records, television series and their own radio shows. Close involvement with the life of the countryside still remains the mainspring of their work, however, and all of them still live near the village which gave them their name.

Who's missing?

b In pairs look at the photo below of the Yetties as boy scouts. Can you work out which one of them is not there? Tell each other.

[13b] Bruce and Rachel did the same. Do you think they were right?

14 Folk singing and other music

[14] You will hear three different groups of people singing. Can you guess where each one is?

a Where do you sing? When did you sing as a child? What kind of songs? What are they about?

b Read to find out if the British are similar to you.

> Folk music is a living tradition and ordinary people are still making and singing songs today. At football matches on Saturday afternoons and in pubs on Saturday nights; on coach outings and at political demonstrations; on the factory-floor and in school playgrounds – people are still singing. And the reason they do it is, as Ralph Vaughan Williams observed: "simply and solely because they want to".

c Desert Island Discs

If you were cast away on a desert island what four songs or pieces of music would you take with you? Make a list.

d Find two or three other people who have similar tastes in music to you. Discuss which singers and musicians you like. Do any of you play an instrument?

▷ Tell the class about your musical tastes. What music have you chosen for the desert island? ◁

15 *Language study*

a **Where?**
Find five phrases which tell us where in section 13 above, and five in section 14. E.g. *beyond Dorset*. Practise saying these phrases with prepositions.

b **When?**
Find four words/phrases which express time in section 13 above, and four in section 14.

c **Why?**
Find one sentence in section 14 which answers the question why?

16 Programme notes

This is a page from the programme of a concert given by the Yetties. Copy the table below leaving plenty of space to fill it in, then read the programme notes and fill in your table.

Bonny Sartin (Vocals, percussion)

Bonny was born about 3 miles from Yetminster and like all the Yetties went to Fosters School in Sherborne. He worked for 7 years in a printing firm before taking up singing full-time. He now lives with his wife and two children in Sherborne, where his main relaxation is gardening.

Pete Shutler (Vocals, accordion, concertina, melodeon, bowed psaltery)

After Yetminster village School and Fosters School, Pete had a number of jobs as a trainee accountant, labourer, window cleaner, salesman and work study expert. He was suspended from the latter job for taking too many days off to play the accordion! His wife is the folk singer Maria MacKenzie, and they have two children.

Mac McCulloch (Vocals, guitar, banjo, auto-harp)

Mac was brought up on a farm and still retains a great interest in country life, particularly old country crafts. Like Bonny, he worked in the printing trade although his original ambition was to be an engine driver like his father. He lives in Sherborne and has two children.

	Name		
	Bonny	**Pete**	**Mac**
School (where?)			
Work			
Interests music other			
Additional details (from section 17)			

WORD STUDY
Match words and phrases similar in meaning.

taking days off	quite a few
original	starting as a career
a number of	joined
handicapped	first, earliest
became a member	unable to live a normal life
taking up	not going to work

Find out similar details about two people in your class. Write a paragraph about each of them in the same style as the programme notes.

17 The Yetties interviewed

17a **a** Listen and discover in which order the Yetties are interviewed. Say how you can tell who it was. Add relevant details to the table above.

17a Listen again. Write a caption for each of the pictures above. Tell each other your captions.

17b **b** Now listen to Roger being interviewed. Take notes so that you can copy and complete this paragraph in the style of the programme notes . Add anything you wish to.

Roger Trim (violin, mandolin, saw)

Roger also _____ as a boy, then after _____ did _____ training and worked as a _____ for the mentally handicapped, and later with handicapped children. He first met the Yetties when _____ . He _____ . He became _____ in 1985.

18 *Language study*

Ways to mark stages in a conversation

17a Listen again, with pauses, and take notes to complete the questions and sentences.

Why ...?
I think, well two reasons why I joined the Scout troop:
one ...
And then ...
When ...?
Well we used to ...
And then ...
and then ...
Eventually ...
And so ...
It was from that ...

Think of an interest you had that developed gradually, in stages, over a period of time. Tell your partner about it, using some of the words above.

19 *Grammar*

Talking about the past
What two-word phrase goes in every one of these blanks? (There is also a single word that would fit most gaps: can you think of it?)

When we were in the Scouts, we _____ sing when we were camping. We always _____ have a camp fire, and sing songs around that. And then, around about the same time, some people in the village started a folk dancing evening, in the village hall ... And all the girls _____ go there as well of course, so all the boys _____ take an interest in it.

16 Programme Notes

Aims: 1 Exposure to brief biographical notes.
2 Reading for and tabulating relevant information.
3 Guessing words from context.

Lexis: ambition, club, crafts, firm, folk, guitar, mentally/physically handicapped, original, printing, singer
Revision: **join, taking days off, taking up singing, trade**

Reading and note-taking   SB16

1 Students copy the table. Give them an idea how much space they need to leave. They should read for the relevant information and fill it in. The last section of the table will not be used until section 17.

Key:

NAME	BONNY	PETE	MAC
SCHOOL	Fosters School, Sherborne.	Yetminster Village School Fosters	Fosters
WORK	Printing firm (7 yrs)	trainee accountant, labourer, window cleaner, salesman, work study expert.	Printing trade
INTERESTS	singing gardening	musician —	musician country life and old crafts

Task, planning and report   SB16

2 Help students to write up their biographies. These could be put up round the walls for others to read at leisure.

17 The Yetties interviewed

Aims: 1 Listening for gist.
2 Listening and sifting information to distinguish familiar and new biographical facts.
3 Writing brief biographical notes.

Lexis: club, dancing, entertain(er), fed up, firm, folk/ dancing, handicapped, institute, instruments, originally, printer, printing, variety
Phrases: **mentally/physically handicapped** (T), **do an apprenticeship, in actual fact**
Note: The **Women's Institute** is a kind of local club for women. They hold meetings afternoons and evenings.
A ceilidh (pronounced /keɪli/) is an informal entertainment at which there is singing, folk music and dancing, mainly in Scotland and Ireland.

Listening   SB17a   17a   PB17

1 Warn students that the Yetties have a local Dorset accent, which may seem a little strange at first, but they do speak quite clearly.
Tell students they will be hearing three of them interviewed one after the other.
If you have a weak group, give them the interviewer's questions first, (see the transcript) and get students to predict what might be said in answer.

2 Make sure students have their completed tables from section 16 to help them.

3 You may want to stop the recording after each interview and find out how much they managed to understand on a first listen. But tell students you will be playing each one again soon for more detailed note-taking.

Key: The Yetties were interviewed in this order: Pete, Mac, Bonny.

Writing   SB17a   17a

4 Play the recording again, with some pauses, to allow students to note down ideas for captions for the photos on this page. They can also add any other relevant facts to their tables.

Sample captions: Singing round the camp-fire/At the printers/Folk-dancing

Listening and note-taking   SB17b   17b

5 Tell students that Roger's interview is a little longer than the first three. Tell students to listen for the interviewer's questions.

6 Play the recording, stopping after each question while students write it down. This may help them predict what is coming.

7 Play the recording a second time with some pauses so students can take notes.

Planning and written report   SB17b

8 Ask students to complete and add to the paragraph about Roger. Allow them to read through the transcript to get more ideas if they wish to.

9 Ask students to summarise what they now know about the Yetties. What do the Yetties have in common? (All started off in other jobs before becoming professional. All keen on music, etc.)

Key: Possible version:
Roger Trim (Violin, mandolin, saw)
Roger also lived in Sherborne as a boy, then after leaving school did medical training and worked as a nurse in hospitals for the mentally handicapped, and later with handicapped children. He first met the Yetties when he took his violin to his local Folk Club. He became a full member of the Yetties group in 1985, and has since travelled all over the United Kingdom, doing a wide variety of shows.

18 Language study

Aims: 1 To highlight staging devices in discourse (ways to mark stages in a conversation).
2 To focus on ways of giving reasons.

SB18   17a

1 Play the recording with pauses while students complete the sentences. Then let students read the first part of section 17a transcript to check what they have written.

2 Ask students to list the staging words and phrases from memory. Can they add any more? (e.g. **First of all, After that, In the end, Finally, We ended up ... + ing**).

3 Interests/hobbies/skills that students might talk about include collecting things (stamps), a sport, learning a language, or a skill like cooking, or playing the piano.

19 Grammar

Aim: To revise ways of talking about habitual actions in the past.

SB19 PB19

1 Let students do this in pairs. They could read the passage out to each other.

Key: used to, also **would**, or **'d**. (Note order: *We'd always have...*) Simple past form could also be used, e.g. *We sang...*

10T

Aims: 1 Discussion of change.
2 Reading a longer text of a historical nature and coping with unknown words and phrases.
3 Understanding habitual actions in the past as expressed by **would** and past simple.
4 Guided summary writing.

Lexis: band, customs, drama, dance, entertain(ment), generation, gypsy, isolated, junior, native, ritual, rural, satisfy, satisfaction, search, seldom, version
Revision: **absorbed, agricultural, involved in, largely, obvious, respect, sense of humour, traditional, World Service** (BBC Radio)

Discussion   SB20a

1 Students in groups could list possible differences. (No radio, television or video, therefore people made their own entertainment, or were entertained by travelling players, village bands... More time for ceremonies, e.g. harvest thanksgiving. Smaller communities, so everyone knew everyone.)

Reading   SB20a PB20

2 This article is from the same programme as the text in section 16. It aims to introduce the audience to a history of folk-music, and to show how the Yetties have helped to keep alive songs that might have died out.
Tell students the text is not easy – they will have to guess a lot of the words. They can use dictionaries to help with essential words, but they should not waste time hunting for words which are unimportant. They can do that after class if they want to.

3 Ask students to read Part 1 and pick out the key points about music and song.

With a weaker class, give students these questions before they read:
(paragraph 1) Is a generation a long time? How do you know? What kind of entertainment would a small village have before the 19th century?
(paragraph 2) How did the performers get new songs to entertain their audiences with? (2 ways.)
(paragraph 3) Why were some songs forgotten? What kind of songs survived?

4 Help students with the Word Study. Encourage students to help each other, and to explain to each other in English if possible.
After guessing, they can look up the words marked [D] in the Dictionary Extracts appendix at the back of the Student's Book, and find which meaning is relevant.

5 Discuss how life changed in the early 20th Century. (Prompt if necessary – growth of transport – trains, cars, motor vehicles; machines in factories, people leaving villages, going to live in towns – the industrial revolution was well underway in Britain). Students' own countries may well be different.

Reading   SB20b

6 Discuss the pictures. What do students think the people are doing? Students then read Part 2, the first paragraph only, and complete the summary. (**Musicologist** is a rare word = specialist in music.)
Possible question to give beforehand:
Why might old songs get lost forever? (because social conditions were changing)

Key: ... the old songs and music would get lost forever, because of changing social conditions. They therefore started to travel round collecting songs (and writing them down). As a result, many of the old songs have been saved/preserved.

Reading   SB20c

7 Explain to students that the sentences in the next paragraph have been mixed up. Can they work out what their original order was?

Key: 3 2 4 1 5

8 Make sure students end the lesson with a sense of achievement. Remind them the article was written for native-speakers, in a formal, historical style. They have done well if they have managed to do most of these activities. (They must not feel they have to learn every word.) You could end up by writing the target words on the board and see how many they now understand.

Society and song

a How is entertainment now different from the 19th century? In what ways? Why?

THE FOLK SONGS OF BRITAIN

Part 1

The folk songs of Britain are part of a rich heritage of music, dance and drama handed on from generation to generation by ordinary people for hundreds, sometimes thousands of years. Until the 19th Century Britain was largely an agricultural society. In its small, isolated communities people made their own entertainments and each village had its singers, story-tellers and musicians. Often there would be a village band made up of self-taught players providing music for every occasion, from the church service on Sunday to the village dance on Saturday night.

Much of their music and song was handed on from generation to generation, as were the ceremonial customs and ritual dances, but the performers were always searching for new material to entertain their audiences. Some would write their own songs or set new words to tunes they already knew. Others would learn songs from the outside world brought in to the village by travelling pedlars, carters, cattle-drovers and gipsies.

Whether the songs came from inside or outside the community they were seldom written down (and even if they were, few of the singers could read) so invariably they were passed on from one to another from memory, with each singer unconsciously developing his own version. Some were soon forgotten, but those that survived did so because they satisfied a need in the people who sang them and heard them.

WORD STUDY

Find these words in the three paragraphs. Guess what they mean.

drama	dance
generation	customs D
band	searching

Match words and phrases similar in meaning.

searching D	cut off, lonely	seldom D	thinking up
isolated	villages	passed on	rarely
agricultural	looking for	developing	did not die out
communities	traditional	survived	handed down
ritual	farming		

▶ In pairs discuss how life changed in the early 20th Century. How might that have affected folk songs?

b Read Part 2. Copy and complete these sentences to make a summary.

At the beginning of the 20th Century some musicologists were worried that...
They therefore...
As a result...

Part 2

At the beginning of the 20th Century a group of composers and musicologists, most notably Ralph Vaughan Williams and Cecil Sharp, felt that, with changing social conditions, the old songs of England would be lost forever. They set about collecting many thousands of songs, variations and fragments from all over the country. Through the work of these collectors, and many before and after them, much of the repertoire of the old singers has been preserved.

Finally, write a caption for the old photograph.

c Rearrange these sentences to show what part the Yetties played in this revival of folk music.

Part 3

1. Their first memory of singing together was during their days as Boy Scouts and their interest in traditional dance stems from the time when they were members of Yetminster Junior Folk Dance Display Team.

2. They take their name from the village of Yetminster in the county of Dorset in South West England which was their childhood home.

3. The Yetties have been actively involved in this revival as professional folk singers for over 15 years.

4. Here in their early years they unconsciously absorbed the songs, music and customs of rural England from their families.

5. They are still actively involved in the life of the village, much in the manner of the village bands of days gone by, and their obvious love of their native Dorset and respect for its traditions, coupled with their boisterous sense of humour, wins them friends where they go.

By Jim Lloyd

Jim Lloyd is a broadcaster and writer on folk music. He presents BBC Radio's only folk programme in Britain and is known to World Service listeners for series such as These Musical Islands and 'Tis My Delight.

21 The gypsy rover

Find these in the pictures:
a gypsy   a valley   a castle gate   woods   a horse

[21] Listen and suggest in what order the pictures should come. Which picture is not about this song? Suggest a better alternative.

A gypsy rover came over the hill
Down to the valley so shady
He whistled and sang till the green woods rang
And he won the heart of a lady.

Chorus
Ar dee do ar dee do dah day, ar dee do ar dee day dee
He whistled and sang till the green woods rang
And he won the heart of a lady.

She left her father's castle gate
She left her own true lover
Left her houses and her estate
To follow the gypsy rover.

Chorus

Her father mounted his swiftest steed*
Searched the valley all over
Sought his daughter at great speed
And the whistling gypsy rover.

Chorus

At last he came to a castle fine
Down by the river Plaidy
And there was whisky and there was wine
For the gypsy and his lady.

'He is no gypsy father dear
But Lord of these lands all over
And I will stay till my dying day
With my whistling gypsy rover.'

* swiftest steed = fastest horse (old-fashioned)

Bonny wrote:
This is a modern version of a traditional song called *The Three Gypsies*. Gypsies and travelling musicians always had a slightly mysterious, magical quality. They were supposed to be able to charm anything from warts to rats (like The Pied Piper) or young maidens. In the original song the gypsy had no castle or money but did have the freedom to roam the country, living an easy life – this is the source of his wealth.

WORD STUDY
Find these words and guess what they mean.
estate version original freedom search/sought
free and easy source wealth

---

22 *Dictionary skills*

Pronunciation and stress
Use the dictionary extracts to check the meanings, pronunciation and stress of the coloured words.

One would assume that the fellow in glasses is the same one as . . . (13)
. . . and work study expert for the local Council. (16)
. . . songs, music and customs of rural England. (20)
They became engaged last week.
The Yetties have many singing engagements.
She left her . . . houses and her estate . . . (21)
He worked for seven years in a printing firm. (16)
He held her arm, not hard but firmly.
She was like all the old folk . . .
. . . they were always searching for new material. (20)

---

23 REVIEW   a   Find and replace

UNIT 2

Find the odd one out and suggest another word to take its place.
1 assuming eventually in the end at last
2 singer entertainer printer further engine driver
3 kingdom freedom republic state
4 searched for sought tried to find found
5 seldom not often frequently on very few occasions hardly ever
6 satisfied happy fed up free and easy
7 boss folk chap fellow guy

b   Missing word?
Which one word is missing from all these?

1 *This seemed like a pretty good _____.* (17)
2 *. . . country dancing . . . and so it really became a _____ for young people, you know.* (17)
3 *_____s were building up. Work was . . . getting in the way of singing.* (17)
4 *. . . and that was work study, you know, sort of time-and-motion stuff and all that sort of _____.*

You can check 1–3 in the transcript for recording 17.

c   Common verbs
Which fits where? (You may need to change the form of the verb.)

do	go	put	take

1 *They _____ their name from the village of Yetminster.* (20)
2 *. . . I'd been to see a show that they'd _____ on in the village hall . . .* (17)
3 *. . . all the boys used to _____ an interest in it.* (17)
4 *I _____ a five-year apprenticeship in printing.* (17)
5 *. . . we had planned to _____ professional for three months . . . through to Christmas, then we were _____ to all _____ back to work again.* (17)
6 *Pete used to _____ a lot of days off work to _____ and play with another group.*
7 *His boss said that, because of all the time he had _____ off, he was suspended.*

NEW WORDS IN UNIT 2

ambition	handicapped
assume D	institute
band	instrument
chap	involvement
club	isolated
council D	junior
countryside	kingdom
craft	mental/ly
custom D	native
dancing	original
drama	print
engaged D	republic
engagement D	ritual
entertain	rural
entertainment	satisfaction
estate D	satisfy/ied
fed up	search D
firm/ly D	seek/sought
folk D	seldom D
freedom	valley
gate	variety
generation	version
guitar	
gypsy	

46 new words
TOTAL SO FAR 72

21 The gypsy rover

Aim: To stimulate evaluative comments.

Lexis: estate, freedom, gate, gypsy, searched, seek, sought, valley, version
Revision: **castle, source, traditional, true, wealth**
Phrases: **win the heart of, at great speed, source of his wealth, free and easy**
Note: **Rover** is an old word for someone who doesn't live long in one particular spot but travels from place to place.

Task SB21 〔21〕

1 Students find the words in the pictures.

2 Before playing the recording of the song, ask students in pairs to guess the story from the pictures. Ask some students to tell their version to the class.

3 Play the song and let students join in if they wish.

4 Go through the song with them and compare their versions of the story. Work out in which order the pictures are used, and identify the odd one out.

Reading SB21

5 Help students read, for interest, what Bonny wrote about this song. How was the original song different?

6 Encourage students to explain the words in the Word Study box.

22 Dictionary skills

Aims: 1 Identifying the relevant meaning in a specific context.
2 Understanding how stress is shown.
3 The abbreviation ADJ. (See *Collins COBUILD Essential English Dictionary* study page 10 for types and positions of ADJ.)
4 Pronunciation: vowels: /uː/ **assume**, /ʌ/ **custom**, /ɜː/ **firm**, /əʊ/ **folk**; consonants: /k/, /g/, /f/, /m/, /j/ as in **yellow**, **assume**.

SB22

1 Students look up the words.

2 Ask students to put the two-syllable words into two groups according to their stress patterns.

Key: Words with stress on first syllable: **council, customs, firmly**. Stress on second syllable: **assume, engaged, estate**.

3 Write the new phonetic symbols on the board and ask students to find the words with these sounds in them. Revise the weak vowel /ə/ which also occurs in these words.

23 Review

Key:
a *Odd words out*   *Extra words*
1 assuming   finally
2 further   teacher/writer/
      listener/farmer
3 freedom   country
4 found   looked for
5 frequently   occasionally/not
      often
6 fed up   contented
7 folk   man
b thing is the missing word.
c 1 take   2 put   3 take   4 did
    5 go, going, go   6 take, go
    7 taken

LEXICAL OBJECTIVES

ambition 1 what you always wanted to be. *His original ambition was to be an engine driver.*
2 the desire to be successful, rich, powerful, famous Adj: *ambitious man* T
assume D
band 1 *a village band providing music for every occasion*
2 Head band, elastic band. T
3 range of numbers/ages. *In her age-band.* T
boss 1 the person in charge. (verb: *Don't boss him about!*)
chap informal word for boy/man. cf bloke, guy. *This fresh-faced chap* . . .
club 1 *joined the local folk club.*
2 a set of golf clubs. T
3 Clubs is one of the suits on playing cards, with hearts, diamonds, spades. T
council D
countryside 1 not town. *The life of the countryside still remains* . . .
crafts 1 making things by hand. *Old country crafts. Craftsmen, carpenters*
2 aircraft, space-craft. T
custom 1 see D.
2 Also: you go through **customs** when arriving from a foreign country (181)
3 = trade. *we get a lot of custom from foreigners.* cf customers. T
dancing singing and dancing
drama 1 music, dance and drama
engage D
engagement D
entertain 1 professional entertaining, to entertain their audiences
entertainment 1 . . . *in the 19th century, people made their own entertainments.*
estate 1 large area of land in the country belonging to one owner.
2 land in/near towns, industrial estates, housing estate. T
3 D
fed up unhappy, bored. *The older ones got fed up and they left.*
firm D
folk D
freedom 1 liberty *political freedom, freedom of speech* T
1.2 being allowed to do what you want. *have the freedom to roam the country*
gate 1 at an entrance *castle gate.*
1.2 at airports. Gate 97
generation 1 a group of people of a similar age or family position. *In my parents' generation* . . . T *music . . . handed on from generation to generation.*

guitar *playing the guitar.*
gypsy a race of travelling people. *Gypsies and travelling musicians.*
handicapped disabled, unable to live totally normal lives. *mentally handicapped / physically handicapped*
institute 1 organisation set up to do a particular kind of work. *Research Institute, Institute of Education. Women's Institutes exist all over Britain, set up mainly for housewives.*
instruments 1 *musical instruments, medical instruments.*
2 means/method. *The Labour Party is the only instrument of change open to them.* T
involvement 1 being involved with, taking part in. *Close involvement with the life of the countryside.*
isolated 1 alone, cut off, a long way from other places. *In its small isolated communities.*
2 lonely. *She lived an isolated life* T
junior 1 not senior, i.e. younger. *the Yetminster Junior Dance Display team,* cf Junior School (for 7–11s)
kingdom 1 a country ruled by a King or Queen, i.e. not a Republic. *United Kingdom. The animal/plant kingdom.*
mental 1 to do with the mind. *mental health, mentally handicapped.*
native 1 where you were born and brought up. . . . *love of their native Dorset.*
2 *He's a native of Dorset.* T
3 native language = mother tongue. *native speakers talking on topics* . . .
original 1 earliest, first. *In the original song the gypsy had no castle* . . . *The original idea.*
print 1 *a printing firm, in the printing trade. I was a printer beforehand. Printed in Hong Kong.*
republic 1 country not ruled by a king. *the Republic of Ireland.* T
ritual 1 customary or regularly followed way of doing things. *ceremonial customs and ritual dances.*
rural to do with the countryside. *music and customs of rural England.*
satisfaction 1 a feeling of pleasure. *She read what she had written with satisfaction. Job satisfaction.* T
satisfied 1 happy because you have got what you wanted. *satisfied customers* T
satisfy 1 *the songs satisfied a need in the people who* . . .
search D
seek, sought 1 to search for. (Formal word). *He sought his daughter at great speed. seek jobs/peace/a solution/ help.*
seldom D
valley 1 *down to the valley.*
variety 1 it has a good variety of . . . = a lot of different kinds of . . .
version 1 *a modern version of the same song / developing his own version.*

12T

Unit 3 Into business

The main theme of this unit is applying for jobs. Students begin by looking critically at letters of application and go on to discuss the essential features of these letters. They then listen to an informal radio interview about the business side of entertainment, before going on to discuss and practise job interviews. Finally there is discussion on retirement, and a light-hearted interview with one of the Yetties on his work experience and his 'early retirement'.

OBJECTIVES

Lexical objectives are in TB33

Discussion topics

a Applying for jobs. (24,25,29,31)
b Running a business. (27)
c Retirement and children's jobs. (32)

Social skills

a Written correspondence – giving the right impression. (24,25)
b The conventions of formal written correspondence. (24,25)
c Giving advice and coming to a decision. (29)
d Expressing attitudes towards people. (29)
e Commenting on the value or relevance of what is said. (30)

Communication skills

Written correspondence:
a Planning the content. (24,25)
b Organising information clearly. (24,25)
Interviews:
c Planning radio interviews and job interviews. (27,29)
d Anticipating questions. (27)

Grammar and discourse

a Imperative and modals for advice. (24,25,29,31)
b Countable, uncountable and mass nouns. (26)
c Two uses of **do**: 1) In positive statements for emphasis. 2) **do/did** etc. with a noun, e.g. *do a course/an appenticeship.* (28)
d Some phrases with **that**: *That's right/interesting.* (30)
e Practice Book Grammar Word: **as**.

Dictionary skills (26)

a Countable and uncountable (and mass) nouns. (26)
b Pronunciation: vowels: /ɛ/ **dress**, /ɛɪ/ **training**, /ɒ/ **job**, /ɔː/ **organise**; consonants: /n/, /ŋ/ **training**, /w/ **well**, **equipment**, /ʃ/ **ship**, **attention**, /dʒ/ **job**, **knowledge**. (26)

24 Letters of application

Aims: 1 Written correspondence – giving the right impression.
2 The conventions of formal written correspondence.
3 Giving advice and coming to a decision.
4 Evaluating the effectiveness of two letters, and comparing them.
Note: Other types of business letters are dealt with in Unit 13.

Lexis: academic, achieve, (achievement T), **application, currently, engineering, enthusiasm, factor, interview, manager, opening, organisation, personality, progress, sign/signature, specific** T, **structure, suitable, superior, training/typing**
Revision: **scheme, nature** (= personality), **success, in view of, limited** = not many), **That's a good point, thinking in terms of...**

1 Discuss the unit title 'Into business' – normally used when someone is going into business with someone else; or when going into business as a career.

2 Find out if any students in your class have ever written (or had to read) letters of application for jobs. Ask what kind of details they would expect to find in such letters.

Reading SB24a

3 Students in pairs help each other to read and understand the letters, evaluating them, and looking for the points listed. Encourage students to guess words if they don't know them. Write up the target words on the board, as required.

4 Discuss their opinions as a class. Which letter did they think the most effective?

Listening SB24a [24a]

5 Explain that Bruce and Edmund had read the two letters. What differences did they find between them? Did they come to the same conclusions as your students? Play the recording, and discuss what they thought.

Key: Letter 1: **academic, success, Finnigan** wrongly spelt. Illegible/unreadable signature. Keeps repeating itself. ('It's a bit airy-fairy' = it is not very specific.)
Letter 2: has more detailed information, a better structure, i.e. organisation of ideas, and shows a willingness to work.

6 Students do the Word Study. Practise any useful phrases.

Task SB24b

7 Explain that **golden** is normally a colour, but it can be used to mean excellent, e.g. **a golden opportunity**. What could it mean in the term **Golden Rules**? Accept all students' ideas for now.

8 Students work in pairs to think of five 'Golden Rules', and write them down. Help them to write accurately. If they need some help, play the beginning of the recording to give them the first few rules.

Report SB24b

9 Students each take turns to tell the class one rule they have thought of. Take notes of students' examples. Build up a list on the board. As a class, choose the ten best as a final list. Number them.

Listening SB24b [24b]

10 As students listen to the recording, they could note down any useful Golden Rules they had not thought of. Then let them adjust the final list. Keep to ten rules, make students justify any changes they want to make to the list.

Unit 3
Into business

Letters of application

a Which of these two letters do you think is more effective, and why?
Say which letter:

    has spelling mistakes. (How many?)
    has an illegible signature.
    has more detailed information.
    shows a willingness to work.
    has the better structure.
    keeps repeating itself.

1

> 26 Araney Rd.
> BRISTOL,
> BS6 51L
> Tel: Bristol (0272) 27603
>
> Mr. A. Finnigan,
> Crestmore Hotel,
> Braymead Road,
> Kingswood,
> Bristol
> BS15 4EW
>
> Dear Mr Finnegan,
>
> I am currently in full time education studying three a level subjects in which I aim to achieve accademic success this summer. I have 7 o level passes including English and Maths.
>
> I have been considering the possabilities within the field of hotel management However training schemes within the town are very limited.
>
> I was recently interviewed by Mr Blake at the White Horse Hotel for the position of trainee assistant manager. In view of my qualifications he told me of the training schemes within your company and gave me your address.
>
> I am very interested in your training scheme and feel sure I would be suitable to do the job.
> This is a career I have come increasingly to feel is suited to my outgoing personality and ambitious nature. As a career is important to me I have always felt that mobility is a necessary factor to success. I hope you can help me.
>
> Yours faithfully,
> P. Asquun

2

> 5 Linacre Avenue,
> Weston-Super-Mare,
> AVON,
> BS23 4QE.
>
> Telephone
> Bristol (0272) 27171
>
> 12th August 1979
> Personnel Manager,
> Mentor (Engineering) Limited,
> 184-186 Carrow Road,
> BRISTOL,
> BS4 1PT.
>
> Ref AS/123
>
> Dear Sir,
> I am interested in the position of wages clerk which you advertised on 4th August in the Bristol Evening Post.
>
> I am 16 years old and I left school at the end of the Summer term. I have passed CSE examinations in four subjects which are Mathematics (Grade 1), English and History (Grade 2) and Art (Grade 3). I studied typing at school and passed the RSA Grade 1 typing examination.
>
> I have always wanted to do office work and I enjoyed mathematics at school. Also I feel a job in an organisation like yours would be likely to lead to further career prospects.
>
> I have had a Saturday job for the last nine months working as a sales assistant in Smith's shoe shop on the High Street.
>
> I shall be happy to provide any further information you require and am available to come for an interview at any time.
>
> Yours faithfully,
> Sally Bright
> SALLY BRIGHT

WORD STUDY
Link the words or phrases that are similar in meaning.

whereas	find, notice
come across	continues
not specific	while
for me anyway	appropriate
structure	saying the same thing
repeating itself	as far as I'm concerned
suitable	plan, organisation
goes on to say	general, a bit vague

24a Listen to what Bruce and Edmund thought about them. How did they answer the questions above? Did you agree with them about which was the most effective letter?

b A magazine produced by the Midland Bank for its younger customers gave ten *Golden Rules* for writing letters of application. Can you guess what five of them might be?

In pairs make a list, then tell the class. While listening, note down other good rules, then choose the ten best rules and make a final list.

10 GOLDEN RULES FOR YOUR LETTER OF APPLICATION

24b Listen to the Golden Rules that Edmund and Bruce wrote down. Were there any you didn't have?

25 Golden rules

a Compare the list of rules you wrote with these. How many of the same ones did you get? Are any of yours more helpful?

---

10 GOLDEN RULES FOR YOUR LETTER OF APPLICATION

1. Write clearly.
2. Keep your letter short and to the point.
3. State what job you are applying for.
4. Make the information you give relevant to the job, and firm, so read the advertisement carefully first.
5. Use plain writing paper and ink, not pencil. Or type your letter if you can do it neatly.
6. Draft out what you want to say in rough first.
7. Give all the information you're asked for.
8. Check your spelling and punctuation.
9. State when you are available for interview.
10. Print your name clearly under your signature.

---

b Dos and don'ts

These specific points were originally written beside the letters in section 24 and arrowed to the text. Here they have been mixed up. Which point was where?

HOW NOT TO DO IT

If you start your letter 'Dear Mr . . .' end with 'Yours sincerely'.

Avoid sounding negative or pessimistic.

State the purpose of your letter in the first paragraph.

Make sure you spell the name correctly.

Unreadable signature.

Avoid sounding over confident.

Don't give the impression you're unlikely to stay long. The employer hopes your training will be followed by a period of faithful service.

HOW IT SHOULD BE DONE

State where you saw the job advertised.

Print your name clearly beneath your signature.

Name and address of firm. Reference number if there is one. Use the person's name if you know it.

Include your phone number if you have one.

State your qualifications in brief.

'Yours faithfully' is correct unless you address the person by name - 'Dear Mr. Black' – then put 'Yours sincerely'.

Name of the person you are writing to if you know it and/or his/her position.

---

c Second draft

▷ Rewrite the first letter making appropriate improvements.

d Write your own

▷ **Either** – if you have a job – decide on one position/job in your present place of work, and write the *ideal* letter of application for it, as if from the *ideal* candidate.

▷ **Or** – if you don't have a job – decide on your *ideal* job and write a letter applying for it.

26 *Dictionary skills*

Count or uncount?
Read carefully the entries for noun count and noun uncount in the Dictionary extracts.

Now say whether the coloured words are COUNT or UNCOUNT:

They want advice on what to do.
She was wearing a short black dress.
More money is spent on dress than on books.
She's had nine months' experience.
She provided me with a very useful piece of information.
I'd like some information about trains.
. . . advances in scientific knowledge.

How do you know?

Look up the following words and say whether they are COUNT, UNCOUNT or can be both.

factor   organisation   job   education   interest
attention   money   equipment   training   ice   luck

27 Radio interview

Bonny Sartin was interviewed recently about the business side of the Yetties folk singing. List the questions you would have asked.

27 What questions did the interviewer in fact ask Bonny? How many of your questions did Bonny answer?

25 Golden rules

Aims: 1 Giving advice in writing and evaluating advice.
2 Understanding evaluative comments.
3 Structuring a letter so the information is clear.
4 Planning the content of a letter.
5 Redrafting and improving a letter.
6 Writing a suitable letter of application.
7 Some conventions of formal letter writing.

Lexis: avoid, golden, sound (vb), **neatly, signature, specific, training**
Revision: **firm, relevant, service**
Phrases: **to the point, in rough, state the purpose, give the impression**

Reading   SB25a PB25

1 Students read and compare lists of rules. Discuss any useful words or phrases.

Reading and task   SB25b

2 Students match points to specific sections of the letters in section 24.

   Key: Letter 1: includes the name of the person written to and the name and address of the firm.
   'Dear Mr . . .' should end 'yours sincerely'.
   Paragraph 2 sounds negative.
   Mr Finnigan is spelt incorrectly.
   The signature is unreadable.
   The last paragraph sounds over confident and 'mobility' suggests he doesn't want to stay long.
   Letter 2: states the purpose of the letter and where the job was advertised.
   Name is printed clearly beneath the signature.
   Includes the name and address of the firm and the job reference number. Ends 'yours faithfully'.
   Ends 'yours faithfully'.
   Both letters: include their phone numbers and state their qualifications in brief.

Writing   SB25c

3 Students singly, in pairs or groups plan and rewrite the first letter. Tell students this letter could be a lot shorter. Then let students compare their letters.

Writing   SB25d

4 Discuss which of the two kinds of letters your students might have to write (or read and act upon) themselves. Suggest that students with similar needs sit together, and plan and write one letter between them.

5 Help students to organise and write their letters accurately. Display the finished letters so that other students can read them. Ask students to find the two letters that are most/least similar in content and purpose.

26 Dictionary skills

Aims: 1 To show that some words in English remain singular in form even though they may seem to have plural meanings, e.g. **furniture**.
2 To show there are some words which have both countable an uncountable forms and that these can have different meanings, e.g. **organisation/s**.
3 Practice in using a dictionary 'Study Page' and understanding a grammatical explanation. (See the entry 'Nouns' in *Collins COBUILD Essential English Dictionary* study pages 532 and 533.)
4 To practise looking up and checking the potential meanings and uses of such words.
5 Pronunciation: vowels: /ɛ/ **dress**, /ɛɪ/ **training**, /ɒ/ **job**, /ɔː/ **organise**; consonants: /n/, /ŋ/ **training**, /w/ **well**, **equipment**, /ʃ/ **ship, attention**, /dʒ/ **job, knowledge**. (26)

SB26 PB26

1 This may well be the first time students have met a lengthy written grammatical explanation. Help and encourage them to read and understand the gist of it. Explain COUNT = countable etc.

2 Give students time to work out whether the coloured words are COUNT or UNCOUNT. Encourage them to refer back to the Study Page if they are not sure.

   Key: All UNCOUNT in the sense in which they are used here, except: **dress** (1) which has the indefinite article – **a** *short black dress*.

   Key: COUNT: factor, job
   UNCOUNT: education, equipment, training, luck
   Can be both: organisation, interest, attention, money, ices

3 Try to get students to relate some of these words to their own lives. e.g. Do they ever wear national dress? What's it like? What organisations do they receive letters from?

4 Write the new phonetic symbols on the board and ask students to find the words with these sounds in them. Again point out the weak vowel /ə/ which occurs twice in **information**. Students can look up some of the other words and practise reading the phonetic script.

---

27 Radio interview

Aims: 1 Preparing to carry out a radio-style interview – choice of possible questions.
2 Listening for what questions were in fact answered, and to see how many questions were actually asked.
3 To promote speculation on how such folk/pop groups find work.

Lexis: agent, contract, gradually, interview, manager, occasionally, permanent
Phrases: **by word of mouth, As far as . . . is concerned . . . , came to a decision**

Lead-in   SB27

1 Remind students that Bonny Sartin is the leader of the Yetties group. Remind them of how the Yetties started out – as workers in the printing trade, a state nurse, etc. before leaving their original jobs, turning professional and going into business as a group.

2 Ask students in pairs or groups to imagine themselves to be in the radio interviewer's position, and think up some serious questions to ask Bonny about how the Yetties find work. Students should write about three or four questions.

Listening and note-taking   SB27 27 PB27

3 Play the recording. Ask students to listen for the answers to the questions they thought of. Which were in fact answered/not answered?

4 Play the recording again. This time ask students:
   a) to list the four ways in which the Yetties find work.
   b) to summarise how they got their first long trip overseas.

   Key: a) By word of mouth (i.e. one person tells another); occasional advertising in folk magazines; foreign tours go through an agent, with a contract; mostly through informal chats on the phone, through Bonny.
   b) Sample summary: Jim Lloyd, their manager, told the British Council about the Yetties. The Council sent someone to some of their concerts around London, and decided they were a suitable group for an overseas tour.

5 Optional summary writing: Ask students to write up a neat final version of the summary from note 4b) above. If they wish, they can check on the facts again before writing by reading the transcript.

28 Grammar

Aims: 1 Emphatic uses of **do**.
2 **Do** used with nouns.

SB28

1 Ask students to read through the four sets of examples and do the first exercise.

> **Key:** a ... I **do** wish he would come to the party. (3)
> b ... we **did** try our best. (1)
> c **Do** please write to us while you're away. (4)
> d The children **do** annoy me when they behave like that. (2)

(Other common phrases in group 4: *Hello – do come in! Do sit down! I'm dreadfully sorry! Do forgive me.*)

2 What other uses of **do/did** with a noun can students think of?
(*a bit of work, the shopping/housework, some walking/ driving/gardening/football practice etc., She did a good job. He does a good deal of talking.*)

> **Key:** It was Roger who did medical training after leaving school.
> It was Bonny and Mac who did an apprenticeship in printing.

3 Ask students if they can remember who (in Unit 1) talked about doing concerts. Who said they didn't do much bathing? (It was Edmund who said 'I do a few concerts and competitions.' It was Bruce who said 'We don't do much bathing now because of the nuclear pollution.')

4 Ask what your students often do/have done/are hoping to do in the way of sports, education etc.

29 Job interviews

Aims: 1 Giving impressions of people.
2 Commenting on the value or relevance of what is said.
3 Summing up general points at the end of stages in discourse.
4 Taking part in interviews.

Lexis: absolute, apparently, avoid, dress, dull, hobbies, interviewer, organisation, sum up
Phrases: **time to spare, in a business-like way, it looks as though, so much the better**
Phrases from the recording: **pay careful attention to ..., generally speaking, living up to the image that you gave ..., that amount to the same thing, in absolute silence, you can get stuck, keep to the point, fall into the same category**

Writing SB29a PB29

1 This can be done singly or in pairs. Students pick one person from the row of candidates in the picture, and describe the person's appearance in an evaluative way. They should write what they can tell about their manner.

2 You may want to give students some useful phrases to start them off. (*He looks as if he's about to ..., a bit casual in the way he dresses; seems a bit 'don't carish' in attitude; too keen and talkative*, etc.)

3 Students pass their reports round the class. They read other people's, and guess which candidate each refers to.

4 As a class, work out how many students wrote about the most popular candidate. Discuss why. Who was the least impressive candidate? Why?

Task   SB29b

5 Students in pairs try to guess what five of the DOs and DON'Ts were. Help them write them down in note form, then read one or two to the class.

6 Pause the recording where required, to allow students to list (in note form) the advice that was given.

7 Students as a class decide on the best five points.

8 Finally let students turn over to section 31 where they can read what the Midland Bank advised. Were all their five points included? What about the other advice?

Interview practice   SB29b

9 You may like to divide your students up on the basis of what experience of interviews/interviewing each person has had. More senior members of the class can form an 'advisory panel' and conduct the interviews, and other students can be interviewees. Or vice versa!

10 Try to ensure that this is a genuinely helpful and constructive session. The groups of three must first agree on the type of job, what it involves, and whether the candidate is to be himself/herself or act a part. Go round to groups as they plan. Get them to tell you what they are planning – in English!

11 Once the 'job' is decided upon, suggest the 'candidate' leaves the group of three, while the 'interviewing panel' decide what questions they will ask. Candidates should sit together and practise answering typical interview-style questions – either as themselves, or acting a person with a different character.

12 After the role-play interview, students are going to evaluate each other's performance. Before the role-play discuss what they might look out for and comment on. (Positive comments are always more welcome! Perhaps suggest students think of two good things about each interview, and one point that could be improved.)

13 Students in their groups of three act out their 'interviews'. Start with the candidate entering the room. Set a rough time limit for each group – two or three minutes? Suggest students write comments as they watch each one.

14 After the interviews allow time for discussion and comments as a class. Wherever possible, dwell on the strong points!

30 Language study

Aims: 1 Spoken discourse – comments with **that**.
2 Commenting on the value or relevance of what is said.

SB30a/b

1 Students read the examples and then do the matching exercise.

> **Key:** 1 c, 2 a, 3 d, 4 b.

2 Further examples from this unit: (Give the first part and see if students can supply a suitable comment with **that**.)

EE: So the aim is to have five.
BB: Oh, that's right, yes.

EE Nerves can make you miss street signs.
BB Indeed, yes. That's true, yes.

Grammar

More uses of do

Bonny said:

> We do .. occasionally advertise in ... one or two folk magazines.

We sometimes use do for emphasis.

1 For contrast or contradiction:
> *I'm not very fond of sport generally, but I do like swimming.*

2 For reinforcement:
> *He plays a lot of games and he does enjoy swimming.*

3 With verbs like **wish, hope, believe:**
> *I do hope you will be able to come round sometime.*
> *I do wish Jim didn't waste so much time.*

4 When you are giving someone advice or an invitation:
> *Do please come round and see us sometime.*
> *Do arrive in plenty of time.*

Put the word do, does or did into these sentences, making any changes necessary, and then say if they belong to group 1, 2, 3, or 4 above.

a *George is great fun. I wish he would come to the party.*
b *I'm afraid we didn't succeed, but we tried our best.*
c *Please write to us while you're away.*
d *The children annoy me when they behave like that.*

Do is often used with nouns like **work:**
> *He does a lot of work at the weekend.*

Can you remember which of the Yetties:
> ... did medical training after leaving school?
> ... did a five year apprenticeship in printing?

29 Job interviews

a What is your opinion of these candidates? Who is most/least likely to get the job and why?

Choose one candidate and write a short report on their appearance and manner. Say whether you would recommend them for a job with an organisation you know.

Can other students guess which of the people you have written about?

b **Advice for candidates attending interviews**
The Midland Bank magazine gave ten DOs and DON'Ts. Can you guess what five of them were?

29b Did you have the same points as Bruce, Edmund and Elizabeth?
Make a list of the points each of them made, and compare it with yours. Now choose the best five points.

Interview practice
In groups of three, plan to act out the first one or two minutes of an interview. Prepare about three or four initial *warming up* questions.
Candidates can choose to play the part as themselves or act the part of someone being over serious, very nervous, etc. Act it for the class to watch and comment on.

30 Language study

Comments with that
We often use phrases with That's ... to comment on what someone has said.

a Look at these extracts from the recordings in this unit:

EE: It looks as if you're interested.
BB: That's it, exactly, yes. (29)
BB: Don't tell lies.
EE: Mm. That's a good one. (29)
EE: They all fall into the same sort of general category really.
BB: That's interesting that, yeah. (29)
BB: Offer to provide any more information if they so wish.
EL: That's a good point, yeah. (24)

b Which comment from a–d below goes best with each of these statements:

1 I've never been as scared like that before or since. (34)
2 ... it's something ... that only I know how to do, and nobody else knows the secret – of how I can fly. (47)
3 ... it's about ... refugees in Hong Kong ... still in the camps there.
4 Have you any particular definite plans or ambitions?

a Well, that's quite exciting.
b Well, that's difficult really.
c That's very frightening.
d That's a terrible business.

31 Dos and don'ts at the interview

Compare this list with yours.

- **Do arrive in plenty of time.** If you think you may have trouble finding the place, set out early. You can always explore the neighbourhood if you've half an hour to spare.

- **Don't let your clothes be too extreme.** Dress in a business-like way.

- **It's polite to knock before you enter an office if the door is closed.**

- **Don't smoke!**

- **Don't put your handbag or briefcase on the interviewer's desk** — it creates a barrier between you.

- **Don't cross your arms and legs** — it looks as though you're withholding information.

- **Do sit still.** Fidgeting with jewellery or shuffling your feet can be very distracting for the interviewer.

- **Don't exaggerate your abilities or achievements.** You're likely to be found out in the end.

- **Be ready with the basic facts and information about yourself** — your education, experience, interests and hobbies.

- **Do make a graceful exit.** Thank your interviewer; walk to the door; don't rush. And if you can give him or her a smile as you leave the room, so much the better.

32 Retirement

a What do you understand by the term 'retirement'? At what age do people retire in your country?

32b b Mac, a member of the Yetties, was interviewed about his early working life. The interviewer found out that Mac had had to retire at the age of ten! How was this possible?

c Find out what jobs other students in your group did as children, or as their very first jobs. Did anyone have any similar working experiences to Mac?

▶ Plan a short summary of your experiences to tell the class.

---

33 REVIEW

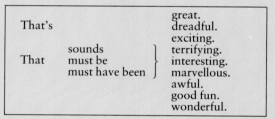
UNIT 3

a Comments with that
Suggest comments from the box on the right for these statements:

We went to London for a holiday.
It was really dark and lonely.
It cost more than £250.
It was the best film I've ever seen.
I thought the plane was going to crash.

That's		great.
		dreadful.
		exciting.
	sounds	terrifying.
That	must be	interesting.
	must have been	marvellous.
		awful.
		good fun.
		wonderful.

b Useful phrases
Complete these sentences with words or phrases from below. Which one is left over?

a *You may well need to accept a _____ before finding a permanent position.*
b *The company or organisation may ask you to sign a _____ for a specific period of time.*
c *Before accepting a permanent job, you should find out about _____, _____, and, if you are interested in promotion, whether a _____ exists.*
d *Some organisations offer _____ for school leavers so that they can learn the job.*
e *It's important to create a _____ at the interview.*
f *Giving parties is fun, but I always forget how much _____ is involved to start with.*

> training schemes
> suitable career structure
> temporary job
> terms of service
> experienced
> contract
> organization
> good impression
> rates of pay

NEW WORDS IN UNIT 3

absolute	knock
achieve	knowledge D
achievement	luck D
agent	manager
apparently	neat/ly
application	occasionally
avoid	opening
contract	organisation D
cottage	permanent
create/d	personality
currently	progress
dress/ed D	rush
dull	signature
engineering	spare
enthusiasm	specific
exaggerate	structure
extreme	suitable
factor D	sum
golden	superior
gradually	temporary
interview	training D

42 new words
TOTAL SO FAR 114

Aim: Grammar revision of forms of the imperative and modals for advice.

Lexis: **achievement**, **apply** T, **create**, **dress**, **exaggerate**, **experience/d**, **extreme**, **interviewer**, **hobbies**, **knock**, **rush**, **spare**, **still**
Phrase: **That applies to your personal life**

SB31

This is the key to section 29. See section 29 note 8 for procedure.

---

 32 **Retirement**

Aims: 1 Understanding an interview.
2 Revision of **would** for past habit: *At weekends you would help. We'd get the cows in for milking every night.*
3 Carrying out a small survey requiring interviews with students.
4 Summarising and writing up a report on the results of the survey.

Lexis: **cottage**, **retire/retirement**
Revision: **involve/involvement**
Phrases: **it was the case of . . .**, **bring in a rule**, **highly illegal**, **high speed races**, **accepted practice**

Class discussion   SB32a

1 Discuss what is meant by retirement, and how it varies from country to country and between the sexes. Do students remember, in Unit 1, that Bruce told us he was a retired teacher? Normally in Britain men retire at 65 and women at 60.

Listening   SB32b

2 Mac talks about his farmwork. Before playing the recording, tell students he had to retire at the age of ten. Ask them to speculate on how this was possible. Get students to list the kinds of farmwork Mac might have done. Finally play the recording.

Key: He started driving tractors (being too small at eight or nine for heavy farmwork, lifting etc.). But the Government brought in a rule to prevent children under thirteen driving tractors, so Mac had to retire from tractor driving at ten years old!

3 Point out the two examples of **would** in Mac's speech – referring to things that happened regularly in the past.

Task and report   SB32c   PB32

4 Students ask each other about their first jobs.

5 Help students write a summary to show or read to the class.

---

33 **Review**

Key and notes:
a Get students to make up some short dialogues using the table and practise these in pairs.
b a temporary job   b contract
c rates of pay, terms of service, suitable career structure   d training schemes   e good impression
f organisation

LEXICAL OBJECTIVES

absolute 1 total. *in absolute silence*
achieve 1 be successful after effort. *I aim to achieve academic success . . .*
achievement *Don't exaggerate your achievements.*
agent 1 someone you pay to do business for you. *Do you actually have an agent yourselves? estate agent, travel agent*
*****amount** 3 adds up to, is worth. *Yeah, that amounts to the same thing.*
apparently it appears that. *Apparently his interview lasted about 30 minutes*
application 1 *a letter of application.*
*****apply** 3 be relevant to. *That applies to your personal life as well*
avoid 1 stop something happening. *How to avoid an accident* T
2 not to do it. *Avoid sounding negative.*
contract 1 legal agreement. *That's all official and done with contracts.*
cottage small house in the country. *one of the farm cottages*
create 1 make, produce, generate. *it creates a barrier between you.*
2 to make a fuss (informal) *Dad's always creating about what I wear!*
currently now, at present. *I am currently in full time education.*
dress, dressed D
dull 1 uninteresting, boring, not lively. *a pretty dull sort of person.*
2 rather dark – of a colour. *a dull grey sky, dull weather* T
3 not intelligent. *dull children* T
engineering 1 *An engineering firm, an electrical/mechanical engineer*
enthusiasm 1 great interest. *Display some sort of enthusiasm for the job.*
exaggerate 1 say something which is more than the true facts, to impress someone. *Don't exaggerate your abilities or your achievements.*
extreme 1 very great in degree or intensity. *Extreme cold.*
2 more unusual or severe than you would expect. *Don't let your clothes be too extreme. extreme conditions/views*
3 far, the furthest point. *the extreme south.* T
factor 1 a single part that combines with others to form the cause of something. *Mobility is a necessary factor to success. social and economic factors.*
golden 1 made of gold, or looks like gold. *Girl with golden hair* T
2 golden rules – important rules.
gradually 1 slow, happening over a length of time. *The whole thing gradually developed.*
interview 1 radio interview. *She was interviewed on TV.* Also: interviewer

2 a job interview. *My son went for an interview . . .*
knock 1 knock on a door. *It's polite to knock before you enter an office.*
2 *He knocked the glass over.* T
3 hit someone hard. *He was knocked unconscious/knocked out/down*
knowledge D
luck D
manager 1 person in charge, boss. *assistant manager*
neat 1 tidy, clean, smart. *Write neatly or type. in neat writing.*
2 clever, efficient. *a neat timetable.*
occasionally sometimes but not often.
*****opening** opportunities for employment. *Say how you heard of the opening.*
organisation D
permanent 1 not temporary. *We don't have a permanent agent.*
personality 1 your character or nature
2 *a famous television personality* T
progress 1 gradually getting nearer to achieving something. *Show an interest in making progress within the firm. technological progress. good progress.* verb: *Health care in the third world has not progressed fast enough.*
2 Meeting in progress = happening
rush 1 do something/go quickly. *Walk to the door. Don't rush. in a rush. = in a hurry.*
2 *a rush of air, the rushing river, The water rushed in to the boat.*
*****sign, signed** 1 a gesture. *She gave a sign and they sat down.* T
2 symbols or notice. *You might miss the street signs. '%' a percent sign.*
3 a sign of something. *No sign of rain*
4 to write your name. *Print your name at the bottom as well as signing it.*
signature the way you sign your name
*****sound** 2 seem, give the appearance of. *Sound motivated for the job.*
spare 1 an extra one you keep in case you need it. *Have you a spare pen?* T
2 with time or money. *If you've half an hour to spare . . .*
3 to make available. *Can you spare me a minute, please?* T
specific 1 precise, exact. *Be specific*
*****still** 3 not moving. *Do sit still!*
structure 1 the way in which something is organised, or made up. *It has a much better structure, that letter.* Verb: *You should structure your life so that . . .*
2 framework or system. *the company developed a good career structure . . .* T
suitable 1 appropriate for. *I feel sure I would be suitable for the job.*
sum 1 *a sum of money, huge sums spent on . . .*
2 a mathematical sum.
3 to sum up – to state very briefly. *So we could almost sum up a lot of our points as being self-discipline.* Phrase: in sum = in short.
summary 1 a short spoken or written account. *Write a summary/Summarise*
superior 1 better, or higher quality.
2 senior, in a higher position. T
3 if you feel superior, you feel more important. *It is a bit 'pushy', being a bit superior about it. cf inferior.*
temporary T 1 not permanent. *a temporary job/arrangement*
training D

16T

Unit 4 — Survivors

This unit is about people's fears, and surviving frightening experiences. The theme is introduced by a poem which is very telling. It leads in to a general discussion of the sorts of things that frighten us. This involves the expression of feelings and attitudes, in contrast to the more factual discussions of the first two units. The unit then looks at two newspaper articles about frightening experiences. Students talk about their own reactions and hear a native speaker talking about his. Finally there is an exercise in summary writing based on versions of the same story from two different newspapers.

OBJECTIVES

Lexical objectives are in TB42

Discussion topics and tasks

a Fears and worries. (34)
b Anecdotes about childhood fears. (34,35)
c Speculating on the outcome of a narrative. (35,36,38)

Social skills

a Telling personal anecdotes. (34)
b Conveying feelings. (34,36)

Communication skills

Narrative:
a Including relevant description. (36)
b Using the title to predict content. (35)
c Telling and summarising a story. (35,36,40)
d Asking questions to elicit specific information. (34,38)
e Using the passive to focus on a sequence of events. (39)

Grammar and discourse

a Expressing similarities and contrasts. (35,36,40)
b Descriptive phrases: relatives, participles, and prepositional phrases. (36)
c Ergative verbs: *He **cooked** the rice./The rice **cooked** slowly. She **grows** flowers./The flowers **are growing** well.* (37)
d Verbs ending in **-ing**. (39)
e Past perfect in narrative. (39)
f The passive in newspaper narrative. (39)
g Some phrasal verbs. (41)
h Practice Book Grammar Word: **in**.

Dictionary skills (41)

Encoding skills – finding suitable phrases. (41)

---

34 Fear

A recording of the poem is on the Student's Cassette only.

> **Aims:** 1 Discussion of emotions.
> 2 Reading a poem.
> 3 Comparing two people's fears.
> 4 Reading out loud with suitable expression.
>
> **Lexis: darkness, downstairs, extent, heights, hide/hid/ hidden, insects, narrow, poem, poetry, scared, shame, sheer, switch, trousers**
> Revision: **deep, fall, fear, blocked it out**
> Phrases: **hold your breath, to some extent, I must admit, to my knowledge** (= as far as I know), **they don't bother me** (= I don't worry about them), **a sheer drop, scared stiff**

Task   SB34a PB34

1 Students discuss the line from the poem, and what it could mean. Who might have said it? Why?

17T

Reading   SB34b

2 Let students read the poem. Encourage them to guess words (like **ripping off**) they don't know. Demonstrate any words that are fun to act out.

3 Students in pairs discuss the poem's title.

4 Students choose two verses (or you can share out the verses round the class) and practise reading them aloud.

Task and class discussion   SB34c

5 Draw attention to the colour pictures. (Notice the parachutist's broken cord!) Students in pairs or groups compare very briefly some of the things they are afraid of.

6 Discuss their findings informally as a class. Do not go into this in too great detail at this stage. They will discuss childhood fears in depth later. If anyone brings up fear of heights, ask what high buildings they have been up. Has anyone been up a lighthouse? (This is in preparation for Bruce's story on tape in section 34e.)

Task   SB34d

7 Give students a minute or so to think quietly and recall their own childhood fears and/or frightening experiences. Then they can tell each other.

Planning and report   SB34d

8 Help students express clearly the story they have chosen to tell the class. After hearing each story, agree on a title for it. Finally vote on the most frightening experience.

Listening   SB34e   34e

10 Students listen to Chris and Bruce and take brief notes of their fears. How many of their fears have already been mentioned by students? Who can remember exactly what happened to Bruce on the lighthouse?

11 Go through the target words and phrases for this section. Make sure students know the meanings of **fear**. Teach (briefly) the informal expression **No fear** as in *Coming for a walk? No fear – not in this rain!* as it comes up as the punchline of a joke in Unit 5.

Writing   SB34e

12 Students use their notes to make three good sentences.

13 Optional writing: Students can use the transcripts to check on the facts in Bruce's lighthouse story, and then write a clear account of what happened to him.

---

35 What's the story?

> **Aims:** 1 Using the title of a news item to predict content.
> 2 To invent and tell their own stories.
> 3 To compare one story with another.
>
> **Lexis: bet, Empire, improve on**
> Phrase: **thinking along the lines of ...**

This is preparation for the next section where students will be reading the actual news story. Don't let them turn over yet!

Task, planning and report   SB35

1 Students follow the instructions. You may need to help with words like **parachute, elastic rope, stunt** etc.

2 Students tell their version to the class. Compare as they finish each story. Tell students to keep their notes safely.

Listening   SB35   35

3 Students listen to Bruce's version, and say whose it was most similar to. In what ways could they improve his story?

The Golden Gate Bridge is in California. The Bristol Suspension Bridge is in the South West of England.

Unit 4
Survivors

34 Fear...

a What can your imagination find in the picture below?
Discuss with each other what this could mean:

'From the light switch to my bed it's the Longest Journey in the World.'

34b **b** Read the poem. Choose two verses and practise reading them out loud.

THE LONGEST JOURNEY IN THE WORLD

'Last one to bed
  has to switch out the light.'
    It's just the same every night.
      There's a race.
        I'm ripping off my trousers and shirt,
          he's kicking off his shoes and socks.

    'My sleeve's stuck.'
    'This button's too big for its button-hole.'
  'Have you hidden my pyjamas?'
'Keep your hands off mine.'

If you win
  you get where it's safe
    before the darkness comes –
      but if you lose
    if you're last
you know what you've got coming up is
the journey from the light switch to the bed.
It's the longest Journey in the World.

'You're last tonight,' my brother says.
  And he's right.

    There is nowhere so dark
      as that room in that moment
        after I've switched out the light.

    There is nowhere so full of dangerous things,
    things that love dark places,
  things that breathe only when you breathe
and hold their breath when I hold mine.

So I have to say:
  'I'm not scared.'
    That face grinning in the pattern on the wall,
    isn't a face –
      'I'm not scared.'
      That prickle on the back of my neck
    is only the label on my pyjama jacket –
  'I'm not scared'.
That moaning-moaning is nothing
but water in a pipe –
  'I'm not scared.'

    Everything's going to be just fine
      as soon as I get into that bed of mine.
      Such a terrible shame
        it's always the same
      it takes so long
     it takes so long
    it takes so long
  to get there.

From the light switch
  to my bed
    it's the Longest Journey in the World.

Michael Rosen

c Which of the following are you afraid of? Ask each other.

    spiders and other insects ghosts the dark·
    the possibility of war heights anything else?

d What were your childhood fears? Exchange experiences with your partner. When in your life have you been really frightened? Describe what happened.

▶ Choose one story, and plan how to tell it to the class. As you listen to other people's stories agree on a title for each one. Write the titles down. ◀

Finally, take a vote on which must have been the most frightening experience.

▶ Write down the story you liked the best. ◀

34e **e** Listen to Chris and Bruce exchanging experiences. What were they each frightened of? Make a list, and note how frightened they were of each thing. Which of them had the most terrifying experience?

▶ Write three sentences comparing Chris and Bruce's fears. ◀

35 What's the story?

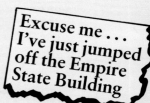

Excuse me... I've just jumped off the Empire State Building

This is the title of a news story. In small groups, make up a story which might have this headline in a newspaper. Write clear notes.

▶ Practise telling one story in your group, then one of you can tell the class. ◀

Clue: the Empire State Building is in New York and is over 86 floors high. There is a picture of it on this page.

35 Was Bruce's story like yours? Could you improve on Bruce's story? How?

17

36 # Excuse me ... I've just jumped off the Empire State building

This is a version of the news report giving only the bare facts of the story. Where something is missing square brackets have been added thus [ ].

a Read the story, and compare it with yours and Bruce's. Summarise the *factual* differences.

Excuse me ... I've just jumped off the Empire State Building

Ayoung artist [   ] decided to kill him-self. He took a lift to the 86th floor of the Empire State Building.

For a few moments, John Helms [   ] clung to the safety fence around the observation floor. He said a short prayer. Then he launched himself towards the specks of cars [   ] [   ].

He awoke half an hour later and found himself on a 2½-foot-wide ledge on the 85th floor [   ]. The unsuccessful artist decided that his prayer had been answered and gave up the idea of committing suicide.

He knocked on a window [   ] and crawled in to safety. Bill Steckman [   ] said: 'I couldn't believe it. You don't see a lot of guys coming in through the window of the 85th floor. I poured myself a stiff drink. ...'

Helms himself found that Christmas was not such a bad time to be alive, after all. Hundreds of families called him to offer him a home for the holidays.

36a Listen to Bruce's reaction. Was it like yours?

b Discuss where the following descriptive clauses fit in. Read the full story to each other, with the missing parts in place. Do you all have the same story?

of the offices of a television station
, where strong winds had blown him
, who was working there at the time,
, aged 26,
moving along Fifth Avenue,
, broke and alone in New York during Christmas 1977,
more than 1,000 feet below

WORD STUDY

Find words or phrases in the full story which are similar in meaning to:

with no money	street	served, got
on his own	powerful	discovered
speak to God	out of danger	telephoned
threw	men	

Practise saying the phrases from the story.

---

c Write your own
Write the bare facts of one of the stories you heard in section 34. Then write it like a newspaper report adding descriptive details.

---

37 # Grammar ....

Verbs with/without objects
a Find the objects of the verbs cook and improve.

'Can you cook rice?' 'This rice will cook in ten–fifteen minutes.'
'My Japanese has improved'. 'I read a lot to improve my Japanese'.

b Look carefully at the scene in the picture. Think too about the weather and the time of day. Find or think of something or someone that:

_____ *will probably drop.*
_____ *has just turned round.*
_____ *is smoking.*
_____ *is pouring out of the engine.*
_____ *is probably about to stop.*
_____ *is/are blowing in the wind.*
_____ *broke into pieces.*
_____ *were growing well.*

c What things can you ... ?

Think of one or two ways to complete these sentences with an object.

Was it you who grew _____?
Can I pour you _____?
Can I offer you _____?
Don't drop your _____!
Be careful not to break that _____.
Mind my drink! Don't knock _____ over!
The wind blew _____ into our eyes.

d Make a list of verbs that appear in **b** and **c**.

Aims: 1 Reading and reacting to a story.
2 Summarising a story, comparing it with other versions.
3 Comparing the reactions of two people.
4 Focusing on descriptive clauses and placing them appropriately back into the narrative to make the original full news report.
5 Writing up the bare outline of a story.
6 Expanding a story by adding suitable descriptive clauses.
7 Descriptive phrases/clauses: relatives, participles, and prepositional phrases.

Lexis: avenue, bet, blow, broke (informal = with no money), **empire, height, kill, launch, observation, pour, prayer, safety, survive, survivor**
Phrases: **commit suicide** T (Unit 16), **a stiff drink** (= a strong drink), **I'll bet**

Reading task   SB36a   36a   PB36

1 Students read the story and summarise the factual differences

2 Students listen for Bruce's reaction.

   Key: Bruce's reaction was 'That's even better isn't it?'

Reading   SB36b

3 Students work in pairs to decide where the descriptive clauses fit. Then they can read the story round the class, together with the replaced clauses. If there is any disagreement, get students to give reasons why they chose the position for the clauses that they did.

   Key: A young artist, broke and alone...
   For a few moments John Helms, aged 26...
   ... specks of cars moving along Fifth Avenue, more than 1,000 feet below
   ... on the 85th floor, where strong winds had blown him.
   ... on a window of the offices of a television station Bill Steckman, who was working there at the time.

4 Help students with the Word Study.

   Key: broke, alone, said a short prayer, launched, avenue, strong, in to safety, guys, poured, found, called.

5 Check students understand the other new target words. Discuss why this unit is called 'Survivors'.

Writing   SB36c

6 Ask students, in pairs, to find the list of titles and any notes they made of each other's stories in section 34. Each pair should choose a story.

7 First they write the bare facts of the story, and show it to you. Correct and rephrase as needed.

8 Then let them imagine they are to write it as a newspaper story, to attract readers' interest. They should include any descriptive clauses that would improve the story, e.g. ... *aged 26, ... who was* ... like the descriptive clauses in the Student's Book. (Students may need to check with the person who first told the story, to ensure the facts are accurate.) Students choose a headline and add that.

9 Students copy their headlines and stories out neatly after checking them with you.
   Either: Get some students to assemble the stories on a larger sheet of paper, to look like a page of a newspaper.
   Or: Display them round the class.

Aims: 1 To highlight and practise the class of verbs which sometimes take an object and sometimes don't. The object can become the subject. e.g. *Can you cook the rice? The rice is already cooking.* (These are known as Ergative Verbs).
2 To show how to recognise these in a dictionary: V + O, V-ERG.
3 to revise other basic verb structures: V + A, V + C etc.

The Study Page on verbs on pages 890–891 in Collins COBUILD *Essential English Dictionary gives very clear explanations of these and all types of verb. This page is summarised below.*

SB37a PB37

1 Make sure students know what a grammatical object is, and that it usually comes after a verb: e.g. *I've read that* **book**. (**read** = V + O). *Have you seen my* **pen**?

2 Go through the two illustrated examples. Show how the words **rice** and **Japanese** can be either the subject or object of the same verb.

   Key: Objects (only in one of each pair of sentences):
   In the first example, first sentence: rice.
   In the second example, second sentence: Japanese.

SB37b/c

3 The exercise is illustrated by the picture of the harbour. Give students time to study the picture and talk about what is happening in it.

4 Move students on to the exercise. Explain to students: The first set in **b** contains sentences with no objects. Students supply the subject, by looking at the picture. The second set in **c** need an object, in this context, which students can supply by looking at the picture, and thinking what the people might be saying.

   Key: b The wind (**drop** = decrease)/The potted plant; The boat; The engine/One of the people/A cigarette; Smoke, The boat near the pier; the smoke/The woman's hair; The flowerpot; The plants.
   c these plants; a drink; a drink; glass/drink; glass; it; smoke.
   d The verbs that appear in both **b** and **c** are: drop, pour, break, blow, grow.
   But the other verbs in **b** can also take an object, e.g. smoking a cigarette, turn the key, stop that car!

Optional

5 This might be a good time to revise the basic verb structures, and teach the common abbreviations used in the Collins COBUILD dictionaries and in the Dictionary Extracts appendix:

   V = Verb which is used without an object (intransitive).
   e.g. *She smiled. My head aches. Are you coming?*
   V + O = Verb which must have an object (transitive). e.g. *I arranged the meeting.* (You can't just say 'I arranged'.)
   V + C = Verb (intrans) which must have a complement, which refers back to the subject. e.g. *James is a teacher. You seem tired. He looks old.*
   V + A = Verb (intrans) which must have an adjunct, which is usually a prepositional phrase. e.g. *He behaved really badly. He lives near London. A car went past.*
   V + REPORT = Verbs of speech, thought, e.g. **say, hope, tell**, that are followed by a clause which tells you what the person said. e.g. *She hoped he would come.* (V + REPORT) *They told me where to go.* (V + O + REPORT)

   Ask students to look up **assume** and **search** in the Dictionary Extracts appendix and explain the abbreviations. (In addition to those above, students may find: OFT = often, USU = usually.)

38 Out from the cold

Aims: 1 To stimulate students' predictive powers.
2 Reading for specific information, i.e. to see whether predictions were fulfilled.
3 Summarising the content of a story.

Lexis: bitter T, **bitterly**, **ice** T, **shirt**, **temperature**
Revision: **accidentally** (= by accident), **playing a joke**,
on the spot (= in one place), **trousers**
Phrases: **cold store**, **freezing point**

Task SB38a

1 Discuss the pictures of the butcher's shop. Introduce the term **cold store**. (Where do butchers keep meat overnight?) Incidentally, the town is Stratford-on-Avon, Shakespeare's birthplace.

2 Ask students to cover up the main news story, and just to read the headline and the first paragraph. They should do this silently, and then write their five questions.

3 Students compare their questions with their partner's and add two more.

Reading SB38b

4 Allow students to uncover and read the whole story. Ask how many of their questions were answered.

5 As a class, find out which questions they wrote were answered, and which were not.

6 Write the target lexis on the board. Add any other words students feel might be useful to them.

Writing SB38c

7 Students in pairs plan and write a summary of this story, in less than 62 words. Help them to write accurately and appropriately. Allow plenty of time for this.

8 Pass students' summaries round, or display them, for others to read and compare.

9 Turn over to section 40, and let students read the original summary, and compare with their own.

Listening [40]

10 Play the recording of Chris and Bruce's questions. Which questions were similar to ones that students had thought of?

39 Language study

Aims: 1 Uses of the **-ing** form of the verb.
2 Uses of **had**.
3 Passive forms (used when we don't know who did something), and practice in some passive verb constructions in the context of a story.

SB39a/b/c/d

Students work through one section at a time, either singly or in pairs.

Key: a (See Student's Book Level 1, 'Grammar Book' page 106.)
1 describing: freezing point, staff arriving* for work, teeth chattering*, Still freezing*, closing time
2 after **is/are** etc: after being locked in, was playing a joke, was wearing
3 reported him missing
4 began shouting
None left over if those marked * are seen as describing.

b had reported, I had gone, staff had all gone home (all for actions that had already happened at an earlier point in time)

c after being locked, Peter Emerson ... was locked, the door was locked. (No, we don't know who locked him in; in fact it isn't important to know who locked him in, which is why the passive form is used.)

d (Encourage students to write corrected sentences using the passive.)
The door was locked when the boy was behind a food shelf.
He wasn't found by the police./He was found by the staff./It was the staff who found him.
He'd been reported missing by his parents, not the police./It was his parents who ...
We assume he was taken home to his parents, but he may have gone home by himself.
He may have been warned about the door – we don't know.

Five more verb phrases: was shut, was not found, had been reported, was taken, must have been warned.

Out from the cold

a Read the first paragraph and write down five questions that you hope will be answered in this report.

▶ Read each other your questions. Add two more to your list. ◀

b Now read the two columns and see how many of your questions were answered.

c There was also a back page summary of this news report, of just thirteen lines in length. It was written just after the boy had gone home to recover. It began:

Night on ice

A 15-year-old schoolboy, Peter Emerson, of Stratford-on-Avon, was recovering at

▶ In pairs, write a summary of this news item in 62 words or less. You can either use the opening sentence shown above, or think up your own. Read each other's summaries. Do any of them answer all your seven questions? ◀

The boy who came out from the cold

A SCHOOLBOY who spent the night trapped in a butcher's cold store after being locked in accidentally ran on the spot for ten hours to stay alive.

Peter Emerson, aged 15, was locked in the store in a Stratford-upon-Avon butcher's shop for 14½ hours, with the temperature around freezing point.

Staff arriving for work at the Wood Street shop found him yesterday morning, his teeth chattering and his face purple with cold. Still freezing, Peter immediately telephoned his parents, who had reported him missing to the police.

Peter, who lives in Banbury Road, Stratford, said: "I help out at the shop after school and I had gone into the cold store just before closing time. I was behind a big food shelf when the door was locked behind me.

"At first I thought someone was playing a joke but when I realised it wasn't and began shouting the staff had all gone home. I tried to kick the door open and to pick the lock but it was no good.

"I was wearing only a shirt, trousers, a thin pull-over and a white butcher's smock. It was bitterly cold and I realised that I might die, so I ran on the spot for about 10 of the 14 hours".

Language study ••••••••••••••••••••••••••

a **–ing**
Find ten clauses with a verb ending in -ing in this story. Find those which:

1 describe something.
2 follow **is/are was/were**.
3 follow a verb like **see, hear, find**.
4 follow another verb like **stop, start**.

How many are left over?

b **had _____**
Find three examples of verbs with had. Why is this form of the verb used?

c **_____ locked**
Find three phrases with the word locked. Do we know who locked the boy in the cold store?

d Which of these are probably true? Correct any that are not true, or that you are not sure about, to make them all true.

The boy was trapped inside a cold store.
The boy locked the door himself.
The door was shut behind him.
He was not found until the morning.
He was found by the police.
He had been reported missing.
The police had reported him missing.
He was taken home to his parents.
The butcher had warned him about the door.
He must have been warned about the possibility of the door closing.

Find five more verb phrases in the sentences above that fit the pattern:

... was/is ⎫ trapped
... been/being ⎭ taken

40 Night on ice

Read the back page report and compare it with your version. What differences can you find?

Night on ice

A 15-year-old schoolboy, Peter Emerson, of Stratford-on-Avon, was recovering at home yesterday after being trapped all night in a cold store at the butcher's shop where he works after school. The door swung shut as he was putting meat into store and he kept warm by jumping for 10 minutes at a time. Staff found him unharmed when they opened the shop.

40 Bruce and Chris read the summary first. What questions did they think of that should be answered in the main story?

41 *Dictionary skills* ·············

Finding useful phrases

Luck   extent

Look up these words and phrases and find one which goes in each gap. You will have two left over.

to the extent that	bad luck
to some extent	the best of luck
to a certain extent	with any luck
to what extent	

a   *Well, I think that _____ it was the boy's fault, going into the cold store at closing time.*
b   *It was just _____ that nobody heard him shouting.*
c   *His parents were worried _____ they called the police and reported him missing.*
d   *_____ can your body temperature drop without you dying?*
e   *_____ it won't happen again.*

42 REVIEW

a   Opposites in conversation
Find pairs of words that can be opposite in meaning. Then think of a phrase or sentence containing one of the words from each pair. Let your partner disagree by saying the opposite. For example:

UNIT 4

'You look nice with short hair.'
'Well, actually, I think long hair is better.'

dark	weak
long	low
strong	narrow
heavy	shallow
deep	light
high	short
wide	

NEW WORDS IN UNIT 4

angle	observe/d
avenue	pity
bet	poem
bitter	poet
bitterly	poetry
blow	pour/ed
darkness	prayer
downstairs	safety
empire	scared
extent D	shame
height	sheer
hide/hid/hidden	shirt
ice D	strength
improve	suicide
insect	survive
kill/ed	survivor
launched	switch/ed
length	temperature
narrow	trousers
observation	

39 new words
TOTAL SO FAR 153

b   Build up a set
Add one or two more words to each set below. Then think up a question to which the answer might include one of the words in that set.

E.g. scared terrified afraid frightened

'Were you afraid of the dark?'
'Yes, terrified.'

fifth   twentieth   thirty-first   forty-second

trousers   shorts   jacket   coat

length   strength   width   weight

mine   ours   his   hers

myself   himself   themselves

c   Verbs with prepositions
You could use a dictionary to help you with this.

down	out	off	up	over

She blew all the balloons _____.
The kids were lighting matches then blowing them _____.
The bomb blew _____ a building in the town centre.
Two trees were blown _____ by the strong winds.
I once nearly got knocked _____ by a car.
He fell _____ the garden wall and knocked himself _____.
$99? Can't you knock $10 _____?

d   Nouns from verbs

a blow	a knock	a fall	a drop	a switch

Which of these can be used in both set A and B below?
A
I hate heights if there is a sheer _____.
The child had a bad _____ going downstairs too fast.
He was hit by a _____ on the back of the neck.
B
There was a sudden _____ in temperature.
Losing his job was the worst _____ he'd ever had.
A _____ in the cost of living would be welcome.
The _____ from Chinese to English in schools caused some problems.
The company went from strength to strength with the _____ in the dollar.

Aims: 1 To compare content and structure of two versions of summaries of the same story.
2 Listening to questions two native-speakers thought should be answered in the full-length news item.

Lexis: angle

SB40

See section 38 notes 9 and 10.

---

41 **Dictionary skills**

Aims: 1 To show students how to identify the parts of an entry which supply phrases useful for their own writing or speaking.
2 To give practice using the phrases.

SB41 PB41

1 Explain to students that each dictionary entry illustrates the most common (and therefore the most useful) phrases and grammatical patterns associated with the word. If they want to know how to use a word, they should read through the whole entry carefully. They will find lots of examples of typical uses and patterns.

2 The extra column also helps students identify the structures used with each word (like v + o and V ERG in section 37.)

3 Ask students to find these phrases in the relevant dictionary entry, and then choose which sentence they would fit into.

Key: a to some extent/to a certain extent b bad luck c to the extent that d To what extent e With any luck Left over: the best of luck

4 Point out that **luck** 1 is N UNCOUNT, and 3.6 is informal. Some uses of **luck** and **extent** are in fact adverbial (and affect the whole sentence (ADV SEN), e.g. **to some extent** (= partly), **with any luck** (= hopefully).

5 Ask students if they have ever been worried to the extent that they have called the police. When might students say 'With any luck'? Or wish someone the best of luck?

---

42 **Review**

Key: a dark – light, long – short, strong – weak, heavy – light, deep – shallow, high – low, wide – narrow
c up, out, up, over/down, over/down, off, out, off.
d Set a): drop, fall, blow. Set b): drop/fall, blow, fall, switch, fall. Set a) words are more physical in meaning than Set b), which are more 'metaphorical'. See Unit 5, section 52.

LEXICAL OBJECTIVES

angle 1 90 degrees = a right angle. T
2 an approach to a topic. . . . *most of it apart from the clothing angle.*
avenue 1 street in a town. *Fifth Ave.*
2 wide road with trees either side.
bet 1 *He bet me $100 I wouldn't do it.*
2 *Perhaps for a bet – he jumped off . . .*
3 in phrases like: *I bet!* (to show you agree.) *It's a good bet* (very likely)
bitter T 1 angry, disappointed.
2 very cold. *a bitter wind*
3 sharp, unpleasant. *It tasted bitter.*
bitterly 1 extremely, intensely. *bitterly cold/angry/disappointed*
blow 1 *strong winds had blown him . . .*
2 with your mouth. T *She blew the dust away.* You can blow up a balloon. SB37
3 a blow is a hard hit, or a problem. *It was a terrible blow for everyone.*
4 *Oh, blow!* to express annoyance.
darkness 1 in the dark.
downstairs 1 on/to the ground floor. not upstairs. *falling downstairs.*
***drop** 4 *a sheer drop of 100 ft.*
5 a small amount of. *A drop of water.*
empire 1 separate nations controlled by one government. *The Empire State Building.*
extent D
height 1 *What height are you?*
2 distance above the ground. *Flying at a height of 8000 metres.*
3 high place. *fear of heights.*
hidden 1 not easily noticed/seen. *hidden danger. hidden valleys.*
hide/hid/hidden 1 *Have you hidden my pyjamas? He used to hide his money*
2 there was nowhere to hide. **Hide and seek** is a game played by children.
ice D
improve 1 get better. *The weather improved. Your English is improving.*
2 do it better. *Can you improve on that?* see SB37
insects 1 a small animal with 6 legs. *I really hate . . . spiders and insects.*
joke 1 noun. something to make you laugh. *Was someone playing a joke?* Phrases: *It's getting beyond a joke! No joke! You must be joking!*
kill 1 *He decided to kill himself.*
2 informal: = hurt. *My back's killing me! They were killing themselves laughing* (informal) *killing time.*
launched 1 to launch a ship is to put it into the water for the first time. T
2 *launch a rocket into space . . . he launched himself towards . . .* = jumped
3 You can also launch an attack, a campaign, a new product, or book T
length 1 measurement. *What length is it? 7m by 4m. Knee-length skirts.* T
2 the whole distance. *They travelled the length of the island.* T
3 size/amount. *A full report, six paragraphs in length. At length.*

narrow 1 not wide. *on this very narrow parapet. narrow streets.*
2 limited. *She is very narrow-minded* T
observation 1 the observation floor of an airport = where you watch the planes. *He's in hospital under observation.*
2 *She made an observation about the way he ate* = said someting critical.
observe 1 to watch or study. T
2 to say. (formal) *reason they do it, as Vaughan Williams observed, . . .*
pity T *It's a pity* = It's a shame
poem
poet someone who writes poetry
poetry poems in general.
pour 1 *poured himself a stiff drink.*
2 *the rain poured down. It's pouring*
3 to stream. *People poured into the hall. They saw smoke pouring out.* SB27
prayer say a prayer = speak to God.
safety 1 *a safety fence. crawled into safety. safety measures. safety belt.*
2 the safety of a product. *worry about the safety of nuclear energy.* T
scared 1 frightened. *If I go up a ladder I'm scared stiff, now.*
2 noun: a fright. *It gave me a scare. There was a nuclear scare.* T
shame 1 uncomfortable feeling of guilt and failure. *a terrible shame* (to be afraid of the dark).
2 to show regret: T *It's a shame these poor kids have nowhere to go.* See **pity**
sheer 1 absolute, complete. *The hotel room was sheer luxury. Sheer beauty.* T
2 a sheer cliff/drop is very steep. *Then a sheer drop of about 100 feet.*
shirt 1 *wearing only a shirt . . .*
strength 1 physical energy. *I hadn't got the strength to go on.* T
2 of a machine, etc. *The car is tested to establish body work strength.*
3 *What strength light bulbs?*
4 greatness, power. *The strength of the Unions. The company went from strength to strength.*
suicide to commit suicide = kill oneself
survived 1 continue to live despite being close to death. *shut in a cold store all night and yet survived.*
survivor someone who has survived.
switch 1 noun: *the light switch.* verb: *Can you switch the light on/off?*
2 change. *a switch from Chinese to English in schools.*
temperature 1 *temperatures dropped/ fell by 20 degrees.*
2 *She's got a temperature* = her body temperature is over 37 centigrade. *I took her temperature and it was 40.*
trousers 1 *wearing only a shirt, trousers and . . .*

Unit 5 — Self-expression

This is another unit dealing with attitudes and emotions rather than facts. There is discussion of the work of an artist and the place of art in society. Students read a short piece by an artist, Suzanne Juta, about her work, and listen to Suzanne talking to concert pianist Edmund Lee about teaching art, the work of an artist, and later about government funding for the arts. There is discussion about the way children express themselves, illustrated by a child's written story and by a short anecdote about a child. This leads into discussion of the way children and adults talk to each other.

OBJECTIVES

Lexical objectives are in TB54

Discussion topics

a Earliest memories. (43)
b Teaching art to children. (43)
c Art as a career. (43)
d Dreams and nightmares. (47)
e Taboo subjects. (49)
f The artist in society. (51)

Social skills

a Comparing memories. (43)
b The effect of status on language. (48,49)
c Awareness of taboo subjects. (49)

Communication skills

a Taking brief notes. (43)
b Distinguishing general from specific. (46)
c Describing past experiences in writing. (43)
d Rewriting a story with illustrations. (45)
e Retelling a well-known children's story. (45)

Grammar and discourse

a Giving examples. (44)
b Punctuation review. (45)
c Signalling changes of direction in conversation. (45)
d Elaborating by moving from general to specific. (46)
e Noun modifiers. (50)
f Adjectives followed by prepositions.(54)
g Phrases qualified by adverbs. (54)
h Practice Book Grammar Word: **the**

Dictionary skills (52)

a Metaphorical use of common words.
b Common words expressing attitudes. (54)
c Pronunciation: vowels: /æ/ **pattern**, /əʊ/ **flow**, /iː/ **stream**, (revise long vowels: /uː/ **pool**, /ɜː/ **firm**); consonants: /p/, /b/, /tʃ/ **approach**.

---

43 Children and art

Aims: 1 To stimulate discussion on childhood memories, children's art, and art as a career.
2 Descriptive writing.
3 Practice in brief note-taking.

Lexis: **architecture**, **ballet**, **bowls**, **freely** ts,
imagination ts, **keen** ts, **leaves**, **nightmare** ts, **patterns**,
project, **railway**, **rough**, **tunnel**, **visual**, **urban**
Revision: **approach** ts D, **concentrate** ts, **drawing**,
forms, **material** ts
Phrases: (all ts) **a certain amount of**, **their own way of
expressing themselves**, **go so far as to . . .**, **in material
terms**, **committed to it**
Understanding only: **curbed** (= brought under control),
romanticise (= make it sound wonderful), **romantic**

21T

Lead-in   SB43 PB43

1 Give students time to comment on the mural in the school playground. Are there any murals in places they know? What do they think about such art projects in inner city areas? Are they a waste of time and money?

Task, planning and report   SB43a

2 Ask students in groups to discuss and then plan how to tell the class.

3 You may like to leave the writing until after they have read Suzanne Juta's piece.

Reading and note-taking   SB43b

4 Students read silently, and take notes to summarise Suzanne Juta's career as an artist.

Class discussion   SB43c

5 Discuss these points as a class or in groups. Possible way to stimulate discussion:
If we had no artists, architects etc., in what way would our lives be different? (e.g. no visual adverts, no pictures in books or papers, no comics or cartoons, no fashion designers, no pretty plates or china, dull food packaging . . . no visual appeal. . . .)

Listening   SB43d [43d]

6 The first time you play the recording, ask students to listen mainly for Edmund's questions, and to jot them down leaving a space between them for notes of the answers. Can students predict or guess Suzanne's answers? Did they catch any words or ideas the first time they heard the recording?

7 Play the recording a second time. Ask students to listen for Suzanne's answers.

Key: Sample summary:
Art in school
Encourage the imagination of each child; let them express themselves as freely as possible. Try to introduce an aesthetic awareness – i.e. an appreciation of beauty, understanding of visual impact. So long as the child is happy with what they are doing, not to interfere, or 'correct', i.e. only offer advice if they need help.

Art as a career
It's no good taking up art as a career if you are keen on making money. Most artists are so committed to their work, they don't question the money side. But the general public romanticise it, and don't realise how difficult an artist's life can be, how poorly paid they are. ('A nightmare in material terms'.)

8 Help students with the Word Study. (Odd word out: **ballet**.) Check that students can understand and use most of the target words and phrases.

---

44 Language study

Aims: 1 To help students recognise how examples can be signalled, and to show that sometimes they are not signalled at all.
2 The position of phrases like **for instance** – they may not come at the start of the example.
3 Additional phrases, in spoken discourse, such as **and things like that . . .**

SB44 PB44

Key: The second half of the sentence contains examples. Other examples in Suzanne's text: The whole of the third sentence exemplifies how visual she is. In the second paragraph, the names of the countries, and the words 'architecture and zen gardens' act as examples. In the last paragraph, the names of the materials.

Man and Dog visiting Mars – mural in school playground, London. It was designed and painted by children with the help of an artist, as part of an inner city art project. Can you find the man and his dog?

43 Children and art

a What are your earliest memories? What kinds of things did you draw or paint as a child?

▶ Find out what other people in your group can remember, then tell the class.

▶ Write a paragraph describing some of your earliest memories.

b Read about Suzanne, then write notes about her career as an artist. List the types of art forms she likes and has been involved with.

Suzanne Juta, artist, Penzance, Cornwall.

I'm interested in all forms of modern art. I always have been a visual person. In fact my very first memory is of lying in my pram in our garden, watching the trees making patterns against the sky. I started drawing and painting at the age of three. My father used to bring large pads of rough paper home from the office, and by the end of the evening they would be full of my pictures and patterns. I loved drawing things that moved, people running, skating, ballet dancing.

I ended up going to art school and university, and travelling — France, Morocco, Japan — to study different art forms, architecture and Zen gardens. Then for a spell I taught art to children in urban schools. We painted pictures all over the school playground, did a huge mural on the walls of a local railway station tunnel. Community art, street art — it was great fun.

The 'paper works' are my latest idea. I make pictures and bowls using paper which I've made myself out of local plants, and adding all kinds of materials — feathers, flower petals, leaves, bits of wood ....

c Do you think art should be taught in schools? At what ages should it be taught, and how much time should be spent? Do artists generally earn a lot?

43d **d** Listen to Suzanne talking to Edmund Lee, the pianist, about teaching art to children and the life of an artist.

Suzanne says:

I wouldn't interfere
– Interfere with what?
This life ... is an absolute nightmare in material terms.
– Which life? What does she mean?

▶ Summarise Suzanne's attitudes towards teaching art to children and art as a career. Say whether you agree with her.

> **WORD STUDY**
> Which is the odd word out?
> modern art   patterns   drawing   ballet   painting
> pictures   images
> Find out what these mean: visual   rough

44 *Language study*

Recognising examples
Sometimes examples are signalled by phrases like 'for example', 'for instance, ...' 'such as ...', 'like ...'.

For example:

... this country has a major ... pool of talent. (51)
Certainly in other spheres – well, theatre for instance and music as well. (51)

This business of paying lots of money for ... paintings like the Van Gogh 'Sunflowers' that went for ... £24 million ... (51)
... I really hate ... fluttering insects. Things like butterflies and moths and things. (34)

Jim Lloyd ... is known to World Service listeners for series such as 'These Musical Islands'. (20)

However, very often, writers give examples without using these phrases to signal them. Which part of this sentence contains examples?

I loved drawing things that moved, people running, skating, ballet dancing. (43)

How many other sentences or parts of sentences act as examples in Suzanne Juta's text?

21

45 My wings

a How would a six-year-old child write in your language? In what ways would it be different from an adult's writing?

b Try to read the child's story *My Wings* out loud, as if it was properly punctuated.

CHEEP CHEEP!

My Wings

I was in the car when I suddenly started groing wings I said daddy why I am groing wings dont speak nonsence I said well I am and I said daddy you have got wings as well and when I looked out and everybody had them I said daddy look out of the window and he did and he said well everybody has got them you did not say in the first place.

We were at home I showed mum my wings she said I cud go flying today I went out and I was flying in the air. I landid in Africa it was very hot. I went a long way. I came to the jungle I met a monky it said cheep cheep. I said monkys dont go cheep cheep the monky said little girls dont grow wings I said can we have some food the monky said that there was no such thing as food only fruit. Then we said that we wud play hide-and-seek I said you count and I wud hide I hid in a tree monky did not come I said monky monky did not say yes as he shoud do I went to look for him I got lost so I climed up a tree and was just about to go to sleep and I saw monky I said where were you monky said I was looking for you I said I was looking for you and they both lafted then we went flying together. Then we went home and mum and dad lafted and I lafted to and monky lafted in his funeey cheep cheep laff and me and monky went to bed.

A story, My Wings, by 6 year old Hannah Dawson, from Young Writers, the anthology of winning entries from the W. H. Smith Young Writers' competition. They were chosen from about 31,000 entries by a panel of judges chaired by the Poet Laureate, Ted Hughes.

THE GUARDIAN

45c **c** Listen to Suzanne reading it. Notice two places where she herself is not sure how to read it.

Discuss how it should be punctuated. If you were a teacher what other alterations would you make? Make a short list and show each other.

d Why do you think this particular piece was chosen for the Guardian feature?

e Discuss what features of the language show that it is written by a small child. Tell each other.

45d/e Suzanne and Edmund discussed the same topics. Did they make any of the points you made? Edmund also told a story about a cigarette, an ash tray and a pot plant. How was this relevant? What phrase does he use to introduce this story? How does he get back to the main topic?

f In groups, write this story again, as if you were a writer writing a children's book. Design the book, planning what words and pictures to have on each page.

Describe what you would have in the pictures.

g What well-known children's stories exist in your language? Plan how to tell one children's story you know well in English.

46 *Language study*

General to specific
After introducing a general concept, people often go on to give more specific details:

GENERAL	SPECIFIC
I taught art to children in urban schools.	We painted pictures all over the school playground, did a huge ...
'Paperworks' are my latest idea.	I make pictures and bowls using paper which I've made myself ...
Some parts of it are rather clever actually.	I think the bit where she finds the monkey and the monkey goes ...

The following consists of three extracts from Edmund's interview with Suzanne Juta. Each speech has been divided in half but the six halves have been mixed up. Put them together and as you do so identify which are the *general* and which the *specific* halves.

a I've taught at all different stages,
b There are so many different approaches to art teaching.
c children right up to Art Schools.
d which is an absolute nightmare in material terms.
e I think that the main thing ... is to encourage the imagination of each child ...
f ... difficult to understand how one can go on ... choosing this life,

47 Dreams or nightmares

What kind of dreams do you have? Have you ever had a dream where you could fly or where you were falling and falling? Tell your group about them.

47 Suzanne Juta often has flying dreams. She says:

Gosh, I'm surprised — (surprised at what?)
I thought everybody ... — (everybody what?)
That actually reminded me of my flying dreams.
— (what did?)

Choose one dream you remember and plan how to describe it to the class.

45 My wings

Aims: 1 To create an awareness of children's writing.
2 To practise reading out loud with expression.
3 To revise some punctuation.
4 To highlight a way of signalling changes of direction in conversation.
5 To give students a chance to discuss style, and improve a text.
6 To encourage students' own creativity and enjoyment – rewriting based on new illustrations.
7 Retelling a well-known children's story.

Lexis: climbed, cigarettes, clever, complex, complexity, complicated T, **dad/dy, dull, feature, imaginative, loud, nonsense, pet, typical, wings**
Revision: **Anyway, . . ., consciousness** (thoughts), **Exactly, yes.** (when agreeing), **hide, images**
Phrases: **a long flow of images, caught up in their own world, pot plant**

Discussion   SB45a

1 Talk about the picture. What do students know about monkeys? Do they make good pets? What do they eat? What noises do they make?

2 Ask students to think about how a six-year-old child would write in their own language. List the features that would make it different from an adult's writing. They could do this in small groups or pairs.

Key: It might differ from an adult's writing in the style of hand-writing, spelling, punctuation, length or lack of sentences and structure. Lost of 'ands' rather than more complex ways of linking ideas. Often written very much from the child's own private point of view.

Reading   SB45b

3 Ask students to find out where this story comes from, who wrote it and how it was published. (They can read the italic notes after the story, and help each other to understand as much as possible.)

4 Students practise reading the story *My Wings* out loud to a partner. Help them with any words or spellings they don't recognise. What are students' first impressions of the story? Try to help them enjoy it, and read it in a lively way.

Listening   SB45c   45c

5 Let them hear Suzanne reading it. The second time you play the recording, pause after each short section and discuss with students what punctuation would help the reader.

6 Students write a list of alterations they might make if they were teachers. They should be able to explain why they would change things. Some may say 'None at all' – so as to encourage the child's creativity and imagination. Others may list spellings, or altering the number of repetitions.

Listening   SB45d/e   45d/e

7 Students in pairs discuss briefly. When they have thought of one or two points, they can tell the class.

8 Students hear the recording of Suzanne and Edmund, and compare opinions.

Key: Points they made:
Chosen because it was fun, imaginative, it has a rhythmic flow, it's quite clever; it has a marvellous sort of liveliness; it's very alive.
Showing that it was written by a small child: the constant repetition, the spelling, a certain lack of grammatical complexity, a lot of sentences with 'I', a 'long flow of images', 'a stream of consciousness' rather than 'grammatical sentences with a structure'.

9 Ask students to retell the ash tray story. First however focus on how it starts: *Reminds me of when I worked in a . . .;* and ends: *Anyway, perhaps, er, shall we go on to . . .* (Point out that **anyway** is a typical way of changing or getting back to a topic.)

Report   SB45f

10 Allow students plenty of time for writing the story again, and designing the children's book. Then each group can present their version to the class, explaining what illustrations they would have.

Planning and report   SB45g

11 Students could begin the presentation of the children's story they know out of class. Next lesson, help them with any problems they may have. They can then either record their stories on tape, or tell them to each other.

46 Language study

Aim: To make students aware of the very common discourse pattern 'general to specific'.

SB46

1 Ask students to read the three examples. Ask which parts give more details. (The parts on the right.) Details of what? (The general concepts – art, paperworks, some parts, lack of grammatical complexity.)

2 Students find three pairs among a–f, with the general idea first followed by a more detailed description.

Key: a–c, b–e, f–d. Point out the general words: **stages, approaches, life.**

47 Dreams or nightmares

Aims: 1 To give students a chance to express their feelings and share experiences.
2 To encourage students to recount an experience in a vivid and imaginative way, to make it lively and interesting for listeners.

Lexis: awake, asleep T, **ceiling, (two-seater) planet**
Notes: **Gosh!** is a colloquial expression of surprise. (Others students may know are: **My goodness! Wow! Really? Honestly?**)
Edmund is joking when he talks about Suzanne levitating. (**levitate** = rise and float in the air, by magic, or like a spirit; a rare word.)

Task   SB47

1 Ask students to think of dreams they can remember and choose one to talk about. Students in groups tell each other about their most vivid dreams.

Listening   SB47   47

2 Suzanne tells Edmund about her dreams.

Key: Suzanne was surprised Edmund didn't have dreams about flying. (Edmund only dreamt about witches flying – he didn't fly himself.)
She thought everybody had dreams about flying.
Going up in a small plane the other day over Cornwall (south-west England, where she lives) reminded her of her flying dreams.

Planning and report   SB47

3 Each group chooses one person's dream to tell the class. Help them prepare to tell it in a lively way.

48 Grimble

Aims: 1 To stimulate discussion about language and status, i.e. what adults may say to a child but children may not say to an adult, e.g. How old are you?
2 Reading narrative with conversation.

Lexis: admitted, embarrassed, extraordinary, leaflet T, peculiar, prefer
Revision: **funny** (= strange), **odd** (= strange)

Lead-in   SB48

Background: Grimble is a small boy who has learnt to be very independent because his parents are very absent-minded (even forgetting his birthday!) and often go away, leaving Grimble on his own. Before this point in the story Grimble realises that Christmas is coming and he has no money for presents and other Christmassy things. So he has the idea of starting a Home Toast Delivery Service, buying sliced bread and using his parents' toaster, making a 2p profit on each slice. He delivers leaflets announcing this new service round the houses in his neighbourhood. At this point, he is going round the houses hoping to collect orders for his toast. This is his third house. He still has no orders.

1 Explain who Grimble is and give students the background. Ask them to look at the picture and discuss which question Grimble might have asked. Which things would be unsuitable for a small boy to ask a grown-up lady?

   Key: (in UK, at least) The second and third ones would be quite unsuitable for a child to ask an adult.

Reading   SB48 PB48

2 Students read the extract by themselves. Ask them why Grimble preferred men. Do they think the story is funny?

3 Students in pairs practise reading it aloud, as if for a child to enjoy. Help them with pronunciation, and show how the conversation in the narrative can be made lively.

4 Ask students to do the Word Study. They must find the words in the text, to get their full meaning.

   Key: People's reactions: put out, embarrassed. To replace **extraordinary**: strange, funny, unusual, odd, peculiar.

49 A question of status

Aim: To make students aware of the way in which someone's status can affect what can politely be said.

Lexis: depressed, depression T, practical T, practically, topic, virtually, whereas
Revision: **otherwise**

***Dole** is an informal word for money given to you by the Government every two weeks when you have no job.*

Class discussion   SB49a

1 Get students to recall what Grimble said. (He asked the lady's age and invited her round to play with his mother.)

SB49b

2 Explain what is meant by status. Give as an example a secretary and a boss or a shop owner and a shop assistant. (Who is higher up, better paid, etc?) Ask students to think of two things a secretary or a shop assistant could not say to their bosses.

   Sample: The boss and the owner can tell their secretary/ assistant what to do, ask why they are late, can criticise what they do, and can also (for instance at an interview) ask them fairly personal questions. But not vice versa.

SB49c

3 Ask students to think of questions that, in normal conversation, would be rude. They can tell each other, and compare.

Listening   SB49c 49c

4 Ask students to list the topics that Bruce and Rachel mentioned. Why was it relevant for Bruce to talk about his son?

   Key: 'Someone said' religion, money, sex, politics (personal political views), but Rachel didn't agree. Just the personal things, and the price of personal things. Also, 'Have you got a job?' is a difficult question in these days of unemployment.

5 Students compare what Bruce and Rachel said with what is inappropriate in students' countries.

50 Grammar

Aim: To show the way nouns can modify each other.

SB50 PB50

1 Start off with some easy examples that you can show or illustrate, e.g. **car/classroom door**, **classroom window** (both 'of' relationships – e.g. the door of the classroom); **light switch**, **board rubber** (both 'for' relationships – e.g. the switch for the light).
   Some examples indicate the place, or the person/people involved, like these from Suzanne Juta's text: **railway station tunnel** (tunnel in the station, the station of the railway), **community art** (paintings done by the local community), **street art** (paintings done on the pavement or on outside walls).

2 Tell students there are many more types of relationship possible between the two (or three or more) nouns. Ask them to read the first set of examples given in the Student's Book to discover what these are.

3 Discuss these examples (some show the time, some the purpose). Then let students try to explain the next set of examples to each other. Some examples they have already met in earlier units. Others will be occurring in later units.

4 Students take turns to explain one example each to the class. There may be different ways of doing so.

   Key: a The school term which lasts the three months of summer (as opposed to autumn/winter term, spring term).
   b The floor (i.e. the main work area) of the factory.
   The playground of the school or the grounds of the school where the children play.
   c The kind of life that people lead in the country.
   d A party where people sit and have dinner together.
   e The fence, the purpose of which is to keep people safe – to stop them falling off or into somewhere.
   f A service which offers delivery of toast to people's homes or a service which delivers toast to . . .
   g An evening where people dance (traditional) folk-dances.
   The hall belonging to the village or the hall used by people in the village or the hall in the village.
   h The engine of the car.
   i A serious injury to e.g. the head.
   j Someone who is training to be the person who assists/ helps the manager.
   k Someone who is learning to drive (who hasn't passed their driving test yet).
   l The seat in the front of a car where the passenger (not the driver) sits.
   m The drop of rain.
   n An article consisting of news.

Grimble

Grimble, the hero of Clement Freud's amusing book, is a small boy who is hoping to start a *Home toast delivery service* to earn some extra pocket money. He is collecting his first orders.

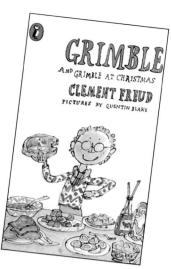

at an extraordinary thing for a boy to ask!'

Which of these questions do you think Grimble has just asked:

Do you like toast?
Do you earn a lot of money?
How old are you?
Could you give me your phone number?
What time shall I come round tomorrow?

This time it was a woman who answered the door. Grimble preferred men. 'Hello,' said the woman, 'you've come about the toast.' Grimble admitted this. 'How old are you?' asked the woman. (This was really why Grimble preferred men.) 'About ten,' he said. 'Oh,' said the woman, 'how nice, I have a little nephew who is coming for Christmas. He is nine and three quarters, you must come and meet him.' There was a short silence. 'Excuse me,' said Grimble, 'how old are you?' The woman looked slightly put out and said, 'What an extraordinary thing for a small boy to ask.' Then she gave an embarrassed giggle and said, 'I-am-in-my-middle-thirties,' all in one gasp. 'How nice,' said Grimble, 'I have a mother at home who is in her middle thirties. I do hope you will be able to come round sometime and play with her. We live two houses up the hill. Now about the toast.' 'Ah yes,' said the woman, 'Toast. Actually we make our own toast.'

Try reading this story out loud as if for a child to listen to.

A question of status

a Think of what Grimble said that embarrassed the lady. Make a list of things that parents and teachers commonly say to children that children cannot say to adults.

b How can differences in status affect people at work? For instance, what things are there that a secretary cannot say to their boss?

c Are there questions that are considered rude in normal social conversations in your country? For example:

How much did you pay for the suit/dress you're wearing?

Make a list, if you can.

49c Listen to the topics that Bruce and Rachel mentioned. Would people in your country talk freely about these things?

Grammar

Noun plus noun
In English we often put two nouns together to express quite complex meanings:

1 *Have a one minute conversation.*
(a conversation lasting one minute)
2 *I have had a Saturday job...* (24) (a job on Saturdays)
3 *What were your childhood fears?* (34) (fears when you were a child)
4 *... a back page summary of this news report.* (38) (summary of a report containing news on the back page of a newspaper)
5 *I was behind a big food shelf when the door was locked behind me.* (38) (a shelf to keep food on)
6 *... his original ambition was to be an engine driver like his father.* (16) (a man who drives engines)

Try to explain what these phrases mean:

a *I left school at the end of the summer term.* (24)
b *... on the factory floor and in school playgrounds.* (14)
c *... a great interest in country life.* (16)
d *You are at a small dinner party.* (59)
e *... John Helms clung to the safety fence.* (36)
f *Grimble's home toast delivery service.* (48)
g *... started a folk-dancing evening, in the village hall.* (17)
h *They must have left the car engine on.* (72)
i *... to prevent serious injury.* (83)
j *... the position of Trainee Assistant Manager.* (24)
k *A learner driver...*
l *He had been put in the front passenger seat...* (72)
m *Listen to the rain drop falling.* (124)
n *This one is a news article.*

WORD STUDY
See what these words mean in the story, then decide which are used to describe people's reaction:

answered   preferred   admitted   put out
embarrassed

Which of these words could be used to replace the word *extraordinary* in this paragraph?

| strange | nice | funny | dreadful |
| unusual | clever | odd | peculiar |

51 Funds for art?

Sunflowers by Van Gogh (1853–1890)
Sold in 1987 by auction
for £24,750,000

51 Listen to Edmund and Suzanne continuing their discussion.

a Find out what country/countries
  i) has a major pool of talent.
  ii) is particularly bad at funding the arts.

b Twice Edmund stopped in mid-sentence because he realised that Suzanne already knew what he was going to say. What was he going to say? Can you finish his sentences?

E: But it seems sad, that it's – it's a famous saying that a painter has to die before he – _____.
S: That's right. It's sad for Van Gogh.
E: But it's a pattern that seems to repeat itself, doesn't it, again and again? People while they're alive – _____.

c What investments gain value well in your country? Land? Houses? Famous paintings? Gold? Stamps? Have you got anything that could prove to be a good investment?

52 Dictionary skills

Words used in a metaphorical sense
Use the Dictionary extracts to find out what the words in colour mean in the phrases below.
Three of the words sometimes have meanings that are to do with water. Which three?

The way that children think, in . . . a long flow *of images . . .* (45)
stream *of consciousness* (45)
. . . so many different approaches *to art teaching* (43)
this life is an absolute nightmare *in material terms* (43)
. . . this country has a major sort of pool *of talent.* (51)
. . . it's again tied up *with the business of . . . the material side (of art).* (51)
. . . it's a pattern *that just seems to repeat itself . . .*

53 Things that children say

Parents often remind their children to be polite and say Yes <u>please</u>/No <u>thank you</u>. But children do not always understand.

Guess the last two words of this story.

No what?
When my sister was at primary school, she was having lunch one day and the dinner lady came round asking who wanted some more semolina for pudding. She came to my sister:
Would you like some more, dear?
No.
No what?
'_____!'

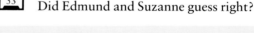

Helen Liebeck

53 Did Edmund and Suzanne guess right?

54 REVIEW

UNIT 5

a Describing people
Think of a relative or acquaintance who might fit each of these descriptions and say why.

practical   peculiar
imaginative   creative
clever   artistic

**NEW WORDS
IN UNIT 5**

admit
architecture
asleep
awake/awoke
ballet
bowl
ceiling
cigarette
clever
climb
complex
complexity
complicated
creative
dad
depressed
depression
drawing
embarrassed
extraordinary
freely
imaginative
investment
keen
leaf, leaves
leaflet

loud
nightmare D
nonsense
pattern D
peculiar
pet
practical
practically
prefer
project
railway
ridiculous
rough
sex
spell
status
talent
technological
topic
tunnel
typical
urban
virtually
visual
wing

51 new words
TOTAL SO FAR 204

b Describing feelings
Think of things you might feel . . .

sad about   delighted with
depressed about   keen on
unhappy with   embarrassed by

c More or less . . .
Make sentences using phrases made up from this table:

absolutely	no English
virtually	everyone in the class
practically	everywhere
almost	all my friends
nearly	tired out
more or less	

d Similar or opposite?
How many pairs of words can you make that could be
1 similar } in meaning?
2 opposite }

town   industrial   village   agricultural   city
urban   rural   country   technological

51 Funds for art?

Aims: 1 To stimulate discussion on ways of funding art, and investment values of art and other things.
2 Practice in listening to and taking part in a complex conversation.

Lexis: funds/funding, investment, ridiculous, talent, technological
Revision phrases: **the material side, a work of art, vast amounts, a famous saying, enough distance** (in time), **judged as such...**

Lead-in SB51

1 Have students heard about famous paintings selling for very high prices? Discuss why this happens.

Listening SB51a

2 Ask students to listen in order to answer the questions in **a**.

Key: England has a major pool of talent, but is bad in funding art.

SB51b

3 Play the rest of the recording and let students suggest ways of ending Edmund's sentences.

Key: ... see transcripts.

Task and report SB51c

5 Students discuss investments in pairs or groups.

52 Dictionary skills

Aims: 1 To show that the metaphorical meanings of words are often among the most common.
2 Pronunciation: vowels: /æ/ **pattern**, /əʊ/ **flow**, /iː/ **stream**, (revise long vowels: /uː/ **pool**, /ɜː/ **firm**); and short vowel /ɪ/ **business**. Consonants: /p/, /b/, /tʃ/ **approach**.

Lexis: All coloured words/phrases.

SB52

1 Students discuss as they do this. Do the same uses of the words exist in their own languages? Discuss which meanings apply here.

Key: flow, stream, and **pool** are all to do with water.

2 Write on the board the new phonetic symbols, and this list of words: **approach, business, flow, material, pattern, pool, stream.** Ask students which words contain the target sounds. They can say the words, guess which symbols, and then look the words up.

3 Point out /ː/ means a long vowel. **material** has two weak vowels /ə/ (no /æ/ sounds). **Business** has two short /ɪ/ sounds.

53 Things that children say

Aim: Reading and anecdote telling.

Reading SB53 [53] PB53

Students read the story and try to guess the ending. Then play the recording.

Key: No fear! (see section 34).

54 Review

Key:
d Similar: industrial – technological; town – city/urban; village – rural; country – agricultural
Opposite: urban – rural; agricultural – industrial etc.

LEXICAL OBJECTIVES

admit 1 agree it's true, reluctantly. *'... toast'. Grimble admitted this.*
2 *He was admitted to hospital.* T
architecture 1 design/style of buildings
asleep 1 sleeping. *He fell asleep.*
awake 1 adj: not asleep.
ballet ballet dancing
bowl 1 a dish. *pictures and bowls...*
ceiling 1 *the ceiling of a room.*
cigarette
clever 1 of a person – intelligent. T
2 of a book/idea etc – skilful. *parts of it are rather clever, actually.*
climbed 1. *So I climbed up a tree.*
2 increase in value or status T
complex 1 complicated. *quite a complex thought for a 6 year-old.*
2 *a shopping/sports complex* T
complexity 1 *grammatical complexity.*
complicated 1 not simple. *Don't write something too complicated.* T
creative imaginative, having the ability to create/develop things. T
dad informal word for 'father'
depressed 1 unhappy. *When my son was out of work he got very depressed.*
2 run-down. *depressed inner city* T
depression 1 the feeling of being unhappy, depressed. T
2 *economic depression*
drawing 1 a picture.
2 the skill/activity. *I like drawing.*
embarrassed 1 feeling shy, ashamed or guilty. *an embarrassed giggle.*
extraordinary 1 *A most extraordinary man.* T
2 surprising. *What an extraordinary thing for a small boy to ask.*
*feature 1 particular part of or characteristics of... *features of the language*
3 in a newspaper ... *chosen for the Guardian feature*
freely 1 in large quantities. *he spends fairly freely on...* T
2 *Would people talk freely about these things?* (= frankly)
funds 1 ... *funding for the Arts.*

*images 1 a mental picture. *children think – in a long flow of images.*
imaginative 1 *imaginative children*
2 *it's a very imaginative story.*
investment *Art as an investment.*
keen 1 want to. *keen on making money.*
2 deep. *He took a keen interest in...*
3 sensitive, sharp, alert. *You need a keen eye to see them. a keen mind.* T
leaf/leaves 1 of a tree. *made of flower petals, leaves...*
leaflet 1 *an information leaflet.*
loud 1 adj = noisy. *the loud disco music kept us awake. in a loud voice.* T
2 not silently. *Read out loud/aloud.*
nightmare D
nonsense 1 words or texts that do not make sense.
2 if a friend says something you do not agree with, you can say 'Nonsense!'
pattern D
peculiar 1 strange, odd, unusual. *maybe I think in a peculiar way.*
2 unique. *the style of decoration peculiar to the 1920s.*
pet 1 a tame animal, bird. *a pet shop.*
2 favourite/personal. *His pet subject...*
practical T EED 1 practical problems/work/ideas/experience are concerned with aspects of a real situation.
2 businesslike. *a practical person.*
practically 1 almost but not completely. *practically everything!*
prefer to like better. *Grimble preferred men.*
project 2 as noun only: an idea or a plan. *an Inner City Art Project.*
railway *railway tunnel*
ridiculous very silly, foolish.
rough T EED 1 uneven. *rough sea.*
2 not gentle. *He grabbed her roughly.*
3 bad, hard, violent. *a rough area.*
4 approximate. *At a rough guess, 200*
5 basic, not well finished. *Do a rough drawing. Write it in rough first.*
sex 1 male/female. *These jobs are open to both sexes.* T
2 to have sex is to make love. T
3 the general topic. *People don't like talking about religion, sex, politics*
spell EED 1 *That word is spelt wrong.*
2 a length of time. *For a short spell.*
3 *magic spells; under his spell.* T
status 1 your position in society. *someone of lower/equal status.*
talent 1 the natural ability to do something well, gift. *He has a great talent for story-telling. talented.* T
2 people, e.g. artists, actors, etc who have this ability. *a major pool of talent in the theatre and music.*
technological 1 to do with technology. *Society is increasingly technological.*
topic 1 subject. *topics British people don't talk about.*
tunnel *a local railway station tunnel*
typical 1 characteristic of... *a good example of... typical child's fantasy.*
2 to complain... *it's raining! Typical!* T
urban belonging to a town or city. *urban areas. urban schools.*
visual relating to sight. *a visual person.*
wings EED 1 insects, birds have wings.
2 *aeroplane wings.* T
3 of a building. *the east wing.* T
4 political. *left/right wing.* T
5 *the wing of his car. a wing mirror.* T

Unit 6 — Revision Unit

The overall aim of this unit is to get students to do as much as possible with the English they now have. It covers again the topics of people's lives and feelings and there are more biographical texts and recordings of people talking about treasured possessions. A Personality Test gives students an opportunity to talk about their own feelings. The theme of childhood is recycled as students talk about their families and listen to others doing the same. Finally there is another poem about childhood – this time rather poignant. There are comparatively few new words in the unit, but in many cases the meanings and uses of familiar lexis are extended. New texts have been used to give students a chance to see what they can now do, and some of the language tasks from earlier units have been repeated with new examples. Much of the recycling inevitably builds on work done in Level 2 of this course as well as Level 3.

OBJECTIVES

Lexical objectives are in TB67

Discussion topics

a Favourite objects, souvenirs etc. (any time after 56)
b Character, and reactions to hypothetical situations. (59,62)
c Personality and position in the family. (63)
d Childen and responsibility. (64)

Social skills

a Talking and writing about acquaintances. (55)
b Making apologies, requests and complaints. (60)
c Giving and responding to compliments and explanations. (60)

Communication skills

a Understanding instructions. (56)
b Asking questions with alternative answers to elicit specific information. (62)
3 Handling numerical information, especially time. (67)

Grammar and discourse

a Present perfect tense. (56)
b **Wh-** clauses for description and definition. (58)
c Past tense and **would** for hypothesis. (59,62)
d Noun modifiers. (59)
e Expressing contrast: **whereas**, **but**, **however**. (61)
f Expressing agreement or similarity: **like**, **so**, **neither**. (61)
g Present tense used for hypothesis. (62)
h Ways of giving the time. (67)
i Practice Book Grammar Word: **do/does/did**.

Dictionary skills

a Character adjectives. (63)
b The prefix **non-**. (66)
c Study section on **time**. (67)

---

55 Writing about people

Aim: Reading and writing brief biographical texts.

Writing task SB55 PB55

1 As preparation, students can read again the biographical texts in Units 1 and 2.

2 Get students to discuss what they can tell about Elizabeth from the photo and the notes on this page, and then to plan and write a paragraph about her.

---

56 The things they brought

Aim: To recycle talking about a specific object in a personal way.

Lexis: cat, description (describe)
Revision: **provided**, **indeed**, **keen on**

Listening SB56a

1 Discuss the things that Bruce, Rachel and Edmund brought from home – as shown in the pictures.

2 Play the recording so that students can draw Elizabeth's object. After they have heard the recording twice, ask them to compare each other's attempts. They can then draw a final version to show the class. (Finally, tell students the actual picture can be seen in section 65.)

Listening and writing SB56b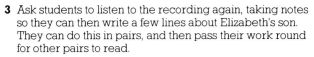

3 Ask students to listen to the recording again, taking notes so they can then write a few lines about Elizabeth's son. They can do this in pairs, and then pass their work round for other pairs to read.

Task SB56c

4 Tell students to choose something interesting to bring next lesson and to tell their group about it. They can write a description of any one of the items to be brought in.

5 Next lesson, when students bring in their objects, display the objects and descriptions, and get students to match them up.

---

57 Language study

Aim: More practice in evaluative comments.

SB57

Refer students back to section 5 in Unit 1 before they do this exercise.

Key: Comments: It isn't a very special picture. (less positive)
But the idea was very nice.
It's lovely.
I think actually it's a cat. (less positive)
... but I like the idea.
That's great, yes indeed.
Very good.

---

58 Grammar

Aims: 1 To revise **wh-** words acting as relatives.
2 To use specific information-seeking questions to find out more details about something.

SB58 PB58

1 Students match the sentence halves using an appropriate relative.

2 Students create similar sentences that are true for them, personally.

Short key: time when/dance team (20); area where/ Colonies (10); moment when/where/Mr Jones (29); village which/name (20); sister who/close (2); boy who/toast (48); dream where/fly (47); machines where/which/read (17); time when/record shop (45)
Ask students to think of sentences which are true for them e.g. *I still live in the town where I was born. I have one sister who lives in X.*

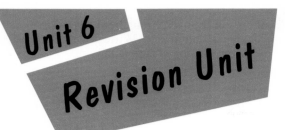

Unit 6
Revision Unit

55   Writing about people

You heard Elizabeth Egerton giving advice about how to do well in job interviews (recording 29b). Using these notes and any clues from the photo, write a short paragraph about her, either like the paragraphs about Rachel, Bruce, Chris and Edmund in Unit 1, or like those about the Yetties in Unit 2.

parents – in Richmond (South West London)

took up health counselling work

recently became a telephone counsellor – on health matters

live in Kingston, near Richmond – two young children – school

works two days a week in London

trained as a nurse (met her husband Richard during training)

for example:

Elizabeth Egerton lives in South-West London with her family, . . .

56   The things they brought

a   We asked Bruce, Rachel, Edmund and Elizabeth to bring something interesting from home to show the others.

Bruce – a medal from South America, given to him by his wife for good luck.
Rachel – her first pen, an expensive green Parker pen her father had given her when she was eleven.
Edmund – a Victorian match box, made of some sort of metal.

56a   Listen to what Elizabeth brought with her. Can you draw it from their description of it?

Show each other your drawings and compare them.

56a   **b**   What do you now know about her son? Listen again and write notes so that you can write a short paragraph about him, and why he gave this to her.

▶ Discuss what to write with your partner, then write it out neatly for the rest of the class to read. ◀

c   If you had to choose one thing to bring to class to talk about, what would it be?

▶ Write a description of it now, then bring it with you next lesson. ◀

57   *Language study*

Comments
Read the transcript for recording 56a and find comments which show what the speaker feels about the object or the whole situation.

For example: It isn't a very special picture.

Which comments are very positive and which less positive?

58   *Grammar*

Clauses with wh- words
We use clauses with **wh-** words to describe or define people and things. Can you make nine sentences from this table? How many of these sentences can you remember from earlier in this book?

Their interest in country dancing stems from the time . . .		. . . a lot of the Colonies are.
That's the sort of area . . .		. . . they say 'Well Mr. Jones, that's the job the way we see it.'
There always comes the moment . . .	WHO	. . . they were members of Yetminster Dance Team.
All of them still live in the village . . .	WHERE	. . . lives quite close.
I have one sister . . .	WHICH	. . . gave them their name.
Grimble is a small boy . . .	WHEN	. . . you could fly.
Have you ever had a dream . . .		. . . you have to read upside-down.
Is that one of those machines . . .		. . . is hoping to start a home toast delivery service.
Reminds me of the time . . .		. . . I worked in a record shop.

Take the beginnings of four of the sentences above. Change and complete them so they are true for you.

25

59 Personality tests

a Read this test. Which alternatives would a very confident person choose? What about a very shy person, lacking in confidence? Write down two lists, (e.g. 1 b 2 c etc.) one for each person.

HOW SELF-CONFIDENT ARE YOU?

'They can do all because they think they can.' VIRGIL 'Aeneid'

If you believe in yourself then others will believe in you too. It's easy to say 'Have confidence in yourself', but not so easy to achieve. Some are born with it, others not, and to those who haven't got it, or have lost it, it takes a long time to build up.

To discover how confident you are, answer the following questions – confidently.

1   Does using the telephone worry you?
a   Yes.
b   Only if I have to speak to someone I don't know.
c   No, it doesn't worry me.

2   Are you afraid of making a complaint if something you have bought is faulty?
a   I keep quiet about it.
b   I'll write a letter of complaint, not a personal one.
c   I don't mind making a scene, as long as I have my rights.

3   If you were travelling by bus but only had a £20 note, would you:
a   Walk home so as not to cause a fuss?
b   Buy something you didn't really want to get some change?
c   Get on the bus and put up with any moans from the conductor?

4   You once knocked over a vase in a shop and broke it and were made to pay for it. Did you:
a   Avoid the shop altogether?
b   Only go in when the manager was not around.
c   Go in as if nothing had happened.

5   You arrive at a party wearing exactly the same outfit as someone else. Do you: (*women only*)
a   Sneak out and change?
b   Avoid the woman and apologise if you meet her?
c   Go up and compliment her on her good taste?

6   You are more than half way to work and you realise you are wearing odd socks – one bright blue, one black. Do you: (*men only*)
a   Continue to work, prepared to laugh it off?
b   Go into a shop and buy another pair quickly, joking with the cashier?
c   Go home and change?

7   You desperately want a day off work to go to the sales or a football match. Do you:
a   Not go because you daren't ask for time off?
b   Ring up and say you are ill?
c   Go to work and pretend to be ill, leaving early?

8   You are at a small dinner party with a host and hostess whom you don't know, and suddenly in the middle of dinner, find yourself desperately wanting to spend a penny. Do you:
a   Ask where the lavatory is?
b   Say you have something stuck in a tooth and it is aching and retreat to the bathroom?
c   Hold it, and wait until after the meal?

9   Your guests compliment you on your excellent dessert, which actually came out of a packet. Do you:
a   Thank them, telling them it is your speciality?
b   Smile graciously, blush and feel embarrassed about it?
c   Tell them it came out of a packet?

10   Your neighbour's dog digs up your best rose tree. Do you:
a   Storm round to the neighbour demanding that the dog be put down?
b   Put the tree back and say nothing?
c   Thump the dog, glare at it each time it looks at you, but say nothing to the neighbour?

59a Find out about Elizabeth by listening to Edmund giving her the test. Write down what alternatives she chooses. Then see if you can work out her score. (See section 65)

b Which questions in this test did you think were inappropriate? Write some alternatives, and try them on your friends.

c Now decide how your teacher would answer. Then give him/her the revised test. Work out his/her score.

60 Coping with embarrassing situations

'Look, I'm very sorry but I've broken this vase – it was right on the edge of that shelf and I was just walking past and it fell off.'
'Oh dear, well...'

In groups choose any two of the situations given in the test.
Imagine what the people involved might say to each other.

▶   Act out one of the situations for the class to watch.

Aims: 1 To practise questions and reactions to hypothetical situations, and also explanations in English. 2 To stimulate personal anecdote telling and talk about character and personality.

Lexis: **appropriate/inappropriate, bathroom, complain** T, **complaint, conscience, daren't, demand/ ing, desperately, excellent, football, honest, honestly** T, **justice, lavatory/toilet/WC/Gents/Ladies/loo**/etc, **neighbour, nerve, overall, prepared to..., pretend to..., rights, score, succeed** Phrases: **cause a fuss, spend a penny** (= **go to the loo**/ **bathroom/toilet...**), **make a scene** (= get angry in public), **avoid a scene, to be honest**

If you have a really good confident class, you may like to let them give each other this test 'cold' before they tackle SB59a. However, most students' language will benefit from the approach suggested here, which may be more tactful if you have some students who lack confidence and may gain a low score.

Lead-in   SB59 PB59

1 Discuss personality tests in general. Do students ever do them in magazines? Read and discuss the introduction to the test about self-confidence. Do students agree with Virgil? (Virgil was an ancient Roman poet.)

Task   SB59a

2 Students do this in pairs. Encourage them to guess and then ask you about words they don't know. (You may need to help with item 8.)

3 After students have completed their lists, go through them as a class and discuss any differences of opinion.

Listening   SB59a   59a

4 Students listen to Elizabeth doing the test with Edmund. Can they work out her score (using section 65)?

Planning and report   SB59b

5 Suggest that students could improve some of the test items. (They were written for an American audience, and some may well be inappropriate for your students.) After finding out which they might like to change, set them a time limit. They must keep in mind the scoring system. Correct any mistakes. One pair can try their items out on another pair.

Task   SB59c

6 Then they can decide in groups *either* how you personally, as their teacher, would answer each one, *and/ or* how to administer the test to you! They will need to revise the scoring system for the items they have changed.

7 Students could give the revised test to you, and/or each other.

Aim: To practise language appropriate to difficult social situations.

SB60

1 Ask students how they might complete the dialogue from the scene in the picture about the broken vase. Sample: Well, there is a notice saying 'All breakages must be paid for.' I'm very sorry, but the manager insists that we do stick to this/ask customers to pay for any items they break. – But it just fell off the shelf./Well, how much would it be... etc.

Planning and report   SB60

2 Students choose two situations, and prepare a short sketch (about two or three exchanges) for each. Help them with their script, and encourage them to rehearse standing up. Get them to use a lot of expression and encourage them to feel/look/sound confident!

3 Groups of students choose one situation to act out to the whole class. Discuss their different ways of handling similar situations.

61 Grammar

Aim: To revise a variety of ways of:
1 Making hypotheses.
2 Making a contrast.
3 Expressing agreement and contrast.

Lexis: appropriate T, **contrast**

SB61a PB61

1 There are basically four ways of setting up this kind of hypothetical problem:

If + present or future tenses (question 2)
If + past tense/would (question 3)
Past tense statement (question 4)
Present tense statement (question 5)

In the examples here, these sentences are being used in the context of a quiz, and such sentences are very common in examinations or tests.

2 With questions 3–10 you can add words to mark the hypothesis: (**what**) **if/suppose/imagine/suppose**. All of these are very common ways of asking someone what they would do in certain circumstances. They are commonly used in discussions of various alternatives where people are trying to reach a decision and are considering possible disadvantages. If, for example, you are wondering what to do at the weekend you would say things like: *What if it rains? Suppose we don't have time?* etc.

SB61b

Key: 1 You've been to Africa, **whereas** I've stuck very largely to Europe.
2 Here the signature's illegible, **whereas** in letter two you can read everything.
Other ways:
... but I've stuck very largely to Europe.
... Africa. I've stuck very largely to Europe however.
... while I've stuck very largely to Europe.

SB61c

Key: 1 and 2 express contrast (**unlike ... but ...**)
3 and 4 express agreement (**same as ... like ...**)
Ask students what other words they know to mark similarity or agreement. (**similarly, Me too, So do I/So does she, Neither do I/Nor does she**, etc.
e.g. Elizabeth feels uneasy about using the phone, and so do I.
Elizabeth doesn't like using the phone and neither do I.

62 Write your own test

Aim: To recycle the language points just practised.
Lexis: appropriate/inappropriate, **ignore**, **score**
Revision: **hurt** (someone's feelings)
Phrase: **Do forgive me ...** (good example of **do** for politeness)

Students should not find this too difficult, since they have already had practice at writing separate items in section 59. However, allow plenty of time for all stages of this task. The language used in the process of planning the test is just as important as the wording and giving of the final test itself.

Writing SB62

1 Use the picture to explain optimist and pessimist. Which man is which? Why? Give students a few minutes to decide which test to work on, and who to work with.

2 Put students in groups of four working pairs, each pair devising half the test. Then each pair can try their items out on the other before finalising the complete test jointly. They may need your help with vocabulary at this stage.

3 They can pass their tests round for other groups to do.

63 First child, middle child?

Aims: 1 Co-operative discussion and opinion sharing.
2 To recycle lexis about families, relationships and feelings.
3 Listening for specific points.

Lexis: benefit, conclusion, joint
Phrases: **put up with something** (= manage in difficult situations), **draw a conclusion**, **outside influences**

Task SB63

1 Students in pairs (or threes) discuss the effects of position in family, and give reasons for their decisions.

Optional report SB63

2 Hear what some groups have to say. Do most students agree?

Listening SB63 63

3 Encourage students to take notes as they listen.

Key: Bruce was the youngest; Rachel was the youngest (of three) for a long time, then became a middle child.
Bruce thinks his youngest has the strongest character; that outside influences have more effect on character than family influences.
Rachel thinks the youngest takes longer to gain a sense of responsibility; the middle child may be more balanced.
Both mention the youngest being spoilt, but this may not be entirely relevant.

Grammar

a Expressing hypotheses

Look at questions 2, 3, 4 and 5 in section 59. What different ways are there of expressing a hypothetical problem? It is very common in arithmetic tests, for example, simply to use the present tense as in question 5:

You have £5 to share equally between three people. How much do you each get?

What is the difference between 2 and 3? You could use the words *suppose, what if, imagine* or *assume* with questions 4 and 5. What other questions could you use these words with? Rewrite question 2 so that it is like 3, and then again so it is like 4 and 5. Now write questions 3, 4 and 5 in three different ways. The meanings are not exactly the same but they are all ways of expressing a hypothesis.

b Ways of making a contrast

Whereas can be used when making a contrast. For example:

I used to be embarrassed about saying I didn't have a job, whereas now I'm not. (49)

Where can the word *whereas* fit in these quotations? Do you know two other words that are similar and can fit in the same place?

1 . . . you've been to Africa I've stuck very largely to Europe . . . (10)
2 . . . the signature's illegible in letter two you can read everything. (24)

c Agreement and contrast

Which of these sentences express agreement and which express contrast?

1 *Unlike Elizabeth I feel a bit uneasy about using the phone.*
2 *Elizabeth is quite happy about using the phone, but some people aren't.*
3 *I'm the same as Elizabeth about using the phone.*
4 *Like Elizabeth, I'm quite relaxed about using the phone.*

Choose three other questions from the test. Write a sentence like 1–4 comparing your answer with Elizabeth's.

Write your own test

Either

How tactful are you?
For example:

At a party you overhear someone talking about something you know is untrue, and could be hurtful if the information was wrongly given. Do you:

a Dash up and say, 'You're telling it all wrong.'
b Ignore it and say nothing.
c Go up and excuse yourself, saying, 'Do forgive me for butting in, but I couldn't help overhearing your conversation, and I happen to know . . .?'

Or

Optimist or pessimist?
If you wanted to find out whether someone was an optimist or a pessimist, what questions could you set? What scoring system could you use?

For example:

If you were planning to go on a picnic in England in the summer would you make alternative plans in case it rained?   *Yes/No*
Do you ever feel that people won't like things that you suggest?   *a Yes, often   b Yes, sometimes   c Hardly ever*

Choose *one* of these tests and set five questions of your own, and work out a scoring system. Give it to another group to try out!

First child, middle child?

Whose family?

Many people say that your personality depends quite a lot on your position in the family.
Find out about your partner's position in the family. From your joint experience of life, what would you say about the effects of being the first child/last child/middle child, etc?

Say which child you think:

. . . is likely to be spoilt.
. . . is likely to have a strong character.
. . . is likely to be more responsible.
. . . is likely to have the most balanced character.

63   Listen to Rachel and Bruce discussing this topic. What position were they in? What conclusions do they draw?

27

64 Poem – arithmetic

Read the poem quickly. Who do you think it was written by? A boy or a girl? Say what leads you to that conclusion.

64 What do you think about the child? Do you agree with the teachers?

▶ Write what you think about the child. Then write what you think Miss Eames might write about him/her.

Arithmetic

I'm 11. And I don't really know
My 2 Times Table. Teacher says it's disgraceful
But even if I had the time, I feel too tired.
Ron's 5, Samantha's 3, Carole's 18 months,
and then there's the Baby. I do what's required.

Mum's working, Dad's away. And so
I dress them, give them breakfast. Mrs Russell
moves in, and I take Ron to school.
Miss Eames calls me an old-fashioned word:
Dunce.
Doreen Maloney says I'm a fool.

After tea, to the Rec. Pram-pushing's slow
but on fine days it's a good place, full
of larky boys. When 6 shows on the clock
I put the kids to bed. I'm free for once.
At about 7 – Mum's key in the lock

**NEW WORDS
IN UNIT 6**

appropriate	desperately
benefit	excellent
cat	football
clock	honest
complain	honestly
complaint	joint
conclusion	justice
conscience	lavatory
contrast	neighbour
dare/n't	overall
demand	pretend
demanding	rights
description	score
	succeed

27 new words
TOTAL SO FAR 231

28

65 Keys (see sections 56a and 59).

The Analysis

1.	c - 3	2. c - 3	3. c - 3
	b - 1	b - 1	b - 1
4.	c - 3	5. c - 3	6. a - 3
			b - 1
7.	c - 3	8. a - 3	9. a - 3
		b - 1	c - 1
10.	a - 3		
	c - 1		

24-30 You have lots of self-confidence and don't mind telling the little white lie to get you out of a spot. You are prepared to stand up for your rights and will go to any lengths to see that justice is done.

15-23 Basically you are a confident person, but sometimes you have a guilty conscience, and probably blush too. Often you fail where you could succeed because your nerve lets you down at the last minute.

14 or less You have little self-confidence and wouldn't say 'boo' to a goose in case it said 'boo' back. You will put up with any situation to keep the peace and avoid a scene.

66 Words with non-

'Why am I growing wings?'
'Don't speak nonsense!'

Non can be used as a prefix added to nouns and adjectives to make them opposite in meaning. Which sentences would these fit in?

non-violent   non-stop   non-alcoholic
non-smoking   non-white   (= racially not of European origin)

What section of the plane do you want, smoking or _____?
The Philippines was a good example of a _____ revolution.
Beer? Wine? Or would you rather have something _____?
It was an easy journey, being a _____ flight.
He talked _____ about politics.
Only 119 members of the whole London Police Force are _____.

67 Ways of giving the time

67 Listen and write down all the times you hear. Decide in which place you might hear them.

Look up the entry on **time** in the Dictionary extracts at the back of the book. Write down in figures all the times written there.

Poem – arithmetic

A recording of the poem is available on the Student's Cassette only.

> **Aims:** 1 To allow students to react personally to a poem about a child.
> 2 To stimulate discussion about eldest children and the effect of position of a child in a family.
> 3 To revise lexis to do with housework, personality, schooldays, childhood routines, teachers' opinions.
>
> **Lexis: draw a conclusion**
> Revision: **even if ..., fool, clock, required**

Reading and preparation SB64 PB64

1 When discussing the picture, introduce the words **pram, Rec** (= **Recreation ground**). Then ask students to read and listen to the poem. You may need to explain '2 times table'; then students can guess that **disgraceful** means very bad.

2 Before students write about the child, you may want to revise suitable adjectives. Here is a list of adjectives and phrases from Units 1–6.

lazy, hardworking, academic, unintelligent, clever, responsible, lucky, dull, imaginative, creative, well organised, successful, bitter, narrow-minded, enthusiastic, strong, peculiar, rough, self-confident, isolated, depressed, honest, prepared to stand up for her rights, easy going, appreciates her small amount of freedom.

Report SB64

3 Students read what others have written and discuss any differences.

 Keys

SB65 This is the key to section 56a and 59.

 Words with non-

SB66

Students can do this exercise on their own, then discuss in pairs.

Key: non-smoking, non-violent, non-alcoholic, non-stop, non-stop, non-white.

67 Ways of giving the time

> **Aims:** 1 To ensure students can understand all ways of giving the time in English, and use one or two ways effectively and fluently.
> 2 To show ways of giving exact and approximate times.
> 3 To revise numbers and some fluency practice with longer numbers.

Listening task SB67 67 PB67

1 Students listen and write down all the numbers referring to time (i.e. no other numbers), and the places where they might hear these announcements.

   Key: See tapescript on page 122T.

2 Students look at the dictionary entry on **time**, and write in figures the times given in words in the first half.

3 Students could write about six times down for their partners to say quickly. Either exactly, or as more commonly used, approximately. Encourage expressions like: just after half past six, nearly eight, just gone twelve, about 5.45 etc.

4 Optional: extend to practise with other numbers if necessary.

5 Useful lexical fields to get students to brainstorm and revise at this point could include:
names of rooms in buildings/houses/hotels/schools etc.
names for people, e.g. **neighbour, fellow, guy, chap.**
Words ending in **-ist** (**artist, pianist** etc.).
Words ending in **-er** (**stranger, singer, entertainer, manager**).
-or (**director, counsellor**).
Others, e.g. **chairman/person.**

You could ask students to go through the wordlists at the end of Units 1–6 to find suitable words.

LEXICAL OBJECTIVES

Sets: ways of asking and stating the time; words used in instructions for tasks and tests: account, contrast, description, etc; words for people in different situations, eg club – **member, president**; game – **player, partner, winner**; football – **goalkeeper, centre forward**, etc

appropriate suitable for a particular situation. *in an appropriate style.*
benefit 1 noun: advantage, a good result. *whether I got a benefit from (being the youngest) I won't admit.*
2 verb: to profit from. T
3 payments from the Government: *Unemployment benefit, child benefit.*
cat (also revise other animals)
clock (also revise telling the time)
complain verb: tell someone about something wrong/unsatisfactory.
complaint 1 a criticism, or formal protest. *Are you afraid of making a complaint if something you bought is faulty? A letter of complaint.*
conclusion 1 opinion, decision. *Say what leads you to that conclusion. What conclusion did you draw?*
2 ending. *Plan the report then write a conclusion. In conclusion, may I say...*
conscience 1 the part of your mind which tells you whether something is right or wrong.
2 When you know you have done wrong – you have a guilty conscience.
contrast a great difference between two or more things. Also as verb.

dare/n't 1 to dare is to have the courage to do something. Mainly used with negative meanings. *You don't go because you daren't ask for time off.*
2 to challenge. *I dare you to spend a night in the graveyard.* T
demand 1 insist on, to ask forcefully. *Would you demand that the dog be put down?/killed?*
2 a firm request. *made a demand for.*
3 require. *Being a nurse demands a lot of patience.*
4 great need for. *no demand for coffee*
demanding 1 tiring. *a demanding job.*
description 1 *Can you draw the picture from their description of it?*
Phrase: *it's beyond description.*
desperately dreadfully. *You desperately want a day off work.*
excellent 1 very good indeed. *Your guests compliment you on your excellent dessert.*
2 to show you approve of something. *"We'll be round by 7." "Excellent!"* T
football (revise other sports and scoring systems)
honest 1 truthful, frank, open. *"I think that is too silly a question to be able to answer it, to be honest."*
2 genuine, trustworthy. *He's totally honest – would never cheat you.* T
honestly to emphasise a point. *I'll do it – I don't mind, honestly.* T
joint 1 shared by two or more people. *from your joint experience... a joint bank account. built jointly by*
2 where two things are joined.
justice 1 fairness in behaviour or the way you are treated. *go to any lengths to see that justice is done.*
2 systems of justice – law/punishments.
3 *The food was lovely, but there was so much we couldn't do it justice.*
lavatory toilet. Also useful: WC, Ladies, Gents, Public Conveniences, cloakroom, bathroom (American); "go to the loo/toilet" = "spend a penny"
neighbours people living in the next door house. Also: neighbouring countries, neighbourhood police.
overall T a situation in general, not specific. *Take three marks off the overall scores. The overall impression*
*prepared 1 prepared to = be willing and able to do something. *Are you prepared to stand up for your rights?*
2 ready for. *Be prepared for power cuts by buying lots of candles.*
pretend 1 to act to make people believe that something is the case when it isn't. *Go to work pretend to be ill and leave early.*
rights 1 something you are morally and legally entitled to have. *to stand up for your rights... have my rights. Equal rights for women.*
*scene 5 to show your anger. *I don't mind making a scene.*
score 1 verb. *who scored that goal?*
2 noun. *the overall scores. What's the score? What method of scoring?*
succeed 1 manage to do or gain something; to get on well/progress. *Often you fail where you could succeed*
2 to follow. *King George was succeeded by his daughter Elizabeth.*
*treated 1 *I was treated like the youngest child.*

The theme for most of this unit is driving. First there is discussion and, no doubt, argument about how men drive in comparison with women. There is work on instructions to do with driving, with anecdotes about driving tests and a short written anecdote about what to do in difficulties. A newspaper story provides scope for discussion and speculation about driving, and students are given two short versions of another news story to compare. The final part of the unit reintroduces the idea of metaphor in everyday language: communication is like 'sending' and words are like 'vehicles' for messages.

OBJECTIVES

Lexical objectives are in TB77

Discussion topics

a Men and women drivers. (68)
b Men and women – character differences. (68)
c Driving tests and regulations. (69)
d Anecdotes about driving. (69, 72, 74)
e Metaphor in language – comparing languages. (76)

Social skills

a Making judgements and offering justification. (68)
b Giving mitigated opinions. (68, 72)
c Offering advice. (69)
d Speculating on and predicting outcomes. (72)

Communication skills

a Instructions and advice. (69)
b Giving precise instructions in speech and writing. (71)
c Writing a short narrative. (69)
d Explaining linguistic differences. (76)

Grammar and discourse

a Making general statements and supporting these with specific examples. (68)
b Expressing contrast. (68)
c Mitigating devices: **may/might**, **sometimes**. (68)
d Modals: **should** (advice/instructions), **have to/must** (obligation). (69)
e Focus on cohesive devices: **a/the**, past perfect tense, **but**, verbs ending in **-ing**, **eventually**. (72)
f Adjectives with – (**for X**) **to . . .**: **polite**, **expensive**, **easy**, **nice**, **possible**, **unusual** etc. (73)
g Metaphorical use of verbs of giving and receiving: **give**, **send**, **take**, **get**, **receive**, **offer**, **accept** etc. (76)
h Practice Book Grammar Word: **have**.

Dictionary skills   70

a Literal and metaphorical meanings. (70, 76)
b Pronunciation: vowels (diphthongs ending in /ɪ/): /aɪ/ **tie**, /eɪ/ **race**, /ɔɪ/ **boy**, **destroy**.

68 Who make the best drivers?

Aims: 1 Prediction and advice.
2 Making general statements and supporting with specific examples.
3 Expressing contrast.
4 Making judgements and offering justification.
5 Giving mitigated opinions.

Lexis: **awkward**, **campaign**, **campaigner**, **cautious**, **comment**, **constantly**, **ditch**, **footpath**, **helpless**, **journalist**, **lane**, **liberation**, **lorry**, **meter**, **motorcyclist**, **motorist**, **motorway**, **naturally**, **panic/ky**, **pavement**, **support**, **supporter**, **van**
Revision: **Anyway . . .**, **careful**, **careless**, **take risks**, **once you get**
Understanding: **show off**, **finds faults about/with** (= finds things wrong with), **old fashioned**, **weighing down on** (= coming very close to)
Phrases: **Women's Liberation**, **Nothing could be further from the truth**, **take too many risks**, **support a campaign**, **have been had up** (= accused of), **an awful lot**, **get into a bit of a panic** ts

Task   SB68a PB68

1 Introduce the pictures very briefly as a class. Use the words **bypass**, **campaign**, **supporters**, **reporter** (bottom right). Students could do the task informally as a class or in twos. It involves prediction and advice, as well as reasoning. Give some examples first:

The most likely thing to happen will be that the car driver gives in and reverses to allow the van to pass, even though the van driver is in the wrong. The motor cyclist ought to get off the pavement or he'll cause an accident. The man by the red car will probably shout at the motorcyclist. The reporter will write up her story for the local paper.

Task   SB68b

2 This involves students making statements which express similarity or contrast, and general opinion backed by specific examples. Students could do this in pairs, and then tell the class which they agreed with.

Reading   SB68b

3 Ask students how they think children feel about this. Students can then read the children's comments.

4 You may want to go over some of the new target words at this point. You could ask students which of these words actually appear in the pictures on this page: **a country lane**, **a path**, **a pavement**, **a ditch**, **a motorway** (there's a sign for one), **a parking meter**, people supporting a **campaign**, someone looking **helpless**. You could also revise names for vehicles. Do you have any Women's Lib. supporters in your class?

5 Expand the discussion to more general statements of character differences between men and women.

Listening   SB68c   [68c]

6 To prepare for the recording, students read the summary and match the phrases from the two sets.

7 Play the recording. Students listen for the complete phrases and summarise in note form the opinions they heard.

8 Play the recording again asking students to notice expressions like 'I think', 'may', 'sometimes' etc. which show that they are mitigating (making their opinions less strong). Notice, too, how often they tend to hesitate.

Planning and report   SB68c

9 Discuss with students how far these opinions might be different with regard to their own country.

Unit 7
Drivers

Mum, why are there so many fools on the road when you're driving?

My dads always putting money in parking meters but he never wins anything!

68 ## Who make the best drivers?

a Choose three people from the pictures on this page. Say what they should do next. Consider two situations. What do you think is likely to happen next in each?

b Are there differences between the way men drive and the way women drive? Which of these statements do you agree with?

Most men drive too fast.

Women are generally more cautious than men.

Men are often careless.

Women have more accidents than men.

Men and women are equally capable.

There's not a lot of difference between the way men and women drive.

Behind the wheel

Dads thinks that they are the greatest drivers in this world. They usually comment on mums' driving. Usually the mums are right because they are naturally cautious and men have to show off. Please do not get the idea that I am a supporter of Women's Liberation, nothing could be further from the truth. Anyway when I drive I will always be right.

Ovenden

My father finds faults about my mother's driving constantly. Go left, go right, your driving is too fast and too slow. But when he is driving he does the same things himself.

Farhad Age 8

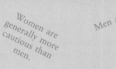

Do you agree with Ovenden and Farhad?
Do you think Ovenden is a girl or a boy?

c Chris and Edmund thought that on the whole women drivers are more cautious than men. However Edmund added that being cautious and taking more time is not always such a good thing, and that women tend to panic occasionally.

These are parts of sentences from their conversation. How might they have completed them?
Try to match the first and second sets of phrases.

I think women may be . . .
I think men tend to . . .
But then a lot of women . . .
I think the main thing is . . .
I think the thing is, though, that sometimes . . .
. . . you know, you need a sort of snappy . . .
I think sometimes women get – when they are in an awkward situation they get . . .
. . . and then, you know, once you get nervous . . .

. . . very panicky . . .
. . . like to drive faster.
. . . being cautious . . . it's actually not such a good thing
. . . a bit more cautious than men
. . . do as well
. . . judgement . . .
. . . you don't do anything right
. . . caution

 Listen and see if you were right.

Would their views apply to drivers in your own country? Write a short paragraph comparing your views with what Chris and Edmund thought.

29

69 Driving test

a Starting the car
In what order should you do these? Start with 4.

1 Put your seatbelt on.
2 Start the engine.
3 Signal your intention of pulling out.
4 Get into the car.
5 Change into first gear.
6 Make sure the road is clear by looking in the mirrors and over your shoulder.
7 Make sure that the handbrake is on and the gear lever is in neutral.
8 Check that the rear-view mirror is correctly positioned so that you can see what is behind you without moving your head.
9 Move steadily away from the kerb and drive off.
10 Let the handbrake off.

b What do you have to do for the driving test in your country? Do you have to do any of these things?

a three point turn
reversing round a corner
parking
motorway driving
a test on the Highway Code
doing an emergency stop
a written test
night driving

c Share your experiences! If you have taken a driving test, or know someone who has, tell your group about it.

▶ Choose one experience to tell the class. ◀

▶ Write about one experience you have heard about. Mention no names.

69c How did Chris and Edmund do when they took their tests?

What was the theory that Edmund told Chris about?

▶ Write down two pieces of advice you would give to someone thinking of learning to drive. Pass them round the class. Finally, make a list of the five most useful hints.

70 Dictionary skills

campaign   race   loose   tie   tight

a Look up the word campaign.
What campaigns have you had in your country? Have you ever campaigned for or against something? Look carefully at the examples given and use them to help you write one or two sentences about campaigns you know about. Read them to each other.

b Look up the words race and racial.
Which meaning of race is connected with racial? What words commonly go with this meaning?

c Skim-read the entries for loose tie tight.
Which of their meanings are concrete and which metaphorical or abstract?
Write down two phrases using these words which you think will come in useful in future. Show your partner.

71 One for the road

a Complete this story using these words.

h_lpl_ss   t_   l__k

ONE FOR THE ROAD

SHORTLY after my daughter passed her driving test, she asked me if she could borrow the car to visit some friends who lived about 70 miles away.

I didn't doubt her driving capabilities, but I was concerned about unexpected emergencies. I asked if she knew how to change a wheel.

"No, Dad," she replied, "but I *do* know how ▮▮▮▮▮▮▮."

—B. Horwitz

b Changing a wheel

Write down exactly what to do if you have a puncture. These words will help you.

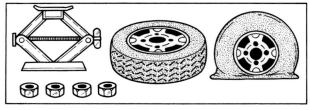

check   make sure   tighten   loosen   spare wheel
jack   wheel nuts

Driving test

Aims: 1 Giving instructions.
2 Obligation/necessity.
3 Writing a short narrative.
4 Modals **should** and **have to**.

Lexis: failed ts, **intention**, **pavement** ts, **reverse**, **theory**
Revision: **engine**, **signal**
Understanding only: **brake**, **gear**, **mirror**, **neutral**,
seatbelt
Phrases: **let ... off**, **first time round** (= the first time I
took the test), **so in other words . . .**, **the first bit**, **in the
bit where you . . .**

Task and planning   SB69a

1 If you have a mixture of drivers and non-drivers in your
class, arrange students in groups of about four, so that you
have some of each in each group.

2 Students do this first on their own and then compare with
the others in their group. Finally discuss as a class what
the correct order is.

   Key: 4 1 8 7 2 6 3 5 10 9

Task and planning   SB69b

3 If you have students from different countries, let them first
discuss and decide on these with others from their own
country. Then each group can go and tell another group
about their particular driving test. Alternatively, students
can discuss in pairs or groups.

Task and planning   SB69c

4 With students in groups, encourage anecdotes – short or
long – about taking driving tests. They should choose the
best one and prepare to tell the class.

Report   SB69c

5 Students listen to other groups' stories and take notes, so
that later they can choose one and write it up. The written
versions can then be passed round to be identified.

Listening   SB69c   [69c]

6 Play the recording twice, or more, so that students can
answer both questions.

   Key: Chris passed first time. Edmund passed second
   time. His theory was that women always passed first time,
   and men never did.

Planning and report   SB69c

7 Get students working together on advice for a non-driver
thinking of learning. Ask students to read and follow the
instructions on their own. Finally they can display their
lists of five useful hints.
Possible hints: Go to an official driving school. Do not have
lessons from a friend or relative. Have lessons regularly.
Get in as much practice as you can.

Dictionary skills

Aims: 1 Literal and metaphorical meanings. (Making L1
comparison.)
2 To show how the dictionary examples can be taken
and adapted for use in the student's own writing.
3 Pronunciation: vowels (diphthongs ending in /ɪ/): /aɪ/
tie, /eɪ/ **race**, /ɔɪ/ **boy**, **destroy**.

Lexis: campaign, **race**, **racial**, **loose** (**loosen**), **tie**, **tight**
(**tighten**), and related phrases

SB70a/b/c PB70

1 Students should do these by themselves, using the
Dictionary Extracts in their Student's Books. Ask them to
read and follow the instructions, and write exactly what is
asked for, using the dictionary examples to help them
with wording. Once they have finished, they can read
their answers to their partner.

2 You may need to help with the concept of metaphorical/
abstract meanings. The picture should help you. Ask
students if he is really tied up, as the lady talking to him on
the phone imagines him to be. (No. It just means he is very
busy so can't do anything extra.)

3 Get students to read out some of their sentences to the
class.

   Key: b race 7 relates to **racial: human race; grounds of
   colour of race; racial discrimination/equality** etc.
   c abstract/metaphorical uses: **loose** 8, 9, **tie** 6, 7 **tight**, 6, 9.

4 Get students to look up **tie up**, and say which of the
categories are metaphorical.

   Key: 5, 6

5 Go over the target sounds and phonetic symbols that
appear in these words. Ask students which words contain
the target vowel sounds; and which sound does not occur
(/ɔɪ/ as in **destroy**, which they can also look up in the
Dictionary Extracts). Revise any other symbols that
appear in the transcriptions of these words.

One for the road

Aims: 1 Speculating on outcomes.
2 Precise written instructions.

Lexis: capable T, **capabilities**, **helpless**
Revision: **concerned** (= worried), **doubt**, **emergencies**,
spare, **wheel**
Understanding: **unexpected**
Phrases: **let her go**, **have a puncture** (= have a flat tyre)

Reading   SB71a PB71

1 Students read the story on their own, and try to complete
the last sentence.

   Key: "No, Dad," she replied, "but I *do* know how to look
   helpless."

Writing   SB71b

3 Allow students to do this in small groups, so that those who
know can help those who don't.

   Sample answer: Park the car in a safe place, and/or put
   up a warning triangle. **Make sure** the handbrake is on
   tight. Put stones under the wheels. **Check** the spare tyre
   and **jack**. **Loosen** the **wheel nuts**, but leave them in
   place. Place the **jack** under the car using the proper
   jacking point, and raise the car so that the tyre is no
   longer touching the ground. Remove the **wheel nuts**.
   Take off the wheel, and put the **spare wheel** on. Put the
   wheel nuts back on loosely, by hand. **Tighten** them a
   little with the key. Lower the car onto the road and
   remove the **jack**. **Tighten** the nuts as firmly as possible.
   Put the tools and the punctured tyre in the boot. Remove
   the stones before you drive away!

72 Any idea how he did it?

Aims: 1 Using context clues to predict outcomes.
2 Focus on cohesive devices: **a/the**, past perfect tense, **but**; verbs ending in **-ing**, **eventually**.

Lexis: article, ditch, drunk, journalist, kilometres an hour (kmh), motorist, motorway, tied, tightly
Revision: **device, set up, speeding**
Understanding only: **adventure, headline, pursuers, road-block, shook off, smashed through, wrists**
Phrases: **try and make sense of it** ts, **the way journalists do**

Reading   SB72a PB72

1 Students should have few problems with new words. They have covered all the important ones earlier in this unit, and the pictures should help with the rest. Begin by discussing how to drive a car with your hands behind your back. Give no opinion as to what the right answer may be.

2 Students read the paragraphs on their own, and then tell their partner what order they think they should be in. Give no help at this stage. Get students to guess the words they don't know. Go round to see how well they are doing.

3 When some pairs have agreed on an order, let them read the article out in order, explaining to the class why they think their order is right. (e.g. 'Summit Colorado' must be first because it gives the place where the journalist was.) Does the class agree? Don't tell them whether they are right. They are going to listen to the article being read to find out.

Listening   SB72b 72b

4 Play the recording. Students see if Edmund and Chris thought the same as them. Discuss any differences of opinion.

Listening task   SB72c 72c

5 Students speculate as a class how Padilla could have driven the car. Then listen to Edmund and Chris's ideas.

6 Discuss very briefly what the Deputy Sheriff may have said. (Three short sentences, which conclude this news story.)

A Sheriff in America is like a police chief, except that he is elected by the people in the area. (Students will have seen Westerns with Sheriffs in them.)

Listening   SB72d 72d

7 Play the ending of the story.

Key: The ending is 'I have no idea how he did it. He was either sitting sideways, or he drove with his knees. His teeth are another possibility.'

73 Grammar

Aim: To practise the pattern:

It	is was might be should be etc.	easy difficult wise good etc.	(for X) to . . .

SB73 PB73

1 Students read the examples and the list of adjectives (check they understand them all), and then complete the sentences.

Key: 1 interesting 2 polite 3 easy, easy 4 nice 5 possible 6 nice 7 difficult
Point out the words 'for me' in 4 and 'for certain individuals' in 5.

2 Ask students questions like: Is it easy/difficult/possible/ impossible/cheap/expensive for you/X to get a bus/taxi home?

3 Get students to ask each other more questions like this. You could write the above table on the board, and get students to suggestion question forms and other prompt words to include in it.

74 Two stories

Aims: 1 Reading for fun.
2 Using the dictionary to find set phrases.
3 Working out what the headlines mean, and why they are funny.

Lexis: Revision: raced, turned out to be

SB74

1 Don't tell students that these stories are virtually identical. It's more fun if they find out for themselves. Tell them they are two stories from different newspapers. Which one is best? (Don't let them stop to worry about the headlines at this point.)

2 Once students have realised they are the same, apart from one slight difference in structure (wait till next section for exploitation of this), let them guess the meanings of the headlines, and then look them up in the Dictionary Extracts. Which do they think is cleverest? And do students like one version better than the other?

3 Do students know any similar stories?

4 Optional: Discuss how two different newspapers had more or less exactly the same report. (Was it the same freelance reporter who sold the story twice?)

75 Language study

Aim: Various ways of linking two events that happen closely after each other in time.

SB75 PB75

1 Get students to read out the whole sentence, using different ways of linking. Notice the change of position for the subject, **police**.

2 Ask why the reporters probably preferred the first two ways for their news stories. (The word **police** early on in the sentence helps to set the scene.)

3 Students do the sentences about Padilla and Edmund. Point out that they must think of the meaning. For instance where there is a longer time delay, **on . . .** is not suitable.

Key: a After driving on . . . Padilla ended . . .; Having driven on . . . Padilla ended
b After reading/Having read a paragraph . . ., Edmund tried to . . .
Another way would be: When he had read . . .

72 Any idea how he did it?

a Is it possible to drive a car with your hands tied tightly behind your back? If so, how?

The paragraphs in this news article have been mixed up. Can you say which order they should be in?

Handcuffed drunk takes police car for a ride

Claude Padilla, 28, had been handcuffed and put in the front passenger seat of the police car, with the seat belt on.

The police eventually set up a device which punctured his tyres, but Padilla still swerved on for another three kilometres before ending his adventure in a ditch, handcuffs intact.

Adventure ended in ditch

Travelling at up to 160 kmh, he shook off police pursuers and smashed through a roadblock.

SUMMIT (Colorado) — A motorist stopped for drunken driving and speeding managed to take a police car and drive it 110 km — even though he had his wrists handcuffed behind his back.

But while the policeman was moving Padilla's car off the road, he drove off the wrong way down a motorway.

72b **b** Write down the order Edmund and Chris suggested. Was it the same as yours?

c So how did he drive the car? Do you think he used his chin? his teeth? knees? feet? How could he have been sitting?
Do you think the police had left the car engine running? Could he have switched it on?
What about the handbrake? (Most American cars have automatic gear change.)

72c Listen to what Edmund and Chris thought.

Now discuss what might be in the last paragraph. It beings:
Deputy Sheriff James Doughty said: _____

72d **d** Listen to the end of the story.

---

73 *Grammar*

it + be + adjective + to
Look at these sentences:

Is it possible to drive a car with your hands tied tightly behind your back? (72)
It's difficult to put my ideas into words. (76)

The pattern **it + be + adjective + to...** is very common with these adjectives:

GOOD/BAD: pleasant/unpleasant; nice/nasty; polite/rude; interesting/boring; useful/useless.
EASY/DIFFICULT: possible/impossible; cheap/expensive; hard.
WISE/FOOLISH: sensible/silly; useful/useless; helpful/pointless; safe/dangerous.

Complete these sentences using the words above.

1 *I should have been studying but I found it more _____ to walk about.* (11)
2 *It's _____ to knock before you enter an office.* (31)
3 *It's _____ to say 'Have confidence in yourself', but not so _____ to achieve.* (59)
4 *It would be very _____ for me to have a picture that I could carry around with me.* (56)
5 *It is _____ for certain individuals to live to ... great ages.* (95)
6 *It's so _____ to have dinner in bed.* (237)
7 *It was very _____ to drive handcuffed the wrong way down a motorway.* (72)

---

74 Two stories

Which version is best?

Joyriding at 80

BRUSSELS: Police stopped a car which raced past a 'halt' sign in Euskirchen, West Germany, and found a man of 84 at the wheel. 'Don't tell my mother I borrowed her car', he begged. She turned out to be 101.

Mum's the word

WHEN police stopped a car which raced past a "halt" sign at Euskirchen, West Germany, they found a man of 84 at the wheel.
"Don't tell my mother I borrowed her car," he begged. She turned out to be 101.

---

75 *Language study*

Linking clauses
Read the first sentence of each story in section 74. Notice how they are different.

Police stopped ... and found ...
When police stopped ... they found ...

Try using these other ways of linking them:
After stopping ..., police found ...
On stopping ..., police found ...
Having stopped ..., police found ...

Find three different ways to write each of these:

a *Padilla drove on for another three kilometres but ended his adventure in a ditch.*
b *Edmund read a paragraph from a book and then tried to explain it to Elizabeth.*

76 We are all postmen...

a In English you can **give** people **things, looks, thoughts, words.** For example:

She gave me a knowing look.

Divide this list into four categories.

a book
some news
a nice smile
a present
some good advice
all the answers
a message from...
a quick glance
an idea

b Here are some other things you can **do** with the following:

– **a message** (give, send, take, get, receive, pass on)
– **some ideas** (give, get, offer, pass on, get across)
– **advice** (give, offer, receive, take, pass on, accept)

What words do you use with messages, ideas and advice in your language? Is it similar to English?

c The concept of metaphor
Communication is sending and receiving.
Ideas are objects...
Linguistic expressions (sentence, phrase) are containers.

Examples:
It's difficult to put my ideas into words.
It's hard to get that idea across to him.
The meaning is right there in the words.
Give me some more examples.
Give him my best wishes.
Could you pass on that message?
He took my advice.
Do you get it, now?
His words were hollow.
He wrote me a letter full of instructions...

76c Edmund tries to explain this concept to Elizabeth. Which of these examples does he use? What does Elizabeth mean when she says:
We are all postmen. Postpeople...?

77 REVIEW

UNIT 7

a What do they do/believe in?

artist	Marxist
capitalist	motorist
chemist	motorcyclist
communist	pianist
dentist	scientist
economist	socialist
journalist	

Look up any words you don't know. Choose seven people. Using a dictionary to help you, write a sentence saying what each person does or believes in.

For example: *An artist is someone who draws and paints as a job or for a hobby.*

b What's the theme?
Give a general name for each set of words. Add one word to each set. The first one is done for you.

van   lorry   motorbike

Car (general term: motor vehicles)

box   tin   packet   cup
lane   avenue   motorway
inches   feet   miles
millimetres   centimetres   metres

c Adjectives
Use one of these to complete each phrase.
awkward   cautious   capable   constant   helpless
loose   packed   tight

1 *They were completely _____ with laughter!*
2 *The child's _____ questions never failed to annoy her – he just went on and on asking.*
3 *The cinema entrance was _____ with Saturday night crowds.*
4 *In my judgement, I'd say she's rather a _____ person; never acts without thinking.*
5 *Oh dear – that's Max's first wife over there – how _____.*
6 *Her long brown hair was _____ about her shoulders.*
7 *Wearing a loose white shirt over a pair of _____ blue jeans...*
8 *She passed her driving test first time – in fact she's a very _____ driver.*
9 *A sports car, _____ of speeds up to 130 mph.*

**NEW WORDS
IN UNIT 7**

article	lorry
awkward	metre
campaign D	motor
capability	motorist
capable	motorway
cautious	mum
comment	naturally
communication	neutral
communist	pack/packed
concept	packet
constant	panic
constantly	path
contain	pavement
container	racial D
ditch	reverse
drunk	seat belt
fail	signal
helpless	supporter
intention	theory
journalist	tie D
judgement	tight/ly D
kilometre	tin
lane	unexpected
liberation	van
loose/ly D	yard

50 new words
TOTAL SO FAR 281

KEY to story in section 71a:
"...to look helpless."

76 We are all postmen ...

Aims: 1 Metaphorical use of **give**, **receive** etc.
2 Explaining linguistic differences.

Lexis: articles, communication, concept, container, packed, passage (= path, corridor), (**packet**)
The concept of metaphor will be familiar to students who have covered CCEC Level 2. Remind them of the concepts:
Your *mind* is a *container* (e.g. A thought came into my mind; I can't get him out of my mind)
Life is a journey (e.g. When you reach the age of 42...) Also remind students of **tied up** etc. in section 70.

Lead-in   SB76 PB76

1 You could begin by brainstorming with students for examples of things that can be containers (**box, tin, bowl, bucket** etc.) and vehicles (**car, motorbike** etc.).

Task   SB76a/b

2 Ask students to read through and consider, and then discuss. Point out that we are not physically giving or passing on by hand when we talk about **ideas, messages, looks, advice** etc. This is what we call the 'metaphorical' (more abstract) use of these words.

Key: a Things: book, present; Looks: smile, glance; Thoughts: an idea; Words: advice, message, answers.

3 Can students use similar words in their own language?

Understanding the concept of communication as a metaphor can help students remember what words (and what sorts of words) and phrases can be used when talking about communicating, e.g. 'Did you get my meaning?' is used to mean 'Did you understand?' It's as if we had sent the meaning (like an object) across to the other person, and were checking it had arrived safely (hence the idea of a postman).

Listening   SB76c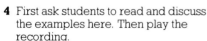

4 First ask students to read and discuss the examples here. Then play the recording.

Key: Elizabeth means that, like postmen, we do a lot of sending and delivering of things, only in our case these are words and ideas rather than letters and parcels etc.
Note: The word 'postpeople' she has coined herself. Some people regularly change words ending in **-man/-men** like **postman/postmen chairman/chairmen** to **-person/people**, like **chairperson/chairpeople**. They believe this is less sexist.

77 Review

Key and notes:
a Students use any dictionary to help them with this.
b container, road, non-metric measurements, metric measurements.
c 1 helpless 2 constant 3 packed
4 cautious 5 awkward 6 loose
7 tight 8 capable 9 capable

LEXICAL OBJECTIVES

Sets: words for roads, paths: **lane, avenue, motorway, pavement, track** etc. distances: **mile, kilometre, yards, metres** etc. Names of vehicles: **lorry, truck, van, motor car/bike** etc. Words for containers: **box, tin, packet** etc.

article 1 *a newspaper article.*
2 an object or item. *You are talking in terms of space and articles and objects ... an article of furniture.*
3 term used in grammar. 'The'/'a' are definite/indefinite articles T
awkward 1 uncomfortable, not elegant. *in an awkward position.* T
2 embarrassed. *I felt awkward at the big formal dances* T
3 embarrassing, difficult. *Women when in an awkward situation – get panicky.*
campaign D
capabilities 1 ability and qualities. *I didn't doubt her driving capabilities.*
capable 1 able to, likely to, having the skill. *She was a capable driver. A poison capable of causing death.* T
cautious 1 careful. *Women drivers are naturally cautious.*
comment 1 verb: to give an opinion. *Dads usually comment on Mums' driving.*
2 noun: make a comment. *No comment!*
communication 1 Communication is sending ... *effective communication systems, eg telephones, satellites.*
communist 1 someone who believes in communism.
concept 1 idea or principle. *Richard tried to explain this concept to Liz.*
constant/constantly 1 all the time. *My mother finds faults with my father's driving constantly.*
2 a constant amount stays the same. *a constant temperature of 76 degrees.* T
contain 1 *a box containing shopping.*
2 *Does this contain sugar?* T
container *a container lorry holds large containers from aeroplanes.* T
ditch 1 narrow channel beside a road. *His adventure ended in a ditch.*
drunk 1 from too much alcohol. *Drunken driving.*
fail EED 1 *fail her driving test*
2 not to do something. *failed to recognise her.* Phrase: *without fail.* T
3 to stop working properly. *The brakes failed and ... His sight is failing.*
helpless 1 with no power or strength to react normally. *I do know how to look helpless! helpless with laughter.*
intention idea or plan *Signal your intention of pulling out.*
journalist a person who works on a newspaper/magazine and writes articles for it. *This is introducing the drunk the way the journalists do.*

judgement EED 1.1 a considered opinion. *My personal judgement is...* T
1.2 a decision made by a judge. T
2 the ability to make sensible guesses or decisions about what do to. *You need a sort of snappy judgement...*
kilometre ⅝ of a British mile
lane 1 a narrow country road.
2 *most motorways have three lanes.* T
liberation freedom. *Women's Liberation*
loose/ly D
lorry large vehicle. (American = truck)
metre just over one yard.
meter *parking meter, gas meter.*
motor car/vehicle
motorist person who drives a car
motorway very wide road.
mum 1 mum = mother; an informal use.
2 keep mum = keep something quiet. *Mum's the word* = agree to keep secret.
naturally D
neutral 1 not supporting anyone in a war/argument, or showing feelings. T
2 in neutral (gear) in a car.
pack 1 *Sending an article across to you packed in a case. We packed all our gear ... into a flightcase* (100)
2 crowded. *The theatre was packed.*
3 full of. *the book is packed full of useful information.*
packet 1 container. *a packet of cigarettes/biscuits/sweets*
panic fear, strong anxiety. *to get into a bit of a panic. Don't panic!*
path 1 footpath, track.
2 the line along which a thing moves. *Stopped the bullet in its path.* T
pavement path (with a hard surface) by the side of a street. (Americans say 'sidewalk')
*race D
racial D
reverse 1 change to the opposite way. *reverse the process. In reverse. The government reversed their decision.* T
2 to drive a car backwards. *Then you have to reverse; in reverse (gear).*
seatbelt *Seatbelts must be worn, by law.*
signal noun and verb. *Signal your intention of pulling out.*
supporter someone who supports a campaign/political party/football team
theory 1 a set of ideas based on a lot of thinking but not completely proved. (theory of evolution) *When I took my driving test there was this theory that women always passed first time.*
2 *Marxist theories, musical theory.*
tie D
tight/ly D Also verb – to tighten. *He tightened his seatbelt.*
tin 1 a soft silvery white metal.
2 a metal container. *a tin of sardines. I rarely eat tinned food.*
unexpected surprising, or unforeseen. *unexpected emergencies*
van a vehicle used to carry goods.
yards There are 1760 yards in a mile.

Problems and solutions

In this unit a variety of texts all illustrate and recycle a very common text pattern in English. There is intensive practice to show how an understanding of such common patterns is of value in spoken and written English.

OBJECTIVES

Lexical objectives are in TB88

Discussion topics

a Shopping – deciding what to buy. (78)
b Solving an ecological problem. (80)
c Scientific research (road safety). (83)

Social skills

a Making choices and giving reasons. (78)
b Telling anecdotes. (78, 83)
c Speculating and hypothesising. (80)
d Discussing problems and advising on solutions. (86)

Communication skills

a Identifying problems and offering solutions. (78,80)
b Marking stages in the development of discourse. (78)
c Identifying and realising the common discourse structure: Situation–Problem–Solution–Evaluation. (79, 80, 83, 85)
d Comparing and evaluating different solutions. (80)
e Summary skills based on recognition of the overall structure of the text. (80, 83, 87)
f Scanning a text for new information. (83)

Grammar and discourse

a The use of **but** and similar words to mark a transition from one stage of the discourse to the next. (78)
b Ways of describing things. (78, 81)
c The use of **that** to introduce a statement or idea, particularly following nouns like **problem**, **thing** etc. (85)
d The use of **to** to introduce an action, particularly following nouns like **answer**, **solution**, **thing** etc. (85)
e Intonation in a complex sentence. (81)
f Practice Book Grammar Word: **of**.

Dictionary skills   84

Finding useful phrases.

---

78 Looking at adverts

Aims: 1 Identifying problems and offering solutions.
2 Recognising stages in the development of the discourse.
3 Identifying the central two parts of the common discourse structure: Situation–Problem–Solution–Evaluation.

Lexis: absent (minded), aware, bulky, combine, combination, container, contemporary, credit card, effective, fold, function, gift, liquid, locate, solid, steel, stone, tough
Phrase: **not only . . . but also**
Revision: **comfort, comfortable, design, elegant, pour, serve you for . . ., space-saving, store** (= keep), **tend to . . ., top quality**
Understanding only: **increasingly, minder** (in the sense of **child minder** from **mind** meaning to look after), **slips** (= goes easily/fits)

Lead-in   SB78

1 Find out if any students have ever bought things from mail-order adverts. The adverts on this page are all from a small mail-order catalogue.

Task   SB78a

2 Students look at the pictures and adverts and discuss in pairs. They list the items in answer to the questions.

Key: Travellers: alarm clock, key-minder. Containers: flask, wallet. Same material: wallet, jacket (not alarm clock – that is just 'leather-look' i.e. not real leather). Gift: key-minder. Cold climate: leather jacket.

Reading task   SB78b

3 Go through the phrases first, explaining any new lexis. Don't tell students which items they could refer to. Students read the text of the adverts to fit in the phrases. If they ask about any target lexis, write it on the board. Later see if any other students can explain it.

Key: flask, wallet, key-minder, jackets, key-minder, alarm clock, jackets.

SB78c

4 Ask students to think about this on their own, before discussing as a class.

Key: But signals a contrast. The first and third adverts begin with a positive statement and the **but** introduces a problem. The fourth begins with a problem, and the **but** signals that the problem is solved. So here it also marks a transition point – a change of direction – in the text as a whole. Other words like **but**: **whereas**, **however**, **while**

Listening   SB78d   78d

5 Students listen to find out which two items are under discussion.

Key: Leather jacket and slimline wallet.
The expression 'you've killed two birds with one stone' is used because with one jacket, you have both warmth (in the padding) and strength (leather is a tough, long-lasting material). (i.e. Two problems are solved, not just one.)

6 Ask students to find phrases which describe and evaluate the products in a very positive way.

Key: solid stainless steel; all the latest functions; most elegant . . . currently available; effective against the cold; combination of style and comfort; space-saving; great gift.

---

79 Language study

Aim: To help students identify the common discourse pattern: Situation–Problem–Solution–Evaluation.

Lexis: solution, evaluation
Revision: **device, empty, structure**

SB79 PB79

1 Ensure that students read the table down each column. Ask students to expand the notes into full sentences.

2 Students think how they would complete the table. First supply the two missing evaluations (do these orally), then get students to copy the table format for the remaining two items and fill it in.

Key:

Situation		travellers need
Topic	flasks	alarm clocks
Problem	break easily	size
Solution	solid steel	3" square, folds flat
Evaluation	serve a lifetime; retain temperature for hours; stopper prevents leakage	inexpensive personalised gift

33T

Unit 8
Problems and solutions

78 Looking at adverts

a Look carefully at these items from the *New Horizons* catalogue. Which things:

– are ideal for people who travel a lot?
– could be classified as containers?
– are made of the same material?
– would be the best gift for an absent-minded person?
– might be useful for a person who lives in or travels to a cold climate?

b Which adverts do these phrases come from?

The fold-away handle makes for easy pouring and storage   wearing a jacket.   a pushbutton light   top quality hand-made   this new version   This is the one they use.   warmth and comfort

c Find the word **but** in the left-hand adverts. What does it signal? Think of other words like **but**.

78d   d Which of the adverts are Edmund and Elizabeth talking about here?
What do they mean:

There you've killed two birds with one stone?

Leather Jackets

Leather jackets have become increasingly popular and fashionable over the last few years, but in the long winter months they just don't keep the cold out. Here's the solution. These beautiful ▆▆ jackets from Somerset combine the suppleness and style of real leather with the unbeatable ▆▆▆▆▆ of genuine 100% British sheepskin...

Time folds flat

Our buyers stay in hotels all over the world, so they are very aware of the need for a good alarm clock that doesn't take up space in the suitcase. ▆▆▆ Just 3″ square with all the latest functions, the soft black leather look case folds flat for travel. An inexpensive and very personal gift. Personalisation: Up to 3 initials.
Fold Away Alarm £6.95 JS3633C*

Designer Shirt Wallet

There are times when you need to carry a wallet but you're not ▆▆▆▆▆ This slim leather wallet (4″ x 2½″) will hold credit cards and notes, and slips discreetly into your shirt pocket. From the house of Pierre Cardin, this is the most elegant shirt wallet currently available at such a low price.
Pierre Cardin Shirt Wallet £6.95 CZ847

The Unbreakable Flask

The problem with flasks is that they tend to break easily, but now we've found one that should serve you for a lifetime. An elegant and contemporary design in solid stainless steel, it will retain the temperature of hot or cold liquid for hours. ▆▆▆ ▆▆▆▆▆ while the threaded stopper prevents leakage.
Unbreakable Flask 1-litre capacity £24.95 JS4046C

Keyminder

Not only does the keyminder bleep when you whistle, enabling you to easily locate your keys, but ▆ also incorporates an LCD clock and ▆ ▆▆▆ to illuminate your lock. A great gift.
Keyminder £4.95 JS4708C

79 *Language study*

SITUATION – PROBLEM – SOLUTION – EVALUATION
Notice the structure of these adverts. Read the notes in the table carefully, then suggest what words or phrases from the texts could go into the empty spaces. Then continue building up the table with notes from the other adverts.

Situation General topic	Leather jackets popular and fashionable	men often carry a wallet	car keys		
The problem is that...	In winter, don't keep cold out (too thin)	when not wearing a jacket (too bulky for shirt pocket)	(people lose them) (difficult to use in dark)		
The solution is to...	line jacket with sheepskin	slim leather wallet 4 x 2½, fits in shirt pocket	bleeper device when you whistle. light		
Evaluation	warmth and comfort combined with style	_____	_____		

80 Seagulls

80a a What sounds can you hear? What possible links can there be between the sounds on the tape? Use the pictures to help you.

What do you think the problem is? What three possible solutions can you think of?

Now look at the first two paragraphs of the article. Were you right about the problem and the solutions? Finally, read the whole article. What information do the last four paragraphs give you? What problems do they present? What solutions are offered? Is the solution likely to be successful?

How a reservoir is gulling the gulls

from ROGER KERR in Glasgow

TAPE-RECORDED squawks of a seagull in distress have enabled water authorities in Strathclyde to cleanse two reservoirs at Milngavie, near Glasgow, by frightening away an estimated 5,000 gulls which were polluting the water.

Although the technique has been used successfully at airports, Strathclyde officials believe this is the first time it has been operated at a reservoir.

Throughout the country, water authorities are plagued, mainly in winter, by roosting seagulls mucking up their reservoirs. Three years ago Strathclyde Regional Council's water department found that seagulls were causing a potential health risk on two reservoirs serving Glasgow.

The cost prohibited covering the two reservoirs at Milngavie or building an improved treatment plant. Instead, Dr Patricia Monaghan, a lecturer at Glasgow University's zoology department, and research student Colin Shedden found the answer—scare them off with a seagull's distress call.

So, during the winter months, a van equipped with a loudspeaker and tape bearing the agonised squawks of a captured seagull held upside down slowly toured the reservoirs for two hours before dusk—a period when gulls fly in to roost.

'When the birds come in looking for a safe place to roost, a fellow bird's distress call will scare them off' said Dr Monaghan.

The Observer

Plan a short four line summary of the article using the framework below. Think of a better title for the article to use for your summary.

The **situation/general topic**...	
The **problem**...	
Two **proposed solutions**...	
Evaluation of the proposed solutions...	
Final solution...	
Evaluation...	

34

in distress — approximate
estimated — making it dirty
polluting — possible
technique — put into action
operated — scared and very worried
potential — method

treatment plant — danger
risk — just before dark
scare off — carrying
equipped with — similar
dusk — frighten away
fellow — factory

80b b Compare the summary that Elizabeth suggested with the summary that you wrote. Did you cover the same points?

80c c What did they say about the headline and the first paragraph?

81 *Language study*

Understanding a complex sentence
Practise reading these sentences quickly. After each one, say what the new information is about.

A van _____ toured the reservoir.

A van equipped with a loudspeaker and tape _____ toured the reservoir.

A van equipped with a loudspeaker and tape bearing the agonised squawks of a _____seagull _____toured the reservoir.

A van equipped with a loudspeaker and tape bearing the agonised squawks of a captured seagull held upside down slowly toured the reservoir.

Look at paragraph 5 of the newspaper article; how many additional phrases are there? Now work out how to read the whole paragraph out loud.

81 Listen to it being read on tape.

82 Peanut butter

Why do you think the boy did this?
This was the **solution** – can you work out what the **problem** was?
Clue: The boy involved was three years old.

▶ Tell the class what you think. ◀

Aims: 1 To encourage speculation.
2 Identifying and realising the common discourse structure: Situation – Problem – Solution – Evaluation.
3 Comparing and evaluating different solutions to a problem.
4 Summary skills based on recognition of the overall structure of a text.

Lexis: **bulk, distress, dusk, operated, plant** (= machinery), **pollution, potential, regional, research, technique, treatment**
Revision: **authorities, birds, cause, fellow, get across** ts, **health, improved, present** (= give), **rather than** (= instead of), **risk, scare, serving, throughout, van**
Understanding only: **equipped with, estimated, loudspeaker, reservoir, prohibited, toured, seagulls, upside down**

Lead-in SB80a `80a`

1 Before you play the recording explain to students that it is a 'mystery' recording of a sequence of different noises, relevant to the pictures. Can they guess what the noises are? Let them compare ideas with each other. Do not tell them whose guesses are actually correct – they will find out when they read the article.

Task, planning and report SB80a

2 Discuss what the problem is. (The reservoir is being polluted by birds (seagulls).) Ask students to discuss in pairs, and find three possible solutions.
(Sample solutions: shoot the seagulls; cover the reservoir; mechanical or human bird-scarers (but how exactly?) treating (= purifying/cleaning) the water before use.)
As they report to the class ask students to evaluate each solution.

Reading and note-taking SB80a

3 Students read the first two paragraphs and see how well they guessed the solution. Go over the new target vocabulary. (In the headline, 'gulling' is a very rare word for 'deceiving'; used as a joke, a play on words.)

4 Ask students to read the whole article, guessing words they don't know, and taking notes of the main points.

5 Check students' notes. Point out the structure of this news report:
Paragraph 1 gives (in this order) the solution, evaluation ('have enabled'), and the problem (5000 gulls polluting . . .) in one sentence. The rest of the report takes each component and expands on it.
Paragraph 2 gives more evaluation; historic detail.
Paragraph 3 – statement of the problem (general – specific area).
Paragraph 4 two solutions and evaluations (one negative, one positive).
Paragraph 5 explains how the solution is put into practice.
Paragraph 6 explains why it works (evaluation expanded).

Summary writing SB80a

6 Encourage students to draft the summary without looking back at the text. (If often helps if they imagine they are trying to explain it orally to someone who hasn't read it.) They need not make a whole new sentence for each section of the framework. About 60–70 words in all.

Sample summary: Reservoirs everywhere are being polluted by seagulls, causing a health risk. Two solutions were proposed. The first, covering the reservoirs, proved too costly. However a research student found that seagulls were scared away if they heard a seagull's distress call. So recordings of a seagull in distress are played daily before dusk and the reservoirs have been cleaned up.

Listening SB80b `80b`

7 Students listen and compare their summaries. (Students' summaries may well be better than Elizabeth's!)

Key: The headline is 'rather useless information' but it 'does draw your interest to the article'. The first sentence, which is 'long and bulky', contains 'the essence of the whole article'.

8 Optional: Play the mystery recording 80a again, and ask students to explain (orally, or in writing) each sound. Which sounds are not actually mentioned in the article? Are these sounds in any way relevant? (Owl, though owls are heard at dusk; rain, though it's rain that fills the reservoirs.) See tapescript on page 000T for detailed key.

81 **Language study**

Aims: 1 To draw attention to ways of describing things, especially clauses beginning with verbs ending in **-ed** and **-ing**.
2 To show students the complexity of noun phrases and how they are built up.

SB81 `81` PB81

1 Students read out loud – quickly – the words printed, ignoring the blank space in each sentence. (For example, 'A van toured the reservoir.') They will notice the blank space gets shorter as additional parts of the sentence are replaced. Make this fun – see how fast they can read each one.

2 When students have identified what information is new, ask them to pick out the verbs ending in **-ed** and **-ing** which describe things, and repeat each separate clause on its own: a captured seagull / a captured seagull held upside-down / tape bearing the agonised squawks of a . . .

3 Read the original paragraph which is even longer, phrasing it clearly. Note how little punctuation there is in the original text.

4 Play the recording of the paragraph being read, and let students read along with it. They should notice how the reader 'punctuates' it with her intonation, and how few words carry a main stress.

82 **Peanut butter**

Aims: 1 Practice in co-operative discussion and decision making.
2 Drafting a concise statement of a problem.
3 More exposure to the text pattern of Situation – Problem – Solution – Evaluation.

It is important that this section is covered and the story is read before students tackle section 85.

Task SB82

1 The solution is illustrated by the photo. You may need to explain that peanut butter is a mixture of oil and ground peanuts. Encourage each group to think of as many possibilities as they can. Do not give them any clue as to the original situation, or let them turn over to section 87a to read the story yet.

Report SB82

2 Students could either tell other groups, or write a paragraph, which can be passed from group to group.

3 Ask them to read the original story in section 87a on page 36, and react to it. The story is also in recording 87a.

4 They could write the summary from section 87a for homework.

83 Airbags and motorcycles

Aims: 1 Writing brief explanations as captions.
2 Summary skills based on recognition of the overall structure of the text.
3 Scanning a text for new information.

Lexis: apparently, automatically, developing, fitted, frame, inflates, instantly, killed, rider, scientists, shot
Revision: **effect, less likely, prevents, receive, injuries**
Understanding only: **breakthrough** (= development/achievement), **on the verge of** (= about to)

Lead-in   SB83

1 Start with some informal discussion. How many of your students can ride a motorbike? Do they have friends with motorbikes? Are crash-helmets necessary by law in students' countries? Allow students to recount informally any opinions about motorbikes or experiences of motorcycling they want to share.

Reading   SB83a

2 Students read the beginning of the report. Ask what they would expect to read in the rest of the report. Then students will need to match notes with pictures. (The notes are jumbled.) Help them to expand the notes accurately and clearly.

Planning and report   SB83b

3 Students use the facts available on this page to plan and write (or present orally) a brief report of this experiment. Basically this entails re-ordering and linking some of the phrases supplied.

Listening   SB83c

4 Students listen once through to compare summaries. Elizabeth's question was 'How would it inflate quickly enough?'

5 Play the tape again and ask students to listen for features which are more typical of a spoken summary than a written one. (Elizabeth uses a question and answer technique for her summary, which is more usual in spoken than written form. Also, note her use of 'you' and 'this', e.g. 'you invent this airbag'.)

Reading   SB83d SB87b

6 Students turn to section 87b on page 36. Encourage students to scan the text quickly to spot extra facts.

Key: balloon bag is fired by gas, developed in Transport Road Research Lab; cannot totally prevent injuries, but makes a difference. 'Theory is proved'. Already used in some cars.

Listening   SB83e

7 Students should be able to write the summary for homework.

84 Dictionary skills

Aims: 1 To show students how examples and definitions illustrate the typical grammatical environment of a word.
2 To help students recognise and adapt phrases relevant to the context in question.

Lexis: dramatic, effect, effective
Revision: **required by law**

SB84

1 Students can do this singly, then compare results.

2 Students practise saying the phrases with prepositions.

Key: a into effect (cat.4)
b an effective way (cat.1)
c effect of... on (cat.1)
d took effect/was put into effect (cat.4)
e more effectively
Point out that category 2 of **effectively** is similar to the phrase **in effect** (category 2 of **effect**).

Other words you may like students to look up (in any dictionary) are **function, operate, solid** and **tough** – all words with several meanings and useful phrases

85 Grammar

Aims: 1 To highlight fronting devices which signal the structure of a text.
2 The uses of **that** to introduce a statement or idea, particularly following nouns like **problem, thing** etc.
3 The use of **to** to introduce an action, particularly following nouns like **answer, solution, thing** etc.

SB85 PB85

1 Discuss the examples with students, bringing out the use of **that** (for a statement or idea) and **to** (for action).

2 Students discuss the phrases in pairs.

Only in context can we be absolutely sure what a phrase introduces. We can, however, often make a good guess even without a context to help us. A phrase like 'The best thing is...' is unlikely to introduce a problem, and something like 'One difficulty is...' is equally unlikely to signal a solution. If a student offers an answer which conflicts with the key, ask them for an example.

Key: The best thing is... (solution)
What worries me is... (problem)
It was too big... (problem)
One possibility might be... (solution)
The answer could be... (solution)
The trouble is... (problem)
The only thing is... (problem: e.g. I'd like to get a new car. The only thing is I haven't enough money. *or* solution: e.g. If you haven't enough money the only thing is to try and save more.)
One difficulty is... (problem)
One way out would be... (solution)
The worrying thing is... (problem)
The disadvantage might be... (problem)

3 Revise these phrases commonly used when speaking, to highlight a situation, problem etc.:
What I said, was, .../What I think is, .../What I thought was, ... (usually without **that**)
For example: What I thought was, you could complete some of these sentences for homework...
(This would act as a solution to the problem: What's for homework? *or* How can you get more practice with these?)

a Read the beginning of the news report and make explanatory captions for the pictures. There are some words and phrases to help you. Add any more you need.

Air bags for m-cycles being tested

By DONALD HIGGS
London Correspondent

LONDON — British scientists believe they may be on the verge of a major breakthrough in saving life and serious injury in motorcycle accidents.

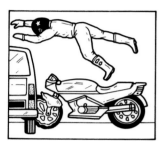

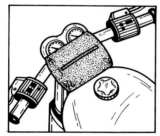

... prevents rider being shot forward

British scientists ... developing ... a balloon bag

... inflates automatically and instantly

Most riders fly over the handlebars ...

... fitted to the frame of the machine ...

... rider less likely to be injured ...

... receive serious, even fatal, injuries.

The airbag has a 'braking' effect on the motorcycle.

.... slows down the speed at which he's shot clear

b Plan a very brief report of this experiment to follow on from the paragraph above. Use some of the phrases in section 83a. As you plan, write down any questions you have about points that are not clear.

83c **c** Edmund and Elizabeth did the same. What points did they include? What question did Elizabeth have?

d Read the full length article (Section 87). What extra facts does it give you?

e Using the Situation – Problem – Solution – Evaluation framework, write a summary of it.

Finding suitable phrases
effect   effective   effectively

Look up these words and make a list of the prepositions that commonly occur with them. Find suitable phrases and adapt them to complete these sentences.

a   *The plan to use tape recordings of a seagull's distress call was first put _____ in the Spring of 1981. (80)*
b   *This had previously proved to be _____ of reducing the number of birds around airports. (80)*
c   *The _____ the seagull's distress call _____ the other seagulls were quite dramatic. (80)*
d   *The law _____ on 21st July last year. (2 ways)*
e   *Traffic police helped to make the system work _____*

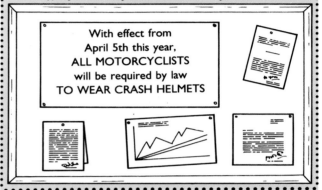

With effect from
April 5th this year,
ALL MOTORCYCLISTS
will be required by law
TO WEAR CRASH HELMETS

---

85 *Grammar*

The problem is that ... the solution is to ...
We use **that** to introduce a situation or problem. We use **to** to introduce the action you would take in finding a solution:

My brother's problem was that he couldn't open the door without using both hands, and he was carrying a slice of bread and peanut butter at the time. His solution was to plaster the sticky side of the bread to the wall while he opened the door.

What bothered the old man was that he had borrowed his mother's car without asking, so he begged the police not to tell her.

If you see smoke the obvious thing is to telephone the fire brigade.

Which of these phrases do you think would introduce **problems** and which would introduce **solutions**? Are there any that might do either?

The best thing is ...
What worries me is ...
It was too big ...
One possibility might be ...
The answer could be ...
The trouble is ...
The only thing is ...
One difficulty is ...
One way out would be ...
The worrying thing is ...
The disadvantage might be ...

86 What's the problem?

a To what problems might these be the solutions?
look it up in a dictionary   try to spend less
hide a key at the bottom of the garden
borrow a bicycle   keep a big dog
buy something you don't really want
use your feet   hang it round your neck

b What might be the solutions to these problems?
you can never remember names
your car has a flat tyre and you don't know how
to change a wheel
you have to rush out to an important meeting
and you can't find your car keys...
... and the phone is not working...
... and it's pouring with rain outside...
... and you haven't got a raincoat or an umbrella.

87 How well did you guess?

a Key to section 82.

STICK AT NOTHING

My three-year-old brother, who had been playing outside all morning, came into the kitchen begging for a snack. I gave him a slice of bread and peanut butter. Holding the bread carefully in both hands, he started to leave, but when he reached the closed kitchen door, a puzzled expression came over his face. He was too small to open the door without using both hands to turn the door knob.

After a moment's consideration, he found a solution. He plastered the sticky side of his bread to the wall, used both hands to turn the knob, peeled his bread off the wall and went out happily to play.

—J. WHITE

Read the whole story again. Can you write notes to complete the table?

SITUATION small hungry child is given bread and peanut butter
PROBLEM...
SOLUTION...
EVALUATION...

b Key to section 83.

Air bags for m-cycles being tested

By DONALD HIGGS
London Correspondent

LONDON — British scientists believe they may be on the verge of a major breakthrough in saving life and serious injury in motorcycle accidents.

They are experimenting with an air bag which is fitted to the frame of the machine and expands automatically in a fraction of a second on impact.

Many motorcyclists killed or injured, fly over the handlebars after their accidents.

The British "balloon bag", fired by gas and now being developed at the Transport Road Research Laboratory in Berkshire, west of London, slows down dramatically the speed at which a rider is shot clear of the bike.

It cannot totally prevent somebody being thrown forward but tests so far show an encouraging braking effect or "rubbing off" of this speed.

This is enough to make the difference between a couple of broken bones and fatal brain or internal injuries, according to a laboratory spokesman.

"We are pretty well convinced that our theory is proved," he said.

The instantly inflatable air bag is already fitted to the steering wheels of some cars, notably in America and West Germany, to prevent serious head injury.

88 REVIEW
UNIT 8

a Sayings
Do you have similar sayings in your language?

You can kill two birds with one stone.
A bird in the hand is worth two in the bush.
People in glass houses shouldn't throw stones.

NEW WORDS IN UNIT 8

absent	function
automatic/ally	gift
aware	inflate
bone	inflation
bulk	instant/ly
bulky	liquid
card	locate
combination	operate
combined	plant
contemporary	pollution
convinced	potential/ly
credit	regional
developed	research
distress/ed	ride
dramatic/ally	shot
dusk	solid
effect D	solution
effective D	steel
effectively D	stone
fitted	technique
fold	tough
frame	treatment

44 new words
TOTAL SO FAR 325

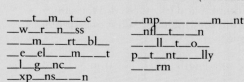

b Related words
The jackets... combine warmth and comfort.
Our buyers... are aware of the need for a good alarm clock.
An elegant and contemporary design.
Seagulls were causing a potential health risk... polluting the water.
... building an improved treatment plant.
An instantly inflatable airbag.
... an airbag which expands automatically...
The British "balloon bag", ... now being developed...

Can you complete these words to show how they are related to the words in blue above?

For example:

___mb__n_t___n = combination (combine)

___t_m_t_c	_mp_____m_nt
_w__r__n_ss	_nfl__t___n
___m___rt_bl___	___ll_t__o__
__e__el___m__t	p_t__nt___lly
_l_g_nc_	___rm
_xp__ns___n	

36

What's the problem?

Aim: To promote discussion.

SB86a/b PB86

Put students in groups to do these. Each group can report back on two.

Possible key:

a Look it up (You don't know the meaning of a word.)
try to spend less (You are short of money.)
hide a key (You often go out and forget the door key
borrow a bicycle (Your car has broken down.)
keep a big dog (You are worried about burglars.)
buy something you don't really want (You only have a ten pound note and you are going on a bus journey.)
use your feet (You are in a car and you want to drive off, but you can't because your hands are handcuffed together. See picture!)
hang it round your neck (You have a lot of things to carry and can't hold the shopping bag with your hand.)

b you can never remember names (Repeat the name when a person is introduced./Listen to see if you can hear someone else using the person's name.)
your car has a flat tyre and you don't know how to change a wheel (Look helpless./Signal another car to stop.)
you have to rush out and you can't find your car keys... (Call a taxi.)
... and the phone is not working (Go to a phone box.)
... and it's pouring with rain outside... (Take an umbrella.)
... and you haven't got a raincoat or an umbrella (Hold your briefcase over your head./

87 How well did you guess?

Lexis: **automatically, bones, convinced, developed, dramatically, effect, encouraging, fitted, frame, inflate/inflatable, instantly, killed, shot, solution**
Revision: **brain, expression, fired by gas, injured, injuries, machine, prevent, speed, theory, totally**
Understanding only: **braking, breakthrough, experiment**

Reading SB87a

1 See section 82, notes 3 and 4.

Reading SB87b

2 See section 83, note 6.

 Review

Key: b automatic, awareness, comfortable, elegance, expansion, improvement, inflation, pollution, potentially, warm.

LEXICAL OBJECTIVES

absent absent-minded = forgetful.
automatic/ally 1 not needing a person to operate it. *automatic gear change* [7] *airbag... expands automatically.*
aware 1 known about, or be conscious of. *Our buyers... are aware of the need for a good alarm clock.*
bones EED 1 *a couple of broken bones*
bulk/y 1 large, thick. *a wallet is too bulky for a shirt pocket.*
2 most of... *that gets across the bulk of what they're trying to get across.*
card 1 *credit card, identity/business card; a card game.*
combination T 1 the mixture you get when two things are put together. *a good colour combination.*
combine *These jackets... combine the style of real leather with the warmth and comfort of.. Combined efforts.* T
***comfort** 1 *the jackets... combine warmth and comfort.* Adj: *comfortable.*
contemporary 1 modern, present-day. *An elegant and contemporary design.*
2 people who lived or events which happened at the same time in the past as something else: *a contemporary account of the life of Henry 8th.* T
convinced 1 to be sure that something is true. *We are pretty well convinced that our theory is proved.*
convince T 1 Verb: to make you believe something is true. *I managed to convince him he'd get well by Sunday.*
credit as in *Credit Card.*
developed 1 form, grow. *Their friendship developed.* T
2 advance. *A country develops slowly.* T
3 build up, evolve. *The British "balloon bag", now being developed at the Transport Road Research Laboratory*
distress/ed 1 a state of great worry. *birds in distress. Distress signals.*
dramatic/ally 1 sudden, impressive. *The air-bag slows down dramatically the speed at which the rider...*
2 connected with the theatre. *She made a dramatic gesture. dramatic works* T
dusk 1 just before night, when it's getting dark. *two hours before dusk – a period when gulls fly in to roost.*
effect D
effective D
effectively D
***elegant** 1 stylish, smart. *An elegant and contemporary design*
***encouraging** 1 hopeful, promising. *Tests so far show an encouraging breaking effect.*
fitted verb: *an air bag which is fitted to the frame of the machine.* Adj: *a fitted carpet/kitchen.* T
fold 1 *the soft black case folds flat for travel. a fold-away handle.*
2 *The business folded* = closed down. T
frame 1 a basic structure on or in which other things can be put. *fitted to the frame of the machine/motor-bike.*
2 ideas, or a set of rules or a plan. *Write a summary using this framework.*
function EED 1 Noun: the role or purpose. *alarm clock with all the latest functions. The function of the heart is to pump the blood round.* T
2 a dinner party or social gathering T
3 Verb: work. *How does it function?* T

gift 1 a present. *A very personal gift*
inflate 1 make something bigger by filling it with air, like a balloon. *An inflatable airbag. Do not inflate your lifejacket inside the aircraft.* T
2 too high. *inflated prices for land.* T
inflation T 1 general increase in prices of goods, the cost of living. *An inflation rate of 17% per annum.*
instant/ly 1 a short period of time. *In an instant. This instant* = now.
2 immediate. *An instantly inflatable airbag. Instant coffee.*
liquid something that can flow or be poured. *Flask for hot or cold liquids.*
locate 1 find. *the keyminder bleeps enabling you to locate your keys.*
2 = positioned. *The house was located in the heart of the city* T
operate EED 1 *operate a business.* T
2 carry out. *first time the technique has been operated at a reservoir.*
***plant** 3 a factory with machinery. *A water treatment plant.*
pollution unpleasant substances that make the air/water dirty and dangerous.
potential/ly 1 possible. *Seagulls were causing a potential health risk...*
2 capability. *That child has potential* T
regional 1 area. *Strathclyde Regional Council Water Department.*
research 1 detailed study of a subject. *research student. Transport Road Research Laboratory.*
ride EED 1 ride a horse. *They rode up to the hills. We loved riding.* T
2 ride a bicycle or a motorbicycle.
3 a ride is a journey by horse, bike, car, bus. *we all went for a ride in the car. A two minute bus-ride away.* T
shot EED (much more common than shoot)
1 fire a gun. *Hands up or I'll shoot!* T
2 be killed or injured. *He got shot in the back. The plane was shot down.* T
3 move very fast. *a rider is shot clear of the bike.*
solid EEC 1 strong, hard, not hollow or liquid. *made of solid stainless steel. Is it solid gold?*
2 continuous in space/time. *a solid yellow line; I read for 3 hours solid.* T
3 worthwhile, good, firm: *solid advice/ evidence/basis/support* T
solution 1 way of dealing with a difficult situation so that the difficulty is removed. *the problem is about... the proposed solution is to...*
2 answer to a riddle/crossword puzzle
steel a very strong metal. *solid stainless steel bridges.*
stone 1 material, like rock. *walls built of stone* T
2 a small piece of rock. *You can kill two birds with one stone.*
3 weight, equivalent to 14 pounds or 6 kilos. *alligator weighing 19 stone.* [9]
technique a particular method of doing something. *The technique has been used successfully at airports.*
tough EED 3 strong and difficult to break, like leather. *A very tough material.*
treatment 3 processing, cleaning by machine. *The cost prohibited building an improved treatment plant.*

This unit deals with wild animals, particularly reptiles, and how people feel about them. The first part is based on the life of a particular individual who works with reptiles. This leads into a factual article about crocodiles and then to a debate about the relationship between man and such 'undesirable' creatures.

OBJECTIVES

Lexical objectives are in TB99

Discussion topics

a Feelings about reptiles. (89)
b The life story of an eccentric. (90,91)
c Man and animals in the environment. (97)

Social skills

a Describing one's feelings, particularly emotions of fear, horror etc. (89)
b Helping one another to build up a story/biography. (90,93)
c Discussing probabilities and giving reasons, usually from one's own general knowledge. (94)

Communication skills

a Definitions. (89)
b Reading informal biographical material. (91)
c Summarizing a biography. (93)
d Skim reading to verify specific statements. (95)
e Practice in deciding which words are vital to the understanding of relevant parts of the text, and which are not. (95)
f Writing contradictory statements and citing evidence. (95)
g Organising information and evidence in a debate. (97)

Grammar and discourse

a Meanings and uses of **it**. (92)
b Expressions like **the more ... the more ...**. (92)
c Opening a topic with a general statement supported by a specific example (discourse pattern: Topic – Illustration). (96)
d **Whose, where** and **which** used to introduce descriptive clauses. (99)
e Practice Book Grammar Words: **is/are/be** etc.

Dictionary skills

a Broad negative adverbs. (98)
b Pronunciation: vowels: /ɑː/ **heart**, (revise long vowel /ɔː/ **more**), /ɛə/ **scare**; consonants: /h/, /v/, (revise /tʃ/ **chain**), /θ/ **thin**, /ð/ **then**.

Aims: 1 Definitions.
2 Feelings about reptiles.
3 Describing one's feelings, particularly emotions of fear, horror etc.

Lexis: **broad, reptile, snake**
Revision: **blood, body, Central China, lays** (eggs), **narrow, skin**
Understanding only: **even** (= regular or equal in size/amount), **giant** (= large), **uneven.**

Lead-in   SB89a

1 Discuss reptiles in general, and how students feel about them. What about giant reptiles such as crocodiles? Get students to describe a local snake. Do any students have any snake stories to tell?

Class discussion   SB89a

2 After reading and discussing the definitions on the page, ask students to define: a mammal, a bird, a leopard. (They could then check them against dictionary definitions.)

---

90   'See you later, alligator'

Aims: 1 Helping one another to build up a story or account.
2 To prepare for the reading text in section 91.

Lexis: **boots, exist, existing** T, **fascinating, giant, own** ts, **owner, pupil, rare, reptiles, zoo**
Revision: **blind, collection, fancy, imagination, on show, welcome**
Understanding only: **farewell** (= a final goodbye), **prize** (= best), **wildlife**
Phrases: **has a way with, struck up a good relationship with, a reptile 'freak'** (= a person who thinks of reptiles and nothing else at all) (all meaning he really likes reptiles and gets on with them); **Don't think I'd fancy ...** (= I wouldn't like to ...)

Don't let students turn over to section 91 yet.

Class discussion   SB90a

1 Speculate as a class about this man, to arouse students' curiosity. Ask students to read the captions.

Task, planning and report   SB90b

2 Encourage students to use the pictures, facts and list of words and phrases here to guess the ideas that Bruce and Rachel had. Students working in pairs can expand the sentences, then each tell the class about one or two of them.

Listening   SB90b   90b

3 Students take notes as they listen. These will be checked by the students themselves after they have done section 91. So ask students to keep them safely.

Writing   SB90c

4 Do this informally in pairs. Don't tell students if they have guessed correctly. Accept all versions. Cover the new vocabulary as it crops up.

Unit 9
Reptiles

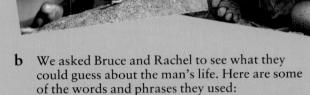

89 Do you like reptiles?

a Find out how people feel about the reptiles on this page. Do you know the difference between a crocodile and an alligator? What kind of snakes do you have in your country? Can you describe one?

alligator /ˈælɪɡeɪtə/, **alligators**. An **alligator** is a large animal similar to a crocodile but with shorter jaws. Alligators live in lakes and rivers in America and China.

crocodile /ˈkrɒkədaɪl/, **crocodiles**. 1 A crocodile is a very large meat-eating reptile which lives in rivers in tropical parts of the world, such as Africa and India. Crocodiles have a broad head, large strong jaws with very sharp teeth, and thick scales that cover their body.

python /ˈpaɪθən/, **pythons**. A **python** is a large, very long snake that kills animals by squeezing them with its body.

reptile /ˈreptaɪl/, **reptiles**. A **reptile** is a cold-blooded animal which has a scaly skin and lays eggs. Tortoises, snakes, lizards, and crocodiles are all reptiles.

See you later, alligator!

In a while, crocodile!

90 'See you later, alligator'

a Who do you think this man is? Have you seen him before? (Maybe in a James Bond film!)

"See you later, Alligator . . ."
John Cheetham bids an affectionate farewell to his grinning chum, Big Boy.

b We asked Bruce and Rachel to see what they could guess about the man's life. Here are some of the words and phrases they used:

an aquarium of some sort
works in a zoo
a keeper . . . I think
that's the term isn't it?
he's got a way with animals.
he collected frogs
a biologist
a bus driver
in the living-room
boots or handbags
special affinity with animals
a researcher
a really good relationship
he's welcome to it, mind
you think he breeds them?
perhaps it's too large
in somebody's house

John in a friendly tussle with Aristotle, a 14ft reticulated python, one of the prize specimens in his collection of giant reptiles on show to the public at Beaver Water World.

Can you guess any of the ideas Bruce and Rachel had?

 90b Listen and write down:

1 What they think he does for a living.
2 Any points they might include in a life story for him.

c Can you add to these words to make sentences which might be in the story of John's life?

glimpse – bus – alligators – sun – zoo – imagination

eleven – baby alligator – local pet shop

Big Boy – magnificent – alligator – North America – 10 feet – 19 stone

giant reptiles – strange hobby – a teacher for the blind – near Sevenoaks

introduces – pupils – pet snake – touch – hold

Finally, read the report on the next page, and see how much Bruce and Rachel guessed.

37

91 Magnificent obsession

a

JOHN Cheetham's magnificent obsession with reptiles began when he was a schoolboy in his home town of Oldham, Lancashire.

A glimpse from the top of a bus of alligators basking in the sun at Manchester's famous Belle Vue Zoo set his imagination racing.

He took every opportunity of visiting the zoo and the more he saw of the creatures that seemed to have stepped out of the remote past, the more his fascination grew until it embraced all reptiles.

When he was 11 he bought a baby alligator from a local pet shop. It was the first step to becoming the only private collector of giant reptiles in Britain.

It was also to lead to John appearing with his own alligators and pythons in films and on television.

And that same pet alligator is with John still, although he's grown a little during the 27 years they've been together.

Big Boy, a magnificent specimen of Alligator mississippiansis found in the southern states of North America, is now 10ft. long and weighs 19 stone.

He and John have appeared with Roger Moore in Live and Let Die and Moonraker. Big Boy has also featured in Clash of the Titans, on TV advertisements and on Top of the Pops.

James Bond fans have seen quite a bit of John without realising it.

It was his legs that did the spectacular dash to safety over the backs of alligators in Live and Let Die.

Most of the giant reptiles in John's collection are housed at Beaver Water World, Tatsfield, which is owned by Jeff Wheeler, his friend and partner.

Among John's other pet reptiles to star in films are Aristotle, a 14ft long reticulated python aged six, and Pythagoras, a 14ft. Indian python, who at 18 is the grand old man among the snakes.

Aristotle and Pythagoras both featured in the underwater wrestling scene in Moonraker with John in a friendly tussle, although the eventual result on film looks deadly serious.

John's collection also includes a giant tortoise, snapping turtles, the largest legless lizard or slowworm found in the world and Nile crocodiles.

Collecting giant reptiles might seem a strange hobby for John, a teacher at Dorton House School for the Blind at Seal, near Sevenoaks.

But John often introduces pupils to his pet snakes, letting them touch and hold them.

John lets blind children and anyone else handle the pythons without any fear that the snakes will attack.

'They are benign creatures. All they want is a quiet life,' he said.

Big Boy, a 10 ft long alligator tipping the scales at 19 stone, grins happily as he slides backwards into his personal pool.

Look again at the sentences you wrote in section 90c. Are they similar in meaning to those in the text?

91b **b** When Bruce and Rachel read this article, what comments do they make?
Listen again and repeat the phrases and sentences which show that they are surprised.

92 *Grammar* •••••••••••••••

a it

1 it for referring back
Find the paragraphs in section 91a containing these phrases with **it** in them. What does **it** mean in each case?

. . . until it embraced all reptiles. (Paragraph 3)
It was the first step to becoming . . . (Paragraph 4)
. . . without realising it. (Paragraph 9)

2 it + who/which/that/–/ for emphasis
Read these examples, then make up two more sentences on this pattern.

It was his legs that did the . . .
It's alligators they have as pets, isn't it?
This time it was a woman who answered the door . . .

b The more . . . the more . . .
True or false? Say what you think.

1 *. . . the more he saw of the alligators in the zoo, the more his fascination grew.*
2 *the more the blind children handle his snakes, the less afraid they will be.*
3 *The bigger it is, the better!*
4 *The more – the merrier!*

93 John Cheetham

Without reading the article again, write **either** about John Cheetham's past life, **or** about what he does now. Include one piece of information that is not true.

Give it to someone else to read to see how well you have remembered, and find one point that is not true.

94 Crocodile quiz

a In pairs, say whether you think the statements are true or false. You must come to an agreement about each one.

a *Most species of crocodile are man-eaters.*
b *Over 2,000 people a year are killed by the Estuarine crocodile.*
c *In Egypt, along the banks of the River Nile, crocodiles kill up to 1,000 people every year.*
d *Crocodiles will eat refuse as well as living creatures.*
e *There are giant crocodiles/alligators living in the sewers in some South American cities.*
f *Crocodiles can grow up to 11 metres in length.*
g *Many crocodiles and alligators live over 100 years.*
h *So many crocodiles have been hunted and killed by man that 16 species are now extinct.*

▶ Tell the class what you decided and why. ◀

94b **b** Did Edmund and Suzanne make the same choices as you?

The Australian Estuarine crocodile has truly terrifying jaws and is a man-eater.

91 Magnificent obsession

Aims: 1 Understanding an informal local news item on the life story of an eccentric.
2 Comparing different versions of sentences conveying similar facts.

Lexis: deadly, fascination, giant, grand, magnificent, owned by, reptiles, scales D, **slide, snakes**
Revision: **among, appearing** (i.e. in films), **attack, blind, creatures, fear, grew, pet, pool, result, safety, strange** (= odd)
Understanding only: **dash** (= rush/race), **eventual** (= final), **featured** (= appeared), **remote** (Unit 19) (= distant)
Phrases: **set his imagination racing, took every opportunity of**

Reading SB91a PB91

1 Students read the text and compare the facts given here with what they had thought when doing section 90. They can go through and compare their sentences from section 90c, too.

Listening SB91b

Lexis: **column, fascinating, Good Lord!, hardly**
Revision: **handle, marvellous!**
Understanding only: **amazing!**
Phrases: **been into all sorts of things** (= done a lot), **in the first/last column, That baffles me** (= I can't understand how . . .)

2 Play the recording. Students should skim the text as they listen, and identify which part Bruce and Rachel are talking about.

3 Play the recording a second time for students to repeat the words and phrases which express surprise.

Key: Where they show their surprise: Good Lord   He actually . . .   It's amazing
Oldham of all places
Seems hardly the place for a future . . .
I didn't know that (at all)
a really amazing life
had a very different life to what I would have thought
seems to have been into all sorts of things

92 Grammar

SB92a PB92

1 Students do this on their own, and then compare with a partner.

Key: his fascination, buying a baby alligator, that you have seen him

2 Explain that we can use the phrase **It is/was . . . who/which/that . . .** when we want to identify something or someone:
His legs did the dash. = it was **his** legs that did the dash.
They have **alligators** as pets. = It's **alligators** they have as pets.

3 Students write two more sentences.

SB92b

4 This is a way of expressing cause:
Because he saw more of the alligators his fascination grew.
Because the blind children handle the snakes they will become less afraid.
etc.

93 John Cheetham

Aim: Summarising a biography.

Writing task SB93

1 Tell students to read the instructions and choose to write either about Cheetham's past or about his present life. Go round and help them write accurately.

2 Students write their names on their summaries, and then pass them round. Other students note down (on a separate piece of paper) what the false information is.

3 After reading a few, they can check with the writers to see if they were right.

94 Crocodile quiz

Aims: 1 Discussing probabilities and giving reasons, from students' own general knowledge.
2 To arouse their interest and give a purpose for reading later on.

Lexis: species, truly
Revision: **banks** (of a river), **killed**
Understanding only: **extinct** (= having died out), **hunted, man-eaters, refuse** (= rubbish)

Task, planning and report SB94a

1 Students do this quiz in pairs. Emphasise that they must come to an agreement about each one, and be able to give a reason for their choice. (This is to stimulate more language use.) Put two pairs together and they too must reach agreement. Do not give any clues at all as to which is correct. In section 95 they will be reading to find out.

2 Each group tells the class what they have agreed. (Number each group and write up in a grid on the board a T or an F according to what they thought.)

Listening SB94b 94b

3 Edmund and Suzanne do the quiz. Students listen to them doing c–h. Students should note down the choices they make. Put them on the board.

Key:

	a	b	c	d	e	f	g	h
SJ/EL	—	—	F/T	F	T	F	T	T

You may want students to become familiar with some of the words that appear in the longer text before they read the whole text to verify their quiz answers. (See Lexis for section 95.) In this case, do section 96b, now.

95 Enemies of man

Aims: 1 Skim-reading a longer text to verify specific statements.
2 Practice in tackling longer texts where only a certain amount of the text is relevant to the reading purpose.
3 Practice in ignoring difficulties which do not hinder the achievement of the reading purpose.
4 Writing contradictory statements and citing evidence.
5 Listening for specific relevant points.
6 Understanding a shift in topic.

Lexis: attractive, devil, enemy, evil, giant, horror, individual, mass, occurred, rare, recorded, rescue, rubber, species, tail, tragedy, tragic, whose
Revision: **attacked, banks, effect of . . ., official** (= recorded), **plain, sank (sink)**
Understanding only: **destroyed** (Unit 16), **twofold effect** (= double effect)
Phrases: **had she not been** (= if she had not been), Would it have been **any less of** a tragedy? **Second World War, oldest official age** (compare **fastest official time**)

Reading   SB95a PB95

1 Get students to go straight into the reading while the quiz questions in section 94a are fresh in their minds. Explain that this is a difficult text, but that they are *only* reading to check specific points from the quiz. (They need to get used to tackling longer texts where only a certain amount of the text is relevant to their reading purpose.) Time them reading.

2 When the class are choosing which three words (in total – the class must agree on which three) to look up or ask you for, make sure that they know whether each comes from a relevant section of the text. In other words, will the understanding of this word give them an answer to one of the quiz questions? If they say yes, ask which one. Discourage them from looking up words that won't help.

   Key: a F b T c T d T e T(?) f F g F h T
   e may be true; h is true but this is not stated until section 97.

3 Students could go back to their notes from section 94b and work out Edmund's and Suzanne's scores. (As far as we know, they got two wrong – d and g, but we don't know about a–b.)

Report   SB95b

4 Help them write the corrections of the untrue sentences from the quiz. Can they explain to you why they are false?

5 Go over any target words from the text. (Students will get another chance to read the whole text in section 95d.)

Listening   SB95c

6 You may need to explain to students the meanings of the words **plain-looking** (i.e. ordinary, not remarkably pretty) and **attractive** before they listen.

7 Explain that Edmund and Suzanne are discussing the last three quiz questions, f, g and h, and that Suzanne goes on to tell a story. She ends with a question. What would the students' answers be? Play the recording and discuss.

Reading   SB95d

8 This is more practice in skim-reading while students find which picture goes with which story.

9 Students choose one picture and find specific facts relevant to the picture to include in their writing.

Written report   SB95d

10 Let students take time over their writing, so they can get it accurate.

11 When they have finished their accurate versions, take them in and number them. You could either read them out loud, asking students to identify which picture each is about (students write down the number and the picture rather than shout out) or students could pass them round the class for others to read and identify, writing the number of the paragraph and the picture it refers to for each one.

12 Further activity – anecdote telling or story writing: You may want to set this after the language work in sections 96 and 99c. Do students have any stories about reptiles? Had they heard about the alligators in the New York sewers?

96 Language study

Aim: To make students aware of the common text pattern Topic–Illustration, i.e. where writers open a topic with a general statement supported by a specific example to illustrate it.

This text pattern is very similar to the General–Specific pattern already focused on in Unit 5. The label Topic–Illustration gives students a slightly different way of looking at it, and may help them to recognise such patterns in later texts.

SB96 PB96

1 Students can do this on their own, and then compare findings with a partner.

   Key: *All* the paragraphs begin with a *Topic* sentence, and are followed by a specific example or *Illustration*.

2 Get students to pick out the key phrases in the topic sentences, e.g. '*tales of huge individuals* living to over 100 years old' (followed by one such tale).

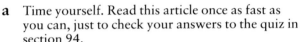

a Time yourself. Read this article once as fast as you can, just to check your answers to the quiz in section 94.
You are allowed to look up or ask your teacher the meanings of *three* words. You can only have *three* words. Choose them carefully.

b Write a corrected version of the false statements in the crocodile quiz. Explain why they are false.

Crocodiles are formidable enemies of man. At least 6 of the 23 species in the crocodile family will attack and eat human beings if they can, and many of the others are large enough to cause serious injury.

The most notorious man-eater of all is the **Estuarine crocodile** which probably kills over 2,000 people each year. There are many individual horror stories about people being eaten by crocodiles and, in at least one case, a mass tragedy occurred. In 1975, 100 people on a holiday trip down the Malili River in Indonesia were attacked by crocodiles when their boat sank. Before they could be rescued 42 people were attacked and eaten.

●

Crocodiles kill up to 1,000 people, mostly women and children, every year, along the banks of the Nile river in Egypt.

●

Those constant rumours about crocodiles growing in the sewers of big cities are true in at least one place in the world. The health officials in Manzini, Swaziland, in Africa decided to capture man-eating crocodiles and put them to work in the sewers gobbling up refuse. This would have the twofold effect of getting the job done cheaply and making it safe for the local people to cross the river. It is not reported whether the sewage workers demanded 'danger money' or not!

Among the many legends about crocodiles and alligators are tales of huge individuals living to be 100 years old and more.

There's a story told by a rubber planter whose plantation lay near the Seguma River in north Borneo. This river was a true crocodile haven and there was one old giant crocodile who lived in the river about 10 miles (16 kilometres) downstream from his plantation who was believed by the local river people to be 200 years old. They never tried to kill him believing him to be the Father of the Devil, and they threw money into the river whenever he appeared to protect themselves from evil. This giant was seen one day sleeping on a sandbank with his tail hanging over at one end and his snout in the water at the other end. When he had moved off, the bank was measured at 32 feet (9.6 metres) making the crocodile himself at least 33 feet (9.9 metres) long!

Although it is possible for certain individuals to live to unexpectedly great ages, most crocodiles and alligators live for about 50 years. The oldest official age recorded is that of an **American alligator** which lived for 56 (and possibly as much as 65) years. This alligator was received at Dresden Zoo in Germany in 1880 and was recorded as being still alive in 1937. In fact it may have lived on until 1945 when the zoo itself was destroyed in the Second World War.

95c **c** Suzanne and Edmund read and corrected their choices. Which did they get wrong?

What was the story that Suzanne told Edmund about? Why was Suzanne cross about the way the story was reported?

d Which photo goes with which paragraph?

Choose one photo and write about it, including some relevant facts from the text about crocodiles or alligators.

96 **Language study**

Topic – illustration
Paragraph 1 starts with a general statement which introduces the topic of the paragraph:

Crocodiles are formidable enemies of man . . .

and then goes on to explain or illustrate this in more detail. Does this happen in the other paragraphs?

97 Debate

Hatred and greed have made the hunting of crocodiles so popular that the world population of them has been drastically reduced. Some 16 species are now almost extinct – among them the rare **Cuban crocodile** which has been reduced to a mere 300 individuals living in a protected sanctuary in Cuba.

In groups, with a chairperson, debate:

Should we try to preserve all species of crocodile, even though they are so dangerous to man?

▷ List two reasons for and two reasons against preserving crocodiles. Present these to the class. ◁

Take a class vote and agree on a decision.

▷ Write down two recommendations you would make. Give reasons. ◁

[97] What solution do Edmund and Suzanne propose? Summarize their solution in one sentence.

98 *Dictionary skills*

Noting meaning and structure

Broad Negative Adverbs: these adverbs are used to give a slightly negative feel to a sentence.

Five of these adverbs are broad negatives. Which ones do you think they are?

barely	scarcely
sometimes	seldom
occasionally	hardly
rarely	

Look them up and find out what effect they have on sentence structure when they come at the beginning of a sentence. Does this always happen?

99 REVIEW

UNIT 9

a Complete the phrases
Look up these words and then complete the phrases below.

chain   exchange/d   exist/s   grand   horror
mass   masses   reserve/d   scale

1   *That word doesn't _____ in English.*
2   *In the early 80s _____ unemployment became a huge problem. It's a problem that still _____*
3   *The _____ of events that occurred after the stock exchange crash was quite expected.*
4   *He had to sell that _____ country-house of his, but he's still got his _____ of supermarkets.*
5   *Do you watch _____ films late at night?*
6   *I can't come – I've simply _____ of work.*
7   *I have an absolute _____ of snakes.*
8   *I'd like to _____ a table for four for dinner tonight, please.*
9   *Could you possibly let me have a blue shirt in _____ for this green one?*
10 *If you went into business on a large _____, you could do well. Small _____ businesses rarely succeed in this area.*

Complete the phrases.

**NEW WORDS
IN UNIT 9**

attractive	occur
barely D	owner
boot	perfectly
broad	preserve
chain D	prize
chairman/person	pupil
column	rare
deadly	rarely D
death	record
debate	reptile
devil	reserve D
disaster	rubber
enemy	scale D
evil	scarcely D
excitement	slide
exist	snake
existence	soil
existing	species
fascinate/ing	tail
fascination	tragedy
giant	tragic
grand	truly
hardly D	vote
horror	whose
magnificent	zoo
mass, masses	

51 new words
TOTAL SO FAR 376

b Find the pairs
Arrange these words as far as possible in pairs in two columns according to their broad meanings.

GOOD   BAD

tragedy   death   horror   birth   joy
rescued   devil   evil   comedy   disaster
deadly   life   god   harmless
loss of life   good   killed

c whose, where or which?
1   *There's a story told by a rubber planter _____ plantation lay near the Seguma River.*
2   *I read ... a short article about a woman being eaten, in _____ the woman was described as attractive.*
3   *They should be kept in special places – special reserves, _____ they won't attack people.*
4   *A species is a group or class of plants or animals _____ members have the same characteristics.*
5   *It was John Cheetham _____ legs appeared in **Live and Let Die**.*
6   *John, _____ own interest in reptiles began in childhood, allows his blind pupils to handle his snakes.*

40

97 Debate

Aim: Organising information and evidence for a debate.

Lexis: chain, death, disaster, excitement, perfectly, preserve, rare, reserves, species, vote
Revision: **approach to . . . , course of** (daily life), **even though, natural** (chain/disaster), **popular, population**
Understanding only: **extinct, hatred** (**hate**), **hunting, mere, reduced**
Phrases: **Do you know what I mean? . . . and so on, What one might call a . . . , give them a vote on it, Take things in your stride** (= take things as they come/not be surprised or upset by events)
Informal use: **chewed up** (= eaten)
Old fashioned: **tilling the soil** (= ploughing, growing crops)

Reading   SB97

1 Students read the paragraph, a continuation of the text in section 95.

Task, planning and report   SB97

2 With students in groups, make sure the chairperson encourages all group members to state their opinions. Each group could then appoint a secretary, who could write down the group's best reasons. A spokesperson could then read these to the class.

Listening   SB97   97

Key: They think that the people who live in areas where there are crocodiles should be free to decide.

98 Dictionary skills

Aims: 1 To show students that, as well as giving the meaning of a word, the examples illustrate common patterns in which it occurs. (This important feature in this case is word order.)
2 Pronunciation: vowels: /ɑː/ **heart**, (revise long vowel /ɔː/ **more**), /ɛə/ **scare**; consonants: /h/, /v/, (revise /tʃ/ **chain**), /θ/ **thin**, /ð/ **then**.

SB98 PB98

1 Students can do this on their own, using the Dictionary Extracts.

Key: The broad negatives are **barely, rarely, scarcely, seldom, hardly**. Normally they come just before the word they modify.
2 Draw attention to **hardly** 2, **scarcely** 3, and **rarely**. When these begin a sentence and are followed immediately by a subject and verb, the verb and subject are inverted:
not: Scarcely we had begun when the alarm bell rang. *but:* Scarcely had we begun when the alarm bell rang. *or:* We had scarcely begun when the alarm bell ran.

99 Review

Key: a 1 exist 2 mass, exists
3 chain 4 grand, chain 5 horror
6 masses 7 horror 8 reserve
9 exchange 10 scale, scale.
Pictures: Foreign Exchange rates; No goods exchanged without a receipt. Grand Hotel; Reserved.
b Good: birth, joy, rescued, comedy, harmless, life, god, good. The rest are usually bad, though if a play is a tragedy, it can be well-acted and therefore good.
c 1 whose 2 which 3 where
4 whose 5 whose 6 whose

LEXICAL OBJECTIVES

attractive 1 a thing, e.g. a salary or a plan or an offer can be attractive. T
2 good looking, not plain. *the woman was described as attractive.*
barely D
***blind** 1 Visually handicapped. *a teacher at a school for the blind.*
boots 1 *boots made out of leather*
2 the boot of a car. Am: trunk.
broad EED 1 wide. *crocodiles have a broad head.*
2 general, a wide range. *a broad negative meaning. broad interests.* Misc: *a broad accent* = strong regional accent. *They did it in broad daylight.*
chain D
chairman 1 You have a chairman/ person to chair a meeting/discussion.
column 1 *The museum had a row of Greek columns. A column of smoke.* T
2 a newspaper column. *In this last column here it says he's a teacher.*
deadly 1 likely to cause death. T
2 extremely. *deadly serious.*
death 1 *different approach to . . . life and death*
debate fairly formal discussion
devil an evil spirit
disaster 1 a bad accident, or failure or mess. *a natural disaster*
enemy 1 not friend. *Crocodiles are formidable enemies of man.*
evil 1 a powerful force believed to cause bad things to happen. *to protect themselves from evil.*
2 T bad, wicked, harmful, or influenced by the devil. *Evil spirits.*
excitement 1 *There's a certain excitement about them . . .*
exist 1 to be present in the world. *Or maybe he's just a reptile freak or something – they do exist. Does that word exist in English?*
existence T 1 *Do you believe in the existence of God? It's the most poisonous snake in existence.*
existing T 1 *find ways of making the existing system work better.*
fascinate/ing 1 *Fascinating business, really. He was fascinated by reptiles.*
fascination 1 the state of being interested and delighted. *His fascination grew . . .*
giant 1 a huge imaginary person T
2 very large. *giant reptiles.*
***grand** 1 *impressive, superior. . . . the grand old man among the snakes.*
hardly D

horror 1 feeling of fear, dismay. *To my horror I saw the fire spreading* T
2 *many individual horror stories about people being eaten by crocodiles.*
***individual** 2 single, separate, specific. (see **mass**). *individual horror stories*
magnificent 1 extremely good, impressive. *Magnificent obsession. Magnificent concert/performance*
mass/es EED 1 a large number, or a lot. *a mass of papers/people.*
2 on a large scale, involving a large number of people. *a mass tragedy. Mass unemployment/communication. Opposite to individual.*
occurred 1 happened. *a mass tragedy occurred.*
2 *a thought occurred to me. It occurred to me that . . . It never occurred to Bruce that he might be a teacher.*
***own** 1 verb = possess. *Beaver Water World, which is owned by Jeff Wheeler.*
owner *the owner is Jeff Wheeler.*
perfectly 1 totally. *perfectly true.*
2 100% accuracy. *No-one speaks English perfectly.* T
preserve 1 keep something the way it is, to protect from change. *Preserve all species of crocodile.*
prize 1 *win prizes in a competition* T
pupil 1 schoolchild. *John often introduces pupils to his pet snakes . . .*
rare 1 not common. *the rare Cuban crocodile.*
rarely D
recorded 2 verb. To keep in writing, to preserve information. *The oldest age recorded is that of an American alligator which lived for 56 years.*
3 recorded on tape, on video. T
reptile 1 cold-blooded animal, e.g. snakes, alligators.
reserve D
rubber 1 a strong elastic substance from the sap of a tropical tree, used to make car tyres. *rubber plantation*
scale D
scarcely D
slide 1 move smoothly. *as he slides backwards into his personal pool*
snake 1 long thin reptile. e.g. python.
soil 1 the top layer of earth in which plants grow. *people along the banks of the Nile, tilling the soil.*
species 1 a group or class of plants or animals whose members have the same characteristics. *Some 16 species (of crocodile) are now almost extinct.*
tail 1 Birds, animals have tails.
tragedy 1 a very sad event/situation involving death, suffering or disaster. *a mass tragedy.*
2 in literature, a sad play, not a comedy.
tragic 1 adj. very sad. *Had she been plain, would it have been less tragic?*
truly 1 completely, genuinely, really. *this crocodile has truly terrifying jaws.*
2 ending a letter: *Yours truly.* T
vote 1 a choice made in a meeting or in an election. *One should give them a vote on it. Do women have the vote?*
whose 1 in a relative clause: *a story told by a rubber planter whose plantation lay near the Seguma River.*
***zoo** park where live animals are kept. *Dresden Zoo.*

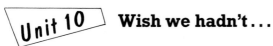

Unit 10 Wish we hadn't . . .

The theme here is misfortunes and misunderstandings. There are both written and spoken versions of a mishap which befell the Yetties on one of their overseas trips. There is a British newspaper article and an American story, both humorous, and each based on chains of unfortunate events that could perhaps have been avoided.

OBJECTIVES

Lexical objectives are in TB108

Discussion topics

a Air routes. (100)
b Things going wrong. (100, 102, 104)

Social skills

a Discussing mishaps and disasters. (100)
b Speculating on possible unfortunate outcomes. (100)
c Sharing personal regrets. (106)
d Telling anecdotes. (104)

Communication skills

a Writing journalistic stories. (100)
b Finding definitions and paraphrases to compensate for lack of linguistic knowledge. (101)
c Predicting the development of an anecdote in which things are going wrong. (102)
d Writing a personal version of a mishap. (102, 104)

Grammar and discourse

a Paraphrases and definitions: **someone who . . .**, **something that . . .** etc. (101)
b Phrases which cover a lack of linguistic precision: **You know what I mean**, **what have you** etc. (101)
c **Had** and **would have** for hypothetical outcomes. (105)
d **Wish + had/would have.** (105, 106)
e Use of **despite**, **although** and **even though**. (107)
f Practice Book Grammar Word: **at**.

Dictionary skills

Words beginning with **mis-**, **un-** and **non-**. (103)

[100] The Yetties in Nepal

Aims: 1 Discussing scheduled arrangements.
2 Understanding an informal interview.
3 Discussing mishaps and disasters.
4 Speculating on possible unfortunate outcomes.
5 Writing a journalistic story.

Lexis: **airliner, borders, costumes, flight, flight-case, gear, meanwhile, sort out, vast**
Revision: **came across, destination, disappeared, enormous, huge, major, packed, on stage, via (go via Rome), lend, borrow**
Phrases: **and you can imagine, to say the least, made enquiries, do for instruments** (= use instead of your instruments), **no point in looking any further, left right and centre, seventy *odd* kilos** (= approximately)
Understanding only: **mend** (= repair), **went comparatively smoothly** (= went off quite well)

The name Yetties is very similar to the word Yeti, the mystery creature which is said to roam the Himalayas in Nepal.

Lead-in SB100a

1 Have any of your students done long journeys by air? Encourage them to tell you their exact routes.

2 Go on to the Yetties' trip. Discuss the pictures. Work out a possible route from the UK. Via which major airports?

Reading SB100b

3 Students read the first part of the interview.

4 Students predict what troubles could have happened en route and share their ideas.

Listening SB100c `100c`

5 Play the recording, and see if any students guessed right.

Key: The airliner stopped in Rome, Cairo and Dehli. The flight case was not taken off at Delhi, but went on to Tokyo, via Bangkok. It crossed about seventeen borders.

6 Ask students what **odd** means in what Bonny said: 'a hundred and seventy odd kilos'. How many other ways could he have said this? (approximately/about/roughly/ around 170 kilos).

Listening SB100d `100d`

7 Play the rest of the conversation. Make sure students know the meaning of **meanwhile/In the meantime** (before they got the instruments back . . .). Ask students to list briefly exactly what the Yetties did (five main things).

Key: found and mended an accordion; Mac was lent a guitar; Bonny borrowed a drum etc.; people from the Embassy made costumes; went to the costumes department of the local drama society for more things.

Reading SB100e

Lexis: **appointed, concert, considerable, costumes, destination, indeed, instruments, residents, splendid**
Revision: **highly, joined in, presented with, provided, total, theatre, traditional**
Understanding only: **clapping, established a rapport** (= formed a good relationship)

9 Point out that the report was written after the end of the Yetties' concert trip. The Nepal Representative had to write a report to send to his Headquarters in London.

10 Many gaps need more than one word. All the necessary facts can be found either on this page or in the transcripts of recordings 100c/d. Students should do this on their own first, and then perhaps discuss with their partner what phrases they have thought of. Some gaps hold many possibilities which are perfectly acceptable.

Task SB100f

11 The odd one out is the US army picture.

Writing SB100g

12 Students write captions for four of the pictures.

[101] Language study

Aim: Finding definitions and paraphrases both to compensate for lack of linguistic knowledge, and to save searching for the right word when talking.

SB101a PB101

1 Students could do this in pairs, and then go over it as a class. Other phrases like this: **and so on, and all that sort of thing, and all that stuff, or something, et cetera (etc.)**

SB101b

2 Tell students that Bonny could not think of the words he wanted, so he described what people do instead.

3 Ask students what they say in their own language for these things.

Unit 10
Wish we hadn't . . .

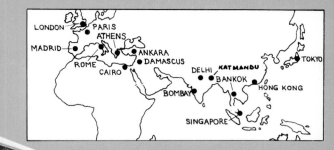

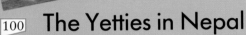

The Yetties in Nepal

a From the map, which route do you think the Yetties took to get to Katmandu?

b We interviewed Bonny about the trip to Nepal. The interview began like this:

INTERVIEWER: You had some troubles on the way to Nepal, didn't you?

BONNY: We certainly did. And you can imagine, a first major, Far Eastern tour, and we were a little bit nervous to say the least about the whole thing. We packed all our gear – we had two of everything, two accordions, two guitars, two this, two that, in a huge flight case, which weighed about a hundred and seventy odd kilos it was. An enormous flight case. And we saw it . . .

How do you think it continued? Think of two things that might have happened, and what they might have done to solve the problem. Tell each other.

100c **c** What actually did happen? Look at the map. Which airports did the plane stop at? What about the flight case? How many borders must it have crossed?

100d **d** What happened in the meantime?

e The British Council representative in Nepal later wrote this report on the Yetties' visit. Can you guess what the missing words and phrases are?

The Yetties arrived on the appointed day but unfortunately their flight case _____ and ended up _____. The case arrived halfway through _____. The Yetties appeared with their own _____ for the second half and gave us a _____ evening. They had been loaned _____ by the Royal Nepal Academy and local _____ and the HAMS Group had _____ them with very good replacement _____.

All three concerts were highly _____. We had a audience of 1700 or so. The Yetties immediately established a rapport and their playing, singing, acting and dancing were very _____. They are real troupers. The Nepalese, generally quiet and inhibited, soon _____ in the choruses, the clapping and the repartee. The Scouts _____ them with traditional khuries (knives), topis and Scout badges and joined the Yetties in camp fire songs.

Many spoke _____ of the concerts. Indeed, a very _____ success.

f There is one picture on this page that has nothing to do with the Yetties' Nepal trip. Can you find it?

g Write a caption for any four of the other pictures, using information from this page and recording 100c and d.

h In not more than 100 words write a description of the Yetties' trip to Nepal. Imagine you are writing for a local newspaper in their home town, to mark the day of their return.

Language study

Thingummies and thingamabobs

a Find these phrases in recording 100 and say which refer to objects and which to places.

two this, two that	and what-have-you
here, there and everywhere	and things
left, right and centre	bits and pieces

These are all phrases we use to indicate a whole list of things without having to mention each one. Do you know any more phrases like this?

b What did Bonny do when he could not remember the words 'Drama Society'? See recording 100. We also have a lot of words which we use when we can't quite think of what to say. How would you say these in your language?

You know what/where/who I mean
or whatever/wherever   what-d'you-call-it
you-know-who   what's-his/her-name

thingamabob /θɪŋəməbɒb/, **thingamabobs.** You can refer to something or someone as **thingama-bob** or **thingummy** when you cannot remember or do not know the proper word or name for them.

41

When the gas man comes

102a **a** This news story is divided into four parts. Stop reading after each part, and discuss what you think will be done next. Write a sentence to summarize what has happened. Then listen to recording 102a to see what Bruce and Edmund thought. Now read the next part. Do the same with the next three parts.

> **WORD STUDY**
> Guess the meaning of the words and then learn them: domestic residence purchase delivery appliance assured delay

b Work singly, then in pairs, then in groups to find which endings best complete the sentences.

1 Both Mrs Bradbrook and Mrs Kerr live in Alton Gardens and a mix-up occurred because
 a Mrs Bradbrook gave the wrong address to a gas board official.
 b Mrs Kerr placed an order for a new gas cooker.
 c Someone at the gas board took the wrong message.
 d Mrs Bradbrook went out to work leaving a message next door for the gas man.

2 Mrs Kerr got home and
 a was pleased to find a shiny new cooker in her kitchen.
 b used the new cooker despite the fact that she knew something was wrong.
 c could not cook her husband's meal because they had taken her cooker away.
 d had to sort out the problem with the new cooker before cooking her husband's tea.

3 The gas board realised they had made a mistake when . . .
 a Mrs Kerr used the new cooker to cook her husband's tea.
 b The gas man got back and said he had taken the cooker to number 14.
 c Mrs Bradbrook pointed out that the cooker had been used.
 d Mrs Bradbrook telephoned to say the cooker had not been delivered.

> Write an account of what happened from the point of view of **either** Mrs Kerr **or** Mrs Bradbrook.

Flare-up with high-speed gas

PART 1

By John Ezard

One of those misunderstandings which sometimes occur when the gasman comes to call has brought puzzlement and ultimate good fortune into the domestic lives of two Essex women.

Mrs May Bradbrook and Mrs Brenda Kerr live in Alton Gardens, Westcliff-on-Sea. Mrs Bradbrook's home is number 40 and the Kerr residence is number 14.

The difficulties began when Mrs Bradbrook decided that the time had come to purchase a new cooker. She placed her order with the North Thames Gas Board but the official who took the details misheard her address.

PART 2

Paperwork duly went through for the delivery and installation of a new gas cooker at number 14, Alton Gardens. When the gasman arrived with it there was nobody at home. They were relieved, however, to find a considerate note saying: "Key next door."

Mrs Kerr was expecting a visit from the Eastern Electricity Board that day and had made arrangements for a neighbour to let them in. When the gas board appeared instead the neighbour assumed that she had misunderstood Mrs Kerr and handed over the key. The new cooker was installed and Mrs Kerr's old one taken away.

PART 3

Shortly after, a politely aggrieved Mrs Bradbrook telephoned the gas board saying that she had waited in all day but the cooker had not come. Inquiries were started.

Meanwhile, Mrs Kerr got home to find the unexpected and gleaming appliance in her kitchen. Clearly, something was amiss: but before Mrs Kerr could get down to deciding how to sort it out she had an urgent priority. She had to cook her husband's tea. There was no other appliance in the house, so she used the new cooker.

The board, having heard from Mrs Bradbrook and contacted its gasmen, was swift to realise the error. It assured Mrs Bradbrook that there would be no further delay in getting the cooker to her. After all, it had only to travel a short way up the road.

PART 4

But — Mrs Bradbrook pointed out — it was no longer the new cooker she had ordered, was it? It had been used.

The gas board saw her point and found that it also had a problem at number 14. It had assured Mrs Kerr that her old cooker would be returned pronto. But it turned out that the cooker had been broken up for scrap immediately after it was taken away.

Both women had clearly suffered "some inconvenience," as the board acknowledged. The upshot of the affair is that Mrs Bradbrook now has the cooker originally intended for her — but at a 20 per cent discount of £30.

Mrs Kerr has been given a re-conditioned "good as new" cooker worth an estimated £350 to replace her scrapped one. And the North Thames Gas Board is some £380 out of pocket.

"We hope we have made up for our earlier error," a board spokesman said yesterday. "Our local manager says it was a one in a hundred chance. All we can do is resolve to listen more carefully in future."

The Guardian

When the gas man comes

> **Aims:** 1 Predicting the development of an anecdote in which things are going wrong.
> 2 Practice in summarising a paragraph.
> 3 Writing a personal version of a mishap.
> 4 Practice in handling multiple choice comprehension questions.
>
> **Lexis: affair, appliance, assure, convenient** T, **delay, deliver** T, **delivery, domestic, electricity, electrical, error, get down to, inconvenience, inconvenient, inform, meanwhile, originally, presumably, priority, purchase, regretted, residence, suffered, ultimate**
> Revision: **good fortune, pointed out**
> Understanding only: **despite, misunderstood, out of pocket, replace**
> Phrases: **made up for, saw her point**

Lead-in   SB102a

1 The pictures and signs will help you to introduce some useful vocabulary. Students discuss the pictures in pairs. Ask them what they can predict about the story from these pictures and signs. (Don't tell them if they are right or not.)

You could also ask students if they know any of the words in the Word Study box. Can they explain them to each other?

Reading, report and listening   SB102a

2 Students summarise each part, then alternately make their own predictions about what will happen next, and listen to hear what Bruce and Edmund predict, before reading on. Between each part, you can ask one or two pairs to tell the class their summary and predictions. The recording is used in three parts for ease of reference.

3 Go over the target vocabulary in context. You may also need to point out that here, **tea** (in 'cook her husband's tea') means evening meal. Get students to guess any other words they want to know.

Reading   SB102b

4 Do not tell the students or groups which answers are correct until the whole class has come to a consensus on each one. Then say which ones are still wrong, and give some clues to help them do them on their own.

   Key: 1 c   2 b   3 d

Writing   SB102b

5 Students read the instructions and do the writing on their own. Suggest they make some notes first. Go round and check their notes, and advise on style and accuracy.

6 Read some of the accounts out, not saying whether they are by Mrs Kerr or Mrs Bradbrook, and see how long it is before students can guess.

Optional role play   SB102

7 Get students to work out where conversations must have happened in this sequence of events. Students choose one situation, work out a conversation, practise it, and then act it out.
Other situations for conversation might be:
When the gas man went next door to get the key from the neighbour who was expecting the Electricity Board.
Mrs Bradbrook telephoning the Gas Board to ask where her new cooker was.
The man at the Gas Board who took her call talking to the man (or the boss of the man) who installed the cooker.
Mrs Kerr explaining to her husband just back from work how she had had to cook his tea on a mystery cooker!
A Gas Board official contacting Mrs Kerr, to apologise and explain how she had got a new oven by mistake.
The same Gas Board official assuring Mrs Bradbrook there would be no further delay, and Mrs Bradbrook complaining it was no longer new.
The same official breaking the news to Mrs Kerr that her old cooker had already been scrapped.
A meeting where the whole affair was settled.
The local manager talking to the reporter who wrote this story.

Dictionary skills

SB103 PB103

1 Students read the dictionary entry, and do the exercise.

> **Key:** ... misheard ... the order ...; ... misled ... advert ...;
> ... mistook ... friend ...; .... mislaid ... address book;
> ... misjudged ... distance ...
> We apologise ... misunderstanding ...; The
> Yetties ... misfortune ...; Our misfortune ... not insured;
> I'm sorry ... misunderstanding.
> The word **misleading** might also be useful (a misleading advert).

2 For extra practice, get students to rephrase the sentences so they mean the same, but without using the **mis-** word (i.e. using another expression). For example: I thought the advert promised a free holiday but when you looked closely, it didn't. I thought he was an old friend of hers, but I was wrong.

3 Brainstorm, and see how many words beginning with **un-** and **non-** students can remember together. Then they can use the Dictionary Extracts to look them up.

---

104 **Just one of those days**

Lead-in SB104

1 Ask students what laws there are about crossing roads in their countries. Are they allowed to cross anywhere? In towns in the USA there are specific places to cross and it is illegal to walk in a road elsewhere. (Introduce the term **jay-walking**.)

2 Are there any features in the pictures which show that this is America?

Reading SB104

3 Get students to read the story silently. When students are trying to guess the ending, you could help them by giving them the clue in section 100 – ask them which picture did not belong on that page.

4 Can students spot something strange about the story, near the end? (Why would Joe have walked home? After all, he had his car nearby, and unless it was out of petrol, it would have cost him nothing to drive it home.)

Report SB104

5 Go round and help as students in pairs or groups write three sentences. Then they can each read one out to the class.
Sample sentences: We think Joe wished he hadn't broken the traffic laws in the first place. Joe must have wished he hadn't driven his car to court.

6 Do students have any stories about diastrous days or even periods in their lives, when everything seemed to go wrong? Or has this happened to someone they know?

---

105 **Grammar**

SB105 PB105

1 Students read one sentence at a time, and then listen to (and possibly repeat) the sentences on tape. After doing three or four like this, see if they are able to predict the form of the one on tape before they hear it.

2 Ask students to make up some sentences of their own, either about Joe, or about one of the disastrous days they talked about in section 104.

> **Key:** See tapescript on page 127T.

Had and ***would have*** *are used for hypotheses about the past. In sentence 1, for example, he* did *break the law and he* did *have to go to court. In 2 he didn't* go by public transport, *etc.*

Had *is also used for wishes about the past:*
He wishes/wished he hadn't broken the law.
... he had gone by public transport.
etc.

103 | Dictionary skills

Prefixes

> **mis-** is used at the beginning of words to indicate PREFIX that something is done badly or wrongly. For example, if you mismanage something, you manage it badly. EG *He had misjudged the situation... ...the risks of miscalculation... ...the misuse of psychiatry.*

Make sentences by matching the two columns and adding a beginning.

misheard	by the advert which promised a free holiday.
misled	him for an old friend of hers.
mistook	the distance and hit the pavement.
mislaid	the order over the telephone.
misjudged	her address book.

Which of these sentences is best completed by the word misunderstanding and which by misfortune?

We apologise for any _____ which may have occurred.
The Yetties had the _____ to lose their flight case.
Our _____ was that the things we lost were not insured.
I'm sorry. These are not my things. There must be some _____.

Now look up the prefixes un- and non-. What other words do you know with these prefixes?

104 | Just one of those days

How many misfortunes had Joe suffered by the end of the story? Suggest what the last line could be. (There is a clue among the pictures in Section 100.)

▶ What do you think Joe wished he hadn't done, or wished hadn't happened? Think of three things and write three sentences. Read them to the class.

▶ Have you ever had a day like this when one thing has gone wrong after another? Tell your group. Write either about your own or someone else's experiences.

Joe Ramirez, 19 years of age, drove to the court house in a New York suburb to face a traffic charge. As his case was about to be called he realised that his parking meter was running out, so he asked the judge for time to feed it. His request was granted.

Joe raced out and was starting across the street when a policeman grabbed him for jay-walking. He gave Joe a ticket – and a long lecture. So long a lecture that a traffic warden got to his car first and gave him a ticket.

When he got back to court, the judge had gone to lunch. Joe had to feed the meter until he returned. He was duly fined $5, as he had expected, but when he took out his wallet to pay, he found that his parking fees had left him with only $2. The court clerk accepted the money on a promise that the remainder would be forthcoming and Joe, now broke, walked two miles home.

When he arrived at his home, he found a letter on the mat. It read:...

105 | Grammar

He would have/he might have/he could have

105 Look at these sentences and listen to the tape. The sentences on the tape mean almost the same as the sentences here. See how well you can remember the ones on the tape.

1 *Joe had broken the law or he wouldn't have had to go to court.*
2 *Joe had gone to court by public transport. That's why he had all the bother of parking and feeding the parking meter.*
3 *He had to wait longer than expected, otherwise the money he had put in the meter might have been enough.*
4 *Joe had crossed the street in the wrong place and that's why he was fined for jay-walking.*
5 *The policeman took a long time giving him a ticket, otherwise Joe might have got back to the court in time.*
6 *Joe was a long time away from court dealing with his parking problem or the judge could have heard his case before lunch.*
7 *Joe would have had enough money to pay the court fines but unfortunately he had had to pay all his other fines on the spot.*

Notice where these words and phrases occur in sentences 1–7: **or, that's why, otherwise, but.**

Make more sentences about Joe like these. Now make some sentences like those on the tape.

106 I wish I hadn't...

a

> Think back over your past life. Is there anything you wish you hadn't done?

Edmund, Rachel, Elizabeth and Bruce discussed this. What do you think they said? Use the pictures to help you guess. Make a guess for each person.

106a See if you guessed correctly. Write down a sentence about each person that summarizes what they wish they hadn't done, giving their reason for their action.

b Notice there are only three illustrations here. What would you suggest for the fourth?

c What do *you* wish *you* hadn't done? In groups of four talk about your past lives, in the same way.

▶ Tell the class. How many of you had similar regrets?

107 Grammar

Despite
The Yetties did not delay their concert despite the loss of their flight case. (100)
(= *Although their flight case was lost,...*)
Despite not having their own instruments, the concert still went ahead. (100)
(= *Even though they didn't have their own instruments...*)

Where should the word despite be in these sentences?

1 *The Gas Board's promise, Mrs Kerr could not get her own cooker back.*
2 *Mrs Bradbrook used the new cooker the fact that she knew something was wrong.* (102)
3 *Ultimately, everyone was satisfied the considerable inconvenience.* (102)

Now write each sentence a different way, using although or even though

108 REVIEW

UNIT 10

a —— or ——?
Guess the two missing words.

1 *But, Mrs Bradbrook pointed ——, it was no longer the new cooker she had ordered, was it?*
2 *Something was clearly amiss. But before Mrs Kerr could get down to deciding how to sort it —— she had an urgent priority.*
3 *But it turned —— that the old cooker had been broken —— for scrap.*
4 *The North Thames Gas Board is some £380 —— of pocket.*
5 *'We hope we have made —— for our previous error,' a Board spokesman said yesterday.*
6 *As his case was about to be called, Joe realised his parking meter was running ——.*

**NEW WORDS
IN UNIT 10**

appliance	inconvenience
appoint	inconvenient
assure	inform
border	judge
concert	lecture
considerable	literally
convenient	meanwhile
costume	originally
delay	presumably
deliver	priority
delivery	promise
depressing	purchase
despite	regret
destination	residence
domestic	resident
electrical	splendid
electricity	suffer
error	thingamabob
everywhere	thingummy
gap	ultimate
gear	ultimately
grant	vast

44

**44 new words
TOTAL SO FAR 420**

b What treatment?
What should you do (or not do) with each of these items?

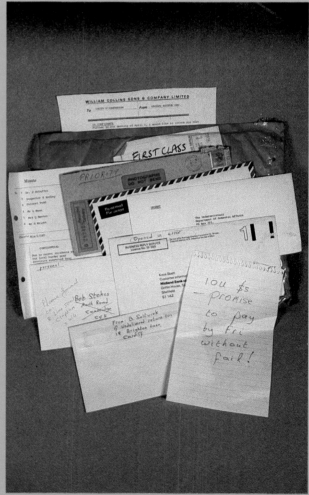

Aims: 1 Talking about regrets.
2 Expressions with **wish** giving reasons.

Lexis: depressing, dropped out (= stopped), **gap, literally, regretted**
Revision: **give up, take up** (the violin)
Understanding only: **shame**
Phrases: **as much as anything, What a shame, What a pity, talked out of it** (= persuaded not to do it), **Shall we put it that way? I've missed out somehow** (= I've not done something that would have been useful)

Listening SB106a PB106

1 Using the pictures for guesswork prepares students for the conversation between Rachel, Elizabeth, Bruce and Edmund. After students have made some guesses, play the recording.

Report SB106a

2 Students write a sentence about each person, with a reason.

Key: See transcripts.

Task SB106b

3 Students discuss the pictures, and may decide the one of Edmund is missing. They could add Edmund as a student!

Task, planning and report SB106c

4 Students in groups of four do the same as Edmund's group. After their discussion, help them to write it up, and prepare to tell the class about each other. As students listen to the various reports, they should take brief notes to help them remember.

107 Grammar

Aim: To introduce **despite** and revise other similar words.

SB107 PB107

1 Students can do this singly, and then discuss in pairs. Point out the variations in structure, especially that **despite** is followed by a noun or a verb ending in **-ing**.

Key: 1 **Despite** the Gas Board's promise . . .
2 . . . **despite** the fact that . . .
3 . . . **despite** the considerable . . .

Key: 1 Although/Even though the gas board had promised . . .
2 . . . cooker, although/even though she knew . . .
3 . . . satisfied, although/even though there had been a lot of inconvenience.

108 Review

Key and notes:
a 1 out 2 out 3 out, up 4 out
5 up 6 out
b Students can make up their own sentences explaining what treatment these should have. e.g. **Priority**: You should deal with this one first as it's very urgent.

LEXICAL OBJECTIVES

*affair EED 1 all aspects of an event. *The upshot of the affair is that . . .*
appliance gas/electrical device used in the home for heating, cooking.
appoint 1 appoint a person to a job. T
2 decided, planned. *The Yetties arrived on the appointed day.*
assure 1 persuade, reassure. *It assured Mrs Bradbrook that there would be no further delay.*
2 be guaranteed. *Assured of a good salary.* T
3 *I can assure you* = believe me! T
border 1 frontier, between countries.
2 edge. *Trees bordered the road.* T
concert 1 performance of music.
considerable 1 large in amount or degree. *A very considerable success.*
convenient 1 suitable, arranged to fit in. *a convenient place to live, near shops and school.* Opp: inconvenient.
costumes 1 clothes worn by performers, actors. *costumes for the Mummers Play.*
delay 1 noun: hold-up, waiting. *It assured Mrs Bradbrook that there would be no further delay.*
deliver EED T 1 take to someone's house. *The gasman delivered the cooker to the wrong house.*
delivery 1 *Plans for the delivery of the cooker . . .*
depressing 1 makes you sad. *A depressing thought.*
despite in spite of. *She used the cooker despite the fact she knew it wasn't hers.*
destination place you're going to. *The flightcase mistook its destination.*
domestic 1 home rather than overseas. *an hour of world and domestic news.* T
2 concerned with the home/household. *the domestic lives of two Essex women.*
electrical *electrical appliances.*
electricity *The Electricity Board.*
error mistake (not very common.) *We hope we have made up for our earlier error.* Also: *in error. an error of judgement. grammatical errors.*
everywhere 1 every place, in general terms. *Everywhere in Asia.* T
2 lots of places, often exaggerating. *Here, there and everywhere.*
*fortune 1 good luck. *. . . brought puzzlement and ultimate good fortune into the domestic lives of two women.*
2 fate. *have your fortune told* = to hear what fate has in store for you. T
gap 1 empty in space or time: *Fill the gaps in the sentences. So I had a big gap and I could've been playing (the violin) all that time.*
2 *the gap between the rich and the poor. The poverty/generation gap.* T

gear 1 *automatic gear change*
2 equipment and special clothing. *We packed all our gear . . .*
*get down to begin. *Before Mrs Kerr could get down to deciding . . .*
grant/ed 1 allowed to have, given. *His request was granted.*
2 a grant is a sum of money given by the government, e.g. for research projects.
3 If you take something for granted you believe it is true without thinking. T
inconvenience 1 problems. *Both women clearly suffered some inconvenience.*
inconvenient *Could I have a word with you? Sorry, it's a bit inconvenient* T
inform 1 tell. *We got to Katmandu and informed the people there . . .*
judge EED 1 Noun. *a judge in a court of law, or in a competition. He asked the judge for time to . . . a good judge of character.*
2 Verb. *She judged the flower show.*
3 to guess. *It's difficult to judge distances.*
lecture 1 an academic talk on a topic.
2 criticism; to tell someone off. *The traffic warden gave Joe a long lecture.*
literally true, even though it sounds surprising. *I went straight from school to university, with literally about two months in between.*
meanwhile while a particular thing is still happening. *. . . Meanwhile, we were panicking all over the place!*
originally 1 first. *She now has the cooker originally intended for her.*
*point out EED 1 cause people to notice an object T
2 to give more information to correct mistaken ideas.
presumably probably, I suppose . . .
priority the most important concern. *She had an urgent priority. Give this letter/case/child priority treatment.* T
promise EED 1 *the court clerk accepted the money on a promise that the remainder would be . . .*
Verb: to say you will definitely do something. *He promised to send it.*
purchase 1 Verb: to buy
2 Noun: an item bought. (formal word.)
regretted 1 to feel sorry. *I went straight from school to university and I've always regretted that.*
residence your home (formal word) *The Kerr residence is number 14.*
residents people who live in a place
*sort out EED verb. 1 to organise or tidy. *Sort out your papers.* T
2 to find a solution to a problem. *Something was amiss . . . before deciding how to sort it out she had . . .*
3 to punish. *I'll sort him out!* T
splendid impressive, of high quality. *The Yetties gave us a splendid evening.*
suffered 1 to suffer pain is to feel pain
2 to be badly affected by something. *Both women had clearly suffered some inconvenience.*
thingamabob see SB101
thingummy see SB101
thingy see SB101
ultimate final, at the very end. *puzzlement and ultimate good fortune.*
ultimately finally, after a long series of events. T
vast huge. *London Airport is so vast.*

44T

Unit 11 Man-eater

This unit deals with an exciting incident in an African game park. A game warden had made a mistake concerning a leopard, which led to dangerous, nearly tragic, consequences for a family staying at the park. The father of the family is interviewed here, and we can piece together the story from his personal account and the subsequent correspondence. Thus the unit recycles spoken and written versions of the same incident and gives students plenty of opportunities to reconstruct their own version of the events.

OBJECTIVES

Lexical objectives are in TB117

Discussion topics

a Game parks. (109, 114)
b Dangerous animals. (109, 114)

Social skills

a Talking about information gathered from various sources (correspondence and radio-style interview). (109, 110, 113, 114)
b Describing reactions and behaviour. (116)

Communication skills

a Understanding a description and the relevance of highlighted information. (110)
b Reconstructing a narrative from deficient information. (109, 110)
c Listening for specific details. (109, 110)
d Predicting the course of a narrative from limited context clues. (110)
e Transferring information from spoken to written narrative, as a letter. (112, 114)
f Writing recommendations for action. (113)
g Writing a formal report drawn from various evidence. (116)

Grammar and discourse

a Modal **would** to state precautions to be taken in a hypothetical situation. (109)
b **Had** and **would have** to identify alternative outcomes to a narrative. (110)
c The discourse framework Hypothesis–Evidence–Conclusion. (113).
d Giving reasons for established behaviour. (113)
e Uses of past simple and past participle. (114)
f Practice Book Grammar Word: **get**

Dictionary skills

a Skimming the longer entries. (111)
b Pronunciation: revision of the vowels /ɪ/ / and /iː/.

109 Such a frightening time

Aims: 1 Reconstructing a narrative from deficient information.
2 Listening for specific details.
3 Modal **would** to state precautions taken in a hypothetical situation.

Lexis: connect, conservation, construct, environment, hut, incident, internal, ministry, outcome, personally, rescued, resources, smell
Revision: **account of, ceiling, companions, conclusion, event, roof, scared away, separating**
Understanding only: **caretaker, chronological order, subsequent**
Phrases: **in the light of** (= using the information we now have), **under the circumstances, set light to, sure enough!, and all the rest of it**

*Get students to guess the words **banda** (hut), **conclude** (finally decide), **gained entry** (managed to get into), **mauled** (injured by biting and scratching), **vacated** (left), as they are not common but can easily be guessed from the situation and in some cases from the basic word form.*

Lead-in SB109a

1 As a class, discuss the questions suggested. Encourage the students to share their knowledge of game parks and animals. Supply any words students feel they need, and write up any target words.

   Key: Possible precautions might be: light a fire/keep a fire burning to scare away dangerous animals; take lots of insect spray so you don't get bitten by mosquitoes; take turns to stay awake at night, on watch; don't leave food where animals can smell it and be attracted by it (hang it in a tree?); go with an experienced game warden, not on your own.

Reading SB109b

2 Students read the letter once. Ask them what they think happened to the Webber family. ('The leopard incident' and 'your experience' are in the first and second paragraphs, and expanded on in the third.) Ask them to read it again and speculate in pairs. Discuss as a class. (Don't give anything away. Don't tell students whether anyone has guessed right.)

Listening and report SB109c/d 109c

3 Before you play the recording, tell students this is only the first part of an interview. The five questions students write down may possibly be answered in the second part which comes later. Students can read each other their questions and discuss answers.

Listening task SB109e 109c

4 Play the recording, with pauses, while students draw a plan of the banda. Ask if anyone could draw the interior of the banda (with walls and ceiling) on the board. This should emphasise that the walls do not connect with the ceiling – there is a space above the walls. The roof goes down past the walls over the balcony on the outside. Understanding this fact is essential if students are going to understand the danger and suspense in the next part of the interview.

Written report SB109f

5 Students should keep their notes about the leopard separately, so that they can add to them throughout this unit. In section 116 they will write a formal report or case study.

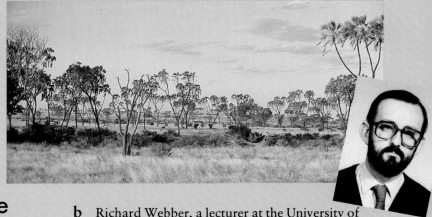

109 Such a frightening time

a What do you know about game parks in Africa from TV or films? Describe two dangerous animals you might find there. What precautions would you take if you were camping in a game park at night?

b Richard Webber, a lecturer at the University of Nairobi, took his family to a game park for a holiday where they had a very frightening experience. Read the letter Richard received after he had returned from his holiday.

MINISTRY OF ENVIRONMENT AND NATURAL RESOURCES
Wildlife Conservation and Management Department
Tsavo National Park (West)
P.O. BOX 71, Mtito Andei

Telegrams: 'Parks' Mtito Andei
When replying please quote reference number

8th April, 1980

Mr. and Mrs. R. D. Webber,
Department of Linguistics,
University of Nairobi,
P.O. Box 30197
NAIROBI

Dear Mr. and Mrs. Webber,

   I was given your address by the Manager of Ngulia Lodge, as I thought you would be interested to hear of the outcome of the leopard incident at the Ngulia Safari Camp.
   Following your experience, the same evening the leopard mauled one of the caretakers who was rescued by his companions, and the following day it was shot dead, as it stood on the verandah of one of the staff houses.
   I would be interested in hearing an account of your experience, and if you have time perhaps you would be good enough to write to me, personally giving me times, how the leopard gained entry into your banda, your reaction, how the leopard behaved and any other relevant facts etc.
   I am sorry that you were subjected to such a frightening time, and I can only conclude that under the circumstances and in the light of subsequent events, it was not more serious as undoubtably your decision to vacate the banda was correct. Can you remember if you closed the door of your banda behind you?

Yours sincerely,

Bill Woodley

(F. W. WOODLEY),
WARDEN TSAVO NATIONAL PARK (WEST)

109c **c** We interviewed Richard about his experience. Listen to him being interviewed and try to work out what must have happened to him and his family.

d You have not got the full story so far. Are you a little puzzled and curious about what exactly happened?

Write down five questions to which you would like answers. Read each other's questions and discuss possible answers.

109c **e** Listen again carefully and draw a plan of the interior of the Banda. What are the inner walls like? Do they connect with the ceiling?

f What do you already know about this particular leopard? As the story continues you will be asked to keep a file recording what happened to the leopard.

Put down, in chronological order, what you have learned about the leopard so far.

45

110 The worst possible thing

a Elizabeth also wrote some questions after she had read the letter. How many of her questions can you now answer?

> 1. What is a 'banda'?
> 2. What was the Webbers' experience with the leopard?
> 3. Where did the leopard come from?
> 4. Did the leopard actually harm either Mr or Mrs Webber?
> 5. Was the leopard still in the banda when the Webbers left?

b Here are some of the phrases that Richard Webber used when talking about the leopard incident. Before you listen try to work out what happened next.

▶ Write a short account in note form. ◀

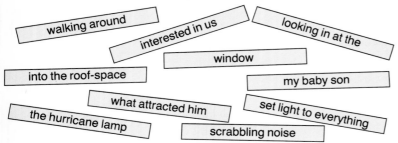

walking around · interested in us · looking in at the · window · into the roof-space · my baby son · what attracted him · set light to everything · the hurricane lamp · scrabbling noise

110b Richard Webber continues his account. As you listen, check your own account and refer to your plan of the banda.

What do you think was 'the very worst possible thing' that had happened?

▶ Write one full sentence. Tell each other. ◀

110c **c** Play the rest of Richard's account, pausing where necessary. Try to understand exactly where the leopard was at each stage. Remember to keep your file up to date.

▷ Think of a good title for this last episode. Compare and discuss titles, giving reasons for your choice.

d Can you now answer all the questions you (and Elizabeth) asked previously?

e What might have happened if the Webbers had run screaming out of the banda rather than walked quietly?

▷ What other things could Richard and his wife have done to scare the leopard away? How would you have escaped? Tell the class.

46

111 *Dictionary skills*

Skimming the longer entries

Beat   hit

a Look up beat and hit. How many numbered sections are there for each? Are they only used as verbs?

Now find a phrase with either beat or hit that fits in these gaps.

1 *I was no good at games – I could never _____ the ball.*
2 *The car stopped dead without _____ me.*
3 *The rain was _____ _____ the windows . . .*
4 *You know that _____ by the Jackson Five? It's got a great _____ – good party music!*
5 *Kent was badly _____ by the storm.*
6 *He was so frightened he could hear his heart _____.*
7 *She'll _____ _____ _____ when she sees what a mess this place is in.*
8 *Football: Liverpool _____ Manchester United three–nil.*
9 *What _____ me is where they get so much money from.*
10 *Ship sinks after a _____ _____. Crew rescued.*

Hold   hold back/down/off/on/onto/out/up

b Do not look up hold yet! In which of the sentences below does the word hold mean to hold with the hands or arms? What does it mean in the other sentences?

1 *Hold tight everyone.*
2 *Still trying to connect you; do you wish to hold the line?*
3 *It grabbed hold of him and threw him around like a doll.*
4 *She's ambitious – don't try to hold her back!*
5 *We should hold an urgent meeting.*
6 *The whole thing was held up by easily half an hour which is why I'm so late.*
7 *Surprisingly, he held down that job for two years.*

Finally, look up hold in the Dictionary extracts and find where each use is explained, and find a category number or headword for each sentence.

112 Write the letter

Mr Woodley asks Mr Webber for an account of his experience. (See the third paragraph of his letter in section 109.)

▷ Write two paragraphs of the letter that Richard Webber might have written to Mr Woodley. It should be as detailed as possible. You may like to listen again to Richard's account on recordings 109c, 110b and 110c. Take notes to help you.

110 The worst possible thing

> **Aims:** 1 Understanding a description, especially the significance of highlighted information.
> 2 Reconstructing a narrative from deficient information.
> 3 Listening for specific details.
> 4 Predicting the outcome of a narrative from restricted context clues.
> 5 **Had** and **would have** used to identify alternative outcomes in a narrative.
>
> **Lexis: harm, impression, internal, scream, smell/smelt**
> Revision: **account, escape, fire, milk**
> Understanding only: **attracted, belief, prepared to, roof space**
> Phrases: **got the impression that ... (gave the impression of/that)**, **set light to** (= set fire to)

Class discussion   SB110a   PB110

1 Students as a class answer Elizabeth's questions. Try to get some suspense going – especially with the three questions they can't answer yet.

   Key: 1 a hut.   2 they saw a beautiful leopard on their veranda early one morning, and it didn't run away, despite the noise they had made.   3 don't know.   4 don't know yet.   5 don't know.

Task, planning and report   SB110b

2 Students in groups work out a possible account of what happened next. The phrases are in the correct order.

3 Help them write notes, from which they can tell each other their versions of the story.

Listening   SB110b   [110b]

4 Play the recording while students compare their stories with what actually happened. They should listen again, and then speculate about what the 'worst possible thing' might be. They can write one sentence each saying what they think, and then tell each other. Keep up the suspense!

Listening and report   SB110c   [110c]

5 Play the recording with pauses, both to keep up the excitement, and to give students time to work out where the leopard was at each point.

6 Students can now add to their files. Play the recording again while they check their facts.

7 Students in groups discuss what would make a good title. They may find it useful to read the transcripts at this point. Encourage short snappy titles.

Task   SB110d

8 Students go back to their questions and see how many they can now answer.

Report   SB110e

9 Encourage sentences like: The leopard might have chased them. The Webbers could have shouted at the leopard/called for help/made a lot of noise/climbed out of the window opposite where the leopard was/hidden under a blanket... etc.

   Students tell the class what they personally would have done.

111 Dictionary skills

> **Aims:** 1 To give students practice in coping with the longer entries.
> 2 Recognising the sounds /ɪ/ and /iː/.
>
> **Lexis: beat, hit, hold**

SB111a   PB111

1 Students do this singly, using the Dictionary Extracts. Using the entry for **hit**, remind them how to use the extra column to recognise noun and verb use. Revise v + o (from Unit 4 section 41.) and N COUNT. Also PHRASE.

2 Ask which meanings of **hit** are physical (1, 2 and 3), and which metaphorical/abstract (4 and 5). Ask them what **hit on** means. What noun commonly goes with it? (**idea**) Can it be used in the passive? (Yes – HAS PASS means it can, e.g. *The idea was hit on after...*)

3 After students have looked at both **hit** and **beat**, they can do the exercise, finding a word or phrase to fit.

   Key: 1 hit   2 hitting   3 beating against   4 hit single, beat   5 hit   6 beating   7 hit the roof   8 beat   9 beats   10 direct hit

SB111b

4 Students think about the meanings of **hold** before they look it up.

   Key: Categories/headwords: 1 1, 2 11, 3 20, 4 hold back, 5 6, 6 hold up, 7 hold down.

5 Students look up **hold** and read the entry. Encourage them to write down any phrases they like or think might be useful.

112 Write the letter

> **Aim:** Transferring information from spoken to written narrative.

Writing task   SB112

Allow plenty of time for the preparation for this letter. In addition to hearing the recording again, students may like to read through the transcripts at home to prepare notes to write up in class. They should write it using 'I' as if they were Richard Webber.

113 Once a man-eater – always a man-eater

> **Aims:** 1 To illustrate the discourse framework: Hypothesis–Evidence–Conclusion.
> 2 Giving reasons for established behaviour.
>
> **Lexis: behaviour, confined, dawn, detailed, director, favour, frankly, fortunate, goats, hut, indeed** (= as you say)**, luckily, outcome, released, pipe, sheep, stock (livestock), strongly, threaten, trapped, victim**
> Revision: **attacked, had it = if it had, matter** (= subject)**, station** (= headquarters or village in game park)
> Understanding only: **attitude, attracted, confined space, reluctant**
> Phrases: **you were indeed very fortunate, did the right thing, as soon as you did, did a fine job**

The whole letter has a slightly old-fashioned ring about it. 'A goner' is slang for 'dead'. The use of 'which' referring to the caretaker is technically ungrammatical, but in the writer's mind he is already thinking of the man in terms of a thing – a rag doll.

Reading   SB113a PB113

1 Students read the whole letter on their own.

2 Before they add to their files on the leopard, they may need to discuss whether to believe Mr Woodley, when he says the two leopards got mixed up. (Introduce the words **hypothesis** and **evidence** at this point.) This hypothesis certainly seems likely – Richard Webber's evidence (the leopard's behaviour) is pretty good. In which case, they would add something about Siaya Location, and instead of 'released in Meru Park' add 'July 79 sent to the Orphanage, from where it was sent to Tsavo for release.'

Key: Two facts: A man-eating leopard was trapped at Siaya in July 1978 and released in Meru park. Another leopard was trapped in 1976 – claimed this was the one sent to Tsavo.

3 Students can do the Word Study, referring back to the letter for the context of the words on the left.

4 Students find words in the third paragraph to match those in the boxes.

Key: In this order: a goner, rag doll, had it not been for the fast reaction, made repeated attempts, rescued, made short work of, commended.

Summary   SB113b

5 Students' attention is here being drawn to a very common discourse structure in which a speaker/writer makes a hypothesis (proposes a theory), considers evidence and then reaches a conclusion. Discuss those parts of the letter which illustrate the discourse framework: Hypothesis–Evidence-Conclusion. See note 2 above.

6 Students could then write the summary singly or in pairs. They read and then answer the questions using full sentences.
They don't need to actually use the words Hypothesis, Evidence or Conclusion in their summaries (just as one doesn't use the words Topic or Illustration in Unit 9 section 96).

Sample: Mr Woodley thinks that it could have been a man-eating leopard. This conclusion was based on Richard Webber's description of the leopard's behaviour and attitude which was typical of a man-eater, especially one that had been held captive and had lost fear of humans.

7 Discuss what various recommendations could be made. Then students can choose one and write it down.

Sample: I would recommend that in future all man-eating leopards that are trapped are shot dead immediately. They should not be released again or placed in the Orphanage, where they could get mixed up and released by mistake, causing danger to our local people and to the tourists who visit our parks.

Students might want to recommend that a man-eating leopard is marked in some way, and then released into an unpopulated area.

114 What makes a man-eater

> **Lexis: crucial, familiar, familiarity, hunt, presence, previously, released**
> Revision: **companion, factor, human, species**
> Understanding only: **game management, human habitation, rounded up** (= caught)
> Phrases: **easy meat** (= easy to catch)**, as it were, crucial factor**
> Note: Students should be able to guess **misbehave** after the **mis-** exercise in section 103).

Task and report   SB114

1 Students discuss the question. Then help them to write their reasons down.

2 Students read and discuss other reasons.

Possible reasons:
They discover that humans are easy to kill.
They can't find any other animals to eat.
They are maybe too old or ill to hunt faster animals.
They are too lazy to hunt.

Listening   SB114   114

3 Students take notes, and then compare their reasons with those Richard gave.

4 Go over the target vocabulary.

113 Once a man-eater — always a man-eater

a Read Mr Woodley's reply, then add two more facts to your file on the leopard.

Explain why he said: 'Luckily you had the approach of dawn in your favour.'

Wildlife Conservation and Management Department, Tsavo National Park (West) P.O. Box 71, Mtito Andei

Dear Mr and Mrs Webber,

Thank you very much for your detailed letter which I found most interesting, and I can only conclude that you were indeed very fortunate. Clearly you did the right thing by leaving the banda as soon as you did, and luckily you had the approach of dawn in your favour. Had it been night you may have been reluctant to leave the banda and had the leopard attacked, (and it may well have been attracted by the child) in the confined space of a room, then one can only guess the outcome. I have known leopard and lion killing large numbers of sheep and goats in the confined space of a hut — on one occasion a lion killed 71 goats in a hut at Tsavo Station.

A man-eating leopard was trapped at Siayu Location in July 79 for killing a young girl, and instead of killing it it was said to have been released in Meri Park. Another leopard trapped for stock-killing in 1976 was held in the orphanage ever since and this is the one that the Orphanage claim was sent to Tsavo for release. Frankly, I do not believe it, and I think that they must have got them mixed up, and the man-eater sent to me in Tsavo. Once a man-eater — always a maneater and the only answer is the bullet. Your description of the animal's behaviour and attitude is so typical of that of a man-eater, and in this particular case, one that has been held captive for months and has lost all fear of humans.

It made very short work of the caretaker, a man weighing 170 lbs. which it threw around like a rag doll. He would have been a goner had it not been for the really fast reaction of his two companions and Angus who hit the leopard with a metal pipe and rescued him and then continued to threaten the leopard whilst it made repeated attempts to recover its victim. They did a fine job and I have strongly commended them in a letter to the director.

I have written to the Director about this matter and have ...

Thanks for writing, and you certainly have a good story to tell your kids — a lucky one and a true one. Best wishes.

Sincerely
Bill Woodley

WORD STUDY
Find pairs which are similar in meaning.

fortunate	result
approach of dawn	caught and held
in your favour	lucky
outcome	daybreak
trapped	set free
released	to your advantage
stock (livestock)	to be honest
frankly	friend
behaviour	person who is hurt
companion	sheep, cows, goats
recover	get hold of again
victim	way he acted

Find words or phrases in the third paragraph which mean:

killed

got him away from the leopard

a child's toy

attacked and injured, very fast

if his friends hadn't acted so very quickly

said how extremely well they did

tried many times

b Summary and recommendation

Discuss, then write answers to the three questions below, to make a summary and a recommendation.

Mr. Woodley offers two hypotheses:

*It could have been a man-eating leopard.
It could have been a leopard which killed livestock.*

Which hypothesis does he think is correct? What evidence does he give for this conclusion?

What recommendation would you make to the National Park Authorities if you were in his position?

114 What makes a man-eater

Work together and try to come up with one good reason why a normal leopard should turn into a man-eating leopard.

Write it down and pass it round the class. Which is the best reason?

114 Richard gives two reasons which he summarizes at the end of his interview. Were they the same? How did Richard explain the concept 'game management'?

115 *Grammar*

Past forms and past participles

a Uses of verbs ending in -ed:

1 Past simple tense, e.g. *He explained why...*
2 As an adjective, e.g. *I was so tired...*
3 To form the present/past perfect tense, e.g. *Have you finished?*
4 To make a passive, e.g. *It was trapped...*

Look at these sentences and say which category each of the words ending in -ed belongs to.

1 *I would be interested in hearing an account of your experience.*
2 *The leopard mauled one of the caretakers, who was rescued by his companions.*
3 *Now listen to Richard being interviewed.*
4 *Thank you for your detailed letter.*
5 *I think they must have got them mixed up.*
6 *They continued to threaten the leopard whilst it made repeated attempts to recover its victim.*
7 *Quite shocked.*
8 *The banda was constructed with a thatched roof.*
9 *We watched it go round.*
10 *The very worst thing that we feared would happen had happened.*

b Verbs with two past forms

The verbs in **a** end in -ed for both past tense (use 1) and past participle (uses 2, 3 and 4). Some verbs have a different form as past participle:

break – broke – broken   take – took – taken

What other verbs have a different past participle?

c More practice with past participles

Rearrange these words to make sentences. Notice which words often go before a past participle.

1 by – your address – was – I – the Manager – given – of Ngulia Lodge
2 never – a hurricane lamp – I've – on the ground – thrown
3 the – shot – it – was – day – following – dead
4 for release – was – to Tsavo – another leopard – sent

Do the same with examples from other Units:

5 by – it – written – who – do you think – was? (64)
6 new cooker – and – was – installed – taken away – old one – the – the (102)
7 had – Mrs Kerr's – old cooker – been – for scrap – broken up (102)
8 clearly – a large number of – spoken – he – people – has – to (188 b)

116 Reaction

Pick three words or phrases Richard might have used to describe his own reaction to his narrow escape.

shocked   relieved   panicky   nervous
couldn't believe it   extraordinary   surprised

 **116** Listen and check. What reason did Richard give for the fact that this specific leopard didn't attack them?

Complete the file on the leopard. Write it up as a report for a local information office.

Before a leopard can be moved it's given a sleeping drug.

117 REVIEW

UNIT 11

a nation
Find the base form **nation** in all these phrases. Find out their meanings.

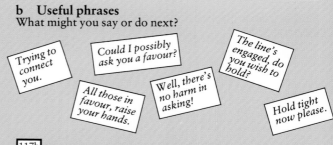

What we as a NATION want is not words but deeds.
NHS = NATIONAL Health Service.
united NATIONS peace keeping force.
NATIONWIDE search for escaped prisoners.
Flight departures! Domestic and INTERNATIONAL.
TSAVO NATIONAL park.
NATIONALITY British.
NATION
Much of the workforce was made up of foreign NATIONALS.
This is the age of INTERNATIONALISM.
there is no room for NATIONALIST feeling.

b Useful phrases
What might you say or do next?

Trying to connect you.

Could I possibly ask you a favour?

The line's engaged, do you wish to hold?

All those in favour, raise your hands.

Well, there's no harm in asking!

Hold tight now please.

117b Listen. What were the situations?

c ———— What one word fills all the gaps?

1 You were ——— very fortunate. (109)
2 Yes, yes, ———. (4)
3 So it's very long ———. (92)
4 Many spoke highly of them. ——— a very considerable success. (98)

NEW WORDS IN UNIT 11

beat D	internal
behaviour	luckily
conclude	ministry
confined	nation
conservation	nationalism
construct	nationalist
crucial	nationality
dawn	outcome
detailed	personally
director	pipe
drug	presence
entry	previously
environment	release
familiar	reluctant
favour	rescue
fortunate/ly	resource
frank/ly	scream
goat	sheep
harm	smell
hit D	strongly
hunting	subsequent
hut	threaten
impression	trapped
indeed	victim

48 new words
TOTAL SO FAR 468

115 Grammar

Aims: 1 Use of past simple tense and past participle.
2 Revision of verbs which have a different form of past participle.

SB115a PB115

1 Go through the uses then let students do the exercise on their own.

Possible key: Past simple tense:
2 mauled   6 continued
9 watched   10 feared
Adjectival forms: 1 interested
4 your detailed letter   6 repeated attempts   7 shocked (this is similar to 'interested') Present/Past perfect:
10 had happened
Passive: 2 was rescued   3 being interviewed   5 mixed up   8 was constructed

SB115b

2 Students can brainstorm on these. If they get stuck give them the present form.

Key: Other common verbs with different past participles (those marked * are often used as adjectives): been, begun, come, done, drunk*, driven, eaten, forgotten, given, gone, known*, run, seen, shown, spoken, taken, worn*, written, broken*, chosen, fallen, flown, grown, risen, shaken*, sung, sunk, swum, thrown, torn, woken, beaten, hidden*

SB115c

3 Students could do these for homework.

116 Reaction

Aim: Describing reactions and behaviour.

Lexis: drug, lead pipe, let go
Revision: **beat, extraordinary, nervous, reaction, shocked**
Understanding only: **recover from** (= get over), **start, feeling better**
Phrases: **couldn't figure out** (= couldn't work out), **grabbed hold of**
Slang: **bump off** (= kill), **chasing after** (= running after), **doped** (= drugged, sleepy from drugs)

Listening   SB116

1 Students write down three possibilities. Check these and then play the recording.

Key: The leopard may still have been sleepy from the tranquilliser drug. Also, the Webbers walked out slowly and silently, so as not to excite it.

Report   SB116

2 Students rearrange the facts in their files, and write them up neatly.

117 Review

Key:
b (*say*) Thank you; (*say*) Yes of course; (*do*) Put your hand up; (*say*) No, I suppose not; (*say*) Yes please/No thanks, I'll ring back later; (*do*) Hold on tightly to a seat.
c indeed

LEXICAL OBJECTIVES

beat D
behaviour 1 way someone/something behaves. *Your description of the animal's behaviour and attitude.*
conclude 1 decide something is true. *I can only conclude that you were...*
2 to end by saying, *in conclusion.* T
confined limited; a confined space is enclosed by walls, e.g. inside a hut.
***connect** EED 1 *the internal walls didn't connect with the ceiling.*
2 Telephone operator: *Trying to connect you, sir.* T
3 *This train connects with the bus*
4 related, linked. *Is good health connected with the food you eat?* T
conservation preservation and protection of the natural environment. *Wildlife Conservation and Management*
construct make, build, create. *banda constructed with a thatched roof.*
crucial essential, vital. *a very crucial factor. training is crucial.*
dawn daybreak. *you had the approach of dawn in your favour.* (opp. to dusk)
detailed *your detailed letter.*
director *I have written to the director about this matter. film director.*
drug EED 2 *illegal drugs* T
3 *a sleeping drug*
entry EED 1 dictionary/diary entry T
2 *the leopard gained entry* = entered
environment 1 the circumstances, people, things, events that surround someone/thing.
2 the natural world in which we live. *Ministry of Environment and...*
familiar not strange, well-known, have an understanding of... *familar with human beings. This familiarity...*
2 too friendly. *He behaved in such a familiar way, the girls got worried.* T
favour EED 1 approval. *Looked on us with favour. All those in favour...*
3 as a help, to your advantage. *had the approach of dawn in your favour.*
fortunate/ly Lucky/luckily. *you were indeed very fortunate.*
frank/ly Honestly, to be frank/truthful. *Frankly, I do not believe it...*
goats domestic animals *Sheep, goats.*
harm 1 verb & noun = hurt, damage. *Did the leopard actually harm them?*
2 Phrases: out of harm's way. *There's no harm in asking. It's alright, no harm done. More harm than good.* EED
hit D
***hold** (get hold of) D
hunting 1 hunt: to kill other animals for food *leopards... are getting old and can't hunt successfully.*
2 to hunt for = to search for. *The hunt for the missing child.* T
3 hunting – the sport of chasing of wild animals/birds.
hut small house with only one or two rooms. *in a hut in the game park.*

impression 1 appearance; the way a person, thing or place seems to you. *I got the impression that it was trying to get in.* See EED for phrases.
***indeed** In fact. *You were indeed very fortunate.*
internal 1 inner (not outer). *the internal walls didn't connect with...*
2 internal policies = home/domestic affairs, not international. T
luckily *Luckily you had the approach of dawn in your favour.*
Ministry 1 a government department. *Ministry of the Environment*
nation country/population. *United Nations peace keeping force.* T
nationalist/sm *nationalist feelings. current trend of Internationalism* T
nationality country you belong to
outcome result. *Had it been night... one can only guess the outcome...*
personally 1 used when giving your own opinion. *Personally, I think they made a mistake.*
2 in person, as an individual; *write to me, personally* T
Phrase: *Don't take it personally.* EED
pipe 1 a piece of lead pipe. Also: *hot water pipes, oil pipeline. He smokes a pipe. piped music.*
presence the state of being there. *familiarity with... human presence.* (opp. of absence) Phrases: *in the presence of... great presence of mind.*
previously at some time earlier. *It had previously killed a little girl.*
release 1 set free. *Instead of killing it, it was said to have been released in Meru Park. After its release...*
2 made public. *the news/record has just been released...* T
reluctant unwilling *Had it been night you may well have been reluctant to leave the banda.*
rescue help someone to get away from a dangerous or harmful situation. *rescued by his companions.*
resources 1 *natural resources e.g. coal, oil, can increase a country's wealth.*
2 money, wealth of a company. *they used all their resources to start a business* T
scream 1 loud high-pitched shout or cry, through fear or excitement. *if they had run screaming out of the hut.*
sheep 1 farm animal. *sheep and goats.*
smell *Maybe the leopard could smell us. Mm, dinner smells good.* T
strongly 1 firmly, highly. *They did a fine job and I have strongly commended them.*
2 *the room smelt strongly of gas.* T
subsequent later. *In the light of subsequent events...*
threaten 1 warn, threaten to harm someone.... *then continued to threaten the leopard while it...*
2 likely to happen. *The dark clouds threatened rain.* T
trapped 1 caught, unable to escape. *A leopard was trapped at Siaya Location.*
2 tricked into doing something. *You're not going to trap me again. It's a trap!* T
victim someone who has been hurt or killed. *the leopard... made repeated attempts to recover its victim.*

Revision Unit

Weather, seasons, landscapes and sunsets are themes explored in a variety of texts from a wide range of sources, specially selected for this revision unit. The chosen texts recycle and extend the discourse patterns and grammar focused on in earlier units, and give students further opportunities to practise summaries. The topics stimulate discussion about reactions and emotions, and form a basis for creative writing and in one case a survey report. More formal writing tasks recycle vocabulary and themes from earlier units, and there is a song for enjoyment.

OBJECTIVES

Lexical objectives are in TB129

Discussion topics

a Films and books. (118)
b The weather, particularly extreme weather. (121)
c The seasons of the year. (124)

Social skills

a Speculating on the outcome of an anecdote. (118)
b Talking about people's feelings. (121,124,126)
c Talking and writing about what you have heard. (121)

Communication skills

a Summarising a story. (119,123)
b Giving instructions. (120)
c Writing letters of reference. (127)
d Understanding poetry and descriptive writing. (124)
e Recognising American spellings and words. (129)

Grammar and discourse

a Using the Situation–Problem–Solution framework to write a summary. (119)
b **To** introducing an action and **that** introducing a proposition. (120)
c Conditional expressions. (122)
d General–specific statements. (122)
e The pattern **The more ... the more ...**. (122)
f The discourse framework Hypothesis–Evidence – Conclusion. (123)
g The uses of present and past participles, verbs ending in **-ed** and words ending in **-ing**. (125)
h Question tags. (128)
i Auxiliaries **do** and **have**. (128)
j Practice Book Grammar Word: **if**.

118 Landscapes and film crews

Aims: 1 Discussing films and books.
2 Speculating on the outcome of an anecdote.

Lexis: according, actors, actress, camera, crew, emotional, grass, hero, heroine T, **landscape** T, **passion, ocean, perform, rocks, romantic, screen, shore, studio**
Revision: **coast, film, rather, rise, scene, set (film-set), shot, sunrise, waves**

Lead-in SB118a PB118

1 Ask students to comment on the pictures.

2 Encourage as much talk as possible while students find pictures that illustrate the words and phrases. Encourage comments on the pictures.

Task and report SB118b

3 Go round and join in as students do this in groups. Then let them tell other groups what they thought.

Reading SB118c

4 Do students know where Hollywood is? (in California – on the West Coast of the USA) Students read the first part of the story, and then close their books (so they don't read the second half of the story too soon).

Task SB118c

5 Students discuss possible solutions. (There are clues in the pictures here.) Hear some of their solutions.

6 Students read to find what solution the director came up with, and whether it was successful.

7 If students are having trouble thinking of the last line, give them some clues: it contains two nouns from this page, and one noun from Unit 8 section 80, which is illustrated on this page. Don't tell them whose answer is closest.

   Key: (See section 129.) All the seagulls were flying backwards, and the waves were moving away from the shore.

8 Go over any target vocabulary.

119 Summary practice

Aims: 1 Revision of the Situation–Problem–Solution– Evaluation pattern. (See Unit 8 section 79.)
2 Summarizing a story.

SB119

1 Go round and advise as students expand the notes to make a summary of the story. Make sure their writing is reasonably accurate. You could limit them to 65 words, which will make them think harder about what to write.

2 They can pass their summaries around, and compare versions.

   A possible summary: The director told his crew to film a sunrise off the coast of California. Unfortunately the sun does not rise off California – it sets. The solution to this problem was to film a sunset and then run it backwards. When they did this, however, they realised that something was wrong. The birds were flying backwards and the waves were going out instead of coming in.

3 Ask some students to read their summaries out. As they do this, draw attention to the way the stages of the discourse are marked.

120 Language study

Aims: 1 To revise Unit 8 section 85: **to** leading to action; (**that**) introducing a statement, idea, or situation.
2 To revise giving instructions (Unit 7 section 71).

SB120a PB120

1 When students read out their completed sentences, go over the functions of **to** and **that**.

SB120b

2 Students can do this by reading the first three lines of the story in secton 118.

3 To revise instruction-giving, getting students to imagine what the director must have said to the various people in the story: hero, heroine, cameramen. What could his actual words have been? e.g. *Could you go and stand next to Y and look passionately into his eyes?*

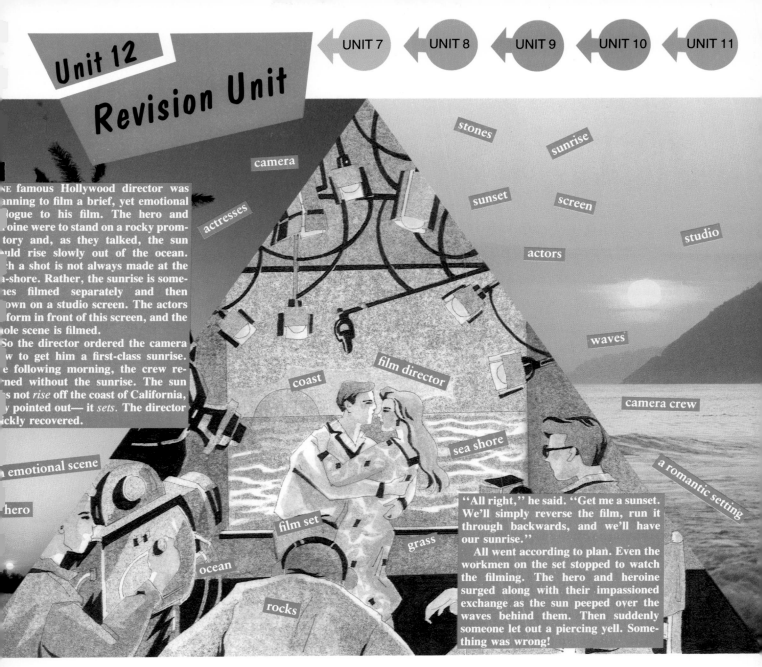

[NE] famous Hollywood director was [pl]anning to film a brief, yet emotional [epi]logue to his film. The hero and [her]oine were to stand on a rocky prom[on]tory and, as they talked, the sun [wo]uld rise slowly out of the ocean. [Su]ch a shot is not always made at the [se]a-shore. Rather, the sunrise is some[ti]mes filmed separately and then [sh]own on a studio screen. The actors [per]form in front of this screen, and the [wh]ole scene is filmed.

[S]o the director ordered the camera [cre]w to get him a first-class sunrise. [Th]e following morning, the crew re[tu]rned without the sunrise. The sun [do]es not *rise* off the coast of California, [the]y pointed out— it *sets*. The director [qu]ickly recovered.

stones *sunrise* *camera* *actresses* *sunset* *screen* *studio* *actors* *waves* *film director* *coast* *camera crew* *sea shore* *a romantic setting* *an emotional scene* *hero* *film set* *grass* *ocean* *rocks*

"All right," he said. "Get me a sunset. We'll simply reverse the film, run it through backwards, and we'll have our sunrise."

All went according to plan. Even the workmen on the set stopped to watch the filming. The hero and heroine surged along with their impassioned exchange as the sun peeped over the waves behind them. Then suddenly someone let out a piercing yell. Something was wrong!

118 Landscapes and film crews

a Match the words on this page to things or people in the pictures.
   Find people who are:
   shooting a film
   performing
   exchanging a passionate look

b If you were asked to choose one book to make into a film, which book would you choose? Why? If you were to make a film of someone's life who would you choose?

c Read the first half of this story and suggest a solution.

d Did the director's solution work?

▶ Guess the ending. Tell each other. ◀

When you have decided on your last line, tell each other. The solution is given on the last page of this Unit.

119 Summary practice

Write a short paragraph to summarize the story. Here are some notes to help you:

SITUATION: film director – planning final scene – sunrise
PROBLEM: Unfortunately...
SOLUTION: Film a sunset – run it backwards...
EVALUATION: ... something was wrong...

120 *Language study*

To and that

a Complete these sentences about the story.

   The director ordered the camera crew to...
   The crew returned and pointed out that...
   So the director told them to...
   In the end, someone noticed that...

b Normally *to* leads to *action*. What action follows these phrases with *to*?

   ... director was planning to...
   ... hero and heroine were to...

121 # Extremes of weather

121a **a** How do Rachel and Edmund feel about thunder and lightning and storms in general? Listen and make notes about each person.

▶ Write two sentences showing their differences. ◀

▶ Write two sentences about Edmund and four about Rachel. Read your sentences out to the class then write a short summary of what Edmund and Rachel say. ◀

Discuss in groups how you and people in your family feel about storms. Have you any stories about storms? Choose one or two things to tell the class, and plan how to tell them.

▶ After listening to other people's experiences, agree on a title for each one. ◀

▶ Choose one to write about. Interview the person concerned if you need to check on facts or feelings. ◀

b What extremes of weather have you experienced? Find someone in your group who has a story to tell about being very hot or very cold. Make notes and tell the story to the class.

Names	hottest	coldest
Maria	38 degrees southern Spain on holiday	Pyrenees-12 degrees c. visiting family one winter
Stephen		

▶ Tell each other what you've found out about two different people. ◀

121b What about Rachel and Edmund? What extremes of heat and cold have they experienced, and where?

▶ Write a report on the results of your survey. ◀

122 ## *Grammar revision*

Revision points
Complete these sentences, taking note of the phrases in colour. Recording 121 may help you with 1–4. Which sentence has a General – Specific pattern?

1 Storms are fine as long as ...
2 Being out in the middle of a storm is lovely provided that ...
3 The air pressure before storms tends to ...
4 Cats always – well, my cat certainly ...
5 The bigger the storm, the more/the ... er ...
6 The higher you go in a ski-lift, the ...
7 The further South you go, the ...

Compare what you wrote with other people's sentences. Did you make up any endings with the same meaning?

123 ## *Language study*

HYPOTHESIS – EVIDENCE – CONCLUSION
Discuss a–c below, rereading the relevant sections from earlier units if you can't remember the facts, so that you can answer the questions. Then write a short paragraph about each one, like the paragraph in **a**.

a See Unit 11 (sections 109–116).
What did Mr Woodley think about the leopard? What did he finally decide? Why?
Mr Woodley thought the leopard could have been either a stock-killer or a man-eater. Because of the way it behaved he concluded that it must have been a man-eater.

b What did Richard Webber and his wife think about the leopard when it was outside their hut looking in the windows?
They thought (that) ...
What did they finally decide?
They decided that ...
What was their reason?
... because ...

c See Unit 10 (section 100).
The Yetties lost their flight case on their way to Nepal. What did the Yetties think could have happened to it? Write a list of possibilities. (For example *it could have been left in London.*)
What had actually happened?

121 Extremes of weather

Aims: 1 Discussing people's feelings.
2 Ways of making a contrast.
3 Transposing from spoken to written form.
4 Summarising a story.

Lexis: psychological, relief, storms
Revision: **extremes, headaches, pressure, relief, shoots, strike, struck, wet, worried**
Understanding only: **lightning, thunder**
Phrases: **caught in a storm/in the rain, the storm breaks**

Listening and writing   SB121a   PB121

1 Talk a little about the weather in the pictures, but not too much because students will discuss this later. Perhaps tell students how you feel about extremes of weather.

2 Play the recording while students take notes. Play it again after a pause, to help students check what they have written. Discuss any words they need.

3 Go round and help them write their sentences. They could refer to the transcripts to help them.

Sample sentences showing differences: Rachel loves storms, and likes to be out in them, as long as there's not too much lightning, whereas Edmund doesn't like getting wet, or being outside in a storm. He thinks a storm is quite fun if he's inside, looking out.

Sample sentences about Edmund: He says storms are fine as long as he's not out in them.
He said he enjoyed a bus-ride through a storm last week.
He asked Rachel if she got headaches in thunder.

Sample sentences about Rachel: She loves storms except for the lightning, because that can be dangerous.
She loves it when a storm breaks after really hot weather, though she's sensible and tends to stay indoors.
She feels tired before a storm, probably as a result of the air pressure, so when the storm breaks it is a relief.
She has a cat who shoots under the bed during a storm.

Task and planning   SB121a

4 Students in groups of four (with a chairperson) exchange feelings and stories about storms. Go round and help when they are preparing what to tell the class.

Report   SB121a

5 After each story, decide as a class on a suitable title for it. Later students will choose one to write about, so they could take notes as they listen, or later go and ask the group that told it for more details, and interview the person concerned.

Task, planning and report   SB121b

6 Students talk to other students (or people outside class) and find out what extremes of weather others have experienced. They can copy out and fill in the survey form and then tell one story to the class.

Listening   SB121b

7 Students write notes about Edmund and Rachel's experiences on the survey form.

Report   SB121b

8 Students write up the results of their survey.

Sample: More people have experienced very hot weather than extreme cold. The person who has been the hottest is _____ who went to _____ and ... etc.

122 Grammar revision

Aims: (All revision points) 1 Conditional expressions.
2 General to specific statements.
3 The pattern 'the more ... the more ...'

SB122 PB122

1 Students think of ways to complete these sentences. If they need help with 5–7, refer them to section 92b.

Key: Sentence 4 has a general to specific pattern.

If you have the Student's Cassette and want some light relief before doing section 123, go on to the song in section 126.

123 Language study

Aim: To extend students experience of the discourse framework Hypothesis–Evidence–Conclusion.

SB123a PB123

1 Students should remember this first example from section 113. Explain that this is a very common pattern:
Hypothesis: The leopard was *either* a man-eater.
                                          or a stock-killer.
Evidence:... the way it behaved.
Conclusion: It was a man-eater.

SB123b

2 If students have forgotten what happened, they can reread transcripts 109c and 110b.

Sample: Richard and his wife thought the leopard would go away, but they finally decided it was trying to get in because they realised it wasn't frightened.
or They thought that the leopard would go away, but when they saw it wasn't frightened they realised it was trying to get in.

SB123c

3 Students can go on and write about the Yetties more independently. Go round and help if they get stuck. Afterwards, they can read each other's and suggest improvements.

A celebration of the seasons

A recording of the poems is available on the Student's Cassette only.

> **Aims:** 1 Discussing the seasons of the year.
> 2 Discussing people's feelings.
>
> **Lexis: fresh, grass, lifetime, rain, raindrop, refer, snow, surprising, theme**
> Revision: **elegant, hide/hidden, leaves, nature, raise, smells, spread**
> Understanding only: **rainbow**
> Note: Teach **fall** = American for autumn.

Reading   SB124a   124a   PB124

1 What different seasons do your students know about, in addition to spring, summer, autumn and winter? (Countries in the tropics usually have only two seasons – hot and wet, then hot and dry.) Do students' countries have strong winds at certain seasons? How do these winds affect people?

2 Discuss *Summer*, written by Karame Sonko from the Gambia (West Africa). Then let students read the other poems and identify which seasons they describe.

   Key: Grant Tennille: probably autumn, since the leaves 'turn into soft colors'. The days don't grow longer in the autumn, but that's not a surprising mistake for a five-year-old to make.
   R. Hunt: Winter.
   Lucia Atanasiu: probably spring, with the reference to 'the grass blade growing'.

3 Play the recording while students read again. They should discuss the poems and say which they like the best and why.

4 From top to bottom the pictures show autumn, summer, winter, spring.

Listening and report   SB124b   124b

5 Play the recording. Students listen for Edmund's and Rachel's opinions. Which students agree with Edmund and Rachel who both prefer 'Listen to the grass blade growing'? Who disagrees?

6 Students write their paragraphs.

7 Encourage students to practise reading their favourite poem out loud with lots of expression.

Writing   SB124c

8 Students write something about their own climate or landscape. Then about how they feel about one of the seasons. There is a lot of help given in the Practice Book for this.

Grammar revision

> **Aim:** To revise and pull together the forms and uses of the present and past participles, and other uses of **-ed** and **-ing** forms.

SB125

Students can do this on their own, and then compare their findings with a partner. Finally go through the exercise with the whole class.

Key: -ed: 1 filmed (passive), thrown (passive)   2 kept (passive)   3 caught (passive)   4 thrown (passive)   5 trapped (passive)   6 happened (present perfect), run (past perfect)   7 returned (past simple)
-ing: adjectives: 6 screaming   7 following   10 thinking, exciting   12 frightening
other: 7 morning (a noun which happens to end in **-ing**)   8 getting wet (verb as noun)   9 being (verb as noun)   11 looking (verb as noun)

A 'verb as noun', or gerund, is usually the subject of a verb (skiing is great fun) or the object (I like skiing).

The life of a man?

The song is available on the Student's Cassette only.

> **Aim:** Some light relief and enjoyment.
>
> **Lexis: easy, gay** (Students should be warned that this use of the word means 'happy' but that 'gay' is now more commonly used to describe someone who is homosexual.), **motion, storm**
> Understanding only: **fade away, frost, viewing**

*There are one or two features that show this is old English, with some poetic licence: 'a walking' (walking), 'had fell' (fallen), 'they did all seem to grow/did fall' (the **did** is to make it scan).*

SB126   126

1 The song writer is obviously comparing the life of a man with the seasons. The song is about autumn and winter when the leaves fall from the trees, and it reminds us we are all humans, and we too must die. The ancient Greek poet Homer also wrote on the same theme.

2 Play the recording of the song. Ask students to listen, and then read along. They may like to join in the chorus. Can they find the lines where the comparison is made?

124 A celebration of the seasons

a Read the poem about summer in the Gambia.

Now read the other three pieces. They are all written by children from different countries. Which seasons do you think they are about?

[124a] Read them out loud, then say which one of the four you like the best and why.

In which order does the artist show the seasons?

Summer

The rains start to come
The plants raise their heads
Fresh flowers appear, elegant smells
A new life has begun

Karamo Sonko, 18, The Gambia

As the days grow longer
The animals play,
And as the colors of the rainbow spread,
The leaves of the trees turn into
Soft colors.
Then the leaves play with each other.
The sun looks down and
Thinks nature is
A good way for the world to be.

Grant Tennille, 5, USA

It always seems surprising when you wake up in the morning and find everything is white with snow. Then, when the sun comes out, the snow sparkles like lots of crystals.

R. Hunt, 13, United Kingdom

Listen to the grass blade growing,
This music is hidden
And heard all day long.
Listen to the black-bird singing,
The song is the same
And new every time.
Listen to the rain drop falling,
Its sound is a moment
In our short lifetime.
Listen to the soft wind blowing,
He's singing a song
For all of mankind.

Lucia Atanasiu, 16, Romania

[124b] **b** What seasons did Rachel and Edmund think each piece referred to, and why? Which was their favourite, and why? Do you agree?

Write a short paragraph expressing what they and you felt about these pieces. Compare or contrast your feelings (See section 61b and 61c). For example:

Unlike X, I thought...
We thought that was about the Spring, whereas...
However we all felt...

c Your climate
What words could you use to describe the climate or countryside in your country?

Write a short paragraph or poem to show how *you* feel about one of the seasons.

125 *Grammar revision*

Past participles and words ending in -ing
Look at sentences 1–6 and find seven past participles. How many of them are in passive verbs? What about the one(s) left over?

Look at sentences 5–12 and find ten -ing forms. How many of them are adjectives? What about the others?

1 ... the sunrise is sometimes filmed separately and then thrown on a studio screen. (118)
2 Do you think they (crocodiles) should be kept in special places... (97)
3 ... storms ... I don't really like being caught in the middle of them. (121)
4 It (the airbag) cannot totally prevent somebody being thrown forward... (83)
5 A man-eating leopard was trapped at Siaya Location ... for killing a young girl... (113)
6 What might have happened if the Webbers had run screaming out of the banda...? (110)
7 The following morning, the crew returned without the sunrise. (118)
8 I don't like getting wet. (121)
9 I remember once being really cold in Japan... (121)
10 ... we went to bed thinking what an exotic place, ... how exciting... (109)
11 ... it started looking in at the window, at my baby son. (109)
12 ... such a frightening time. (109)

126 The life of a man?

The Yetties have a song which begins 'What's the life of a man any more than a leaf?' What do you think the song will be about?

[126] Bonny sings this song. Find the lines where the life of a man is compared to a leaf.

As I was a-walking one morning with ease
Viewing the leaves that had fell from the trees
All in full motion appearing to be
Those that had withered, they fell from the tree.

Chorus:
What's the life of a man any more than a leaf
A man has his seasons so why should he grieve
For although through this life we appear fine and gay
Like a leaf we must wither and soon fade away.

If you had seen the leaves just a few days ago
How beautiful and bright they did all seem to grow
A frost came upon them and withered them all
A storm came upon them and down they did fall.

Chorus

If you look in our churchyard there you will see
Those that have passed like a leaf on a tree
When age and affliction upon us have called
Like a leaf we must wither and down we must fall.

Chorus

127 Write a reference

If you had to write a reference for *one* of the
following people, what would you say? In your
group, think carefully about the person himself, the
circumstances, the demands of the new job, and how
capable you think he would be of doing it. Prepare
some notes.

Either John Cheetham who wanted to leave teaching
as a career to take part in a series of films dealing
with the conservation of reptiles. (89)

Or Bill Woodley, who wanted promotion to Head
Warden of the whole Tsavo National Park, which
would mean a move to Headquarters. (At present he
is warden of Tsavo Park, West.) (110)

▶ Write the reference, then tell other groups
what you have said. ◀

128 *Language study*

Question tags

a All these examples are from the transcripts of
spoken conversations. Why do the speakers use
question tags? Do you have question tags in your
language? What do you have?

Which tags fit where?

can't it? didn't it? doesn't it? isn't it? mustn't
it? wasn't it? wouldn't it? can it? does it? is
it? was it? would it?

Sorry, no, that one must come before, _____. (72)
Well it's just the steering _____. I suppose maybe
he . . . (72)
. . . . that was when they punctured his tyres, _____.
(72)
BB: It seems likely, _____.
RS: Or perhaps – I don't know. A 'keeper' then. I
think that's the term _____, they use? (90)
Ah, now it says 'an affectionate farewell', _____ so
does that mean . . . (90)
Looks like they're all true, _____. (95)
. . . it was no longer the new cooker she had ordered,
_____ (102)
. . . flight case . . . Nothing that big. No. Can't be that
big, _____. (100)
That's the way to do it, _____ (106)
But you're right, it goes up to June, _____, then it
starts getting shorter. (124)

. . . it does, _____. (124)
BB: The ship would slow down, _____.
EL: Yeah . . . exactly. (207)

Read the sentences aloud, paying attention to stress
and intonation.

b Now what about these?
Choose one of the verbs below, then add he/she/
it/they/you as needed to complete the sentences.

didn't/doesn't/don't/did/has/have/was

EE: Because people had them as pets _____ and
then . . . (94)
BB: I've never seen him before. _____? (90)
RS: No, I've heard of him. (90)
BB: He obviously lives in Kent, _____, so that er –
according to the . . . (90)
INT: You had some troubles on the way to Nepal,
_____? (100)
EL: Ah you took it up earlier, _____? (106)
RS: Yes, I was playing it . . . (106)
EL: . . . used. People have small minds _____?
(102)
BB: Mm. Dear oh dear. (102)
BB: It was as bad as that _____? (204)

129 American English

a Spelling

British	American
colour	color
behaviour	behavior
favour	favor
TV programme	TV program
travelling	traveling
kilometre	kilometer

Can you work out any rules to
explain some of the differences
between British and American
spelling?

b Words
Match each English word with
the correct American word
below.

British	American
pavement	fall
lorry	truck
autumn	elevator
lift	sidewalk
trousers	check
bill	pants
petrol	purse
toilet	gas
shop	freeway
motorway	store
handbag	bathroom

**NEW WORDS
IN UNIT 12**

according	motion
actor	ocean
actress	passion
camera	passionate
crew	perform
ease	psychological
emotion	refer
emotional	rock/y
fresh	romantic
gay	screen
grass	snow
hero	storm
heroine	studio
landscape	surprising
lifetime	theme

30 new words
TOTAL SO FAR 498

KEY to section 118
All the seagulls were flying backwards,
and the waves were going away from the
shore.

127 Write a reference

Aim: Writing and understanding letters of reference.

Since students do not have direct experience of either person mentioned, they will need a lot of help with this. They will also need to use their imaginations, and perhaps add a few facts and figures.

Lead-in SB127

1 Find out if anyone in your class ever has to write references. What advice can they give?

2 Has anyone recently had to ask someone if they would mind writing a reference for them? What kind of things does one write or expect to read in references? What does one not write?

Class discussion SB127

3 Brainstorm with the whole class on adjectives and phrases that could be used about either John Cheetham or Bill Woodley. e.g. hard-working, very able, understanding with people and animals, good with people, caring, both have a great love of animals. Ask students what evidence they have for each opinion.

4 Discuss the possible future jobs, and how good each person would be at doing them. Students should think up reasons.

5 Discuss ways of expressing recommendations. Read these two examples to students and ask them which person each is about:

1 I would imagine that, given his great knowledge of animals, and his obvious patience with humans, he would be an excellent candidate for this post/job. (John Cheetham)

2 He can express himself very clearly in writing, which is essential for such a post, and is extremely fair in his judgements of other people and situations. (Bill Woodley.)

Planning and report SB127

6 Group students according to which person they would prefer to write about. Go round as they plan what to write, and help them draft a first version. Groups writing about the same person could then exchange drafts and comment on the accuracy and appropriacy of each other's style and content.

7 You may have to help them make up a first line. For example: 'I have known x for the last three years, during which time he has been working with me at ... Before this, he ...'

8 Groups prepare final drafts, laid out correctly, and pass these round for comment. Which one do students think is the most tactful? positive? vague? exaggerated?

128 Language study

Aim: To review auxiliaries and question tags, especially the auxiliaries **do** and **have**.

SB128a PB128

1 Discuss why question tags are used. (Often when a speaker wants feedback from the listener, e.g. when reaching an agreement.) Sometimes people in Britain just say **Mm?**

2 Students on their own do one set at a time, and then discuss with a partner. Go round and see how they are doing. For key, see transcripts.

SB128b

3 Follow the same procedure as 128a.

129 American English

Aim: To highlight some differences between British and American English.

SB129a

1 Students may have noticed that some stories in the course are by American writers. Examples of the spelling differences between British and American English are given here. Help students to deduce the rules. Ask students if they know any other examples. e.g. How do Americans spell neighbour? (neighbor)

SB129b

2 Some students may have met some of these American words. Many words can be guessed, e.g.
sidewalk = pavement.

Key: *British – American:*
pavement – sidewalk; lorry – truck; autumn – fall; lift – elevator; trousers – pants; bill – check; petrol – gas; toilet – bathroom; shop – store; motorway – freeway; handbag – purse.

LEXICAL OBJECTIVES

according 1 to show the source of your information. *According to the weather forecast, it's going to rain.* T
2 depending on. *according to age.* T
3 *All went according to plan.*
actors/actresses people who perform in films and plays.
camera *TV/film camera*
crew group of people with technical skills who work together. *camera crew.* Also: *crew of a ship/plane.* T
ease 1 with ease = easily
2 comfort. *lived a life of ease and luxury. at ease* = relaxed.
emotion feeings like fear, jealousy.
emotional *emotional problems.*
fresh 1 new, recently made or acquired. *fresh flowers. a fresh drink. Fresh information.* T
2 original. *a fresh look at the subject*

gay 1 T homosexual. *A friend of mine who's gay had difficulty getting a job. Many gays are worried about AIDS.*
2 lively and happy. (now slightly oldfashioned.) ... *through this life we appear fine and gay.*
grass 1 cows eat grass. *blade of grass*
hero/heroine main character in a film
landscape T scenery
lifetime *in our short lifetime. a once in a lifetime opportunity.* T
motion 1 movement, continually moving. *all in full motion. in slow motion*
2 idea, argument in a debate. *he supported the motion that women should have equal rights.* T
3 *he motioned us to sit down.* T
4 to pretend to be serious about. *he went through the motions of clapping* T
5 set something in motion.
ocean 1 the sea. *the sun rose slowly out of the ocean. the Atlantic Ocean.*
passion very strong feeling/belief or sexual attraction. T
passionate full of passion
perform 1 carry out a task, an action or a service. *200 heart operations are performed every year at ...* T
2 to perform in a play/film/concert. *actors perform in front of a screen.*
psychological 1 mental, concerned with the mind, not physical. *It is like a psychological relief when the storm breaks.*
refer 1 mention or talk about. *In his letter he referred to recent events.* T
2 to relate to. *Which season do the poems refer to?*
*rise rose risen EED 1 move upwards. *The sun would rise slowly out of the ocean.* (Things like prices also rise)
rocky covered with rocks
romantic a romantic film or story is one with a love affair.
screen 1 a flat vertical surface. *TV/Film screen.* Also **to screen a film**.
2 screens round a hospital bed. T
*set 8 verb: *the sun does not rise off the coast of California, it sets.*
9 film set – place ready set up with scenery etc ready for filming in.
snow white with snow. *It snowed a lot*
storm 1 bad weather, with wind, rain and often thunder and lightning.
2 *a storm of criticism/laughter.*
studio 1 workshop where artists work.
2 film studio
surprising remarkable, unexpected. *It always seems surprising when ...*
theme 1 main idea or subject in a conversation.
2 an idea that an artist develops throughout a work. *It's got a theme through it of sounds and music.*

52T

Unit 13 Plans for a tour

In this unit we find out how the Yetties set up and prepare for an entertainment tour abroad. Students hear the Yetties talking about planning their concert programmes and focus on the language used in decision making. A light hearted anecdote from Roger gives an example of the confusions that can arise through language problems, a topic which students then expand on. The language of planning and the conventions of business correspondence are recycled through a sequence of letters and minutes exchanged in the process of finalising and following up the tour. The theme of touring abroad is introduced again through a narrative.

OBJECTIVES

Lexical objectives are in TB138

Discussion topics

a Cultural appropriacy of programme contents. (130)
b Language problems. (131)

Social skills

a Evaluating and recommending habitual procedures. (130)
b Anecdotes about language problems. (131)
c Speculating on a narrative. (137)

Communication skills

a Listing procedures. (130)
b Skimming letters for specific information. (133)
c Giving a verbal report of the contents of a letter. (133)
d The conventions of formal letter-writing. (134)
e Letters of complaint. (135)
f Writing a memo. (135

Grammar and discourse

a Referring back to a context in the form of an advertisement, a previous letter, or an oral encounter. (134)
b Conventional expressions of thanks in formal letters. (134)
c References to enclosures or attachments in formal correspondence. (134)
d Expressions of attitude in formal correspondence. (134)
e Requests with **would** and **could** in correspondence. (134)
f Recognising ways of referring to future time. (134)
g Relative clauses introduced by, and ending with, prepositions. (136)
h Optional revision of uses of the present continuous and the present perfect tenses. (134)
i Practice Book Grammar Word: **to**.

Dictionary skills

a Verb patterns: v + o, v + o USU PASS, etc. (132)
b Use and exemplification of grammatical notation. (132)
c Dipthongs: /aɪə/ **require**; /ɪə/ **near**; /aʊə/ **power**.

130 Planning the programme

Aims: 1 Discussing how one would go about selecting a programme of folk songs for another country.
2 Evaluating habitual procedures in this context.

Lexis: crops, harvest, load of rubbish, offend/be offensive to, relate to, selecting (selection), tour, tremendous
Revision: **join, popular, radio stations, suit, therefore**
Understanding only: **beforehand, records (record covers), taboo** (= things you don't talk about)
Phrases: **We're lucky in as much as our . . .** (= lucky in that our . . ./lucky because . . .), **join in with us** (= sing along with us), **In actual fact, . . .**

53T

Lead-in SB130a PB130

1 Explain that the Yetties were planning a concert tour abroad. Ask students to guess from the pictures and the map where the Yetties were going. (The Far East.)

2 Ask students to match the quotations with the pictures and discuss the people and events shown.

3 Topics to exploit as a class: foreign groups/pop stars on tour; liveliest festivals; harvest traditions.

Task and report SB130b

4 Ask students to think in groups of things they might do in advance, if they had to plan a programme for a number of countries. Students can then read their ideas to the class.

Samples: Find out as much about the country as possible; climate, agriculture, taboo subjects (politics/religion?).

Listening SB130b 130b

5 The Yetties were interviewed as a group. Divide this listening activity into two parts, stopping at the interviewer's question 'Do you find that audiences in different countries are in fact very different?'

6 Then ask them to speculate on the answer to the interviewer's question before playing the last part.

Key: All audiences like to join in and sing together.

131 Language problems

Aim: Anecdotes about language problems and misunderstandings.

Task, planning and report SB131

1 Students in pairs read the quotations and guess what must have happened. Ask the groups to give you their version.

Listening and report SB131 131

2 Tell students they are to write a short summary of what actually happened. They can listen with pauses and take notes to help them.

3 Students read and compare their summaries.

132 Dictionary skills

Aims: 1 To show that the entries give information about the patterns of use of words as well as their meanings.
2 To show how the information in the extra column relates to the entry, e.g. that the explanation/example illustrates the pattern abbreviated in the extra column.
3 Dipthongs: /aɪə/ **require**; /ɪə/ **near**; /aʊə/ **power**.

Lexis: attach, enclose, load, settle
Revision: **require**

SB132 PB132

1 Students look up the words and answer questions 1–4.

Key: 1 **attach** (cat. 1); **enclose** (cat. 2); **require** (because it is formal).   2 **require** has the word FORMAL in the extra column. The word **need** is given in the explanation.
3 **Load** can also be a noun. Point out its informal uses.
4 The examples can be taken directly from these entries: v + o **settle** (cats. 1,3); v + o OFT + TO **attach** (cat. 1); v + o USU PASS **settle** (cat. 2); v + o USU PASS + TO **require** (cat. 2).

2 Go over the target vowel sounds.

130 Planning the programme

a Match the quotations to the pictures.

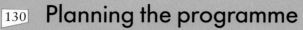

> ...o get...someone who knows bout the tradition of that untry...so that we can ind things which are very similar.

> It's not a problem at all to find something where you can immediately make contact with the local people. Because we all dance and sing at harvest time...

> We try to get songs with very easy choruses so that they can actually pick up the song and join in with us.

> They try to get them on the radio stations and get 'plays' on certain songs.

b How do you think the Yetties decide what songs to put on the programme when they are going to a country they haven't visited before?

▷ Work in groups and see how many ideas you can come up with between you.

130b Listen to the recording. Did you think of everything? Listen again, making brief notes of the points made.

131 Language problems

The Yetties told us about how they set up a tour to Frankfurt in Germany, where they had been asked to sing outside a department store.

Look at these quotations:

> They also ay that my other spoke erman very well though

> Roger's mother is German.

> So we had a German this end speaking to an English (person) the other end.

> They spent ten minutes running round the store trying to find someone that spoke English.

Something funny happened to them when they had to make a phone call to arrange the trip.

▷ Can you guess what happened? Tell the class what you guessed.

131 Listen and see if you were right.

▷ Write a short summary of what happened.

▷ Have you ever had any amusing experiences caused by language problems? Tell each other.

132 *Dictionary skills*

Verb patterns: V + O ...
Enclose Attach Settle Require Load

Look up these words and discuss:

1 Which three words would you consider most likely to appear in business letters?
2 Which word is formal? What word would you normally use instead of this word?
3 Which word can also be a noun?
4 Which verbs have which of the following patterns? Write down an example for each verb which illustrates one of the patterns.

v + o	= VERB followed by an OBJECT
v + o OFT + TO	= VERB followed by an OBJECT, OFTEN with TO
v + o USU PASS	= VERB followed by an OBJECT, USUALLY found in the PASSIVE
v + o USU PASS + TO	= VERB followed by an OBJECT, USUALLY in PASSIVE followed by TO

133 The Yetties to South East Asia – April/May 1982 a

Quickly read the extracts from letters and internal correspondence and say which order they were written in. Which dates fit which extracts?

20 November 1981
16 December 1981
26 Feb '82
9 March '82
5 May '82
6 May '82

Who's who?
James Lloyd was the Yetties' manager.
Caroline Dacey was in charge of organising the Yetties' tour on behalf of the British Council Music Dept.
Ivor Sussman was dealing with the Yetties' travel arrangements.

Choose one letter, read it carefully, then prepare to tell the class, in general terms, what it was about. Don't mention who wrote it. Can the class recognize which one it is?

James Lloyd
PO Box 254 Croydon CR9 7AH   01-654 0743

Miss Caroline Dacey,
Music Department,
The British Council,
11 Portland Place,
LONDON W1N 4EJ

Dear Caroline,

Thank you for your letter of 20 November. I am glad that you found the visit to Sherborne so useful – I'm sure it was helpful to The Yetties, they now have a clear picture of what is required of them.

I am collecting together the list of songs, synopses, photographs, etc, and hope to have these to you by the end of next week. The same applies for the passport photographs and serial numbers.

I am seeing The Yetties this evening and will point out that you need the vaccination certificates by the beginning of February.

Many thanks for your help and efficient support for The Yetties. I'm sure they are a lot more comfortable about the trip now that they've met you.

All good wishes.

Yours sincerely,

JAMES LLOYD

b

Our ref
Your ref
Tel ext

251 Travel Service
Brompton Road
London SW3

10 Spring Gardens
London SW1A 2BN
Telephone 01-930 8466
Telex 8952201 BRICON G
Fax 01-839 6347

Dear Ivor

The Yetties to Far East

Many thanks for making all the travel arrangements for this tour. It has all gone extremely well and the only problem was the initial loss of the instruments on the way to Kathmandu. I would be grateful if you would ask XAL for an explanation and an apology for this. Considering the enormous fuss they made of the group at Heathrow on departure and the fact that our Delhi office had had two lots of assurance from the local XAL representatives that the transfer was all in hand, I feel that they owe us some sort of explanation. It was certainly a bad start to the tour for the Yetties to have to give half their first concert on borrowed instruments with no assurance that their own would appear before they were due to move on.

134 *Language study*

Writing letters – common phrases in correspondence

a Referring back to a letter, or an advertisement, or the last time the two parties met
This provides a context for the letter:

I am interested in the position of wages clerk which you advertised on 4th August in the Bristol Evening Post.

Look at the correspondence in this unit and find:
– a reference to a previous letter.
– two references to previous meetings.

b Thanking someone for a previous letter or for providing a service of some sort:

Thank you for your letter of 20 November.

Can you find five more expressions of thanks?

c Referring to documents enclosed or attached:

I now enclose our cheque for £50.

Find one more reference to something being enclosed and two references to something being attached.

d Phrases expressing the writer's attitude:

I am glad that you found the visit so useful.

Make up sentences which might come in a letter using these phrases:

I am looking forward to . . .
I was delighted to hear that . . .
We were very sorry to hear that . . .

e Polite requests with could and would

Would it be possible to have the details . . .
Could I please have details of starting times . . .
Could I stress once more that all transport arrangements should take into account the flight case . . .

How might you politely ask someone to:
reply to your letter by the end of the month?
let you know the date of your next meeting?
pass on a message to someone else?

f References to the future

Read these sentences. How many ways of referring to the future can you find?

I am collecting the songs . . . and hope to have these to you by the end of next week.
I am seeing the Yetties this evening.
We will meet when we have time.
Would it be possible to have details . . . by then?
Let me know if any flights are impossible.
The group will be paid full subsistence.
A list of the songs most likely to be included.
I would be grateful if you would ask XAL . . .

Write down five time expressions from these letters. Say which refer to the future. For example:

now that they've met you.

Aims: The overall aims of sections 133, 134 and 135 are to get students to process first rapidly, then in more depth, a complete sequence of correspondence, and finally to write a further letter and memo in the sequence. Students should end up with the view that a letter is not a single, one-sided piece of writing. It is one link in a chain of related interactions, each letter referring both back and forwards in time. In business nowadays, there will often be phone-calls and telexes in addition to letters, to which correspondence may well refer.

1 Skimming letters for specific information.
2 Reading for more detail and giving a verbal report of the general contents of a letter.
3 Understanding some of the conventions of formal letter writing.

Lexis: **arrange, arrival, balance, behalf, considering, departure, efficient, fuss, grateful, greatly, helpful, initial, nevertheless, organising, outstanding, representatives, reviews, sincerely, stress, tour, transfer, translations**
Revision: **article, attach, enclose, loading/unloading, material** (= songs etc.), **required, settle, support, printing**
Understanding only: **fees** (= pay/wages), **vaccination, certificates, venues** (= places they will give concerts at)
Phrases: **on behalf of, the same applies to..., arrival and departure times, as follows, an outstanding success** (= tremendous success)
Note: **pointers** (informal) = suggestions.

Part of SB133 is on page 55.

Lead-in   SB133

1 Make sure students know which countries make up South-east Asia (Thailand, Malaysia (which includes Sarawak and Sabah), Singapore, Indonesia, Philippines, Japan, China, Hong Kong, Taiwan, Vietnam etc.) Students may remember that the Yetties also went to Nepal. Get them to recall what happened there, as this is referred to in this correspondence. (See section 100.) Ask if any students have links with these places.

Reading   SB133

2 Explain that the first task is to read through all the correspondence quickly just to find out in which order the letters were written. The 'Who's who?' section explains who the writers are. Allow students time to read and do this ordering task, but make sure they do not worry about understanding every word at this stage.

3 Get students to compare the order they have, until the whole group can agree on an order. Then draw the class together and get each group to read out the order they consider most likely. Ask them to identify the clues which enabled them to order the letters. Get the class to discuss any they don't agree on and justify their decisions. Don't tell them the right answer yet. Wait until the end of section 134. Write any target words on the board as they are asked about.

Planning and report   SB133

4 You could allot (quietly) one letter to each group to prepare as a spoken summary – students should imagine they have to tell someone else the basic message quickly.

5 Students can either tell each other their summaries, or record their summary, as if for a telephone answering machine. The class should listen, and then say which letter is being summarised.

6 Go over and practise the target words and phrases that are new to students.

Key: The original order was E, A, C, D, B, F.

Aims: 1 Referring back to a context in the form of an advertisement, a previous letter, an oral encounter etc.
2 Conventional expressions of thanks in formal letters.
3 References to enclosures or attachments in formal correspondence.
4 Expressions of attitude in formal correspondence.
5 Polite requests with **would** and **could** in correspondence.
6 Recognising various ways of referring to future time.
7 Optional revision of some uses of present continuous and present perfect tenses.

Part of SB134 is on page 55.

SB134 PB134

1 Students work at each small section at their own speed, ending with a class recap.

2 If you have students who are in business, or who already handle correspondence in English, ask them to bring several copies of a short series of their letters in for others to read, discuss and analyse for similar language points in a later lesson.

Key: a Thank you for your letter of 20 November.
Many thanks for coming in the other day.
Thank you so much for arranging the visit to Sherborne on Wednesday and for taking me down and looking after me so well.

b Thank you for your letter of 20 November.
Many thanks for coming in the other day.
Thank you so much for arranging the visit to Sherborne on Wednesday and for taking me down and looking after me so well. (It is common to combine referring back with an expression of thanks.)
Many thanks for your help over this tour.
Many thanks for your help and efficient support.
Many thanks for making all the travel arrangements for this tour.

*It is worth pointing out that if **thanks for...** is followed by a verb it is followed by the **-ing** form.*

c I now enclose our cheque for £150.
I enclose copies of the two reviews.
I attach our final itinerary.
Attached is a list of the countries.

Common forms are:
I enclose...
I attach...
Enclosed is/are...
Attached is/are...
Much less common but still possible:
I am enclosing/attaching...
I have enclosed/attached...

e Useful phrases: Would you mind + **-ing**...
I would be grateful if you could/would...
Could you please tell me/let me know...

f I am collecting the songs (this is present reference, see the extra exercise below) and hope to have these to you by the end of next week. (Future introduced by **hope**, **expect**, **look forward to** etc.)
I am seeing the Yetties this evening. (Present continuous. See below.)
We will meet when we have time. (**will**. Present simple.)
Would it be possible to have details . . . by then? (**would**. See exercise **e** above.).
Let me know if any flights are impossible. (Present tense with future reference after **if**.)
The group will be paid full subsistence. (**will**. This example is passive.)
A list of songs most likely to be included. (**To be** in this phrase refers to the future.)
I would be grateful if you would ask XAL for an explanation. (Polite request.)

3 Optional revision of present continuous: Write examples a–c on the board and ask students to look at these three uses of the present continuous:

  a I am collecting together the list of songs.
  b I am seeing the Yetties this evening.
  c I am sending you a cheque made out to the Yetties.

Do they refer to present or future time? (a and c – present, i.e. not at this actual moment, but as part of her present work. b – future.)

4 Present perfect: Point out the example 'now that they've met you' in the last paragraph of letter A. This is a good example of a past action in the present perfect tense because it is affecting the present/future. Ask students to find three more examples of this tense in letter B. Ask what other tense appears in other parts of the same sentence. (Future with **will** and present. The co-occurrence of the present perfect and the future is very common.)

135   A letter of complaint

> **Aims:** 1 To get students to write a letter as part of the same series, but adding relevant facts derived from the situation in section 100.
> 2 To draw attention to style, layout, position of address, date, reference, and greetings at the end of letters.

Planning   SB135 PB135

1 Begin by giving instructions on the layout of business letters of this kind.

2 Ask students to look at the letters on this page and see whether the sentences are long and complex or short and simple. Ask students how many sentences have commas in them. (Only four, apart from the commas in lists.) Point out that in business correspondence (as opposed to personal letters) each sentence normally covers one single item of information or asks one simple question.

3 Ask students to work in groups, drafting the letter in rough. Give them plenty of time to think and discuss how to make the complaint. (Remind them to use the information they already have from section 100.) It should obviously be polite throughout, explaining the situation, and requesting the relevant action (refer students to section 134e.)

Writing   SB135

4 Suggest that groups share their ideas and compare their plans at an early stage, before finalising their first draft.

5 Groups discuss any relevant changes they wish to make, and then one student in each group writes out a final draft for other groups to read.

Planning and report   SB135

6 Finally, they can write the memo to Caroline Dacey. The purpose of this is to communicate to her that her request to write to XAL has been carried out. A personal comment could of course be added.

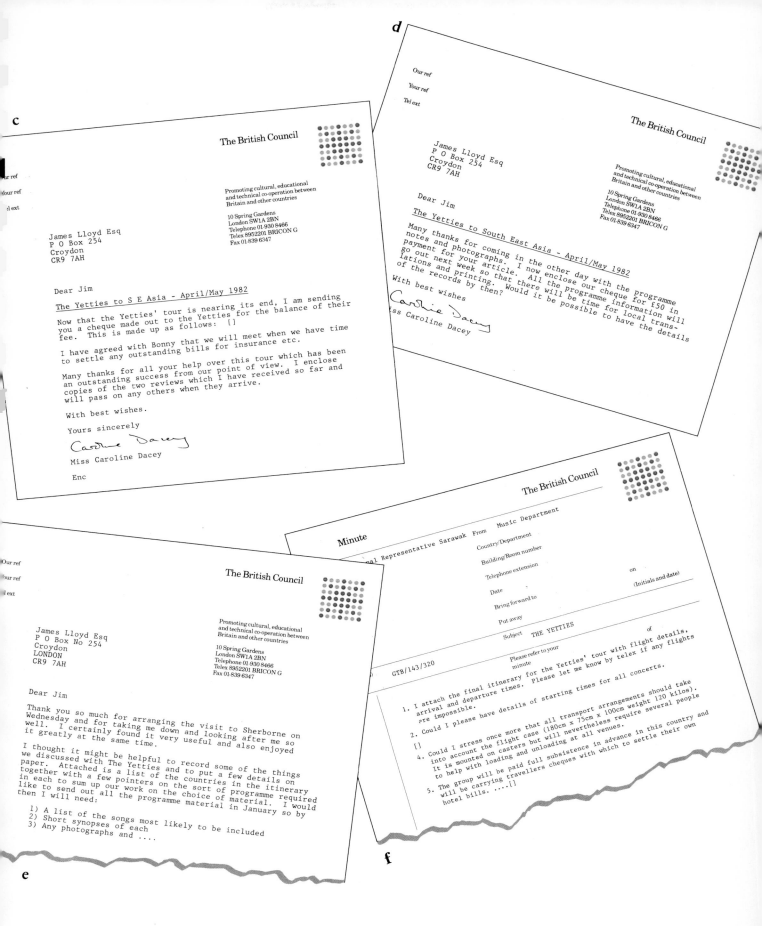

A letter of complaint

135

In her letter to Ivor, above Caroline Dacey says
'... the only problem was the initial loss of the
instruments on the way to Kathmandu. I would be
grateful if you would ask XAL for an explanation and
an apology for this.'

Write a polite letter to XAL doing this. You
could suggest they write a personal apology
directly to the Yetties, via their manager. Take
care with the layout and wording of your letter.

Write a memo to Caroline Dacey, referring to
her letter, and attach a copy of your letter to
XAL.

[136] *Grammar* ....

_____ which

> The group will be carrying traveller's cheques **with which** to settle their own hotel bills.

a It is quite common to have a preposition + which like this. What preposition goes in each of the following sentences?

1 *I am studying three A level subjects _____ which I hope to achieve academic success this summer.* (24)
2 *It slows down the speed _____ which he's shot from the bike.* (83)
3 *You don't always want to wear a jacket _____ which to put a wallet.* (78)
4 *There was a short article about a woman being eaten, _____ which the woman was described as attractive.* (95)

b Someone once said 'You should never use a preposition to end a sentence with'. What's wrong with saying that? What could they have said?

In fact native speakers do use prepositions to end sentences. For example, 'He didn't say which country he thought we were from'.

Use prepositions to end these sentences:

1 *This is the room we keep our papers _____.*
2 *Use this cloth to wipe the windows _____.*
3 *Warrington is the town John comes _____.*
4 *Hello! You're the very person we were talking _____.*
5 *List the points you think listeners would like further explanation _____.*

[137] A trip to Germany

Bonny and Roger talked about their trip to Germany. Here are some of the things they said:

It was actually playing for one of the big department stores.

When we arrived . . . no-one really seemed to know what we were supposed to do.

That was their hit tune at the time, so that went down very well.

It was great because he entertained us for twenty minutes.

In fact a couple of weeks before, their number one in their hit parade actually was The Wild Rover which is a popular English song.

As we don't know very much German that was quite useful really.

You're much more in contact with people there.

March. In March and it was quite cold.

Promoting British goods.

This was in February I think was it?

He borrowed Mac's guitar and started singing German folk songs.

Using the information from these quotations write about 150 words describing the Yetties' trip to Germany. Read each other's reports.

[137] Now listen to the tape and see whose story was the closest to what actually happened.

[138] REVIEW

UNIT 13

a Matching
Each word in **A** is often found with one of the words in **B**. Can you match them? Use a dictionary if you wish.

A	B
book	of rubbish!
take into	review
load D	account
balanced	stage
totally	view
initial	different

NEW WORDS IN UNIT 13

arrange	nevertheless
arrival	offend
balance	offensive
behalf	organise
collect	outstanding
consideration D	related
considering D	representative
crop	review
departure	rubbish
efficient	select
enclose D	selection
fancy	settle D
fuss	sincerely
grateful	stress
greatly	tour
harvest	transfer
helpful	translation
initial	tremendous
load D	

37 new words
TOTAL SO FAR 535

b Filling the blanks
Fill the blanks with a word from the box. Which word is used more than once? Which word is not needed?

> balance   consideration D   considering D
> facts   loads D   require D   review   settle D
> stress   tour

1 *For people in the West, New Year's Eve is often a time to _____ the past year.*
2 *It's only Tuesday. We've got _____ of time.*
3 *_____ he received no help, his exam results are very good.*
4 *The report is full of _____ and figures.*
5 *He always treated her with great kindness and _____.*
6 *Is there anything you _____, Mr Heissman?*
7 *Our holiday ended with a three day _____ of Wales.*
8 *When organising a holiday, cost is often an important _____.*
9 *It takes some time to _____ down well in a foreign country.*
10 *On _____, I consider the tour was very successful.*

c Which one is wrong?
Which of these cannot fit either sentence?

nevertheless   even so   in spite of this   therefore   still

1 *The flight case is mounted on castors (wheels) but will _____ require several people to help with loading and unloading.*
2 *He had not slept the night before. _____ he arrived at work full of his usual energy and drive.*

136 Grammar

Aim: Relative clauses introduced by and ending with prepositions.

SB136a PB136

Sentences 1–4 are all from former units. Students should be able to remember them. If they are not sure, encourage them to look back and check in the relevant sections.

Key: 1 in 2 at 3 in 3 in
Other prepositions, for example **of**, **to** and **with** are also found with **which**, but **in** happens to be nearly ten times more frequently used preceding **which** than **to** or **with**.

SB136b

*It is far more common in English to avoid clauses beginning Preposition + **which**, and use prepositions to end the sentence with. This is the purpose of exercise b. Note that, apart from example 1, it would actually be very strange, even incorrect, English if you were to transform these into clauses using preposition + **which/whom**.*

Key: 1 in 2 with 3 from 4 about
5 of/on/about

137 A trip to Germany

Aim: 1 Speculating on a narrative on the basis of limited information.
2 Reporting a story.

Lexis: fancy
Revision: **department store, products, would gather around/ join in** (**would** for past habit), **totally**
Understanding only: **hit tune, hit parade, promoting**
Phrases: **more in contact with people, no-one seemed to know what we were supposed to do, Don't fancy that very much!**
...went down well (= was popular, was well liked)

Task, planning and report SB137

1 Remind students they have already heard about how this trip was set up (section 131). Students could read the transcript again if they wish.

2 Students read the jumbled quotations, speculate (in pairs) about what happened, and then build up and write their own version. Ask them to imagine they are writing for a local newspaper, and to add some linking details. They may not need to use every quotation. They could begin: 'The Yetties are just back from Germany where they have been entertaining shoppers. When they first arrived, however, nobody seemed to know what they .../they couldn't find anybody who knew what they ...'

Listening SB137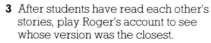

3 After students have read each other's stories, play Roger's account to see whose version was the closest.

4 Optional: Discuss other ways of promoting products. (Free gifts/ samples in shops, advertising leaflets through the door, door-to-door Sales Representatives (Reps), TV, radio and cinema advertising, adverts on buses/tubes, helicopters with banners etc. Ask students if any of them or their families are in the sales business. What and how do they sell?

138 Review

Key: a book review, take into account, load of rubbish! (informal), balanced view, totally different, initial stage
b 1 review 2 loads 3 Considering
4 facts 5 consideration 6 require
7 tour 8 factor 9 settle
10 balance. Word not needed: stress.
c therefore (Note that in 1, the word order should preferably change when using **in spite of this**: ... but in spite of this it will require ...)

LEXICAL OBJECTIVES

arrange 1 make plans, organise. *Thank you for arranging the visit.*
2 T put in order. *arrange the flowers*
arrival 1 *flight details – arrival and departure times*
2 T something or someone new. *the latest arrival; the new arrival*
balance EED 3 money owing to you. *a cheque for the balance of their fees*
consideration D
considering D
crops plants like corn/rice, grown for food, collected at harvest time.
departure see **arrival** 1 above
efficient done well, not wasting time or energy. *your efficient support ...*
enclose D
fancy EED 1 want, be attracted to. *Don't fancy that much.*
2 to imagine. Phrase: *Fancy that!*
3 lot of decoration. *a fancy hat*
fuss to behave in an unnecessarily anxious, excited, angry way. *so as not to cause a fuss* [6]; *considering the enormous fuss they made ...*
grateful thankful. *I would be grateful if you would ask XAL ...*
harvest *harvest time* see **crops** above.
helpful 1 useful *I'm sure it was helpful to the Yetties.*
initial 1 early on, at the beginning. *the initial loss of the instruments*
2 T capital letters representing a name. *E L are Edmund's initials.*
load D
nevertheless in spite of what has just been said. *mounted on castors but will nevertheless require several people ...*
offend EED 1 to upset, embarrass, or cause offence. *You don't want to go on the stage and offend the audiences ...*
2 T to break a law, commit a crime.
offensive 1 rude, insulting, upsetting. *To say 'Get stuffed' is offensive.*

organised 1 verb: *C Dacey was in charge of organising the Yetties' tour.*
2 adj: very efficient. *She's a very organised person.*
outstanding 1 very good indeed. *an outstanding success.*
2 T *money outstanding* = money still owed.
relate 1 used to show a connection or link. *the story may relate to some of their songs ... Two related questions* T
2 to communicate, interact. *children need to relate to other children.* T
3 to relate a story T
representative 1 *The XAL representative assured the Yetties ...*
review 1 an article giving opinions as in a book or film review. *two reviews of the Yetties' concerts.*
2 T to look back over, examine. *The situation is under review.*
rubbish 1 T unwanted things, or waste material. *rubbish bin/dump.*
2 you can say a foolish idea is rubbish. *What people say ... is an absolute load of rubbish.*
select 1 to choose. *How do you go about selecting a programme?*
selection T 1 *she stood little chance of selection for the job.*
2 range of goods. *a large selection of school books*
settle D
stress 1 emphasise the importance of. *Could I stress once more that all ...*
2 T tension/strain. *examination stress*
3 *Which words should be stressed? Where does the stress fall here?*
tour 1 T journey round a place. *Coach tour of Scotland. Go on a bus tour.*
2 a series of performances. *The Yetties' tour of South East Asia.*
transfer EED 1 move. *XAL informed them the transfer of the instruments was in hand. He was transferred to a new job* T
translation T *Can you do a quick translation into English for me?* verb: *roughly translated, it means ...*
tremendous 1 important *a tremendous lesson that was for everybody.*
2 T large, vast. *a tremendous noise*

Unit 14 — BBC Foreign correspondent

This unit focuses on broadcasting and on the BBC in particular. There is a reading passage on the BBC World Service and students are introduced to Bob Jobbins, a BBC correspondent, who writes and talks about his career. He shows how he works from short notes when broadcasting, and students' attention is drawn to the way he expands these notes. Students discuss the question 'What is news?' and speculate about how reporters actually get their news. Bob Jobbins then explains how radio news items are written. The unit ends with an old folk song Lillibulero, which is also the signature tune of the BBC World Service. This provides material for a note-taking exercise leading on to story-telling.

OBJECTIVES

Lexical objectives are in TB147

Discussion topics

a Careers and qualifications. (139)
b News stories – good news and bad news. (143)
c The work of a foreign correspondent. (143)

Social skills

a Reconstructing a story. (145)
b Story-telling. (146)

Communication skills

a Reading for gist. (139)
b Expanding outline notes. (140,146)
c Understanding the role of intonation in the weighting of information. (141)
d Listening for precise wording. (143)
e Summarising main points. (143)
f Distinguishing illustration from main point. (143)

Grammar and discourse

a Adverbs showing speaker's attitude. (141)
b Noun modifiers. (142)
c **of + -ing** for reports. (144)
d Practice Book Grammar Word: **can/could**.

Dictionary skills

Finding and explaining a dictionary definition. (143)

Things needed:
Ask students to bring in a newspaper (either in their own language or in English) for section 143.
For section 146 you will need at least one cassette recorder with recording facilities (microphone) and blank cassettes, for groups to record themselves telling a story.
If possible, get hold of a copy of London Calling, the BBC World Service monthly publication which gives details of all programmes worldwide. (Your local British Council, Embassy or Consulate should have some. Or you can write direct to the BBC in London for a copy, from BBC World Service, Bush House, PO Box 76, Strand, London WC2B 4PH.)

139 Bob Jobbins BBC correspondent

Aims: 1 To discuss students' own radio listening habits, and the role/purpose of the BBC World Service, in general.
2 To discuss qualifications and careers, homing in on the media and journalism.

Lexis: broadcast, correspondent, economics, editor, external, financed, foreign policy, headquarters, media T, **reputation, parliamentary, peak, politics, precise, weekly**
Revision: **on the air** (= being broadcast by radio), **aspect, control, grants, rests with** (= belongs to, is the responsibility of)
Understanding only: **continuously, reporter, specialise in, specialist in**
Phrases: **at peak times (peak travelling hours, off-peak travel), gaining experience**

Lead-in SB139 PB139

1 Allow students time to browse over the page and ask any questions they wish to. Ask them to identify the themes of the unit (radio news, the work and career of a foreign correspondent).

2 Ask students if they have ever heard the BBC World Service. Tell them about the magazine *London Calling* which gives all the World Service programmes. Ask them what kind of programmes they like to listen to, and what they find difficult about British radio.

3 Explain that this is the first of three units in this block (13–18) which aims at helping them understand radio broadcasts in English.

Reading SB139

4 Ask students to read the leaflet *The Job of External Services* quickly for the gist. Then ask:

Who pays for the BBC? (The British Government through Parliamentary grants.)
Who controls the content of the programmes? (Note that the content is not controlled by the British Government.)
What is the aim of the BBC External Services? (See middle paragraph.)

Reading and note-taking SB139a/b/c

5 Students read about Bob Jobbins and then try to answer the interviewer's questions on the basis of what students now know about Bob, as well as their own personal knowledge. Their short notes for the first two questions should be written from the point of view of Bob Jobbins himself. The other notes about qualities etc. are students' own personal opinions.

6 Students can either pass their notes round and read each other's, or you can ask students to tell the class what they thought, and write the main ideas up on the board for class discussion.

7 The Word Study here is, unusually, a preparation exercise, designed to help students understand some of these words when they hear Bob using them later on. Encourage students to ask each other and you for explanations of words they cannot guess. Finally get students to practise pronouncing them, and saying them quickly.

Key: Areas/topics: cultural affairs, economics, foreign policy, politics.
All the others are people except: reputation.

Unit 14
BBC Foreign correspondent

BBC Broadcasts to the World

*Bush House, London,
the headquarters of
the BBC External Services*

0600 Newsdesk
- 30 Meridian
- 30 African News
- 35 Saturdays Only

0700 World News
- 09 Twenty-Four Hours: News Summary
- 30 From the Weeklies
- 30 African News
- 35 Saturdays Only

The Job of External Services

BBC External Services broadcast to the world in English and 36 other languages for over 100 hours every day. They are financed by parliamentary grants. The government prescribes the languages which are broadcast and the length of time each one is on the air, but editorial control of what is broadcast rests with the BBC.

Programmes are designed to give news and reports of world events, and project a broad picture of Britain's life and thought.

The main programme in English is the World Service, on the air continuously for 24 hours a day and addressed at peak listening times to all parts of the world.

139 Bob Jobbins BBC correspondent

a For fourteen years, until his promotion in 1987, you would hear Bob Jobbins reporting from different parts of the world on the BBC World Service. Read and find out how he became a foreign correspondent for the BBC.

> I left school at the age of 18 and got a job as a reporter on the local newspaper, The Watford Observer. After three years I joined the Swiss Broadcasting Corporation in Berne, where I worked for four years as a sub-editor on the news desk. Then I did four years in Paris with Agence France Presse on the African desk. After that I travelled around a great deal gaining experience and finally joined the BBC in 1973.

b We asked someone who was interested in journalism as a career to interview Bob about his job. These are the questions she planned to ask him:

How do you become a foreign correspondent?

What qualifications do you need? For example, a degree?

Does a foreign correspondent, when he's actually working, specialize in one aspect of the country? In economics, for example, or politics, or foreign policy?

c Taking his personal experience into account, how do you think he replied to the first two questions? What precise qualities do you think a journalist needs? Name two.
What do you think is the answer to the third question?

Write short notes, then read each other's. You will find out later how Bob replied.

> **WORD STUDY**
> Find eight words that are people, and four that are areas or topics often covered in news reports. Which word is left over?
>
> colleagues
> correspondent
> cultural affairs
> economics
> editor
> expert in local affairs
> foreign policy
> politics
> politicians
> producer
> programme producer
> reputation
> specialist

Bob Jobbins, BBC World Service correspondent, at work on a communiqué

57

140 Notes for a broadcast

```
Q/A How to become a foreign correspondent.

Q: How do you become a foreign correspondent?

A: usually you have to start at the beginning -- as a
journalist -- local newspapers/radio etc. or can be
what we call a stringer, if already living abroad.
some people its their burning ambition others just
drift into it.

Q: what qualifications do you need? A degree, for
example?

A: I dont know: xxxx obviously a degree in languages
or politixcal science or economics could be very
useful -- but in itself probaly not the key. it's
difficult to define the precise qualities, apart
from stamina, and the ability to assimilate inform-
ation quickly and accurately and then produce stories
which fit the style of the newspaper or radio or
television station you work for: i mean it's no good
writing a very detailed economic assessment for a
newspaper which is more interested in purely polit-
ical news.

Q: xxxx does a foreign correspodent specialise then
in economics, or politics or foreign policy?

A: not really -- it's more a question of specialising
in the country in which you work -- or the countries,
since many foreign correspondents actually "cover" a
region -- for example the middle east or south america
or south east asia. within those geographical limits,
you have to try to know everything on every subject -
which is of course impossible.
```

a It is important for news despatches to sound spontaneous. If a correspondent wrote out the despatch in full and then read it out the spontaneity would be lost. For this reason experienced correspondents like Bob Jobbins work from short notes which they then expand in front of the microphone.

On the right are the notes Bob wrote for the recording of the interview. Does he include anything you thought of? At what points do you think he might expand on his notes, when actually recording his interview?

140b **b** Listen to the interview very carefully and notice where and what he adds to his notes. Why do you think he adds these things? Was there anything he omitted?

141 *Language study*

Attitude markers and intonation

a Attitude markers
There are some very common words in English, as in most languages, which can be omitted without affecting the meaning very much, but which are very important because they show the speaker's attitude to what he is saying, for example, how sure he feels about it.

141a Listen to the tape and see where these words go:
as such – fairly – I mean – really – particular – precise – probably

I don't _____ know what qualifications _____ _____ obviously a degree in modern languages or political science or economics would be very useful but in itself _____ wouldn't be the key it wouldn't be enough to get you the job it wouldn't be enough to make an editor decide to send you abroad erm so it's difficult to define the _____ qualities . . . but there's no list of qualifications that an editor is going to be looking for when he's trying to appoint a new correspondent to a _____ place and so it often becomes a _____ personal – a _____ personal choice I think.

Can you think of words like this in your language?

b Intonation
We have deliberately put no punctuation in the transcript opposite. When you are listening as opposed to reading, there are no commas, full stops or new paragraphs to help break up the text. But there are other things to help. For example, when Bob Jobbins' voice falls down to a fairly low level, this usually tells you he has reached the end of a point or section of what he is saying.

141a Without reading, listen to where this happens. Then read the extract as you listen, and note the words where this happens.

What other features help you understand what he is saying?

Listen again together to decide what punctuation the transcript should have had.

142 *Grammar*

Noun before noun
We have seen that English often puts two nouns together and leaves the reader or listener to work out the relationship between those two nouns. Thus an **ice cube** is a cube made of ice, but an **ice tray** is not a tray made of ice. It is a tray which is filled with water and put into the refrigerator to make ice cubes.

Which is which?

Try to explain what these expressions mean:

a government success   press conferences
opposition politicians   a newspaper reader
the radio listener   a news programme
a news item   a programme producer
The World Service   world events   the mass media
Choose any four and write sentences explaining them.

Aims: 1 Expanding outline notes.
2 Understanding a monologue.

Lexis: aim, colleague T, **continent, cover, cultural** ts, **define, economics, editor, enable, limits, nowadays, politics, precise, precisely** T, **purely, rely/ied upon**
Revision: **fit the style, upon** (= on)
Understanding only: **assessment** (= balanced description/evaluation), **assimilate** (= understand and get a balanced view), **spontaneous** (= natural, unrehearsed), **stamina** (= energy and strength)
Phrases: **drift into** (= start doing something in an unplanned way), **geographical limits, burning ambition, cultural terms of reference (to understand the culture of the area), to be honest, a (journalist) of some sort, work your way up** (= start at the bottom of the promotion ladder, with the aim of moving up it)

The recording of Bob's interview will not be easy for students to understand, so there is quite a bit of preparation to help them. You may want to leave the actual listening until the next lesson.
Part of the test of the interview appears in section 141. Try to avoid bringing this to students' notice, or they will read it and be less motivated to think for themselves.

Reading and discussion   SB140a PB140

1 Discuss what students think is happening in the picture. (Bob Jobbins in a BBC studio broadcasting a news bulletin.)

2 Explain that news reports must often be given out at great speed and that they must be as accurate as possible. So short notes are vital. Bob wrote these notes as if he were writing speech. They do not represent typical written English – he writes them to help him speak naturally, hence no concern for capital letters or spelling.

3 After reading the notes through once, and reacting to them, students can compare what Bob wrote with their own short notes from section 139c. Discuss these as a class. For example, what qualities does Bob mention?

4 Students can work in pairs or small groups to decide what parts of the notes might be expanded upon in his broadcast. Give some ideas, e.g. he may add more examples instead of the 'etc.'. Don't evaluate their ideas at this stage. Accept them all as possible.

5 Help as students draft their own ideas for expansion. Each group can then explain them to another group.

Listening   SB140b 140b

6 You will need to play the recording several times; it is at normal radio speed. Pause after each reply to discuss what additional information is given, and other changes.

7 Play the recording again allowing students to read the transcripts, checking what changes Bob Jobbins made.

Key: Things added: There are not many organisations with numbers of foreign correspondents; the majority just drift into being correspondents; it's the editor who decides which correspondents to send abroad; there's no precise list of qualifications. (Bob finally omits the example about fitting the style in his broadcast.) He names some of the bases from which a correspondent may cover a region; he talks a lot about the tricks and techniques of finding out reliable information from other people, and learning to understand the country in cultural terms – which is the basic skill of journalism.

Aims: 1 To highlight words that show the speaker's attitude to what he is saying.
2 To focus students' attention on the way that pitch and intonation help listeners to follow spoken language (comparing their function with that of punctuation in a written text).

SB141a 141a

1 Point out that it is quite easy to understand the gist of the message even without these words in the spaces.

2 Perhaps some students can remember where some of the words go, before they listen (but this is unlikely, since they were not vital to meaning).

3 Play the recording, asking students to listen for, and then repeat, the phrases with the words in them.

4 Students in groups can think of words in their language(s) that work in the same way, and try to explain what they are and what attitude they convey.

SB141b

5 You could make photocopies of this transcript so students can write on it, and punctuate it, after doing the intonation exercise. But get students to listen first (perhaps with their eyes shut!) and to signal when they hear Bob's voice falling to a low level.

Key: His voice falls to a low level on these words/phrases: as such, very useful, the key, send you abroad, particular place, fairly personal/personal choice I think.

You may like to point out how the intonation system works here. If, after a low fall (i.e. at the end of a sentence) the speaker continues on the same note, or slightly higher, he is likely to be adding another similar point. If, after a low fall, he starts again on a higher note, it is likely to be a new point or topic, like the beginning of a new 'paragraph'. In this interview, it is the interviewer who starts again on a high note, because Bob only speaks about one topic (like one paragraph) in answer to each question. But in his next piece (section 143c/d) you could remind students to listen for this low fall going on to a high tone marking something new.

---

142 **Grammar**

Aim: This is similar to the exercise in section 50, but with different nouns. Explaining the relationship gives excellent practice in expressing new meanings and formulating precise sentences in English, as well as practice with noun modifiers.

SB142 PB142

1 Go through the examples with the class, pointing out there are many different kinds of relationships (made of, containing, consisting of, happening in).

2 Students can try to explan to a partner what the expressions mean, then choose four to write about.

3 They can read their sentences out to each other, and compare explanations.

4 You could ask students how they express some of these noun groups in their language(s). Do they use more or less words than in English? Are the relationships clearer or less clear?

5 Ask students if they know any more noun phrases. (Other examples from nearer home are: car door, windscreen wipers, gas cooker, soup bowl, cheese board, kitchen cupboard, desk drawer, address book, credit card, cheque book, alarm bell, fire alarm, emergency exit, bus conductor.)

What is news?

Aims: 1 Listening for precise wording.
2 Summarising main points.
3 Distinguishing examples etc. from main points.
4 General discussion about what makes news.
5 Understanding how news stories for the radio are researched, written and structured.
6 The Word Study prepares students for the new words they will be hearing in Bob Jobbins' talk.

Lexis: **conference**, **confuse**, **defend**, **denial** (**deny** T), **development**, **establish**, **gossip**, **item**, **opposition**, **politicians**, **producer**, **reader**, **rumour**, **sadly**, **scandal**, **vital**
Revision: **the authorities**, **had up for** (= arrested and accused of), **issue statements**, **keep secret**, **rare**, **trust**, **while** (= whereas)
Understanding only: **an eye-witness**, **alert** (= to make aware), **cheerful** (= happy)
Phrases: **drink and drive** (= driving while under the influence of alcohol)

This activity will be richer if students have brought their own newspapers.

Lead-in SB143a PB143

1 You could begin by letting students look at the headlines in their own newspapers to see what news is good news, and what is not. They can give the class a rough outline of some of the stories, with their comments on them.

2 Students think of types of news that people may want to spread, or keep quiet about. For example, good examination results, or fall in the cost of living, as opposed to a motorway accident, failure to prevent strikes etc.

3 Discuss the headlines on this page. The pictures show the World Cup crowds celebrating, and a driver being given a breathalyser test.

4 The aim of the Word Study is to help students to understand these words when they occur in Bob Jobbins' recording in section 143b/c. Students try to match the headings to the sets of words.

Key: The left hand top set are possible contents of news items. The left hand bottom set are sources of news. The right hand middle set are types of news items.

5 Ask students to choose a word or phrase and to look up and explain it to the class. They can explain it by giving examples, or by rephrasing it, perhaps using and adapting their dictionary definition.

6 Students in groups could be asked to add extra words to each set, and to justify their choice of extra word.

Listening SB143b [143b]

7 The words in the Word Study box should help give students ideas for this discussion. Do this quickly and informally, to tune students in to what they will hear on tape.
(Some ideas: Ask a colleague (another reporter) who is nearer the place to go there and report back. Telephone someone who lives near where the story happened. Get there as soon as possible and interview eye-witnesses. Listen to what the local radio is reporting. Interview people responsible for the event. Listen to rumours and then check them out. Read government statements.)

8 Play the tape. Students take very brief notes. They can check their notes later, using the transcript.

Listening SB143c/d [143c]

9 Students should guess that the other half of a reporter's job is informing the public, communicating the news to an audience, writing up a good story or planning a lively broadcast. Play recording 143c so students can check.

10 After discussing and writing two points of their own, students should have fewer problems understanding the main points that Bob makes in the second half of his talk.

11 Play the recording. Once students have heard the six points, ask them to identify the two points for which Bob gives a reason (easy to understand because the listener has only one chance to hear; vital facts at beginning, because the report might be cut), and the point for which he gives an example (the style).

Report SB143d

12 If any students find this really difficult, even after listening several times, allow them to use the transcripts. Remind students that in a summary like this one, the examples and reasons can be omitted.

Key: The six points are: must be interesting and easily understood (these should be counted as two); only a limited number of facts per sentence; some repetition; vital information should come at the start of a report; style of presentation must match the subject matter.

---

144 **Grammar**

Aim: To highlight more words commonly followed by **of** plus a verb ending in **-ing**.

SB144

1 Students on their own make a list of words followed by **of**. They could practise saying the whole phrase with **of**; e.g. 'Another way of doing it . . .'

Examples 9–12 come from later units. Don't spend too long explaining them at this point. (POW stands for Protect Our Water.)

Key: way, question, memory, idea, fear, effect, opportunity, thought, risk, accuse . . ., chance, plan.

2 Students rewrite sentences 5, 7 and 12 in different ways. Check their sentences orally.

Key: 5 fear that I would fall . . .   7 opportunity to visit . . .
12 plan to jump . . .

---

145 **Signature tune**

Aims: 1 Informal discussion in order to reconstruct a story.
2 Telling their own version of the story to the class.
3 Enjoyment from singing a chorus.

Lexis: **devil**, **farmer**
Revision: **hell**
Understanding only: **dwell** (= live), **torment** (= to cause extreme mental or physical pain), **nag** (= complain continually)

This section acts as preparation for the song in section 146, and will help students understand the story of it. But don't tell students this yet. It's more fun if students make up their own stories first.

SB145 [146]

1 Play the chorus of the song. Ask if any students recognise it. The words: 'Lero lero lilliburlero' etc. are nonsense words and mean nothing. But they should be fun to sing.

2 Help students with the new words. They can find them in the pictures.

Task, planning and report SB145

3 Students in groups work out a possible story using all the pictures, in any order. Any story is acceptable. When they have finished, they can tell their stories to another group, or read them to the class, and compare versions.

143 | What is news?

a 'News can be something that people want you to know, or it can be something people want to hide, or keep quiet.'

Think of examples of both types of news.

What about these?

> **WORD STUDY**
> These words and phrases have been divided into three categories. Match one of the headings below with each category.
>
> **Possible contents of news items**
> **Types of news item**
> **Possible sources of news**
>
> outline of a new policy
> latest developments
> denial
> secret scandal   press reports
> explanations   statements
>   communiqués
> authorities   announcements
> press conferences despatches
> local newspapers
> local officials
> eye-witnesses
> rumour
> gossip
>
> Use any dictionary to look up three things from these lists that you are not sure about. Explain them to the rest of the class.

143b **b** **Getting the news**

How do you think reporters actually get their news? Can they always be at the right place at the right time? What if they can't get to the scene of the crime or the place or person involved, and report as an eye-witness? See what Bob Jobbins says about this.

143c **c** 'Just getting the news is only half the job.' What's the other half? Can you guess, before you listen?

In order to do the other half of his job well, Bob lists six main points to remember. Write two things you think he might say. Listen a few times until you have six points.

▶ Write a summary of the points he makes about the way radio news should be written. ◀

144 | *Grammar*

Of + _____ing
Some words are very commonly followed by *of* + _____*ing*. Look at these examples and make a list of words followed by *of*:

1 *Another way of doing it is to work abroad.* (140)
2 *I think it's more a question of specializing in the country in which you work.* (140)
3 *Their first memory of singing together was during their days as Boy Scouts.* (13)
4 *His prayer had been answered and he gave up the idea of committing suicide.* (36)
5 *I always had this fear of falling downstairs.* (34)
6 *This would have the twofold effect of getting the job done cheaply and making it safe for the local people to cross the river.* (97)
7 *He took every opportunity of visiting the zoo.* (91)
8 *So the thought of competing with a three year old is quite difficult.* (106)
9 *... how to reduce the risk of falling a victim to violent crime.* (150)
10 *The POW Group also accuse the government of refusing to provide water as a deliberate policy.* (163)
11 *It would have to keep right on going if he was to have any chance of winning it now.* (229)
12 *And then he hits on this crazy plan of jumping overboard ...* (243)

This is another way of talking about ideas and actions. You could rewrite sentence 4 like this:

... he gave up the idea that he would commit suicide.

Can you rewrite sentence 5 in the same way?
Sentence 1 can be rewritten like this:
Another way to do it is to work abroad.
What about sentences 7 and 12?

145 | Signature tune

145 This song should remind you of the signature tune for the BBC World Service. But what is the story? Look at the pictures and see if you can sort them out and make them into a story.

▶ Tell your version of the story to another group. ◀

146 Lilliburlero (the farmer's cursed wife)

146 Read the words to see how far you guessed the story.

There was an old farmer in Dorset did dwell
Lilliburlero bullenala
And he had a wife that many knew well
Lilliburlero bullenala
Lero lero lilliburlero, lilliburlero bullenala
Lero lero lilliburlero, lilliburlero bullenala

The devil came to the old man at the plough
Lilliburlero bullenala
'One of your family I must have now'
Lilliburlero bullenala
'It's not your oldest son that I crave
But 'tis your wife and she I will have'
Lero lero lilliburlero, lilliburlero bullenala
Lero lero lilliburlero, lilliburlero bullenala.

▶ How do you think the farmer will react to the devil's demand? ◀

'Now welcome good Satan with all of my heart
I hope you and she will never more part'
Now Satan has got the old wife on his back;
He's lugged her off like a pedlar's pack.

He trudged her away till they came to his gate:
'Come and take in this old farmer's mate.'
She saw thirteen imps all dancing in chains,
She ups with her boots and beats out their brains.

She knocked old Satan against the wall.
'Let's turn her out or she'll murder us all.'
He's bundled her up on his back and then
To her old husband he's took her again.

'I've been a tormentor the whole of my life,
Lilliburlero bullenala,
But I've never tormented like this farmer's wife.'
Lilliburlero bullenala

Lero lero lilliburlero, lilliburlero bullenala
Lero lero lilliburlero, lilliburlero bullenala.

Write brief notes telling this story in modern English. Begin: – story told in Dorset – old farmer with wife who continually nagged/ shouted at him. One day, farmer was ploughing . . .

Either Tell your version of the story to another group.
Or Get a cassette recorder with a blank cassette and record your partner telling the full story.

---

147 REVIEW

UNIT 14

a Odd word out?
Find the odd word out and replace it with a better word or phrase.

1 essential crucial vital reliable
2 politician programme producer news editor newsreader
3 build up establish develop confuse
4 purely sadly simply only merely
5 rumour gossip truth lies scandal
6 the press headquarters radio TV the media
7 degree modern languages politics economics

b Matching words
Find words from **A** that often go together with words from **B**. You can combine them in several ways. What does each combination mean? For example: foreign policy, foreign correspondent.

A	B
press	policy
foreign	conference
newspaper	politicians
political	correspondent
opposition	events
world	science
geographical	affairs
current	limits
cultural	developments
latest	facts
vital	

c Matching phrases
Match columns **A** and **B** below to make phrases you have heard or read in this unit.

A	B
based in	the entire Middle East
build up	a whole continent
establish	Cairo
cover	Parliamentary grants
rely on	your reputation
financed by	the truth
	your sources

d Find the appropriate form of each of the pairs of words to fit the sentences. One pair is not used. Which?

precise   reliable   denial   defend   terms
precisely   rely   denied   defence   term

1 *Being new to the area, she had only herself to _____ on.*
2 *The government was forced to _____ its policies against opposition attack.*
3 *In court, the defendant's _____ of the charge was met with disbelief by the media.*
4 *Good morning! You are 37 minutes late, to be _____!*

NEW WORDS IN UNIT 14

aim	headquarters
broadcast	item
colleague	journalism
conference	limited
confused	media
continent	murder
correspondent	nowadays
cultural	opposition
culture	parliamentary
defence	peak
defend D	precise
define	precisely
denial	producer
deny	purely
development	reader
economics	reliable
editor	rely
essential	reputation
establish	rumour
external	sadly
farmer	scandal
finance	vital
gossip	weekly

46 new words
TOTAL SO FAR 581

146 Lilliburlero

The song is on the Students' Cassette only.

> **Aims:** 1 Enjoyment.
> 2 Making notes for a story.
>
> **Lexis: murder**, **part** (verb) (= leave each other)
> Understanding only: **torment**, **tormentor**

SB146 146

1 Play the first two verses while the students read the words. The pictures in section 145 can still be used to help students identify who is who.

2 Some words are used in an old fashioned way here: **dwell** = live, **crave** = want badly, **she I will have** = it's her that I want, **lugged** = carried roughly. A **pedlar** used to be a man who travelled round selling things. **Trudges** = walks in a tired and heavy footed way. **Mate** = wife.

3 Check students understand the story line. Then discuss what the farmer will do. (Do they think the farmer and his wife get on well?)

4 Sing the rest of the song, with the tape, and then check students understand the funny ending. Ask students to compare this story with their own versions from section 145.

The image of the 'nagging wife' is (happily) rather out of date now, but has traditionally been a source of humour. You could ask students what types of man–wife relationships are more commonly portrayed in up-to-date songs, literature, advertisements etc.

Planning and report SB146

5 Students in groups write notes to help prepare them for telling a version of the story in modern English.

6 If possible, get students to record each other telling the story, as if to a radio audience. They should use the notes, but sound as lively and spontaneous as they can. If you have a big class, students can tell one part of the story each. If they don't like their first recording, they can record a second attempt.

7 Optional: Students think of a folk tale from their own country and write notes in English, planning how to tell it. Help them practise telling any parts of it that need rehearsal. Then they record that, and play it back to the class.

147 Review

Key:

a 1 reliable (replace with: very important) 2 politician (presenter, correspondent) 3 confuse (get, help to improve – i.e. words that can be used with things like school, institution, company, reputation etc.) 4 sadly (just) 5 truth (misleading information) 6 headquarters (newspapers, journals) 7 degree (history, science)

b press conference, foreign policy/correspondent, newspaper correspondent, political correspondent/science, opposition politicians/policy, world events. geographical limits, current affairs/developments, cultural affairs, latest developments, vital facts.

c based in Cairo, build up your reputation, establish the truth, cover the entire Middle East/the whole continent, rely on your sources; financed by Parliamentary grants.

d 1 rely 2 defend 3 denial 4 precise. Not needed: terms

LEXICAL OBJECTIVES

aim 1 T *he aimed the gun at him.* 2 something you hope/plan to achieve. *you have to work with that aim in mind.*
broadcast *The BBC broadcasts to the world. British Broadcasting Corporation*
colleague someone you work with.
conference 1 T a formal meeting, several days long.
2 a press conference, where reporters question a famous person.
confuse 1 T mix things up. *He confused me for my sister.*
2 make it difficult to think clearly. *This would confuse the listener.*
3 make it difficult to understand. *Rumour and gossip confuse the situation.*
continent 1 T the mainland of Europe. 2 Africa, Asia are continents.
correspondent 1 person who writes news. a foreign correspondent.
cultural 1 see culture. *in cultural terms or reference.*
culture T 1 the ideas, art and customs of a country. *the great cultures of Japan and India.*
defence EED 1 action taken to protect someone against attack. *What can you say in defence of your position?*
defend D
define 1 describe. *It's difficult to define the qualities a foreign correspondent needs.*
2 explain a word meaning. *It depends how you define 'refuse'*
denial see deny. 1 *News can be... a denial of a failure*
2 *denial of the right to vote.*
deny T 1 say something is not true. *He denied being involved in the murder.*
2 to refuse to let someone have something. *Women were denied the right to vote.*
development EED 1 T slow growth
2 T improvement
3 a recent event, likely to affect the present. *the latest developments*

economics e.g. specialise in one aspect of a country... *in economics or politics?*
editor person in charge of a newspaper or magazine.
essential T 1 very important. See **vital**. *Essentials such as food and clothing.*
establish EED 3 discover the facts. **check** information to help establish what is the truth.
external outside. *BBC External services broadcast to the world. For external use only = not to be swallowed. (medical)* T
farmer *a farmer in Dorset*
financed paid for. *financed by parliamentary grants.*
gossip informal talk about people. *Rumour and gossip confuse... She loves to gossip.* T
headquarters 1 *Bush House, headquarters of the BBC external...*
item EED 1 *a wallet can be a bulky item to carry around.*
2 *two items of business to attend to*
3 article in a newspaper. *news item.*
journalism job of writing news items. *The basic skill of journalism...*
limit EED 1 T *speed limit, time limit.*
2 boundary of an area. *within those geographical limits...*
media T television, radio, newspapers as a group. *The media are more interested in bad news than good.*
murder 1 unlawful killing of a person. 2 (informal) hard, unpleasant. *That was murder!*
nowadays these days, as opposed to the past. *Nowadays, you have to...*
opposition 1 T strong disagreement. *His ideas faced strong opposition.*
2 *the opposition politicians/party.*
parliamentary to do with parliament.
peak EED 1 T *reached a peak of fitness* 2 busiest. *peak listening times.* 3 T top of a mountain.
precise exact. *the precise qualities*
precisely T 1 *Let me explain precisely* 2 for emphasis. *He was furious precisely because he had not been...*
producer 1 *film/programme producer.* 2 T *Russia is a producer of crude oil.*
purely completely, entirely. *a newspaper interested in purely political news*
reader *a newspaper reader can re-read*
reliable T person/thing you can trust. *Reliable information/sources of news.*
rely to trust/depend on. *finding who can be relied on to provide good...*
reputation *hoping to build up a reputation.* (= a good name)
rumour information that may or may not be true. *Rumour and gossip...*
sadly 1 unhappily.
2 regrettably. *a cheerful voice would be sadly out of place for a report of a plane crash.*
scandal an event that people think is wrong or very bad. *a secret scandal...*
vital 1 necessary, essential, important. *vital information.*
2 T very lively, full of energy.
weekly *a weekly news programme.*

Unit 15 — Newspapers

The emphasis shifts from broadcasting to newspapers. There is a general discussion of the press, the kinds of news contained in the papers, and students' own preferences. Students go on to speculate on newspaper headlines and use these as a basis for their own news stories. They give their reactions to news stories and hear Bruce and Rachel doing the same. After focusing on common words and patterns used when reporting, they look at how information can be presented diagramatically in the press. After examining how short news stories are developed, students write more stories of their own.

OBJECTIVES

Lexical Objectives are in TB159

Discussion topics

Newspapers. (148, 152)

Social skills

Discussing the content of news stories. (154)

Communication skills

a Predicting content from headlines. (149, 154, 156)
b Comparing spoken and written versions of a story. (150)
c Summarising information by means of a chart or diagram. (152)
d Interpreting figures from a diagrammatic source and then writing an explanation of them. (152)
e Writing short news stories. (156)
f Composing headlines for news stories. (156)

Grammar and discourse

a Noun modifiers in headlines. (149)
b Evaluative comments in spoken interaction. (150)
c Reporting words in news stories. (151)
d Impersonal reports. (151)
e Devices for hedging on the truth of a story. (151)
f Complex noun groups in newspaper stories. (155)
g The pattern **wh- + to**. (157)
h Practice Book Grammar Word: **must**.

Dictionary skills

Metaphorical uses of common headline words. (153)

Encourage students to bring in recent newspapers while you are going through this unit. If they are in a language you don't understand, so much the better. You can ask students to explain about one article or item that looks as though it could be interesting.

148 Which newspaper?

Aims: 1 To give students an idea of the range of newspapers available in Britain.
2 To draw comparisons with those from their country.

Class discussion SB148a/b

1 Discussion on both points can be done in pairs and then informally as a class. Students can use the dictionary definitions to help them. They should already know the meanings of other names, like **Times** and **Independent**.

Key: Newspapers which aim at mass circulation: *Daily Mirror, Daily Mail, Daily Star, The Sun, Daily Express,* also *Today* (the newest).

Planning and report SB148c

2 Get students to divide into groups on the basis of what newspaper, or what style of newspaper they have in common. Students could work in groups of two or three, to prepare an oral presentation, while you walk round and help.

3 A spokesperson from each group reports to the class, who listen to find out how many different types of newspaper have been covered by the end.

4 Ask each group to summarise in one sentence the general findings of the report. They can read out or write up their sentences and compare them.

Written report SB148d

5 Students could write a short paragraph about the newspaper they know best, saying why they like it, and comparing it with a British paper.

149 Mystery headlines

Aims: 1 Predicting content from headlines.
2 Understanding noun groups in headlines (e.g. kangaroo target).
3 To show students that headlines are often deliberately ambiguous or mystifying, to make you want to read what follows (e.g 60 mph walk).

Lexis: act, chief, cracked, critical, feat, guide, headlines, refugees, target, urged, violence
Understanding only: **slump** (= sudden fall in business), **visas, CIA** (= Central Intelligence Agency (USA))

SB149 PB149

1 Explain the several possible different meanings of some of the target words such as **critical**, **target**. Discuss the play on spelling of **feet/feat**; and that '**guide on**' could either mean how to be violent or how to avoid violence. Headlines are often deliberately mystifying, or shocking, to make people buy the paper. Students should now be able to work out what the whole headline could mean.

Task, planning and report SB149

2 Students in groups decide what they think three of the headlines could be about. Help them to prepare what to say, and then a spokesperson can report to the class.

If you realise that students have actually gone ahead in the course book, and read the whole news items already (they are in section 150), ask them what two things they think Rachel and Bruce will come up with for each headline.

Listening SB149

3 Play the recording of Bruce and Rachel. Pause after they have dealt with each headline, to allow students to compare their views with those of Bruce and Rachel and comment. Note that Bruce and Rachel missed out *60 mph walk* by mistake.

Written report SB149

4 Help students to write three complete sentences in the style of a news item. They can read each other's work.

5 Go straight on to section 150, to compare versions.

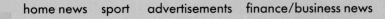

Unit 15
Newspapers

letters

features

editorial

international news

cartoons

gossip column

horoscopes

human interest stories   weather reports   weather forecasts   book/film/music/   play reviews

148 Which newspaper?

a Find out what the names of the newspapers originally meant. Do any newspapers in your country have similar names?

Which name do you think is the most suitable for a newspaper nowadays?

1 When you **express** an idea or feeling or when you **express** yourself, you show people what you think or feel by saying or doing something. **6** An **express** service is one in which things are sent or done faster than usual.

1 Mail is the letters and parcels that the post office delivers to you. **2** The **mail** is the system used by the post office for collecting and delivering letters and parcels. EG *Send it to me by mail.*

1 A star is a large ball of burning gas in space. Stars appear to us as small points of light in the sky on clear nights. **3 Stars** are star-shaped marks that are printed against the name of something to indicate that it is of high quality. EG *...a four-star hotel.* **4** Famous actors, musicians, and sports players are often referred to as **stars**. EG *...a tennis star...*

A **guardian** is **1** someone who has been legally appointed to look after a child, usually when the child's parents have died. EG *He became the legal guardian of his brother's daughter.* **2** someone who is considered to protect or defend a person or thing.

A **mirror** is a flat piece of glass which reflects light, so that when you look at it you can see yourself reflected in it. **2** If water **mirrors** something, it reflects it, like a mirror. **3** If one thing **mirrors** another thing, it has similar features to it, and therefore seems like a copy of it.

An **observer** is **1** someone who spends time studying the latest news about a subject or an area of activity. EG *...political observers.* **2** someone who sees or notices something. EG *A casual observer*

The **telegraph** is a system of sending messages over long distances by means of electrical or radio signals, and printing them at the other end.

b Choose two newspapers which you think aim at mass circulation with a lot of human interest stories, and few political or cultural themes. Choose two which are aimed at a more educated audience.

c Which sections of a newspaper interest you most – Sport? Fashion? Politics? TV and radio? Why do people buy newspapers? Find out different people's reasons.

d Describe the newspaper you normally read at home. Which of the British papers shown above do you think it is most like?

149 Mystery headlines

What could each of these news items be about?

Home Office urged to act on refugees

CIA chief 'critical'

Kangaroo target

60 mph walk

Cat's feat

Jaguar slump

Women's guide on violence

149 What did Bruce and Rachel think the news items would be about? Compare their ideas with yours.

Bruce and Rachel suggested one or two things for each headline. What do you think they said?

▷ Tell the class what you thought about three of them.

Select one headline and write two or three sentences that you think could appear in the news item. Read other students' ideas and compare them with yours.

150 Mystery solved

a Read the news items and check your intuitions.

150a Listen to Bruce and Rachel talking about the items. Which one did they fail to mention?

What additional stories did Bruce tell Rachel about?

Cat's feat

A 16-WEEK-OLD kitte named Mor jumped 200 fe from a balcony of her 22n floor apartment in Britis Columbia to the street an walked away without scratch.—AP.

With more than 8,000 Vietnamese refugees still behind barbed wire in Hong Kong's closed camps, the Home Office is coming under pressure to reach a decision on the number allowed into this country.

By David Burbidge
The British Refugee Council

By Martin Wainwright
A free booklet of advice to women on how to reduce the risk of falling victim to violent crime has been issued by the Home Office. It ranges from tips on jogging (use well-lit populated routes) to hints about fighting.

SYDNEY – Queensland wants to increase the quota of kangaroos that can be culled in the state by half a million to provide work for professional hunters and protect farming and grazing areas, a senior state official said yesterday.
Exports of kangaroo products earn Australia more than A$12 million (S$15.8 million) a year – Reuter.

A man was arrested last night after allegedly walking on the roof of the Holyhead-Euston 60mph express train.

New York (AP) – M William Casey, the forme CIA head, was in a critic: condition yesterday at th Glen Cove Communit Hospital in a suburb c New York, a hospit: spokesman said.
Mr Casey, aged 74, wh underwent brain surger for cancer in Decembe was admitted in the inte: sive care unit.

JAGUAR's American subsidiary reported yesterday that US sales had collapsed in April. Sales fell from 2159 cars in April 1986 to 1460 cars last month.

150a How did Bruce and Rachel feel about the stories? Play the tape again and make a list of the comments they made which showed their attitudes. For example:

RS: Got my doubts actually.
RS: – at all. That's incredible.

150b **b** Listen to their cat stories again. Do you know of any similar stories?

WORD STUDY

a Find the phrases in the news items which include these words.

act on	refugees
apartment	risk of
chief	sales
critical (in)	violent
former	wire
guide on	
increase ... by	
pressure (under)	
ranges from ... to	
reduce	

b Find the words in the left-hand column below in the new items. Match each word with one of the meanings given on the right.

quota	hunted and killed
reduce	numbers
hints	do something abou
target	make less/smaller
culled	make more/bigge
increase	bits of advice
act	number aimed at

151 *Language study*

Reporting words

Newspapers often make it clear that they are simply reporting what they have heard from some other source:

... a senior state official said yesterday.
... a hospital spokesman said.
Jaguar's American subsidiary reported yesterday ...

Sometimes they use words which show that they are not certain of the truth of what is said:

A man was arrested last night after allegedly walking on the roof of the Holyhead-Euston 60 mph express train. (150)
Three million Somalis face starvation because of drought, according to the country's Interior Minister. (158)
Incomes have never been higher, a ministry spokesman claimed last night.

When they do not want to name a source they often use the it form with a passive verb:

It is reported/believed/alleged that ...

or the there form:

There is speculation that ...
There are rumours that ...
There are signs/indications that ...

Some reporting words like report and announce imply that the source of the story has some official status:

It was announced yesterday that the Prime Minister would speak on television that evening.

Find three reporting expressions in the stories on this page and change them so that:

you show you are not sure of the truth of the story.
you conceal the source of the story.
you imply some official status for the story.

Look in a newspaper to find some reporting words. Explain to your teacher what they mean.

150 Mystery solved

Aims: 1 Reading with the specific aim of comparing accounts of a news story.
2 Practice in guessing meanings from context.
3 Intonation and stress in evaluative comments.

Lexis: act, allegedly, apartment, chief, concrete, cracked, critical, decision, earth, feat, former, guide, hunter, increase, latter T**, pressure, ranges from, refugees, sales, target, urged, violence**
Revision: **minister, ministry, protect, products, reduce, risk**
Understanding only: **arrested, exports**
Phrases: **in a critical condition, intensive care unit, falling victim to ..., reach a decision, express train**
Words students should be able to guess: **without a scratch** (= unharmed), **collapsed** (= fallen/dropped a lot), **behind, barbed wire** (see picture)

Reading   SB150a

1 Students read the news items, and compare their versions. Allow time for them to react and comment.

2 For the item *60 mph walk* ask students (in groups perhaps) to consider the possible reasons why the man was walking on the express train roof. (What does the word **allegedly** add? – Perhaps he just told someone he had! And why was he arrested? – Is it a crime?)

Listening   SB150a   150a

3 Students listen to see how Bruce and Rachel reacted to the complete stories. Ask students to listen out for two additional anecdotes that Bruce tells (one about a cat in Paris, and one about Vietnamese refugees).

Key: They fail to mention the *60 mph walk.*

4 Play the recording again with pauses, and ask students to make a list of the phrases where Bruce or Rachel make evaluative comments. Students could also repeat them after the tape. This should be fun, as well as giving intonation and stress practice.

Key: Got my doubts actually, ...
22nd floor!
Sure it's a cat?
at all. That's incredible.
Concrete's terrible.
That's a terrible business that, really.
Lovely people. They really were ...
Absolute disgrace it was.
Terrific. And then they went ...

5 Word Study
a Students simply read out and practise pronouncing the phrases which commonly go with these words, e.g. urged to act on refugees; increase the quota ... by half a million.
b Key: The left-hand column should be in this order, to match the right-hand one: culled, quota, act, reduce, increase, hints, target.

Listening   SB150b   150b

6 Students listen again to both Rachel's and Bruce's cat stories. This time ask students to compare them. What facts are different?

7 Find out if students have any similar stories about cats. They can tell each other. They could write up one of these stories for homework.

8 In conclusion, discuss as a class which news item students found – the most serious? the least likely? the most interesting?

151 Language study

Aims: 1 Reporting words in news stories.
2 Impersonal reports.
3 Devices for hedging on the truth of a story.

Lexis: allegedly, rumour
Revision: **according to, announced, believed, claimed, source, signs that**
Understanding only: **conceal** (= hide), **imply** (**implications**), **indications, speculation, spokesman**

SB151 PB151

1 Help students to read the explanations for themselves.

2 Students work in groups to find reporting expressions that could be changed. Help them say whether the present ones sound official or not.

3 Read the article *Kangaroo target* with students. The reporting phrase is already official-sounding. You could make it less certain by changing it to: 'a senior state official *claimed* yesterday'. Note that the changes may have to occur elsewhere in the item, e.g. 'There are rumours that Queensland will be increasing the quota ...' (in which case the original reporting phrase will be omitted altogether).

4 Get students to look at any newspaper, in any language they understand, and pick out the reporting words and phrases. They could read them in their language and then explain to you in English what kind of reporting words were used. (Which of the four categories given here were they most like?)

152 Charts and diagrams

Aims: 1 Summarising information by means of a chart or diagram.
2 Interpreting figures from a diagrammatic source and then writing an explanation of them.

Lexis: represents
Revision: **crimes, a rate of**
Understanding only: **at a glance, toll** (e.g. **death toll** = number of people who died. A **toll road/bridge** is one where you have to pay to travel on it, like some motorways in Europe.)

Task, planning and report   SB152a

1 Students read the report *Road toll* on their own. Can they work out roughly what number of people are killed per day in crimes, and then fires? (About 35 in crimes, 7 in fires. You begin by dividing 110 by 3, and then by 15.)

2 Students in groups design some sort of diagram or chart to show these figures clearly. They should think of labels, titles etc. and present their ideas to another group.

Task, planning and report   SB152b

3 Either: Students use the information given in the pie chart (surprising though the figures are!) to write a short report. It could either be for a popular newspaper with mass circulation, like the *Daily Mirror*, or for the more educated audience of a newspaper like *The Times*.
Reporters can add personal comments to suit the style of the newspaper.

Or: Students do their own survey to find out why people buy newspapers, and write a report based on their findings.

4 Possible survey topics: ways of passing leisure time; hours spent watching television/doing homework; sporting interests; musical tastes, reading habits.

Students in groups could devise a simple questionnaire to carry out a survey outside class. Allow at least an hour of class time to help with questionnaires. (Students can try them out on each other before finalising them.) Students then spend some time outside class, interviewing other students, or members of the public (between 15 and 30, depending on the survey). Finally students plan and write up the survey results, with a diagram (half an hour of class time needed), which they later present to the class.

153 Dictionary skills

Aim: To give students more insights into metaphorical uses of common headline words.

Lexis: act, context, increase, strike

SB153 PB153

1 Ask students to think first of the physical action or meaning of these words. (Some students might enjoy demonstrating them, or acting them out.)

2 Students then find the appropriate dictionary entry for each headline word. These give the metaphorical meanings. Discuss with students and find out if the same happens with these words in their own language.

Key: rise, cut, fall, act, increase, strike, lose, drop. In this order:

154 News in brief: who, what, when, where, why?

Aims: 1 To help students develop a questioning technique when reading which can help them make useful predictions and thus lead them to understand texts more easily.
2 Practice in formulating concise and relevant questions.
3 Awareness that writing is an interactive process. The writer's aim must be to answer the questions that will occur in most readers' minds.
4 Listening to distinguish relevant information.

Lexis: aid, bomb, elderly, exploded, explosion, former, identified, identity, interior, refused, responsible, responsibility, starvation, strike, underground
Revision: **face** (verb), **response of the authority, supporters**
Understanding only: **Somalis** (= people from Somalia in Africa), **blast** (bomb), **planted** (= put there)
Phrases: **I was going to say that!** (future in the past), **former president, Interior Minister**

Task, planning and report   SB154 PB154

1 Students on their own read and write three questions for each item. For example: When did the strike happen? Is the strike still on? What effects did it have?

2 In groups, they discuss each other's questions. Then ask them to tell the class their questions. Write the most popular ones on the board.

Listening   SB154

3 Play the recording of Bruce and Rachel drafting questions. Stop the tape after each one so students can quote Bruce and Rachel's questions and compare with their own. They can write down any that are different.

Reading and report   SB158

4 Ask students to turn over to section 158 and read the original items, ticking off their questions as they are answered. They can ask you for new words as they read. They can then report to the class which questions were not answered at all. The class can speculate as to why this information was missing.

5 Check that students understand and have a list of the target lexis for this section, and revise verbs like **cut, rise, affect** etc. These words are very common in newspapers, and will be useful.

155 Grammar

Aims: 1 Understanding the relationships in complex noun groups.
2 Preparation for section 156.

If your students want more information on adjectives, you can refer them to the Collins COBUILD Essential English Dictionary, study page 10. Order of adjectives: qualitative – colour – classifying – noun, as in 'small brown wooden box' may be useful here.

SB155a/b

1 Students read quickly the examples about the London policeman. After students have got the idea, ask them to make up their own. They could work in groups and write about other people in their class, as well as people in their families. Keep this light-hearted – it should be fun, especially when students read their examples out.

SB155c

2 Students practise phrases from the table referring to sources. For example: An official French trade union spokesman.

152 Charts and diagrams

a Together work out how to draw a suitable diagram or chart to show the following information at a glance. Draw it, giving a title etc.

Road toll

TRAFFIC accidents in China last year killed more than 42,000 people – a rate of more than 110 a day, the People's Daily said yesterday. The figure represents slightly more than three times the number killed in crimes and 15 times the number killed in fires.—AP.

b *Main reasons for buying a newspaper*

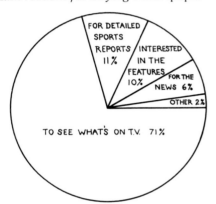

FOR DETAILED SPORTS REPORTS 11%
INTERESTED IN THE FEATURES 10%
FOR THE NEWS 6%
OTHER 2%
TO SEE WHAT'S ON T.V. 71%

Either Write this up as a short report for a popular newspaper.
Or Do your own survey and present your results.

153 Dictionary skills

Meanings for headline words
The following words often appear in headlines.

Fall Drop Strike Rise Cut Lose Increase Act

Look at the dictionary definitions and examples and say which goes with each word.

If a sound [ ] from a group of people, it comes from them. EG *A loud gasp [ ] from the boys.* `v:usu+from`

If you [ ] the amount of something, you reduce it. `v+o`

If something [ ] in amount, value, or strength, it decreases. EG *The value of the dollar has [ ]...*

When you [ ], you do something for a particular purpose. EG *We have to [ ] quickly... He [ ] alone in the shooting.* `v:usu+a`

An [ ] is a rise in the number, level, or amount of something. EG *At the meeting they demanded a sharp [ ] in wages.* `n count`

If something such as an illness or disaster [ ], it suddenly happens. EG *When disaster [ ], you need sympathy and practical advice...* `v or v+o`

If you [ ] a close relative or friend, he or she dies. EG *I [ ] my father when I was nine.* `v+o:no cont`

If a level or amount [ ], it quickly becomes less. EG *The temperature of their bodies [ ] ten degrees.* `v:oft+a`

154 News in brief: who, what, when, where, why?

Read these headlines and first lines.

Train cut
A STRIKE by Madrid underground workers

Kabul blast
A CAR bomb exploded

Starvation fears
THREE million Somalis face starvation

Woman wins £1m
A WOMAN aged 60 has won

Write three questions that you would expect to find answered in the rest of the seven–eight line news items.

154 Did you think of the same questions as Bruce and Rachel? Write down the questions that were different.

Then read the whole items and see which of your questions were in fact answered (section 158).

155 Grammar

Noun phrases   Who's it about?

a Newspapers pack a lot of information into a short space. One way of doing this is by expanding the noun phrase when introducing the person the story is about:

Mr. William Casey, the former CIA head...(150)
A 16 week old kitten named Mor...(150)

A common pattern is:

NAME	AGE	PLACE	JOB
John Brown, a forty-five year old London policeman.			

Sometimes the name comes at the end:

Forty-five year old London policeman, John Brown...

Write descriptions like this for some of your family and friends.

b Sometimes the description can be even more extended:

Handsome smiling forty-five year old former London policeman, John Brown...

Can you write some like this?

c The same thing often happens when the newspaper refers to the source of a story. Make some examples from this table:

DESCRIPTION	PLACE/ NATION	EMPLOYER	STATUS
senior official	British	government	spokesman
	French	hospital	official
	London	prison	representative
	Paris	school	
		trade union	

156 Story and headline

Write a short news item of not more than 75 words. (It can be for a school, local, or national newspaper.) Then, on a separate piece of paper, write a headline for it.

Pass your headline to someone who has not read your story.

Write a second story which fits the new headline. Then find the person who wrote the original story; exchange stories and compare them.

157 Grammar

Wh- + to
It is very common to have wh- words (who, which, when, where, what, why, how) followed by to with a verb:

A free booklet of advice to women on how to reduce the risk of falling victim to violent crime... (150)

Use seven of these eight phrases to fill the gaps in the sentences below.

how to do; what to do; how to look helpless; who to ask; how to sort it out; how to draw; how to find somebody; how to change a wheel.

1 *It's something... that only I know _____, and nobody else knows the secret.* (47)
2 *I asked if she knew _____. 'No, Dad,' she replied, 'but I do know _____!'* (71)
3 *Before Mrs. Kerr could get down to deciding _____ she had an urgent priority.* (102)
4 *... you really just have to know _____ who does know...* (140)
5 *Together discuss and work out _____ a suitable diagram or chart...* (152)
6 *I really didn't know _____, so I left there and just got a job.*

As you can see the most common word in this pattern is how, but there are other common phrases, especially:

I don't know | where to go. / what to do/say. / when to start. / which to have. / who to ask.

158 More News in Brief

Train cut
A STRIKE by Madrid underground workers demanding a pay rise yesterday cut the number of morning rush-hour trains by half, affecting an estimated 500,000 people, company officials said.—AP.

Kabul blast
A CAR bomb exploded in a central bazaar of the Afghan capital, Kabul, on Tuesday and a loud blast was heard across the city yesterday, Western diplomats said. There is speculation that the bazaar bomb might have been planted by supporters of the former president, Mr Babrak Karmal.—Reuter.

Woman wins £1m
A WOMAN aged 60 has won £1,032,088.40 on Littlewoods Pools. The woman, who lives with her husband in Bexley, Kent, told Littlewoods that she was "a quiet, shy type of person" and refused to be identified.

Starvation fears
THREE million Somalis face starvation because of drought, according to the country's Interior Minister, Brigadier-General Ahmed Suleiman Abdalla. About 600 Somalis, mostly children and elderly people, had already died of starvation over the last two months, Brigadier Suleiman said.—Reuter.

159 REVIEW

UNIT 15

a Odd word out?
Be prepared to explain why, or add a more appropriate word to 1–6 opposite.

1 chief head target leader director
2 represent act on behalf of speak for criticize
3 protect preserve pressure save
4 reduce increase rise go up get bigger grow
5 refused admitted said no to wouldn't allow
6 inner incredible interior internal inside

b Colloquial and idiomatic expressions for emphasis
Find the words or phrases that add emphasis. (Some are done for you.) Then imagine whether the listener would be worried or happy.

1 *You know that problem with the car? Well – I've cracked it!*
2 *I've been wondering how on earth to break the news to you...*
3 *Where on earth have I put your keys?*
4 *Oh, you haven't cracked that vase, have you? It'll cost a bomb to replace! They really do cost the earth! – Well, the last one I bought cost peanuts!*
5 *She simply exploded last time that happened.*
6 *Why the hell didn't you tell me earlier?*
7 *Our hospital staff are just cracking under the pressure – which is why nurses are going on strike.*

NEW WORDS IN UNIT 15

act, aid, alleged, apartment, arrest, bomb, chief, concrete, context, cracked, critical, criticize, earth, elderly, expand, explode, explosion, feat, former, guide, headline, hunter, identified, identity, increase, incredible, indication, interior, latter, pressure, refugee, refuse, represent, responsibility, responsible, sales, star, starvation, suburb, target, underground, urge, violence, wire

44 new words
TOTAL SO FAR 625

64

Unit 15

Story and headline

Aim: To give students a chance to create their own news story.

Planning and written report SB156

1 Help students with their first drafts. They can write about anything that has happened either in their own countries, or in the school, or where they live, or a story they have heard on TV or the radio, funny or serious.

2 Encourage students to 'edit' i.e. improve and correct each other's stories, and then discuss and decide on a good headline. Students keep their own story but pass on their headline.

3 Students write a short item about the headline they have received. You could allow others to ask the writer one or two or maximum three questions.

4 They then exchange and read the other person's story and compare stories.

5 Mix up all stories and headlines and put them up on a wall. Can others link them?

If students can think of a mystifying or ambiguous headline, the chances of the stories being quite different are far higher.

 Grammar

Aim: To highlight the pattern **wh- + to + verb.**

SB157 PB157

1 Students try this on their own. Several different phrases could quite easily fill one gap. If students are keen to know the original, they can look back at the relevant sections.

2 Ask them what is the most commonly used phrase like this in their own language(s). What gestures may accompany it?

3 Point out that this pattern is very common after **know.** Also that **know how to** is much the same as **can** in examples like 'something only I know how to do'. 'Can you ride?' is much the same as 'Do you know how to ride?'

Key: 1 how to do 2 how to change a wheel; how to look helpless/who to ask 3 what to do/how to sort it out 4 how to find somebody 5 how to draw/who to do 6 What to do

 More News in Brief

This section acts as key to section 154.

Review

Key: a 1 target (not usually a person) 2 criticize (the others are supporting roles) 3 pressure (the others are ways of keeping things safe) 4 reduce (the only one that means get smaller) 5 admitted (the only positive one) 6 incredible (the only one that does not refer to an inside of something)
b Happy: 1. All the rest the listener would be worried about.

LEXICAL OBJECTIVES

act EED 1 to do something. *Home Office urged to act on refugees.*
2 acting in a play.
3 one action. *a superstitious act*
4 an Act of Parliament
aid EED 1 help given to poor countries. *getting aid to Somalia.* Phrase: **in aid of** (charity)
alleged without proof, so people doubt it's true. *A man was arrested after allegedly walking on the roof...*
apartment American = a flat.
arrested caught by police. *A man was arrested last night...*
bomb *a car bomb exploded in Kabul.*
chief 1 leader, head. *CIA chief* 2 T most important. *the chief cause of the famine was...*
concrete 1 hard building material. *whether he fell on concrete or grass.* 2 T not vague. *concrete evidence*
context 1 T ideas, information, situations that make something easier to understand fully. *to put the oil crisis in context...*
2 in text. other words/sentences round a word that help you understand.
cracked EED 1 split, broke, open. *The cat cracked its palate. crack an egg.*
critical EED 2 dangerous. *in a critical condition* = very ill.
3 disapproving. *critical speech against...*
criticize EED T 1 to show disapproval.
2 to make a judgement on a film, book.
earth EED 1 T the planet we live on.
2 substance of the land surface. *Concrete and earth.*
elderly polite way of saying old. *children and elderly people*
expand T *Expand these sentences...*
explode 1 *a car bomb exploded*
2 T *he exploded with anger.*
feat an impressive act. *Cat's feat. the feat of a cartoon character*
former 1 previous. *former CIA chief*
2 the first of two.
guide EED 1 T *a guided tour; our guide*
2 *Women's Guide on Violence* – a free booklet of advice.
headlines *new headlines*
hunter someone who hunts wild animals
identified EED 1 T recognised.
2 named. *the woman refused to be identified.*
3 associated with. *identified with...*
identity T 1 *He hid his identity.*
2 beliefs, feeling of belonging. *Our identity as black people...*
increase get more or larger.
incredible 1 amazing, very unusual.
2 unbelievable T

indication *There are signs/indications that... He gave no indication of...* T
interior 1 T inside, centre. *the interior of China.*
2 *Interior Minister* – deals with internal/domestic affairs.
latter T 1 the second of two.
pressure 1 force. *air pressure.*
2 strain and stress. *pressure of work.*
3 persuade strongly. *The Home Office is under pressure to reach a decision*
refugee 1 someone forced to leave a country for political reasons. *Vietnamese refugees.*
refuse 1 say you will not do or allow something. *The woman refused to be identified. They refused permission* T
represent EED 1 T act on behalf of.
2 T be a symbol for.
3 amount to. *The figure represents more than 3 times the number...*
responsibility 1 T authority, duty. *mothers have a lot of responsibility.*
2 admit you are to blame. *accept responsibility for... Who claimed responsibility for the car bomb?*
responsible 1 T to have a duty. *responsible for cleaning up... a responsible job.*
2 to be blamed for. *Who was responsible for the car bomb?*
3 trustworthy, wise. *responsible parents* T
sales 1 amount a company sells. *Jaguar reports that US sales collapsed*
2 T *the sales department*
star
starvation death, suffering due to lack of food. *3 million Somalis face starvation because of drought.*
suburb an area not close to the centre of a city. *A suburb of New York*
target 1 person, place, thing being aimed at. *Kangaroo target. My first shots missed the target.* T
2 result you hope to achieve. *Sales target for the year...*
underground 1 T underground car park.
2 T not official or legal, e.g. an underground newspaper/movement.
3 transport system. *By underground* = on the tube.
urge EED 3 advise/persuade strongly. *Home Office urged to act on refugees.*
violence words/actions meant to hurt. *robbery with violence* T *Women's Guide on Violence.* (**violent**)
wire EED 1 thin metal used for fences. *Vietnamese refugees behind barbed wire.*

64T

What style radio news?

More about radio and newspaper news stories. Students are given examples of different kinds of news bulletins and stories and look particularly at how intonation is used to structure information in news broadcasts. Bob Jobbins develops one story in detail, and shows how it might be treated in different ways. Finally students are given a chance to write their own stories and develop their own news programmes.

OBJECTIVES

Lexical objectives are in TB170

Discussion topics

Broadcasting services and radio programmes. (160)

Social skills

Co-operative discussion in planning and putting together a bulletin of news and current affairs. (167)

Communication skills

a The structure of a news story. (161)
b Predicting the broad content of a story from the introduction. (161)
c Identifying sources for a story. (161)
d Recognising different styles of news report. (161, 163)
e Writing a brief news story. (161)
f Identifying questions to highlight the main points of a news story. (163)
g Identifying topic words in the sentence. (164)
h Producing a news story from brief notes. (166)

Grammar and discourse

a Contrast and classification. (162)
b Intonation pattern for comment and introduction. (164)
c Prepositional phrases, noun phrases, and other devices to condense information in introductory sentences. (165)
d Nouns used to introduce reports. (169)
e Practice Book Grammar Word: **by**.

Dictionary skills

To show that many words concerning physical warfare, e.g. **battle**, are used just as often in their metaphorical senses, e.g. 'winning arguments', 'battle of wits'. (168)

You will need (if at all possible) a cassette recorder with blank cassette, and microphone; preferably one set for each group of about 4–6 students.

160 Different programmes, different styles

Aim: To get students thinking and talking about different styles of news broadcasts, e.g. casual and chatty on a pop station/channel, formal and serious on another.

Lexis: casual T, **TV channel**

Class discussion   SB160a

1 Although the main aim of this unit is to help students understand news broadcasts, begin by discussing the kind of programmes they listen to and watch.

2 Go on to discuss the way that news is presented on different TV channels and different radio stations.

Task   SB160b

Key: Short and snappy: Newsbeat, News Briefing
Longer, more serious: 9.00 am News
More analytical: Today

161 Songs into news . . .

Aims: 1 The structure of a news story.
2 Predicting the broad content from the intonation.
3 Identifying sources for a story.
4 Recognising different styles of news report.
5 Writing a brief news story.

Lexis: adequate/inadequate, announcement, argue/ argument T, **dispute, female, fetch, incident, male** T, **mysterious, pop, row** (= argument), **shortage, supplies**
Revision: **connected with, admitted (to hospital)**
Understanding only: **investigating, pail, piped water, tumbled, well**
Phrases: **take X seriously, receive head injuries, not believed to have been . . ., medical checks**
Note: 'Broke his crown' is very old fashioned and means cracked his head.

Bob Jobbins illustrates his explanations of different styles of news items by taking the story of the child's nursery rhyme, Jack and Jill as the basic theme for all of them. To give students the idea of a nursery rhyme or song turned into a piece of news, they start with a 'news report' of the Lilliburlero song (see section 146). The picture and the name Yorrick Etty act as clues (Y Etty is like the Yetties.)

Reading   SB161a

1 Students read the news report about Mrs Etty. They should recognise that this is the story of the song *Lilliburlero* (see section 146).

Listening   SB161b   161b

2 Play both versions of *Jack and Jill*, giving no clues as to their difference. Most students should immediately recognise that the first version is a father telling his child a nursery rhyme. The second is read as a news item.

Key: Differences are mainly in intonation and stress.

Class discussion and listening   SB161c   161c

4 Remind students how the song *Lillliburlero* was turned into a news story, by changing the style and adding background detail. Ask students (in pairs or groups) to think of ways to expand *Jack and Jill* into a news story.

5 Listen to and accept all their ideas. Students then look at the beginning of Bob Jobbins' report, and listen to recording 161c. Help with lexis as needed.

6 Get students to speculate as to what might follow.

7 Play the rest of recording 161c. It is quite fast and formal, so students will probably need to hear it twice.

Key: Two sources: hospital sources; opposition party spokesmen. The question is – did Jack fall, or was Jack pushed?

Listening   SB161d   161d

8 Ask students to note down what two styles Bob Jobbins mentions first. Pause the tape before he goes on to 'straightforward official announcement'. Then ask which style he gives an example for later, and play the rest.

Listening   SB161e   161c

9 Play the tape and get students to hear the tones on the words in colour. A rising tone denotes information that the speaker considers the hearer knows already. A falling tone denotes new information.

Key: well f, companion r, injured r, checks f, opposition r, spokesmen r, calling r, push f, inquiry f, accident f, reports f, pushed f.

Unit 16
What style radio news?

5.30am Adrian John

7.00am Simon Mayo
with the Breakfast Crew

9.30am Simon Bates

12.30pm Newsbeat
with Ian Parkinson

12.45pm Gary Davies

3.00pm Steve Wright
Today's lucky numbers are
2, 13 and 87.

5.30pm Newsbeat
with Ian Parkinson

5.45pm Bruno Brookes

6.00am News Briefing

6.10am Farming Today

6.25am Prayer for the Day
with ROSEMARY FOXCROFT. *Stereo*

6.30am Today
Presented by Sue MacGregor
and Brian Redhead
6.30, 7.30, 8.30 News Summary
6.45* Business News
with PETER DAY
7.00, 8.00 Today's News
Read by BRYAN MARTIN
7.25*, 8.25* Sport
with GARRY RICHARDSON
7.45* *Thought for the Day*
8.35* *Yesterday in Parliament*

9.00am News

---

160 Different programmes, different styles

a How many stations does the radio have in your country? What station do you listen to most? What kind of programmes do you like?

b How many news programmes can you find in the extracts above? Which are likely to be short and snappy? Which longer and more serious? Which might offer analysis of events or situations, with different people giving different opinions?

161 Songs into news...

a Gone to the devil?
Listen to and read this news story. Does it remind you of something you have heard before?

Police investigating the mysterious disappearance in Dorset of Mrs. Etty, a local farmer's wife, believe that the disappearance may be connected with devil worship. The woman's husband, Mr. Yorick Etty, says that black magic is still common in some parts of the county and that his wife had threatened more than once to leave him and 'go to the devil'. Up to now, however, Mr. Etty had not taken these threats seriously. He now feels that his wife may indeed have left him to join some religious sect.

▶ Can you explain what you already know about this story? ◀

b Jack and Jill

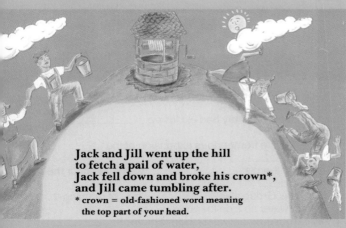

Jack and Jill went up the hill
to fetch a pail of water,
Jack fell down and broke his crown*,
and Jill came tumbling after.
* crown = old-fashioned word meaning
the top part of your head.

[161b] Listen to these two versions of *Jack and Jill*. Why are they different? What are the differences?

c Read the news story in section 161a. Can you expand *Jack and Jill* to make a full news story?

Bob Jobbins produced a story about a water shortage and Jack being injured in a serious scuffle with members of POW – the Protect Our Water group. The report began like this:

[161c] Newsreader: A local man was badly injured today in an incident connected with the long running dispute over water supplies. Bob Jobbins reports:

The row over inadequate water supplies flared up again today with the announcement that a local man, identified only as Jack, received serious head injuries...

▶ How do you think he went on? ◀

[161c] Listen and find out. What were his two sources? What question does the report end with?

d What styles?

[161d] Bob Jobbins talks about different styles of reports.

e What intonation? Rise or fall?
Look at this example from recording 161c. The arrows show how the speaker's voice rises and falls on the stressed words.

inadequate **water** *supplies*...

[161c] Listen and add the arrows here.

... *close to the main* *well. His female companion* ... *seriously* *injured*, ... *for medical checks. Opposition* *party* *spokesmen, who have been* *calling for* ... *say they will* *push for an official* *inquiry into the* *accident, and in particular into* *reports that Jack did not fall but was* *pushed*.

65

162 *Language study*

Classifying

Bob Jobbins talks about different kinds of news broadcast. He begins by pointing to the difference:

Different radio programmes require different styles of writing and broadcasting . . .

Then goes on to describe types and examples:

. . . some programmes, for example on a pop music channel, like short snappy reports. Others on more serious channels want more details and perhaps some analysis.

Can you expand these opening sentences in the same way? There are some notes in 1 to help you. Write notes, then full sentences.

1 Not all jobs require the same kind of qualifications.

Some - eg teaching - academic qualifications - eg a degree. Others - eg newspaper reporter - personal qualities - eg stamina, the ability to assimilate information quickly and accurately.

2 Different sports appeal to different people . . .
3 Different countries seem to enjoy different kinds of food . . .
4 Different means of transport offer different advantages . . .

Read one of your completed paragraphs out to the class. Find out who has thought of a similar way to continue. Listen to their report and continue in the same way.

163 Current affairs – the Jack and Jill story

The area under threat

a   Having demonstrated a short snappy report of this story, Bob goes on to explain:

163a   In a longer current affairs programme following the news, he or she [the correspondent] might be asked a number of questions by the programme's presenter to try to explain even further just what is going on.

In this case, the programme presenter needs to know the background to this area; there has been a lot of new building, and the local farmers are worried about water shortages due to the construction work and an increase in the local population.

If you were the presenter, what questions might you ask the correspondent about the incident at the well?

In groups make a list of points you think listeners would like further clarification of. (Look back at section 161). Then write three questions.

 Tell the class your questions. Take a vote on what questions and points you think will be covered in this current affairs item.

163b   **b**   Listen to the questions that Bob was asked. Take brief notes as you listen for the answers.

 Compare your notes with other students'.

163c   **c**   Bob ends by discussing this style of report. What could a follow-up report consist of? Who might he interview?

164 *Language study*

Intonation practice

164   Listen for the missing words. Try to repeat each phrase after the tape in a newsreader tone of voice.

a Well, the official version definitely says _____ _____

b – and implies that his companion Jill _____ _____ . . .

c and I think that is probably _____ _____ of a coincidence.

d Jill is _____, but the press are being _____ _____ . . .

e Possibly members of the Protect Our Water Group, _____ as POW.

f . . . until recently they had exclusive _____ well . . .

g but since the tremendous expansion of the _____

h they say there's _____ water, even for their _____

i The POW Group also _____ of refusing to provide water as a deliberate _____ . . .

j say the government wants to drive them off _____

k which would solve the current land _____

Aim: To give practice in building up a text expressing contrast and classification.

SB162 PB162

1 Discuss the example. Students then work singly or in pairs on 1–4. Walk round and help. Finally students read some out to the class to compare their ideas.

2 Further examples and patterns to try out:
Not all holiday makers want the same kind of holiday . . .
Not all holiday resorts offer the same facilities . . .

3 You could also revise and extend the pattern:
Many/Most/The majority of/A large number of/xxx . . .
Some/A few/A small number, however/on the other hand,
. . . because . . .

Aims: To show the difference in style between the short report and a longer but slightly more casual treatment of the news topic, where the programme producer 'interviews' the reporter.

Lexis: **accuse, alternative, casual, committed to, construction** (firms), **crisis, current** (affairs), **deliberate, fight, formula, implies, nearby, ordinary, permission, slipped**
Revision: **denied, drive them off, due to, as a policy, refusing, settle** (the fight), **solve, supporters, tremendous**
Understanding only: **exclusive use of** (= only they used it), **expansion, militants** (= people who will fight for justice), **unconvinced**
Phrases: **land/water shortage, minimum needs/ requirements, All the signs are that . . .**
Note: Many of these words will be recycled in section 164.

Task   SB163 163a PB163

1 Remind students they have already heard demonstrated a short snappy news report. Current affairs programmes go into more detail.

2 Play the recording, which is very short. Students read and follow the rest of the instructions.

3 Make sure students use the picture and the background information to help them think of questions that the presenter might ask. Be careful to accept all possible ideas, not just the ones that are finally used! This stage is vital to prepare students for the recording that follows, to help them predict and listen intelligently.

Planning and report   SB163a

4 Help students phrase their questions. When they read them to the class, write the most popular questions on the board.

5 Warn students they may not understand everything first time. Get them to listen once straight through, and then once with pauses, while they take very brief notes of questions and main points in the answers. There is no need to study the text in detail at this stage. This will be done in section 164. Explain only the target lexis that holds students up. (The rest can be covered in section 164.)

6 Students compare notes and discuss which of their questions were answered. Ask if students agree with the water supply expert.

With a weak class, for the second half of this recording you could let them listen and follow the text as given in the Practice Book, where they have to fill in the names of the people concerned.

Listening   SB163 163c

7 Students should listen and answer the questions.

164 **Language study**

Aims: 1 To highlight useful phrases containing the target lexis in context.
2 To give further practice in recognising the communicative value of intonation and stress over stretches of monologue.
3 Distinguishing rising and falling intonation on the main stressed styllable.

This note refers to both section 161e and 164.
It is important to be able to hear whether a speaker's voice rises or falls on the stressed words. Often the most important parts are spoken with a falling tone. A falling tone denotes new information. A rising tone occurs when the speaker thinks the information is already shared information, i.e. not new.

SB161e SB164 164 PB164

1 Revise briefly section 161e, by letting students read out Bob Jobbins' news with the correct intonation. Then explain how the rising and falling tones have different meanings (see the note above).

2 Play the recording. Stop after each example. Students listen for the missing words and then practise saying them. Play the example again, asking students to identify which words are stressed, and which intonation they have. Then students can practise repeating the whole phrase.

Point out to students that there are sometimes very many unstressed words between two stressed ones.

3 This whole exercise should be done in a light-hearted fashion. Copying the 'newsreader tone of voice' highlights the use of stress and falling/rising tone, and should be fun. If some students can be encouraged to 'mimic' the newsreader, so much the better.

The repetition practice is not designed to turn students into newsreaders! It is purely a way of raising their awareness of the meaning that stress and tone can give in English.

4 Explain, revise and practise the target words and phrases (as given in TB163) as they occur.

Grammar

Aims: 1 Prepositional phrases, complex noun phrases and other devices to condense information in introductory sentences.
2 To show that 'packing' or 'fronting' of information in news items also occurs when introducing events or situations as well as when introducing people (see section 155 in Unit 15).

SB165 PB165

1 Read through the explanations with students. Then they work through the exercise individually and finally compare their sentences with a partner.

2 At some stage, you may like to point out to students how few main verbs there are in sentences like these. Nouns made from verbs are often used instead. Students could find the following examples for themselves: disappearance, action, advice, negotiations, treatment.

3 Point out the phrase 'through lack of equipment' where **through** means 'because of'.

Key: Students can check 1 and 2 themselves (see sections 150 and 158).

3 All 91 passengers on board a Dutch plane hijacked to Rome were released unharmed last night after brief but intense negotiations.

4 Up to 20 children a month are refused treatment at Great Ormond Street Hospital, London, through lack of equipment and a shortage of nursing staff, says Professor Lewis Spitz, a pediatric surgeon.

---

166 **Write a news report**

Aims: 1 Writing a communiqué from brief notes.
2 Listening for details in order to check essential facts.
3 Writing an explanatory caption (using complex noun phrases).

Lexis: **destroyed, drown, guards, record, revealed, so-called, sweep**
Revision: **estimated, sank, stated**
Understanding only: **auctioneers (auction rooms,** where things are sold by auction), **the late** (= recently died), **swept (sweep)**
Phrases: **radio-active fall-out, world record, just what I was going to say! I didn't really make sense of it.**

Task and listening   SB166a

1 Students working in pairs find a heading for each set of notes in the box. The pictures should help.

2 Hear what some students have decided, but don't say if they have guessed correctly or not.

3 Play the recording to compare their ideas with what Bruce and Rachel decided.

Written report and listening   SB166b

4 Students construct a possible sentence for each one, then compare theirs with other students. Go round and help.

5 Play the recording. Students compare their own sentences with those that Bruce and Rachel thought of. Tell students before they listen that Bruce and Rachel found this quite difficult and did not do them in the same order. Pause the tape after each one, and discuss their wording.

Listening   SB166c

6 Finally play the recording of Bruce and Rachel reading out and commenting on the original newspaper reports. If you wish, you could use one or two of the items as a dictation exercise – students listen, tell you when to pause the tape and write only the actual news item. (They can check by reading the transcripts. The news items do not appear anywhere in the book in their original form.)

Writing   SB166c

7 Students now have enough information to write a full explanatory caption for the pictures and diagrams on this page.

Sample: Firemen fighting the fire in which eight people died as it swept through the annexe of this Paris hospital early yesterday.

---

167 **Make your own news programme**

Aim: To encourage students to use whatever language resources they now have, to write and record their own news or current affairs programme.

This could be worked on in the same way as the Newspaper Project in Unit 15 section 156. Each group of students takes responsibility for one news item. It may take them a few days to plan and draft their pieces, based on local or national news.

Task, planning and recorded report   SB167

1 Students could plan either a straightforward announcement, or a question and answer interview, with questions for the presenter to ask. Remind them of Bob's advice in section 143. Help with language problems.

2 After drafting their news stories, students should practise reading them to each other, and then discuss what order they should go in, and why. (Which are the most important? How can they be classified? e.g. as world news, domestic news, or local news?)
This is the stage where you can help perfect the language, and encourage the 'readers' to practise.

3 Appoint a news presenter to introduce the news programme, and link items if necessary. Get groups to rehearse this carefully. Help where you are needed.

4 Record each piece of news, one item at a time, in the correct order.

5 Play the recording back to the class for comments. If they want to rerecord it, with improvements, so much the better.

6 Optional: Video recording – 'TV' news.
If you have the use of a portable video camera, or a video studio, and a video expert to advise you, you could at this point start a more ambitious project – planning and producing a simple TV news programme. Students could collect items, make their own stills, and put it all together for recording in one sitting later on.

Fronting information

In Unit 15 we saw how newspaper articles pack a lot of information into descriptions of people:

Handsome smiling forty-five year-old London policeman . . . (155)

They do the same with events. Opening sentences particularly highlight a lot of information to set the scene for what follows:

Police investigating the mysterious disappearance in Dorset of Mrs. Etty, a local farmer's wife . . . (161)

Opposition party spokesmen, who have been calling for government action to bring piped water into the centre of the town . . . (161)

Rearrange the following phrases to make opening sentences which you have seen before:

1 *on how to reduce the risk – A free booklet – of falling victim – of advice to women – to violent crime – . . . has been issued by the Home Office.* (150)

2 *yesterday – by Madrid underground workers – A strike – demanding a pay rise – . . . cut the number of morning rush-hour trains by half . . . (158)*

Now rearrange these phrases which you *haven't* seen before:

3 *and crew members – on board a Dutch plane – last night – All 91 passengers – were released unharmed – hijacked to Rome . . . after brief but intense negotiations.*

4 *at Great Ormond Street hospital, – Up to 20 children a month – London, – through lack of equipment – are refused treatment – and a shortage of nursing staff – . . . says Professor Lewis Spitz, a pediatric surgeon.*

166 Write a news report

a Look at the headlines and then the sets of notes.

Each set in the box below contains about six words/phrases (in the correct order) from the main sentence of a **News in Brief** item from a newspaper.

Decide which headline goes with each group of words. Say why.

166a Did Bruce and Rachel work it out in the same way as you?

b In groups try to reconstruct a possible version of the sentence in the news item. Write it down.

166b Listen to Bruce and Rachel doing the same thing. Stop the tape after each sentence and compare what you wrote.

166c **c** Finally Bruce and Rachel were allowed to read the original items and compare them with their versions. Listen and compare yours.

> Using the facts you now have, write explanatory captions for three of the photographs. Pass them round for others to identify.

died injured swept through hospital Paris early	Italian concert world record Christie's London Stradivarius
investigating fire damage Oxford night	number Italy estimated 10% February because of radio-active fallout Chernobyl new study
Zambia's Kafue River Southern town Namwala hippopotamus sank canoe police	

167 Make your own news programme

What might you hear about on the news tonight? It could be local, national or international news.

As a class, think of five or six possible news items. Decide on the style of news programme you would like to make.

In groups, choose one item. Remembering what Bob said about how to plan a news item for broadcasting, plan your news story and prepare to record it.

> Put your stories in a suitable order to make up a complete news programme. Record the whole programme, and play it back.

168 Dictionary skills

Conflict, war, debate
Use any dictionary and the pictures to help you
understand the new words in the sets below.

Classify each set of words according to whether you
would expect to find them in a report on:

– the kind of conflict Bob describes between the
  farmers and the Government over water supplies
  (C for conflict)
– a war (W for war)
– a parliamentary debate (D for debate)

a war   civil war   fighting   battle   revolution
b attack   defend   defence
c win   lose   defeat   beat   overcome   victory

d soldiers   military   troops   army   guards
  revolutionary forces
e conflict   row   dispute   argument   protest
f civilians   citizens   general public
g tanks   bombs   explosion   nuclear missiles
h crisis   disaster   tragedy   violence   destruction
i support   criticize   accept   reject   agree

Find which words are illustrated in the pictures
below. Make up some phrases about the people,
things, and happenings in each picture using some of
the words from the sets.

Pass these round. Write a short paragraph about two
of the pictures.

169 Grammar

Reporting verbs and reporting nouns
Make nouns from these verbs and
use some of them to fill the gaps
(for example, state – statement):

accuse   allege   announce   believe   claim
deny   doubt   imply   refuse   threaten

1 'It is our _____ that Mrs. Etty's disappearance may be
connected with devil worship,' a senior police
spokesman announced last night.
2 Mr. Etty's _____ that black magic is still common was
being investigated by the police.
3 Up to then Mr. Etty had not taken seriously his wife's
_____ to leave him and 'go to the devil'.
4 The row flared up again with the _____ that a local
man had been seriously injured.
5 There may be some truth in the government _____ that
Jack fell.
6 A police official expressed his _____ that the couple fell
after a scuffle near the summit.
7 It is the farmers' _____ that until recently they had
exclusive use of the well.
8 Our reporter expressed _____ about the official _____
that Jack fell, and the _____ that his companion, Jill
also slipped.

Rewrite the coloured phrases in sentences 1, 2, 3 and
5 using a verb from above rather than the noun.
Make any necessary changes.

170 REVIEW

UNIT 16

NEW WORDS IN UNIT 16

accuse
adequate
alternative
announcement
argue
battle
casual
channel
citizen
civil (war) D
civilian
committed
conflict
construction
crisis/es D
current
defeat D
deliberate
destroy D
destruction D
dispute
drown
female
fetch
formula
guard

imply
incident
male
military
missile
mysterious
nearby
ordinary
overcome D
permission
pop
protest D
rebel
rejected
reveal
revolution
row
shortage
slipped
so-called
soldier
supplies
tank
troops D
victory D

51 new words
TOTAL SO FAR 676

68

Odd one out?
Which word has a very different meaning from the others?
1 won   crisis   beat   victory   overcame
2 battle   fight   war   civil   conflict   revolution
3 slipped   fell   tumbled   swept
4 accused   revealed   announced   made it known
5 alternative   casual   different   other
6 current   present-day   existing   former   modern
7 intended   deliberate   doubtful   planned   on purpose

Dictionary skills

Aims: 1 To revise and extend students' understanding of words to do with conflict, war and debate.
2 To show that many words concerning physical warfare, e.g. **battle, fight, win, victory, defeat** etc. are used as often in their metaphorical sense (winning arguments, battle of wits) as they are to describe actual physical violence.

Lexis: battle, citizens, civilians, civil D (war), **conflict, defeated** D, **destroy** D, **destruction** D, **military, missiles, overcome** D, **protest** D, **rebels, reject, revolution/ revolutionary, tanks, troops** D, **victory** D
Revision: **defend** D, **fight, guards**
Note: Most of this lexis will also occur in Unit 18.

Task   SB168   PB168

1 Discuss the three pictures, using as many of the target words as possible.

2 Make sure students know which words they can find in the Dictionary Extracts (see the Unit 16 word list below). Help students apply the words from the dictionary entries to the pictures.

3 Students look at the sets of words and see which of the pictures they could apply to. The pictures from left to right show war, debate, conflict. Discuss the key as a class.

Key: (W = War, D = debate, C = conflict)
a W b W D C c W D d W
e C D f W C g W h W i C D

Planning and report   SB168

4 Help students write some phrases and sentences about the situations in the pictures, using some of the words above.

5 Students pass their work round, and discuss each other's phrases.

6 Help students draft a paragraph as if they were writing a news report based on the happenings from two of the pictures. Students can then read and compare each other's interpretations of the scenes.

 Grammar

Aim: To show that nouns are used to introduce reported speech and thought, as well as verbs.

SB169

1 Do the first two examples with the class. Then check they know the nouns from the verbs. (A few, like **allegation** and **implication** may be quite new.)

2 Students do as many as they can on their own.

---

3 **Key:** 1 belief 2 belief/claim/ allegation ('accusation' is not acceptable since there is no-one to accuse. Compare 9.) 3 threat 4 allegation/claim ('accusation' is not acceptable – see note on 1 above. But it would be if you added the words 'by the police' to show that it was an accusation against the police.) 5 allegation/announcement/claim 6 belief 7 claim 8 doubt; claim/ announcement; implication/ allegation/claim.

Key to phrases:
1 We believe that Mrs Etty's disappearance... or Mrs Etty has disappeared and we believe that this... may be connected with devil worship.
2 Mr Etty claims that black magic is still common and this is being investigated by the police.
3 His wife had threatened to leave him and go to the devil, but up to then Mr Etty had not taken her seriously.
5 The government claimed that Jack fell, and this may possibly be true. or ... there may be some truth in this.

---

170 **Review**

Key:
1 crisis 2 civil 3 swept 4 accused 5 casual 6 former 7 doubtful

LEXICAL OBJECTIVES

accuse say someone has done wrong. *The POW group accuse the Government of refusing to provide water.*
adequate large enough. *adequate water supplies.*
alternative other. *alternative sources of water/energy sources.*
announcement public statement. *an official announcement.* (**announce**)
argue T 1 give your opinion and the reasons for it. *The POW argues that the government is reducing water supplies... their argument is...*
2 disagree, debate. *children arguing over which TV programme to watch.* T
battle EED 1 fight, in war. *soldiers killed in battle.*
2 verbal fight, struggle. *battling against pollution... battle for control*
casual informal in dress, relaxed in manner. *in a slightly casual style.*
channel 1 wavelength for radio/TV. *pop music channel.*
2 T The English Channel.
citizens *British citizens.*
civil D
civilian person who is not in the armed forces. *soldiers were facing unarmed civilians.*
commit EED 1 *commit a crime/suicide*
2 decide on a course of action. *The Government is publicly committed to protecting...*
conflict EED 1 serious disagreement
construction building of roads, bridges, etc. *construction companies.*
crisis D

---

current 1 T flow of electricity.
2 happening now. *current affairs*
3 T commonly accepted. *current beliefs*
defeat D
deliberate 1 intentional, planned. *refusing to provide water as a deliberate policy.*
2 slow, careful action. *treading the deck in a deliberate... fashion*
destroyed D
destruction D
dispute 1 argument. *the long-running dispute over water supplies.*
drown *Ship sinks. Eight drown.*
female 1 not male. *Jack's female companion.*
2 a woman.
fetch to go and get. *fetch a pail of water. Can you fetch the children?* T
2 T to fetch a high price.
formula EED 1 T *mathematical formulae.*
2 plan or set of rules. *using this formula of question and answer...*
guard 1 soldiers guarding the palace.
2 security guards, armed guards.
imply suggest without saying. *He implied that Jill was pushed.*
incident unpleasant/violent event. *injured today in an incident near...*
male T see **female**.
military armed forces. *military forces ... military spending.* T
missiles weapons. *nuclear missiles*
mysterious 1 curious, unexplainable. *the mysterious disappearance of Mrs Etty*
nearby not far. *the nearby city area*
ordinary 1 T The ordinary public
overcome D
permission *No further permission to be given for building on farmland.*
pop EED 1 modern music. *a pop station.*
2 a short sharp sound. T
3 put. *I'll just pop that there.* T
4 *pop in/out/round/up* etc. T
protest D
rebel person fighting their own government, or against society.
reject 1 refuse to accept, turn down. *Requests for interviews with Jill have been rejected.*
reveal 1 make something known. *reveal your feelings. fall in number of births was revealed by a new study.*
revolution attempt by revolutionaries to change the political system
2 T revolutionary changes
row EED 1 /rəʊ/ near *rows of chairs*
2 noisy argument. /raʊ/ *the row over inadequate water supplies*
shortage *water/land/staff shortages*
slip EED slide and fall. *Jill slipped and tumbled down the hill.*
so-called used to show you think a word is misleading. *Stradivarius's so-called golden period.*
soldier person who works in the army.
supplies amount of something available. *water/medical supplies*
*sweep, swept EED 1 T with a brush. *he swept the kitchen floor*
2 move quickly. *Fire swept through a school in Paris.*
tank 1 T container. *a petrol/water tank*
2 military vehicle. *tanks and troops.*
troops D
victory D   68T

All for the love of...

Students begin by discussing personal relationships. This leads in to a look at two kinds of human-interest story that commonly appear in the popular press. A research report demonstrates how language is used to show readers how seriously a story is to be taken. Within the context of one story students discuss different possible courses of action.

OBJECTIVES

Lexical objectives are in TB181

Discussion topics

Relationships within the family. (171)

Social skills

a Describing people's behaviour. (171,176)
b Talking about personal relationships. (171,172,176)
c Discussing alternative courses of action. (176)

Communication skills

a Reading popular newspaper articles. (171)
b Recognising the tone of an article. (173)
c The use of informal lexis. (173)
d Rewriting an informal report in a formal style. (174)
e Retelling a story from another point of view. (176)
f Concluding a story. (176,178)

Grammar and discourse

a Logical relationships between paragraphs. (176)
b **Would/should have** for hypothetical past. (176)
c Past participle at the beginning of a sentence. (177)
d **Had** + inversion for hypothetical past condition. (180)
e Practice Book Grammar Word: **for**.

Dictionary skills

a Metaphorical and informal uses of words. (174)
b Guessing which word in a prepositional phrase to look up in a dictionary. (179)

171 Influence

> **Aims:** 1 To get students thinking and talking about relationships, change and spheres of influence in the family – parents to children, and between couples.
> 2 Describing people's behaviour.

This section acts as an introduction to topics that appear in this unit, and can be covered quite informally.

Discussion SB171a/b/c PB171

1 Take **a**, **b** and **c** one at a time, and discuss informally as a class, or get students to talk in smaller groups, while you walk around. If there is a popular TV soap opera that most students watch, you could begin with the couples that star in that.

2 Ask students to speculate about the backgrounds and relationships of couples in the photographs, and then choose one couple to tell the class about.

If you know your class well, you might feel you could ask them to talk about their own families.

3 Other possible points for group discussion: Have they ever been influenced or forced to do things they didn't want to do? Or banned from anything? How did their parents' behaviour towards them change as they grew older? Can they give examples?

172 Effects of marriage?

> **Aims:** 1 Talking about personal relationships, and change.
> 2 Metaphorical meanings of adjectives used to describe varying degrees of intelligence.
>
> **Lexis: basis*, competition*, dim, dumb, equally, intellectual, intelligent, marriage, rubs off*, shortly, smart, survey*, wedding**
> Revision: **academic, bright, clever, dull, thick, sharp** (all denoting degrees of intelligence)
> Understanding only: **brainy**
> Phrases: **as far as intelligence goes, shortly after, on a different basis***

Task and listening SB172a

1 This serves as preparation for the quiz in section 172b. Dividing the words into two categories helps students to become familiar with the new words they will need to help them with both the quiz and the story in section 173, and gives further practice in recognising metaphorical meanings: e.g. **bright**, **dull** and **dim** used of both light and intelligence. This is dealt with in depth in section 174.

2 After students have divided the words into categories, and explained their reasons, they can listen to the recording to check how Bruce and Chris did this.

3 Discuss the next set of words, which are all more formal. Ask students to explain what they mean.

   Key: dull and **slow** are the only words meaning unintelligent.

You may want to do section 174 at this point instead of later.

Task SB172b

4 Students can do the quiz in pairs, discussing and deciding which statements they would agree with. They must commit themselves, writing down T or NT for each.

5 Two pairs can join up, and compare and decide again. They must agree and commit themselves to T or NT, giving reasons where they can. *Do not tell them if they are right or wrong.* The point of the exercise is that they can find out for themselves by reading the survey in section 173.

6 Point out that if this were a more formal quiz, the words 'more intelligent' would have been used instead of 'smarter'.

Report SB172b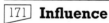

7 As they tell the class what they think, make a grid on the board as follows, and write T or NT for each group.

   Sample grid with key:

group 1	group 2	group 3 etc.	Bruce	Chris
a				
b				
c				
d				
e				
f				

8 Play the recording. The class listens and tells you whether to write T or NT in the Bruce and Chris columns.

9 After listening and completing the grid, take a class vote on each quiz question, and record those figures too.

10 Students can check their response straightaway by reading section 173.

171 Influence

a Think of a couple you know well, or watch regularly on TV. How do they get on together? Say what you know about their relationship. Which one has more influence over the other? How can you tell?

b How far have you followed in your parents' footsteps? How far did they (do they still) influence you? In what areas? Have they influenced your choice of friends/partners? clothes? career? books? films? food?

c Talk about people who have had the most influence over you. Perhaps a teacher? a parent? a friend or relation?

▷ Tell each other. ◁

172 Effects of marriage?

a Divide these words into two categories according to meaning.

bright dim stupid brainy smart sharp
dumb thick intelligent

Explain how you did it.

172a Listen to how Bruce and Chris did it.

Now what about these?

academic dull quick slow clever
intellectual

b What do you think about these statements? Work with a partner and say which you think might be true, and which not.

1 *The wife will get smarter if her husband is really smart.*
2 *If the husband is less smart than the wife, she will also get less smart as the years go by.*
3 *During the course of marriage, both the wife and the husband change equally, as far as intelligence goes, and get more like each other.*
4 *Your ability to do Maths increases or decreases according to how good your spouse's Maths is.*
5 *The happiest time of a marriage is shortly after the wedding.*
6 *The worst time is when the children have grown up and are leaving home.*

▷ Tell the class. Then have a class vote on each statement. ◁

172b What did Bruce and Chris think?

69

173 Marriage can make a dimwit brainier!

From WILLIAM LOWTHER
in Washington

WHEN a bright woman marries a dim man she will eventually sink to his level.

And if a stupid woman marries a smart man, she will become as sharp as he is, according to a scientist. 'So the dumb blonde who marries a professor has everything to gain,' says Dr Warner Schaie after a 30-year study.

'Women who marry men brighter than themselves get brighter, and women who marry losers get worse,' says the Washington University psychologist who tested the same 175 couples throughout the study.

Happier

They tended to quickly adopt each others' personality traits and intellect during the first seven years of marriage and then levelled off for another seven years. But as the couples grew older and their children had left home, they became increasingly similar.

Marital bliss mirrors these changes says Dr Schaie. 'Couples are happiest shortly after marriage, become less happy when the children are small and happily married again when the children grow up and move out.

At the last stage even their ability to do mathematics increases or decreases, depending on their spouse.'

But his studies show it is the wife who changes for better or worse, and not the husband. 'Probably for economic reasons, because in the couples we've been studying men are the primary breadwinners,' says Dr Schaie.

Daily Mail

The psychologist at work

The University

Do you think Dr. Schaie's work was a serious piece of research?

How serious is the Daily Mail report of his work? (See section 174.)

▶ How far do you agree with his conclusions? ◀

WORD STUDY
Can you guess what these words mean?

adopt	gain
basis	increasingly
course	level off
economic	shortly

174 Dictionary skills

Informal and other uses

informal /ɪnˈfɔːməl/. You use **informal** to describe behaviour or speech that is relaxed and casual rather than correct and serious. In this dictionary, language of this kind is indicated by the word 'Informal' in the Extra Column. EG ...*a relaxed and quite informal discussion.* ◇ **informally.** EG ◇ ADV ...*people talking informally together.* (ADJ QUALIT)

brainy   dim   dumb   thick   loaded   smart

a Look up these words and find which have informal uses.
Which word has a different use in American English?
Which can be offensive?

b Which word is the odd one out, as far as meaning is concerned?
Do you have informal words for these meanings in your language, too?

c Rewrite the headline for the article in section 173 and the first three sentences in a more formal style.

175 Language study

Comparison and change
Which of these phrases imply a change for the better and which a change for the worse?

make a dimwit brainier
sink to his level
become as sharp as he is
get brighter
get worse
grew older
become less happy
ability to do mathematics increases

Which words indicate change in these examples?

Her hair's turned grey. Well, I've gone grey, too.
She went mad! I'd never seen her get so angry!
It grew colder and colder.
The weather's turned quite nasty. Hope it'll improve by tomorrow.
It was awful – he fell ill whilst on holiday.
Get well soon!

173   Marriage can make a dimwit brainier!

Aims: 1 Reading popular newspaper articles.
2 Recognising the tone of an article.
3 The use of informal lexis.

Lexis: adopt, dumb, economic, gain, happily, increasingly similar, intellect, level, mirrors, professor, psychologist, shortly after, stupid
Revision: **sharp** (= clever), **sink**
Understanding only: **bliss** (= great happiness), **losers** (= not-so-bright men), **primary breadwinners** (= main wage earners) .
Phrases: **has everything to gain, for economic reasons, for better or worse**

Reading   SB173 PB173

1 Students read and check their responses to the quiz. Allow time for reactions and encourage comments. How far did the class vote tally with the research findings?

2 Before discussing how serious Dr Schaie's work etc. is, you may like to go ahead to section 174, which focuses on 'informal' uses of the words used in the article, and so gives students help with recognising the tone of such a piece (which emerges largely through the type of lexis used).

   Key: The use of so many informal and colloquial expressions, e.g. 'dimwit/brainier' in the headline and 'dumb blonde', show that this is not a particularly serious report of Dr Schaie's work.
   Although Dr Schaie studied 175 couples, he admits himself that his findings may have economic causes – the men were the primary breadwinners. A really serious study would have taken a greater range of couples.

3 Word study: Get students to find the phrases with these words in the article above, and then try to explain their meanings in context, guessing if necessary. Finally discuss these words as a class.

4 Check students now understand all the target lexis.

174   Dictionary skills

Aims: 1 To compare the metaphorical uses of adjectives with their basic or physical meanings.
2 To help students recognise informal uses of adjectives (often in their metaphorical use).
3 To extend students' knowledge of social registers, e.g. American, literary, informal, offensive, and how to recognise labels for these in the *Collins COBUILD Essential English dictionary*.

SB174a/b

1 Ask students to follow exactly the instructions given, and use the Dictionary Extracts to look up these words. They can discuss their findings with a neighbour.

   Key: a informal uses: brainy, dim, thick, loaded.
   American: smart (= clever).
   Offensive: dumb. (Warn students never to use a word or phrase marked 'offensive'.)
   b Odd word out: loaded – nothing to do with degrees of intelligence.
   Point out that 'sharp' in paragraph 2 is also used in a metaphorical way (a sharp person is quick to understand and see what needs doing etc.)

2 Ask students if words like these can be used in a similar way in their own language(s) (i.e. words referring to light as well as to degrees of intelligence).

3 Ask students what **smash** can mean in English. (The driver in section 72 who stole a police car, smashed into a road block.) Get them to look up **smash** in the Dictionary Extracts and find out what **smashed** and **smashing** can mean, and how/when students might use them appropriately (only with close friends – they are both informal).

4 What informal words do students have in their own language for: very clever, unintelligent, rich, having no money/broke, drunk, really good.

5 Summarise by saying that if students want to find out if an article is a serious one or not, they can look up the words they think might be less formal in use, and check to see if they are labelled 'informal'.

Writing   SB174c

6 Discuss with students which words and phrases need changing, and help them rewrite the first three sentences in a formal style.

   Sample: When a bright woman marries a man who is much less intelligent (*or* of a much lower intelligence), she will eventually sink to his level. And if an unintelligent woman marries an intelligent man, she will become as clever as he is, according to a scientist. 'So, if a less intelligent girl (*or* a girl of lower intelligence) marries a professor she has everything to gain.'

7 Optional writing: Students could write a serious report of Dr Schaie's research, as if for a journal rather than a newspaper. To do this they will need to put the facts into chronological order, select less informal lexis, and discuss a serious title. You coud give students part of the first sentence of this sample as an example of the style to follow.

   Sample: (Title) A study of patterns of change in married couples.
   Dr Warner Schaie, a psychologist from Washington University, USA, has just completed a 30-year study of patterns of change in 175 couples.
   His research dealt with intelligence, personality, behaviour and the success of the relationship. He tested the couples at intervals throughout their marriage. He found that . . .

175   Language study

Aim: Expressing the notion of change in English.

SB175 PB175

1 Students could discuss these in pairs, and then you can go through them with the class.

   Key: Better: make a dimwit brainier; become as sharp as he is; get brighter; ability to do maths increases.
   Worse: sink to his level; get worse; become less happy.
   Either: grew older.
   Words indicating change: turned, gone, went, get, grew, turned, improve, fell, get.

2 Ask students to practise the phrases with these words in them, e.g. 'turned quite nasty', 'fell ill'.
   Also point out **become**, and then words like **increase, decrease, rise, sink, drop** etc.

3 Point out that the concept that **up** often has the meaning of more, better, happy whereas **down** often means less, worse, unhappy. (The wet weather really got me down. Sun always cheers me up.) Ask if it is the same in students' own language(s).

176 Love story

Aims: 1 Logical relationships between paragraphs.
2 **Would/should have** for hypothetical past.
3 Discussing alternative courses of action.
4 Retelling a story from another point of view.
5 Speculating about future relationships.

Lexis: **adventure, banned, desperate, executive, friendship, furious, independent, hired, let in for, luxury, marriage, mere, merely** T, **proposed, prospect, track, undeterred, ward** (of court), **wedding**
Revision: **assuming, basis, set (on)**
Understanding only: **detectives** (police), **smuggle, outright**
Phrases: **proposed marriage, trouble struck, prison/ jail sentence, attractive prospect**
Notes: **Roedean** is one of the most expensive fee-paying girls' schools in Britain.
A Levels = Advanced level exams, which you have to pass with good grades in order to get a university place.
Jumped bail = failed to turn up for his court case for driving while disqualified (with no licence).
Made a ward of court = put in the care of a court of law (usually happens only if both parents have died).

Reading and listening   SB176a/b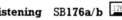

1 Discuss the headlines. (See notes above.) Have students heard of Shakespeare's play *Romeo and Juliet*?

2 Students read and discuss in pairs which order the paragraphs should be in. Don't tell them if they have guessed the correct order or not. When all students have finished, play recording 176a to see if Chris and Bruce had the same order.

3 Students in pairs can summarise the story and read their summaries to the class.

   Key: a, e, c, f, b, g, d

Task, planning, report and listening   SB176c SB178   176c

4 Students, first singly and then in pairs, think what they would have done as parents in those circumstances.

5 Help them to summarise their course of action, so they can tell the class.

6 Students listen to the recording to see what Chris and Bruce would have done. Allow time for reactions.

7 Discuss with students what they think Selina's parents did.

8 Let students read the end of the story in section 178. You can also play recording 178, with the reactions of Chris and Bruce.

Listening   SB176d   176c

9 These phrases are all useful ones from the recording. Students could do this on their own, and then listen to check.

   Key: 1 kept 2 mere 3 assuming 4 best 5 basis
   6 position 7 rest

Task, planning and reports (oral and written)   SB176e/f

10 This is a chance for students to air their own views on three connected topics. The first one about Selina could be prepared briefly in groups and reported orally.

11 Get students to write only the part of the letter where Paul gives an account of how he met and married Selina. This can be slightly informal in style, since the letter is to a friend. Encourage students to use their imaginations and add any details they wish to. Go round and help with any language problems. They then read each other's.

12 Discuss as a class what they think may have happened in ten years' time, and in what ways the relationship may have changed.

177 Grammar

Aim: Use of phrases beginning with past participle or adjective to start a sentence.

SB177 PB177

1 When going through the examples, point out that the order of clauses may need to change. Also that the subject must be the same in both clauses.

   Extra example: 'He called the police because he was worried about the noise next door.' becomes 'Worried by the noise next door, he called the police.'

2 Students rewrite sentences 1–4 individually, then compare versions.

   Key: 1 Asked what he had...
   2 Excited at the news...
   3 Informed that he was under arrest he...
   4 Delighted with the result he...

3 Draw students' attention to the words **because, when** and **so** in sentences 1–4. These show the relationships between the clauses more clearly, but are omitted when the clause starts with a past participle or adjective. The relationship must still be understood by the reader or listener.

4 After doing the exercise, you could remind students of sentences beginning with a present participle (section 75). For example:
Realising what he had done...
On realising...
After...

176 Love story

a Look at the two headlines. What can you guess about the story?

Read the first part of this news report, then decide in what order the following paragraphs originally appeared.

ROMEO PAUL SWEEPS ROEDEAN BEAUTY OFF HER FEET

All for the love of Selina

WHEN Paul Burdell met the girl of his dreams, he could never have guessed just what he was letting himself in for.

Things normally went according to plan for the 28-year-old American City executive who had just about everything he wanted — good looks, money, fast car, luxury flat in Chelsea.

So when he proposed marriage to beautiful blonde Selina Rigden-Hodge and she accepted, he could not have been happier.

Undeterred, however, he jumped bail and drove to the school in Brighton where he collected his sweetheart and the pair jetted off to Mexico and married two days later.

By ADRIAN LITHGOW

c   **Trouble**

Set on a career, they banned any prospect of marriage outright. Paul therefore decided to smuggle Selina out of the country to marry in Mexico.

d   **Career**

By now Mr and Mrs Burdell were in hiding in New York. But eventually Paul had to come back to Britain to his lucrative career — and the less attractive prospect of a seven-day jail sentence.

e That, however, was until he found out that his beloved was a mere 17 and still studying for her A-levels at Britain's top girls' school, Roedean: which might perhaps have been less of a problem had Selina's parents and teachers not had other, more independent, plans for her.

f But trouble struck on the day of the elopement. Just 100 yards from his flat in Cadogan Street, police arrested Paul for driving while disqualified.

g Selina's furious parents — they live in Kent, and her father is a company director — hired detectives to track her down and made her a ward of court in a desperate attempt to bring her home.

The Mail on Sunday

176b **b**   Did you get the same order as Chris and Bruce?

▶ Summarize what has happened so far. ◀

c What course of action would you have taken had *you* been in the situation of Selina's parents? Compare your course of action with your partner's, giving your reasons.

▶ Decide on the best course of action to take in similar circumstances. Come to an agreement and summarize what you would have done.

176c See what Chris and Bruce would have done in similar circumstances.

▶ What do you think Selina's parents finally did? Discuss, then turn over and find out. ◀

d   **Phrases with common words**

assuming	basis	best	kept	mere	position	rest

176c Decide where you think the words in the box fit. Check by listening to Bruce and Chris again. For example:

. . . one would presume one could do that on an international __basis__ .

1 *. . . something that should be _____ in the family rather than . . .*
2 CB: *It depends, I mean she's almost eighteen.*
   BB: *Well, quite . . . a _____ seventeen is a bit much isn't it really . . .*
3 *I think _____ there was no note, . . . I would contact the police . . .*
4 *I would make the _____ of a bad job perhaps . . .*
5 *not a very good _____ for friendship between . . .*
6 *And he is . . . in a _____ to support her.*
7 *He's got a good salary and all the _____ of it.*

e What do you personally think Selina should/ shouldn't have done? What do you think she should do next? (Remember her husband is out at work all day.) Tell each other.

▶ **f**   Write an account of what happened from Paul Burdell's point of view. Imagine that he was writing to explain to a good friend why he had not got in touch for so long. ◀

How do you think things will be for Paul and Selina in ten years' time? Why?

177 *Grammar* . . . .

Past participle
In English we quite often use a past participle (asked; told; given etc.) at the beginning of a sentence:

Set on a career, they banned any prospect of marriage outright. (They banned marriage because they were set on a career . . .)
Questioned by reporters . . . Mrs Etty replied . . . (When she was questioned by reporters Mrs Etty replied . . .)

Rewrite these sentences with a past participle or an adjective as the first word:

1 *When he was asked what he had done he claimed that it was all an accident.*
2 *They were excited at the news so they rang Selina's parents at once.*
3 *He asked for a lawyer when he was informed that he was under arrest.*
4 *He went out to celebrate because he was delighted with the result.*

178 Happy ending

Now, with the adventure some months behind them, even Selina's parents have decided to forgive and forget.

'I've had lunch with them and everything is all right,' said Selina — now 18 — this weekend.

'We've been through an awful lot ... but it's all been worth it.'

Paul added: 'You could certainly write a good book about what we've been through, but I have to be careful what I say because I've got my career to think about. We just want to be left on our own now.'

178 What comments did Chris and Bruce make about the ending?

179 *Language study*

Phrases with prepositions
Try to remember which preposition is needed.

about   behind   down   in   of   on
through   to   with

1 He could never have guessed just what he was letting himself _____ for.
2 Things normally went according _____ plan.
3 He proposed marriage _____ beautiful blonde Selina Rigden-Hodge.

180 *Grammar*

When 'had' equals 'if' ...
We can say:
It might have been less of a problem if Selina's parents had not had *other plans for her.* **Or**
[It] might have been less of a problem had Selina's parents not had *other plans for her.* (176)

Can you change these sentences in the same way?
1 *Would it have been any less of a tragedy if she had not been attractive?* (95)
2 *If it had been night you may have been reluctant to leave the banda.* (116)
3 *If the leopard had attacked in the confined space of a room, then one can only guess the outcome.*

And can you change these the other way?
1 *Had an adult written it it would probably have sounded a lot more dull.* (45)
2 *What course of action would you have taken had you been in the situation of Selina's parents?* (176)

4 *Set _____ a career, they banned any prospect _____ marriage.*
5 *... hired detectives to track her _____.*
6 *... made her a ward of court _____ a desperate attempt to bring her home.*
7 *Now, _____ the adventure some months _____ them, ...*
8 *We've been _____ a lot, but it's been worth it.*
9 *I've got my career to think _____.*

Now use a dictionary to check your answers. What word will you look up for 1? let? himself?

181 REVIEW

UNIT 17

a What's the situation?
In what context would you be likely to hear or read these phrases?

1 GOODS TO DECLARE   Red channel   Green channel   Shall we risk it? Anything to declare, sir?

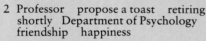

2 Professor   propose a toast   retiring shortly   Department of Psychology friendship   happiness

3 Ward Ten   nurse   patient   desperate for a cigarette   banned
4 car hire company   good economic prospects   luxury cars   assuming not much competition   stand to gain
5 the pound sterling   gained some ground   prospects look brighter   competition from the Yen

b Noun, verb or adjective?
Arrange these words into three columns according to their parts of speech. You will need to write some words more than once.

ban   proposed   compete   equal   gain
independent   independence   intelligent
intelligence   mirror   intelligent
competition   hire   level   equality   proposal

NO PROSPECTS NOW OF PARK PROPOSAL

BAN ON SMOKING IN TUBE

The British Council is an equal opportunity employer.

RACIAL EQUALITY   BA EXECUTIVE CLASS

HIRE CAR

INSURANCE PROPOSAL   COMPETITION!

... is an independent body dealing with complaints ...

NEW WORDS IN UNIT 17
adopt
adventure
assuming
ban/banning
basis
competition
declare
desperate
dim D
dumb D
economic
equality
equally
friendship
furious
gain
happily
happiness
hire
increasingly
independence

intellectual
intelligence
intelligent
luxury
marriage
mere
merely
mirror
professor
propose
prospect
psychologist
psychology
rub
shortly
smart D
stupid
survey
track
ward
wedding

42 new words
TOTAL SO FAR 718

Happy ending

This is the ending of the article in section 176, so students should have already read this, and heard Chris and Bruce's comments. (See TB176 note 8.)

 Language study

Aims: 1 To highlight some useful phrases from the story in section 176.
2 To extend students' exposure to verbs with prepositions.
3 To give practice in using a dictionary to look up phrases and check usage.

SB179

1 Students first try to fill these blanks without a dictionary.

2 Which word would students look up in a dictionary, to check which preposition to use? For example:
1 Look up **let...for** (not **himself**), to find **in**.

Key: 1 in 2 to 3 to 4 on, of
5 down 6 in 7 with, behind
8 through 9 about

 Grammar

Aim: To help students recognise that the sentence-initial or clause-initial **had** + inversion of subject and verb, can be used for hypothetical past condition (i.e. **had** can mean the same as **if**.)

SB180 PB180

Key: 1 ... had she not been attractive.
2 Had it been night...
3 Had the leopard attacked in...

1 If an adult had written it...
2 ... if you had been in the same situation...

 Review

Notes and key: a These phrases illustrate other meanings of words used in this unit.
1 going through British customs
2 speech at a farewell dinner party on the retirement of a Professor of Psychology 3 in a hospital ward – a patient is desperate for a cigarette, but smoking is banned! 4 somebody considering the prospect of starting or buying a car hire company 5 financial news broadcast, or stock market report

b Discuss the uses of the target words that appear in the headlines, signs and quotations illustrated in the lower box. Ask students where they might see each of these signs, headlines etc. Other forms are given in brackets.

NOUN	VERB	ADJECTIVE
ban	ban	(banned)
competition	compete	(competing)
equality	(equalise)	equal
gain	gain	
independence		independent
intelligence		intelligent
	hire	hire/(hired)
level	level	level
mirror	mirror	
proposal	(propose)	proposed

LEXICAL OBJECTIVES

adopt 1 T to adopt a child is to make someone else's child legally your own. 2 take on. *married couples adopt each other's personality traits.*
adventure unusual/exciting series of events. *with the adventure some months behind them...*
assuming if; on the understanding/assumption that. *assuming there was no note I would've contacted the police.*
ban prevent. *her parents banned the marriage. Ban on smoking on the Tube.*
basis EED 1 *not a very good basis for friendship*
2 *on the basis of/that*
3 system. *on an international basis.*
competition 1 two/more people trying to get one thing. *foreign competition for sales.* T *no competition or motivation between partners.*
2 event where people try to win a prize. *annual competition*
declare 1 *Nigeria declared independence in...*
2 T *'I will not' he declared angrily.*
desperate a desperate action is one you take in a situation that is so bad you will try anything to change it. *made a desperate attempt to bring her home.*
2 T *desperate for the money*
dim D
dumb D
economic financial. *for economic reasons, for men are the breadwinners.*
equality EED T *equality of the sexes.*
equally 1 T evenly. *money was divided equally between them.*
2 to the same degree. *husband and wife change equally.*
3 T to introduce another comment. *You could equally well say...*
friendship friendly relationship. *friendship between parents and son-in-law.*
furious 1 very angry. *furious parents*
2 with great energy. *worked furiously.*
gain EED 1 T get more of. *to gain experience.*
2 benefit, profit from. *she has everything to gain...*
3 increase T *gain in weight/popularity*
happily satisfied. *happily married*
happiness T *Does money bring happiness?*
hire 1 *car hire companies. For hire.* T
2 pay someone to do a job. *They hired detectives to track her down.*
increasingly more and more
independence *24 years of independence*
intellectual 1 intelligent; intellect is the ability to think and understand ideas. *an intellectual conversation.* T

intelligence 1 ability to think, understand, learn. *Husband and wife change equally as far as intelligence goes.*
2 CIA = Central Intelligence Agency
intelligent clever
luxury 1 T great comfort. *a life of luxury.* (**luxurious**)
2 T something not essential but nice.
3 expensive, often specially designed. *a luxury flat in Chelsea.*
marriage 1 relationship between husband and wife. *seven years of marriage.*
2 the marriage ceremony itself. *banned any prospect of marriage.*
mere EED 3 to emphasise how small an amount is. *Selina was a mere 17.*
merely EED just, only, used to show it's not important, or small. *She was merely 17. She merely nodded, saying nothing.*
mirror 1 *driving mirror*
2 verb: reflect. *the water mirrored the blue sky.* T
3 have similar features to. *Marital bliss mirrors these changes.*
professor 1 T a very high ranking lecturer in a British university
2 a lecturer in an American university
propose EED 1 T to suggest, e.g. a plan.
2 T intend (formal). *what changes have been proposed?/are in the proposal?*
3 propose marriage *when Paul proposed marriage to Selina... she accepted.*
prospect 1 possibility. *Her parents banned any prospect of marriage.*
2 something you know will happen. *Paul came back to the prospect of a 7-day prison sentence.*
3 T *he had good business prospects.*
psychologist person who studies the human mind and behaviour.
psychology the study of the human mind and behaviour.
rub 1 T *He rubbed his eyes.*
2 rub off on – If someone's characteristics rub off on you, you develop the same qualities as the other person. *You think it rubs off?*
3 rub out = erase T *Shall I rub this out now?*
stupid not clever. *If a stupid woman...*
survey 1 T to inspect or look carefully. Also: house/land survey
2 detailed investigation into something, often behaviour. *I don't care what the survey says, I don't agree. Carry out a class survey.*
track 1 T a narow path or unmade road. Also race-track.
2 T footprints or marks left by someone. *follow his tracks.*
3 track down = search for. *hired detectives to track her down.*
ward 1 T section of a hospital. *emergency ward.*
2 ward of court = person put in the care of a law court. *Selina's parents made her a ward of court.*
wedding marriage ceremony

Unit 18 Revision Unit

This unit brings together what students have discussed in connection with planning travel and also broadcasting and journalism. They talk about stories which have caught their attention and hear Bob Jobbins talking about his own favourite story. The Yetties provide the stimulus for students to plan a programme of entertainment. Bob Jobbins reports an earlier story in a different style, and students get their chance to write a report and develop a story. They write two letters planning and finalising a journey.

OBJECTIVES

Lexical objectives are in TB194

Discussion topics

a News stories: good news and bad news. (182)
b Selection of songs/stories for an entertainment. (186)
c The metaphorical uses of words in different languages, especially in relation to war and argument. (187)

Social skills

a Sharing recollections to reconstruct a story. (182, 184)
b Evaluating judgements, and supporting opinions. (183)
c Co-operating over the planning of a project. (186b)
d Making joint recommendations for a plan of action. (190)
e Making arrangements for a future trip, writing a letter about them, and responding to such a letter. (193)

Communication skills

a Writing in an informal style (a letter). (182)
b Giving an account of a hectic/rather tense day. (185)
c Translating a story or song. (186)
d Planning a programme for a class concert. (186)
e Understanding a serious radio news item. (184, 188)
f Writing a report and recommendations for action. (190)
g Writing and recording a sequel to a news bulletin. (191)

Grammar and discourse

a Recognising the difference in style between a short news communiqué, an interview with a correspondent, and a detailed news commentary. (188)
b Complex noun phrases, fronting information, and relations between clauses. (189)
c Recognising less explicit future reference. (192)
d Revision of adjectives and adverbs (Units 13–18). (194)
e Revision of intonation and stress in bulletins. (184b)
f Practice Book Grammar Word: **will**.

Dictionary skills

The metaphorical uses of words about war. (187)

182 News round-up

Aims: 1 To get students chatting about recent events in the news, summarising and evaluating them.
2 Sharing recollections to reconstruct a story.
3 Writing in an informal style (a letter).

Task, planning and report SB182a PB182

1 Students could do this in groups of three or four.

2 After the reporting stage, discuss together what kinds of stories they were. How many had happy endings?

Writing SB182b

3 Students help each other to write about one story, as if it were part of a letter. They can then read each other's.

183 Events which make the headlines

Aim: To get students to evaluate a judgement, and to give and back up their own opinions.

Lexis: **crash**
Revision: **crises, disasters, covering, positive developments**

Reading and discussion SB183 PB183

Give students time to read the headlines on this page. Help them plan how to express their opinions.

184 Overthrow of a president

Aims: 1 Sharing recollections to reconstruct a story.
2 Understanding a serious in-depth radio feature.
3 Identifying stressed words, and their significance.
4 Past narrative in a summary.

Lexis: **bill** (= proposed new law), **congress, entirely, palace, surrounded, tension**
Revision: **army camp, citizens, civilians, defeated, drama, guards, ordinary, popular** (= of the people), **protest, rebels, revolution, tanks, troops, violent/non-violent**
Understanding only: **exile, overthrow, regime, take-over**
Phrases: **get out of control, against all the odds, military force**

Planning and report SB184a

1 Students work out what happened from the pictures and headlines, and reconstruct the story. Students then tell each other.

2 To prepare for the next listening task, revise the vocabulary from section 168.

Listening SB184b

3 Bob Jobbins is talking to a wide international audience, who can remember this revolution, and will know about the people involved. Students will need to know this, so they can guess which words are likely to be key words and will thus carry the main stress. Can they guess the word that follows on after 'almost entirely . . .'? (non-violent – to contrast with 'recipe for disaster'.)

4 Once students have guessed where the main stresses will come, play the recording once or twice.

Key: 'The overthrow of a **Pres**ident, with tanks and troops on the street **sounds** a recipe for disaster – particularly when the soldiers were facing **unarmed** civilians, including **children** and old people.
'But the revo**lut**ion in the **Phil**ippines, which led to the exile of President Marcos, and the **take**-over by Mrs Cory Aquino was **al**most en**tire**ly . . .

Listening SB184c

5 Discussing the phrases will help students with the next listening task. List them on the board in three columns as students suggest.

PRO-MARCOS	ANTI-MARCOS	OTHER
colleagues	unarmed civilians	large city (Manilla)
loyalist guards	the rebels	
defeated president	ordinary citizens	a regime

6 Play the feature at least twice, and help with lexis.

Key: The surprising thing was that it was non-violent.

73T

Manneke Pis 600 jaar

Σε ευρωπαϊκούς ρυθμούς Λάρισα, AEK και ΠΑΟΚ

Martedì le misure sui rifiuti tossici

Inculpée d'assassinat
Simone Weber a été confrontée à sa fille, qui l'avait accusée

افتتاح قرية سياحية بالعلمين
تضم ٤٠ شاليها وحمامات سباحة وملاعب
العلمين ــ مصطفى البدوى وجابر المجعاوى

182 News round-up

a What is the most interesting news story you have heard or read lately?

▶ Tell each other and then tell the class about it. ◀

As you listen to other students' stories, note down which of them are good news; bad news; violent; concern sport; politics; foreign news; local news.

b Choose one recent story that interests you. Discuss with a partner how you would write about it in a letter to an overseas friend who is interested in such things. Include details like source of story, what happened, the effects of it on others, as well as your own feelings about it.

▶ Write the part of the letter describing the story. ◀

183 Events which make the headlines

183 In the real world, a lot of news is bad news: disasters, wars, crashes, and crises. These are the events which make the headlines, and which a foreign correspondent spends a lot of time covering; although we also . . . in specialist programmes, do also report positive developments.

Look at the news stories from the newspapers on this page, and consider the stories people have just told. To what extent is it true that most news is bad news?

184 Overthrow of a president

Mrs Aquino Takes Over in Manila
Marcos Flees in Exile
'BILLS IN CONGRESS 'MARCOS MUST GO' CALL
High-con pledges Marcos

Army Chief leads Philippines Revolt

a Do any of you remember the overthrow of this president which happened in 1986? If so, tell the others what you know about the situation. Do you think the overthrow of President Marcos was violent or non-violent? Popular or unpopular? Do you know how things have gone in the Philippines since 1986?

b From our own Correspondent . . .
For Bob Jobbins one of the most interesting news stories in recent years was a non-violent revolution.

Read this first part of the feature by Bob Jobbins. Can you guess where the main stresses will occur? He was talking quite rapidly, so there are only four in the first paragraph and five in the second. The first two are given in bold print for you.

184b Listen and check where the main stresses occur. Why are they on these words and not others? How do you think he'll continue? What could his next few words be?

The overthrow of a **Pres**ident, with tanks and troops on the street, **sounds** a recipe for disaster, particularly when the soldiers were facing unarmed civilians, including children and old people.

But the revolution in the Philippines, which led to the exile of President Marcos, and the take-over by Mrs Cory Aquino, was almost entirely . . .

c Bob uses these phrases later in his report. Who or what do you think each of them refers to? Who were pro-Marcos and who anti-Marcos?

unarmed civilians   colleagues   a large and sprawling city
the rebels   loyalist guards   the defeated President
ordinary citizens   a regime

184c Listen to the whole of the feature. What was surprising about the revolution?

73

185 A hectic time...

a Read again what Bob said:

For several days my colleagues and I raced around Manila, a large and sprawling city, between the army camp where the rebels had their headquarters, to the Presidential Palace, surrounded by loyalist guards, and back to our hotels to send our reports back to London.

> **WORD STUDY**
> How many prepositions can you find above? Do they refer to time or place or neither?
> Find three phrases which describe places.

b Think of a hectic day you had recently. Tell your partner what you did, where you went, and why.

▶ **c** Make notes about your partner's hectic day and tell the rest of the class. ◀

186 An entertainment

a For their tour of South East Asia, the Yetties added two songs to their programme that were in the local language, Bahasa Malaysia. Listen to both the songs, and then decide which you like best, and why.

186 A song called *Burong kakak tua*, which roughly translated means, 'I've got a parrot and my grandmother's got two teeth.'

Gelang si-paku gelang is a song in praise of Sarawak, saying: 'Let us return home, let us return home together.'

▶ Think of a simple song or rhyme you know and tell the others what it means in English. ◀

b **Plan your own entertainment**
Imagine you are planning a programme of entertainment for a group of English visitors. You are going to include a number of songs, poems and readings from your country, mainly in your own language or languages.

▶ Plan the programme and write programme notes, explaining the items you have chosen. Give any necessary cultural or background information and make the ideas or story clear. ◀

187 Argument is war

a Can you use some of these words to say what seems to be happening in this picture?

attack   defend   armed   position   strong   weak

What do the coloured words mean in these sentences?

He made a strong speech attacking the opposition.
What can you say in defence of your position?
You cannot produce a strong argument unless you are armed with the facts.
I agree with his basic position but I still think his arguments are weak.

Look at these words:

> **attack**
> If you **attack** a person, belief, or idea, you criticize them strongly. EG *The senator attacked the press for misleading the public.* ▶ used as a noun. EG *...attacks on apartheid... Burt's work came under violent attack.*
>
> **defend**
> If you **defend** someone or something, you argue in support of them when they have been criticized. EG *The bank has defended its actions in these cases.*
>
> **strong**
> If the arguments for something are **strong**, they are supported by a lot of evidence. EG *There is a strong case for an Act of Parliament.*
>
> **weak**
> If an argument or reason is **weak**, it does not convince you that it is right or logical. EG *That was an incredibly weak answer...*

▶ What words do you have for attack, defend etc. when you are talking about war in your language? Can these words be used to talk about ideas and arguments in the same way as in English? ◀

187a Elizabeth has just read about the concept 'Argument is War' and tries to explain it to Edmund. She begins by talking about aggression. What examples does she give?

> **WORD STUDY**
> aggression   implies   military   war-like   attack   defend   indefensible   strategy
>
> 187a Listen and repeat the phrases with these words in.

187b **b** What other words do they suggest here that we often use in a metaphorical way?
What does Elizabeth mean when she says:
... the tools for fighting are different?

The Fight Against Famine

185 A hectic time...

Aims: 1 Analysis of prepositional phrases and descriptions of place to highlight the internal structure of a report.
2 To encourage students to create a similar piece, about a hectic or tense day that they remember experiencing.

Reading   SB185a

1 Students read the report and do the Word Study.

Key: Time: **for**. Place: around, between, to, back to. Neither: by, to (= purpose).
Phrases describing places: a large and sprawling city; where the rebels had their headquarters; surrounded by loyalist guards.

Task, planning and report   SB185b/c

2 Get students to follow the instructions by themselves. Help if really necessary.

3 Students report to the class.

Sample: Throughout the morning, I rushed round town – which was very crowded being market day – from the business district, where I had a meeting, to the Holiday Inn – packed with overseas tourists – for a quick lunch with a friend, and then back to the main street to do some food shopping for dinner that night. I finally reached home at 2 p.m. just in time to welcome some other friends, newly arrived from Australia.

186 An entertainment

Aims: 1 Some relaxation and entertainment.
2 Giving opinions and stating preferences about songs and music.
3 Translating a story or song from the student's own country for the benefit of an audience.
4 Drafting and designing a programme for a class entertainment.
5 Co-operating over the planning of a project.

The fact that the songs are in a foreign language that most students will not understand should make it easier for students to react effectively to them. There is no need to be worried about the words.

SB186a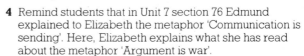

1 The large photo shows a family scene in a long house in a Sarawak village, in eastern Malaysia. Students may like to comment on Pete's translation of the song. Play both songs and see which one most students like best.

2 Students talk about a song they like, explaining what it is about.

Task and planning   SB186b

3 Decide with students when you could have an entertainment. They might like to invite students from other classes.

4 Encourage students to think of a song, poem, piece of music or dance they could either bring on cassette or sing or perform themselves, either in English or in their own language.

5 Help students plan how to introduce their item in English, and explain what it is about. (Explaining about things written only in their own language is a useful skill.)

6 Help students design a programme, and check their programme notes before they make a final copy.

187 Argument is war

Aim: Recognising the metaphorical use of words about war, as they are used in arguing. This revises and extends section 168.

Lexis: **awfully, backed up by, logical, weak**
Revision: **argument, attack, convince, criticised, defend, evidence, implies, literally, military, supported by**
Understanding only: **aggression, famine, strategy, tools, warlike, wipe you out** (= kill everybody)
Phrases: **Fair enough.**

SB187a   PB187

1 Use the picture to get students using words like **attack**, **defending**, etc. in a warlike context. (If you haven't done so already, revise Unit 16 section 168.) Brainstorm with students on other military words they know; perhaps some connected with sport (**goal defence, wing attack, reserves** etc). (Note that we say 'Can I **reserve judgement** on that point?')

2 Discuss the meanings of the coloured words in the sentences. Then students read the dictionary extracts on this page. These however only give the meanings related to argument. The full entries for these and other military words are in the Dictionary Extracts, and should have been referred to in Unit 16.

Report   SB187a

3 Give students time to think about their own language(s). Then they can explain to you how they talk about argument and war in their language. (If you have a multi-lingual class, group students according to their mother tongue.)

Listening   SB187a   187a

4 Remind students that in Unit 7 section 76 Edmund explained to Elizabeth the metaphor 'Communication is sending'. Here, Elizabeth explains what she has read about the metaphor 'Argument is war'.

5 Play the recording and ask students simply to try to write down some of the examples she uses. Then play it again for them to listen to what is said in between the examples.

6 Do the Word Study. Play the tape and get students to repeat the relevant phrases.

Listening   SB187b   187b

7 Play the recording.

Key: Apart from 'Fight against famine' (where the tools for fighting would be money, food and transport), they mention only a story 'lifted' from another book.

News and comment

Aims: 1 Understanding a serious radio news programme.
2 Recognising the functions and general contents of a serious more detailed news and comment broadcast, with political/social background and further developments in addition to actual events and details of sources.
3 Recognising the difference in style between a short news communiqué, an interview with a correspondent, and a detailed news commentary.

Lexis: intense, in spite of, rapid/rapidly, severe
Revision: **incident, judge, political, pressure, rejected, in shock** (medical term), **urban areas**
Understanding only: **crops**
Phrases: **background information, further developments, take urgent/direct action, on the grounds that** (giving the reason that), **a full-scale crisis, current limits on spending**
Also: **a tense moment, she felt very tense, a state of tension, intense pressure/feelings, an intensive care unit**

Listening   SB188a/b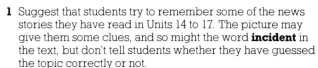

1 Suggest that students try to remember some of the news stories they have read in Units 14 to 17. The picture may give them some clues, and so might the word **incident** in the text, but don't tell students whether they have guessed the topic correctly or not.

2 Play recording 188a. Students listen to see which story he is covering. Once they realise which story it is, tell students to wait until the end before they say. Don't go into detailed explanation at this stage.

3 Read Bob's comment with students, and then play recording 188b while they read.

4 Before they listen to the whole story again, make sure students understand what the four types of information are.

5 Play recording 188a again, pausing while students identify which parts of the report contain what type of information. Stop the tape after each 'paragraph' of transcript, and ask students to say what they have just heard.

Key: (P refers to paragraphs in transcript 188a.)
P1: Political background.
P2: Source: statements by ministry, official statement, then report of events.
P3: Report of events, including four sources: police, the Authorities, unconfirmed reports, the hospital.
P4: Possible further developments.
P5: Further developments with two sources: the Government and spokesmen for the local farmers.

(If students can do this with 75% success, they have done very well indeed – remember to tell them this is normal speed BBC World Service reporting, and is not easy for learners to follow.)

6 Play the tape again while students read the transcripts. Ask them to listen for the intonation, and say which words are stressed. Also to note how Bob's voice falls at the end of each 'paragraph', and then goes to a higher note to start the new paragraph – if it is a change of focus. (An example of how intonation in spoken language fulfills the role of punctuation in written text.)

Report   SB188b

7 Suggest that students read through earlier transcripts 161 and 163, and then identify what information is new in this current affairs report. They can make notes and then tell the class.

Key: This is the third serious injury by the well; Jack has had an operation (surgery) and is in intensive care; Jill is still in shock; the Government has imposed limits on spending, so developments to the water supply system are impossible in the near future.

Language study

Aim: Patterns in typical news bulletin sentences: complex noun phrases, fronting information, relations between clauses.

SB189a/b PB189

1 Help students work through this on their own or in pairs. They may find it fun to read each example out loud.

2 Point out how the link is made. (**In spite of**, plus the verb **stated** changing to the noun **statements**, and adverb **repeatedly** changing to adjective **repeated**.)

SB189c/d

3 They will need to look at transcript 184c for the facts from which to build their sentences. Show students how to write full sentences each time.

Sample key: 1 This revolution was in the Philippines.
2 The revolution in the Philippines which led to the overthrow of President Marcos.
3 The revolution in the Philippines which led to the overthrow of President Marcos and the take-over by Mrs Cory Aquino.
4 The revolution in the Philippines which led to the overthrow of President Marcos and the take-over by Mrs Cory Aquino was almost entirely non-violent.

1 There was always the risk of shooting.
2 There was always the risk of shooting or of the situation getting out of control.
3 Throughout the drama, there was always the risk of shooting or of the situation getting out of control.
The two sentences fit together with the word **although**. and so on . . .

Bob Jobbins's final report covers a news story you have met in one of the last five units. It begins:

A slightly more detailed version for a more serious news programme might well include more facts and more background information to help the audience judge the real importance of the incident . . .

188a **a** Listen very carefully and say which story it covers.

188b **b** At the end, Bob comments:

Now this gives much more of the political background to the incident, and makes it clear that there could be further developments. The correspondent has clearly spoken to a large number of people, on all sides, involved in the dispute.

188a Listen again, pausing after each sentence, and say which of these he has just mentioned:

political background
descriptions of further developments
identification of sources of news
straightforward report of events

▶ Note down any new facts and information that you had not been given earlier, either in the communiqué or in the interview. ◀

 189 *Language study* •

Sentence building

a We have seen how news reports pack a lot of information into a single sentence. See how this sentence is put together:

A young man was seriously injured.
(What young man?)
A young man, identified as Jack, was seriously injured.
(Who identified him?)
A young man, identified in an official statement as Jack, was seriously injured.
(How was he injured?)
A young man, identified in an official statement as Jack, was seriously injured when he fell down the hill.
(What hill?)
A young man, identified in an official statement as Jack, was seriously injured when he fell down the hill where the well is located.

b Now look at this sentence:

The ministry stated repeatedly that there was no danger.
(No danger to whom?)
The ministry stated that there was no danger to the public.

How is sentence **b** related to the first sentence? Now see how the two sentences fit together.

In spite of repeated statements by the Ministry that there is no danger to the public, a young man, identified in an official statement as Jack, was seriously injured when he fell down the hill where the well is located.

c Now read the second paragraph of Bob's feature on the Philippines. (Recording 184c.)

Start with this sentence:

The revolution was non-violent.

Then answer these questions, writing out the new sentence after each question:

1 Where was this revolution?
2 Which revolution in the Philippines?
3 Who took over when Marcos left?
4 Was this revolution completely non-violent?

There was always the risk . . .

1 The risk of what?
2 Were there any other risks?
3 When were these risks present?

How do the two sentences fit together?

d Now look at the fourth paragraph and start with this:

The President left . . .

1 Which president?
2 When did he leave?

The world's press poured into the Presidential Palace . . .

1 Was anyone else involved?
2 Why did they go to the palace?
3 What had happened to the regime?
4 Had this been expected?
5 Why had it fallen?
6 Was military force used?

How do the two sentences fit together?

190 Detective work

Imagine that the correspondent who broadcast the story about the water dispute disappeared immediately after broadcasting it at noon that day.

If you were the team of detectives who had to track down the correspondent, where would you go, and who would you talk to? Begin by working out what the correspondent must have done the morning before he broadcast this news item. End by giving your recommendations for a search. You may add any extra details you wish to.

▶ Write a brief report and a recommended plan of action. Pass your reports round and compare plans of action. ◀

191 Lady Angela disappears

191a **a** Look at this story. Have you heard anything like it before?

It is rumoured that Lady Angela Fitzbrian, the daughter of the Duke of Birmingham, and a distant cousin of the Queen, has disappeared shortly before her marriage to the London businessman Lord Drinkwater. A good deal of mystery surrounds this disappearance. For example Miss Mary Bonnington, a close friend of the family, claims to have seen Lady Angela on the day of her disappearance riding in a gipsy caravan just beyond her father's estate. It is difficult to offer any explanation for this bizarre report. It is said that police suspect foul play.

▶ Write a second news bulletin to show how the story ends. ◀

191b **b** This may remind you of the story.

▶ For each story make up some newspaper headlines suitable for three different types of newspapers. ◀

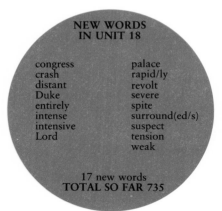

NEW WORDS IN UNIT 18

congress palace
crash rapid/ly
distant revolt
Duke severe
entirely spite
intense surround(ed/s)
intensive suspect
Lord tension
weak

17 new words
TOTAL SO FAR 735

192 *Grammar*

Talking and writing about the future
Which of the phrases in blue refer to the future?

a *But if Jack's injuries* do turn out *to be the result of a deliberate attack,* it will not only increase *the government's embarrassment, but* could provoke *a full-scale parliamentary crisis.* (188)

b *... unless* there is urgent action *to find* new sources of drinking water for the urban areas, they will take *direct action to protect...* (188)

c *... current limits on spending* make *further developments in the water supply system impossible...* (188)

d *This gives* more background and *makes it clear that* there could be further developments. (188)

What about these?

e *... farmers are worried about water shortages due to ...* an increase in the local population. (163)

f PRESENTER: *... alternative sources of water?*
BJ: *Well. I think that* must be the hope *of everyone involved in this crisis.* (163)

g *'We just want* to be left *on our own now.'* (178)

193 Plans for a journey

Imagine you are about to make a journey somewhere, for instance a business trip, or a visit to friends, some distance away. Work out how you would travel, and what you would need to tell the people expecting you at the other end.

▶ Write a final letter explaining your plans to the person responsible for meeting and entertaining/looking after you. You will find some useful words and phrases to help you in the letters in section 133.

Give your letter to someone else in the class. ◀

▶ The people you give it to should write a reply which acknowledges and/or queries the details set out. It should also confirm exactly what you and they will be doing. ◀

194 Similar or opposite?

The first word or phrase gives you a possible context for the two words below it. Which of the pairs of words are similar and which opposite in meaning?

a village	a headache	the way he spoke
distant nearby	severe slight	casual deliberate

light or heat	a journey	gunfire
strong intense	rapid fast	intensive occasional

his proposals	a feeling of	the police
rejected accepted	tension worry	suspect are nearly su

the results	titles	to what extent?
revealed showed	Duke Lord	entirely partly

190 Detective work

Aims: 1 Understanding the previous report so as to be able to make sensible inferences about the journalist's day and speculations about his possible whereabouts.
2 Writing a brief report and recommendations for action.

Lexis: suspect T, **track down**

Task, planning and report   SB190 PB190

1 This should be treated in a light-hearted way, and be done for fun.

2 Try to get the class to think like detectives. Has the journalist been kidnapped? Why? Who by?

3 Students in pairs or groups complete the report and recommendations for action. They can read each other's, or give their recommendations orally.

191 Lady Angela disappears

Aim: Producing a sequel to a short news bulletin.

Lexis: distant, duke, Lady/Lord, surrounds, suspect
Revision: **it is rumoured that, shortly before**

Listening and reading   SB191a

1 Students read and listen to the news bulletin. Do they recognise the story? They will remember The Gipsy Rover from Unit 2 section 21.

Writing   SB191a

2 In pairs write the next day's news report, about the father finding her at the wedding feast, and realising the gipsy was the real 'Lord of these Lands'.

3 Students read each other's stories, and make up headlines.

192 Grammar

Aim: Talking and writing about the future: recognising less explicit future reference, including nouns.

SB192

Key: a do turn out, will not only increase, could provoke   b there is urgent action to find, will take direct action to...   c further developments... impossible
d could be further developments   e water shortages ('Worried about water shortages' taken *in context* implies future shortages.)
f alternative sources, the hope of
g want to be left

193 Plans for a journey

Aim: Making arrangements for a future trip, writing a letter about them, and responding to such a letter.

Letter writing   SB193

1 Try to get students to think of a real journey they could actually make.

2 Students should work on their own. They can refer to Unit 13 sections 133 and 134. Walk round and help them draft their letters.

3 Before they pass their letters on, students should attach a brief memo stating the purpose of their journey, giving enough background for the recipient to reply with sensible suggestions.

4 Students read the memo and letter they have received, and write a reply.

194 Similar or opposite?

Aim: Revision of adjectives and adverbs from Units 13–18.

SB194

1 Explain that the top word gives the context. For example, a village could be a distant village or a nearby village. (The adjectives here are opposite in meaning.)

2 Students should do this on their own. They could use a dictionary if necessary. Then compare with a friend.

Key: (in this order, from left to right)
opp   opp   opp
sim   sim   opp
opp   sim   sim
sim   sim   opp

LEXICAL OBJECTIVES

congress 1 T large meeting, usually of representatives of a national or international organisation, held to discuss ideas, policies etc. *The second Congress of Negro Writers and Artists*
2 elected group of politicians responsible for making the law in the USA. *Bills in Congress*
crash 1 accident. *car/plane crash.*
2 T loud noise. *I heard a big crash.*
3 financial or business failure. *Wall Street crash in '29... stock market crash*
distant 1 T far away in space or time. *a distant part of the country... At some point in the distant future...*
2 distant relative = one you are not closely related to. *a distant cousin*
3 *He behaved very distantly* = coldly.
Duke a nobleman. *daughter of the Duke of Birmingham...*

entirely completely, totally. *The revolution in the Philippines was almost entirely non-violent...*
intense 1 strong, deep. *The Government is under intense pressure from Opposition Parties...* Also 'intense emotions' 'intense colour'
2 T serious, concentrated. *an intense person... an intense lecture.*
intensive T 1 involves concentrating on a particular task in order to achieve a lot in a short time. *intensive preparation for exams.*
2 intensive care unit = place in hospital where very ill people are given extremely thorough care.
Lord title used in front of the name of British earls. *the London businessman Lord Drinkwater.*
Palace large, richly decorated house. Usually the home of a king, queen or president. ... *the world's press poured into the Presidential Palace... Buckingham Palace* T
rapid T very fast. ... *the rapid and massive increase in public spending.*
rapidly very quickly. *water...is now being consumed rapidly by the growing number of people...*
revolt a violent attempt by a group of people to change their country's political system. *Army chief leads Philippines revolt. the Peasants' Revolt.*
severe 1 very bad. *Jack is now in an intensive care unit after surgery for severe head injuries.*
2 T strict, harsh, grim. *severe discipline... a severe expression*
spite 1 'in spite of' is used to introduce a fact that makes the other part of the sentence surprising. *In spite of repeated statements by the Ministry that there is no danger, ... a young man was seriously injured...*
2 T a feeling that makes you behave in a nasty way. *He teased the cat out of pure spite.* Also: *do something to spite someone* = do something deliberately to annoy them.
surrounded/s 1 positioned all around something. ... *the Presidential Palace, surrounded by loyalist guards...*
2 exist all around or closely associated with something. *A good deal of mystery surrounds this disappearance.*
suspect 1 think something is likely to be true. *It is said that the police suspect foul play.*
2 T doubt that something can be trusted. *She suspected her husband's honesty.*
3 T suspect = person thought to be guilty of a crime.
tension 1 feeling of uneasiness or worry which occurs in a situation where there is a possibility of conflict. *after days and nights of tension, the defeated President left...*
2 T the degree to which something is stretched tight. *The tension in the wires/guitar strings.*
weak 1 T delicate, not strong. *He was weak from hunger. That chair's got a weak leg.*
2 powerless, inneffective. *a weak government.*
3 *weak argument* = one that is not right or logical.

Unit 19 Spot the hoax

Units 19–24 offer a final opportunity to build up students' confidence in handling long stretches of unsimplified English and a chance to review the major language features covered in Level 3, particularly in the context of written tasks.

In this unit, three newspaper stories on widely differing topics provide a stimulus for discussion, explanation, narrative and summary, as well as practice in using general knowledge to infer the meaning of unknown words. The texts provide a basis for a study of tense patterns, complex sentences and cohesion in narrative. In deciding which is the 'hoax' story, students are encouraged to read with a healthy scepticism, and discuss how far the stories are credible.

OBJECTIVES

Lexical objectives are in TB203

Discussion topics

a News stories which stretch belief. (195, 196, 201)
b Hoaxes. (196, 201)

Social skills

a Expressing belief, doubt and disbelief. (196, 198, 201)
b Personal anecdotes. (195, 196, 198)
c Expressing a change of mind. (201)

Communication skills

a Stating an opinion as to the truth or falsity of a story and giving evidence for that statement. (196, 201)
b Handling long texts containing a lot of new words. (200)
c Summarising a news story, spoken and written. (196, 200)

Grammar and discourse

a Lexical reference – understanding the variety of ways of referring to characters in a narrative. (196, 198)
b Practice in building complex sentences. (197)
c Topic coherence – following the development of a story. (198)
d Contrastive stress. (198)
e Habitual states and actions in past and present time. (199)
f Practice Book Grammar word: **that**.

Dictionary skills

a To help students consider and judge which 'difficult to guess' words are sufficiently important to look up. (200)
b To find additional uses and meanings of new words. (202)

---

195 Heroic rescue

Aims: 1 Speculating about an unlikely news story.
2 Telling anecdotes.

Lexis: block, cartoon T, **cope, mid-air, threaten**

Task, planning and report SB195

1 Discuss the headlines as a class. (Spiderman is an American cartoon character who can fly, and who uses his strength and his gift of flying to help people.)

2 Ask students in pairs or groups to work out a possible story. Help them to plan it.

3 One student from each group presents their story to the class. Encourage student comments.

---

196 Hero

Aims: 1 Reading to compare information from two sources.
2 Lexical reference – the variety of ways in which the people in a story can be referred to.
3 Expressing belief, doubt and disbelief.

Lexis: block, cartoon, chat, grabbed, leaped, lover, rope, swing, terrible T, **threat, threaten**
Revision: **awful, colleague, commit suicide, feat**
Understanding only: **fruitless** (= useless), **hailed** (= praised publicly), **harness**

Reading and class discussion SB196 PB196

1 Students read the whole newspaper story silently, then comment on it.

2 Do the Word Study exercises. The first focuses on the new words (left hand column). Ask students to find them in the text, and then match each with a word from the right.

3 The second makes the point that in a narrative characters can be referred to in a variety of ways.

   Key: Six ways: a suicide girl, a lovesick woman, Jeanne Charmean, Jeanne, the woman, she

Class discussion SB196a

4 Explain the title of the unit, and what a **hoax** is. Discuss, as a class, if this story could be true. (Is the person who jumped off the roof likely to fall faster than the girl and catch her?) Accept all students' opinions.

Summary SB196b

5 Make it clear the sentences must be in the order in which the events happened, not the order in which they appear in the news item. Tell students they will probably get between nine and eleven short sentences.

   Key: (The first three are given in the Student's Book.)
   She leant out of the window and threatened to jump.
   The priest, police and firemen arrived.
   The priest and police tried to talk her out of it.
   Firemen climbed up on to roof (6th floor).
   One fireman put on a harness and tied it to a pillar.
   After five hours Jeanne jumped and so did Lovisio.
   Lovisio caught her 30 feet above the ground.
   Firemen pulled them both up to safety.
   Later Jeanne said she must have been out of her mind and Lovisio was called a 'spiderman hero'.

Planning and report SB196c/d

6 Get students to follow the instructions, working on the description and the personal account in pairs. Choose the best versions to be presented to the class or acted out.

---

197 Language study

Aims: 1 Practice in building complex sentences with or without explicit markers of clause relations (e.g. **because, as a result of, so**).
2 Summarising a news story.

SB197a

1 Try to get students to do this without looking back at the story. (Sections 75, 125, 155 and 189 may help here.)

SB197b

2 Challenge students to tell the story in the least number of sentences.

3 Students read their accounts out to compare versions.

Unit 19
Spot the hoax

Spiderman to rescue
Fireman jumps and grabs suicide girl

195 ## Heroic rescue

Look at these headlines and the picture. What do you think the story is about? Make up a possible story.

Here are a few words to help you: threatening to jump – fifth-floor window – small baby – couldn't cope – police – fire brigade – the roof of the block – safety harness – mid-air

Tell your story to the class.

196 ## Hero

a Read the full story. Do you believe it? Is it possible?

Tell each other.

FIREMAN Lionel Lovisio was being hailed as a spiderman hero last night.

He leaped from the roof of a Paris apartment block to save a lovesick woman who had jumped out of her fifth-floor window.

It was the kind of feat that normally belongs to the pages of the cartoon character. Lovisio, wearing a harness and line, actually caught 25-year-old Jeanne Charmean before she hit the ground.

Jeanne had been leaning out of the window for several hours threatening to jump. "My lover has left me," she shouted. "I'm

Daily Express

EXPRESS FOREIGN SERVICE

alone with a small baby, and I've lost my job."

As a priest and policemen talked to her through loud-hailers from the street, Lovisio and a colleague, Jean Ferrier, quietly made their way up the stairs of the six-storey building to the roof.

Harness

Lovisio put on his harness and attached it to a pillar. Then he leaned over a low wall to listen to the woman's threats.

After five hours of fruitless

chatting with the priest and the police, the woman climbed out on to the window sill.

Lovisio was watching her every movement. Then she jumped to what would have been her death. The fireman jumped too.

Heavier than Jeanne, he fell faster. By the time she was level with the second floor—and only 30 ft. from the ground—he grabbed her.

Lovisio said: "We were swinging in space. Luckily, she was so surprised that she did not try to pull herself from my grasp."

As police raced to the roof, the other fireman hauled them up to safety.

Later Jeanne said: "I must have been out of my mind."

b **Factual summary**

Can you write a list of the events in chronological order. For example:

Jeanne Charmean's lover left her.
She lost her job.
Decided to commit suicide by jumping...

c **Description**

Describe the scene from the point of view of one of the people waiting on the roof.

Either write or record your impressions, as if for an informal news programme. For example:
'It was awful, up there on the roof...'

d **Personal account**

Now imagine you were a passer-by who had stopped to see what was happening. What might you say to a neighbour when you got home? In twos, plan and act out a short dialogue.

WORD STUDY

a Find the pairs that are similar in meaning.

leaped	block of flats
apartment block	talking informally
threatening	jumped
attached	mad
chatting	got hold of
grabbed	saying she would
swinging	tied
out of my mind	hanging

b Find these words in the story. Who do they refer to?

Spiderman Fireman Fireman Lionel Lovisio
spiderman hero He Lovisio The fireman

Now write down the different ways Jeanne Charmean is referred to, in order. What do they tell you about her?

197 ## Language study

Complex sentences

a Look at these sentences:

Fireman Lionel Lovisio was being hailed as a hero last night.
He leaped from the roof of a Paris apartment block.
He saved the life of a woman.
She was lovesick.
She was threatening to commit suicide.
She had jumped out of her fifth-floor window.

Put them together to make two sentences, or one single sentence. Compare your sentences.

b Look at the sentences you wrote in 196b. Join them to make a chronological account of the story.

198 Reincarnation

a Do you believe that we have all had other lives, before this one?

> **1 Reincarnation** is supposed to happen when someone is born again after death and lives again in the body of another creature.

Have you ever seen a hypnotist at work? Or seen someone hypnotised? What do you know about hypnotism? Share your knowledge.

b The three sentences in the box below the article have been taken out of the story opposite. Can you put them back in the right place?

> **WORD STUDY**
> **People and places**
> Angie's mother is referred to as follows:
>
> Little Angie's parents – her mother – Angie's mother – she.
>
> How is *Angie* referred to?
> How is the *bank* later referred to?

c **Mysterious feelings**
Have you ever heard of any stories like this? Have you ever had the feeling Angie had?
Or have you ever had the feeling that you have been to a place or done something before, when you know you couldn't have?

▶ Discuss in groups then tell the class. ◀

Have these children lived before?

LITTLE Angie's parents were mystified. When the three-year-old passed a bank on the way to the shops with her mother she would say: "That's where I used to be a nurse."

"I wore a long dress and a funny-shaped hat," Angie said. "Not like nurses wear now. And the place wasn't near the shops like it is now.

Angie's mother decided to trace the history of the building. She found that 200 years ago it had been a workhouse and hospital and was outside the town boundary.

The clothes Angie described were the uniform the nurses wore.

Many psychic researchers today believe in reincarnation. They say most of us have lived before, perhaps several times.

But children sometimes seem to remember previous existences without outside help.

Researchers say it is because their minds are more open, and not crammed with memories of this life.

Titbits

(a) It was in the country."

(b) Hypnosis is often used to help people recall their past lives.

(c) At first her mother put it down to vivid imagination, but she became less certain as the little girl's story became more detailed.

199 *Grammar* ....

When (ever)

a Look at paragraph 1 in the article above.
Which three of the words or phrases below could be used instead of *when*?

Whenever... Every time... One day when...
Each time... Once when... If...

Can you rewrite each of the sentences below using one of the words or phrases above?

1 *When we were in the Scouts, we used to sing when we were camping.* (17)

2 *... because I used to sleepwalk, perhaps, and I always had this fear of falling downstairs when I was sleepwalking.* (34)

3 *I used to be embarrassed about saying I didn't have a job.* (49)

4 *My eldest son was out of work for about 15 months I think and if people said to him 'What are you doing?' he was virtually speechless.* (49)

5 *a picture ... and I could get it out and remind myself of him when he was at school.* (56)

6 *We – always when we arrive in a new country, we get somebody ... who knows about the traditions...* (130)

7 *During songs people would come up and try to speak to you.* (137)

8 *It was great because the people would gather round us and they would join in and, I remember on one occasion...* (137)

9 *It's explaining that when we talk about – when we argue, that the words that we often use... are war-like.* (187)

b How many ways can you find of referring to actions that happened repeatedly or regularly in the past? Which sentence refers to present time, but implies that this would also happen in the past?

198 Reincarnation

Aims: 1 Ways of expressing belief and disbelief.
2 Personal anecdotes.
3 Contrastive stress.

Lexis: hypnosis, hypnotise, imagination, memories, mystery, mystified, put down to, recalled
Revision: **nurse, vivid, uniform**
Understanding only: **crammed** (= full of), **reincarnation, a workhouse** (where poor people (children or adults) use to go if they had no means of support)
Phrase: **trace the history**

Class discussion   SB198a PB198

1 Discuss the dictionary definition and the whole concept of reincarnation. What do students believe?

2 Find out whether students have had any experience of hypnosis. Do any believe that hypnosis can help people recall previous existences?

Reading task   SB198b

3 Students read on their own and find where the lost sentences fit. They could check their final ideas with a partner, and plan how to explain their answers.

Report   SB198b

4 Pick some students to explain to the class what goes where. They could read the completed paragraph out loud. (See note 7 below.)

Key: Number the paragraphs 1–6. (At first her . . .) at end of paragraph 1; a (country) at end of paragraph 2; b at start of paragraph 6.

5 Help students to do the Word Study. First they find the references to Angie's mother in the story. Then they find which phrases refer to Angie, and read them out in order. They can do the same with the bank.

Key: Angie: the three-year-old, she, (I, nurse), the little girl. Bank: the place, the building, workhouse and hospital.

Task   SB198c

6 If students have no direct experience, they may have read about something similar, or seen something on TV they could talk about.

7 Optional exercises on contrastive stress: The second paragraph is suitable for identifying where the main stresses are likely to occur when being read out loud.

Key: the main stresses will occur (mainly in pairs) on: I wore a LONG DRESS / and a FUNNY-shaped HAT Angie said /, NOT like nurses wear NOW. / and the place WASN'T near the SHOPS / like it is NOW. / It was in the COUNTRY.

8 To show how intonation can actually change the meaning of a sentence, try this. Write this sentence on the board:
'I wanted you to phone me on Tuesday morning, not...'

Underline one of the words, e.g.
I wanted you to phone me on Tuesday morning, not...

and ask students to read what you have written stressing the word underlined and completing the sentence:
I wanted YOU to phone me on Tuesday morning, not JOHN.

Similarly they can do:
I wanted you to PHONE me on Tuesday morning, not... (WRITE.)
I wanted you to phone me on TUESDAY morning, not... (MONDAY.)

Continue in this way with other words: **I, me,** and **morning,** with students thinking of contrasting words.

199 Grammar

Aims: 1 To draw attention to **when** and **if** meaning 'whenever'.
2 To review ways of referring to repeated actions in the past.

SB199a PB199

1 Draw attention to the **When** in paragraph 1 in the story in section 198. Ask students if this is something which happened once or many times. (The word **would** in 'she would say' shows that it is something which happened many times.)

2 Ask them which of the words and phrases could be used instead of **When**, given that the sentence is about something which happened many times. (**Whenever, Every time, Each time, If**.)

3 Ask them to rewrite (or read out loud) sentences 1–9, using one of the words/phrases, and making any other necessary changes. In sentence 1, it is the second **when** they can change. (The first **When** means 'all the time when'.) Give weak students a clue: tell them there is one sentence where they need to use **Once when/One day when**.

Key: 1 . . . whenever/every time/each time/if we were camping.
2 . . . whenever/every time/each time/if I was sleepwalking.
3 . . . whenever/every time/each time/if I said I didn't have a job.
4 . . . whenever/every time/each time people said to him . . .
5 . . . whenever/if he was at school.
6 . . . whenever/every time/each time/if we arrive in a new country . . .
7 Whenever/Every time/Each time/If you were singing . . .
8 . . . I remember once when/one day when . . .
9 . . . whenever/every time/each time/if we argue . . .

SB199b

4 Remind students of the phrase 'she would say' (from the story) which means it is a repeated or regular or habitual action in the past.

5 Ask them to read through sentences 1–9 again and find other ways of expressing this concept.

Key: 1 used to sing   2 used to sleep walk/always had
3 used to be   4 if people said   5 could get it out
6–7 would come up and try to . . .   8 would gather round/would join in   9 –

*To summarise: **Used to** plus verb, **would** (or **'d**) plus verb: simple past form – as in 2 and 4. In this respect, the simple past is like the simple present form – see sentences 6 and 9.*

Sentence 6 is present in form, (denoting habitual action), but implies this has also happened regularly in the past.

Aims: 1 Handling a lengthy text with a high proportion of unknown words.
2 To make students consider how important the meaning of a given word is in inferring the meaning of another word.
3 Summarising a news story.

Lexis: bearing, belongings, cave, courtesy, directly, display, elements, examine, experiment, expose (exposure), faint, gallery, outer, peasants, philosopher, precious, principles, remote, silver, stunned
Revision: **a find** (noun), **leads experts to believe, lay hidden, concern** (= worry)
Understanding only: (only as needed)
Phrases: **came to light**

Lead-in   SB200a

1 What do your students know about archaeology? Are there any archaeological sites in their country/ies? How do they find out how old things are?

Carbon dating is a way of calculating the age of an object by measuring how much radioactive carbon it contains.

Key: Other tests: studying the earth or environment the object is found in; comparing with similar objects found elsewhere.

2 Are any students in your class photographers? What do they know about the history of photography? What was used before camera film was invented? Make your 'experts' into group leaders, and let them use English to talk about photography and cameras with the rest of their group.

The faint black and white picture in the centre of the newspaper feature is of an ancient photographic plate (a thin sheet of glass, covered with chemicals that react to the light, and on which an image can be formed). Plates were used before modern photographic film was invented.

Reading   SB200b/c

3 Ask students to find out as much as they can about the picture in the centre by reading this article once fairly quickly. They should try to understand the main theme without worrying about words they don't understand or the missing words. They will talk about these later.

This text may appear to be very difficult. Nevertheless students should be able to make good sense of it if they do not get too worried about specific words. The exercise is designed to demonstrate to them that they can understand quite a bit of text even if many of the words are unknown.

4 Find out from students what they have managed to understand. Write on the board what students tell you about the picture in the centre. For example: found in a box belonging to Yorimoto Hishida. Found in a cave last September. Glass plate which bears a faint image. Perhaps the first picture ever taken.

5 Now explain about the eleven blanks and nine words underlined. Students have to guess the meanings of the words or phrases that go in the blanks. To help, they may, as a class, ask you for the meanings of three, but only three, of the words underlined. The class must decide amongst themselves which three words would be best to ask for. (See Aim 2 above.)
Give these two examples to help students choose.
1 It is unlikely that the meaning of the word **lacquered** is going to help them much with the blank in:
The new evidence was _____ in a lacquered box.
The blank fairly clearly means something like 'found' or 'discovered' (the actual word is **unearthed**). **Lacquered** is simply an adjective describing **box** and for our purposes it doesn't matter what it means.
2 On the other hand it is very difficult to guess what might go in the blank in:
. . . his execution following the peasant _____.
The meaning of the word **peasant** might be useful here. Students must therefore think carefully about the process of inference before they decide which three words to ask you for.

6 Give students time to read and to discuss amongst themselves which three underlined words they want to know.

7 After supplying the three meanings, ask students to read the piece again to guess the meanings of all the blanks.

8 Discuss these with the class. Help them suggest words that could fit. Having guessed, for example, that the first blank is **found/discovered**, they will be able to understand **unearthed** when they hear it.

Key: Blanks: 1 unearthed
2 carbon dating
3 establish (be sure of the truth of)
4 exiled (forced, as a punishment, to live away from one's home)
5 shrouded (covered. A shroud is the cloth used to cover a dead body.)
6 sorcerer (wise man; magician)
7 grisly (very unpleasant; horrifying)
8 uprising (rebellion)
9 hailed (acknowledged; accepted)
10 courtesy of (thanks to; as a result of the generosity of)
11 exposure (leaving uncovered or unprotected)

Underlined words:
a lacquered – covered with a hard shiny varnish
b image – picture
c alerted – informed urgently
d stun – amaze; astonish
e lost favour with – offended so that he was no longer respected by
f mystery – ignorance; lack of knowledge
g archives – historical records
h peasant – poor farmer; poor countryman
i on display – put out for people to see

Planning and report   SB200d

9 The purpose of the final A/B exercise is to get students to give the general gist of the story very briefly, and to compare the language used in a formal written account (A) with that used in an informal spoken account (B). Divide the class into halves, A and B. Help them plan what to write or say.

10 Get each B student to move next to an A student, who can take on the imaginary role of the photographer friend. Ask B students to tell A about the find, in not more than 30 seconds, using their notes.

11 B students can then read A's written report. How do they compare?

12 Finally, go through the meanings of the target lexis with students and help them to understand some of the alternative meanings (e.g. **precious** = valuable). It may help to do section 202 at this point.

200 Photography

a How do archaeologists find out how old things are? Historical knowledge? Carbon-dating? Other tests?

What do you know about the history of photography?

Do you have a simple camera or a complicated one? What advantages does yours have?

b Read this article quickly. Find out what you can about the picture without worrying about the missing words.

c There are eleven blanks and nine words or phrases underlined. You have to guess the possible meanings of the words or phrases that were in the blanks. Suggest a word or phrase that could fit each one. To help, you may ask your teacher for the meanings of three, but only three, of the words underlined.

The history of photography as we know it may soon be history itself.

A recent find on Japan's North Island now leads experts to believe that the basic principles of the process were understood and in use many years before previously supposed.

The new evidence was _1_ in a lacquered box containing the belongings of Japanese philosopher Yorimoto Hishida.

For almost 2 centuries it lay hidden in a cave high in the remote Outer Fokus Mountains. Last September it finally came to light.

It contained not only detailed accounts of experiments of the effect of light on silver salts but also a glass plate bearing the faint image you see here.

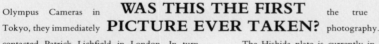

WAS THIS THE FIRST PICTURE EVER TAKEN?

When news reached Olympus Cameras in Tokyo, they immediately contacted Patrick Lichfield in London. In turn, he alerted George Hughes, editor of Camera Weekly.

Together with a team of Olympus experts, they flew directly to the area of the find.

They were the first Westerners to examine the most historic photographic development of the century.

The plate was immediately transferred to Tokyo for _2_ . The results are sure to stun the camera world. The picture was taken no later than 1782.

Almost a full half century before the earliest work of either Fox Talbot or Nicéphore Niépce.

Suddenly everyone is asking the same question: Who was Yorimoto Hishida?

Information is hard to find. To date we have been able to _3_ precious few facts.

After early successes in the field of medicine, it appears Hishida lost favour with the Japanese aristrocacy and was _4_ to the North Island in 1771.

The years that followed are _5_ in mystery.

Local archives speak of a _6_ in the mountains. But the only other positive reference so far uncovered is a _7_ account of his execution following the peasant _8_ of 1792.

A sad end indeed for a man now being _9_ as the true father of photography.

The Hishida plate is currently in London for further tests, _10_ Olympus Cameras.

But due to scientific concern that _11_ to the light could weaken the already faint image, it will be on display to the public for one day only.

If you would like to see the historic Hishida plate for yourself, visit The Photographers Gallery at 5 Great Newport Street, London WC2 between 11 am and 7 pm today.

OLYMPUS CAMERAS

---

d Your teacher will tell you what words were used originally in the blanks. Do they mean the same as the ones you suggested?

A students: Write *two* sentences which summarize the main points of this feature, as if for a **News In Brief** report.

B students: Plan how you would tell a photographer friend of yours about this find, in not more than 30 seconds. Write short notes.

As and Bs in pairs together: compare your pieces.

79

201 Spot the hoax

unusual doesn't ring true strange April Fool!

genuine? *unlikely* impossible true

common enough possible suspicious a load of rubbish

exaggerated ridiculous **a complete hoax**

a One of the stories in Unit 19 is in fact a hoax, published on April Fool's day to trick readers. Which do you think it is? Say why you think so.

The other two stories were reported by the newspapers as true stories. Do you believe they are really true? Give at least one reason.

▶ After discussing all three, present a short report on your decision and how you reached it. ◀

b We asked Elizabeth Egerton and Edmund Lee to do the same. Which of the words and phrases above do you think they might have used about each story?

`201b` Listen to the first part of their discussion. See which words they did in fact use.

`201c` **c** Do you agree with what Elizabeth and Edmund finally thought? Edmund admitted to changing his mind over this. What had he originally thought when he read them previously?

202 *Dictionary skills*

Guess before you look up

a Examine the coloured words carefully in their context. Can you think of a word or phrase with a similar meaning? The words in the box opposite may help you.

1 ... *except that there are one or two* elements *that don't ring true.*
2 *The basic* principles *of the process (of photography) were understood ...*
3 ... *box containing the* belongings *of Japanese philosopher Yorimoto Hishida.*
4 ... *a glass plate* bearing *the* faint *image you see here.*
5 *Last September it finally* came to light.
6 *The plate was* immediately transferred *to Tokyo.*
7 To date *we have been able to establish* precious *few facts.*
8 ... *plate is currently in London, ...* courtesy *of Olympus Cameras.*
9 ... *exposure to the light could* weaken ...
10 ... *will be* on display ... *visit The Photographers Gallery ...*

general rules	taken directly
not being protected from	thanks to
on show to the public	up to now
one or two	was found/revealed
parts of it	weak/unclear
possessions	with

b **Elements   principles   bearing   faint**
Look up these four words which were coloured in the sentences above, and find some of the other meanings they have. Choose one example for each word that you think may be useful.

Write the examples out leaving a blank space for the word. Give them to another student. Can they guess which word fits before looking it up?

203 REVIEW

UNIT 19

Find the stranger
In each set of words opposite, there is one word that is very unlikely to fit. Can you find it?

1 I'm just popping out to the library! I'll be back directly/effectively/immediately/straight away/shortly.
2 So much noise! I can't cope with it/stand it/bear it/imagine it any longer.
3 The piece of rope/string/wire/silver was now fully extended but still wouldn't reach the water.
4 The cave was in the distant/remote/vague/far away mountain range above a stunningly beautiful valley.

5 It was in principle a crazy/ridiculous/stupid/faint plan to go there in winter.
6 A wide range of mysterious/precious/costly/valuable metals are to be found there, for instance, silver/gold/iron
7 He can't set out until he's entirely/fully/completely/100%/directly recovered from his illness.
8 She arrived late, bearing/blocking/carrying/swinging/holding a simply huge bouquet of flowers.
9 The weather forecast threatened deep snow/sunny periods/storms/gale-force winds

NEW WORDS IN UNIT 19

bear D	imagination
belongings	leap
cartoon	lover
cave	mystery
chat	mystified
cope	outer
courtesy	peasant
directly	philosopher
display	precious
element D	principle D
examine	recall
experiment	recover
expose	remote
exposure	rope
extend	silver
faint D	stunned
fully	swing
gallery	team
grab	terrible
hoax	threat
hypnosis	uniform
hypnotise	

43 new words
TOTAL SO FAR 778

80

201 Spot the hoax

Aims: 1 Assessing the credibility of a story by reading critically.
2 Expressing belief and disbelief.
3 Expressing a change of mind.

Lexis: elements, exposure, extended, display, fully, hoax, ridiculous, rope
Revision: **genuine, suspicious, whereas**
Understanding only: **namely, a hell of a jolt** (informal, = violent bump)
Phrases: **one or two elements that don't ring true** (= sound true), **It's not that unusual to find . . .**

Lead-in SB201

1 Discuss the meanings of the words and phrases at the top of the page. Ask students which they could use if they did not believe a story.

Key: Phrases expressing definite disbelief: impossible, ridiculous, a complete hoax, a load of rubbish (informal), April Fool!

It is a custom in UK that on April 1st every year people play jokes on each other, to try to get them to believe things that are not true. Once the person seems to believe it, the other person shouts 'April Fool!'

Task, planning and report SB201a

2 Ask students in groups to recall and discuss all three stories in this unit and decide which they think is the hoax. They should then prepare a short report.

3 Hear or read out their reports. Write very briefly on the board what each group has decided about each story.

Listening SB201b/c

4 Students decide which of the words and phrases at the top Elizabeth and Edmund might have used about each story. Then play recording 201b.

5 Check which words they did use.

6 Play recording 201c.

Key: Edmund first thought only the photography one was genuine. He finally thought the reincarnation one was common enough to be true; that the spiderman was a complete hoax, and the photography one was probably true. Elizabeth still has doubts about the photography one.

7 Tell students the real answers: the photography one was published on April Fool's Day, and was a complete hoax, thought up by Olympic Cameras as an advertising gimmick. (Note the clue in using the name Outer Fokus – to sound like 'out of focus'.) The other two were reported as true stories. However, the spiderman story cannot be true, because both the fireman and the girl would fall at the same speed – he would never have caught up with her in mid-air!

202 Dictionary skills

Aims: 1 To focus on the more common of the new words that occurred in the text in section 200, and to find what other uses and meanings they have.
2 To help students read an entry selectively, and pick an example that they may find useful.

SB202a PB202

1 Students guess and match each coloured word with a word or phrase from the box.

SB202b

2 Students look up these four words in the Dictionary Extracts to find other useful meanings and phrases.

3 Students write down the phrases leaving a blank instead of the headword. They pass these round for other students to fill in. This amounts to students writing their own cloze test, and trying it out on the others. Discuss the results as a class. Did anyone pick the same examples?

203 Review

Key: 1 effectively   2 imagine
3 silver   4 vague   5 faint
6 mysterious   7 directly
8 blocking   9 sunny periods.
Note: Draw attention to the use of the word **recover**.

LEXICAL OBJECTIVES

bear D
belongings things that you own. *a box containing the belongings of Yorimoto*
cartoon funny drawings.
cave large hole in hillside or underground. *it lay hidden in a cave.*
chat talk in an informal way.
cope cope with = deal successfully with a problem or difficult situation. *Alone with a small baby, she couldn't cope.*
courtesy 1 T polite behaviour.
2 by courtesy of = with permission of.
directly 1 T to show exact position. *directly overhead; directly behind me.*
2 immediately, very soon. *They flew directly to the area.*
display 1 for people to see. *on display to the public. Fireworks display.* T
2 T to show an emotion. *displayed her feelings of affection.*
elements D
examine 1 to look carefully at. *first Westerners to examine the historic photograph.* Also: **medical examination** examine an idea = think deeply about.
2 be examined by a teacher
experiment 1 scientific test. *detailed experiments on the effects of light . . .*
2 T to try out a new idea. *Businesses experimenting with computers.*
expose EED T to uncover something to make it visible or well-known.
exposure EED T exposure to the light.

extend EED continue to a point in time or distance. *fully extended.*
faint D
fully 1 completely, to the greatest degree. *fully extended/recovered.*
gallery place for exhibitions. *The Photographers' Gallery. Art galleries*
grab, grabbed take hold of quickly. *By the time she was level with the second floor he grabbed her.*
hoax a trick. *Which story is a hoax?*
hypnosis see hypnotise. *Hypnosis is often used to help people recall their past lives.*
hypnotise a hypnotist puts someone into a state where they seem to sleep but can respond to things they see and hear. *Have you ever been hypnotised?*
imagination 1 creative ability. *At first her mother put it down to vivid imagination.*
2 pictures/things in your mind that don't exist in real life. *It's your imagination!* T
leap EED 1 jump high or far. *He leaped from the roof of an apartment block.*
lover 1 someone you have a sexual relation with, but are not married to.
2 *Young lovers* = people in love.
mystery T EED 1 something that cannot be explained. *His death is a mystery.*
mystified *Little Angie's parents were mystified* = they could not understand
outer 1 T not inner. *outer walls.*
2 things situated near the edge. *the remote Outer Fokus Mountains.*
peasant poor low-class farm worker. *in the peasant uprising of 1792.*
philosopher person who studies thought, existence, knowledge.
precious 1 T important, valuable, rare. *precious metals, like silver or gold.*
2 precious little = a small amount. *able to establish precious few facts.*
principle D
recall 1 remember. *recall their past.*
2 T make someone return. *He was recalled to the army.*
recover 1 get better. *fully recovered from an illness. a speedy recovery.* T
2 T to get back. *to recover the money*
remote 1 far away in time or distance. *remote mountains. the remote past.*
Phrases: **there's a remote possibility; I have not the remotest idea.**
rope very strong thick string. *If he fell to the end of the rope.*
silver valuable metal. *a silver necklace. silver coins.* Also used in photography: *silver salts*
2 T colour. *long silver hair.*
stunned 1 shocked, astonished. *The results were sure to stun the camera world.*
2 T knocked unconscious. *Stunned by the fall.*
swing EED 1 move back and forward. *We were swinging in space.*
team 1 *football team*
2 group of people working together. *a team of experts.*
terrible awful. *a terrible experience*
threat 1 warning. *the woman's threats*
2 T something harmful. *threat of floods*
uniform 1 special clothes. *nurses' uniform, school uniform.*
2 T even, regular, or identical. *uniform tall white buildings.*

80T

Unit 20 Off to sea!

This unit contains the first two chapters of A Dip in the Pool, *a short story by Roald Dahl which is serialised in the last five units of the course. It is set on an ocean liner, so there students discuss travel by sea before reading. The story provides the basis for a written narrative, and draws attention to the use of verb forms ending in* **-ing** *in setting the scene for a literary narrative. The second chapter of the story provides for practice in spoken narrative. A final exercise describing an auction, which is a central part of the story, gives practice in giving instructions and advice.*

OBJECTIVES

Lexical objectives are in TB214

Discussion topics

a Travelling by ship. (204)
b Difficulties of travel – sea-sickness. (204)
c Songs about the sea. (209)

Social skills

a Exchanging anecdotes about travel. (204)
b Talking about songs: explaining theme and content. (209)

Communication skills

a Reading a narrative. (206,210)
b Scene-setting in a narrative for pleasure. (206,208)
c Inferring meanings from context. (207)
d Writing informal narrative. (207)
e Speculating on the possible interpretation of an obscure sentence. (210)
f Understanding a weather forecast. (211)
g Explaining a sequence of events. (213)

Grammar and discourse

a The use of verbs ending in **-ing**, especially with reference to a literary context. (208)
b Adverbs modifying verbs and adjectives. (212)
c Practice Book Grammar Word: **on**.

Dictionary skills

a Finding meanings appropriate to a given context. (205)
b Compound words with **sea-**. (214)

204 Big ships, small ships

Aims: 1 To introduce the themes of sea travel, life on board a big ship, sea-sickness.
2 To encourage anecdote-telling about journeys by sea.

Lexis: cabin, calm, deck, float, ghastly, moderately, naval officer, navy, sailor, smooth, steward
Revision: **captain, the Channel, concentrate on, rough, ship, spread like the..., waves**
Phrases: **spread like the plague**

Lead-in SB204a–d PB204

1 Begin by asking students to tell you all the words they know about the sea. Write them on the board. Divide them into categories – objects, people, feelings, verbs (movements, actions), adjectives etc. Underline any that are target words for this unit.

2 Work through questions a–d, which are intended partly to expose students to the lexis which follows in the story, and partly to encourage general discussion on the theme of sea voyages.

Listening SB204 [204b]

3 First find out how many of your students are 'good sailors'? And how many tend to get seasick?

4 Play the recording for students to hear some more tales of sea travel. Students should take brief notes in answer to the questions. Pause between the two conversations and discuss.

Key: Rachel says she's quite a good sailor and has only been seasick once. Chris seemed to manage a journey back from France all right. Bruce says he's an 'average sailor' unless it's really rough, but Edmund says he's an 'earth person' and is pretty bad. So he's probably the worst.

Types of ships: Rachel: a very small boat (with a cabin, as she talks about being inside). Chris: a big boat from France. Edmund: a hovercraft; a Sealink which is a European cross-channel car ferry.

205 Dictionary skills

Aims: 1 To prepare students to speculate on the title of the story in section 206.
2 To encourage students to read an entry critically, and find meanings appropriate to a given context.

Lexis: coloured, dip, pool, raw, surface
Revision: **liquid**

SB205 PB205

1 Students find **dip** and **pool** in the Dictionary Extracts and read the definitions, thinking which of their meanings could possibly be linked in a story title.

2 Help students to speculate on the various possible meanings of the two words in combination (e.g. going for a swim in a pool; doing the football pools etc.). Accept all their ideas as possibles. Don't tell students what the title actually means because that will spoil their enjoyment of the story. A final discussion of this title comes in Unit 24.

206 Dip in the pool

Aims: 1 Reading for pleasure.
2 Understanding the background and scene-setting to a story.

Lexis: cabins, chapter, crept, calmed, deck, delicate, emerged, novel, sailors, stewards, rows
Revision: **atmosphere**
Understanding only: **heatless, upturned, seasoned** (= experienced)
Phrases: **with the air of, moderately rough, (moderate winds** T)

Lead-in SB206

1 Explain that up to now in this course, students have had a lot of practice in reading useful texts like correspondence and news reports. Now they have a chance to read for pleasure.

Reading and listening SB206 [206]

2 Students read, then listen to the opening paragraphs and discuss the pictures. Ask them how the weather had changed.

3 Go through the target lexis, seeing which words they can guess from context.

204 Big ships, small ships

a Which picture shows sea that is: moderately rough? reasonably calm? quite smooth? really rough?

b What experience of boats or ships have you had? Are you a good sailor, or do you get seasick?

c Which of these ships might cross a large ocean like the Atlantic?

d What do you think these people do on board ship? What part of the ship would they work in?

Captain Navigating Officer Purser Chief Steward
Deck steward Cabin steward Naval Officer Sailor

204b Listen to Rachel and Chris talking about their experiences of travelling by sea.
Edmund and Bruce do the same. Compare their experiences. Which of the four is probably the worst sailor? What types of ship do they refer to? Are there any that are not in the photographs here?

205 Dictionary skills

Look up the words dip and pool. The two words together form part of the title of a story. What possible meanings could they have in the title?

206 Dip in the pool

Roald Dahl is a famous writer of short stories and novels, many of which have been dramatised for television and translated into other languages. One is included in this book as a ten part serial.
Read the opening paragraphs and see which of the pictures on this page best illustrate them.

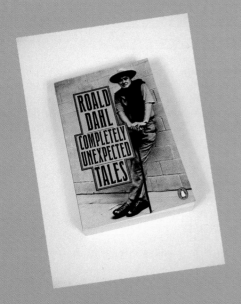

CHAPTER ONE

A CHANGE IN THE WEATHER

On the morning of the third day, the sea calmed. Even the most delicate passengers – those who had not been seen around the ship since sailing time – emerged from their cabins and crept up onto the sun deck where the deck steward gave them chairs and tucked rugs around their legs and left them lying in rows, their faces upturned to the pale, almost heatless January sun.

It had been moderately rough the first two days, and this sudden calm and the sense of comfort that it brought created a more genial atmosphere over the whole ship. By the time evening came, the passengers, with twelve hours of good weather behind them, were beginning to feel confident, and at eight o'clock that night the main dining room was filled with people eating and drinking with the assured, complacent air of seasoned sailors.

206 Now listen to the story being read.

207 # Mr Botibol

Mr Botibol is on his way back home to America, on a British ship . . .

a The missing words are not vital to your understanding of the story. Read the text once to get the general idea of the story.
Later, you could try to guess what kind of words might go in the blanks.

CHAPTER ONE *continued*

The meal was not half over when the passengers became aware, by a slight _____ between their bodies and the seats of their chairs, that the big ship had actually started rolling again. It was very gentle at first, just a slow, lazy leaning to one side then to the other, but it was enough to cause a subtle, immediate change of mood over the whole room. A few of the passengers glanced up from their food, hesitating, waiting, almost listening for the next roll, smiling nervously, _____ _____ _____ _____ in their eyes. Some were completely _____, some were openly _____, a number of the _____ ones making jokes about food and weather in order to _____ the few who were beginning to suffer. The movement of the ship then became rapidly more and more violent, and only five or six minutes after the first roll had been noticed, she was swinging heavily from side to side, the passengers _____ themselves in their chairs, leaning against the pull as in a car cornering.

WORD STUDY
What phrases describing the movement of the ship and the reaction of the passengers can you find? Can you guess (and demonstrate) what they all mean?

b Now answer the questions below.

1 Which points in the story do the pictures illustrate? Write a caption for each picture.

2 Make a list of the characters and try to remember what they each did. How was each of them feeling by the end?

3 Why did the steward sprinkle water on the table?

4 What do you think the last two sentences mean? – 'What I want to know is, will the captain already have made his estimate on the day's run – you know, for the auction pool? I mean before it began to get rough like this?'

207b What do Rachel and Chris, then Bruce and Edmund say in answer to questions 3 and 4?

WORD STUDY
Find these words and guess their meanings.

slight rolling gentle lazy subtle glanced
roll heavily hurrying concealed approval
grave vacant whisper anxious affect

At last the really bad roll came, and Mr. William Botibol, sitting at the purser's table, saw his plate of _____ _____ _____ _____ _____ sliding suddenly away from under his fork. There was a _____ of excitement, everybody reaching for plates and glasses. Mrs. Renshaw, seated at the purser's right, gave a little scream and _____ that gentleman's arm.

'Going to be a dirty night,' the purser said, looking at Mrs. Renshaw. 'I think it's blowing up for a very dirty night.' There was just the faintest suggestion of _____ in the way he said it.

A steward came hurrying up and sprinkled water on the tablecloth between the plates. The excitement _____. Most of the passengers continued with their meal. A small number, including Mrs. Renshaw, got carefully to their feet and _____ _____ _____ with a kind of concealed haste between the tables and through the doorway.

'Well,' the purser said, 'there she goes.' He glanced around with approval at the remainder of his _____ who were sitting quiet, looking _____, their faces reflecting openly that extraordinary pride that travellers seem to take in being recognised as 'good sailors'.

When the eating was finished and the coffee had been served, Mr. Botibol, who had been unusually grave and thoughtful since the rolling started, suddenly stood up and carried his cup of coffee around to Mrs. Renshaw's vacant place, next to the purser. He seated himself in her chair, then immediately leaned over and began to whisper urgently in the purser's ear. 'Excuse me,' he said, 'but could you tell me something please?'

The purser, small and fat and red, bent forward to listen. 'What's the trouble, Mr. Botibol?'

'What I want to know is this.' The man's face was anxious and the purser was watching it. 'What I want to know is, will the captain already have made his estimate on the day's run – you know, for the auction pool? I mean before it began to get rough like this?'

207c **c** Listen to the chapter being read.

> Imagine you were one of the passengers.
> Write an account of the day – either as a letter to a friend, or as a diary entry.

208 # *Language study*

Verbs ending in -ing
The first two paragraphs, in section 206, give us the background to the story. The next two paragraphs on this page set the scene in the dining room for the first part of the action. There are fourteen -ing forms in these two paragraphs. Find:

– two examples of the past continuous tense.
– one -ing form following the verb see.
– one -ing form after start.
– one used as a noun.
– nine other examples.

Why is the -ing form used so much in these paragraphs?

Mr Botibol

Aims: 1 To help students not to worry about words they don't know – to show them they can still understand the story even when quite a few of the words are missing.
2 Inferring meanings from context.
3 Writing informal narrative.

Lexis: affect, anxious, approval, concealed, fork, gentle, glance, grave, heavily, hesitating, hurry, lazy, reflecting, roll, slight, subtle, vacant, whisper
Revision: **competition, faint, mood, scream, swinging, suffer, urgently, violent**
Understanding only: **freshen up*, haste, noon, take pride in** (being a good sailor)
Phrases: **a change of mood, a small number of, the remainder of, a faintest suggestion of, coffee is/had been served, affect the mileage**

Reading SB207a

1 Explain Aim 1 to students. Make sure they know the words **passengers** and **roll**. Remind students of what happened in the first part of this Chapter (section 206) and where the passengers are (in the dining room).

2 Students can read the first paragraph silently, and then try the Word Study.

Key: Movement of ship: rolling, gentle, slow, lazy leaning, to one side then to the other, roll, more and more violent, swinging heavily, from side to side.
Reaction of passengers: became aware, a subtle immediate change of mood, smiling nervously, making jokes, beginning to suffer.

3 Ask students to pick out the words and phrases referring to the passengers (a few, some, a number of the . . . ones, the few who, the whole room (means the people in the room)). Point out the (literary) use of **she** for the ship.

4 Students read on to the end of the chapter, and discuss the story-line. Can students summarise it in two sentences? (For example: It got much rougher and some people felt ill and left the dining room. During coffee, Mr Botibol moved next to the purser and asked him a question.) (The ending is meant to be mysterious, so keep students in suspense.)

Task SB207b

5 Ask students in groups to consider questions 1–4 in turn, and then to skim-read to write the captions and discuss possible answers.

6 Students read out their captions. Discuss these and the answers to 2–4 informally as a class.

Listening SB207b

7 Students listen and compare the answers of Rachel and Chris, and then Bruce and Edmund. Clarify, if necessary, that the captain's 'estimate on the day's run' refers to what distance the captain thinks the ship will travel during the next 24 hours (up to noon the next day). The captain obviously knows the ship's speed, the weather forecast and sea conditions, and thus can calculate accordingly. The exact distance the ship has actually covered is always announced the following day at noon.

8 Word Study: This second box focuses on the target words, some of which students will by now have understood. They should find the words in the story, and practise saying them in phrases.

9 Get students to suggest what meanings might be expressed by the unknown words in the blanks. They are not common enough words for students to learn, but if they can guess the meanings from context, that is excellent practice.

Listening SB207c

10 Students listen once or even twice for enjoyment.

Written report SB207c

11 Students take the details from the story and write a personal account, with added comments. Suggest that they use their imagination to express their own feelings. If they were bad sailors and were frightened of being seasick, they would write very differently from a passenger who enjoyed the rough weather and the empty dining room, feeling proud at being a seasoned traveller!

Language study

Aim: Revision and consolidation of uses of verbs ending in **-ing**, with special reference to narrative use.

SB208 PB208

Students find and classify the words ending in **-ing** in the first two paragraphs of the episode on this page – section 207. (From 'The meal . . .' to 'gentleman's arm'.)

Key: Past continuous: . . . she **was swinging** heavily from side to side . . . the few who **were beginning** to suffer
Following **see**: . . . Bobitol . . . **saw** his plate **sliding**
After **start**: had **started rolling**
Noun: slow, lazy **leaning**
Nine other examples (these are all used like adjectives to *describe* the passengers): **hesitating, waiting,** almost **listening** for the next roll, **smiling** nervously . . . a number of the smug ones **making** jokes . . . the passengers **bracing** themselves in their chairs . . . **leaning** against the pull as in a car **cornering**. Mr William Botibol, **sitting** at the purser's table . . .

*There are a lot of **-ing** forms here because they are used to describe the scene, either as past continuous, telling us what everyone was doing when the action commenced, or in the adjectival form which describes people **hesitating, waiting, smiling** etc. to conjure up in our minds a picture of the scene.*

209 Song

The song is available on the Student's Cassette only.

> **Aims:** 1 To provide some light relief.
> 2 To stimulate explanation and rough translation of theme and content of songs from the students' own country.
> **Lexis: roughly**
> Revision: **bound** (for a place), **miss** (someone), **traditional**
> Understanding only: **Fare you well** (old-fashioned = fareware, hope things go well for you)
> Note: The language in this song is slightly old-fashioned.

Listening   SB209

1 Discuss the picture and listen to (and sing) the song.

2 Ask students how they would explain (to someone who hadn't heard it) what this song is about. (For example: An old traditional song sung by sailors as they set off to sea, to sail back to their own country, saying goodbye and farewell to the people they are leaving.)

Task, planning and report   SB209

3 Students in groups of about four discuss similar themes in songs from their own country/ies. They can choose one or two, and prepare a rough translation/explanation of them to tell the class.

210 Dip in the pool

> **Aims:** 1 Reading more rapidly for general meaning and enjoyment.
> 2 Speculation on the possible interpretation of an obscure sentence.
> 3 Retelling the story from another point of view.
>
> **Lexis: anxious, lowered** (his voice), **patiently, roll, steady himself, straining, sun deck, whisper**
> Revision: **automatically, driving at** (= wanting to know), **estimate**
> Understanding only: **frowning, half-hypnotised look**
> Phrases: **gets any worse/any better, take a lot of trouble, to allow for, a little conference** (= discussion/chat), **It might be worth -ing, Straight from the horse's mouth** (= from the expert)

Reading   SB210a PB210

1 Get students to remind each other of what happened at the end of Chapter One. (It got very rough during dinner and Mr Botibol was asking the purser when the captain would have made his estimate on the ship's run – before it got rough? But we don't know why he is asking this.)

2 Explain the phrase **driving at** (= wanting to ask, but not directly). Students read the chapter silently. Help with any really problematic words. Do students realise 'the old man' (in a middle paragraph) refers to the Captain? The talk about buying numbers will probably mystify most students. Get them to speculate on what it could mean, to prepare for hearing Bruce and Edmund giving a clear explanation of this later on tape. Don't explain anything yet.

   Key: Mr Botibol wanted to know which number he should buy, and which number might be the winning one.

3 Ask students why Mr Botibol was whispering. And what did he want the purser to tell him?

   Key: He wanted to be told what number might win, i.e. which number to buy in the auction. And perhaps he didn't want other people to hear the number in case they wanted to buy the same one.

Listening   SB210b

4 Let students hear the story being read.

5 Ask students to discuss questions 1 and 2. Discuss what they think, but give no right answers yet.

Listening   SB210c

6 Students hear Rachel and Chris's, and then Bruce and Edmund's answers to the same questions. (Bruce and Edmund's are more helpful. Students may like to read the transcripts to clarify things.)

Report   SB210c

7 Remind students that the purser must have done many journeys on this ship and met many passengers who wanted inside knowledge on the ship's run. The crew probably gossip about the passengers at their table. What might the purser have said? Students could work on this informally in groups, and then act it out to each other.

   Sample: Well, Mrs Renshaw didn't stay long (thank goodness!) She must have been feeling ill, what with the weather getting so rough again! Anyway, during coffee, Mr Botibol came and sat by me, and was trying to get me to tell him what number to buy in the auction. Same old thing – desperate to win! Wanted to know if the Captain had already made his estimate before this storm – would he be better off buying low numbers. I finally had to tell him they don't announce the range till the auction starts. And when I said I wasn't any good at it anyway, he got up and left! I wonder what he'll do. Poor chap!

211 Mystery recording

> **Aims:** 1 To set the scene for talking about predicting weather, especially bad weather and storms at sea.
> 2 Understanding key words in a broadcast weather forecast.

Listening   SB211

1 Students may need help to identify this as a weather forecast. If so, give them a number of key words one by one (e.g. **showers, breeze, temperatures, frosty, ice**) asking them after each word what they think the recording will be about. Once they have focused on the idea of weather, play the recording as far as '. . . ice in many areas'.

2 Gather as many words as you can from them about the weather. When you play the rest of the recording, ask one group of students to listen to statements about the south of England and others to listen to reports about the north. Explain that the report was given on a Thursday. Ask them if the weather will be good or bad in their part (north or south) on Thursday night, Friday and Saturday. If you want you can play through the recording again and ask them when there will be rain, sleet and snow.

Report   SB211

3 Students in groups could write a very short weather forecast for the sea area Mr Botibol's ship is in. They should practise reading it out loud.

4 Preferably, get each group to record their forecast. Play the forecasts back to the class. Later in the story, students will find out whose weather forecast was the nearest to what happened in the story.

83T

209 Song

209 The Yetties sing a traditional song about the sea called *Homeward Bound*.

> Think of a song about the sea, or a journey, or missing someone, in your language. Explain it or translate it quickly so the others can understand roughly what it means.

210 Dip in the pool

a Read and find out what Mr Botibol is really driving at. In other words, what does he want the purser to tell him? Don't worry about any words you don't know.

CHAPTER TWO

IF THIS GETS ANY WORSE...

The purser, who had prepared himself to receive a personal confidence, smiled and leaned back in his seat to relax his full belly. 'I should say so – yes,' he answered. He didn't bother to whisper his reply, although automatically he lowered his voice, as one does when answering a whisperer.

'About how long ago do you think he did it?'

'Sometime this afternoon. He usually does it in the afternoon.'

'About what time?'

'Oh, I don't know. Around four o'clock I should guess.'

'Now tell me another thing. How does the captain decide which number it shall be? Does he take a lot of trouble over that?'

The purser looked at the anxious frowning face of Mr. Botibol and he smiled, knowing quite well what the man was driving at. 'Well, you see, the captain has a little conference with the navigating officer, and they study the weather and a lot of other things, and then they make their estimate.'

Mr. Botibol nodded, pondering this answer for a moment. Then he said, 'Do you think the captain knew there was bad weather coming today?'

'I couldn't tell you,' the purser replied. He was looking into the small black eyes of the other man, seeing the two single little sparks of excitement dancing in their centres. 'I really couldn't tell you, Mr. Botibol. I wouldn't know.'

'If this gets any worse it might be worth buying some of the low numbers. What do you think?' The whispering was more urgent, more anxious now.

'Perhaps it will,' the purser said. 'I doubt the old man allowed for a really rough night. It was pretty calm this afternoon when he made his estimate.'

The others at the table had become silent and were trying to hear, watching the purser with that intent, half-cocked, listening look that you can see also at the race track when they are trying to overhear a trainer talking about his chance: the slightly open lips, the upstretched eyebrows, the head forward and cocked a little to one side – that desperately straining, half-hypnotized, listening look that comes to all of them when they are hearing something straight from the horse's mouth.

'Now suppose you were allowed to buy a number, which one would you choose today?' Mr. Botibol whispered.

'I don't know what the range is yet,' the purser patiently answered. 'They don't announce the range till the auction starts after dinner. And I'm really not very good at it anyway. I'm only the purser, you know.'

At that point Mr. Botibol stood up. 'Excuse me, all,' he said, and he walked carefully away over the swaying floor between the other tables, and twice he had to catch hold of the back of a chair to steady himself against the ship's roll.

'The sun deck, please,' he said to the elevator man.

210b **b** Listen to it being read.

1 What do you think the purser means when he says 'They don't announce the range till the auction starts after dinner.'

2 Why is Mr. Botibol so concerned about the weather? Why do you think he wants to go out on the sun deck?

210c **c** Whose explanations are the most helpful, Rachel and Chris's or Bruce and Edmund's?

> Tell the story of what happened over dinner as the purser might tell it to another member of the crew.

211 Mystery recording

211 You might hear this on the radio. What is it? Listen carefully and write down the key words. As a class, compare the words you wrote down.

212 Grammar

Adverbs

a Some adverbs are used to modify adjectives:

It had been moderately rough the first two days . . . (206)
Some were completely unruffled, some were openly smug . . . (207)

Put the adverbs in the right place in these sentences:

Mr. Botibol . . . had been grave and thoughtful since the rolling started . . . (207) unusually
I doubt the old man allowed for a rough night. (210) really
It was calm this afternoon when he made his estimate. (210) pretty
I think that anybody who thumps the dog has to be stupid. (59) pretty

b Some adverbs are used to modify verbs:

A few of the passengers glanced up, smiling nervously.
The movement . . . became rapidly more and more violent.

Put these adverbs back in their sentences:

She was swinging from side to side . . . (207) heavily
He saw his plate . . . sliding away . . . (207) suddenly
Mr. Botibol . . . stood up and carried his cup of coffee round to Mrs. Renshaw's vacant place . . . (207) suddenly
He does it in the afternoon. (210) usually
'I don't know what the range is yet,' the purser answered. (210) patiently
. . . he walked away over the swaying floor. (210) carefully
The great ship was moving. (228) fast
It had killed a little girl. (114) previously
. . . he came out on deck . . . (234) cautiously

213 For sale by auction

FREEHOLD HOUSE Vacant
AUCTION SALE
18th/19th/20th JULY 1988
barnard marcus
01 602 6111

What's happening here?

Arrange sentences c–h to continue the instructions and advice about how to buy something in an auction:

a You begin by selecting what you want to buy, and check what number it is. (There is usually a catalogue of items for sale.)
b Decide beforehand what your top price would be, i.e. what it's worth to you, and, if you open the bidding, what price you would start at.
c Bid – by calling out, nodding your head or waving your programme.
d Write out a cheque and give it to the auctioneer's assistant who will take down your details.
e Wait until your number comes up.
f If everyone stops bidding before you, the auctioneer says 'Going . . . Going . . . Gone for £x to the lady/gentleman with the . . .' and bangs his hammer.
g Tell him whether or not you want it delivered.
h If other people continue bidding and the price goes up, don't be tempted to go over your top price.

Think of something you have bought, but not in a shop, for example second-hand from an advert, from a catalogue, or a market. Explain precisely how you bought it (did you bargain? test it?). Write advice for someone thinking of buying something in a similar way.

214 REVIEW

UNIT 20

a Words beginning with sea-
Choose the correct word(s) to complete each sentence.

seasick   seaside   seabed   seashells
seamen   seagulls   seashore
sea level   seafood   seaweed

e.g. She sells *seashells* on the *seashore*.
(Try saying this quickly!)

1 *It's at 5000 feet above _____.*
2 *A member of the National Union of _____.*
3 *The journey was ghastly – I was so _____.*
4 *Eating _____ reminds me of lazy holidays by the sea.*
5 *Our boat was followed by a whole flock of _____.*
6 *Looking below the surface, you could see fish, half concealed by the _____, and crabs creeping along the _____.*
7 *The tide had turned, and the waves were breaking gently on the _____.*
8 *The few remaining swimmers left the beach and gathered in the _____ café.*

b Odd word out?
Which word in each set means something entirely different?

1 *He had a _____ look on his face.*
grave   anxious   worried   serious   ridiculous   strained
2 *Are any of the changing rooms _____?*
vacant   empty   occupied   free   not in use
3 *I hope the sea crossing will be nice and _____!*
smooth   steady   calm   rough
4 *Didn't he join the _____?*
sailors   army   navy   airforce
5 *Sssh. Be quiet, don't _____ again!*
shout   scream   whisper   call out
6 *The fish lay still, _____ between the rocks.*
hidden   concealed   impossible to see   exposed
7 *The divers put their masks on and all _____, out of sight.*
sank   went under   floated   swam underwater
8 *The captain emerged from his cabin and _____ around.*
looked quickly   glanced   hurried   took a brief look
9 *The colours she chose were really _____ and met with approval.*
ghastly   subtle   delicate   gentle

NEW WORDS IN UNIT 20

affect
anxiety
anxious
approval
auction
cabin
calm
chapter
coloured
concealed
creep/crept
deck
delicate
dip D
emerge
float
forecast
ghastly
glance
grave
heavily
hesitate
hurry
lazy
lower

moderate
moderately
naval
navy
novel
patient/ly
pool D
raw
remaining
roll
roughly
sailor
shell
shore
slight
smooth
steady
steward
strain
subtle
surface
thoughtful
tide
vague
whisper

50 new words
TOTAL SO FAR 828

Grammar

Aim: To focus on adverbs modifying adjectives and verbs.

SB212a/b

Key: a unusually grave (it could also start the sentence, and be more general), really rough, pretty calm, pretty stupid (**pretty** here means 'quite a lot', nearly the same as **very**)
b swinging heavily, suddenly saw/ sliding, suddenly stood up, usually does, answered patiently, carefully walked/ walked carefully, moving fast, previously killed, Cautiously he/He came cautiously

---

213 For sale by auction

Aims: 1 Explaining a sequence of informal instructions, with advice.
2 To stimulate discussion about buying and selling things (not in a shop).
3 To prepare students for the next chapters of *Dip in the pool*.

Class discussion and reading   SB213

1 Discuss what is happening in the big photograph. Ask if any of your class have ever been to an auction of any kind. (This one is a famous Art Auction at Sotheby's.) If more than one student has, divide students into groups so you have one 'auction expert' in each group. Other students can interview him/her to find out what the procedure is, and what this person bought.

2 Explain any difficult vocabulary in the sentences. Students read them and decide on the best order. Discuss their choices.

   Key: a b e c h f d g

3 In Britain, you can buy pictures, furniture, antiques, farm animals, farm machinery, old cars, and occasionally land and houses, by auction. Ask students about their countries.

Writing   SB213

4 Help students choose something (it could even be a house or a car, or an animal) to write about. At the planning stage, encourage them to read, comment on and 'edit' each other's work. Finally they can exchange advice, and discuss whose advice was the best.

Review

Key:
a 1 sea level 2 Seamen 3 seasick 4 seafood 5 seagulls 6 seaweed, seabed 7 sea shore 8 seaside
Note: Point out new target words: **shell**, **tide**, **remaining**.
b 1 ridiculous 2 occupied 3 rough 4 sailors 5 whisper 6 exposed 7 floated 8 hurried 9 ghastly

LEXICAL OBJECTIVES

affect cause something to change. *rough weather could affect the mileage*
anxiety T nervousness. *his anxiety over the weather.*
anxious 1 nervous, worried. *the anxious frowning face of Mr Botibol.*
2 T to want to. *anxious to go abroad.*
approval 1 T agreement. *the decision met with the committee's approval.*
2 admiration. *he glanced around with approval at the rest of his flock.*
auction sale where goods are sold to the person who offers the highest price.
cabin small room on a ship.
calm 1 T not worried or excited. *Keep calm, don't panic.*
2 state of peacefulness. *this sudden calm and sense of comfort . . . created a more genial atmosphere.*
3 calm sea or weather without wind, not rough. *It was pretty calm . . .*
chapter section of a novel or story.
coloured 1 not just black or white. *Pool is a game using coloured balls.*
2 T if you are coloured you belong to a race who do not have pale skins.
concealed 1 T hidden from sight.
2 kept secret, not letting others know. *a kind of concealed haste.*
creep, crept 1 move quietly and slowly. *passengers emerged from their cabins and crept up on to the sundeck.*
deck 1 top part of a ship that forms a floor in the open air. *the sun deck.*
delicate EED 1–4 T a delicate smell/ movement/hint/situation
5 of a person – not strong, often ill. *Even the most delicate passengers . . .*
dip D
emerge EED 1 come out from a place, a situation or experience. *passengers emerged from their cabins.*
2 T to become known. *It emerged that . . .*
3 T emergence of new ideas
float T lie on the surface of a liquid, not sinking below.
forecast *weather forecast*
ghastly very unpleasant. *It was ghastly*
glance look quickly. *He glanced around.*
2 T recognise immediately. *You can see at a glance that they're good friends.*
grave 1 T where a dead person is buried. *flowers on the grave.*
2 T serious. *a grave mistake.*
3 quiet and serious. *Mr Botibol, who had been grave and thoughtful . . .*

heavily EED 1 T in great quantity.
2 solidly. T *heavily built.*
3 move with force. *the ship was swinging heavily from side to side . . .*
hesitate 1 pause slightly. *glanced up from their food, hesitating, waiting . . .*
2 T be unwilling to. *I'd hesitate to say*
lazy 1 T not wanting to work.
2 T without effort. *gave a lazy smile.*
3 slow, gentle movement. *a slow, lazy leaning to one side then to the other*
lower 1 T move downward. *lowered his eyes. Lower the lifeboats.*
2 make less, reduce. *lowered his voice.*
moderate T 1 not extreme. *moderate views; moderate behaviour/winds.*
2 verb: *the bad weather had moderated*
moderately fairly. *moderately rough*
naval T *naval officer, naval base.*
navy 1 military force which fights at sea.
2 T *navy blue* is dark blue.
novel 1 story. *novel by Roald Dahl.*
2 T new, not done before. *a novel idea*
patient/ly calm, without annoyance. *. . . the purser patiently answered.*
pool D
raw 1 uncooked food, substances. *raw vegetables for a party dip.*
remaining left over, still existing. *the few remaining swimmers.*
roll EED 1 T *the ball rolled under the car.*
2 T *Roll up your trousers.*
3 *The big ship started to roll again.*
4 a bread roll = small loaf of bread.
roughly 1 T without gentleness.
2 approximately. *roughly translated*
sailor 1 person who works on a ship. Also – a good sailor is someone who does not get sea-sick at all.
shell 1 sea-shell, eggshell, nutshell.
2 T explosive shells fired from a gun
shore 1 land by a sea, lake etc. *Waves going away from the shore*
2 on shore = on land rather than on board ship. *telephone shore, go ashore*
slight 1 small in degree or quantity. *a slight friction between their bodies.*
2 T slim. *He's slightly built.*
smooth EED 1 T not rough or lumpy. *a smooth surface.*
3 even, steady, comfortable. *hovercraft . . . is OK if it's smooth.*
steady EED 1 T without interruption. *a steady rise in prices.*
2 T *Hold it steady.*
3 stop something moving. *He had to hold the back of a chair to steady himself against the ship's roll.*
steward man who looks after passengers *the deck steward.*
strain EED 1 T force or pressure. *the bridge cracked under the strain . . .*
2 T nervous strain, anxiety.
3 making a great effort. *desperately straining, half-hypnotised look.*
subtle 1 faint, not noticeable. *a subtle change of mood.*
surface 1 outside or top part of something. *surface of the sea/road.*
thoughtful *grave and thoughtful*
tide 1 regular change in level of the sea. *I'll take a dip before the tide comes in.*
2 T *the tide of fashion etc.*
vacant 1 empty, available. *Mrs Renshaw's vacant place.*
whisper talk very quietly. *began to whisper urgently in the purser's ear.*

Unit 21 Family relationships – past and present

This unit begins with a discussion of life in an earlier generation and of family relationships. In Chapter Three of Dip in the pool, *Mr Botibol is considering a present for his wife Ethel. A song by The Yetties picks up the theme of grandparents and family life in an earlier generation. Chapter Four of the story, the beginning of the auction, provides practice in summarising, and the reading of the story focuses attention on stress and intonation.*

OBJECTIVES

Lexical objectives are in TB222

Discussion topics

a Old times and family stories. (215)
b Parents and grandparents. (215,219)
c Family relationships – the effect of absences. (216)

Social skills

a Talking about old times. (215)
b Telling family stories. (215)
c Comparing old times and modern times. (215)

Communication skills

a Talking and writing about differences and contrast. (215,219)
b Finding out and writing about a personality. (215,219)
c Following a narrative. (217,221)
d Inferring meaning from context. (217)

Grammar and discourse

a **Would** and other ways of expressing the future in the past. (218)
b Conjunctions expressing addition, contrast, time, result, cause, and condition relationships. (220)
c Practice Book Grammar Word: **with**.

Dictionary skills

Identifying the meanings of conjunctions. (220)

215 In the old days

Aims: 1 Talking about old times.
2 Telling family stories.
3 Comparing old times and modern times.
4 Identifying and talking about differences and contrast.

Lexis: ancestors, conscious of, space
Revision: **(space) shots, consciousness**
Understanding only: **incredulous**
Phrases: **making up for years of . . ., make own amusements up** (two different uses of **make up**),
If only I'd had . . .

Lead-in SB215a PB215

1 Give students time to write down the names and details of any of their ancestors. They can then tell each other about them.

Task, planning and report SB215a

2 Students make lists of differences in pairs. (For example, in the old days, nothing was made of plastic. There were no fast food restaurants.) Pass their lists round the class for others to read and comment on.

3 Ask students what they think the main differences are.

Planning and report SB215a

4 Ask whether students would rather have lived fifty years ago. Take notes of all their ideas on the board, correcting any inaccuracies.

5 Get students to walk around to find other people with similar ideas, and then sit with them to write a paragraph.

6 Students read each other's paragraphs and find one like their own.

Reading SB215a

7 Students read the story and react in groups. Can they guess the words they don't know?

Listening and report SB215b 215b

8 Ask students to listen for three main points.

   Key: 'all we had was the radio', 'make our own amusements' i.e. no television; things they didn't have, i.e. advantages of being young today; education.

9 Ask students in groups to do the same as Elizabeth and Rachel, making lists of things their parents used to tell them about the old days. Then they can choose some aspects and tell the class.

Writing SB215c

10 Help students to draft their ideas about an old person. Students exchange their work and read each other's to find a piece about a similar person.

216 Bonny and family

Aim: To talk and write about the effect of absences on family relationships.

Lexis: bother, colloquial, routine
Revision: **fair enough, get used to me + -ing**
Understanding only: (all colloquial) **had a whale of a time, mates** (= friends), **piled** (= rushed/poured into)

Task, planning and report SB216

1 Students in groups exchange experiences of family members travelling or being away, e.g. on business. They prepare to tell the class the main things.

2 Students listen to find someone who has had a similar experience to themselves.

Listening SB216 216

The photograph shows Yetminster Primary School.

3 Students listen to Bonny Sartin (of the Yetties) talking about trips away from home and family. Suggest students take brief notes in answer to the questions.

4 Do the Word Study. Phrases 1–7 contain useful words. Encourage students to read and repeat the phrases as they look them up in the transcripts to see who said them.

   Key: 1,3,5,6,7 – Bonny. 2,4 – Elizabeth.

Writing and report SB216

5 'Travel' here means people going away from home, for example on business, or to visit distant relations. Students write their pieces individually. Help if needed.

6 Students could exchange pieces with someone they don't know very well, and 'edit' each other's. Suggest they write questions about any point they find interesting, for their partner to answer.

Unit 21
Family relationships — past and present

---

215 | In the old days

a What do you know about your ancestors? What did your grandparents or parents tell you about the old days?

Write down five striking differences between those days and the world of today. Compare lists.

Would you rather have been born and lived fifty years earlier? Write a paragraph giving reasons for your opinion.

A FATHER was discussing life with his nine-year-old son and the talk turned to the olden days, in the late 1930s, when Dad was young. The son was incredulous that his father could have enjoyed life way back there during the Dark Ages when there were no TV dinners, pizza pies, transistor radios, space shots or color television.

"You know, Dad," he mused, "when I think of you as a little boy, I always think of you in black and white."

Fun & Laughter.

---

dark age, dark ages. 1 A **dark age** is a period in which there is a lack of culture and progress in a society and people are ignorant. EG *We may be entering a new dark age.* 2 The **Dark Ages** are the period of European history between about 500 A.D. and about 1000 A.D.

215b **b** Elizabeth told Rachel about her parents. Did your parents say similar things to you? Can you give an example?

c Choose one old person you know or used to know well. Write what you can remember about the things they used to say and do. Exchange pieces. Try to find another piece about a person who is similar to the person you wrote about.

---

216 | Bonny and family

Have you or any of your family had to be away from each other for any length of time? Describe what happened and why it came about.

Travelling makes big demands on family life and can affect relationships.

216 We talked to Bonny about this. He talked first about short trips, then about longer trips. How did his boys react to his going off on tour? What about his wife?

WORD STUDY
Can you remember who in recording 215b and 216, said these and in what context?

1 I think they've got used to it.
2 … very conscious of not having television …
3 … and didn't bother to say goodbye …
4 … it's not fair, I didn't have that.
5 Oh well. Fair enough then. Be like that.
6 … gets into a routine …
7 … you break that routine …

Colloquial expressions
Guess what Bonny meant by these phrases. Can you write them in more formal English?

8 … get used to me breezing in and out all the time.
9 … tremendous party … We had a whale of a time
10 … and he saw his mates, piled into the playground …

Who in your family travels or has travelled most? Do you know anyone else who travels a lot?

Write a short piece explaining where they went, what for, and how long for. Also describe the effect it had on the family left behind.

85

217 Dip in the pool

a What meaning?
Can you work out the meanings of the words or phrases that were originally in the numbered spaces? Then guess the actual words and phrases.

217a Did you get the same words as Chris and Rachel guessed?
Write the words Edmund and Bruce guessed. Which are the best?

CHAPTER THREE
PRESENT FOR A WIFE?

The wind caught him full in the face as he stepped out onto the _____1_____. He staggered and _____2_____ ____ the rail and held on tight with both hands, and he stood there looking out over the darkening sea where the great waves were welling up high and white horses were riding against the wind with plumes of spray behind them as they went.

'_____3_____ out there, wasn't it, sir?' the elevator man said on the way down.

Mr. Botibol was combing his hair back into place with a small red comb. 'Do you think we've _____4_____ at all on account of the weather?' he asked.

'Oh my word yes, Sir. We slackened off considerable since this started. You got to slacken off speed in weather like this or you'll be throwing the passengers all over the ship.'

Down in the smoking room people were already gathering for the auction. They were grouping themselves politely around the various tables, the men a little stiff in their dinner jackets, a little pink and overshaved and stiff beside their cool, white-armed women. Mr. Botibol took a chair close to the auctioneer's table. He _____ _____5_____, folded his arms, and settled himself in his seat with the rather desperate air of a man who has made a tremendous decision and refuses to be frightened.

---

b Read and find out how Mr. Botibol hopes to get seven thousand dollars.
What one single word will fit all the spaces in the next part?

The pool, he was telling himself, _____ probably be around seven thousand dollars. That was almost exactly what it had been the last two days with the numbers selling for between three and four hundred apiece. Being a British ship they did it in pounds, but he liked to do his thinking in his own currency. Seven thousand dollars was plenty of money. My goodness yes! And what he _____ do he _____ get them to pay him in hundred dollar bills and he _____ take it ashore in the inside pocket of his jacket. No problem there. And right away, yes right away, he _____ buy a Lincoln convertible. He _____ pick it up on the way from the ship and drive it home just for the pleasure of seeing Ethel's face when she came out the front door and looked at it. _____n't that be something, to see Ethel's face when he glided up to the door in a brand-new pale-green Lincoln convertible! Hello Ethel honey, he _____ say, speaking very casual. I just thought I'd get you a little present. I saw it in the window as I went by, so I thought of you and how you were always wanting one. You like it, honey? he _____ say. You like the colour? And then he _____ watch her face.

Now can you work out when you think this story took place: 1929? 1952? 1971? 1987?

217b Take notes on how the others answered the same questions. Compare your answers.

217c **c** Listen to the chapter being read. Did the words you chose have the same meanings as the original ones? Use a dictionary to find out.

---

218 *Grammar* •••

Future in the past
Now see how **would** is used in these sentences:

The pool... **would** probably be around seven thousand dollars.
And right away... he **would** buy a Lincoln convertible.
He **would** pick it up on the way from the ship.

The story is set in the past. But Mr. Botibol is thinking about the future. Would is often used when people in the past are described talking or thinking about the future.

Now look at these sentences. How many other ways can you find of expressing the future in the past?

1 *What were you going to do for instruments?* (100)
2 *As his case was about to be called he realised his parking metre was running out.* (104)

3 *It stopped at Cairo, and Delhi. It was going on to Bangkok.* (100)
4 *The gas board assured Mrs. Bradbrook there would be no further delay.* (102)
5 *What I was prepared to do was to throw the hurricane lamp on the ground.* (110)
6 *The director was planning to film an emotional epilogue.* (118)
7 *No-one really seemed to know what we were supposed to do.* (137)
8 *Yeah. Just what I was going to say!* (166)
9 *And I thought, this is going to be terrible. You know, that I really was going to miss them, and I did. And I thought that they would probably feel the same.* (214)

Write about two things that you were hoping to do but never did.

Dip in the pool

Aims: 1 Understanding narrative.
2 Inferring meaning from context.
3 Understanding the hypothetical meaning of **would**.
(don't explain this to students beforehand.)

Lexis: comb, convertible, (**convert** T), **currency, horse, rail, spray, stepped, stiff**
Revision: **casual/ly, considerably, gathering, refuses to be, sir, right away, terrible**
Understanding only: **apiece** (= each), **brand-new, elevator** (American for **lift**), **slackened speed** (= slowed down). A **Lincoln convertible** is a really smart car. **kitty** ts (= pool of money)
Phrases: **white horses** (= white topped waves), **on account of** (= due to/because of), **Oh my word, yes! My Goodness yes.**

Reading SB217a PB217

1 Ask students to remind each other about what happened last. (Mr Botibol has just left the dining room to take the lift up to the sun deck – possibly to see if the bad weather is likely to continue, so he can decide which number to buy in the auction.)

2 Students read the first half quickly, and then read it again (perhaps in pairs) and guess the meanings of the missing words – either two or three for each blank. (It doesn't matter if they don't get the actual words, so long as they have the general meaning of the whole sentence.) The pictures of the rough sea will help with the first paragraph.

3 Can students guess that 'slackened off speed' means going more slowly, reducing speed? (This will have the effect of reducing the number of miles covered in one day, so a low number might win, since the Captain's estimate of mileage was made when the weather was good, and the speed faster.)

Listening SB217a

4 Students listen and write down what words the four thought of. Exploit the useful lexical sets (for example: **terrible, fierce, awful, ghastly/pretty rough, very windy; grabbed, took hold of, got hold of**). Students compare with their own choices, and select the best.

Optional listening SB217c

5 This really comes later, but you could play just the first part of the recording at this point, so that students can listen and hear what words were originally used, while the memory of the text is still fresh in their minds.

Reading SB217b

6 Read the first sentence with students and ask them which use of the word **pool** this must be (a pool of money collected together). Students read the two questions first, and then read the story.

7 Give students time to discuss answers, and then consider the date question. Discuss these as a class.

Listening SB217b

8 Students listen to both pairs of native-speakers, take notes, and then discuss their ideas. The explanations should be quite helpful to students.

Listening SB217c

9 The whole chapter is read aloud. Encourage students to read along while listening.

Key: Part a: 1 open deck 2 grabbed hold of 3 pretty bad 4 slackened speed 5 crossed his legs
Part b: would
He would get $7000 from winning the auction pool, based on the previous two days.
Written in 1952. You can tell by the rate of the pound against the dollar – the price for a smart car (the Lincoln convertible).

Grammar

Aim: To revise **would** and draw together other ways of expressing the future in the past.

SB218 PB218

1 Help students with the explanation if necessary.

2 Then help them remember the contexts of the sentences. For example, when the Yetties' instruments got lost, they didn't know if they would arrive or not, and somebody later asked them 'what were you doing to . . .'. (The whole story is about the past, but this is referring to the future in the past.)

A 'time line' may help:

```
                    V                      V
PAST ———————————————————————————————— >> FUTURE
         story      future in     present
         here       past          (you now)
```

Key: 1 were you going to 2 was about to 3 was going 4 would 5 was prepared to 6 was planning to 7 were supposed to 8 was going to 9 thought this is going to, really was going to, would feel. (Note the thought 'this is going . . .' is like direct speech/thought.)

Samples: I was always planning to learn Spanish, but never did. I was hoping to go to university . . . I had always intended to . . . When I was a child I thought I would . . . My parents said I would . . .

219 My grandfather's clock

Aims: 1 Light relief.
2 To stimulate comment and talk about grandfathers (and/or grandmothers).
3 To explore the possible logical relationships between the clauses and an initial revision of conjunctions.

Lexis: alarm, bride, (**bridegroom** T), **chart, departure, grandfather/mother/parents, grief, pride, shelf, silent/ly, soul** T, **spirit,** (**spiritual** T), **treasure**
Revision: **joy**
Understanding only: **dumb** (deaf and dumb), **slumber** (= sleep), **life seconds** (= seconds of his life)
Phrases: **stopped short, kept the time, in the dead of the night** (= in the middle of)

SB219

1 This song is sung by the Yetties. Students can read what Bonny wrote about it.

Listening SB219a [219a]

2 Ideally, play the song early on, telling students not to worry about the missing words. The words and the way it is sung will help students to understand the basic story.

3 Ask students what was strange about this clock. (It seems human; it seems to share his feelings and know what's happening to him, changing the way it strikes according to the occasion.)

4 Students discuss what words could fill the blanks. To do this they will have to explore the possible logical relationships between the clauses. There are several possibilities for some of them. Get students to make a list of possible conjunctions in order. (They will need this for section 220.) Deal with the target lexis as you go through.

5 Play the song again, so they can hear which words are used.

Key: (Point out that other words may fit equally well – see next section.) So, Though, But, When; But; And When, For, But, When; But, when; And, As, But, When; But, When.

Task, planning and report   SB219b

6 Students interview someone in the class, and take notes about their grandparents. For example, where they lived, size of family, what work they did, their personalities, how they travelled . . . If they don't remember them or don't want to talk about them for personal reasons, any other elderly person they know will be suitable.

7 They organise and write what they have found out, drawing comparisons with people in their own family.

8 After finishing a first draft, they can give it to the person whose grandparents it is about, to check both for accuracy of factual detail and language. Be prepared to help if you are needed.

9 Students write a final draft. They can display these on the wall.

220 Language study

Aims: 1 To recycle and consolidate conjunctions, and the relationships they may express.
2 To remind students that some have more than one possible meaning.

SB220a PB220

1 Students copy the table allowing plenty of space in each column. They first use the list of conjunctions they prepared when reading the song in section 219, and discuss which column they should go in. Explain that the column headings are only intended to give a broad general area of meaning, hence **though** and later **despite** will fit into the contrast column (**despite** = in contrast to what I said thought . . .).

Key: Meaning 'and'; (**and**)
Meaning 'but'; **though**, (**but**)
Meaning 'when'; (**when**), **as**
Result: **so**
Cause/reason: **for**
Condition: –

2 Students now read and discuss the next two sets of conjunctions. They could use dictionaries to check meanings and uses of any conjunctions they are not sure about, so that they can write them in the appropriate columns.

Strictly speaking, in some of these meanings (especially the 'time' column), some words are not always used as conjunctions, but as adverbs, or prepositions. However, do not worry students with this now. They need only to get a general picture of the potential of each word at this stage.

Key: Meaning 'and'; **in addition, moreover, what's more**
Meaning 'but': **though, although, on the other hand, however, whereas, while, yet, despite, in spite of, even though**
Meaning 'when' (time): **as, since, while, yet, now** (**that**)
Result: **so, therefore, thus, now that, otherwise, or else**
Cause/reason: **for, because, since, considering that, seeing that, given that, what with**
Condition: **in case, unless, provided that, so long as, given that, assuming, considering that, otherwise, whether or not**

3 Optional: Students could write down any useful examples given in the dictionary for some of these, and read them to each other afterwards. This gives added exposure and more chance to discuss meanings.

SB220b

4 Explain that very often the relationship between sentences or clauses is not signalled by a conjunction. This can make reading quite difficult.

5 Students discuss how to change sentences 1–3. Point out that adding a conjunction can make them easier to understand. They could write out the sentences using a conjunction from above.

Sample: 1 Because/Since/As/Seeing that/Given that it was a British ship, they . . . *or* It was a British ship and so they . . ./as a result of which they . . .
2 If/Assuming/Provided that he got them to pay him . . . he would take it ashore . . . So/Therefore there would be no problem there.
3 And sometimes, when you come home/on coming home . . .

My grandfather's clock

Bonny: This song was very popular in the 20s and 30s. If there had been a pop chart in those days then it would have appeared in them regularly over a long period.

a Read the words of the song. There's a word missing at the beginning of some of the lines. Can you work out what each one could be?

My Grandfather's clock was too large for the shelf
_____ it stood ninety years on the floor
It was taller by half than the old man himself
_____ it weighed not a pennyweight more
It was bought on the morn of the day that he was born
It was always his treasure and pride
_____ it stopped, short, never to go again
_____ the old man died.

Ninety years without slumbering tick tock, tick tock
His life seconds numbering tick tock, tick tock
_____ it stopped short never to go again when the old man died.

In watching its pendulum swing to and fro
Many hours he had spent while a boy
_____ in childhood and manhood the clock seemed to know
_____ to share both his grief and his joy
_____ it struck twenty four when he entered in the door
With a blooming and beautiful bride
_____ it stopped short never to go again
_____ the old man died.

Ninety years without slumbering tick tock, tick tock
His life seconds numbering tick tock, tick tock
_____ it stopped short never to go again
_____ the old man died.

It rang an alarm in the dead of the night
An alarm that for years had been dumb
_____ we knew that his spirit was pluming for flight
That his hour of departure had come
Still the clock kept its time with a soft and muffled chime
_____ we silently stood by his side
_____ it stopped short never to go again
_____ the old man died.

Ninety years without slumbering tick tock, tick tock
His life seconds numbering tick tock, tick tock
_____ it stopped short never to go again
_____ the old man died.

Henry C. Work

---

220 *Language study*

Uses of conjunctions

a Look at the words missing from the song. They are all conjunctions. They link two phrases, clauses or sentences and help to express or signal the relationship between them.

Which column would each one fit in?

meaning 'and' (additional)	meaning 'but' (contrast)	meaning 'when' (time)	to express result	cause or reason	condition

How many columns could **and** and **as** fit in?

b Look at these. Which column(s) could they fit in?

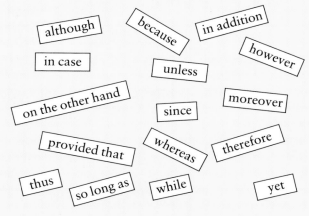

although   because   in addition
in case   unless   however
on the other hand   since   moreover
provided that   whereas   therefore
thus   so long as   while   yet

What about these?

assuming
considering that
despite   even though

219a

As   And   But   For   So   Though   When

b Find out anything you can about your partners' grandparents. Write about them. If you can, compare them with your own grandparents.

otherwise   in spite of   now that
seeing that   what with…   given that   what's more…
or else   whether or not…

Use a dictionary to help you.

c Sometimes – in fact very often – we don't use conjunctions at all. We leave others to infer the relationship. For example:

Being a doctor, she's on call every other week-end. She can never be too far away from a phone.
= As/Because/Since she's a doctor, …
= So she can never be too far …
OR And/As a result she can never be too far …

What conjunction could the writer or speaker have used in these sentences? (Change the sentences accordingly.)

1 Being a British ship, they did it in pounds, …
2 … get them to pay him in hundred dollar bills and he would take it ashore in the inside pocket of his jacket. No problem there.
3 And sometimes, coming home, you break that routine …

221 # Dip in the pool

a Spot the two extra sentences
Someone wrote a summary of this chapter, then
two sentences were added that didn't belong.
Read the summary first, then the story. Now can
you spot the two extra sentences in the summary?

> The auctioneer announced the captain's estimate, 515 miles, Mr Botibol was
> very pleased. He explained that the range was from 505 to 525 and that other
> mileages would come under 'low field' or 'high field'. The first four numbers
> went for about £110 each. When the low field was called Mr. Botibol knew
> that it would fetch a high price because the weather was so bad. He wanted to
> buy number 525. He was prepared to bid up to £200 but decided to wait for
> others to bid first.

b What is the auctioneer auctioning? What do you
think the 'high field' and 'low field' are?

▶ Tell each other your answers to the questions. ◀

221b Whose answers are the clearest, Edmund's and
Bruce's or Chris and Rachel's?

221c **c** Practise reading one paragraph out loud.
Mark the words you feel should be stressed. Listen to
the chapter being read and compare.

CHAPTER FOUR
LAST BID

The auctioneer was standing up behind his table now. 'Ladies
and gentlemen!' he shouted. 'The captain has estimated the
day's run, ending midday tomorrow, at five hundred and fifteen
miles. As usual we will take the ten numbers on either side of it
to make up the range. That makes it five hundred and five to five
hundred and twenty-five. And of course for those who think the
true figure will be still farther away, there'll be 'low field' and
'high field' sold separately as well. Now, we'll draw the first
number out of the hat... here we are... five hundred and
twelve?'

The room became quiet. The people sat still in their chairs, all
eyes watching the auctioneer. There was a certain tension in the
air, and as the bids got higher, the tension grew. This wasn't a
game or a joke; you could be sure of that by the way one man
would look across at another who had raised his bid – smiling
perhaps, but only the lips smiling, the eyes bright and absolutely
cold.

Number five hundred and twelve was knocked down for one
hundred and ten pounds. The next three or four numbers
fetched roughly the same amount.

The ship was rolling heavily, and each time she went over, the
wooden panelling on the walls creaked as if it were going to split.
The passengers held on to the arms of their chairs, concentrating
upon the auction.

'Low field!' the auctioneer called out. 'The next number is low
field.'

Mr. Botibol sat up very straight and tense. He would wait, he
had decided, until the others had finished bidding, then he would
jump in and make the last bid. He had figured that there must be
at least five hundred dollars in his account at the bank at home,
probably nearer six. That was about two hundred pounds – over
two hundred. This ticket wouldn't fetch more than that.

---

222 **REVIEW**

UNIT 21

a Opposite or similar?
Are these pairs opposite or similar in
meaning? (The words on the left are
in the story.)

high	low
raise	lower
game	joke
fetched	cost

split	break apart
held on	let go
tense	stiff
figured	worked out

b Converting currencies
Work these out, then learn the coloured words.

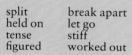

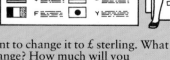

You hold US$50. You want to change it to £ sterling. What
is the current rate of exchange? How much will you
receive?
If you go to Eastern Europe, you may find, on departure,
that the local currency is non-convertible. So what must
you do, prior to departure?

Complete the sets
c Two possible opposites are given for each headword.
Can you complete them with six of these words?

> clear   conscious   lively   loudly   lower   pride   routine   sadness

united
split divided

silently
noisily _____

relaxed
stiff tense

joy
grief _____

body
spirit soul

lazy
_____ full of spirit

unusual/one-off
_____ regular

arriving
departing leaving

confusing
_____ straight-forward

raise
drop _____

NEW WORDS
IN UNIT 21

alarm	grandmother
ancestor	grandparent
bid	grief
bother	horse
bride	pride
bridegroom	rail
chart	routine
colloquial	shelf
comb	silent
confusion	soul
conscious	space D
consciousness	spirit
convert	spiritual
convertible	split
currency	spray
estimated	step
figure	stiff
grandfather	tense
	treasure

37 new words
TOTAL SO FAR 865

221 Dip in the pool

Lexis: **bid, confusion, confused, estimated, field, figured, nearer, split, tense**
Revision: **basically, draw** (= pull), **except that..., fetch** (= be sold for/cost), **lower, raise** T, **range, specific, tension, term** (= call/use a word)
Understanding only: **mileage, gets the kitty** (= wins all the pooled money from the sale of the tickets)
Phrases: **Ladies and gentlemen, in the air** (= atmosphere), **maximum and minimum**

Reading SB221a

1 Reading the summary first will help students understand this chapter more easily. Make sure students realise they will need to read both the summary and the story before finding the extra sentences.

Key: Mr Botibol was very pleased. (No reason for him to feel pleased or otherwise, as he was only interested in low field.)
He wanted to buy number 525. (False! That's not low field.)

Report SB221b

2 **Key:** The auctioneer is auctioning twenty numbers (denoting distances in miles) and two others – high and low field. High field is any number higher than 525; low field is any number lower than 505.

Listening SB221b

3 Students listen and compare explanations. (Most students will probably think Bruce and Richard's are fuller and clearer.)

Pronunciation and listening SB221c

4 Go through the target lexis in the story. Get students to practise pronouncing new words in their phrases. Allot sections of the story to different students, to practise reading out loud.

5 Play the chapter being read aloud. Then let students read it out loud again to each other.

222 Review

Key: **a** opp, opp, sim, sim, sim, opp, sim, sim.
b Find what the current rate is. In mid-December 1988, the rate was about 1.83 dollars to the pound, so you would have got £27.32.
You have to spend all your local currency in Eastern Europe before you leave.
Also ask students if they know how to convert kilometres to miles. (divide by 8, multiply by 5).
What other things/people can you convert? (buildings, e.g. houses into flats; systems, e.g. computer systems; you can also convert people's religious beliefs)
c Words needed in this order: loudly, sadness, lively, routine, clear. Not needed: conscious, pride.
Note: New target words: **soul, tense**.

LEXICAL OBJECTIVES

alarm 1 fear, anxiety. *rang in alarm*
2 an alarm clock, a burglar alarm. *An alarm that for years had been dumb.*
3 *She would probably give the alarm* = warn people of danger
ancestors grandparents etc.
bid 1 T an attempt. *a bid for power.*
2 offer to pay a certain amount of money to buy something. *As the birds got higher, the tension grew.*
bother EED 1 *he didn't bother to say goodbye.*
2 T trouble. *Sorry to be a bother.*
3 upset. *thunder doesn't bother me at all*
bride woman getting married.
bridegroom man getting married.
chart 1 T diagram showing information.
2 *pop charts* = lists of hit records.
colloquial informal words, phrases used only in conversation.
comb *combing his hair back into place with a small red comb.*
confusion unclear situation, or muddled state of mind. *I think this is where the confusion is. I'm confused.*
conscious 1 thinking about. *very conscious of not having television.*
2 T politically/socially conscious.
3 T deliberate. *a conscious act.*
4 T awake, aware. *fully conscious during the operation.*
consciousness T your mind/thoughts, or ideas/attitudes shared by a group.
2 *Political consciousness.*
3 *lose consciousness* = be asleep.
convert T 1 change, alter. *Power stations convert energy into electricity.*
2 *convert dollars to pounds sterling*
convertible 1 car with a roof that folds down.
2 currency (money) that can be changed internationally. Also: **non-convertible**
currency system of money used in a country. *thinking in his own currency.*
estimated calculated approximately.
figure 1 verb (informal American) to think or guess. *He had figured there must be at least $5000 in his account*
grandfather
grandfather clock is a very tall clock
grandmother
grandparents, great-grandparents T

grief 1 extreme sadness. *to share both his grief and his joy.*
Phrase: **Good grief** to express surprise
horse the animal. **White horses** are large waves with white spray blowing.
pride 1 T feeling of satisfaction. *She pointed with pride to the horses she had trained.* Phrase: **take pride in**.
2 a treasured possession. *it was always his treasure and pride.*
rail 1 horizontal bars, such as the rails round the ship's deck.
2 T *by rail* = by train
routine 1 T normal. *routine problems.*
2 way of organising yourself so you do the same things at the same time each day. *My wife gets into a routine... break that routine.*
shelf e.g. book shelf.
silent 1 not speaking. *the others at the table had become silent and were trying to hear.*
2 T making no noise. *the guns fell silent. a silent film.*
silently *as we silently stood by his side.*
soul EED T 1 spiritual, non-physical part of a person.
2 *the soul of the American people*
3 person. *she was a kind soul. Not a soul. I never saw a soul!*
space D
spirit EED (compare with entry for **soul**) 1 non-physical part. *His spirit was pluming for flight. ghosts and spirits, evil spirits.*
2 T energy, feelings. *the kids were in high spirits. a spirited performance.*
spiritual EED T relating to people's deepest thoughts. *spiritual instruction.*
split 1 T divide. *split into two groups. The split between the two countries = caused by a disagreement.*
2 crack or tear. *the wooden panelling creaked as if it was going to split. He split his jeans.*
spray 1 fine drops of liquid forced upward and scattered, such as spray from passing cars on the wet road. *...with plumes of spray behind them.*
2 T *fly spray, hair spray* = aerosols.
step verb: *he stepped out on to the deck.*
stiff EED 1 T firm. *a stiff brush.*
2 not easy to move. *I'm too stiff!*
3 formal behaviour. *the men a little stiff in their dinner jackets.*
Also: *a stiff drink, scared stiff*
tense 1 not relaxed. *Mr Botibol sat up very straight and tense.*
2 T situation causing anxiety. *a long, tense silence.*
treasure 1 T valuable item/s. *the sale of valuable art treasures.*
2 something important, a treasured possession. *The clock was his treasure and pride.*

If you had three wishes...

The general theme of this unit is the future of the world we live in, and environmental issues. Five young people express their hopes and pleas for the future, and students discuss environmental problems that affect their countries, recommending a course of action. Later, we hear different people comparing their more personal wishes for the future. Meanwhile, in Chapter Five of Dip in the Pool, *Mr Botibol retires happily to bed after the auction, but – in Chapter Six – when he wakes up, he finds he has a big problem, which could seriously affect his future.*

OBJECTIVES

Lexical objectives are in TB 231

Discussion topics

a Pollution of the environment. (223)
b Hopes and ambitions. (226)

Social skills

a Expressing attitudes towards ecology and pollution, in spoken and written form. (223)
b Expressing hopes for the future. (226)

Communication skills

a Writing different styles of appeal, and recommending action. (223)
b Reading a narrative. (224,228,229)
c Describing and explaining procedures. (224)
d Providing illustrative examples. (223,224)
e Practice in formulating explanations and definitions. (227)
f Narrative coherence. (228)
g Evaluating plans and strategies. (228)

Grammar and discourse

a Expressions of hope, intention etc. (226)
b Revision of noun phrases. (227)
c More practice in the use of relative clauses. (227)
d The language of prediction and speculation, especially modals and adverbs of probability. (228)
e Revision of three uses of **would**. (229,230)
f Practice Book Grammar Words: the **wh-** words (**who, what, which** etc).

Dictionary skills

a Formation of nouns with common suffixes. (225)
b Meanings of suffixes. (225)

---

223 **Hopes and pleas for the future**

> **Aim:** Expressing attitudes towards ecology, pollution and conservation.
>
> **Lexis: aspect, creation, cement, cry, extinct** T, **extinction, jungle, plea, poster, roots** T, (**uprooted**), **teenager**
> Revision: **ancestors, appealing, concerned** (= worried), **dirt, drown, effective, energy, favour, generation, species, waste**
> Understanding only: **pollution, revel** (= really enjoy), **urbanisation**
> Phrases: **get to** (= am able to (future)), **do me a favour, take action**

Lead-in   SB223   PB223

1 The pictures illustrate some aspects of the state of the world today. Ask students to look at the pictures and see which relate to the words and phrases around them. Can they offer explanations of terms like 'concrete jungle'?

Reading   SB223a

2 Students read the pieces on the right. Once they have found the lost endings, they could read some of the pieces out loud to each other. Go through any new target words.

Key: There are no trees... – Greece; By the time I... – USA; Please leave... – Bermuda; Look! Man!... – Australia; I think a country... – Korea.

Task, planning and report   SB223b

3 Ask students individually to note down their personal order of preference, beginning with the one they like best.

4 In groups of four, students must agree on a joint order of preference. Encourage them to justify their choices. Finally each group tells the class which piece got first place and why.

Writing   SB223c

5 Students could do this on their own or as a group activity.

Sample: These young people are concerned about the polluted state of the world today. They want adults to appreciate how necessary it is to stop wasting energy, to conserve nature and stop the spread of urbanisation, to make the world a better place for the next generation.

Task, planning and report   SB223d

6 Begin by brainstorming about other forms of pollution: traffic noise and fumes, chemical pollution of rivers, (industrial waste), chemical spraying of crops, litter, and other possible worries of people from all over the world.

7 Students then find out about each other's worries and concerns. This could either be done in class as a small survey, or even better, with students interviewing three or four people from outside their own class. They might need help to plan questions and an introductory chat.

8 Students present their reports orally, and compare findings.

Writing   SB223e

9 As a class discuss what action could be taken in some of the cases reported in step 8 above. Write any useful phrases on the board.

10 As the composition component of a test will always provide students with a choice of topics, alternatives are given here. It is sensible for students to practise choosing the topic that is most suitable for them. Help students to see that the letter to the newspaper needs to be more factual, and the magazine piece more expressive.

11 Students could write either on their own or in groups, while you help as needed. Then display or pass round their pieces.

Task and report   SB223f

12 Students design a poster. It must be eye-catching and have a slogan that people can remember. Try the two slogans out on other people. If it is possible to find card/paper, coloured pens, and pictures from magazines, students could produce some finished products (to be displayed in the school?).

Unit 22

If you had three wishes . . .

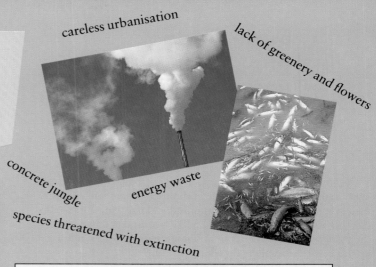

careless urbanisation

lack of greenery and flowers

concrete jungle

energy waste

species threatened with extinction

Cry for our beautiful world

Young people from over 30 countries plead for the survival of our natural world.

Edited by Helen Exley

pollution

Hopes and pleas for the future

Children and teenagers from all over the world were asked to write a short piece for a book called *Cry for our Beautiful World*, the aim of which is to bring to adults' notice how serious the state of the world is today.

a Read and find the 'lost' endings from those given below the poems on the right.

b **Which is best?**
In groups, put the pieces in order, the best one first.

▷ Tell the class which you chose to come first, and why.

c **Summary**

▷ Write two or three sentences about the worries these young people have about the future. Compare your sentences.

d **What are your worries?**
Find out from other students what aspects of pollution people in their region should be most concerned about.

▷ Report to the class about what you have found out. Compare your findings.

e **What action to take?**
Write a short piece:
Either like those above for a magazine or book such as *Cry For Our Beautiful World*.
Or in the form of a letter to the Editor of a newspaper, recommending action that could be taken in your country, or in Britain, to help solve one of these problems. Make an appeal to your readers.

f **Design a poster**
Design a poster suitable for a place you know. Think up two alternative slogans that would be suitable for the poster.

There are no trees in my town. They were uprooted by huge buildings. There are no flowers outside my house. They were killed by cement.

By the time I get to drive a car there won't be any gas. By the time I get to own my own house I won't be able to turn the light switch on because there won't be any electricity.

Please leave something for us.
Our generation needs a home too.
We can't live in this dirt and grime
  left for us by you.
Your ancestors left the world OK.

Look
Man!
Look out
From yourself.
Look out at life!
Stop drowning yourself
In your own creations.

I think a country where flowers grow beautifully is good to live in. We should know the beauty of flowers, and grow many flowers and make a mountain of flowers.

Please do the same for us.
          Melanie Boyd, 11, Bermuda

Open your eyes; look outside;
Revel in the beauty you find.
          David Robinson, 14, Australia

There are no birds gathered on my windows. They were turned away by smog.
          Vania Tsigaridi, 14, Greece

Then the minds of the people who look at the flowers will become beautiful, won't they?
          Jae Yong Lee, 11, Korea

Please do me a favour and don't waste energy.
          Donna Jean Stevens, 14, USA

89

Dip in the pool

224a **a** Will Mr. Botibol buy his low field number even if the price goes up? Listen to the dramatised version, then read this chapter to find if he succeeds. How much may he win?

CHAPTER FIVE

TWENTY-ONE HUNDRED-ODD POUNDS

'As you all know,' the auctioneer was saying, 'low field covers every number below the smallest number in the range, in this case every number below five hundred and five. So, if you think this ship is going to cover less than five hundred and five miles in the twenty-four hours ending at noon tomorrow, you better get in and buy this number. So what am I bid?'

It went clear up to one hundred and thirty pounds. Others besides Mr. Botibol seemed to have noticed that the weather was rough. One hundred and forty . . . fifty . . . There it stopped. The auctioneer raised his hammer.

'Going at one hundred and fifty . . .'

'Sixty!' Mr. Botibol called, and every face in the room turned and looked at him.

'Seventy!'

'Eighty!' Mr. Botibol called.

'Ninety!'

'Two hundred!' Mr. Botibol called. He wasn't stopping now – for anyone.

There was a pause.

'Any advance on two hundred pounds?'

Sit still, he told himself. Sit absolutely still and don't look up. Hold your breath. No one's going to bid you up so long as you hold your breath.

'Going for two hundred pounds . . .' The auctioneer had a pink bald head and there were little beads of sweat sparkling on top of it. 'Going . . .' Mr. Botibol held his breath. 'Going . . . Gone!' The man banged the hammer on the table. Mr. Botibol wrote out a cheque and handed it to the auctioneer's assistant, then he settled back in his chair to wait for the finish. He did not want to go to bed before he knew how much there was in the pool.

They added it up after the last number had been sold and it came to twenty-one hundred-odd pounds. That was around six thousand dollars. Ninety per cent to go to the winner, ten per cent to seamen's charities. Ninety per cent of six thousand was five thousand four hundred. Well – that was enough. He could buy the Lincoln convertible and there would be something left over, too. With this gratifying thought he went off, happy and excited, to his cabin.

---

b Could you write a summary of the way the ship's run auction pool works? Discuss and then draft an outline explanation in groups. Explain how much Mr. Botibol stands to win.

224c **c** Listen to Edmund and Bruce doing the same, and compare drafts.

WORD STUDY

Which of the words below each sentence have similar meanings to the words in blue?

Others besides Mr. Botibol seemed to have noticed that the weather was rough.
on account of   apart from   in addition to   as well as

Mr. Botibol wrote out a cheque . . .
made out   cancelled   signed   withdrew   prepared

He could buy the car and there would be something left over, too.
knocked off   remaining   in addition   on top

. . . five thousand four hundred. Well — that was enough.
ample   plenty   sufficient   all right   adequate

---

225 ## Dictionary skills

Suffixes

a -ation -tion -ion
Use one of these suffixes to make nouns from the verbs below, then check your answers by looking up -ation or the nouns themselves.

adopt   alter   cancel   consider   destroy   educate   organise

Now do the same with these:
create   explain   inform   introduce   intend   pollute   reduce   select   solve   produce   starve

Check their spellings and other meanings by looking in any dictionary.

b -able -ibility -ness -ment -less -ous
Look up these suffixes and discuss their meanings.

c Which of the suffixes from **a** and **b** can you add to the words below? What do they then mean? Use any dictionary.

courage   profit   establish   realize   connect   hope   happy   responsible   value   improve

Aims: 1 Reading a narrative.
2 Describing and explaining procedures.
3 Providing illustrative examples.

Lexis: ample, banged, besides, cancel, charities, cheque, hammer, noon, still, sweat
Revision: **adequate, cabin, covers** (= includes), **came to** (= added up to), **left over, raise, range, remaining, seamen, settled back**
Understanding only: **beads of sweat, sufficient**
Phrase: **As you know ...**

Listening and reading   SB224a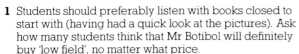

1 Students should preferably listen with books closed to start with (having had a quick look at the pictures). Ask how many students think that Mr Botibol will definitely buy 'low field', no matter what price.

2 Explain to students that they will be hearing a 'play' (a dramatised version), rather than a simple reading of the story. Play the recording. Ask students to imagine how Mr Botibol must be feeling at the end.

3 Students can now read the story on their own.

Writing   SB224b

4 Students could tackle this in groups. Suggest they read again the first paragraph of Chapter Four (section 221) and then add the relevant facts from the present chapter. Ask students to explain it as if to someone who has not read the story. You may want to give them a first sentence or two. Alternatively, with a weak class, do the listening in section 224c first.

Sample answer: Every evening, the captain announces his estimate of the distance the ship will cover during the 24 hours up to midday the following day. This is called the ship's run. People taking part decide what number of miles they think will be the correct distance, and plan to try to buy that number. Obviously factors like the weather will affect the distance actually travelled.
The auctioneer sells a range of 20 numbers, 10 on either side of the captain's estimate, plus low and high field. People bid for the numbers and the highest bidder gets the number. The money from the sale of the numbers goes into a pool. They wait until the next day at midday, when the captain announces the exact mileage the ship has covered. The person who has that number is the winner. Ninety percent of the money in the pool goes to the winner, and ten percent to seamen's charities. Since the pool in this case was £2100, or $6000, of which 10% goes to charity, Mr Botibol stands to win $5400; but he has already paid about £200 or $600 for his number, so that makes his clear winnings $4800.

5 Encourage groups who finish before others to read and check each other's.

Listening   SB224c

6 Let the class hear Edmund and Bruce's summary. (They calculate his clear winning, after deducting what he paid for his number.)

7 Help students with the Word Study, and go over any target words which have other meanings.

Key: apart from/in addition to/as well as.
made out/signed/prepared.
remaining/in addition/on top (colloquial).
ample/sufficient/adequate. ('Plenty' and 'all right' could also be used in this sense, depending on the speaker's intonation.)

Aims: 1 To make students aware that suffixes can be looked up in the dictionary, where students will find suitable examples.
2 To help students generalise what they know about suffixes, familiar and unfamiliar.
3 To revise work already done on suffixes in earlier units, where the following have been covered, mainly in Review sections: **-ion** (12b), **-ment, -tion, -able, -ness** (88b).

SB225a   PB225

1 Students could do these on their own. When they look up **-ation**, they will find the first three words given as examples (**alteration, cancellation**). The remaining four nouns can be looked up separately in the Dictionary Extracts.

2 The second set are all words that students should already have met, but can be checked in any dictionary. (They do not appear in the Dictionary Extracts).

3 Get students to work out the rule about verbs ending in **-uce** becoming **-uction** (e.g. **reduce, produce, introduce; reduction, production, introduction**).

SB225b

4 If you are short of time, you could divide the six suffixes up between groups, who then report their findings, with examples, to the whole class.

SB225c

5 This could be set for homework. Ask students to find and write an example for each word they make, or to prepare an explanation.

6 Optional: Other less common suffixes (attached to common words) that you might like to cover are:
-dom (freedom, kingdom, boredom)
-ship (relationship, friendship, ownership, hardship)
-hood (childhood, adulthood, parenthood)
-ism (communism, socialism, racism)

-ful (but this is far more complex:
hopeful = full of hope   *but* **pitiful** = to be pitied
beautiful = full of beauty   **fruitful** = useful
peaceful = full of peace etc.   **hateful** = to be hated)

-full is also used in nouns (with any kind of container):
cupful, teaspoonful, mouthful etc.

Aim: Hopes and intentions: **I hope**, **I'd like** etc.

Lexis: ambitious T, **ample**, **classical**, **conservative** T, **courage**, **courageous** T, **elect**, **election**, **leak**, **leakage**, **mould**, **peaceful**, **piles of** (= plenty of), **production**, **redundant**, **ugly**, **warfare**, **weapons** T
Revision: **connected/connect**, **feature**, **nuclear energy/warfare/arms**, **peace**, **prospects**, **skills**, **starvation**, **wealth**
Phrases: **being at the heart of it** (= because we are in the middle of it), **Labour to get in** (at the next election) (= be elected to Government), **Conservative/Labour Party** T

Lead-in SB226 PB226

1 Students discuss and classify the words and phrases according to whether they could be hopes, or fears etc.

Task, planning and report SB226

2 Students think of three wishes and write them down.

3 Students discuss their lists with a partner. They decide on one wish each and prepare to tell the class.

Listening SB226

4 Note that we only hear Bruce's third wish (his first two are for health and peace throughout the world).

5 Students take brief notes, and then compare with what people in the class said earlier.

Key: Rachel wants: 1 to teach jazz violin in schools, 2 the Labour Party to get in at the next general election, 3 something done about starvation in the Third World. Elizabeth: 1 courage in general, 2 courage to learn new skills and more about the world around her, 3 to work as a volunteer health worker. Bruce: 3 no more nuclear warfare/armaments, no more nuclear energy.

Listening and writing SB226

6 Students can refer to the transcripts to help them with their summary. Then they should add their own opinions.

 Grammar

Aims: 1 Practice in formulating explanations and definitions.
2 Revision of sections 50 and 142.
3 More practice in the use of relative clauses.

SB227 PB227

1 Point out the use of the relative clauses in the explanations. Review sections 58 and 136 if necessary.

2 Students prepare explanations for one set and pass these round to students who have done different sets.

3 Students look up some of the phrases in a dictionary.
Key: 1 **Third World country** – refers to the underdeveloped countries of Africa, Asia and South America. **Health workers** – nurses and others who look after the sick. **Health clinics** – places to which sick people go for treatment. 2 **Nuclear warfare** – a war in which nuclear weapons are used. **Nuclear energy** – energy is released as a result of splitting the atom. **Nuclear power station** – a station which generates electricity from nuclear power. 3 **Smoking room** – a room in which people are permitted to smoke. **Smoking gun** – a gun which has just been fired so that smoke is coming out of the barrel. **Hundred dollar bills** – bills or notes, each one of which is worth a hundred dollars. **Three dollar bills** – three notes, each of which is worth a dollar.

4 **Sports clothes** – clothes people wear when playing sports. **Sports stars** – famous sportsmen and sportswomen. **Sports report** – a news bulletin about sport. **Deck tennis** – a game played on board ship which resembles tennis in some ways. **Deck-hand** – a worker on a ship who is responsible for keeping the decks clean. **Tennis shoes** – shoes worn to play tennis. **Tennis court** – area where tennis is played. 5 **Life-boats** – small boats carried on a ship to be used in an emergency if the ship sinks. **Life-jacket** – a special jacket which will help someone keep afloat in the water. **Life-belt** – a circular device which can be thrown to someone who is drowning to help them keep afloat. **Life insurance** – a form of insurance in which a person makes regular payments to an insurance company. In return, a sum of money is paid to them when they reach a certain age, or to their wife, husband or children when they die. 6 **Arrivals hall** – the room to which people are directed when they arrive at an airport. **Departure lounge** – the room in which people sit while waiting to board their plane. **Customs post** – a place at which arrivals in a country report to customs to have their bags checked. **Border guards** – soldiers or police who stand at the border of a country to check people who come into the country. **Check-point** – a place, usually on a border, where people are examined to make sure they are not dangerous in any way.

 Dip in the pool

Aims: 1 Focus on narrative coherence.
2 The language of prediction, especially modals and adverbs of probability.
3 **would** for hypothesis.

Lexis: anger, **cast**, **matter**, **peered**, **stomach**, **strategies**, **withdraw**
Revision: **smooth**
Understanding only: **drawing cheques**, **bunk** (= bed), **monthly instalments**
Phrases: **keep the matter secret**, **making up for lost time**, **hadn't a hope**, **Oh my God!**

Listening SB228a

1 Remind students that Mr Botibol has just bought the 'low field' and left the auction to go to his cabin.

2 Explain that they will be hearing a dramatisation of the story, with sound effects. Play the tape pausing as necessary to allow students in groups to speculate on what the sound effects are, and what is happening.

3 Get the class to summarise the story, so far as they can predict, and to suggest what might happen next.

Reading SB228b

4 Students read then discuss where the sentences could go.

Key: ... ship was not rolling. He jumped up and peered out...
... win it after this. Mr Botibol turned away...
... drawing cheques. And what about the monthly installments...

Task, planning and report SB228c

5 Students in groups discuss what they would do. They should compare strategies and then write notes to compare with what Bruce and Edmund, and Chris and Rachel thought.

Listening SB228c

6 Ask students to note down only the new ideas they hear.

If you had three wishes...

Hopes? Ambitions? Wishes? Fears?

New car   Better job prospects

Courage   *Starvation*   new skills

Piles of food   Peace

Use of natural energy   peaceful nuclear energy

Nuclear Warfare   Health   Wealth

Happiness

What wishes could you add to those above?
What wishes for the future do you have, either
personal or general?
Write down three things, then compare them with
your partner's.

▶ Choose one of your wishes, and tell or write it
briefly for the class. ◀

226 Listen and see what three wishes Rachel,
Elizabeth and Bruce had. Write notes. Are any of
them the same as yours?

226 Listen again, then choose one of
the three people and write a short
summary of one of their wishes, adding
your own opinions. Use one of the pictures
to help explain your ideas, if you wish.

227 *Grammar* ·············

Explaining noun phrases
Choose one set of phrases below and write a full
sentence with a verb to explain what the phrases
mean. For example:

A light switch is the switch which operates the light.
Or the switch which turns the light on and off.
A time limit is the time or date before which
something must be completed.
A family party is a party to which mainly members of
your family are invited.

See sections 50, 142 and 136.

1 third world country   health workers   health
   clinics
2 nuclear warfare   nuclear energy   nuclear power
   station
3 smoking room   smoking gun   hundred dollar
   bills   three dollar bills
4 sports clothes   sports stars   sports report   deck
   tennis   deck hand   tennis shoes   tennis court
5 lifeboats   lifejacket   lifebelt   life insurance
6 arrivals hall   departure lounge   customs post
   border guards   check-point

Read each other's sentences. Finally look up some of
the words in any dictionary and compare
explanations.

 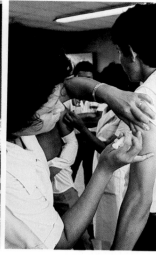

Sellafield nuclear power station   A health clinic in Nicaragua

228 Dip in the pool

228a **a** Listen to the dramatisation of the story.
What do you think has happened? What will happen?

▶ Tell each other. ◀

b These three sentences have been taken out of the
story. Read it and see where they fit.

And what about the monthly instalments on the television set
and the Encyclopaedia Britannica?
He jumped up and peered out of the porthole.
Mr. Botibol turned away and sat slowly down on the edge of his
bunk.

CHAPTER SIX A

SMOOTH AS GLASS

When Mr. Botibol awoke the next morning he lay quite still
for several minutes with his eyes shut, listening for the sound of
the gale, waiting for the roll of the ship. There was no sound of
any gale and the ship was not rolling. The sea – Oh God – was
smooth as glass, the great ship was moving through it fast,
obviously making up for time lost during the night. A fine
electricity of fear was beginning to prickle under the skin of his
stomach. He hadn't a hope now. One of the higher numbers was
certain to win it after this.
   'Oh my God,' he said aloud. 'What shall I do?'
   What, for example, would Ethel say? It was simply not
possible to tell her that he had spent almost all of their two years'
savings on a ticket in the ship's pool. Nor was it possible to keep
the matter secret. To do that he would have to tell her to stop
drawing cheques. Already he could see the anger and contempt
in the woman's eyes, the blue becoming grey and the eyes
themselves narrowing as they always did when there was anger in
them.
   'Oh my God. What shall I do?'

c What would you do if you were Mr. Botibol?
Think of two alternative strategies. Discuss in
groups.

▶ Agree on the best two plans and tell the class
about them. How many of you had the same
ideas? ◀

228c See what Chris and Rachel thought, then compare
their ideas and yours with Bruce and Edmund's. Take
a vote on the best idea.

229 Dip in the pool

a Read on. What did Mr. Botibol think of doing?

CHAPTER SIX B

SMOOTH AS GLASS continued

There was no point in thinking that he had the smallest chance now – not unless the goddam ship started to go backwards. They'd have to put her in reverse and go full speed astern and keep right on going if he was to have any hope of winning it now. Well, perhaps he should ask the captain to do just that. Offer him ten per cent of the profits. Offer him more if he wanted it. Mr. Botibol started to laugh. Then very suddenly he stopped, his eyes and mouth both opening wide in a kind of shocked surprise. For it was at this moment that the thought came. It hit him hard and quick, and he jumped up from his bed, terribly excited, ran over to the porthole and looked out again.

We have changed seven words in the first paragraph of chapter six B. Can you guess which of the words in the story we replaced them with? The seven original words were:

chance   giggle   maybe   pretending   slightest
began   idea

b What could Mr Botibol's idea be? Discuss, then read on and see.

Well, he thought, why not? Why ever not? The sea was calm and he wouldn't have any trouble keeping afloat until they picked him up. He had a vague feeling that someone had done this thing before, but that didn't prevent him from doing it again. The ship would have to stop and lower a boat and the boat would have to go back maybe half a mile to get him, and then it would have to return to the ship and be hoisted back on board. It would take at least an hour, the whole thing. An hour was about thirty miles. It would knock thirty miles off the day's run. That would do it. 'Low field' would be sure to win it then. Just so long as he made certain someone saw him falling over; but that would be simple to arrange. And he'd better wear light clothes, something easy to swim in. Sports clothes, that was it. He would dress as though he were going up to play some deck tennis – just a shirt and a pair of shorts and tennis shoes. And leave his watch behind. What was the time? Nine-fifteen. The sooner the better, then. Do it now and get it over with. Have to do it soon, because the time limit was midday.

 Listen to the dramatised version.

c Discuss the answers to questions 1, 2 and 3. What do you think Bruce and Edmund, then Chris and Rachel said?

1 So what was it that Mr. Botibol decided to do?
2 What could go wrong? Do you think the plan will work?
3 What precautions will Mr. Botibol need to take?

229c What did the others think?

d What could happen next? Discuss in groups.

▶ Write one paragraph to continue the story. ◀

230 *Grammar* ....

Three meanings of would
Would can be used
1 to express a hypothesis, for example:
   What would you do if you were Mr. Botibol? (228)
   (See Units 10, 12 and 17)
2 for future in the past, for example:
   I thought that they would ... feel the same. (216)
   (See Unit 21)
3 for past habit, for example:
   When the three-year-old passed a bank on the way to the shops with her mother she would say: 'That's ...' (198)

Read the second paragraph again (from Well, he thought, ...). What does would mean here?

 Listen again to the dramatised version. What differences are there between this and the story.

231 REVIEW
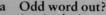
UNIT 22

a Odd word out?
1 ruined   improved   damaged   spoiled   split
2 definite   imprecise   unclear   vague
3 withdraw   paint   take out   take back   remove
4 in connection with   on the subject of   about   on account of
5 connected   linked   divided   joined
6 silent   still   ample   peaceful   quiet

b Extreme or not so extreme?
totally redundant   not particularly difficult
smooth as glass   absolutely incredible
terribly excited   well over forty

NEW WORDS IN UNIT 22

ambitious	leakage
ample	link
anger	midday
aspect	mould
backwards	noon
bang	peaceful
besides	peer
cancel	pile
cast	plea
cement	poster
charity	production
cheque	profit
classical	redundant
conservative	root
courage	ruin
courageous	stomach
creation	strategy
elect	sweat
election	teenager
extinct	tennis
extinction	ugly
hammer	vague/ly
jungle	weapon
leak	withdraw

48 new words
TOTAL SO FAR 913

229 Dip in the pool

Aims: 1 Focus on **would** as the past tense of **will**.
2 To encourage students to enjoy their reading.

Lexis: backwards, knock...off (= reduce), **measure, midday, profits, ruin, tennis, vague,** (**vaguely** T)
Revision: **no point in pretending..., keep afloat**
Understanding only: **in reverse** (= backwards)
Phrases: **had a vague feeling, the sooner the better, get it over with** (= do it now and quickly), **...is one thing, ...that's the impression I've got**

Reading and listening SB229a/b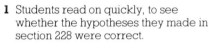

1 Students read on quickly, to see whether the hypotheses they made in section 228 were correct.

2 Stop after the first paragraph for students to discuss what his idea could be.

3 Students read the second paragraph. Can they explain his idea?

4 Play the dramatised version.

5 Students go back to the first paragraph to find the replaced words.

Key: chance – hope, giggle – laugh, maybe – perhaps, pretending – thinking, slightest – smallest, began – started, idea – thought.

Listening SB229c

6 Students discuss questions 1–3 and tell each other what they think. Then play the tape and ask students to note down any different ideas they hear.

Writing SB229d

7 Help if needed as they work in groups to write a continuation of the story. They can read each other's.

8 Keep the suspense up. Do not be tempted to let them know who has guessed the actual ending.

230 Grammar

Aims: 1 To review the use of **would** for the future in the past.
2 To draw together other uses of **would**: for hypothesis and past habit.

SB230

1 Students will be asked to compare the dramatised 'here and now' version with the past tense narrative of the story to highlight the use of **will** and **would**. Ask them to reread the paragraph beginning 'Well, he thought, why not?' and think about the meanings of **would**.

2 Play the second half of recording 229a again while students read the narrative. What differences do they notice? (Most of the **would**'s have become **will**, because he is talking about the future from a present standpoint.)

Key: Written version: 'wouldn't have any trouble keeping afloat until they picked him up' – Mr Botibol is probably thinking 'If I jumped overboard, I wouldn't etc., i.e. this is still hypothetical.
But as he gets more and more determined to do it, the element of hypothesis disappears. The **would**'s in the written story simply show he is talking about the future in the past.

231 Review

Key: a 1 improved 2 definite
3 paint 4 on account of 5 divided
6 ample
Note: Target word: **link/ed**
b All extreme except **not particularly difficult**

LEXICAL OBJECTIVES

ambitious 1 someone with ambition, who wants to be successful. *my ambitious nature.*
ample enough and some extra. *ample natural energy.*
anger *He could see the anger and contempt in the woman's eyes.*
aspect one of the parts of the nature of something. *What aspects of pollution concern you most?*
backwards in reverse. *not unless the ship started to go backwards.*
bang loud noise. *he banged the hammer on the table. a loud bang*
besides 1 in addition to. *Others besides Mr Botibol had noticed...*
cancel 1 T stop something happening. *The match was cancelled due to rain.*
2 *Could you cancel the cheque?*
cast EED 1 T the actors in a play
2 *cast around for* = look for
cement 1 used for concrete.
2 T *cement a relationship* = strengthen
charity organisation that raises money *for the seamen's charity.*
cheque *He wrote a cheque.*
classical 1 serious music
2 T *classical Greece*
conservative T 1 unwilling to accept change.
2 cautious. *It's a conservative guess.*
3 politically right wing. *member of the Conservative Party.*
courage bravery. *I'd like to have the courage to learn new skills.*
courageous brave
creation EED 1 T *a job creation scheme*
2 T the entire universe
3 something made. *Man – stop drowning yourself in your own creations.*
elect T 1 choose by voting. *Elect a president.*
election event where people vote to choose a leader. *I wish Labour would get in at the next election.*

extinct no longer existing
extinction *species threatened by extinction may well die out.*
hammer EED 1 a tool. *he banged the hammer on the table. hammer and nails.*
jungle 1 tropical forest.
2 T *the jungle of real politics*
leak T 1 *a leak in the roof where the rain came in.*
2 *the story was leaked to the media.*
link T EED 1 *What's the link between these ideas?*
2 physically connected. *a bridge linking the two buildings. Link these sentences...*
mould 1 T shape or influence. *mould a child; mould clay to make a model.*
2 container for moulding jelly etc. *have the courage to break out of the mould* = to change your way of life.
peaceful 1 T quiet, calm, untroubled.
2 non-violent, not war. *peaceful nuclear energy* (i.e. not for weapons).
peered looked carefully. *peered out of the porthole.*
pile EED 1 T *a pile of sand/papers*
2 T to pile things up; pile into etc.
3 *piles of* = lots of. (informal) *I just see piles of food.*
plea 1 emotional request. *Pleas for the future. plea for help.*
poster *Design a poster.*
production 1 act of manufacturing, growing or creating something. *food production...*
2 T play/opera performed at a theatre
profits 1 money gained in business or trade. *Offer him 10% of the profits.*
2 T gain. *I profited from his advice.*
redundant 1 T no longer employed. *25 made redundant at local chicken farms.*
2 unnecessary. *the production of nuclear energy is totally redundant.*
root EED 1 roots of a tree. *trees uprooted.* Also: *roots of a problem.*
ruined 1 severely damaged. *leave his watch behind so it doesn't get ruined.*
2 T someone who has lost all his money. *a ruined man. business in ruins*
3 what is left after it's been destroyed. *ruins of an old building.*
stomach where your food is digested; where you feel uncomfortable if you are afraid. *fear... under the skin of his stomach.*
strategies plans you adopt to be successful. *Think of two alternative strategies.* Also: **military tactics**.
sweat perspiration – if you are very hot. *little beads of sweat sparkling*
teenagers people aged from 13 to 19.
tennis the game. *deck tennis.*
ugly 1 very unattractive to look at. *Power stations – ugly dangerous things*
2 T an *ugly situation* could be violent
vague 1 T not clear or precise. *The terms of the agreement were deliberately left vague.*
2 unclear in your mind. *a vague idea. He had a vague feeling that someone had done this thing before.*
weapons T guns, missiles etc. used in wars to kill people. *nuclear weapons.*
withdraw 1 T remove, take out. *withdraw money from a bank account.*
2 take back a statement or offer. *Can you withdraw your offer?*

Unit 23 Hopes and plans

The Yetties talk about future developments in their entertainment business, including travel plans, while students discuss points in their lives where they have felt under stress. Chapter Seven of the story involves us in Mr Botibol's immediate plans, which concern another passenger. Next comes a light-hearted task describing personality and physical characteristics. Students then plan and conduct interviews on the subject of long-term plans. Chapter Eight of the story takes us towards the climax. Students are asked to speculate on a dramatic ending.

OBJECTIVES

Lexical objectives are in TB240

Discussion topics

a Future plans. (232,238)
b Insecurity and stress. (233)

Social skills

a Changing the subject. (232,238)
b Describing people's physical appearance and character. (235,236)
c Talking about stressful experiences. (233)
d Asking specific questions to keep people to the point, and redirecting a conversation that has gone off the point. (238)
e Practice in hedging, avoiding the question, and changing the subject. (238)

Communication skills

a Narrative coherence. (234)
b Giving precise physical descriptions. (236)
c Inferring meanings from context. (239)
d Listening for specific detail. (239)
e Planning and conducting an interview. (238)

Grammar and discourse

a Adverbs which modify a whole sentence. (237)
b The predictive nature of words like **thought**, **reason**, **difficulties**. (234)
c Practice Book Grammar Word: **would**.

Dictionary skills

Checking formation of opposites with **in-**, **im-** and **un-**. (240)

---

232 Trying to diversify

Aims: 1 Discussion of other people's career developments, hopes and ambitions.
2 Changing the subject.
3 Talking about times of stress.
4 Practising questions in 'interviewer style'.

Lexis: broaden, diversify, divorced, fun, insecure, novel, novelist, rates, secure, stress, tone
Revision: **achieve, taking on** (= accepting, letting themselves in for), **turn up** (= happen, arrive, occur)
Phrases: **day by day, week by week, take the future day by day** (Also: **take things as they come**), **turned professional, a fun thing to be in, ... we have that to be thankful for, ... make a lot of money**

Lead-in SB232 PB232

1 Discuss the possible meanings of the section title 'Trying to diversify' which is a quotation from the interview with Bonny, the leader of the Yetties group. What could Bonny mean? Ask students to speculate, using the pictures. In what ways could the Yetties diversify?

Listening SB232a

2 Students listen and take notes. Ask students which of the things that Bonny talks about are illustrated.

Key: To write a book about Thomas Hardy and his music, and make a recording; he implies more radio and TV work; to write songs for films or plays, with the others writing the music. Generally, to broaden their horizons.

Listening SB232b 232b 232c

3 Students should think of things Pete might say before they listen to recording 232b.

Key: In fact Pete does not actually answer the question, apart from saying he would still like to be rich. He could have said things like: get his own TV or radio programme; run a Dorset Folk Festival; write or arrange more old music; learn to play more old instruments.

4 Play recording 232c. What else do they talk about?

Key: Mac says he'd like to do more foreign work, as well as Germany. But it's difficult to plan far ahead. The interviewer switches topics slightly on hearing that Mac is divorced – away from how the family feels about his future career, to how travel used to affect the family, and the insecurity of singing as a career.

Task SB232c

5 While designing the table in pairs, students can think of other questions the interviewer could have asked, to get better, more specific responses from Pete and Mac.

Sample table: *Plans/hopes for the future*

	Bonny	Pete	Mac
General	Diversify, broaden out	Difficult to plan ahead. Get rich?	Difficult to plan ahead.
Specific	Book and recording on Thomas Hardy. Write songs for films, plays. (More radio/TV.)	—	More work overseas.

Possible questions: What specific personal ambitions do you have, apart from just making some money?/travelling overseas?
What could you do to promote the spread of folk music?
Will you be making any more tapes, or records?
Might you write/collect some modern folk songs?

Listening SB232d

6 As you play the interview with Mac again, students should listen for how the interviewer's voice reaches quite a high note on the key word every time there is a change of subject, near the end, we have:

> YETminster? (*high*)
> INT: Erm. What about
>   Yea, right. (*low*)

---

233 Insecurity and stress

Aim: To give students opportunities to talk, or avoid talking, about times when they have been under stress.

There is deliberately no lead-in or report phase, as students may not want to talk in public about personal situations that have caused them stress.

Task SB233

Students read and follow the instructions. Point out that they will not be reporting back. Monitor tactfully.

Unit 23
Hopes and plans

Thomas Hardy (1840–1928) was one of Britain's greatest writers. He spent most of his life in Dorset where his novels are set. In later life he turned to poetry, which he often set to music.

Thomas Hardy's cottage, Dorset.

Yetties in concert

Yetties in pantomime

232 Trying to diversify

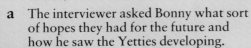

a The interviewer asked Bonny what sort of hopes they had for the future and how he saw the Yetties developing.

232a Bonny talked about the past and present, as well as the future. What hopes does he have for the group? Write brief notes.

b Pete was asked what he would like to achieve, both as an individual entertainer, and as one of the Yetties. What kind of things might Pete say?

Tell each other two things you thought of.

232b What does Pete actually say in answer to the question?

232c **c** What about Mac? What hopes does he have? At what point does the interviewer switch topics? Why do you think he does this?

Work in groups to design a table to include the relevant answers to the interviewer's questions.

What other questions could the interviewer have asked to get a more complete picture?

232c **d** Intonation

Listen to the last part of Mac's interview. How can you tell from the interviewer's tone of voice that he is changing the topic?

> **WORD STUDY**
> Choose any four of these words and try to explain them in context. They are all from the transcripts.
>
> broaden (horizons)   insecurity
> diversify   rates
> divorced   secure
> fun

233 Insecurity and stress

Insecurity at work (e.g. changing jobs, becoming unemployed) or in the family (e.g. illness, death, or events leading to separation or divorce) can lead to severe psychological stress. Moving house, preparing for a festival, or examinations can also result in a heavy stress load.

Find out from your partner at what points in their lives they have felt under most stress.

93

[234] Dip in the pool

a One sentence has been taken out of this part of the story – from somewhere in the three paragraphs. Read carefully and discuss at what two possible points it could fit in.

> Nervously he looked around him.

CHAPTER SEVEN PART A

A CAUTIOUS MAN

Mr. Botibol was both frightened and excited when he stepped out onto the sundeck in his sports clothes. His small body was wide at the hips, tapering upward to extremely narrow sloping shoulders, so that it resembled, in shape at any rate, a bollard. His white skinny legs were covered with black hairs, and he came cautiously out on deck, treading softly in his tennis shoes. There was only one other person in sight, an elderly woman with very thick ankles and immense buttocks who was leaning over the rail staring at the sea. She was wearing a coat of Persian lamb and the collar was turned up so Mr. Botibol couldn't see her face.

He stood still, examining her carefully from a distance. Yes, he told himself, she would probably do. She would probably give the alarm just as quickly as anyone else. But wait one minute, take your time, William Botibol, take your time. Remember what you told yourself a few minutes ago in the cabin when you were changing? You remember that?

The thought of leaping off a ship into the ocean a thousand miles from the nearest land had made Mr. Botibol – a cautious man at the best of times – unusually advertent. He was by no means satisfied yet that this woman he saw before him was absolutely certain to give the alarm when he made his jump. In his opinion there were two possible reasons why she might fail him.

What words in the last sentence tell you what to expect in the next paragraph?

[234a] Listen to Part A being read. Listen for where the lost sentence went originally.

b Discuss how you think Mr. Botibol will check up on the elderly woman. What do you think Edmund, Bruce, Rachel and Chris thought?

[234b] Listen to what they do say.

94 **c** Now read Part B and see what Mr. Botibol did.

PART B

Firstly, she might be deaf and blind. It was not very probable, but on the other hand it might be so, and why take a chance? All he had to do was check it by talking to her for a moment beforehand. Secondly – and this will demonstrate how suspicious the mind of a man can become when it is working through self-preservation and fear – secondly, it had occurred to him that the woman might herself be the owner of one of the high numbers in the pool and as such would have a sound financial reason for not wishing to stop the ship. Mr. Botibol recalled that people had killed their fellows for far less than six thousand dollars. It was happening every day in the newspapers. So why take a chance on that either? Check on it first. Be sure of your facts. Find out about it by a little polite conversation. Then, provided that the woman appeared also to be a pleasant, kindly human being, the thing was a cinch and he could leap overboard with a light heart.

How well did you guess? Compare your guesses.

[234c] How well did Bruce and Edmund feel they had done? Who did they say was under a lot of stress?

d Look up any two words that are new to you, and use the phonetic symbols to work out how they should be pronounced. Tell the class.

[234d] Listen to this part being read. Check the pronunciation of the new words.

> **WORD STUDY**
> Find words or phrases which mean:
>
> | | |
> |---|---|
> | in advance | very good |
> | show | so long as |
> | he had realised | very easy thing to do |
> | have a high number | without worrying |

[235] *Language study*

Physical looks or personal qualities?
With two or three other students, draw two large circles like these. Discuss which circle to write each word in. You may use a dictionary, but do this quickly and see which group finishes first.

What other words can you think to add?

234 Dip in the pool

Aims: 1 Narrative coherence.
2 The predictive nature of words like **thought** and **reason**.

Lexis: **ankles, beforehand, by no means, deaf, demonstrate, demonstration** T, **hips, immense, provided that, resemble, sloping, sound, stress, sufficient**
Revision: **blind, coat, give the alarm, fail him, nervously, suspicious**
Understanding only: **collar, leaping** (**advertent** = attentive to detail – very rare word)
Phrases: **from a distance, under a lot of stress, Why take a chance? All he had to do was . . . , the thing was a cinch** (informal)

Reading   SB234a PB234

1 Students recap on the last chapter. What had Mr Botibol decided to do? (Jump overboard, to slow the ship down.)

2 Students read Part A and find where the lost line could fit. They tell each other, saying why they think so. Replacing the lost sentence should make students read and process the text in a detailed and analytical way.

   Key: After 'in his tennis shoes' or 'see her face'. It's unlikely to be the second position, since we have a description of how he feels followed by a description of what he looks like. (The lost sentence is action, not description.)

3 Students should have no trouble finding the words 'two possible reasons'. Ask students what other words they can think of like **reason** which must be followed by an explanation (here, of what the reason is) unless it has already been explained beforehand.

   There is one example in the third paragraph: 'The **thought**' followed by 'of leaping off a ship . . .'.
   Other words like this: **difficulty, problem, idea, solution, situation, question, fear** etc.
   (e.g. If you say 'I've got an idea!' or 'I've found a solution' and stop there, you will certainly be asked to continue and explain further.)

Students can look out for three of these in Chapter Eight in section 239. (It was a question of . . . , a few difficulties . . . , a new fear.)

Listening   SB234a

4 Students can read along while listening. Tell them to raise a hand when they hear the lost sentence.

Task and listening   SB234b

5 Students can discuss this in pairs. Even if some students have read ahead, they still have to predict what Edmund and Bruce, and then Rachel and Chris will say. Play the recording of the two pairs discussing. Can students remember or quote what they said?

Reading   SB234c

6 Students read silently, and then discuss in small groups how well they guessed.

Listening   SB234c

7 Students listen to Bruce and Edmund's personal evaluation of how well they guessed. It's interesting to note what Edmund says: When one is under a lot of stress, one does think of every detail.

Listening   SB234d

8 Students choose words to look up and tell each other about them, trying to pronounce them. Get students to read them out together with the other words in the same phrase, deciding where to put the main stress.

9 Play the recording. Students can ask you to pause the tape as necessary, so they can repeat the phrases which contain their words.

10 Do the Word Study. The words are in the right order to be found easily in the story.

   Key: beforehand, demonstrate, it had occurred to him, be the owner of . . . , sound, provided that, cinch (very colloquial), with a light heart.

235 Language study

Aim: To revise and extend lexis used to describe people's physical appearance and character.

Lexis: **brave, determined,** (**determination** T), **faithful, fun, generous, generosity** T, **optimistic, optimism** T, **self-sufficient, sensible**
Revision: **kind, kindness** T, **plain** (= ordinary looking), **thick** (= wide and unintelligent) (others as needed)
Understanding only: **outgoing** (= lively, extrovert), **skinny** (= thin), **broad-minded,** (cf **absent-minded**)

SB235

1 First ask students to consider why some of the words are written as they are. (For example, can they guess the meaning of **skinny** from the way it is written?)

2 Once they have got the idea, check that they understand how to choose which circles to write the words in. (The overlapping part is for words that can refer to both physical looks and personality.) Tell them they must be able to explain why they have chosen which circle.

3 Time the groups to see which group can allot all 25 words fastest. With the groups that finish first, test them on some words to see they really understand them.

   Key: Personal qualities: ambitious, brave, (broad-minded), cautious, deep, determined, efficient, faithful, generous, insecure, kind, nervous, optimistic, outgoing, self-sufficient, sensible, sound.
   Some words could refer to both: attractive, broad, narrow (-minded – or in outlook), sound.
   The rest are physical attributes; **deaf** and **sound** referring to health/physical condition rather than looks.

4 Draw two large circles on the board, and get students to tell you where to write each word. Ask them to say why the word fits, or give a phrase which includes the word.

5 Students suggest other words to add, explaining why. If they choose words like **fat, pessimistic, mean**, ask them how you could write them to show the meaning.

6 Optional: If you are able to get hold of newspapers (any language) with large job adverts in them, get students to bring some to class, and skim through for adverts which ask for particular types of people. Students then explain – in English – the personal qualities they are looking for.

Describe ... and draw

Aims: 1 Talking about one's own personality. (See Unit 6.)
2 Describing the personality of a character in a story.
3 Giving and understanding precise physical descriptions.
4 Reacting and commenting.
5 Fun.

Task and report   SB236a/b PB236

1 Students could work from the words they wrote in the circles in section 235. Get students to read and follow the instructions, without too much help from you. You could also appoint a student to 'chair' the two reporting sessions, leaving yourself free for linguistic queries.

Task   SB236c

2 As a class, or in groups, students describe all the features of the man in the cartoon.

Task   SB236d

3 Students will need either large pieces of paper or – even better – OHP transparencies. Then at the end, you can display students' pictures.

4 Optional writing: Students could take one picture home and write a description of it for a matching game next lesson. (Mix up pictures and paragraphs, and students find the pairs.)

 Grammar

Aim: To show how some adverbs affect the meaning of the whole sentence, not just an adjective or verb (as in section 212).

SB237 PB237

1 Help students work through the exercise. In some sentences there are two possible places for the adverb.

2 To check where the adverbs originally went, give each pair of students two or three sentences to find in the section marked. (4, 29, 204, 140, 244 are in the transcripts.) Students can then read out their sentences to the class.

*If the adverb is to apply to the whole sentence, there is a slight tendency for it to be either at the beginning or the end (except that here, with **basically**, **nevertheless** and **actually** this is not the case).*

In the long term ...

Aims: 1 Talking about future hopes and ambitions, especially as regards career, family security etc.
2* Asking specific questions to keep people to the point, and redirecting a conversation that has gone off the point. (B students)
3* Practice in hedging, avoiding the question, changing the subject. (A students)

Lexis: long-term, in the long term
Revision: **in terms of**

*This whole activity depends on concealing these aims from the students. Do NOT let them know the real aims until the end. Be careful not to let B students know what A students will be trying to do.

Planning   SB238

1 Divide the class in half, with A students sitting together but well apart from B students. (Later they will be working in pairs, with one A student and one B student in a pair.)

2 Tell B students to prepare a range of relevant questions, and give them a little help to start with.

3 Then go to the As, and explain to them that the purpose of this exercise is to practise *avoiding* answering questions, without the other person realising. Discuss any strategies they could use.

Examples: In order to do this politely, A students could:
– skirt round the question, answering other things instead. (B: What is X going to do when she leaves school? A: Well she's in her last year at present. She's doing mainly history and geography I think.
– or keep asking for clarification of the question. (B: What is X going to do when she leaves school? A: Do you mean school or university? B: I mean school. A: Oh, I see. Do you mean what exams and so on or do you mean is she going to go to university?)
– or misunderstand the question. (B: What is she going to do when she leaves school? A: Sometime next year I think. That must be about right. You see she's about seventeen now, so she'll be leaving some time next year . . .)
– or change the subject. (While answering a question, give your opinion about it rather than the facts: 'I don't think she should have stayed on at school – if she had got herself a job at 16 like the others . . .')
– or introduce another person. (I had a friend once who did that and it didn't work out at all.)
– and/or ask the interviewer questions. (Do you now anyone in that line of business/students doing similar subjects?)

Task   SB238

5 Once both A and B students are ready, pair them off, so there is one A and one B in each pair, and the interview can begin. Give them three minutes.

Planning and report   SB238

6 After the interview, B students prepare to tell the class *or* write a paragraph about the person concerned. While B students are doing this, A students also write a paragraph about the same person, but this time, in full, not hiding anything. They will not show this to B students until B students have finished their reports.

7 Form larger groups of about two or three original A/B pairs, and B students give their reports or pass their reports around. Then they read A students' reports, which will of course be much fuller. Alternatively, with a small class, B students can report to the whole class.

8 At the end, let A students explain to the B students what they were trying to do.

236 Describe ... and draw

a Choose five words from section 235 that you might use to describe your personality, and three words that would not give a true impression of you. Be prepared to justify your choice.

▶ Tell each other. Do the others agree? ◀

b Write five words you might use to describe Mr. Botibol's character. What makes you choose them?

▶ Take turns to give the class one of your words. It must be a word no-one else has said. If you hear someone else say a word that is on your list, cross it out. Who has the most words left at the end? ◀

c Which words could you use to describe this man's arms; shoulders; neck; chin; nose; forehead; etc?

d Tell people in your group exactly how to draw a silly man, barefoot, wearing sports gear. For example:
Starting from his feet. Very broad flat feet. Thin ankles, long skinny legs with hairy knees, and tight shorts; average waist, very broad strong chest, huge square shoulders and a ...

237 *Grammar*

Adverbs
Sometimes adverbs comment not on an adjective or verb but on a whole sentence or clause:

Nervously he looked around him. (234)
Firstly she might be deaf and blind. (234)
His wife may indeed have left him to join some religious sect. (161)

Here is an unusual example:

Actually – funnily **enough** originally **when I read them yesterday, I thought that that one was** ... possibly **the only one that was genuine** ... (201)

Put these adverbs back in their sentences (some may have more than one possible place):

We don't do much bathing now. (4) unfortunately
His interview lasted about 30 minutes. (29) apparently

You are a confident person. (65) basically
The flight case is mounted on castors, but it will require several people to help with loading and unloading at all venues. (133) nevertheless
... the big ship had started rolling again. (207) actually
... I'm quite a good traveller. (204) normally
A degree in modern languages or political science or economics would be very useful. (140) obviously
She was so surprised that she did not try to pull herself from my grasp. (196) luckily
You did the right thing by leaving the banda. (109) clearly
It had occurred to him that the woman might herself be the owner of one of the high numbers in the pool ... (234) secondly
She's the – the ... nurse of this one with the fat ankles. (244) presumably

238 In the long term ...

Divide into A students and B students.

A students:
Write down the name of a friend or relative whose long-term plans you are prepared to talk about.

You are going to give the name to your B student partner who will interview you about him/her for about three minutes.

B Students:
Prepare some ideas for questions. Interview your A student partner. Find out about the plans of the person they know. Make notes so you can tell the class what you have found out after the interview.

239 Dip in the pool

a Read on and guess the words.

CHAPTER EIGHT

EVERYTHING IN ORDER?

Mr. Botibol advanced __1__ towards the woman and took up a position beside her, leaning on the rail. 'Hullo,' he said __2__.

She turned and smiled at him, a surprisingly lovely, almost a __3__ smile, although the face itself was very __4__. 'Hullo,' she answered him.

Check, Mr. Botibol told himself, on the first question. She is neither __5__ nor __6__. 'Tell me,' he said, coming straight to the point, 'what did you think of the __7__ last night?'

'Auction?' she asked, frowning. 'Auction? What auction?'

'You know, that __8__ old thing they have in the lounge after dinner, selling numbers on the ship's daily run. I just __9__ what you thought about it.'

She shook her head, and again she smiled, a sweet and pleasant smile that had in it perhaps the trace of an apology. 'I'm very lazy,' she said. 'I always go to bed early. I have my dinner in bed. It's so __10__ to have dinner in bed.'

Mr. Botibol smiled back at her and began to edge away. 'Got to go and get my exercise now' he said. 'Never miss my exercise in the morning. It was nice seeing you. Very nice seeing you . . .' He retreated about ten paces, and the woman let him go without looking around.

239a Compare lists of words with your partner. Then listen and write the words that Edmund and Bruce, Rachel and Chris suggested.

239b b Listen to this part being read and see what words were in the original.

c As you read this second half, imagine what Mr. Botibol must have been thinking.

Everything was now in order. The sea was calm, he was lightly dressed for swimming, there were almost certainly no man-eating sharks in this part of the Atlantic, and there was this pleasant kindly old woman to give the alarm. It was a question now only of whether the ship would be delayed long enough to swing the balance in his favour. Almost certainly it would. In any event, he could do a little to help in that direction himself. He could make a few difficulties about getting hauled up into the lifeboat. Swim around a bit, back away from them surreptitiously as they tried to come up close to fish him out. Every minute, every second gained would help him win. He began to move forward again to the rail, but now a new fear assailed him. Would he get caught in the propeller? He had heard about that happening to persons falling off the sides of big ships. But then, he wasn't going to fall, he was going to jump, and that was a very different thing. Provided he jumped out far enough he would be sure to clear the propeller.

Mr. Botibol advanced slowly to a position at the rail about twenty yards away from the woman. She wasn't looking at him now. So much the better. He didn't want her watching him as he jumped off. So long as no one was watching he would be able to say afterwards that he had slipped and fallen by accident. He peered over the side of the ship. It was a long, long drop. Come to think of it now, he might easily hurt himself badly if he hit the water flat. Wasn't there someone who once split his stomach open that way, doing a belly flop from the high dive? He must jump straight and land feet first. Go in like a knife. Yes sir. The water seemed cold and deep and grey and it made him shiver to look at it. But it was now or never. Be a man, William Botibol, be a man. All right then . . . now . . . here goes . . .

239c Listen to the story being read.

239d d Note what Rachel and Chris, Bruce and Edmund think is going to happen.

▶ Write two sentences to continue the story dramatically. Read them to the class. ◀

240 REVIEW

UNIT 23

a Changing things
Which of the things listed below might someone deliberately:

deepen strengthen lengthen shorten broaden darken tighten?

a door lock   a journey
their experience   a sickroom
a skirt   their attitudes
a harbour channel   security

Which of these things listed below might, of their own accord: darken weaken deepen strengthen quicken:

your affection or love   the sky
feeling of doubt   someone's sight
feeling of depression   the beat of the music
the pace   your determination

NEW WORDS IN UNIT 23

ankle	illness
beforehand	immense
brave	insecurity
broaden	kindness
coat	long-term
deaf	lounge
demonstrate	optimism
demonstration	optimistic
determination	pace
determined	resemble
dive	retreat
diversify	secure
divorce	sensible
faithful	separation
feature	shiver
generosity	slope
generous	sufficient
hips	tone
	trace

37 new words
TOTAL SO FAR 950

b Opposites with in- im- un-
Use a dictionary where needed to make these adjectives opposite in meaning by adding **in-** **un-** or **im-**. Choose five and think of a context for them. What others do you know?

direct	conscious	ambitious
possible	faithful	intelligent
kind	fair	patient
secure	moderate	delicate
certain	connected	steady
sufficient	sound	polite

239 Dip in the pool

Aims: 1 Inferring meanings from context.
2 Listening for specific detail.
3 Understanding the predictive nature of words like **reason**, **difficulties** etc.

Lexis: advanced, apology, dive, exercise, lounge, paces, provided that, retreated, shiver, trace
Revision: **deep, in order, split (open), stomach, by accident** (= without intending to)
Understanding only: **sharks, belly flop** (= dive flat onto your stomach), **propellers, hauled up**
Phrases: **It was a question of whether . . . , in any event** (= in any case, no matter what happened), **Come to think of it . . . , swing the balance in his favour, 'a bit floored' on that one** (= found that one more or less impossible to do) (coll.), **. . . loses his nerve**

Reading   SB239a

1 Students guess the words by themselves, make a list, and then compare with their partner's list. See if they can retell the story briefly – despite the missing words.

Listening   SB239a

2 Students listen to see which words the native-speakers suggested.

Listening   SB239b

3 Play the recording so students can check the original words. If they sound very different from those students guessed, do they have a similar meaning?

Key: 1 slowly   2 pleasantly
3 beautiful   4 plain   5 deaf
6 blind   7 auction   8 silly
9 wondered   10 restful

Reading and listening   SB239c

4 Students read and then listen to the second half, to enjoy the story. Can they imagine how they would feel if they were Mr Botibol?

5 See TB234 note 3. Ask students to find three words like **reason**, **thought** and **problem**. (Three in the first paragraph, one at the beginning of the second paragraph.)

Key: It was a question of . . . , a few difficulties . . . , A new fear . . . , a position.

Listening and writing   SB239d

6 Ask students for their own ideas before they listen. The listening may give students some more ideas about what to write. Play the tape, and then ask students to write two dramatic sentences and read them out.

240 Review

Key: a deepen a harbour channel; strengthen a door lock/attitudes; lengthen/shorten a skirt/journey/channel; broaden experience; darken a sickroom; tighten security.
Point out with these you could paraphrase: make X deeper/stronger etc.
the sky might darken; affection/sight/determination – weaken; affection/love/depression – deepen; affection/love/determination/doubt – strengthen; the pace/beat of the music – quicken.
Here you could paraphrase: X grew deeper/darker etc.
Note: Ask which of these could apply to the picture of the steel band.

LEXICAL OBJECTIVES

Lexical sets: words describing personality and physical qualities. Revision of parts of the face and body.

ankle where your foot joins your leg. *an elderly woman with very thick ankles.*
beforehand earlier than something. *All he had to do was check by talking to her a moment beforehand.*
brave EED T 1 courageous. Also: *put a brave face on it; brave a situation.*
broaden 1 T become wider.
2 to include or become involved with a larger number of things. *We've broadened out to doing things like pantomime. broaden our horizons.*
3 T *broaden your mind* = to become more willing to accept other's beliefs.
coat 1 *a coat of Persian lamb.*
2 T a thin layer. *a coat of paint; my face was coated with dust.*
deaf unable to hear.
demonstrate 1 to show, make clear. *This will demonstrate how . . .*
2 T take part in a march or meeting to show opposition or support.
demonstration 1 see **demonstrate** 2. *political demonstrations*
2 T talk given by someone to show how something is done or works.
3 T *demonstration of affection*
determination T quality you show when you won't let anyone stop you.
determined T having made a firm decision to do something, you stick to it. *Mr Botibol is determined to win.*
dive EED 1 jump head-first into water. *a high dive.* Also: *deep-sea diving.*
2 T *he dived after the ball.*
diversify increase the variety of things you do. *trying to diversify.* Also: *diversity.* = variety.
divorced 1 no longer married. *I did have a family. I'm divorced now.*
2 T treat two things as separate. *Is it possible to divorce sport from politics?*
faithful T 1 remain firm in your support. Also: *a faithful husband.*
2 *the film was faithful to the book.*
feature EED T 1 a part/characteristic something has. *One feature of our work is that . . . safety features.*
2 *physical features* = parts of the face.
3 articles in a magazine/newspaper. *a feature on . . .*
4 *a news story which featured . . .*

generosity T quality of being generous
generous T 1 someone who gives more of something than is usually expected. *a generous donation to charity.*
2 kind, helpful. *She's a generous soul.*
hips sides of your body between the tops of your legs and your waist. *wide hips. She put her hands on her hips.* T
illness 1 experience of being ill.
2 T a particular disease.
immense extremely large, massive. *an elderly woman with thick ankles and immense buttocks.*
insecurity 1 T feeling unsure of yourself. *Divorce often creates feelings of insecurity.*
2 state of being unsafe, unprotected. *decided to give up a secure job for the insecurity of singing.*
kindness T caring, helpful act or attitude. *he treated his workers with kindness and consideration.*
long-term *long-term plans. In the long term* = over a long period of time
lounge 1 room where you sit and relax.
2 *airport lounge*
3 lounge about. *relax in a lazy way.*
optimism feeling of being hopeful and positive about the future.
optimistic T people were optimistic and hopeful. *Are you an optimist or a pessimist?*
pace EED 1 T speed. *at a brisk pace.*
2 *keep pace with.*
3 a step of normal length. *He retreated about ten paces.*
resemble be similar to. *it resembled, in shape at any rate, a bollard.*
retreat 1 move away from. *He retreated about ten paces* – the woman let him go
2 T *the enemy forces retreated.*
secure EED 3 something you are certain not to lose. *a secure job.*
4 T firmly fixed.
sensible T 1 able to make good decisions based on reason not emotion. *She was far too sensible to believe these ridiculous lies.*
2 *sensible clothes/shoes* are practical and strong rather than fashionable.
separation 1 state of being apart or away from someone.
shiver You shiver when you are cold. *The water seemed deep and cold and it made him shiver to look at it.*
slope 1 T side of a mountain, hill or valley. *Ski slopes.*
2 sloping = at an angle. *sloping shoulders. sloping handwriting.*
sufficient enough. *sufficient noise to attract attention.*
tone EED 1 tone of voice is a quality in their voice which shows what the person is thinking. Also: *ringing tone* (telephone); *tone of an instrument, colours tone in well*
trace EED 1 T find, discover. *trace a missing person.*
2 to outline a pattern or argument.
3 T a sign that shows someone has been there. *vanish without trace.*
4 very small amount. *traces of poison. a pleasant smile that had in it perhaps the trace of an apology.*

96T

Unit 24 — Revision Unit

This revision unit contains a wide variety of tasks for both speaking and writing, to take students back over important features of the whole course (not just the preceding five units). Many sections give students specific section references where they can find something to help them with the task. You may need to allow extra time for this preparation and revision.

In this unit we are more concerned with getting students to do a lot, and realise how much they can now do, rather than to learn new words. They are also encouraged to consider ways to help them continue to learn English in the future. The first part of the unit reviews the common text patterns students have covered. Practice in written summary is followed by Chapter Nine of the story which then leads on to the denouement. Revising Bob Jobbins' analyses of different types of news story, students then prepare reports on the events in the short story – one in the form of a radio news item, one as a newspaper report. There is practice in letter writing and a short book or film review. Finally there is a competition that gives students the opportunity to win a dictionary.

OBJECTIVES

Discussion topics

Ways to keep up a foreign language. (248)

Social skills

a Recalling previous events. (241)
b Describing people and places. (241)

Communication skills

a Writing short notes about people and places. (241)
b Scanning texts to check on specific details. (241,251)
c Skim reading to check the sequence of events. (243)
d Producing oral and written summaries. (243)
e Reading a narrative. (244,246)
f Speculating on the outcome of a story. (244)
g Preparing and writing a news bulletin. (246)
h Preparing and writing a newspaper story. (246)
i Discussing and recommending possible courses of action. (248)
j Writing letters of application. (249)
k Reading and assessing book reviews. (250)
l Expressing personal opinions in writing. (251)

Grammar and discourse

a Recognising discourse patterns in text (242):
    situation–comment/evaluation
    sequential
    general–specific
    situation–problem–solution–evaluation
    toipic–illustration
    hypothesis–evidence–conclusion
b **Had** in past narrative (past perfect). (245)
c Reporting thoughts, opinions, speech etc. (247)

You would find useful:
a selection of English newspapers and magazines (246).
English Language School Brochures (249).
publishers' catalogues of readers (250).

241 How observant are you?

Aims: 1 Recalling and describing previous events.
2 Scanning a text quickly to check for specific details.
3 Describing people and places.
4 Writing short notes about people and places.
5 Writing explanatory captions (using noun phrases).

Task, planning and report SB241 PB241

1 Ask students to form groups of three or four, and see how many of the bits of pictures they can identify.

2 Students can share out the writing of notes so that each student writes on four or five of the pictures. They may well need to go back through Student's Book texts, and check on details, so allow time for this.

3 Ask students to check each other's notes, and practise talking about one or two of their pictures.

4 Each group in turn tells the class about one item, but without stating the section number or exactly which it is or where it is on the page. Go on taking turns, until all pictures have been identified and described.

Key: subjects and sections (from top left): sun 65, cat 150, Mr Botibol writing cheque 224, lighthouse 34, cooker 102, disc jockey 130, peanut butter 82, flight case 100, Bruce 4, Yetties 20, Selina 176, 3 wishes 226.

242 Language study

Aim: Recognising discourse patterns in text.

SB242 PB242

1 Divide the class into six groups. Allot each group one text pattern, which they look up in the appropriate section and then explain to the class, with an example.

2 Students do examples 1–5 on their own and then discuss any problems in pairs. Go over them with the class.

Key: 1 General–specific (*or* Topic–illustration)
2 Situation–problem–solution 3 Hypothesis–evidence–conclusion 4 Situation–comment 5 Sequence

243 Summarising

Aims: 1 Preparing oral and written summaries.
2 To encourage skim-reading.

Listening SB243a 243a PB243

1 You may need to play each summary through twice.

Sample comments:
The first summary is very concise, but almost too short to be understood by someone who had not read the story. The second summary is much clearer, but too long – it includes details which are not necessary in a summary, e.g. one of the passengers leaving the table feeling sick is merely an illustration of the topic so could be omitted.

Both summaries are obviously unplanned. They contain colloquial expressions, for example 'grill' the purser (= ask demanding detailed questions). Also, some facts are in the wrong order, e.g. 'He goes to bed after the auction – he has managed to get the number he wants.'

Reading SB243b

2 Students could do this on their own or in pairs.

Writing SB243c

3 Using the information in their tables, students write a summary of the story, and include one extra detail, or piece of false information. They can add the ending they thought of in the last unit (section 239).

4 Students read each other's summaries and find the extra detail.

97T

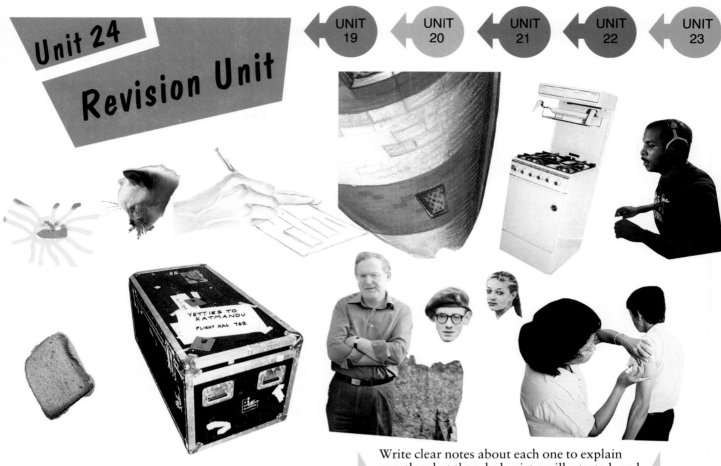

241 How observant are you?

All the above are pictures from somewhere in this book. How many of these can your group recognise?

▷ Write clear notes about each one to explain exactly what the whole picture illustrated, and what the writer or speakers were talking about.

▷ Take turns to choose one and tell the class about it. Do they think what you say is right?

242 *Language study*

Different patterns in text
You have studied the following text patterns:

SITUATION – COMMENT/EVALUATION
A SEQUENCE OF EVENTS/STAGES (18)
GENERAL – SPECIFIC (46)
SITUATION – PROBLEM – SOLUTION – EVALUATION (79, 119)
TOPIC – ILLUSTRATION (86)
HYPOTHESIS – EVIDENCE – CONCLUSION (123)

Look up one of these patterns in the section given and write down one or two examples so that you can explain the pattern to the rest of the class.

Which pattern do these texts fit?

1 *Most big cats can turn man-eater. The leopard is no exception.*
2 *He wanted to drive off up the highway, but unfortunately he was handcuffed. The only thing was to steer with his feet.*
3 *It is possible that another source of water could be found. If there is a well at the top of the hill there is a good chance that there is water at the bottom too.*
4 *He managed to jump from the roof and catch the girl as she was falling. It was an incredible feat.*
5 *We started singing together in the Scouts and then, when we all started work, we made a bit of money as entertainers in our spare time, until eventually we decided to go fully professional.*

243 Summarising

243a **a** Rachel and Chris, then Edmund and Bruce, were asked to summarise 'Dip in the Pool'. Listen to their summaries and say which one is clearest.

b Skim quickly back through the chapters of 'Dip in the Pool', from section 206 onwards, then fill out a table like the one on the right:

Mr. Botibol's movements throughout the story

Where he was/went	How he felt	Who he spoke to	Result

▷ **c** In no more than 120 words, write your own summary of the story so far, then add the ending you thought of. Include an extra detail that is not in the original story.

Swap summaries. Can you spot the extra detail?

97

244 Dip in the pool

a Read on and answer the questions that follow.

CHAPTER NINE

HELP!

He climbed up onto the wide wooden toprail, stood there poised, balancing for three terrifying seconds, then he leaped – he leaped up and out as far as he could go and at the same time he shouted 'Help!'

'Help! Help!' he shouted as he fell. Then he hit the water and went under.

When the first shout for help sounded, the woman who was leaning on the rail started up and gave a little jump of surprise. She looked around quickly and saw sailing past her through the air this small man dressed in white shorts and tennis shoes, spread-eagled and shouting as he went. For a moment she looked as though she weren't quite sure what she ought to do: throw a life belt, run away and give the alarm, or simply turn and yell. She drew back a pace from the rail and swung half around facing up to the bridge, and for this brief moment she remained motionless, tense, undecided. Then almost at once she seemed to relax, and she leaned forward far over the rail, staring at the water where it was turbulent in the ship's wake. Soon a tiny round black head appeared in the foam, an arm was raised above it, once, twice, vigorously waving, and a small faraway voice was heard calling something that was difficult to understand. The woman leaned still farther over the rail, trying to keep the little bobbing black speck in sight, but soon, so very soon, it was such a long way away that she couldn't even be sure it was there at all.

After a while another woman came out on deck. This one was bony and angular, and she wore horn-rimmed spectacles. She spotted the first woman and walked over to her, treading the deck in the deliberate, military fashion of all spinsters.

'So there you are,' she said.

The woman with the fat ankles turned and looked at her, but said nothing.

'I've been searching for you,' the bony one continued. 'Searching all over.'

'It's very odd,' the woman with the fat ankles said. 'A man dived overboard just now, with his clothes on.'

1 Did the fat woman see him fall into the sea?
2 Has she reported what has happened?
3 Do you think Mr. Botibol will be rescued?
4 Do you think he will win the pool?

Tell each other what you think.

244a Who do you agree with most – Edmund and Bruce or Rachel and Chris?

244b **b** Listen to this chapter on tape then read the ending. Your teacher will tell you where it is.

Tell each other how you feel about it.

5 Do you think the title 'Dip in the Pool' is a good one? What themes does it relate to?
6 What do you know about the thin woman, Maggie, and the other woman?
7 When the Captain finds out what has happened, he is bound to ask for exact details. What do you think Maggie might say?

244c **c** Listen to what Rachel and Chris think. (Note that they wrongly think Maggie is the fat woman.) Then listen to Edmund and Bruce.

Write a description of the two women. What do you think is the relationship between them?

245 Grammar

Had in past narrative

Read these sentences summarising 'Dip in the Pool':

1 *The sea was very rough on Mr. Botibol's voyage to the States.*
2 *Thinking that the bad weather would slow the ship up Mr. Botibol decided to buy the low field in the daily auction.*
3 *He paid two hundred pounds for the ticket, hoping to win enough money to buy a new car.*
4 *When he woke up next morning he was horrified to find that the sea was calm and the ship was moving quickly.*
5 *Mr. Botibol was terrified of losing all his savings so he had to find some way of slowing the ship down.*
6 *Finally he hit on the crazy plan of jumping overboard.*

What happens if you start the story at sentence 4?

When Mr. Botibol woke up he was horrified to find that the sea was calm and the ship was moving quickly. At the start of his voyage to the States the sea had been very rough. Thinking that the bad weather would slow the ship up Mr. Botibol had decided to . . .

Try telling the story, starting with the words:

Mr. Botibol was terrified. Unless he could find a way of slowing the ship down he would lose all his savings.

OR

Mr. Botibol stood on the deck ready to jump overboard.

244 Dip in the pool

Aims: 1 Reading a narrative.
2 Speculating on the outcome of a story.

Lexis: judging from that, there's something about the way...
Understanding only: **disturbed** ts, **moral** ts, **get rid of** ts, **spread-eagled** (= with legs and arms out)
Colloquial expressions: **a bit fishy** (= suspicious), **a mental case** (= mentally ill//handicapped), **tied up with** (= involved in)

Reading and listening   SB244a

1 Explain that this is the last but one Chapter. Students read it for the story, and then discuss answers to questions 1–4 in pairs.

2 Ask students to share their opinions with the class.

3 Play the recording, and discuss who students agree with most, and why.

Listening and reading   SB244b   SB250

4 Play the recording, for students to enjoy.

5 The last Chapter has been deliberately 'hidden' to prevent students reading the end too soon. It is in section 250, entitled 'Such a nice man'. Let students read it now, and react to it informally. Ask if they thought it a good ending. What did they think of the last line?

6 Ask students to discuss answers to questions 5–7. (Remind them of section 205 where **dip** and **pool** appear in Dictionary Skills.)

7 Discuss the title with the class. Ask what students feel about questions 6 and 7.

   Key: Themes the title relates to: dip – the idea of a quick 'dip' (in a metaphorical sense), into a gambling situation; he ended up having a longer 'dip' (but in the sea, not in a swimming pool); the pool refers to the ship's pool of money from the sales of the mileage tickets.

Listening   SB244c

8 Explain that Rachel and Chris, and then Edmund and Bruce, discuss questions 6 and 7, and make general comments on the ending. Also make sure that students know that Maggie is the thin woman, who came to find the woman with the fat ankles. Rachel and Chris got the two women mixed up.

9 Play the recording. Ask students to summarise what Chris and Rachel felt about the two women. Bruce and Edmund in fact only discuss question 7, and the ending.

Writing   SB244c

10 The description can include both physical appearance and personality. Students will need to re-read the descriptions in the last Chapters. Encourage students to contrast the two women. (Refer them to sections 61b and 220.) A further paragraph could explore and speculate on the relationship between them, i.e. who the women are.

11 Students might enjoy reading each other's descriptions.

245 Grammar

Aim: Had in past narrative (past perfect).

SB245

1 Read through sentences 1–6 with students. Make sure students realise they are in the correct sequence, and that the verbs denoting the main action are in the past simple tense.

2 If you start at sentence 4, all the verbs referring to earlier events (sentences 1,2,3) go into the past perfect. Ask students to do sentence 3 so it fits this account. (*He had paid...*)

3 Ask students to work on the third version (*Mr Botibol was terrified...*) on their own. Then get them to start the narrative with the last sentence.

4 Point out the same thing happens with a present tense narrative; it can switch to present perfect. See transcript 243, where Bruce forgets to mention that Mr Botibol bought his number, and adds it later: 'He goes to bed after the auction – he has manged to get the number he wants –...'

246 Disappearance at sea

> **Aims:** 1 Preparing and writing a radio news bulletin.
> 2 Preparing and writing a newspaper story.

Lead-in   SB246 PB246

1 First ask students to guess what letters are missing from the section title (written with gaps to prevent students guessing too soon what happened to Mr Botibol).

Planning and recorded report   SB246a

2 Explain that students will be asked to write and record a news story – either about Mr Botibol (hence the headline 'Disappearance at Sea') or about a local event or story that has just happened.

To do this well, students may need to revise what Bob Jobbins explained about different types of news broadcast: Unit 16, transcripts 161, 163; SB165 and SB169, and Unit 18 transcript 188; SB189.

3 With students in pairs, ask them first to choose a topic for a news despatch, and then to decide on the type of broadcast to prepare. (Your weaker students could do a simple News Summary, while your better students could tackle a Current Affairs style interview, or even a News and Comment report.

4 Go round and help students plan and rehearse their dispatches. Those that finish early can go round and write a list of topics of broadcasts, and decide what order to record them in, or help to 'edit' other items.

5 Students record their reports, in turn, and then play them back as a news broadcast.

Before going on to section SB246b, you may find it useful to do section 247.

Planning and written report   SB246b

6 For the planning of the newspaper story, follow a similar procedure to SB246a above, allowing time for students to review especially the Grammar and Language sections.

7 Optional alternative: create a newspaper.

Rather than writing their own, students could select interesting items (stories, short features, radio/TV/Film reviews, cartoons) from any English newspapers or magazines, copy them out or photocopy them, and use them to make up a newspaper page to display on the wall.

247 Grammar

> **Aims:** 1 Reporting thoughts, opinion and speech.
> 2 To show that reporting what people think or feel is even more common than reporting what people say.
> 3 To show that (**that**), **to** and **of** are also used very commonly after words which have a function other than reporting.

SB247

1 Go through the first few with the class. The first one, 'risk of falling', is strictly neither saying nor thinking, but it does show how people feel – that there is a danger of falling victim. The second, 'sure that', is to do with thinking. The third and fourth ones, 'the answer is to' and 'sure way of', do not actually report. They are ways of giving advice.

Key: 5 The thing is (that) it's so expensive – neither saying nor thinking, a way of emphasising the point.
6 expect to – thinking   7 believed to – thinking
8 found that – thinking (**found** here means 'realised' or 'discovered')   9 privilege of – neither   10 Nice to – neither (opinion)   11 clear that – neither   12 been told – saying (**told** is very common in the passive)   13 assumed that – thinking

2 Ask students to read through transcripts of both conversations in section 244c and see what examples they can find of reported thought, opinion, or speech, with and without **that** (about 12).

Key: I don't think either that they'll really believe her / They may think she's just imagining things. / I don't think they'd believe her / she didn't think that he was... / She just thought he was going out for a swim. / I don't think she actually understood what he was doing / when they found out he's missing / have to pretend she knows nothing / reveal that this other woman / she therefore thought that there couldn't be... / she says she couldn't possibly believe the word of Miss X

Further examples:
14 *The other thing I felt was that the second letter was much more detailed.* (opinion)
15 *The official version says that Jack fell.* (speech; could be writing)
16 *The unsuccessful artist decided that his prayers had been answered.* (thought)
17 *He would be able to say afterwards that he had slipped and fallen by accident.* (speech)
18 *She'll have to be honest and reveal that this other woman is not to be trusted.* (speech)

248 Keep up your English

> **Aims:** 1 Discussing possible courses of action.
> 2 Recommending particular courses of action.

Task   SB248

1 Students working in groups discuss ideas and write notes. They should have some rough idea of how much each alternative will cost.

2 Ask students to agree on the best ideas to tell the class about. If they don't know how to begin, point out there are some ideas in the picture.

Report   SB248

3 A spokesperson from each group reports back to the class. How many groups had similar ideas? Which ones are the most practical, and therefore the most likely to be followed through and carried out?

4 Take the opportunity to discuss this seriously with your class.

249 Letter writing

> **Aim:** Writing letters of application.

You may want to let your students choose which of these two, a or b, to write.

Writing   SB249a PB249

1 Students could begin preparing this at home, revising the relevant sections and thinking of what to say.

2 Help students write a final version of this in class. They can exchange letters and read each other's and suggest improvements.

Writing   SB249b

3 Students should by now be able to do this with little help from you. When they have finished their letters, take them in, and give them out again to different students.

4 If you have some Language School brochures, now is the time to give them out. Students can read them for relevant details to include in their replies.

D*s*p*e*r*n*e *t *e*

a Radio News
Look again at what Bob Jobbins said about how to write news stories. He explained and demonstrated three main types of radio news report:
– **News Summary**: the short factual news communiqué, where the announcer summarizes what's happened, then asks the correspondent for a brief report. (161)
– **Current Affairs** programme: the presenter interviews the correspondent on the air. (163)
– **News and Comment**: a longer, more detailed report for the serious news programme. (188)

Select one of these three formats. Plan and record a news despatch in one of these styles, **either** about Mr. William Botibol, **or** about some recent local event. Play them to each other.

b Newspaper news story
Plan how to write a piece for a newspaper about Mr. Botibol, under the headline that forms the title of this section.

Decide what type of newspaper you wish to write for – serious, or popular; a local newspaper, or an international one – and on the length of the piece: **News in Brief,** (see section 154) or a back page summary, (section 40) or a full feature (see sections 173 and 196).

You will find that the Grammar and Language Studies in sections 151, 155, 165 and 169 will help you.

Write a report and pass it round the class.

Grammar ··················

Reporting   Thoughts, opinions and speech: What people think, feel and say
How many nouns, verbs and adjectives can you find that introduce clauses with (that), to and of?
How many of them are to do with *saying* or *thinking*?

1 *… advice on how* to *reduce the risk* of *falling victim to serious crime.*
2 *I'm not sure* that *I want to go.*
3 *If you want to lose weight the answer is* to *give up all fatty food.*
4 *Giving up all fatty foods is the only sure way* of *losing weight.*
5 *It's certainly a good one. The only thing is, it's so expensive.*
6 *Write three questions you would expect* to *find answered.*
7 *His female companion is not believed* to *have been seriously injured.*
8 *He found* that *his parking fees had left him with only two dollars.*
9 *We have had the privilege* of *entertaining guests from overseas.*
10 *Nice* to *meet you.*
11 *It is clear* that *there could be further developments.*
12 *We've been told many times* that *audiences in many countries … will appreciate what you are doing.*
13 *The neighbour assumed* that *she had misunderstood Mrs. Kerr.*

Keep up your English

In groups discuss the best ways to keep up your English and carry on learning on your own, after finishing this course. What possibilities are open to you? What do you intend to do?

Tell the class what most people in your group intend to do, and how. How much it will cost?

Letter writing

Before you start, revise sections 24, 25 and 134.

a Applying for a scholarship or travel grant
Imagine that you get a chance to apply for a scholarship or travel grant to enable you to improve your English.

Write not more than 250 words applying for a travel award which allows you to travel to Britain and take a course in English, all free.

Say why you feel you deserve this money – what you have done in the past and why you need good English in the future.

b Letter to a language school
Plan a letter to a language school, telling them how much English you already know, and in what areas you wish to improve. Ask them what they can offer you in the way of language tuition. Ask for any other information about cost, size of class, other students, accommodation, entertainment, travel etc, that you'd like to have.

Write your letter.

Exchange letters with someone else in your class and reply to their letter. (You could use a Language School brochure to help you.)

[250] Read more widely?

Marilyn Monroe *Peter Dainty* The sad story of the life and death of one of the cinema's most controversial stars. 80pp

Is That It? *Bob Geldof* The life story of a modern day hero. 80pp

The Canterville Ghost *Oscar Wilde* A comic short story in which an American family in Europe meet their first ghost. 48pp

Chariots of Fire *WJ Wetherby* A moving tale of the courage and determination of 2 men who 'ran for gold' in the 1924 Olympics. Based on the smash hit British film. 48pp

Tina Turner *Stephen Rabley* This is the story of Tina Turner – grandmother, actress, Buddhist and queen of rock and roll – From her early days in America, through hard times, to her present day position as one of the world's most exciting singers. 48pp

---

Such a nice man *Roald Dahl*

'Nonsense.'

'Oh yes. He said he wanted to get some exercise and he dived in and didn't even bother to take his clothes off.'

'You better come down now,' the bony woman said. Her mouth had suddenly become firm, her whole face sharp and alert, and she spoke less kindly than before. 'And don't you ever go wandering about on deck alone like this again. You know quite well you're meant to wait for me.'

'Yes, Maggie,' the woman with the fat ankles answered, and again she smiled, a tender, trusting smile, and she took the hand of the other one and allowed herself to be led away across the deck.

'Such a nice man,' she said. 'He waved to me.'

▶ Write a review of a book you've read, or a film or show you've watched. ◀

[251] Annual competition

GREAT PRIZES TO HELP YOU IMPROVE YOUR ENGLISH EVEN MORE!

WIN A FREE DICTIONARY!

RUNNERS UP WIN A COLLINS READER

Collins Publishers offer five first prizes and twenty runner up prizes TO THE BEST ENTRIES

All you have to do is find the answers to the eight quiz questions below – they are all to be found in Level 3 Student's Book or Transcripts – and then write a short piece – not more than 150 words – about what you liked best about Level 3.

Copy out this entry form and fill it in (don't forget to include your name and address!).
Send it to Collins ELT (Cobuild Competition Entry) 8 Grafton Street, London W1X 3LA, to reach them by 30th September. Please enclose an addressed envelope. All entries received after 30th September next will be saved for the following year's competition.

ENTRY FORM

Name _____

Date _____

Full postal address _____

_____

_____

Where have you been studying English?

_____

_____

Section A

1 If you like poetry, you will remember that the longest journey was from _____ to _____.
2 A man of 84 once borrowed a car from _____ who was _____.
3 Whose legs appeared in the James Bond film 'Live and Let die'? _____.
4 What did the Yetties lose on their trip to Nepal? _____

5 Bob Jobbins wrote a news report about a row over inadequate _____.
6 Is it true that if an unintelligent woman marries a bright man she will become more intelligent? _____
7 Mr. Botibol was on a ship going to _____.
8 Who wanted to go and work in a Third World country as a health worker when the children had grown up? _____

Section B
The things I most enjoyed about the Collins Cobuild English Course:

_____

_____

_____

_____

_____

Number of words in **Section B**: _____ (NOT MORE THAN 150)

Read more widely

> **Aims:** 1 Reading and assessing book reviews.
> 2 Writing a review of a book or film.
> 3 To encourage students to read in English.
> 4 To encourage students to listen to more songs in English.

Class discussion   SB250

1 Reading is one very good way of continuing to learn English. Ask students which of the books described here appeal to them. Have some students already read other books in English?

2 Suggest that students join a library where they can borrow books in English. Show them some publishers' catalogues so they can find out what is available, and what to ask their library for. Magazines and newspapers are also worthwhile.

Writing   SB250

3 Discuss with the class what a review should contain.

For example: Enough of the story to whet the appetite, but not too much; details of some of the main characters; the style and length; whether it is slow or fast-moving, funny, exciting, full of action . . . mysterious, or moving; the kind of person who would enjoy it; where you can see/ find it.

4 Optional: If your students have enjoyed the songs on the student's cassette, play some again. The song from Unit 1, section 9, *Come Stranger Come Friend*, fits the 'end of course' theme.

5 What other songs do students know in English? Passing on words of pop-songs is also a good way to continue learning.

'Such a nice man' – see TB244 note 5.

 Annual competition

This is something that students should do as individuals, without your help, but possibly with a dictionary. Make sure they know it is real, and that they do stand a chance of getting a prize.

Dictionary Extracts Index

Dictionary Extracts

These Dictionary Extracts, taken from entries in the *Collins COBUILD Essential English Dictionary*, accompany the Dictionary Skills sections which appear in all units except revision units.

The extracts have been carefully selected and provide material to practise a variety of reference skills. In some extracts you will notice the category numbers are not consecutive. This is because we have only included categories which are helpful and relevant to the skill being practised in a particular unit.

Early use of an English learner's dictionary will help you make progress at intermediate level. We hope that you will go on to exploit the dictionary skills you have learned, by using the *Collins COBUILD Essential English Dictionary* both in and out of class.

-able is added to some verbs to form adjectives. SUFFIX These adjectives describe someone or something as able to have the thing done to them described by the verb. For example, something that is identifiable can be identified. EG *They are both immediately recognizable... Only the titles were readable.*

ADJ CLASSIF stands for **classifying adjective**
Adjectives which have the label ADJ CLASSIF in the Extra Column classify a noun as being of a particular type. Classifying adjectives do not have comparative and superlative forms, and do not have words like 'very', 'more', or 'rather' in front of them.

ADJ PRED stands for **predicative adjective**
Adjectives which have the label ADJ PRED in the Extra Column are normally only used after a verb such as 'be', 'become', 'feel', and 'seem'.

ADJ QUALIT stands for **qualitative adjective**
Adjectives which have the label ADJ QUALIT in the Extra Column describe features of a noun that can vary in amount or intensity, so that you can have more or less of the feature described. They can show this by comparative and superlative forms, or by words like 'very', 'more', and 'most'.

advice /ɔ³dvaɪs/. If you give someone **advice**, you tell them what you think they should do in a particular situation. EG *She promised to follow his advice... They want advice on how to do it.* N UNCOUNT : USU+SUPP

allowance /ɔlauɔns/, **allowances**. 1 An **allowance** is money that is given regularly to someone, in order to help them pay for the things that they need. EG *...a maternity allowance.* N COUNT+SUPP
2 If you **make allowances** for something, you take it into account in your plans or actions. EG *They make no allowances for a child's age.* PHRASE

approach /ɔprɔutʃ/, **approaches, approaching, approached.** 1 When someone **approaches** you, they come nearer to you. EG *He opened the door for her as she approached.* ▶ used as a noun. EG *The dogs began to bark as if aware of our approach.* V+O OR V / ▶ N COUNT +SUPP
2 If you **approach** someone about something, you speak to them about it for the first time, often making a request or offer. EG *They had approached us about working with their party.* ▶ used as a noun. EG *I had an approach to join the staff of the Daily Mail.* V+O : OFT+A / ▶ N COUNT
3 When you **approach** a situation or problem in a particular way, you think about it or deal with it in that way. EG *Governments must approach the sub-* V+O+A

ject of disarmament in a new spirit. [   ]
6 An **approach** to a place is a road or path that leads to it. N COUNT : OFT + to
7 An **approach** to a situation or problem is a way of thinking about it or of dealing with it. EG *We need a new approach to this problem.* N COUNT : OFT + to

assume /ɔ³sjuːm/, **assumes, assuming, assumed.** 1 If you **assume** that something is true, you imagine that it is true, sometimes wrongly. EG *I assume you don't drive... I was mistakenly assumed to be a Welshman because of my surname.* V+REPORT : ONLY *that* OR V+O+*to*-INF
2 If someone **assumes** power or responsibility, they take power or responsibility. EG *Hitler assumed power in 1933.* V+O

-ation, -ations. -ation, -tion, and **-ion** are added to verbs to form nouns. These nouns usually refer to an action or to the result of an action. For example, 'alteration' can refer to the altering of something or to the result of altering something. Nouns like these are often not defined in this dictionary, but are treated with the related verbs. EG *He was annoyed by the cancellation of the visit... The majority of adoptions are highly successful.* SUFFIX

attach /ɔtætʃ/, **attaches, attaching, attached.** 1 If you **attach** something to an object, you join it or fasten it to the object. EG *He attached some string to the can... Attached to the letter was a list of hotels.* V+O : OFT + to
2 If someone **is attached** to an organization or group of people, they are working with them, often only for a short time. EG *Hospital officers would be temporarily attached to NHS hospitals.* V+O : USU PASS + to

attack /ɔtæk/, **attacks, attacking, attacked.** 1 If you **attack** someone, you try to hurt them or to get them in your power using physical violence. EG *He attacked and mutilated two women... She was attacked by a shark.* ▶ used as a noun. EG *There were more attacks on women going alone in the street... There were no defences against nuclear attack.* V+O OR V / ▶ N COUNT OR N UNCOUNT
2 If you **attack** a person, belief, or idea, you criticize them strongly. EG *The senator attacked the press for misleading the public.* ▶ used as a noun. EG *...attacks on apartheid... Burt's work came under violent attack.* [   ] V+O / ▶ N COUNT OR N UNCOUNT
4 If you **attack** a job or a problem, you start to deal with it with energy and enthusiasm. EG *He attacked his task with determination.* V+O
5 When players **attack** in a game such as football or hockey, they try to score a goal. V

attention /ɔ³tɛnʃɔ⁰n/, **attentions.** 1 If you give something your **attention**, you look at it, listen to it, or think about it carefully. EG *When he felt he had their attention, he began... He switched his attention back to the magazine... They were listening with close attention... She was the centre of attention.* N UNCOUNT
2 If someone brings something important or interesting to your **attention** or draws your **attention** to it, they point it out to you. EG *I feel it is my duty to bring to your attention the following facts.* N UNCOUNT

101

3 If something **attracts** your **attention** or **catches** your **attention**, you suddenly notice it. EG *How can I attract the captain's attention?* `PHRASE`

barely /beəli[1]/. If something is **barely** true or possible, it is only just true or possible. EG *He was so drunk that he could barely stand... It was barely two months old.* `ADV BRD NEG`

bear /beə/, **bears, bearing, bore** /bɔː/, **borne** /bɔːn/. **1** A **bear** is a large, strong wild animal with thick fur and sharp claws. ● See also **polar bear.** ● **teddy bear**: see **teddy.** `N COUNT`

2 If you **bear** something somewhere, you carry it there or take it there. EG *Camels and donkeys bear those goods inland... She arrived bearing a large bunch of grapes.* `V+O : USU+A` `Formal`

3 If something **bears** the weight of something else, it supports the weight of that thing. EG *His ankle now felt strong enough to bear his weight.* `V+O`

4 If something **bears** a particular mark or characteristic, it has that mark or characteristic. EG *...a petition bearing nearly half a million signatures... The scene bore all the marks of a country wedding... The interpretation bore no relation to the actual words spoken.* `V+O`

5 If you **bear** something difficult, you accept it and are able to deal with it. EG *It was painful of course but I bore it... Their policies are putting a greater strain on the economic system than it can bear.* ● to **grin and bear it**: see **grin.** `V+O`

6 If you **can't bear** someone or something, you dislike them very much. EG *I can't bear weddings.* [   ] `PHRASE`

8 When a plant or tree **bears** flowers, fruit, or leaves, it produces them. `V+O`

beat /biːt/, **beats, beating, beaten.** The form **beat** is used in the present tense and is the past tense of the verb.

1 If you **beat** someone or something, you hit them very hard. EG *His stepfather used to beat him... The rain beat against the window.* `V+O OR V : OFT+A`

2 When a bird or insect **beats** its wings or when its wings **beat**, its wings move up and down. EG *It was trying to escape, frantically beating its wings.* ▶ used as a noun. EG *Flies can move their wings at 1000 beats per second.* `V-ERG` `▶ N COUNT`

3 When your heart or pulse **is beating**, it is continually making movements with a regular rhythm. EG *His heart beat faster.* ▶ used as a noun. EG *He could feel the beat of her heart.* `V` `▶ N COUNT : USU+SUPP`

4 The **beat** of a piece of music is the main rhythm that it has. `N SING : the+N`

5 If you **beat time** to a piece of music, you move your hand or foot up and down in time with the music. `PHRASE`

6 If you **beat** eggs, cream, or butter, you mix them thoroughly using a fork or whisk. `V+O`

7 If you **beat** someone in a game, race, or competition, you defeat them. EG *He's going to be a tough candidate to beat.* `V+O`

8 If someone or something **beats** a particular thing, they do better than it or are better than it. EG *He'll be trying to beat the world record... To my mind nothing beats a bowl of natural yogurt.* `V+O`

9 If you intend to do something but someone **beats** you **to it,** they do it before you do. EG *The Italians beat them to it by about 36 hours.* `PHRASE`

10 You use **beat** in expressions such as **'It beats me'** to indicate that you cannot understand or explain something. EG *What beats me is where they get the money from.* `PHRASE` `Informal`

11 A police officer **on the beat** is on duty, walking around the area for which he or she is responsible. `PHRASE`

12 If you tell someone to **beat it,** you are telling them to go away. `CONVENTION` `Informal`

brainy /breɪni[1]/, **brainier, brainiest.** Someone who is **brainy** is clever and good at learning. `ADJ QUALIT` `Informal`

business /bɪznɪs/, **businesses. 1 Business** is work relating to the production, buying, and selling of goods or services. EG *...firms that do business with Britain... There are good profits to be made in the hotel business... Are you in San Francisco for business or pleasure?... He had a business appointment.* `N UNCOUNT`

2 A **business** is an organization which produces and sells goods or which provides a service. EG *He set up a small travel business.* `N COUNT`

3 If a shop or company goes **out of business,** it `PHRASE`

has to stop trading because it is not making enough money. EG *Umbrella sellers went out of business.*

4 If you have some **business** to deal with, you have something, especially something important, to deal with. EG *She got on with the business of clearing up... Let's get down to business now.* [   ] `N UNCOUNT`

8 You use **business** to refer in a general way to an event, situation, or activity that you are talking about. EG *The whole business affected him profoundly... This assassination business has gone far enough.* `N SING+SUPP`

campaign /kæmpeɪn/, **campaigns, campaigning, campaigned. 1** A **campaign** is a planned set of activities that people carry out over a period of time, in order to achieve something such as social or political change. EG *...Labour's election campaign... ...the campaign against world hunger.* ▶ used as a verb. EG *He campaigned for political reform.* ◊ **campaigner, campaigners.** EG *...anti-apartheid campaigners.* `N COUNT` `▶ V+A` `◊ N COUNT`

2 In a war, a **campaign** is a series of planned movements carried out by armed forces. EG *...bombing campaigns.* `N COUNT`

chain /tʃeɪn/, **chains, chaining, chained. 1** A **chain** consists of metal rings connected together in a line. EG *She wore a silver chain around her neck... ...a length of chain... ...bicycle chains.* [   ] `N COUNT OR N UNCOUNT`

3 A **chain** of things is a group of them existing or arranged in a line. EG *...the island chains of the Pacific.* `N COUNT+SUPP`

4 A **chain** of shops or hotels is a number of them owned by the same person or company. EG *...a chain of 970 food stores.* `N COUNT+SUPP`

5 A **chain** of events is a series of them happening one after another. EG *...the brief chain of events that led up to her death... ...a nuclear chain reaction.* `N COUNT+SUPP`

civil /sɪvə[0]l/. **1** You use **civil** to describe events that happen within a country and that involve the different groups of people in it. EG *...a society in which wars or civil disturbances happen.* **1.2** people or things in a country that are not connected with its armed forces. EG *...the civil authorities... ...a supersonic civil airliner named the Concorde.* **1.3** the rights that people have within a society. EG *...the defence of civil liberties and human rights.* `1.1 ADJ CLASSIF : ATTRIB`

consider /kənsɪdə/, **considers, considering, considered** [   ] **2** If you **consider** something, you think about it carefully. EG *He had no time to consider the matter... I had begun to consider the possibility of joining a new company.* `V+O`

consideration /kənsɪdəreɪʃə[0]n/, **considerations. 1 Consideration** is **1.1** careful thought about something. EG *After careful consideration, her parents gave her permission.* [   ] `N UNCOUNT`

3 If you **take** something **into consideration**, you think about it because it is relevant to what you are doing. EG *The first thing one has to take into consideration is the cost.* `PHRASE`

considering /kənsɪdə[0]rɪŋ/. You use **considering** to indicate that you are taking a particular fact into account when making a judgement or giving an opinion. EG *Considering that he received no help, his results are very good... Considering her dislike of Martin, it was surprising that she invited him.* `CONJ OR PREP`

council /kaʊnsə[1]l/, **councils. 1** A **council** is **1.1** a group of people who are elected to run a town, borough, city, or county. EG *...Wiltshire County Council... ...council meetings.* **1.2** a group of people who give advice about a particular subject or who run a particular organization. EG *...the Arts Council.* `N COLL` `British`

2 A **council** house or flat is owned by the local council. You pay rent to live in it. EG *...council estates... ...a council tenant.* `ADJ CLASSIF : ATTRIB`

coverage /kʌvə[0]rɪdʒ/. The **coverage** of something in the news is the reporting of it. EG *They put an immediate ban on all television coverage of their operations.* `N UNCOUNT`

covering letter, covering letters. A **covering letter** is a letter that you send with a parcel or with another letter in order to give extra information. `N COUNT`

crisis /kraɪsɪs/, **crises** /kraɪsiːz/. **1** A **crisis** is a serious or dangerous situation which could cause death or hardship to many people. *I was in Munich* `N COUNT OR N UNCOUNT OFT+SUPP` during the 1938 crisis... *They've still got an economic crisis on their hands.*

custom /kʌstəˀm/, **customs.** 1 A **custom** is 1.1 a traditional activity or festivity. EG *My wife likes all the old English customs.* 1.2 something that the people of a society always do in particular circumstances because it is regarded as the right thing to do. EG *It is the custom to take chocolates or fruit when visiting a patient in hospital.* N COUNT / N COUNT OR N UNCOUNT / N COUNT : USU + POSS

defeat /dɪˈfiːt/, **defeats, defeating, defeated.** 1 If you **defeat** someone, you win a victory over them in a battle, game, or contest. EG *Arsenal were defeated on Saturday... Labour was defeated in the General Election of 19 June 1970.* V+O
2 If a proposal or a motion in a debate **is defeated**, more people vote against it than vote for it. EG *The motion was defeated by 221 votes to 152.* V+O : USU PASS
3 If a task or a problem **defeats** you, it is so difficult that you cannot do it or solve it. EG *...a complex sum which defeats many adults as well as children.* V+O

defend /dɪˈfɛnd/, **defends, defending, defended.**
1 If you **defend** someone or something, 1.1 you do something in order to protect them. EG *The village had to defend itself against raiders.* 1.2 you argue in support of them when they have been criticized. EG *The bank has defended its actions in these cases.* V+O OR V-REFL / V+O OR V-REFL
◊ **defender, defenders.** EG *...a defender of right-wing views.* ◊ N COUNT : USU + SUPP
2 In a court of law, when a lawyer **defends** a person who has been accused of a crime, he or she tries to prove that the charges are not true or that there was an excuse for the crime. V+O
3 If a sports champion **defends** his or her title, he or she plays a match or a game against someone who will become the new champion if they win. V+O OR V

destroy /dɪˈstrɔɪ/, **destroys, destroying, destroyed.** 1 To **destroy** something means 1.1 to cause so much damage to it that it is completely ruined. EG *Several buildings were destroyed by the bomb.* 1.2 to cause it not to exist any more. EG *They want to destroy the State... I don't wish to destroy a life-long friendship.* V+O

destruction /dɪˈstrʌkʃəˀn/ is the act of destroying something. EG *It will cause pollution and the destruction of our seas and rivers.* N UNCOUNT

dim /dɪm/, **dimmer, dimmest; dims, dimming, dimmed.** 1 Something that is **dim** is 1.1 rather dark because there is not much light in it. EG *The room was dim.* ◊ **dimly.** EG *...the dimly lit department store.* [   ] ADJ QUALIT / ◊ ADV
2 If your memory of something is **dim**, you can hardly remember it at all. EG *I only have a dim recollection of the production.* ADJ QUALIT
3 If you describe someone as **dim**, you mean that they are stupid. ADJ QUALIT Informal

dip /dɪp/, **dips, dipping, dipped.** 1 If you **dip** something into a liquid or powder, you put it into the liquid or powder and then quickly take it out again. EG *He dipped his pen in the ink.* V+O : OFT +in/into
2 If something **dips**, it makes a downward movement. EG *The plane's nose dipped.* V
3 If a road **dips**, it goes down quite suddenly to a lower level. EG *The railway dips between thick forests.* V
4 A **dip** in a surface is a place in it that is lower than the rest of the surface. EG *...a small dip in the ground.* N COUNT
5 A **dip** is a thick creamy mixture which you eat by scooping it up with raw vegetables or biscuits. EG *...tasty cheese dips.* N COUNT OR N UNCOUNT
6 If you have a **dip**, you go for a quick swim. N COUNT

district /dɪstrɪkt/, **districts.** A **district** is 1 an area of a town or country. EG *...doctors in country districts... ...a working class district of Paris.* 2 an administrative area of a town or country. EG *...district councils... ...the Southall district of London.* N COUNT + SUPP

dress /drɛs/, **dresses, dressing, dressed.** 1 A **dress** is a piece of clothing worn by a woman or girl. It covers her body and extends down over her legs. EG *She was wearing a short black dress.* N COUNT
2 You can refer to clothes worn by men or women as **dress**. EG *He was in evening dress.* N UNCOUNT

dumb /dʌm/, **dumber, dumbest.** 1 Someone who is **dumb** is completely unable to speak. EG *She was deaf and dumb from birth.* ADJ CLASSIF

2 If someone is **dumb** on a particular occasion, they cannot speak because they are angry, shocked, or surprised. EG *We were struck dumb with horror.* ADJ PRED

3 **Dumb** also means stupid; an offensive use. EG *Get out of the way, you dumb idiot.* ADJ QUALIT Informal

education /ɛdjəˀkeɪʃəˀn/ consists of teaching people various subjects at a school or college. EG *...the government's policy on higher education.* N UNCOUNT

effect /ɪˈfɛkt/, **effects, effecting, effected.** 1 An **effect** is 1.1 a change or event that is caused by something or is the result of something. EG *This has the effect of separating students from teachers... ...the effect of noise on people in the factories... These measures did have some effect on rural poverty.* 1.2 an impression that a speaker or artist deliberately creates. EG *Don't move, or you'll destroy the whole effect.* ● If you do something **for effect**, you do it in order to impress people. EG *...a pause for effect.* N COUNT OR N UNCOUNT : OFT + on / N COUNT / ● PHRASE
2 You add **in effect** to a statement to indicate that it is not precisely accurate but it is a reasonable description or summary of a situation. EG *In effect he has no choice.* ADV SEN
3 You use **to this effect, to that effect**, or **to the effect that** when you are summarizing what someone has said, rather than repeating their actual words. EG *...a rumour to the effect that he had been drunk... He said, 'No, you fool, the other way!' or words to that effect.* PHRASE
4 When something **takes effect** or **is put into effect**, it starts to happen or to have some result. EG *The tax cuts take effect on July 1st... Signing the agreement was one thing, putting it into effect was another.* PHRASE
5 If you **effect** something, you succeed in causing it to happen. EG *Production was halted until repairs could be effected.* V+O Formal
6 See also **sound effect**.

effective /ɪˈfɛktɪv/. 1 Something that is **effective** works well and produces the results that were intended. EG *...the most effective ways of reducing pollution... In order to be effective we need your support.* ◊ **effectiveness.** EG *Methods vary in effectiveness.* ADJ QUALIT / ◊ N UNCOUNT
2 **Effective** also means having a particular role or result in practice, though not officially. EG *He assumed effective command of the armed forces.* ADJ CLASSIF : ATTRIB
3 When a law or an agreement becomes **effective**, it begins officially to apply or be valid. EG *...a ceasefire, to become effective as soon as possible.* ADJ PRED

effectively /ɪˈfɛktɪvliˀ/. 1 If something works **effectively**, it works well. EG *...an attempt to make the system work more effectively.* ADV
2 You can also use **effectively** to indicate that what you are saying is a reasonable summary of a situation, although it is not precisely accurate. EG *The television was on, effectively ruling out conversation.* ADV

element /ɛləˀməˀnt/, **elements.** 1 An **element** of something is a single part which combines with others to make up a whole. EG *...the different elements in the play... ...the basic elements of a job... Surprise would be an essential element in any such action.* [   ] N COUNT + SUPP
4 If something has an **element** of a particular quality or emotion, it has a certain amount of this quality or emotion. EG *It contains an element of truth... to add an element of suspense and mystery to my novels.* [   ] N PART
8 If you say that someone is **in their element**, you mean that they are doing something that they enjoy and do well. PHRASE

enclose /ɪˀnˈkləʊz/, **encloses, enclosing, enclosed.** [   ]
2 If you **enclose** something with a letter, you put it in the same envelope. EG *I enclose a small cheque.* V+O
◊ **enclosed.** EG *The enclosed list gives details of the courses available.* ◊ ADJ CLASSIF

engaged /ɪˀnˈgeɪdʒd/. 1 When two people are **engaged**, they have agreed to marry each other. EG *A week later, Tony became engaged to Caroline.* ADJ CLASSIF : OFT + to
2 If a telephone or telephone line is **engaged**, it is already being used, so you cannot speak to the person you are trying to phone. ADJ CLASSIF : USU PRED
3 If a public toilet is **engaged**, it is already being used by someone else. ADJ PRED

103

engagement /ɪ²ŋ¹geɪdʒmə²nt/, **engagements**. N COUNT
An **engagement** is **1** an arrangement that you Formal
have made to do something at a particular time. EG
I phoned my wife to cancel our lunch engagement.
2 an arrangement that has been made for a
performer to perform somewhere on a particular
occasion. EG *He is much in demand in America for
television engagements.* **3** an agreement that two
people have made with each other to get married.
EG *Their engagement was officially announced on
5th August.* **4** the period of time during which two
people are engaged. EG *...a letter which she wrote
to Harold during their engagement.*

equipment /ɪ¹kwɪpmə²nt/ consists of the things N UNCOUNT
which are needed for a particular activity. EG
...kitchen equipment... ...fire-fighting equipment.

estate /ɪ²steɪt/, **estates**. [   ]
3 Someone's **estate** is all the money and property N COUNT
that they leave when they die. EG *She left her estate
to her grandchildren.*

experience /ɪ²kspɪərɪəns/, **experiences, experi-** N UNCOUNT :
encing, experienced. **1** Experience is **1.1** the USU+SUPP
fact of having worked at a particular kind of job for
a period of time. EG *I had no military experience...
She's had nine months experience.* **1.2** the act of
seeing, doing, or feeling something or the fact of
being affected by it. EG *...his experience of nature
and natural forms... The new countries have no
experience of democracy.* **1.3** the things that have
happened to you or that you have done. EG *Everyone learns best from his own experience... ...speak-
ing from personal experience.*
2 An **experience** is something that happens to you N COUNT+SUPP
or something that you do, especially something
unusual. EG *Moving house can be a traumatic
experience... I was enjoying the experience of
working with Tony.*
3 If you **experience** a situation or feeling, it v+o
happens to you or you are affected by it. EG *Similar
problems have been experienced by other students...*

extent /ɪ²ksten̪t/. **1** The **extent** of something is its N SING+POSS
length, area, or size. EG *...to expand the empire to
its largest extent.*
2 The **extent** of a situation or difficulty is its size or N SING+POSS
scale. EG *The full extent of the problem is not yet
known.*
3 You use phrases such as **to a large extent**, **to** ADV SEN
some extent, or **to a certain extent** in order to
indicate that something is partly true, but not
entirely true. EG *Well I think to a certain extent it's
true.*
4 You use phrases such as **to what extent, to that** PHRASE
extent, or **to the extent that** when you are
discussing how true a statement is. EG *To what
extent are diseases linked with genes?... A computer is intelligent only to the extent that it can store
information.*

factor /fæktə/, **factors**. A **factor** is one of the N COUNT+SUPP
things that affects an event, decision, or situation.
EG *Confidence is the key factor in any successful
career... ...social and economic factors.*

faint /feɪnt/, **fainter, faintest; faints, fainting,**
fainted. **1** Something that is **faint** is not at all ADJ QUALIT
strong or intense. EG *There was a faint smell of
gas... Her cries grew fainter... ...a faint hope.*
2 A **faint** action is one that is done without much ADJ QUALIT
effort or enthusiasm. EG *...a few faint protests... Her
lips parted in a faint smile.*
3 If you **faint**, you lose consciousness for a short v
time. EG *He nearly fainted from the pain.*
4 Someone who feels **faint** feels dizzy and un- ADJ QUALIT
steady.

firm /fɜːm/, **firms; firmer, firmest**. **1** A **firm** is N COUNT
an organization which sells or produces something
or which provides a service which you pay for. EG
He was a partner in a firm of solicitors.
2 Something that is **firm** **2.1** does not change its ADJ QUALIT
shape much when you press it, although it is not
completely hard. EG *...a firm mattress.* **2.2** does not ADJ QUALIT
shake or move when you put pressure on it. EG *...a
firm ladder.* ◊ **firmly**. EG *Each block rested firmly* ◊ ADV
on the block below it.
3 If you have a **firm** grasp of something, you are ADJ QUALIT
holding it tightly. EG *I took a firm hold on the rope.*
◊ **firmly**. EG *She grasped the cork firmly.* ◊ ADV
4 A **firm** push or pull is done with quite a lot of ADJ QUALIT
force but is controlled. EG *...firm pressure.*
◊ **firmly**. EG *She closed the door firmly.* ◊ ADV

5 A **firm** decision or opinion is definite and unlike- ADJ QUALIT
ly to change. EG *...a person with firm views.*
◊ **firmly**. EG *His sister was firmly of the belief that* ◊ ADV
he was crazy.
6 **Firm** evidence or information is definitely true. ADJ QUALIT
EG *No firm evidence had come to light... By the
weekend came firm news.*
7 Someone who is **firm** behaves in a way that ADJ QUALIT
shows that they will not change their mind or that
they are in control. EG *Our present state of affairs
demands firm leadership... 'No,' said Mother in a
firm voice.*

flow /fləʊ/, **flows, flowing, flowed**. **1** If a liquid, v+A
gas, or electrical current **flows** somewhere, it
moves there steadily and continuously. You can
also say that a number of people or things **flow**
somewhere. EG *The river flows south-west to the
Atlantic Ocean... European scientists are flowing
into the United States.* ► used as a noun. EG *The* ► N COUNT
blood flow is cut off... There's a good flow of +SUPP
information.
2 If someone's hair or clothing **flows** about them, it v+A
hangs freely and loosely. EG *She let her hair down
so that it flowed over her shoulders.* ◊ **flowing**. EG ◊ ADJ CLASSIF
...women in long flowing robes.
3 If a quality or situation **flows** from something, it v+from
comes from it or results naturally from it. EG *The* Literary
love for one another flows from that unity.
4 If there is a **flow** of conversation, people are N SING+SUPP
talking without stopping. EG *She can keep up a non-
stop flow of baby talk.*

folk /fəʊk/, **folks**. **1** You can refer to people as N PLURAL :
folk. EG *...old folk... ...country folk.* OFT+SUPP
2 Your **folks** are your close relatives, especially N PLURAL
your parents. EG *I don't even have time to write* Informal
letters to my folks. American
3 You can use **folks** to address a group of people. VOCATIVE
EG *That's all for tonight, folks.* Informal
4 **Folk** music, art, and customs are considered to ADJ CLASSIF :
be traditional or typical of a particular community ATTRIB
or nation. EG *...Russian folk songs.*

hardly /hɑːdlɪ¹/. **1** You use **hardly** to say that ADV BRD NEG
something is only just true. EG *I was beginning to
like Sam, though I hardly knew him... The boy was
hardly more than seventeen... She had hardly any
money... Her bedroom was so small that she could
hardly move in it.*
2 If you say **hardly** had one thing happened when ADV BRD NEG
something else happened, you mean that the first
event was followed immediately by the second. EG
*Hardly had he uttered the words when he began
laughing.*

hit /hɪt/, **hits, hitting**. The form **hit** is used in the
present tense and is the past tense and past
participle of the verb.
1 If you **hit** someone or something, you deliberate- v+o
ly touch them with a lot of force using your hand or
an object. EG *He hit the burglar on the head with a
candlestick... He never hit the ball very far.*
2 When something **hits** something else, it touches v+o
it with a lot of force. EG *The truck had hit a wall...
Enormous hailstones hit the roof of the car.*
3 If a bomb or other missile **hits** its target, it v+o
reaches it. EG *Three ships were hit.* ► used as a ► N COUNT
noun. EG *The tanks were designed to withstand
anything except a direct hit.*
4 If something **hits** a person, place, or thing, it v+o
affects them very badly. EG *Spectator sport has
been badly hit by the increase in ticket prices.*
5 When a feeling or an idea **hits** you, it suddenly v+o
affects you or comes into your mind. EG *The shock
of her death kept hitting me afresh... Suddenly it hit
me: my diary had probably been read by everyone
in the office.*
6 A **hit** is a record, play, or film that is very N COUNT
popular and successful. EG *The play became a
tremendous hit... ...a hit single.*
7 If you **hit the roof**, you react to something very PHRASE
angrily. Informal

hit on or **hit upon**. If you **hit on** an idea or **hit** PHRASAL VB :
upon it, you think of it. EG *He hit on the idea of* V+PREP,
cutting a hole in the door to allow the cat to get in HAS PASS
and out.

hold /həʊld/, **holds, holding, held** /held/. **1** When v+o : USU+A
you **hold** something, you have your fingers or arms
firmly round it. You can also **hold** things with
other parts of your body, for example your mouth.
EG *He was holding a bottle of milk... I held the
picture up to the light... He held her in his arms.*

▶ used as a noun. EG *She resumed her hold on the* ▶ N SING
rope. ● If you **hold tight**, you hold something very ● PHRASE
firmly, especially so that you do not fall.

2 If you **hold** someone or **hold** them prisoner, you V+O : USU+A;
keep them as a prisoner. EG *I was held overnight in* ALSO V+O+C
a cell.

3 If you **hold** your body or part of your body in a V+O+A
particular position, you keep it in that position. EG OR V-REFL+A
Etta held her head back... Mrs Patel held herself
erect.

4 If you **hold** power or office, you have it. EG *...one* V+O
of the greatest Prime Ministers who ever held
office. [   ]

6 If you **hold** an event such as a meeting or a V+O
party, you organize it and it takes place. EG *He had*
promised he would hold elections in June.

7 If you **hold** a conversation with someone, you V+O
talk with them. [   ]

11 If someone asks you to **hold** the line when you V+O OR V
have made a telephone call, they are asking you to
wait until they can connect you.

12 If you **hold** someone's interest or attention, you V+O
do or say something which keeps them interest-
ed. [   ]

15 If something **holds** a particular amount of V+O
something, it can contain that amount. EG *The*
theatre itself can hold only a limited number of
people.

16 If an offer or invitation still **holds**, it is still V
available for you to accept.

17 If your luck **holds** or if the weather **holds**, it V
remains good. EG *If my luck continues to hold, I*
think I've got a fair chance. [   ]

20 If you take **hold** of something, you put your N UNCOUNT :
hand tightly round it. EG *She took hold of my wrist...* OFT+*of*
He still had hold of my jacket.

21 When something takes **hold**, it starts to have a N UNCOUNT
great effect. EG *Then the fire took hold.*

22 If you **get hold of** something or someone, you PHRASE
manage to get them or find them. EG *Can you get*
hold of a car this weekend?

23 Hold is also used in these phrases. **23.1** If you PHRASES
say to people **'Hold it'** or **'Hold everything'**, you
are telling them to stop what they are doing. **23.2** If
you **hold still** or **hold steady**, you do not move. EG
'Oh! do hold still!' she cried.

hold back. 1 If you **hold back** or if something PHRASAL VB :
holds you **back**, you hesitate before you do some- V-ERG+ADV
thing because you are not sure whether it is the
right thing to do. EG *Police have held back from*
going into such a holy place. **2** If you **hold** V+O+ADV
someone or something **back**, you prevent them
from advancing or increasing. EG *If she is ambi-*
tious, don't try to hold her back... The rise in living
standards has been held back for so long. **3** If you V+O+ADV
hold something **back**, you do not tell someone the
full details about something.

hold down. If you **hold down** a job, you manage PHRASAL VB :
to keep it. EG *He was surprised to find her holding* V+O+ADV
down a successful job in high finance.

hold off. 1 If you **hold off** something such as an PHRASAL VB :
army, you prevent it from coming too close to you. V+O+ADV
2 If the rain **holds off**, it does not rain although you V+ADV
had expected it to.

hold on. 1 If you **hold on**, you put or keep your PHRASAL VB :
hand firmly round something. EG *He tried to pull* V+ADV
free but she held on tight. **2** If you ask someone to V+ADV, OFT+A
hold on, you are asking them to wait for a short
time. EG *Hold on a moment, please.*

hold onto. If you **hold onto** something, **1** you put PHRASAL VB :
or keep your hand firmly round it. EG *He has to hold* V+PREP
onto something to steady himself. **2** you keep it. EG V+PREP
Politicians want to hold on to power at all costs.

hold out. 1 If you **hold out** your hand or some- PHRASAL VB :
thing that you have in your hand, you move it away V+O+ADV
from your body, usually towards someone. EG
'John?' Esther held out the phone. **2** If you **hold** V+ADV,
out for something, you want it and refuse to accept OFT+*for*
anything else. EG *Women all over the country are*
holding out for more freedom. **3** If you **hold out**, V+ADV
you manage to resist an enemy or opponent. EG *I*
can't hold out forever.

hold up. 1 If someone or something **holds** you PHRASAL VB :
up, they delay you. EG *The whole thing was held up* V+O+ADV
about half an hour. **2** If you **hold up** something as V+O+ADV+A
being good or bad, you mention it to other people
in order to influence their opinions. EG *Their ways*
are held up to scorn... What do you hold up to the

children as being desirable goals? **3** See also **hold-**
up.

-ibility, -ibilities. -ibility is added in place of SUFFIX
'-ible' at the end of adjectives to form nouns. These
nouns are often not defined in this dictionary, but
are treated with the related adjectives. EG *...the*
need to provide flexibility... ...the impossibility of
any change.

ice /aɪs/, **ices, icing, iced. 1 Ice** is **1.1** water that N UNCOUNT
has frozen and become solid. **1.2** pieces of ice that
you use to keep food or drink cool. EG *...two tall*
glasses of pineapple juice, soda and ice.

2 If you **ice** cakes, you cover them with icing. V+O

3 An **ice** is an ice cream. EG *He bought ices and* N COUNT
lollipops for the children.

4 If you do something to **break the ice**, you make PHRASE
people feel relaxed and comfortable, for example
at the beginning of a party. EG *A cigarette was often*
the means of breaking the ice.

information /ɪnfəmeɪʃəⁿn/. If you have **informa-** N UNCOUNT
tion about something, you know something about
it. EG *I'm afraid I have no information on that... She*
provided me with a very interesting piece of
information about his past.

interest /ɪntəⁿrə²st/, **interests, interesting, in-**
terested. 1 If you have an **interest** in something, N SING OR
you want to learn or hear more about it. EG *None of* N UNCOUNT
them had the slightest interest in music... Brody
was beginning to lose interest.

2 Your **interests** are the things that you spend N COUNT
time on because you enjoy them. EG *He had two*
consuming interests: rowing and polo.

3 Something that is of **interest** attracts your N UNCOUNT
attention because it is exciting or unusual. EG *There*
was nothing of any great interest in the paper
today.

4 If something **interests** you, you want to learn V+O
more about it or to continue doing it. EG *Young men*
should always look for work which interests them.

job /dʒɒb/, **jobs. 1** A **job** is **1.1** the work that a N COUNT
person does regularly in order to earn money. EG
Gladys finally got a good job as a secretary. **1.2** a N COUNT
particular task. EG *There are always plenty of jobs*
to be done round here... ...a repair job.

2 The **job** of a particular person or thing is their N COUNT+POSS
duty or function. EG *It's not their job to decide what*
ought to be the law.

3 If you say that you had a **job** doing something, N SING
you are emphasizing how difficult it was to do. EG *I* Informal
had a job sneaking into the house unnoticed.

4 If you say that someone **is doing** a good job or **is** PHRASE
making a good job of something, you mean that
they are doing something well. EG *Daddy thought*
we'd made a very good job of the bathroom.

knowledge /nɒlɪdʒ/. **1 Knowledge** is information N UNCOUNT :
and understanding about a subject, which someone USU+SUPP
has in their mind. EG *...advances in scientific knowl-*
edge... All knowledge comes to us through our
senses... He is the only person I know with a real
knowledge of income-tax legislation.

2 If you say that something is true **to your knowl-** ADV SEN
edge, you mean that you know that it is true. EG *Of*
these thirty-seven couples, thirty-five, to my knowl-
edge, are still married.

-less is added to nouns in order to form adjectives SUFFIX
that describe something or someone as not having
the thing that the noun refers to. EG *...meaningless*
sounds... ...landless peasants.

load /ləʊd/, **loads, loading, loaded. 1** If you **load** V+O OR V+O+
a vehicle or container or **load** things into it, you A
put things into it. EG *...when they came to load the*
van with their things... They were ordered to begin
loading the lorries... We started loading the pheas-
ants into the sacks.

2 A **load** is something which is being carried N COUNT
somewhere. EG *We took up our heavy load and*
trudged back... Its load of minerals was dumped at
sea.

3 When someone **loads** a gun, they put a bullet in it V+O
so that it is ready to use.

4 When someone **loads** a camera, computer, or V+O
tape recorder or **loads** film or tape into it, they put
film or tape into it so that it is ready to use.

5 If people talk about **loads** of something or a **load** N PART
of something, they mean a lot of it. EG *We talked* Informal
about loads of things.

6 People say that something is **a load of rubbish** PHRASE
or **a load of junk** as a way of expressing their Informal

disapproval of it. EG *You paid twenty pounds for a load of junk like this?*

loaded /ˈləʊdɪd/. **1** If something is **loaded** with ADJ QUALIT: things, it has a large number of them in it or on it. OFT+*with* EG *...a truck loaded with bricks... ...waitresses with loaded trays.*

2 If you are **loaded** with things or **loaded down** ADJ PRED: with them, you are carrying a lot of them. EG *A man* OFT+*with* *precedes him up the stairs, loaded with bundles... She was loaded down with parcels.*

3 If you say that someone is **loaded**, you mean that ADJ PRED they have a lot of money. Informal

loose /luːs/, **looser, loosest. 1** Something that is **loose** is **1.1** not firmly held or fixed in place. EG *The* ADJ QUALIT *doorknob is loose and rattles... ...loose strands of copper wire.* ◊ **loosely.** EG *Willie held the phone* ◊ ADV *loosely.* **1.2** not attached to anything else. EG *...a* ADJ CLASSIF *few loose sheets of paper.*

2 Loose clothes are rather large and do not fit ADJ QUALIT closely to your body. EG *...a loose cotton shirt.* ◊ **loosely.** EG *His black garments hung loosely* ◊ ADV *from his powerful shoulders.*

3 When a woman's hair is **loose**, it is hanging ADJ CLASSIF freely round her shoulders rather than being tied back. EG *She shook her hair loose.*

4 If you set animals **loose**, you release them when ADJ CLASSIF they have been tied up or kept in a box or cage. EG *He had taken some white rats into church and let them loose on the floor.* [   ]

8 A **loose** organization or administration is not ADJ QUALIT strictly controlled. EG *A loose grouping of 'radicals' was formed which met once a week... The country has a loose federal structure.*

9 If you are **at a loose end**, you have nothing to do PHRASE and are bored.

luck /lʌk/. **1 Luck** or good **luck** is success that N UNCOUNT does not come from your own abilities or efforts. EG *I had some wonderful luck... He wished me luck.*

2 Bad luck is lack of success or bad things that PHRASE happen to you, that have not been caused by yourself or other people. EG *One spring we had a lot of bad luck.*

3 Luck is used in these phrases. **3.1** If you say **'Bad** CONVENTION **luck'** or **'Hard luck'** to someone, you are expressing sympathy when they have failed to do something or failed to get something. EG *Tough luck, Barrett. You played a great game.* **3.2** If you say CONVENTION **'Good luck'** or **'Best of luck'** to someone, you are saying that you hope that they will be successful. EG *Good luck to you, my boy... Best of luck with the exams.* **3.3** If you say that someone is **in luck**, you PHRASE mean that they are lucky on a particular occasion. **3.4** If you say that someone **is pushing** their **luck**, PHRASE you mean that they are taking a risk and may get into trouble. **3.5** When someone **tries** their **luck** at PHRASE something, they try to succeed at it. EG *He came to England to try his luck at a musical career.* **3.6** ADV SEN You can add **with luck** or **with any luck** to a Informal statement to indicate that you hope that a particular thing will happen. EG *This one should work with a bit of luck... With any luck they might forget all about it.*

material /məˈtɪərɪəl/, **materials. 1** A **material** is N COUNT OR a solid substance, especially one which can be used N UNCOUNT in making things. EG *We need a cheap abundant material to make the electrodes... ...synthetic substitutes for natural materials.*

2 Material is cloth. EG *The sleeping bags are made* N UNCOUNT *of quilted or acrylic material.* OR N COUNT

3 Ideas or information that can be used as a basis N UNCOUNT for a book, play, or film can be referred to as **material**. EG *She hoped to find material for some articles... They researched a lot of background material.*

4 You use **material** to describe something which is ADJ CLASSIF: concerned with possessions, money, and conditions ATTRIB in which people live, rather than with their emotional or spiritual life. EG *...the material comforts of life... ...material possessions.* ◊ **materially.** EG ◊ ADV *...conditions which they found materially adequate but spiritually impoverished.*

5 Materials are the equipment or things that you N PLURAL: need for a particular activity. EG *I packed all my* USU+SUPP *books and writing materials... ...cleaning materials.*

-ment, -ments. -ment is used to form nouns that SUFFIX refer to actions or states. For example, 'bombardment' refers to the bombarding of a place, and 'disenchantment' refers to the state of being disen-

chanted. When these nouns are formed from verbs, they are often not defined in this dictionary, but are treated with the related verb. EG *...the commencement of the flight... ...disillusionment with politics... Tree diseases are largely a result of mismanagement.*

money /ˈmʌnɪ/. **1 Money** consists of the coins or N UNCOUNT bank notes that you use when you buy something. EG *I spent all my money on sweets... I had very little money left... They may not accept English money.*

2 If you **make money**, you obtain money by PHRASE earning it or by making a profit. EG *To make money you've got to take chances.*

-ness, -nesses. -ness is added to adjectives to SUFFIX form nouns. These nouns usually refer to a state or quality. For example 'sadness' is the state of being sad and 'kindness' is the quality of being kind. Nouns formed in this way are often not defined in this dictionary but are treated with the related adjectives. EG *The aim of life is happiness... ...the smallness of the school... He was aware of his weaknesses.*

nightmare /ˈnaɪtmɛə/, **nightmares.** A **night-** N COUNT **mare** is **1** a very frightening dream. EG *He rushed to her room when she had nightmares and comforted her.* **2** a very frightening or unpleasant situation or time. EG *The first day was a nightmare.*

non-. 1 non- is used to form adjectives that de- PREFIX scribe something as not having a particular quality or feature. For example, a non-nuclear war is a war fought without nuclear weapons. EG *...non-violent demonstrations... ...non-industrial societies.* **2 non-** is also used to form nouns. These nouns PREFIX refer **2.1** to situations in which a particular kind of action is not taken. *...a non-aggression pact... ...non-payment of fines.* **2.2** to people who do not belong to a particular group. EG *...non-car-owners... ...non-Christians... To the non-angler this can be very puzzling.*

N COUNT

The most common nouns in English are countable nouns (N COUNT). These are nouns that have both a singular and a plural form. The plural is usually made by adding **-s** to the singular.

When countable nouns are used in the singular, they must have a determiner, such as **a, the,** or **my** in front of them. So you say: *...the house... ...a friend... ...his dog.*

When you want to use an adjective to tell you more about the noun, you put the determiner before the adjective: *...a clean shirt... ...that little boy... ...her pretty green dress.*

When a countable noun is used in the plural, it can have a determiner, but only when you want to pick out some rather than all of the particular item. So you can say: *...tables... ...the tables... ...those tables... ...her tables.*

Countable nouns go with the same number choice in verbs. For example: *The house is on fire... The table is dirty... Those flowers are lovely.*

N UNCOUNT

Many nouns are uncountable nouns (N UNCOUNT). These are nouns which have only one form. Examples are: *hatred, rice, information, news, furniture.* You cannot put numbers in front of an uncountable noun, so you cannot say *'one furniture'.* You have to say *'one piece of furniture'* or *'two items of news',* and so on.

Uncountable nouns are not usually used with the determiners **a** and **the**, unless extra information about the noun is being given. So you would normally say: *They sell furniture.* But you can also say: *...the furniture I want for my bedroom.*

Uncountable nouns take a verb in the singular. For example: *The furniture is needed urgently.*

---

occasional /əˈkeɪʒənl, -ʒənəl/ means happening ADJ CLASSIF: or being present sometimes, but not regularly or ATTRIB often. EG *...an occasional trip as far as Aberdeen...* [   ]

◊ **occasionally.** EG *Friends visit them occasional-* ◊ ADV *ly... He was arrogant and occasionally callous.*

organization /ɔ:gənaizeɪʃəⁿn/, **organizations;** N COUNT
also spelled **organisation**. **1** An **organization** is a
group of people who do something together regularly in an organized way. Businesses and clubs are
organizations. EG *...student organizations... ...the
World Health Organisation.*

2 The **organization** of a system is the way in N UNCOUNT:
which its different parts are related and how they USU+SUPP
work together. EG *There has been a total change in
the organization of society.*

3 The **organization** of an activity or public event N UNCOUNT:
involves making all the arrangements for it. EG *I USU+SUPP
don't want to get involved in the actual organisation of things.*

-ous is added to some nouns to form adjectives that SUFFIX
describe qualities. For example, someone who is
courageous shows courage and someone who is
envious feels envy. EG *...scandalous stories... ...a
mountainous region... ...a hazardous journey.*

overcome /əuvəkʌm/, **overcomes, overcoming,**
overcame /əuvəkeɪm/. The form **overcome** is
used in the present tense and is also the past
participle.

1 If you **overcome** a problem or a feeling, you V+O
successfully deal with it or control it. EG *I was still
trying to overcome my fear of the dark... We tried
to overcome their objections to the plan.*

pattern /pætəⁿn/, **patterns, patterned. 1** A **pat-** N COUNT:
tern is a particular way in which something is OFT+SUPP
usually done or organized. EG *Over the next few
months their work pattern changed... ...behaviour
patterns... It fits in with the pattern of her family
life.*

2 A **pattern** is also **2.1** an arrangement of lines or N COUNT
shapes, especially a design in which the same
shape is repeated at regular intervals over a
surface. EG *Jack was drawing a pattern in the sand
with his forefinger... ...a frock with a pattern of
little red apples.* **2.2** a diagram or shape that you
can use as a guide when you are making something
such as a model or a piece of clothing. EG *...sewing
patterns.*

pool /pu:l/, **pools, pooling, pooled. 1** A **pool** is **1.1** N COUNT
a small area of still or slow-moving water. EG *...long
stretches of sand with rocks and pools.* **1.2** a
swimming pool. EG *She went swimming in the hotel
pool.*

2 A **pool** of liquid or light is a small area of it. EG *He* N COUNT+of
*was lying dead in a pool of blood... A spotlight
threw a pool of violet light onto the stage.*

3 A **pool** of people, money, or things is a number of N COUNT+SUPP
them that are collected together to be used or
shared by several people or organizations. EG *...car
pools... ...a pool of agricultural workers.*

4 If people **pool** their money, knowledge, or equip- V+O
ment, they allow it to be collected and used or
shared by all of them. EG *We pooled our money,
bought a van, and travelled... Families pooled their
food resources in a common kitchen.*

5 Pool is a game. Players use long, thin sticks to N UNCOUNT
hit coloured balls with numbers on them into six
holes around the edges of a table. EG *...a pool table.*

6 If you do the **pools**, you take part in a gambling N PLURAL:
competition in which people try to win money by the+N
guessing correctly the results of football matches. British
EG *...pools coupons... They won £300,000 on the
Pools.*

principle /prɪnsɪpəⁿl/, **principles. 1** A **principle** N COUNT OR
is a general belief that you have about the way you N UNCOUNT
should behave, which influences your behaviour. EG
*...a man of high principles... She abandoned her
principles... Our party remains a party of principle.*
● If you do something **on principle**, you do it ● PHRASE
because of a particular belief that you have. EG *I
had to vote for him, of course, on principle.*

2 A **principle** is also **2.1** a general rule about how N COUNT+SUPP
something should be done. EG *...the principles of
formal logic... ...a party organized on Leninist principles.* **2.2** a general scientific law which explains
how something happens or works. EG *...the principle of acceleration.*

3 If you agree with something **in principle**, you PHRASE
generally agree to the idea of it but may be unable
or unwilling to support it in practice. EG *We are
willing, in principle, to look afresh at the 1921
constitution.*

protest, protests, protesting, protested; pro-

nounced /prətest/ when it is a verb, and /prəutest/
when it is a noun.

1 If you **protest** about something or against some- V : USU
thing, you say or show publicly that you object to it. +about/
EG *Labour MPs took to the streets to protest against against/at
government economic policy... ...a group protesting
at official inaction... I was shoved, protesting, into a
side room.* ◊ **protester, protesters.** EG *The pro-* ◊ N COUNT
*testers surrendered to the police after about an
hour.* [   ]

4 A **protest** is the act of saying or showing publicly N COUNT OR
that you object to something. EG *They joined in the* N UNCOUNT
*protests against the government's proposals...
There was a wave of student riots, in protest at
university conditions.*

race /reɪs/, **races, racing, raced. 1** A **race** is a N COUNT
competition to see who is the fastest, for example
in running, swimming, or driving. EG *She came
second in the race... The race is run through the
streets of London... ...a horse race.*

2 A **race** for power or control is a situation in N SING+SUPP
which people or organizations compete with each
other for power or control. EG *The race for the
White House is now on.... ...the arms race.* ● See
also **rat race.** [   ]

4 If you **race** somewhere, you go there as quickly V+A
as possible. EG *He turned and raced after the
others... She raced down the stairs... We had to race
across London to get the train.*

6 You describe a situation as a **race against time** PHRASE
when you have to work very fast in order to do
something before a particular time.

7 A **race** is also one of the major groups which N COUNT OR
human beings can be divided into according to N UNCOUNT
their physical features, such as the colour of their
skin. EG *The law prohibits discrimination on the
grounds of colour or race.* ● See also **human race.**

racial /reɪʃəⁿl/ describes things relating to peo- ADJ CLASSIF:
ple's race. EG *...racial discrimination... ...racial* USU ATTRIB
prejudice... ...racial equality... ...racial harmony.

rarely /reəliⁱ/ means not very often. EG *We very* ADV BRD NEG
*rarely quarrel... I'd rarely seen a man look so
unhappy... Rarely has so much time been wasted
by so many people.*

require /rɪkwaɪə/, **requires, requiring, re-** V+O : OFT+for
quired. 1 If you **require** something or if some- Formal
thing **is required**, you need it or it is necessary. EG
*Is there anything you require, Mr Heissman?...
Parliamentary approval would be required for it.*

2 If you **are required** to do something, you have to V+O : USU PASS
do it because someone says you must do it. EG *All* +to-INF, of,
the boys were required to study religion... He was OR REPORT,
doing what was required of him... The course ONLY that
requires you to be bilingual.* ◊ **required.** EG *Check* Formal
that the machines meet required standards. ◊ ADJ CLASSIF
OR ADJ AFTER N

reserve /rɪzɜ:v/, **reserves, reserving, re-**
served. 1 If something **is reserved** for a particu- V+O : USU PASS
lar person or purpose, it is kept specially for that
person or purpose. EG *The garden is reserved for
those who work in the museum... I had a place
reserved at the Youth Hostel...* [   ]

6 A nature **reserve** is an area of land where the N COUNT :
animals, birds, and plants are officially protected. USU+SUPP

scale /skeɪl/, **scales, scaling, scaled. 1** If you N SING+SUPP
refer to the **scale** of something, you are referring
to its size, especially when it is very big. EG *The
scale of change is so enormous... ...the sheer scale
of the United States.*

2 You use **scale** in expressions such as **large** N UNCOUNT :
scale and **on a small scale** when you are indicat- OFT+SUPP
ing the size, extent, or degree of one thing when
compared to other similar things. EG *The district
grew peas on a large scale... The plan was never
very grand in scale... ...small scale methods of
getting energy.*

scarcely /skeəsliⁱ/. **1** You use **scarcely** to say ADV BRD NEG
that something is only just true or is not quite true.
EG *I can scarcely remember what we ate... They
were scarcely ever apart... ...a very young man,
scarcely more than a boy.*

2 You can use **scarcely** in an ironic way to say ADV BRD NEG
that something is certainly not true. EG *There could
scarcely be a less promising environment for children.*

3 If you say **scarcely** had one thing happened ADV BRD NEG
when something else happened, you mean that the
first event was followed immediately by the second. EG *Scarcely had the car drawn to a halt when
armed police surrounded it.*

search /sɜːtʃ/, **searches, searching, searched.** 1 V+A OR V+O: If you **search** for something, you look carefully for OFT+*for* it. If you **search** a place, you look carefully for something there. EG *He glanced around the room, searching for a place to sit... He searched through a drawer and eventually found the photo... I searched the city for a room.*

2 If the police **search** you, they examine your V+O clothing because they think that you may have something hidden in it. EG *We were stopped by the police and searched.*

3 A **search** is an attempt to find something by N COUNT looking for it. EG *I found the keys after a long search... ...the search for oil.* ● If you go **in search** ● PHRASE of something, you try to find it. EG *We went round the town in search of a place to stay.*

seldom /sɛldə⁰m/. If something **seldom** happens, ADV BRD NEG it happens only occasionally. EG *It seldom rains there... The waiting time was seldom less than four hours... He seldom feels confident.*

series /sɪəriˈz/. **Series** is both the singular and the plural form.

1 A **series** of things or events is a number of them N COUNT: that come one after the other. EG *He was arrested* USU+*of* *in connection with a series of armed bank robberies... ...a series of lectures on American politics.*

2 A radio or television **series** is a set of pro- N COUNT grammes of a particular kind which have the same title. EG *...the popular television series, 'Yes, Minister'... ...a new 6 week series on Europe.*

settle /sɛtə⁰l/, **settles, settling, settled.** 1 If V+O someone **settles** an argument, they end it by making a decision about who is right or about what to do. EG *The strike went on for over a year before it was finally settled.*

2 If something **is settled**, it has all been decided V+O: USU PASS and arranged. EG *Good, well, that's settled then.*

3 If you **settle** a bill, you pay the amount that you V+O owe.

4 When people **settle** in a new country or area, or V+A when they **settle** somewhere after moving around a lot, they start living there permanently. EG *He had settled in England.*

smart /smɑːt/, **smarter, smartest; smarts, smarting, smarted.** 1 Someone who is **smart** is ADJ QUALIT pleasantly neat and clean in appearance. EG *The boys looked smart in their school uniforms.*
◊ **smartly.** EG *...a smartly dressed executive.* ◊ ADV

2 You can also describe someone as **smart** when ADJ QUALIT they are clever. EG *She's one of the smartest* American *students in the whole school... ...a smart idea.*

3 A **smart** place or event is connected with ADJ QUALIT wealthy and fashionable people. EG *We met at a very smart lunch party.*

4 A **smart** movement or action is sharp and quick. ADJ QUALIT: EG *...the smart crack of a whip... ...moving along at* ATTRIB *a smart trot.* ◊ **smartly.** EG *Grabbing the bottle,* ◊ ADV *she hit him smartly on the head.* Written

smash /smæʃ/, **smashes, smashing, smashed.** 1 V+O If you **smash** something, you break it into many pieces by hitting it, throwing it, or dropping it. EG *Some windows have been smashed... I nearly smashed the TV set.*

smashed /smæʃt/. Someone who is **smashed** is ADJ PRED extremely drunk. Informal

smashing /smæʃɪŋ/. If you describe something as ADJ QUALIT **smashing**, you mean that you like it very much. EG Informal *We had a smashing time.*

sometimes /sʌmtaɪmz/. You use **sometimes** to ADV say that something happens on some occasions. EG *Sometimes I wish I was back in Africa...*

space /speɪs/, **spaces, spacing, spaced.** 1 Space N UNCOUNT is 1.1 the area that is empty or available in a place, building, or container. EG *There was just enough space for a bed... Belongings take up space... I did not have the space to store the bricks... ...the luggage space at the back of the car.* 1.2 the vast area that lies beyond the Earth's atmosphere and surrounds the stars and planets. EG *...the first human being to travel in space... ...space research.*

2 **Space** in a talk or piece of writing is the amount N UNCOUNT of the talk or writing that is available for a particular thing to be discussed. EG *There is no space in this book to argue the alternative viewpoint... I shall devote some space to describing my own experiences.*

3 If a place gives a feeling of **space**, it gives an N UNCOUNT impression of being large and open. EG *The low hills give a feeling of great, intense space... A*

mirror can add space to a room.

4 If you are looking or staring **into space**, you are PHRASE looking straight in front of you, without actually looking at anything in particular.

5 A **space** is 5.1 a gap or empty place in something solid or crowded. EG *The door had spaces at the top and bottom... ...an open space in the jungle.* 5.2 a place or area that is empty and available for people to use or fill. EG *There were two spaces on the morning plane to Canton... We spent half an hour looking for a parking space... There is no official space for it on the form.*

6 A **space** of time is a period of time. EG *It* N SING+*of* *happened three times in the space of five months... He should arrive in a very short space of time.*

spacecraft /speɪskrɑːft/. **Spacecraft** is both the N COUNT singular and the plural form.

A **spacecraft** is a rocket or other vehicle that can travel in space.

Space Invaders is the name of a computer game N UNCOUNT in which players use control buttons and levers to try to shoot and destroy spaceships that move and attack them on a computer screen.

stream /striːm/, **streams, streaming, streamed.** 1 A **stream** is a small, narrow river. EG N COUNT *He led us along the bank of the stream.*

2 You can also refer to a narrow moving mass of N COUNT liquid, gas, or smoke as a **stream**. EG *Horace blew out a stream of smoke.* ● See also **bloodstream**.

3 A **stream** of people or vehicles is a long moving N PART line of them. EG *A steady stream of workers left the* OR N COUNT *factory... ...the stream of cars.*

4 A **stream** of things is a large number of them N PART occurring one after another. EG *...a steady stream* OR N COUNT *of questions... The stream of insults continues.*

5 If a liquid **streams** somewhere, it flows or comes V-ERG: USU+A out in large amounts. EG *She stood in the doorway, tears streaming down her face... His back was streaming with sweat.*

6 If people or vehicles **stream** somewhere, they V+A move there quickly and in large numbers. EG *The doors opened and the audience began to stream out... The cars are streaming by at sixty miles an hour.*

7 When light **streams** somewhere, it shines strong- V+A ly there after passing through or between things. EG *The sun was streaming in through the windows.*

8 A **stream** in a school is a group of children of the N COUNT+SUPP same age and ability who are taught together. EG *...pupils in the top streams.*

9 To **stream** pupils means to teach them in groups V+O according to their ability. ◊ **streaming.** EG *Our* ◊ N UNCOUNT *new headmaster says he's going to end streaming.*

stuff /stʌf/, **stuffs, stuffing, stuffed.** 1 You can N UNCOUNT: refer to a substance, a thing, or a group of things as USU+SUPP **stuff.** EG *What's that stuff in the bucket?... Quite a lot of stuff had been stolen... She was reading the travel stuff in the colour supplement.*

2 If you **stuff** something somewhere, you push it V+O+A there quickly and roughly. EG *Willie gathered up the bills and stuffed them carelessly into his pocket... Nora stuffed a cigarette into her mouth.*

3 If you **stuff** a place or container, you fill it with V+O: material or other things until it is full. EG *...stuffing* OFT+*with* *a toy dog.* ◊ **stuffed.** EG *He'd got a big rucksack,* ◊ ADJ CLASSIF *stuffed with notes, on his back.* [   ]

6 If a dead animal **is stuffed**, it is filled with V+O: USU PASS material so that it can be preserved and displayed. ◊ **stuffed.** EG *...a stuffed parrot.* ◊ ADJ CLASSIF

7 If you say that someone **knows** their **stuff**, you PHRASE mean that they are good at doing something be- Informal cause they are experienced at it and know a lot about it. EG *These union negotiators know their stuff.*

8 If you are angry with someone for something that EXCLAM they have said or done, you might say **'Get** Informal **stuffed!'** to them; a rude expression.

> **SUPP** stands for **supporting word or words**
> Many nouns have the label +SUPP in the Extra Column. This means that the noun is not usually used on its own in this sense, but is used with other words, phrases, or clauses which give extra information about it or which add to its meaning in some way.

thick /θɪk/, **thicker, thickest.** 1 Something that is

thick has a large distance between its two opposite surfaces. EG ...*thick slices of bread... We were separated by thick concrete walls... ...a thick sweater... Last winter the snow lay thick on the ground.* ◊ **thickly.** EG *She buttered my bread thickly.* `ADJ QUALIT OR ADV` `◊ ADV`

2 If something that consists of several things is **thick**, the things in it are present in large quantities and are grouped very closely together. EG *She had a lot of thick black hair... They were on the edge of the thick forest...* `ADJ QUALIT`

4 If you say that someone is **thick**, you mean that they are stupid or slow to understand things. EG *He's a bit thick... They were too thick to notice it.* [   ] `ADJ QUALIT Informal`

6 Smoke or fog that is **thick** is difficult to see through. EG *The fog seemed to be getting thicker.* [   ] `ADJ QUALIT`

11 If you continue to do something **through thick and thin**, you do it even though the conditions or circumstances have become very bad. EG *She stayed with her husband through thick and thin.* `PHRASE`

tie /taɪ/, **ties, tying, tied. 1** If you **tie** one thing to another or if you **tie** it in a particular position, you fasten it to the other thing or fasten it in that position, often using string or rope. EG *one of those labels you tie onto the handle of your suitcase.* `V+O+A`

2 If you **tie** a piece of string or cloth round something or **tie** something with the string or cloth, you put the string or cloth round it and fasten the ends together in a knot or bow. EG *...a little dog which had a ribbon tied round its neck... ...a parcel tied with string...* [   ] `V+O+A`

5 A **tie** is a long, narrow piece of cloth that is worn around someone's neck under their shirt collar and tied in a knot at the front. Ties are worn mainly by men. EG *He took off his jacket and loosened his tie.* ● See also **bow tie.** `N COUNT`

6 Something that **is tied** to or into something else is connected to it or linked closely with it. EG *Canada is more tightly tied into the American economy.* `V+O+to/into USU PASS`

7 A **tie** is also a connection or feeling that links you with a person, place, or organization. EG *Family ties are often very strong... They want to loosen their ties with Britain.* `N COUNT : USU+SUPP`

tie down. A person or thing that **ties** you **down** restricts your freedom, for example by making you live, behave, or act in a particular way. EG *You're not tied down to a date.* `PHRASAL VB : V+O+ADV`

tie up. 1 If you **tie** something **up**, you put string or rope round it so that it is firm or secure. EG *Clarissa came in, carrying some canvases tied up in brown paper.* **2** If someone **ties** you **up**, they fasten ropes or chains around you so that you cannot move or escape. **3** When you **tie up** your shoelaces, you fasten them in a bow. EG *Tie up your laces. Hurry!* **4** When you **tie up** an animal, you fasten it to a fixed object with a piece of rope or chain so that it cannot run away. **5** If you **tie up** something such as money or resources, you do something with it, so that it is not available for other people or for other purposes. EG *People don't want to tie their money up for long periods.* **6** Something that **is tied up** with something else or **ties up** with it is closely linked with it. EG *It tied up with her interest in dance.* `PHRASAL VB : V+O+ADV` `V+O+ADV` `V+O+ADV` `V+O+ADV` `V+O+ADV` `V-ERG+ADV, OFT+with`

tied up. If you are **tied up**, you are busy. EG *I'm tied up right now, can you call me back later?* `ADJ PRED Informal`

tight /taɪt/, **tighter, tightest; tights. 1** Clothes or shoes that are **tight** fit closely to your body. EG *He was wearing tight cream-coloured trousers.* ◊ **tightly.** EG *...a tightly fitting suit.* `ADJ QUALIT` `◊ ADV`

2 If you hold something or someone **tight**, you hold them firmly and securely. EG *Ann was now clutching the letter tight in her hand.* ▶ used as an adjective. EG *His fingers were tight on Thomas's arm.* ◊ **tightly.** [   ] `ADV AFTER VB` `▶ ADJ QUALIT`

4 Something that is shut **tight** is shut very firmly. EG *He closed his eyes tight.* [   ] `ADV AFTER VB`

6 You use **tight** to describe things that are very close together. EG *They stood in a tight group... Her hair was arranged in tight curls.* ◊ **tightly.** EG *...houses tightly packed together.* [   ] `ADJ QUALIT` `◊ ADV`

8 A **tight** plan or arrangement allows only the minimum time or money needed to do something. EG *We have a tight schedule.* `ADJ QUALIT`

9 A **tight** rule or system of control is very strict. EG *Security has become visibly tighter over the last year.* ◊ **tightly.** EG *...a society which is very tightly controlled.* `ADJ QUALIT` `◊ ADV`

TIME
This entry shows some of the ways in which you can refer to time in English.
There are a number of ways of asking the time or of saying what time it is. EG *'What time is it, Gordon?' – 'Just after five.'... 'What's the time now?' – 'It's quarter past nine.'... 'Can you tell me the time?' – 'It's twenty-five past twelve.'... 'Have you got the time?' – 'It is nearly one o'clock.'... 'What time does the boat leave from Weymouth?' – 'At a quarter past three in the afternoon.'... The time is six forty-five... My watch says six thirty... It's five to eight and breakfast's at eight o'clock...*

twelve o'clock	twelve in the morning	
twelve	12 a.m.	`12:00`
12 o'clock	midday	
	noon	
	twelve at night	`00:00`
	12 p.m.	
	midnight	
a quarter past twelve		`12:15`
quarter past twelve		
twelve fifteen		`00:15`
a quarter after twelve		
ten to eight		`07:50`
ten minutes to eight		
seven-fifty		`19:50`

---

training /treɪnɪŋ/. **1 Training** for a particular job involves learning or teaching the skills that are needed for the job. EG *I had a great training as a gardener... ...giving people training in computer programming.* `N UNCOUNT`

2 Training also involves doing physical exercises and eating a special diet in order to be fit for a sports match or a race. EG *Are you in training for a cross-country run?* `N UNCOUNT`

troop /truːp/, **troops, trooping, trooped. 1 Troops** are soldiers, especially ones taking part in military action. EG *They have more than 11,000 troops in Northern Ireland... ...reports on troop movements.* `N PLURAL`

un-. 1 un- is added to the beginning of many adjectives, adverbs, and nouns in order to form words with the opposite meaning. For example, if something is unavailable, it is not available. EG *...undemocratic regimes... ...an uncomfortable chair... She may unintentionally have caused suffering... He regretted his unkindness.* `PREFIX`

2 When a verb describes a process, **2.1** you can add **un-** to the beginning of it in order to form a verb describing the reverse process. EG *He unlocked the door... She untied the rope and rowed back to shore.* **2.2** you can add **un-** to the past participle in order to form an adjective indicating that the process has not been carried out. For example, if your hair is uncombed, it has not been combed. EG *Everywhere hedges remain uncut... ...unconvicted prisoners.* `PREFIX`

victory /vɪktə⁰riʰ/, **victories.** A **victory** is a situation in which you gain complete success, for example in a war or a competition. EG *In A.D. 636, an Arab army won a famous victory over a much larger Persian force... Nobody believed he had any chance of victory... The final agreement was a victory for common sense.* `N COUNT OR N UNCOUNT`

109

Words followed by a star (*) occurred in Level 1 and 2 of the Course, but further new uses are covered here. Words followed by 'D' are defined in the Dictionary Extracts on pages 101–109. Figures refer to sections where examples of the word can be found, either in the Students' Book or in the transcripts. 'T' after a reference means students may need to be given the word to complete the section as it does not actually appear in the text. To locate each unit, refer to the table at the top of the page.

absent 78T
absolute 29
academic* 24
according 118
account* 110
accuse 163
achieve 24
achievement 24
act 150
actor 118
actress 118
adequate 161
administration 2
admit 48
adopt 173
advance* 239
adventure 178
advice*D 31
affair* 102
affect 207
agent 27
aid 154
aim 140
alarm 219
alleged/ly 151
allowance D 8
alternative 163
ambition 16, 226
ambitious 226T
amount* 29
ample 224
ancestor 215
anger 228
angle 40
ankle 234
announcement 161
anxiety 207
anxious 207
apartment 150
apparently 29, 83
appliance 102
application 24
apply* 31
appoint 100
approach*D 52
appropriate 59
approval 207
architecture 43
argue 161
arrange 133
arrest 150
arrival 133
article 72
asleep 47T
aspect 223
assume D 22
assuming 176
assure 102
atmosphere* 206
attach*D 132
attack*D 187
attention*D 26
attractive 95
auction 207
automatic/ally 83
avenue 36
avoid 25
awake/awoke 47
aware 78
awfully 187

awkward 68
backwards 229
balance 133
ballet 43
ban/ning 176
band 20
bang 224
barely D 98
basis 172
battle 168
bear D 202
beat D 111
beforehand 234
behalf 133
behaviour 113
belongings 202
benefit 63
besides 224
bet 35
bid 221
bitter 38
bitterly 38
blind* 90
block* 34, 196
blow 36, 37
bomb 154
bone 87
boot 90
border 100
bother 216
bowl 43
brave 235
bride 219
bridegroom 219T
broad 89
broadcast 139
broaden 232
bulk 80
bulky 78
bush 4
business*D 52
cabin 206
calm 206
camera 118
campaign D 70
cancel 224
capable 68, 77
capability 71
card 78
cartoon 195T
cast 228
casual 161
cat 56
cautious 68
cave 200
ceiling 47
cement 223
chain D 99
chairman/person 97T
channel 160
chap 13
chapter 206
charity 224
chart 219
chat 196
cheque 228
chief 150
cigarette 45
citizen 168
civil D 168

civilian 168
classical 226
clever 45
climb 45
clock 64
club 17
coat 234
colleague 139
collect 133
colloquial 216
coloured 205
column 91
comb 217
combination 78
combined 78
comment 68
committed 163
communication 76
communist 77
companion* 113
competition 181
complain 59
complaint 59
complex 45
complexity 45
complicated 45T
concealed 207
concentration 12
concept 76
concert 100
conclude 109
conclusion 63
concrete 150
conference 142
confined 113
conflict 168
confused 143
confusion 221
congress 184
connect* 109
connection* 225
conscience 59
conscious 215
consciousness 45, 215
conservation 109
conservative 226T
consider*D 138
considerable 107
consideration D 138
considering D 133, 138
constant 68
constantly 68
construct 109
construction 163
contain 76
container 76
contemporary 78
context 153T
continent 140
contract 27
contrast 61
convenient 102
conventional 4
convert 217
convertible 217
convinced 87
cope 195
correspondent 139
costume 100
cottage 32

council D 22
countryside 13
courage 226
courageous 226
courtesy 202
cover* 140
cracked 149, 159
craft 16
crash 183
create 31
creation 225
creative 54
credit 78
creep/crept 206
crew 118
crisis D 163, 168
critical 149
criticize 159T
crop 130
crucial 114
cry* 223
cultural 140
culture 140T
currency 217
current 163
currently 24
curtain 10, 12
custom D 20
dad 45
dancing 17
dare/n't 59
darkness 34
dawn 113
deadly 99
deaf 234
death 97
debate 97
decent 4, 5
deck 206
declare 181
deep* 239
defeat D 168
defence 147, 168
defend D 143, 168
define 140
delay 102
deliberate 163
delicate 206
deliver 102
delivery 102
demand 59
demanding 59
demonstrate 234
demonstration 234
denial 143
deny 143
departure 133
depressed 49
depressing 106
depression 49T
description 56
desperate 176
desperately 59
despite 107
destination 100
destroy D 166
destruction D 168
detailed 115
determination 235T
determined 235T

Tapescripts and Transcripts

Collins COBUILD English Course 3 is accompanied by a set of three cassettes. These include both unscripted and scripted recordings. There is a booklet containing the transcripts of the unscripted recordings in the back cover of the Student's Book. Complete tapescripts and transcripts are given here. (* denotes an unscripted recording.)

UNIT 1

`2` *

EL: Erm, well, your name's Chris.
CB: Chris Bates, yes.
EL: Chris Bates. Edmund Lee.
CB: Hello.
EL: Hi. Erm, whereabouts do you live?
CB: I live in Forest Hill, south east London.
EL: Oh yeah. I used to live near there.
CB: Where did you live?
EL: Erm, Brockley. About six years.
CB: Not far away.
EL: No. Very near. It's – I really enjoyed it there actually. Are you working near there?
CB: I work in London. I work as an administrator for a small charity. Erm, that's only part-time. I also work in a wine-bar. That's part-time.
EL: What, in the evenings?
CB: Erm, yeah, two evenings a week.
EL: Right. Yeah. It's quite a long way in from Forest Hill, mm?
CB: It's quite a journey into erm, Central London. It's Hatton Garden I work.
EL: Yeah. That's right. But you get the mainline in?
CB: That's in to Charing Cross, and, erm, I tend to walk from there, yes. Trying to get fit.
EL: Right. I'm quite lucky. I work at home.
CB: What do you do?
EL: I'm a pianist. So I spend most of the day practising. Trying to er, get as many recitals as possible.
CB: Do you teach?
EL: Er I don't at the moment, no. I'm just concentrating on playing sort of, six hours a day, that kind of thing.
CB: Mm.
EL: Five days a week. But erm, getting yourself established is pretty difficult.
CB: Yes, so do you – are you actually working, playing at the moment?
EL: Erm. Yeah, well I've just done two concerts, in the North. And er, I now trying to er, enter for a competition, in Austria, next January. So erm, maybe something 'll come out of that.

`4` *

BB: Well I've got some family photos here. Let's start with an easy one. Erm. That's me obviously, and my wife, standing in front of our semi-detached box. As you can see it's fairly conventional stuff, garden in the front, garden at the back, and er, double glazing. You know, what more could you want?
RS: I like the erm, the yellow flowers.
BB: Mm. Yes. I don't know what it's called. My wife's the gardener and er – She er – She took a cutting actually from my aunt's garden, about – ooh, a couple of years back I suppose and it's grown like mad. It's – As you can see, it's quite a decent-sized bush now.
RS: Very nice photo.
BB: You think?
RS: Yes. It's very clear, in the foreground. The background's sort of nice and shimmery.
BB: Yes. It was a German friend of my wife's who took it, so maybe that had something to do with it because er, normally we – our photos are absolutely terrible. You can't tell who's who and the background disappears. But er, it's not too bad is it? Er, what's yours like? Oh you've got one as well of your family then have you?
RS: Well, erm. In fact I lied earlier on when I said I had five sisters, in fact what I meant was there are five girls in the family.
BB: Ah, I see.
RS: I've got four sisters. In the front here, with the long hair, and ear-rings, is Sarah-Jane. She's the oldest. Er. On the right here is er my sister Emma. And er she's the next. Just slightly older than me, a couple of years, twenty-nine. And this is me here with a slightly different hairstyle. And, here's my younger brother. Although he looks a little older cause he's taller.
BB: Mm. Yes. How tall is he?
RS: I think he's about five foot ten inches.
BB: He looks fairly tall there. Yes.
RS: Erm. That's my little half sister Lucy. She's an absolute sweetie. She's much taller than that now. That's – this was taken a couple of years ago. Erm. And this is Kate, who's also, er, younger than me. She's nineteen.
BB: I can see the family resemblance all round.
RS: Yes, there is isn't there? The actual colour – we are – I'm red-headed, and er so's my sister Kate, and Sarah-Jane. Erm, but I think it's to do with the light – makes everybody look slightly reddish. This is the British Museum.
BB: I should have recognised that really I suppose. That's a good photo though. You can really see who the people are.
RS: Yes.
BB: That actually looks like you, doesn't it. Don't you think?
RS: Yes it does actually. Yeah, it's not bad.
BB: You obviously take a good one.
RS: We – But this is the erm, the – about the fourth in a series of several photos. We started off very erm, po-faced and –
BB: Yes. And then you relaxed a bit.
RS: Yeah.
BB: No, it's very good that.
RS: It's lovely. It's one of my favourite photos.

113T

BB: Yes I'm sure it must be. Yes. Indeed. Yeah. Well there's another one. I don't know as – That's my middle son. He's at university at the moment, and er – we were doing – That's my wife's aunt. We were doing her garden for her. She has a marvellous garden, it really is a terrific place. She has this little summer house so we collapsed in a chair with a cup of tea and so on. Because it was a really hot day. Earlier this year, in that little hot spell that we had. And we practically wore ourselves out cutting trees down and so on. Er, you can't really tell from that but he's about six foot five.
RS: Really?
BB: Yeah, enormous. He really is. It's frightening. I'm the midget of the family now.
RS: So, which part of the country is this?
BB: This is up in the north-west.
RS: North-west.
BB: Erm, Barrow, which is on the edge of the Lake District.
RS: Oh lovely.
BB: On the coast. So it's quite a nice area. You hop in the car and ten minutes and you're in the Lakes, so that er – That's if you want to go that way. If you want to go the other way, ten minutes you're in the sea, so it's er, you know you have a bit of each really. It's quite a nice area to be. Unfortunately we er – we don't do much bathing now because of the erm, nuclear pollution, which er, has not er, improved matters really.
RS: Yeah.
BB: Because we're just down the coast from Sellafield.

---

 *

BB: Now how about erm – travel? Have you been anywhere at all?
RS: Erm. Yeah. My parents used to work abroad.
BB: Did they?
RS: In Africa, yes. I lived in Malawi, er, Botswana. Erm . . . I've also visited Greece and Spain on holiday –
BB: Yeah.
RS: And France. Erm. I think I like Spain best actually.
BB: Yes, I like Spain very much. I went there as – ooh when I was nineteen. I was still a student and er . . . in those days of course it was so cheap it was unbelievable. So I went all over the place for a very little and really enjoyed it. I thought it was a terrific place. But I must admit France is my favourite country, but that's perhaps because I er – I lived there for a couple of years er, partly at university and partly teaching and you grow to like a place when you do that. Erm, I've been over most of Western Europe, I think. Erm . . . Last year, I went to East Germany which I found very interesting. Have you been behind the Iron Curtain?
RS: No I haven't. I'd love to. Do you speak erm, German or French?
BB: No, my wife speaks German and I speak French so we er, we manage fairly well.

BB: You've been to France, er, you said.
RS: Yes.
BB: Whereabouts?
RS: I went to erm Paris, for a few days, and er, I walked around for hours. Went to Notre Dame and the Sacré Coeur, erm and I just loved walking round and seeing all those different lovely streets and different buildings.
BB: Yes. It is the place to walk around, I think, isn't it, really. I lived there as I said, for a while and er, I used to spend hours, I must admit, walking about when I should have really been studying but er – I found it more interesting to walk about.
RS: I went to erm Brittany too. I helped erm, in a holiday camp for children.
BB: Did you?
RS: It was called a 'Colonie de Vacances', and that was very erm, strenuous.

BB: Yeah, I'm sure it was. Whereabouts was that?
RS: In – it was er, in a place called Laporette . . . I'm not pronouncing it correctly.
BB: Mm. Now. Where's that exactly?
RS: Erm. It's just along – It's on the Brittany coast, I think it's further – quite southwards.
BB: Yeah. Because I had a year in Vannes er, in er college there. That's on the southern coast, which er – I was wondering if it was near there, because that's the sort of area where a lot of the 'colonies' were.

BB: Have you any plans to go abroad? – in the coming years?
RS: Erm, yes, I'd like to go to Spain again. My brother's staying there at the moment – teaching English. And erm, I love Spanish music and I'd really like to have the chance to . . . play it.
BB: Of course, yes indeed. Yes. We're hoping to go to France and Germany this time. Er, we are going, actually. We've lined it up to take a couple of the children with us. Erm. So, you've been to erm, well, more places really than me, haven't you? Let's face it. I mean, you've been to Africa.
RS: I don't know about that.
BB: That's way off my er – off my experience, that really is. Whereas I've stuck very largely to Europe I think.

UNIT 2

---

 *

BB: Well, we've got a photo here. Now – Which of them is not in the Boy Scout photo? Have you any ideas on that? Because quite honestly, they seem to have changed tremendously. One would assume that the fellow in glasses is the – is the same one as the one in glasses in the original photo.
RS: Ah, yes. I'm afraid my photo's not very clear. I'll have to look at yours. Yes, I would think so. And erm, the one on the left-hand side, I would imagine is the violin player. Something about his face . . . it's fairly plump.
BB: So that this fresh-faced chap you think's the one with the other guitar?
RS: Yes. So it must be the accordion player who's not there.
BB: The accordian player, you think. Yeah.

Fragments of songs:
Football fans singing at match.
Someone in the bath or shower.
Auld Lang Syne.

---

 *

INT: Pete, when did you first meet Bonny and Mac?
PS: When I joined the Boy Scouts. In Yetminster. So I must have been then about eleven or twelve. And – I think – Well, two reasons why I joined the Scout troop. One, I'd been to see a show that they'd put on in the village hall, and I thought this was great, you know. This seemed like a pretty good thing. And then I'd met erm, Mac at school. This was when we both went er, from the village into the town of Sherborne to go to Grammar School. And er, he was in the Scouts you see and so er, I thought well, this would be a good thing to join.
INT: And when did you start making music together?
PS: Well we used to sing – When were in the Scouts, we used to sing when we were camping. We always used to have a camp-fire, and sing songs around that. And then, er, around about the same time, some people in the village started a folk-dancing, er –
INT: Right.
PS: evening, in the village hall. And er – I think originally it was the Women's Institute, and there were

all these older ladies going to this country dancing. And then some of us younger children got interested, and eventually I think there were so many kids interested in the dancing that the older ones got fed up and they left, and so it really became a thing for young people, you know.
INT: Yeah. Yeah.
PS: And all the girls used to go there as well of course, so all the boys used to –
INT: That helps.
PS: take an interest in it. That got us interested in folk-dancing and folk music. And it was from that we actually started playing instruments and then singing.

INT: You weren't always an entertainer were you?
MM: No, I was a printer, beforehand.
INT: And how long was that?
MM: I did a five-year apprenticeship in printing. And then we did a – well er we were sort of singing while an apprentice, you know, so it was really – I mean I did the five-year apprenticeship but the actual singing started during that time. And er at the end of the apprenticeship, we just turned professional. That was it. Things were building up. Work was getting – You know it was really – it was getting in the way of singing. I was finding it very difficult working a day job and then working evenings, weekends and everything, so –
INT: Were you worried about leaving your full-time job and taking a gamble on singing?
MM: Erm. I suppose yes. There was a certain worry at the time. But not – only in as much as I'd finished my apprenticeship. And we had planned to do – go professional for three months. So I finished in September, through to Christmas, then we were going to all go back to work again. We were at that sort of stage where we thought, if we didn't give it a go at that time we may look back in years to come and regret it, so we said right, let's do it for three months, have a look around the country, do some professional bookings, and then go back to work again. And that snowballed on steadily ever since.

INT: Well what did you do before you – before you became a full-time musician? Because erm, Mac was telling me he was a printer.
BS: That's right. Well Mac and I used to work – We did our apprenticeship with the same firm in fact.
INT: I see. You were both printers together?
BS: Yes. He er, worked the machines, to actually do the printing, and I was a typesetter. I used to typeset by hand and also work a typesetting machine.
INT: Yeah. Yeah. That's one of those machines where you have to read upside-down and back-to-front isn't it?
BS: That's the one. You've got it, yes.
INT: How long does it take to learn?
BS: Erm. I don't really know. I can't remember. I suppose six months or so before you've really got the hang of doing it at any speed. Yes. But it is a five-year apprenticeship, so there's er, plenty of time to learn.

 17b *

INT: Roger when did you join the group? When did you become a Yetty?
RT: Ah, I became a full member of the Yetties I suppose about, erm, it was just over two years ago now. I'm the newest member of the group.
INT: And how did it happen?
RT: Erm. Well, there used to be a folk club which in fact we still run here in Sherborne where we live, and erm, it was really open to anyone who wanted to come and play or sing at the club. And the Yetties at the time were running the club. And I went down with my violin under my arm. And er, played a few tunes and sang a few songs. And then it really started from there. And er, they eventually asked me to sort of come out and join in a few dances and ceilidhs that we used to play around the country. Erm. And it became more and

more and eventually I left my job, erm, which was actually working with handicapped children at the time, and went full-time.
INT: So you didn't suddenly join the group, you gradually became more and more a part of the group.
RT: That's right, yes. I erm – As I said the bookings sort of became more and more. And I became quite involved with music and song, which I had done for a number of years anyway. Erm. And sort of, you know, as the singing increased, I didn't seem to have much time for my full-time job.
INT: Right. And so before that you were working with handicapped children.
RT: Yes. I've worked with handicapped – well adults and children for about ten, eleven years altogether. And er, I did training as a state enrolled nurse. And I've worked, well, mainly in the southern part of England with handicapped children.
INT: So you've worked in different parts of England?
RT: Yes. Yes.
INT: Erm. And, what travelling have you done? Because we've heard a bit about travelling in Sarawak and other parts of the world. What about you? What travelling have you done?
RT: Well since I've joined the group we haven't had any extensive tours as they have done in the past. But certainly we travel all over England, Scotland and Wales. Erm. And also a variety of venues as well. Erm. Not just concerts but open-air events – ceilidhs, sort of folk dances . . . .

21

Song: **The gypsy rover**

UNIT 3

24a *

BB: Er well. Letter one I – Erm – I noticed several spelling mistakes in it.
EL: Mm.
BB: I think success and –
EL: Mm.
BB: and the chap's name Finnigan was spelt in two different ways.
EL: Oh. Oh yes. Well done.
BB: Erm. Which I thought would be a little bit annoying for the person concered.
EL: Mm.
BB: Er, the signature's illegible. And the writing isn't marvellous.
EL: Mm.
BB: Whereas erm, in letter two you can read everything –
EL: Mm.
BB: and I didn't come across any actual mistakes.
EL: Yeah.
BB: Erm. The other thing I felt was that letter two had much more detailed information.
EL: Yes. Yes.
BB: You know, personal and the question of qualifications and so on. Er. There was a specific enquiry for a job.
EL: Mm.
BB: And a particular job. Er, there was a willingness to work shown.
EL: Mm.
BB: And erm, the thing, for me anyway, was correctly written.
EL: Yeah, it has a much better structure that letter. The first one just keeps repeating itself, doesn't it? Because it says, I'm very interested in – it takes a whole paragraph, towards the bottom to say I'm very interested in your training scheme, and feel sure I'd be suitable to do the job. And I sort of feel that – I don't know. Perhaps he'd almost said that already. Maybe he hadn't.
BB: Mm. Well that is the important –
EL: Sorry, and then he goes on to say this is a career

115T

I've come increasingly to feel is suited.
BB: That's right, yes.
EL: Erm. He's not really – As you say – He's not giving them anything very specific to go on.
BB: No. No. It's very airy fairy, isn't it? Er –
EL: Yeah.
BB: Not the sort of letter I would like to receive, I think, if I was er, looking for people.
EL: Mm.

---

 *

EL: Well do you think we should talk about these ten golden rules?
BB: Mhm. Yes. Surely. Erm –
EL: Erm –
BB: Well, go on, let's hear yours.
EL: I'll give a few of them. Write neatly or type.
BB: Yes.
EL: Er. Don't repeat yourself. Keep it brief as possible.
BB: Yes.
EL: Plenty of paragraphs.
BB: Mhm.
EL: Erm. And then other things just like, you know, address, phone number, date, make sure you get all that right. Erm. Print your name at the bottom as well as signing it.
BB: Yes, that's a good point. Certainly. Yes.
EL: And then be sure about the rules about yours faithfully or yours sincerely.
BB: Yes.
EL: Which – I think there do seem to be rules about that. Erm. Be clear.
BB: Yes.
EL: Erm. You know, be confident about your aptitude for the job you're going for.
BB: That's a good point, certainly, yes. That's true.
EL: And the last one, I think, is make it clear at the beginning of the letter, er what – what you're writing about. I mean, where you saw the advertisement, you know, that sort of thing.
BB: Mm. Yes. Yes. I have that one as well.
EL: Have you got any extra ones?
BB: Erm, let's see. Correct – Well, I put head it correctly.
EL: Yeah.
BB: I'm just thinking in terms of what you were saying.
BB: Write legibly. Provide accurate information, rather than make things –
EL: Make things up again. Yeah. Don't lie.
BB: And that applies to your personal life as well, I would think.
EL: Yes.
BB: Erm. Try and display some sort of enthusiasm. I think you more or less said that actually, didn't you?
EL: Mm. Mm. Mm.
BB: Erm. Offer to provide any more information if they so wish.
EL: Yes.
BB: I think that's –
EL: That's a good point, yeah.
BB: Erm. Perhaps say how you heard of the opening. I mean sometimes newspapers like you to sort of quote their er, adverts, sort of things.
EL: Mm. Mm. Well. I'm sure they do.
BB: And erm, indicate your interest in making progress.
EL: Mm.
BB: Within the firm presumably.
EL: Mm.
BB: Erm. And be polite.
EL: Yeah.
BB: You know, I think that - that letter there isn't really polite, is it? It's –
EL: This first one? No it's a bit pushy, isn't it?
BB: It is. Being a bit superior about it. Yeah.
EL: Mm. I don't think any job will – I think we'll manage every one actually. We – we –
BB: Mm. Yes, indeed.

EL: Nothing too difficult after that lot.
BB: No problem at all . . . .

---

 *

INT: Erm. How does the business actually work, Bonny? Erm. How do you go about finding work? Or if someone else wants a folk-group to open a store in Germany or something like that, how do they go about it?
BS: Well, erm. Most of it really is done by word of mouth. We do actually occasionally advertise in some – one or two folk magazines. But generally we just wait for the work to come in. As far as erm, the foreign tours are concerned, and some – most of the theatres, they would go through another agent. And there are various agents up and down the country, who er, have got our address. And someone rings up and says, er, I want a folk-group, or I want the Yetties, they just then get in touch with me. And er, that's all official and done with contracts. But most of our work comes through me, and it's a friendly chat on the phone and er, how much can you afford? and – So it's fairly easy-going really.
INT: Do you actually have an agent yourselves?
BS: Well not a permanent agent, no. We used to. For about twelve years we had a manager, in fact, who handled all our work. But er, that got rather expensive. And er, so now we do it ourselves.
INT: Uhuh. Some of your overseas tours are with the British Council.
BS: That's right. Yes.
INT: How did that contact begin?
BS: Well. That started – That's a long time ago now. Erm. That started through Jim Lloyd who was our manager at the time. He had another group that did one or two trips for them. And he mentioned us. And they came to various of our concerts in – around London area, Croydon and the Queen Elizabeth Hall. And sat back in the audience and hummed and ha'd. And eventually came to the decision that we were quite personable and would probably get on quite well in these countries. And the whole thing gradually developed. Erm. Then one day they rang up and said, you know, would we like to go to Nepal? Whereon we laughed. You know, Yetties going to Nepal? Yes. Big laugh. But it happened to be true. And so er, we started on the first large tour – the first seven-week tour.

---

 *

EE: What advice would you give a young person leaving school or university? So the aim is to have five –
BB: Oh that's right. Five.
EE: – five things that – five bits of advice that you would give. Erm. Would you like to –
BB: Yeah, okay, I'll read mine out and see how many of you – of them you have. Er. Pay careful attention to dress – appearance. You know generally speaking in the interview. I think this is very important.
EL: Yeah. I've got that as my number one as well.
EE: Yes. Yes. I hadn't put that one, but I do agree with you. Erm. But I think there's also – You need to be yourself.
BB: Yes. You mean natural, er, rather than erm, putting on some sort of an act.
EE: Yes. Yes.
BB: I'd certainly agree with that.
EE: It'd be very difficult to go through your working life –
BB: Yeah. Mm. True enough. Yeah.
EE: – living up to the image that you gave at your interview, if it isn't you.
EL: Right.
BB: Yes. Er, so. Have a clear idea of the – if it's a university one – have a clear idea of the subjects you wish to take and then of your possible career. And if it's a job interview, er, show that you're interested in the job, and have tried to find out something about it before

you actually get to the interview.

EE: Yes. I put erm, find out a little about the organisation, so you can make a comment.

BB: Yeah. That amounts to the same thing really.

EE: Erm. So – Yes. It looks as if you – you're interested. And also it's very flattering to the organisation.

BB: Yes. Of course. Indeed. That's it exactly, yes.

EL: There always comes that moment when they say well er, you know, well Mr Jones that's the job as we see it. Er. Would you like to ask us anything about it? You just sit there in absolute silence, you don't get the job.

BB: That's it, exactly, yes. Erm, right. Third. Have at least one topic or hobby which you can really talk about, and show that you know a lot about. Erm, I think this is important because if, you know, if you get stuck, erm, that this is the sort of question which can be asked, erm, and if you have no erm, interests or hobbies or whatever you like to call them then it shows you are a pretty dull sort of person. Er, and I think it would go rather badly for you.

EE: Yes.

BB: Erm. I had one or two examples of that. My son went for an interview. He - His erm – He builds model planes. And er, in the course of the last few years he's become a real expert on them, so that er, apparently his interview lasted about thirty minutes and twenty-nine and a half were spent talking about model planes.

EE: Did he get the job?

BB: Oh yes, he got the – well yes – position in university and er, such – he got it, yeah. So, it worked very well for him.

EE: Yes, I'm sure there's an element of luck – that the interviewer, erm, was interested in model planes.

BB: I don't think he was really, no. I think he was trying to find out about things, er, from what Michael said – that er, he was picking up information all the time. Mm.

EE: Have you got any others?

BB: Yes er. Don't tell lies.

EL: Mm. That's a good one.

BB: You're always liable to be found out. And er – You know, it's something to avoid I would think.

EE: Yes. I think, erm, something to include in that one is not to try and cover up when you don't know something. Which isn't quite the same thing as telling a lie. Erm, I've found in interviews that it's actually better to say, I'd like a moment to think about that. I hadn't thought of that before. I'd like a minute – to digest the information and think of an answer.

BB: And finally, be on time.

EE: Yes.

EL: Yes. I've got that one too.

EE: Yes. I put do allow plenty of time to make the journey and find where you are going to. Nerves I think can make you miss street signs and –

BB: Indeed, yes. That's true, Yes. Mm.

EE: Yes. I've noticed that we've all been putting dos rather than don'ts.

EL: Well I've got a don't here. Er, which is don't gush too much. Er. Which is like, you know, I think you can have – be tempted to have a sort of verbal diarrhoea really. You know, in your interview, because you think the more I say the more they'll think I'm – and I think that erm – I think there's a danger of saying too much as well as too little.

EE: Yes. And keep to the point.

BB: That's right. Yeah.

EE: I mean gushing can include getting right away from the subject that you're meant to be talking about.

EL: Right.

BB: That's true enough that, yes.

EE: So we could almost sum up, erm, a lot of our points as being self-discipline.

BB: Yes. Yes. I would agree with that, certainly. Mm. Have you any others er – ?

EL: Well no. I mean three of mine were exactly the same as yours. Er. I put sound motivated for the job,

but that's pretty obvious really isn't it? I mean we've included that anyway. It – they all fall into the same sort of general category really.

BB: That's interesting that, yeah.

32b *

INT: I think before you were a printer, you did a certain amount of farmwork, didn't you?

MM: Erm, yes. But that was really – er – Yeah. I mean that was – Everyone did farmwork. They lived in the villages really. It was the case of if you lived in the villages you helped out on the farm, and I lived on a small farm in the farm cottages there, and at weekends you would help. I mean I did milking every night, get the cows – home from primary school. We'd get the cows in for milking in the evenings.

INT: Even from primary school. That was what sort of age?

MM: Well that would be nine. Eight or nine I started there. And you drove the tractor as well. Because you were –

INT: At the age of eight or nine?

MM: Yeah. Because you weren't – you couldn't lift a bail. You couldn't help with the actual manual work, so they stuck you on the tractor.

INT: Highly illegal.

MM: It wasn't then.

INT: It wasn't?

MM: No, in fact I had to give it up because the government did bring in a rule, saying that children under thirteen I think it was weren't allowed to drive tractors. So I had to take a couple of years off.

INT: So that you had to retire at the age of ten or something like that from tractor driving?

MM: That's right. But I mean there was no – it was very slow. There was no high speed racing round the fields or anything. And er, it was just accepted practice I think.

INT: Right.

UNIT 4

34c *

BB: Er, as a child, were you frightened of the dark? Erm. I certainly was.

CB: Were you?

BB: Yeah. Still am to some extent, I must admit. Erm. Quite why I don't know. It's just the –

CB: Did you use to sleep with the light on?

BB: No, I never had the light on. My parents wouldn't allow it. But erm – It erm – I suppose because I used to sleepwalk, perhaps, and I always had this fear of falling downstairs when I was sleepwalking. I've grown out of that fortunately.

BB: You had nothing like that?

CB: I was never really frightened of the dark, I don't think. I think I liked to know there were people around me. Erm – that weren't far away, but I was never frightened of the dark. Erm. And I don't think I ever slept – sleepwalked, to my knowledge.

BB: No, well it's a frightening thing. You know, you er, find yourself out in the street or something and er, when you wake up it's er, something you remember all your life.

CB: I've never quite understood it.

BB: No, neither have I. No. But er – It just happened. Yeah. Anything else that's er, frightened you? Or frightens you?

CB: Erm, I think I'd – I'd – looking at the list, I don't like – actually like erm, spiders.

BB: Mm.

CB: Going on to the next one. Erm. One of the things I really hate is spiders and insects. Erm.

BB: Yeah.

CB: Fluttering insects. Things like butterflies –

BB: Mhm.

CB: And erm, moths and things.

BB: No they don't really bother me, at all er. I think I've got some sort of irrational fear of ghosts, but I don't really believe in them. It's er, just one of those er, deep feelings that you have I suppose. Erm. Anything else. Certainly afraid of war. Yeah, that is something that er, I have thought about and the idea of a war now –
CB: Yes.
BB: is very frightening.
CB: I don't particularly like heights. Erm. Heights, er, at the top of a mountain, or a hill, where it's possible to fall. Erm. The top of something like a lighthouse or something I don't mind because there's a barrier around you. But heights where you think you may be able to fall.
BB: Yeah. I was okay until I had a rather nasty experience about er, height. Until then I was okay. I could go anywhere but er, I was er, on a lighthouse actually. We were being taken round it. We went up all the stairs and to the light, er, room. And then the chap says oh come on right we'll go out here. I went through the door. And I was on this very very narrow little parapet.
CB: Yep.
BB: With a rail about – perhaps eighteen inches high.
CB: Mm.
BB: And then a sheer drop of about a hundred feet or something. I was absolutely petrified. I've never been as scared like that before or since.
CB: That's very frightening.
BB: And, you know I sort of edged round. I couldn't go back through the same door. I edged round and managed to find the other door. And that's it. Ever since then if I go up a ladder I'm scared stiff now. It's really is, it's er, changed my whole life, you know. Absolutely frightening, that.
CB: I don't think I've ever had a really frightening experience, or one that I can actually remember. Erm. Because I think possibly if I have had a bad experience I may have blocked it out of my memory.
BB: Mm. Yes. Mm.
CB: Erm. But I haven't really got anything that was really terrifying to me.
BB: Oh yeah. You've been very lucky then, haven't you?

---

35 *

BB: Oh, do you think it's possibly someone with a parachute erm, one of those stunts. You know, like jumping off the erm, suspension bridge in Bristol on the end of an elastic or something, or the Golden Gate Bridge, that sort of idea? Er . . .
CB: Someone – what? – someone that had been attached to a rope, do you think?
BB: Mm. That's possible. Er. I was thinking on the lines – you know – perhaps the erm – for a bet, he'd er, jumped off, parachuted down and erm, perhaps landed on somebody's car, you know.
CB: Yes.
BB: Excuse me, I've just jumped off the Empire State Building. Er. Can you improve on that?
CB: I don't know.
BB: No. No it's –

36a *

CB: There's the real Empire State Building.
BB: Yeah. Here we are. Oh no. Mm . . .
CB: He woke up on a ledge.
BB: Mm. That's even better isn't it, that, yes. Mm . . . Bill Steckman, I couldn't believe it. I'll bet. I poured myself a stiff drink. Mm. No that's one I –
CB: So he's fallen one floor.
BB: Mm. That's one I would never have believed in really.

---

40 *

BB: Now. Night on ice. Have you got that one?
CB: Read this back page summary of a news report.

BB: Fifteen-year-old school boy was recovering at home. Mm. Well. Can we – Can we think of five questions that –
CB: Five questions that you think will be answered in the full story.
BB: Mm.
CB: Erm . . . What he did while – to keep warm.
BB: Well it says that he kept warm by jumping for ten minutes at a time. Er. Did he ever feel he was never going to get out?
CB: What – What was – What did he think about all night?
BB: Yes, that's right. What did he think about? Mm. Er. Was I going to die? I suppose. I think I would think like that. Erm. Has it put him off working for a butcher? Mm.
CB: Wonder if he was thinking how can he get out?
BB: Mhm.
CB: I should think he was.
BB: – he was. Yes. How can I get out? Mm.
CB: Methods of escape.
BB: Yeah.
CB: Do we have five questions?
BB: Er. One, two, three, four so far. Erm. Will he be a vegetarian? No. Er. Mm.
CB: Shall we go on, and have a look at it?
BB: Shall we go on? Yes. That's it. Mm. Oh, I thought someone was playing a joke eh? Mm. That's it. I tried to kick the door open, to pick the lock – So that's obviously one of the – answers one of ours.
CB: Yes.
BB: Erm. I realised I might die. That's another one.
CB: Did we say what he was wearing?
BB: No we didn't. Perhaps we should have thought of that, yeah. Erm. What did he think about?
CB: He ran on the spot for ten out of the fourteen hours.
BB: Mm. Good Lord. Yeah. How can I get – Yes, we've had how can I get out. Mm. Ah well. Seem to have covered most of it, apart from the clothing angle there, I would think. Yeah.

UNIT 5

43d *

EL: Well there are various topics, and the first one is art in school. I think –
SJ: Mm.
EL: you do a certain amount of teaching. Do you –
SJ: I have done, yes.
EL: Do you actually teach art yourself at the moment in school, or is it –
SJ: Erm. I'm not doing much of it at the moment. I've done quite a bit in the past. I mean I've taught in all – at all different stages.
EL: Mm.
SJ: Children right up to art schools.
EL: And how – It's very difficult to teach art in a way, because children especially have got their own way of expressing themselves, and how much do you feel they – that –
SJ: Well, hopefully –
EL: That has to be curbed and –?
SJ: Erm. No I mean, there are so many different approaches to art teaching, but erm, I think that the main thing is not – is to encourage the imagination of each child, and erm, allow them to express themselves as freely as possible. But at the same time, introducing erm, an aesthetic awareness they might not have had time to concentrate on. I think it's really –
EL: So you might see little Johnny doing a drawing which – Would you then say now I think – Wouldn't it be better if it went a bit that way? Would you actually sort of, go so far as to erm –
SJ: Mm. No, only if the child asked. All the while they were happy with what they were doing and I would constantly say are you happy with the way it is? And all the while the child was happy with the way it was, I

wouldn't erm interfere.

EL: Mm. Right. Yeah. And how about art as a career?

SJ: Forget it unless you – Er, I mean if – if – Forget it if you're keen on making money. Erm. But if – Art is a, erm, a vocation if you like. It's something in inverted commas, vocation. Erm. I mean if you are committed to it then you do it and you don't question it.

EL: Right. Yeah. I think that's very true and – I think people often find it difficult to understand how one can go on just voluntarily choosing this life which is an absolute nightmare in material terms, but –

SJ: Yes, I think people romanticise it.

EL: It is its own reward, isn't it?

SJ: Yes, people romanticise it and they say oh how lovely it must be to be an artist. But of course they don't see the other side of it. You know.

EL: Mm. Right.

SJ: You know, as an artist one is something of an outsider.

EL: Yes.

SJ: And erm, our society is getting increasingly technological and that's what's seen as the important thing.

EL: Right . . . .

45c

SJ: My wings. I was in the car when I suddenly started growing wings. I said, Daddy, why am I growing wings? Don't speak nonsense. I said, well I am, and I said, Daddy, you've got wings as well and when I looked out, and everybody had them, I said Daddy, look out of the window, and he did, and he said, well, everybody has got them. You did not say in the first place. We were at home. I showed Mum my wings. She said I could go flying today. I went out, and I was flying in the air. I landed in Africa. It was very hot. I went a long way. I came to the jungle. I met a monkey. It said, cheep cheep. I said, monkeys don't go cheep cheep. The monkey said, little girls don't grow wings. I said, can we have some food? The monkey said that there was no such thing as food, only fruit. Then we said that we would play hide-and-seek. I said, you count, and I would hide. I hid in a tree. Monkey did not come. I said, monkey, monkey. – Did not say 'yes' as he should do. I went to look for him. I got lost, so I climbed up a tree, and was just about to go to sleep, and I saw monkey. I said, where were you monkey? Said – I was – Monkey said, I was looking for you. I said, I was looking for you, and they both laughed. Then we went flying together. Then we went home, and Mum and Dad laughed. And I laughed too. And monkey laughed in his funny cheep cheep laugh, and me and monkey went to bed.

45d/e *

SJ: It's a wonderful little story, isn't it?

EL: Yeah, it's fun.

SJ: Why do you think they chose that for the Guardian feature, rather than any of the others?

EL: Erm. Well. It's got a lot of charm. And er, I – you know, it's very imaginative and – Takes you off into er, Africa and -

SJ: That's right.

EL: around a bit.

SJ: Mm. A sort of typical child's fantasy. And I think just the whole rhythmic flow of it, you know.

EL: Yes.

SJ: The sort of repetition. And I think some parts of it are rather clever actually. I think the bit where she finds the monkey, and erm, the monkey goes cheep, cheep.

EL: Yeah.

SJ: And she says, monkeys don't go cheep, cheep.

EL: Yeah. That's good.

SJ: And the monkey says, Little girls don't grow wings. I think that's quite erm complex – Thought, actually, for a six year old. Don't you?

EL: Yeah. I agree with you. Yes. Yes. It's very good that. Reminds me of when I worked in a record shop, and erm, people kept on er, stubbing their cigarettes out in a pot – in a pot-plant. And er – so somebody put a sign up saying er, this pot-plant is not an ashtray. And the next day I went into work and somebody had put a sign in all the ashtrays saying this ashtray is not a pot-plant. Anyway. Perhaps er – shall we go on to five B?

SJ: Oh. Yes. So how can you tell it's written by a small child? Well. I think the constant repetition. Apart from the obvious spelling mistakes, but then some grown-ups don't spell so well. Erm. And er, certain kind of lack of, erm, grammatical complexity. The way it's very simple sentences. Sort of I did, I said.

EL: Yes.

SJ: A lot of sentences beginning with I because children are so caught up in their own little world and, it's all I isn't it? Experiencing things. And sentences obviously that all flow into one another. The way that children think, in sort of a long flow of images rather than in grammatical sentences with structure.

EL: Yes. So stream of consciousness stuff really.

SJ: Stream of consciousness. Yes. That's exactly what I thought. Gertrude Stein would have loved it. Have you read any Gertrude Stein?

EL: I haven't, no.

SJ: She imitates this sort of childlike style, actually.

EL: Oh, right. I suppose monkey, monkey, you know, if it was an adult it would be the monkey the whole time, wouldn't it?

SJ: Exactly, yes. In fact in a way, it gives it erm, I mean a marvellous sort of liveliness. You know, it's very alive.

EL: Yeah. Oh it is.

SJ: If an adult had erm, written it it probably would have er, sounded a lot more dull.

EL: Right.

---

47 *

EL: Well, shall we go on to er, the next one?

SJ: Yes. Ah. Have you ever had a dream where you could fly? Where you had wings?

EL: I don't think I have, no.

SJ: You haven't?

EL: I used to have a lot of dreams about witches, but er, that was them rather than me, I think.

SJ: Ah. Gosh, I'm surprised. Because I dream I'm flying all the time.

EL: Do you?

SJ: Usually just under the ceiling. Right at the top of a room and I – and erm, it's something I know that only I know how to do, and nobody else knows the secret – of how I can fly. I thought everybody had flying dreams – actually.

EL: Well, that's quite exciting.

SJ: Mm. I don't know what it means, but –

EL: Does it – Does it ever happen while you're awake?

SJ: No, but actually I did go up in a plane, a little plane the other day, which was a bit like my fly – it was – it reminded me of my flying dreams. You know, I was in a little two-seater plane, flying over Cornwall. Just high enough to see things quite clearly. And erm, that actually reminded me of my – my flying dreams. Very unreal sort of feeling.

EL: Well. Perhaps you'll start levitating one day.

SJ: Yes. I'm not sure I'd want to, actually.

49c *

BB: Well I suppose as I say British people are fairly reserved really aren't they? Even now. I mean you don't normally go and ask people personal questions, do you?

RS: That's funny actually because the other day somebody said that English people don't like talking about erm, religion, money, er sex, politics – What was the other one? I can't remember, but it was practically everything. I didn't agree of course.

BB: No, no, it's er – I think it's just the really personal things, perhaps that people tend to shy away from now. Yeah.

RS: Yes. I'd agree.

BB: I mean I wouldn't go and ask you you know how much did you pay for your jersey or you know your dress or what have you.

RS: Well I didn't actually because somebody gave it to me, but er –

BB: Somebody – That's even better isn't it? I suppose you might if you knew them well, yes, that's right, mm. But otherwise, no. Erm. Er – Even – what – have you got a job? is a difficult question these days, isn't it, too.

RS: Yes. I think it's becoming less, actually.

BB: You think people are getting used to the idea do you?

RS: Yes. I used to be embarrassed about saying I didn't have a job whereas now I don't. Because although I'm on the Enterprise Allowance Scheme it's actually like another type of dole scheme. And, yeah I think, some of that – I think depends on – people get used to a certain way of being.

BB: That's right, yeah. No my eldest son was out of work for about fifteen months I think when he left school and he – he got very depressed and er, if people said to him what are you doing? he was virtually speechless for a while because er, he really felt it. But fortunately he's got a job so it's er – that's disappeared but – I think there's still some people who feel it that badly.

RS: I think they do.

BB: They must do, you know. It must be a terrible er, experience to – to have no job when you want one.

RS: Yeah. I think it is.

BB: I suppose there are those the other way. What about other countries? I don't know. I've never found much difference, quite honestly, have you? between British people and foreign people, or any other sort of people.

RS: No. No, I don't think so either. Maybe it's the way people put things. Or perhaps erm, er, perhaps English people phrase things – differently.

Yeah well quite, obviously . . . .

 *

SJ: You know, as an artist, one is something of an outsider.

EL: Yes.

SJ: And erm, our society is getting increasingly technological and that's what's seen as the important thing.

EL: Right.

SJ: But in fact, you know, I think this country has a major sort of pool of talent.

EL: Mm.

SJ: Certainly in other spheres – well, theatre for instance and –

EL: Yeah.

SJ: and music as well.

EL: Yeah. But a lot of people say that England is particularly bad compared with even other European countries in this –

SJ: In the funding, you mean?

EL: Yes, in the funding.

SJ: Well yes, it certainly is.

EL: Yeah. And that a lot of people find it easier to go to Germany and France.

SJ: Yes. And I've just read the Royal Shakespeare Company are running out of money.

EL: Mm.

SJ: And they must be one of the most venerated.

EL: Mm. Yeah. Right. Mm. Finally, you know, it's again tied up with the business of – you know, the material side. This business of paying lots of, erm, money for, erm, you know – paintings going for absolutely ridiculous sums nowadays.

SJ: Oh yes. Yes, like the Van Gogh, er –

EL: Yeah. Exactly.

SJ: Sunflowers that went for a record –

EL: Seven million or something?

SJ: No much more than that. It was something like twenty-four million actually.

EL: Uhuh.

SJ: it was a vast amount. Mm.

EL: Mm. But it seems sad, that it's – it's a famous saying that a painter has to die before he er –

SJ: That's right. It's sad for Van Gogh.

EL: Yeah. Erm. But it's a pattern that just seems to repeat itself doesn't it, again and again? People while they're alive –

SJ: Mm. Mm. Mm. Mm.

EL: I don't suppose there's enough distance to judge whether it's a great work of art or not.

SJ: Partly that – well, not so much that it's a great work of art, but that it's a great investment. Because art in the terms of the Sunflowers and so on is an investment, and it can't be judged as such until later on.

EL: Do you think the people who buy these things appreciate them? Or do you think it's like the bottle of wine which is – goes for twenty thousand pounds, and no-one's actually going to drink it?

SJ: I don't really know because I've never met anyone who could afford to pay that amount of money. I hope that they er – I suspect that they could easily have bought, erm, something else. You know, a non-artistic product and therefore because they've chosen to buy a painting perhaps, I imagine they would have a sensitivity towards it, yes.

[53] *

EL: Well. I think that's pretty obvious, isn't it?

SJ: Well, I think that it's fairly obvious, but I suppose there are different – different er – slightly varying answers, you know?

EL: Well, what would you say?

SJ: Well I – I said, no more of that horrible semolina.

EL: Oh I see.

SJ: Maybe I think in a peculiar way. What did you – what did you think?

EL: Oh well, I just thought, no thank-you.

SJ: Oh no. She's supposed to say no thank-you, but, because it's called things that children say –

EL: Oh I see.

SJ: You see because grown-ups always say to children, no what? and the child's supposed to say no thank-you. But I think the child was supposed to say no thank-you and he's said no semolina or no more horrible semolina.

EL: Aha.

SJ: Because I think the child has taken – taken it literally, the question, rather than has forgotten to say thank-you.

EL: Okay. Shall we turn over and find out what the answer is?

SJ: Oh. Oh, I haven't got an answer.

EL: Well here it is.

SJ: Oh. Key. No what? No fear. Oh well yes. That's – There we are. No fear, that horrible semolina. I mean, how many children actually like semolina anyway? It always has lumps in it when it's in school dinners.

EL: Yes . . . .

UNIT 6

 *

EE: I've brought a picture – that my five-year-old son did for me. It isn't a very special picture. I think it's a cat. I think this might be a balloon. But the idea was very nice because he decided that it would be very nice for me to have a picture that I could carry around with me in my purse and I could get it out and remind myself of him when he was at school. I told him that I missed him when he was at school during the day. So he did

this picture so I could keep it with me. It's lovely.
EL: Mm. There's a tree isn't it? on the left? Or isn't it?
EE: Erm. I think it is, yes.
BB: It's not a gardens is it?
EE: The sun.
RS: And this looks like a very happy sheep actually.
EE: I think it's actually a cat.
RS: It's actually a cat yeah.
EL: I can't remember the details of, erm, what it's about but I like the idea. And he did one for his father, who has a wallet that has erm, a piece where you can put a photograph in and my husband's put it in – in that place.
BB: Is this totally unsolicited, or is it –
EE: Yes. Oh yes. These were presents, and he very much enjoyed cutting – cutting out these little pictures. And he provided all the family with their own picture.
BB: That's great. Yes. Indeed. My kids never did that for me. Where did I go wrong?
EE: He's very keen on writing letters as well.
BB: Very good.
EL: Perhaps you – you should have been a mother.
BB: Yeah. Probably that's it.

59a *

EL: Erm. How self-confident are you? Erm. First of all, does using the telephone worry you? And there are two – three possible answers. Yes. Only if I have to speak to someone I don't know. Or no, it doesn't worry me.
EE: No it doesn't worry me.
EL: Right.
EE: I'm only able to answer that recently after becoming a telephone counsellor I can tell you.
EL: Ah. Okay. Erm. Are you afraid of making a complaint if something you have bought is faulty? A. I keep quiet about it. B. I'll write a letter of complaint. Not a personal one. C. I don't mind making a scene as long as I have my rights?
EE: C.
EL: Three. If you were travelling by bus, but only had a twenty pound note, would you – A. Walk home so as not to cause a fuss. B. Buy something you didn't really want to get some change. C. Get on the bus, and put up with any moans from the conductor.
EE: I think I'd buy – B. I'd buy something that I didn't particularly want. Probably a newspaper or something.
EL: Er four. You once knocked over a vase in a shop and broke it, and were made to pay for it. Did you. A. Avoid the shop altogether? B. Only go in when the manager was not around? C. Go in as if nothing had happened?
EE: C. I might wait six months first though.
EL: Right. Five. You arrive at a party wearing the same outfit as someone else. This is women only by the way. Do you – A. Sneak out and change? B. Avoid the woman and apologise if you meet her? C. Go up and compliment her on her good taste? That's the women who's wearing the same –
EE: I – Yes. I don't – If I was living near to home I think I would go home and change. Erm. Otherwise C.
EL: C. Right. Erm. Six. You're more than half way to work, and you realise you're wearing odd socks, one bright blue, one black. Do you – A. Continue to work prepared to laugh it off? B. Go in to a shop and buy another pair quickly, joking with the cashier? C. Go home and change?
EE: Well it depends what I was wearing at the – at the same time. I think B.
EL: B. Right.
EE: That is, go and buy another pair of socks isn't it?
EL: Er, that's the one, yeah. Right. Seven. You desperately want a day off work to go to the sales or a football match. Do you – A. Not go, because you daren't ask for time off? B. Ring up and say you're ill? C. Go to work and pretend to be ill, leaving early?
EE: I find that one very difficult to answer. Erm –
EL: Well I don't suppose you have to answer it if you don't want to. Just –

EE: I suppose I wouldn't go. A. I wouldn't – I wouldn't go to whatever it was I was hoping to have the time off for.
EL: Right. Okay. Erm. Eight. You are at a – there are only three more by the way. You are at a small dinner party with a host and hostess whom you don't know, and suddenly in the middle of dinner find yourself desperately wanting to spend a penny. Do you – A. Ask where the lavatory is? B. Say you have something stuck in a tooth, and it's aching, and retreat to the bathroom? C. Hold it, and wait until after the meal?
EE: A.
EL: Yeah. Nine. Your guests compliment you on your excellent dessert which actually came out of a packet. Do you – A. Thank them, telling them it is your speciality? B. Smile graciously, blush, and feel embarrassed about it? C. Tell them it came out of a packet.
EE: C.
EL: And er. Last one – Your neighbour's dog digs up your best rose tree. Do you – A. –
EE: Shoot the dog?
EL: Coming up, yeah. Storm round to the neighbour demanding that the dog be put down? B. Put the tree back and say nothing? C. Thump the dog, glare at it each time it looks at you, but say nothing to the neighbours?
EE: Oh gosh I don't think I'd do any of those. Erm. Well, I wouldn't thump the dog.
EL: Mm.
EE: I wouldn't say nothing.
EL: Would you ask –
EE: And I wouldn't demand for the dog to be put down. That's – that's er –
EL: Right. So.
EE: I think anybody who thumps the dog has to be pretty stupid. Erm.
EL: You wouldn't put the tree back and say nothing?
EE: I think that's too silly a question to be able to answer it, to be honest.
EL: Okay. Right.

EL: Erm. Which is – Do you want to hear what it is?
EE: Go on. Tell me the worst.
EL: Basically you are a confident person. But sometimes you have a guilty conscience, and probably blush too. Often you fail where you could succeed, because your nerve lets you down at the last minute.
EE: I'd agree with that except that I don't blush.
EL: You don't blush. Right.

---

63 *

RS: A lot of people say that your personality depends quite a lot on your position in the family. Erm. And this begins with middle child.
BB: Mm. Yes.
RS: Where do you – Where did you come in your family?
BB: I was the youngest. So I was always being accused of being the spoilt member of the family, you see. My brother would say, oh your mother spoils you and I have to suffer as a result. And my sister used to say er, the same thing about my father. It's not true of course. I think the youngest member can actually have a pretty thin time of it. Erm, if er, they haven't got erm, a particularly strong character. Erm. Whether I suffered or not I don't know, erm. Maybe I won't admit it. Erm, or whether I got benefit from it, perhaps I won't admit that either. But er, I know looking at my children the youngest one there has er – he's had to put up with a lot from the elder ones er. And he has certainly come out of it as possibly the er – the strongest character in the family.
RS: It's funny that because er, I was the youngest of three girls originally. In fact I was treated like the youngest child –
BB: Mm. Yeah.
RS: for a long time. And then I had a brother and two

121T

other sisters.
BB: Yeah.
RS: And so I became the middle child, which was quite strange.
BB: Yes. Yes.
RS: Erm. Because I – Well in a sense it was quite good because then I could tell my brother and my two younger sisters that they'd been spoilt rather than it was just being me.
BB: You've seen both worlds then there, yeah.
RS: Yeah. So er –
BB: Well, what conclusion did you draw from that?
RS: I think er – I definitely think that being a youngest child affects you a lot because you're usually looked after by the oldest.
BB: Mm. Yeah.
RS: Erm. And I think er – You know, you're usually not so responsible. It takes you a lot longer –
BB: Mm.
RS: to be more responsible. Erm, because you're allowed to get away with a lot of things. And perhaps as your parents perhaps get a bit richer you receive more goodies.
BB: Mm. Yeah, yeah. I suppose that's possible. Yes. Yeah.
RS: If that's what happens.
BB: Yeah. If that's what happens. Indeed.
RS: Erm. And I think er, a middle child in a – in a way has erm – It's – You experience both ends.
BB: Mm.
RS: Of being an older sibling, and a younger sibling.
BB: Yeah, you get it from each side. I suppose that's true. Yeah.
RS: So you have more – er – I think possibly it balances out your character more. I wouldn't say that for certain.
BB: Mm. Mm. I think outside influences perhaps have er, more effect than being in a particular position in a family. I mean I grew up during the war. And er, as a result, there were lots of things I never got which my elder brother and sister of course had had.
RS: Mm.
BB: And er, I used to feel a bit er – a bit narked about that at times but er, when I got a bit older I understood it of course.

Listen, and write down all the times you hear.

[STATION]
ANNOUNCER: The train now standing at platform 13 is the 21.15 to Manchester.

[FERRY TERMINAL]
M: Oh dear. When's the next ferry? Let's see. It says 17.00 hours here.
F: Oh, but that's Saturdays only.
M: Oh, right. Erm, so ... 18.35, that's just after half six.
F: That's two and a half hours to wait.

[STATION]
ANNOUNCER: The train from Leeds due in at 14.40 is running approximately 15 minutes late. We apologise.

[AIRPORT]
ANNOUNCER: British Airways regret to announce the late departure of flight BA21 to Singapore. This will now be leaving at 01.45 hours from gate number 47.

[RADIO]
ANNOUNCER: BBC World Service. It's nineteen hundred hours Greenwich Mean Time. Here is the news.

UNIT 7

68c *

EL: We're on to the next one now.
CB: What differences are there if any between the way

women and men drive? I think this is the old-fashioned argument of women drivers.
EL: Yes. That's right, yeah.
CB: I think women may be a bit more cautious than men.
EL: Mm. I think you're probably right.
CB: I think men tend to like to drive faster. But then a lot of women do as well.
EL: Yes. Yes. Erm, I think you're right. I think the main thing is, er, caution.
CB: I think that's why women drivers have been, erm, had up in the past for being, erm, made to be bad drivers, because they're more cautious than men and possibly taking more time.
EL: Yeah. Yeah. I think the thing is, though, that sometimes being cautious and taking time, it sounds like it's a good thing, but sometimes it's actually not such a good thing, –
CB: Yes.
EL: when there's an awful lot happening in the middle of a road.
CB: Yes, that's right.
EL: Erm. You know, you need, sort of snappy judgement, really, And er, I think sometimes women get erm – when they are in an awkward situation they get very panicky. And there are lots of men, you know, with erm, bulging biceps, er, you know, weighing down on them, out of articulated lorries or something, and they get into a bit of a panic. Erm. And then, you know, once you get nervous, you don't do anything right, really.

69c *

CB: Shall we talk about the driving test?
EL: Erm, yes.
CB: Did you pass first time?
EL: Er, no. Second time.
CB: I passed first time.
EL: You passed first time. Well, er, going – you can relate that back to the last er, question a bit.
CB: Caution.
EL: No, not that. It was just – when I took my test, which was quite a long time ago, erm, there was this theory that women always passed first time, and men never passed first time. Erm.
CB: I think I was lucky to pass first time. It was a very good day, and it was a sunny day and, the driving conditions were right, and erm, I felt very happy about it all. I think it was just a good day for me.
EL: Right. Well er – You know the three-point turn?
CB: Yeah.
EL: Erm, I think my main mistake first time round was I went the first bit fowards – up the pavement, and then I put it into reverse. And I came back exactly the same way. Instead of turning to come back this way, so in other words it had –
CB: Doing a triangle. Yeah.
EL: And then I had to start all over again, and then it was a five-point turn instead of a three-point turn. And I don't think that went down very well. And then I – in the bit where you have to reverse, I backed onto the pavement.
CB: Yes.
EL: Erm, so, I think, when we were up on the pavement I knew I'd failed.

72b *

CB: Handcuffed drunk takes police car for a ride.
EL: Mm. I think you have to read those cuttings and then try and make sense of it. Erm. Well. I think the first one is the one with the erm, the headline. Do you see? Summit Colorado.
CB: Yes.
EL: That's obviously the beginning of the article. So if we read that we'll get the – Mm. The second one looks like Claude Padilla at the top. This is introducing the drunk the way journalists do, you know, they tell you

what happened and then – this is the name of the chap.
CB: Who he was.
EL: Who he was. Erm. What about the next one? Could it be that one?
CB: Is it the bottom one? While the policeman was moving the police car off the road he drove off the wrong way down a motorway.
EL: Yeah. Right. And then, this. Because once he's going they've got to stop him. So they set up a device which punctured his tyres. But he still went on, before ending his adventure in a ditch. Handcuffs intact. Do you think that's it? But then why is this erm – Oh hang on. Sorry, no, that one must come before, mustn't it? Because you get this new smaller headline.
CB: Yes.
EL: And you get that. And then that's the end of it. Ends his adventure in a ditch. So erm –
CB: So how did he manage to drive the car?
EL: Oh yes. Er. Well. Erm. He's got his wrists behind his back. So he can't use his – Well you can – Ah.
CB: Well it's just steering isn't it? I suppose maybe he used his chin to –
EL: Could have used his chin. Yes.
CB: to steer on the, erm, on the wheel.
EL: They must have left the car engine on. Because he couldn't have turned it on. And then just used his feet.
CB: Possibly he was going in a straight line.
EL: Yes. He ended up in a ditch. Oh no, that was when they punctured his tyres, wasn't it? Well, it could only happen in America.
CB: They thought he used his teeth.
EL: All American cars are automatic, yeah, so he wouldn't need that.
CB: Ah, yes.

72c *

CB: Well it's just steering isn't it? I suppose maybe he used his chin to –
EL: Could have used his chin. Yes.
CB: to steer on the, erm, on the wheel.
EL: They must have left the car engine on. Because he couldn't have·turned it on. And then just used his feet.
EL: Yes. He ended up in a ditch.

72d

M1: Deputy Sheriff James Doughty said: "I have no idea how he did it. He either was sitting sideways, or drove with his knees. His teeth are another possibility."

76c *

EL: It's like – I – He's trying to say that I'm – You know if I'm trying to get an idea across to you, quite a good way of putting that business – process is to see it in terms of, I'm sending an article across to you, packed in a – in a case. I mean. You know –
EE: I see.
EL: And he – he says that a lot of the way we use language actually erm, seems to show that, you know, he might have a point. And he uses phrases like it's hard to get that idea across to him. You see.
EE: Yes.
EL: Or, erm, it's difficult to put my ideas into words. Like you put something in –
EE: Yes. Yes.
EL: You know. Or, erm, your words seem hollow. You know. All phrases like that which are –
EE: Yes.
EL: You are talking in terms of space and articles and objects and this sort of thing. So er, do you begin to see what he's trying to get at?
EE: Yes, I do.
EL: It's just er – It's a way of erm, er – And he calls these things conduit metaphors.
EE: Mhm.

EL: For what it's worth. Er, because it's like a passage. You're just sending – I'm sending this information in a container to you –
EE: Yes.
EL: and you're sending it back to me in another container. You know, so it's like a – there's a passage between us. Well that's about the best I –
EE: We're all postmen. Postpeople.
EL: We're all po- – we're all postpeople. Yeah.

UNIT 8

78d *

EL: Which is that the winter months are long, basically. Therefore, one needs something.
EE: Oh. Or isn't it that the winter months are cold?
EL: Ye – Long and cold. Yes. Okay. Cold. Yeah. Erm. The problem then is that okay yes you wear a leather jacket. But, it hasn't got anything padding. Therefore it's not really very effective. Er, although it's a very good material. It's very tough material. And so the solution is, er, to fill – to pad it out with sheepskin and there you've killed two birds with one stone, sort of thing. Do you want to take the next one? . . .
EE: . . . Yes, the problem is that the – a wallet can be bulky.
EL: Yeah.
EE: The situation is that you don't always want to wear a jacket in which to put a wallet.
EL: Mm. Mm.
EE: So the solution is to have a slimline wallet.
EL: Right. Absolutely.

80a

Sounds of: rain; water running into reservoir; happy seagulls; owl; van revving up; distressed seagull cry broadcast from loudspeaker; seagulls flying away into the distance.
M2: Great! It really works!

80b *

EL: Erm. If we look at the first sentence – of each one. And see whether all – these four components are mentioned. The background situation, the problem, the proposed solution, an evaluation of the proposed solution.
EE: Yes. Shall I – Shall I give you the, erm, summary of my article about – about seagulls, and pollution, so that we can do them all together?
EL: Oh. Right. Sure. Yeah. Mm.
EE: Erm. The article is about seagull pollution in reservoirs. The background to it is that airports have been very successful in using tape recordings of a distressed seagull.
EL: Yeah.
EE: To keep the area clear of – clear of seagulls.
EL: Right.
EE: Er, which can be a problem for airports.
EL: Mm.
EE: The problem is about pollution in reservoirs in Scotland, and the proposed solution is that they use tapes of distressed seagulls –
EL: Yes.
EE: as a cheap way to cut down seagulls in the area and polluting the reservoirs rather than having to use filtering methods.
EL: Right.
EE: For cleansing the water before it can be used.
EL: Yes. I see.

80c *

EE: So –
EL: Well, I think what we've got to decide is whether these four texts present satisfactorily –
EE: Yes.
EL: erm, the er – you know, the information that one

123T

needs to know.

EE: Yes.

EL: And erm, they say that's – I think that's why they say look at the first sentences, and the headline and see if you think that that gets across the bulk of what they're trying to get across.

EE: Yes.

EL: What do you think about your seagulls? Do you think erm –

EE: Erm. Yes. I would say so. The first – The headline is actually –

EL: Mm.

EE: rather useless information. How a reservoir is gulling the gulls.

EL: Yeah. It's a bit of a crack, isn't it?

EE: It doesn't – It doesn't say very much –

EL: Mm.

EE: except that it does draw your interest to the article. The first sentence is: tape recorded squawks of a seagull in distress have enabled water authorities in Strathclyde to cleanse two reservoirs at Milngavie nor – near Glasgow by frightening away an estimated five thousand gulls –

EL: Yeah.

EE: which were polluting the water. It's actually a very long bulky sentence. But it does actually contain –

EL: Yes. But it does tell you most of –

EE: the essence.

EL: Right. Right.

EE: Of the whole article.

EL: Mm.

EE: So I would say –

EL: Mm.

EE: Yes.

EL: Mm.

EE: That does.

F2: So during the winter months, a van equipped with a loudspeaker and tape bearing the agonised squawks of a captured seagull held upside down slowly toured the reservoirs for two hours before dusk – a period when gulls fly in to roost.

__83c__ *

EL: This is airbags and motorcycles. And erm, motorbikes, okay, so a lot of people have accidents on motorbikes, and how do you stop them? The problem is that they – often they fly over the handlebars. How do you stop them killing themselves? Or prevent them killing themselves so easily? You, er – You invent this airbag, which goes off immediately that the – the crash happens, and it inflates, and somehow that sort of, erm –

EE: It stops the person from going over the handlebars. Is that right?

EL: Yes. Yeah. That seems to be what happens. To prevent serious injury.

EE: How would it inflate — quickly enough?

EL: Erm. Well – I don't know. I mean that must be the way it's made. I'm not very good at the scientific side of it. Erm –

EE: My –

EL: It slows down the speed at which he's shot clear of the bike. That's what it says. It can't prevent him being completely thrown forward, but it has a sort of breaking effect, apparently. Erm. So. We seem to have done that . . .

EE: . . . Yes.

EL: The third one is a bit obscure, isn't it? It's hard to know quite how it works. The motorbikes, I mean. Mm.

EE: Yes. Erm. It doesn't seem very – as if there's enough information.

EL: Right.

__90b__ *

BB: Okay.

RS: Right.

BB: See you later alligator. Who do you think this man is? Well, he's John Cheetham, isn't he? Erm. I've never seen him before. Have you?

RS: No, I've heard of him.

BB: You've heard of – ah.

RS: Erm, but I can't think from where.

BB: No.

RS: Some – Some stor- – Some big story, I'm sure.

BB: Mm. No, it means nothing to me at all. Erm. Does he run a – an aquarium of some sort, or a zoo perhaps do you think?

RS: I would imagine.

BB: Yeah. It seems likely, doesn't it?

RS: Or perhaps – I don't know, something about the picture that makes me think that he's actually, erm, somebody who works in a zoo rather than owning it because . . . something of – his relationship with the reptile in question.

BB: Mm. Yes, yes.

RS: Looks very sort of much like he looks after it.

BB: A keeper then. I think that's the term isn't it, they use? Er.

RS: Yeah. I imagine he's quite – I imagine he's got a way with animals.

BB: Mm. Yes obviously.

RS: Probably from the time he was a little boy.

BB: Mhm. You feel he collected frogs and er –

RS: Yeah, I'm sure.

BB: – that sort of business.

RS: Or perhaps if he was brought up in erm, in a different country.

BB: Mhm.

RS: Erm. He probably spent a lot of time, er, in places with lots of wildlife. And he –

BB: Yes. That seems a possibility. And he's sort of carried this interest over into his career.

RS: Maybe his erm, father or mother was a biologist or . . . something else to do with –

BB: Mm. That's possible I suppose, yes. Or maybe he's just a reptile freak or something. They do exist.

RS: Mm. He might – He possib- –

BB: Or a bus driver or something who keeps a – an alligator in the living room. Er.

RS: There might – That – I mean there could be another side of the story. It could be all a big erm, ruse. And in fact he likes making erm . . . rep- – erm alligator purses or boots or handbags. I mean I hope not actually.

BB: No. Quite. I'd never – I'd never have thought of that one, no. He obviously lives in Kent, doesn't he, so that er – according to the caption there.

RS: Yes, there is a zoo down there.

BB: Is there? Ah. I see.

RS: Erm. So it could – may not be the same one.

BB: Mm. I would reckon he's some sort of keeper then in a zoo, or, er, reptile house or whatever, and that erm as you say he has a special affinity with animals so that he's able to er – well these reptiles anyway – so that he's able to er – to get close to them like that.

RS: He may possibly be erm – just be a researcher who – who's really struck up a really good relationship with one of his erm, subjects.

BB: Mm. Yes. Yes. Yes, well that's certainly a possibility. He's welcome to it mind.

RS: Yes.

BB: I don't think I'd fancy getting that close to a – No. Erm.

RS: Could possibly be –

BB: Ah, now it says 'an affectionate farewell', doesn't it so – does that mean he's leaving or the alligator's leaving? Er, do you think he breeds them?

RS: Could do.

BB: Mm. And that er he then has to say goodbye. Or

possibly he himself is moving. Er. Mm.

RS: Yes I'd imagine the alligator's probably going to erm, another place. Perhaps it's too large for where it is now.

BB: Mm. That might imply that he keeps it in a private residence then. Do you think?

RS: Ooh. Now. That's – That could be something that – Looks pretty large to be in somebody's house actually. It doesn't look like a small one.

BB: It does, yeah. From the background it looks very big.

RS: It's not exactly terrapin size.

BB: Well you do read about people who keep snakes and reptiles of one kind or another in the living room, but er, that does look a little bit big. Yeah. Er. So. Well. Any other ideas on that one? Shall we turn over and see . . . .

91b *

BB: Ah. One of the prize specimens in his collection of giant reptiles on show at Beaver Water World. John Cheetham. At his home town of Oldham. Good Lord.

RS: He actually bought it in – his first alligator in a pet-shop.

BB: Mm. Mm. Ah, was the first step to becoming the only private collector of giant reptiles in Britain.

RS: It's amazing, and he was born in erm – he was in – living in Oldham in Lancashire of all places. Seems hardly the place for er, a future – erm.

BB: Well there is quite a big zoo though, isn't there, in Belle Vue. Or there was. I don't know if it's still there.

RS: Oh I don't know. I didn't know that actually.

BB: No. Obviously you can see them from outside if er – You can see the alligators from the bus. That's interesting. Mm. I didn't know that at all.

RS: I must say he's had a really amazing life. He's been in erm – in Live and Let Die.

BB: Oh yes. Mm.

RS: James Bond film.

BB: Clash of the Titans and so on.

RS: Top of the Pops.

BB: Yeah. Marvellous really.

RS: In fact he's had quite – It's interesting because he's had a completely different erm – very different life to what I would've thought he'd had.

BB: You don't – No connection really with –

RS: Far from the sort of erm, spaced-out biologist or – or erm, zoo keeper. He seems to be into all sorts of things.

BB: Well in this last column here he says he's a teacher at the school for the blind.

RS: Mm.

BB: Yeah. Yes. Fascinating business really. He lets blind children and anyone else handle the pythons eh? Mm? Well, that baffles me I must admit. Mm.

94b *

SJ: Erm. Do they have crocodiles in Egypt?

EL: I'm not sure they do.

SJ: I think they might do actually.

EL: Mm.

SJ: No, I'm not sure. This is where I get muddled between alligators and crocodiles.

EL: Mm.

SJ: Erm. It's possibly true.

EL: So, you're saying yes?

SJ: I'll have a don't know.

EL: Don't know. I don't think you're allowed to actually.

SJ: We're not allowed. Well I'll say – I'll say, mm yes. Up to a thousand people every year. Well then if it kills one people – one person every year, that counts as up to a thousand, doesn' it?

CB: Well.

SJ: I'm going to say yes. What are you going to say?

EL: Erm. Well I'll go for the fact that there aren't crocodiles in Egypt, so I'll say no.

SJ: Ah, right. You could probably be right. D.

EL: D. Er.

SJ: Crocodiles will eat refuse.

EL: No, I don't think so.

SJ: Erm. I don't know. It depends what you mean by refuse. Erm. As well as living creatures. Erm. It depends on how you define refuse. I'll say no actually.

EL: No.

SJ: I should think they just like living things.

EL: Right. Erm.

SJ: E.

EL: Sewers – Living in the sewers.

SJ: Oh yes, definitely.

EL: Right. Yes, I – I'll agree with you there.

SJ: Because people had them as pets didn't they and then they flushed them down the loo. Have you not heard that story?

EL: No, I haven't. No. Do you actually know that?

SJ: Well, there was a great craze. Well, I'm not sure. I mean – I saw it – I must have read it in a newspaper and I don't believe everything I read in newspapers.

EL: Mm.

SJ: But erm, I seem to remember reading that people had kept them as pets – I don't know about in South America but in New York.

EL: Mm.

SJ: And then they'd gone off them because the fashion had died and so they flushed them down the loos, and that's how they live down there.

EL: Right.

SJ: So that's true, I should say.

EL: Okay. Er, what about this G one.

SJ: Gosh, there's a lot of these.

EL: Yes, have you got – two more I think.

SJ: Crocodiles can grow up to eleven metres. I'm hopeless on metres and I have to know what something is in feet to understand it at all.

EL: Well a metre is more or less a yard.

SJ: Right, so that's –

EL: So it's very long indeed.

SJ: eleven yards. That is rather long isn't it?

EL: Mm.

SJ: Well I hope they don't grow that long.

EL: So – I'm not sure.

SJ: Began up to you see. Up to.

EL: Yes, but I mean that means –

SJ: Oh that means that's the longest one ever been recorded.

EL: Yeah. Yeah. Could be, yes. I'm not sure. I think that's too long myself, so I think I'd say no to that.

SJ: Mm. I think I'd say no as well.

EL: And G I think, er, is possible because they always look so old.

SJ: Yes, they do look old. I'll accept that.

EL: And H?

SJ: Sorry?

EL: What about H?

SJ: That's what I mean. I'm saying I accept that.

EL: Ah. The hunted one?

SJ: Oh sorry. H, sorry, I thought you said age. H. So many crocodiles have been hunted. Erm. Probably true.

EL: Sixteen species – Yes. I agree with you there. Yeah.

SJ: That sounds very true.

EL: Right. Now we've got to turn over and read –

SJ: Check by reading the text overleaf.

EL: the real story.

95c *

SJ: Looks like they're all true, doesn't it?

EL: Ah yeah. The refuse er –

SJ: I haven't got that far. Where's that?

EL: Hm.

SJ: We stop at believing him to be there – do we? if you see what I mean.

EL: Erm, no.

SJ: Father of the devil business.

EL: No. That.
SJ: Is that ...
EL: This is the continuation.
SJ: Mm. Oh I see. Believing him to be the father of the devil. Sorry. Oh, it's nine point nine metres long as opposed to eleven.
EL: Mm. Pretty near.
SJ: Yes it is. Oh they only live fifty years.
EL: Well, as you say, a lot of them are true.
SJ: Certainly the age one isn't. – Not.
EL: Erm. The age one. No, that's right.
SJ: Mm.
EL: Erm, and there are crocodiles in the Nile.
SJ: I did actually read erm, – That's right, erm, I read this very funny letter in the Times, actually, recently, which was erm, about a woman being eaten by a crocodile in Australia and erm, well it was replying to a write-up about it – an article – a short article about a woman being eaten, in which the woman was described as attractive. It said a crocodile ate an attractive woman, and erm, this was a tragedy, and erm the letter said, would it have been any less of a tragedy had she not been attractive? Had she been plain, erm, you know, would it have been less tragic? And erm –
EL: Right.

---

97 *

EL: Now we've got to go on to the debate.
SJ: The debate.
EL: Which is erm –
SJ: Should we try to preserve all species of crocodile? Oh dear. Even though they're dangerous to man. Oh I see.
EL: Right.
SJ: Mm. Mm.
EL: Well. I don't know. I mean, it seems – I tend to think they must be there for a reason.
SJ: Yes.
EL: Presumably as well as eating er, humans –
SJ: Mm.
EL: they probably eat other things which –
SJ: They're part of a natural chain.
EL: Exactly. Yes.
SJ: Mm.
EL: So er – And they do have a certain er – ... I mean as long as you're not in their jaws, erm –
SJ: Mm.
EL: There's a certain excitement about them, I suppose. You know, which – you know – is probably worth having. So, I would say, erm, we should try to preserve them.
SJ: Even though they're dangerous.
EL: Yeah. Mm.
SJ: So what would – what should one do about the fact that erm, crocodiles kill all these people in Egypt and so on along the banks of the Nile where people have to go in their natural course of –
EL: Mm.
SJ: tilling the soil and that sort of thing? Do you know what I mean?
EL: Yes.
SJ: Do you think they should be kept in special places – special reserves, where they won't attack people? I mean should they be sort of zooed off into nature reserves?
EL: Well, I don't think so.
SJ: Or allowed to just wander about?
EL: I think, you know, you probably find this is some statistic which is, you know, perfectly true, but, you know, if you went out there and lived there and were a person living on the banks of the river Nile, you would take things like this in their stride – in your stride.
SJ: You wouldn't if –
EL: No, well I mean, you would, I mean –
SJ: if you just –
EL: It's rather like –
SJ: if your brother or sister had just been chewed up.

EL: Well I know. Yes. But I think – I think they probably have a different approach to this sort of, what one might call natural disaster.
SJ: To life and death?
EL: Yes. Than what we have. And erm, you know, perhaps it's just rather interfering to go and say they should do this and they should do that, but –
SJ: I think perhaps one should give them a vote on it. See if they want the crocodiles – kept or –
EL: Well I'm sure they can give themselves a vote on it, without us interfering.
EL: Erm. Well what's our summary. Ah. Well I think that's the end of that one then.

UNIT 10

100c *

INT: You had some troubles on the way to Nepal, didn't you?
BS: We certainly did. And you can imagine, a first major, er, Far Eastern tour, and we were a little bit nervous to say the least about the whole thing. We packed all our gear – we had two of everything, two accordions, two guitars, two this, two that – in a huge flight case, which weighed about a hundred and seventy odd kilos it was. An enormous flight case. And er, we saw it disappear at Heathrow Airport, and we had to change flights at Delhi, you see, to go on to Nepal. And er, when we got off the plane, no flight case. Disappeared. Couldn't find it anywhere.
INT: Completely.
BS: Yes. Absolutely. And er, we made enquiries here and there. And er nobody – No, no. No flight case. Nothing like that at all. Nothing that big. No. Can't be that big, can it? And eventually we gave up. And decided to go on to Nepal and get the British Council to er, sort the problem out.
INT: What were you going to do for instruments?
BS: Well. We didn't know. We were absolutely lost and er, there was no point in looking any further in Delhi airport, and we didn't know whether it was in London. Because you never see anything get on an airliner. London airport is so vast. Er. We didn't know – The plane had stopped also at Rome. And it stopped at Cairo, and Delhi. It was going on to Bangkok, and then to – off to Japan, to Tokyo, you see. So we didn't know where this flight case was.
INT: Any one of six or seven capitals.
BS: That's right. Yep. So, eventually we got to Katmandu, and er, informed the people there what had happened. And there was telexes flying left right and centre all round the world. And nobody could find this flight case, until about a day and a half later somebody came across – stumbled over it in a hanger in Tokyo Airport.
INT: Gone all the way to Tokyo.
BS: Yes, that's right.

100d *

BS: Yes, that's right. So er, they quickly put it on a Thai Airlines flight and got it back to Nepal half way through the first concert we were doing. Meanwhile – Meanwhile, we were panicking all over the place. We did actually manage to find an accordion, which we had to mend. We had to take it apart, and put it all back together and mend it you see. Er, somebody lent Mac a guitar, and er, I borrowed one or two bits of things to bash. You know, a drum and what-have-you. And erm, we had the er, people at the Embassy, the British Embassy in Katmandu, running round making us costumes for our Mummers' Play, which we do, with all the swords and helmets and shields and things. And we raided the er, costumes department of the local little er – people that get together and do little plays and things like that.
INT: Drama society. Yes.
BS: Yes. And er – For a few more bits and pieces.

And we went on stage armed with this. Now er, after that experience, we thought well look, if we can handle this, we can handle anything.
INT: You've arrived. That's it.
BS: And from there on, you know, everything went comparatively smoothly.

102a *

BB: Er. Yes. Mm. Forty, fourteen.
EL: Mm.
BB: Mm. Well, presumably the er – the person with the new – who came with the new cooker went to the er – the wrong address.
EL: The wrong address. Yes. That's – looks like what happened. Okay. Shall we go on?

BB: Yes. So they arrive at the wrong house and put in the – in the cooker then presumably.
EL: Yes.
BB: Yeah. Erm. Well Mrs Kerr presumably what? comes back and er, wonders what's happened? Erm.
EL: Erm. I don't quite understand the key business. Which – Which one – Oh I see, yep. Yep.
BB: Mm. Yes, its – The neighbour had left the key er and been left with the key hadn't she? So that er –
EL: Yes. That's right. Because of this other thing, the electrical thing, right.
BB: Yeah. So –
EL: Yeah. So she comes back and says, er, erm –
BB: Why have I got a new gas cooker?
EL: Yeah. Exactly. That's it. Right. On we go.
BB: Right. Now . . . .

EL: Ah. I think I can see what's happening in part four now. Looks like they're going to arrive and say oh sure. Erm, I can see the mistake, but because you've already used it, we're not allowed to take it away.
BB: Yes. Yes. I see what you mean. Yeah. If they're going –
EL: Probably a legal thing. Saying as long as you don't use it we'll change it.
BB: Could be. Could be. Erm. Now. Let's see where we are.
EL: It's the other one., The other one complaining that it's already been used. People have small minds don't they?
BB: Mm. Dear oh dear.

105

Listen carefully to these sentences.
1 If Joe hadn't broken the law in the first place, he wouldn't have had to go to court.
2 If he had gone to the court by public transport, he wouldn't have had the bother of parking and feeding the parking meter.
3 If he hadn't had to wait so long, the money he had put in the meter might have been enough.
4 If Joe had crossed the street in the proper place, he wouldn't have been fined for jay-walking.
5 If the policeman had taken less time giving him a ticket, Joe might have got back to the car before the traffic warden.
6 The judge could presumably have heard his case before lunch if Joe hadn't been so long away from the court dealing with his parking problem.
7 Joe would have had enough money to pay the five dollar fine if he hadn't had to pay all the fines on the spot.

106a *

EL: Okay. Who'd like to start? Rachel. Something you hadn't done.
RS: Erm. Something I wish I hadn't done?
EL: Something you wish you hadn't done, yeah.
RS: Yeah. Well, I wish I hadn't given up the violin when I was in my teenage years.

EL: Ah you took it up earlier, did you?
RS: Yes, I was playing it for about er, four years. Erm. Then I had lots of exams. And also the exams in the erm, Royal Schools of Music were quite hard.
EL: Right.
RS: So I gave it up. And then I took it up a few years ago.
EL: So you didn't – you didn't do the grade exams?
RS: Er, only about up to about grade three.
EL: Mm.
RS: So I had a big gap and I could have been playing it all that time.
BB: Ah. Shame.
EL: Still, there's plenty of time.
RS: Yes.
EL: What about you, Liz?
EE: I wish I hadn't given up learning French. I gave in, erm, because I was afraid of the pronunciation, as much as anything, and now I find it very difficult because various family members speak French, and I have a friend who lives in France, and her three-year-old son intimidates me with his French speaking. Erm. So the thought of competing with a three-year-old is quite difficult.
EL: Yeah.
EE: – to go back and try to do that.
BB: Yes indeed. Yes. Mm.
EL: Well maybe you could spend a month out there or something, one day. That's the way to do it isn't it?
EE: Yes. But I – If I go to France or Switzerland or somewhere that they speak French, with family it's very easy to hide behind them and let them do the ordering and do the hard work.
BB: How much did you actually do?
EE: Well I actually went up to O level. Erm. And I dropped out at the mock O level exams.
EL: Mm. Bruce. What about you? Something you wish you hadn't done.
BB: Well there's so many things really. Er. Oh dear. I wish I hadn't given up mathematics. There we are. Shall we put it that way, yeah. Erm. When I reached the sort of A level stage er, erm, I wanted to do maths, and – but at the same time I wanted to go on the arts side, you see. I'm one of these people who wanted to mix things. And in those days it was very much frowned on. You weren't supposed to sort of cross over the lines. And I was talked out of it by the headmaster and er I've always regretted that really because I felt I could well have made something of it.
EL: Oh I see, yeah. It's not just that you can't add?
BB: No, no. No, it's always been something that's, er, interested me, and er, I feel I've missed out somehow on that.
EL: Mathematicians seem to burn out, don't they?
BB: Yes, that's true. I think really, erm – Well they do say once you get past about eighteen actually you're on the way down. I don't know whether that's true or not but er – If it is, it's perhaps it's just as well.
EE: A depressing thought.
EL: Well I suppose in my case er, the thing I – it's not something I wish I hadn't given up, but it's when I was, erm – when I was at school I went straight from school to university. And er – With literally about two months in between. And er, I've always regretted that. Erm. Because I think I'd have got a lot more out of university if I hadn't you know been fed on the erm – the sort of meat-market production line, just straight from school to university. If I'd gone away for nine months like a lot of friends were doing I think I would have had a much better time.
EE: Do you mean you would have had some more life experience?
EL: More life experience. I'd have been less manic about the whole thing. Just let some air in, you know. Instead of which, I – it meant I was – I didn't have a very good time at university, so – That was one thing. Let's move on to . . . .

*

RW: But Erm – on this occasion, er, we went to Tsavo Park.
INT: Was it with your family?
RW: Yes that's right. With my wife and er, baby son. He was just, oh, I think about one at the time. And we er – I forget exactly where we went, but we stayed in a – what's called a banda, which is a type of hut, in er, somewhere called Ngulia, within the park. Erm. And the banda was constructed with a thatched roof, and erm, walls inside it separating, er, a bedroom, a bathroom, and a kitchen. But the – there was no ceiling, it was just a roof above. So the internal walls didn't connect with the ceiling. This is an important detail. I have to make it clear.
Well, the very first night we were there, as I describe we went er, to bed thinking what an exotic place, you know, how exciting, and all the rest of it. And the following morning, my wife woke me up and er, said er, Richard, there's a – there's a leopard on the veranda. So we got up, and er, very quiet, because er, we'd heard that these animals were very, er secretive and very, very, er, easily scared away. So, I got out of bed, and went to look at the animal, which was on the veranda, and sure enough there was a leopard on the veranda. And we watched, and we thought oh what a wonderful animal, how beautiful, how pretty, and all the rest of it. Sun coming up over the plain. A very very beautiful sight. And er, it went round the banda, and we watched it go round. And then it stayed, it didn't run away. And we thought it probably should have run away because we'd made some noise, or maybe it could smell us.
INT: Mm.

 *

INT: Mm.
RW: And it went round, and around. And I began to think that in fact it was walking around, er, perhaps interested in us. And in fact it started looking up into the roof-space between the wall and the roof. So I lit a hurricane lamp. And er, as the animal came by, I switched the hurricane lamp at it, in the mistaken belief that it would be afraid of fire. And it wasn't. And er, eventually – and I don't exaggerate at this point – it started looking in at the window, at my baby son. Actually looking at him. And er, he was young enough to be drinking milk, so the place probably smelt very milky. I don't know, maybe that's what attracted him.
INT: How old was your son at this time?
RW: He was just a bit less than one. Er. So, eventually – One of my plans – I got the impression that it was trying to get in, and we were in danger. One of my plans which I never had to do, but what I was prepared to do was to throw the hurricane lamp on the ground, and try and set light to everything, in an attempt to frighten it off. But I don't know if that would really work. I've never thrown a hurricane lamp on the ground. You see it in films.
INT: Yes.
RW: Anyway, looked around, and couldn't see the animal, then heard a scrabbling noise. And the very worst possible thing that we feared would happen, had happened.

 *

RW: And the very worst possible thing that we feared would happen, had happened. It had got up onto one of the internal walls. I asked my wife to get the key to – so that we could get out of the banda. She couldn't get it. She couldn't find it. I began to get very panicky. But she did find it. Then I unlocked the door but kept it locked because we still weren't – shut – kept it shut, because we still weren't sure where it was – whether it

was inside or outside. And then, there were – we actually saw it over the wall, on the top of the door, where we had to get out. And we – My wife took the baby in her arms, holding the baby, erm, very close, so it didn't appear to be a separate thing.
INT: Mm.
RW: And we walked out of the banda underneath the leopard. The leopard was above us.
INT: Yes.
RW: So we were walking towards it. And we walked very slowly, and we didn't say – make any noise at all. As soon as we were out of the banda, my wife wanted to run, but I told her to walk. So we walked slowly to another banda where some German people were. And so we escaped.

 *

INT: I was going to ask you what turns a normal lepoard into erm, a man-eating leopard?
RW: I'm not an expert, but I understand that erm, if they're getting old, and they can't hunt easily, they'll start – hunt in the wild – they'll prey on, you know, easy meat as it were, like er, goats or whatever, that have been tethered. And er, so they get used to er, being near human habitation and that maybe kill – In fact this tig- – this leopard that erm, we escaped from, it had previously killed a little girl. Which is why it had been rounded up and why it was released.
INT: So, it had already killed –
RW: Yes. Yeah. A little girl.
INT: a human. And it was released into the –
RW: They'd made a mistake. They move these animals around, erm, for game management, you know, if one area hasn't got enough –
INT: Yes.
RW: of a certain species, they'll move it. They also round animals up, erm, if they kill people or they misbehave. And they mixed up one that had misbehaved with a – they thought it was just one that they were moving from one area to another.
INT: Mm.
RW: So this one already had it's er – already had been a man-eater.
INT: So this familiarity with sort of human presence which er –
RW: Yes.
INT: is a very crucial factor.
RW: And also I think that they're getting old, and they can't er, hunt successfully.
INT: Mm.
RW: And in the case of this one it had been kept in Nairobi for some time, in the, er, park there, so it was completely familiar with human beings, which makes them much more dangerous rather than less dangerous.
INT: Yes.

 *

INT: It must have taken a good few days to recover from the experience.
RW: Yes. Yes.
INT: Quite shocked.
RW: I am interested in my own reaction, because I'm a very nervous person. And yet I w- – I reacted erm, really very well, and did the right things, and got it all right. Erm. But I was very, very nervous afterwards. I couldn't believe that we'd escaped.
INT: Mm.
RW: Because of course the leopard would easily bump off three people, and bump off a large number of people in a confined space.
INT: In a way it's quite extraordinary that it didn't pounce on top of you as you were walking underneath. On the way out.
RW: Yes. I think the way we behaved was lucky, because walking towards it, rather than – if we'd've run away, then I think it would have pounced but perhaps

because we walked towards it, and we walk- – we were absolutely silent, we didn't make any noise at all, it couldn't figure out what was going on.
INT: Because it was half light, half dark?
RW: No, it was light.
INT: It was light.
RW: Yeah. It was light. I think it may have been doped from the – for the journey, so maybe the tranquilliser was still wearing off.
INT: Because it had been brought to the park quite recently.
RW: Right. But er – What was I going to say? Later it definitely wasn't doped because the following night it came back and it grabbed hold of a big chap, and dragged him off. And his comrades had to beat the leopard off of him with a lead pipe. Can you believe it? Chasing after the leopard and it let go.

[ON PHONE]
M1: Trying to connect you.

[LOW HUBBUB OF VOICES AT MEETING]
F1: All those in favour, raise your hands.

[LOW VOICES]
F2: Could I possibly ask you a favour?
M2: Well, there's no harm in asking.

[ON PHONE]
M1: The line's engaged, do you wish to hold?

[BUS PULLING OUT]
F2: Hold tight now please!

UNIT 12

---

 *

RS: So, how d'you feel about storms?
EL: Well, they're fine as long as – I don't really like being caught in the middle of them. I mean, as long as you're at home or even in a train. I like storms when you're in a train.
RS: Mhm.
EL: I was just, erm, going up north in a bus to Durham last week and er, it was absolutely pitch black outside and really pelting down. And that was quite fun. But if you're actually out in it, I find that – I don't like getting wet.
RS: Right. Yeah. I actually like storms. I love them except for the lightning, because I know it can be dangerous.
EL: Right.
RS: But erm, I think particularly if you've had a really hot, steaming weather and then the storm breaks, it's just something.
EL: And you like being out in the middle of it?
RS: Lovely, if it's – as I say if it's not much lightning or anything that'd be fine.
EL: Mm.
RS: But it's a bit – I tend to sort of be sensible and stay indoors.
EL: Right.
RS: Erm. Thunder can be quite scary sometimes but I'm not too worried.
EL: Do you get headaches in thunder? Some people get really bad headaches.
RS: No. No.
EL: Before it, or as it's happening.
RS: Mm. No I mean, I think the erm, sort of – the air pressure before storms tends to make me rather tired and a bit bad tempered.
EL: Yeah. Right.
RS: So it is like psychological relief when the storm breaks.
EL: Yes. I think animals get quite erm, uppity too.
RS: Oh yes. Cats always – Well my cat certainly

shoots under the – under the bed.
EL: Right.

---

 *

EL: Have you ever been in extremes of erm – real extremes of –
RS: Weather. Yeah. Very hot, and very cold.
EL: Where was the hot?
RS: Erm, in Africa.
EL: Oh, you've been to Africa?
RS: Yeah.
EL: Mm.
RS: Erm. Also in erm, Greece.
EL: Right. Yes it can get really – really hot there.
RS: It was. We just had to stay indoors and lie down.
EL: Mm.
RS: Erm.
EL: Mhm.
RS: Probably about a hundred and something.
EL: Yeah. Yeah. I remember once being really cold in erm, Japan it was. It was erm – went ski-ing in the north, and you – it was – you couldn't really erm – you took a ski-lift up just five hundred feet, and the skin just about came off your face –
RS: Urgh!
EL: It was so cold. It was really unpleasant. Same as Siberia I suppose. It's on the same latitude as Siberia.
RS: Mm.

---

 *

EL: Well shall we try and nail the seasons down? Which ones they refer to?
RS: Yes. Er, well there's erm – one's – the next one must be summer, as the days grow longer.
EL: Ah, yeah. I thought that erm – I thought that was autumn.
RS: No, the days grow shorter in autumn.
EL: Oh yes, they do. Sorry I was thinking of the trees turning to soft colours. I was thinking sort of brown and –
RS: That's true, yeah. Could be late summer.
EL: Mm. But you're right, no it goes up to June doesn't it, then it starts getting shorter.
RS: Mm.
EL: It's coming up now.
RS: Yeah.
EL: Yep.
RS: Then it's er, must be winter.
EL: That must be winter, yep. And that last one is erm, spring? . . . the grass blade growing.
RS: It does, doesn't it?
EL: Mm. I quite like that, listen to the grass blade growing.
RS: I think that's probably my favourite one actually because it's got – it's got quite a strong form, you know, it's got a theme through it of sounds and music.
EL: Yes. Yes.

UNIT 13

130b *

INT: How do you go about selecting a programme for a foreign tour?
PS: Well we're lucky in as much as our records and cassettes usually go to the country beforehand. They try to get them on the radio stations, and get plays on certain songs. And it depends really on the local – probably just the producer really. If he listens to the record and thinks that song will suit his audience, he will play it on the radio. Therefore the public get to hear it and become familiar with it. When we get out there they – we get a list of songs that were found to be popular from our records and cassettes, and build a programme around that, you know. But we still have plenty of choice really.
BS: We also try to, er, get songs that have stories

which we think, you know, the people in a particular country will understand the story of the song, and perhaps sometimes the story may, er, relate to some of the songs and customs they have in their own country. Songs about erm agriculture er – about er, harvesting, sowing the seeds, and those sorts of things. And often too we try to get er, songs with very easy choruses so that they can actually join – pick up the song and join in with us. Or even songs with hand actions that they can join in.

PS: We er – Always when we arrive in a new country, we er, get somebody, erm local staff or someone who knows about the traditions of that country, and we corner them, and we badger them for a couple of hours, er, asking them really what their traditions are, so that we can find things which are very similar. In actual fact it's amazing. It's not a problem at all to find something where you can immediately make contact with the local people. Because we all dance and sing at harvest time. And all dance and sing to make the crops grow – in the country, being simple folk. You know. Everybody does it. And er, it worked out okay.

BS: And also – And the other thing too about erm doing concerts in, erm other countries, is that you don't want to go on the stage and offend the audience that you're you know trying to entertain. So therefore you need to find out some of the sort of – I suppose sort of perhaps religious erm, things of that country. Er. Or maybe some of the sort of taboo areas that you don't – you know you wouldn't want to mention, or sing about. Er. So that you don't actually end up offending the people that you want to please.

INT: Mm. Do you find that audiences in different countries are in fact very different?

BS: Well er, no. Not really. Erm. We've been told many many times that er, the audiences in a lot of countries in – particularly in the Far East, they will appreciate what you're doing, they'll be quiet, but they wo- – and they won't join in. Which is an absolute load of rubbish because you give people the opportunity to join in, and they're in there, and we've never had any problems with that at all, in fact.

PS: No. Even in, you know some countries where we've done shows and there have been, er, people from many nationalities actually in one concert, and they all join in together. You know. And it's er, one of those strange things that I suppose people are just people wherever they are.

BS: I think er one or two of the schools we've been to, the international schools, have been very special in this way. And there's one school, er, in Ethiopia that we've been to a couple times, er, where there's forty-six different nationalities at the school. And er they all muck in together and they all sing together and they're all great mates. And er, a tremendous lesson that for everybody I think.

INT: Mm.

---

 131 *

BS: But I think in setting up the tour we have a few problems with er, trying to get communications from them. And er, Roger's mother is German, so we thought great we can telephone the store direct to Germany, we have someone here that speaks German, they can converse. And as soon as they realised it was a call from England they spent ten minutes running round the store trying to find someone that spoke English. So we had a German this end speaking to an English the other end –

RT: They did say that my mother spoke German very well though, so that's one compliment.

BS: I think that – a lovely bit of organisation that. Frankfurt, which is where we were, is actually twinned with Birmingham. And er, they had an information desk there, to tell people all about Birmingham and what a wonderful place it is. And er – which we thought was funny. Er. And erm, they were really efficient the English people. They – True, the lady who was on the information desk, er, did live in Birmingham. But she was French and she didn't speak German.

---

 137 *

INT: Mm. What about your last trip to Germany? Roger, can you say a bit about that?

RT: Yes that was something different from our usual trips abroad. It was actually playing, erm, for one of the big department stores there, who were having a er – who were promoting British goods actually, that week. Trying to get the Germans to buy good British products you see. And er, we were actually over there singing and playing our traditional songs. And er the German people do like English, Scottish and Irish music very much. And er in fact a couple of weeks before, erm, their number one in their hit parade actually was er The Wild Rover which is a popular English song. They'd altered the words and er, that was their hit tune at the time, so that went down very well.

INT: Mm. Did you have any problems on – on the German tour or did it all go through as planned?

RT: Well. Yes, it went – As I said it was something totally different that we'd never actually done before. And you're much more in contact with people there and then we were playing outside the store actually. And er, you know during songs people would come up and try to speak to you. They like to speak English. And as we don't know very much German that was quite useful really.

BS: I think on that trip we thought there were going to be problems, because when we arrived and no-one really seemed to know what we were supposed to do and then someone said well you have to sing outside the store in this big shopping centre and we thought, don't fancy that very much, you know, because it was – this was in February I think was it?

RT: It was March.

BS: March. In March and it was quite cold. And wet. And then once we – we'd done sort of one or two shows, er, we thought it was great because the – you know the people would gather round us and they would join in and, I remember on one occasion when there was that man who came up and he stayed to watch the whole show that we did and then afterwards he came up and he started talking and he borrowed Mac's guitar and started singing, er, German folk songs to us.

RT: It was great because he entertained us for twenty minutes. It was really nice.

INT: Yes. Yes.

UNIT 14

140b *

[BBC World Service signature tune (Lillibulero)]
Announcer: This is the BBC World Service.

INT: How do you become a foreign correspondent?

BJ: Usually you have to start at the beginning. That's, you have to begin as a journalist of some sort on a local newspaper, a local radio station, maybe on a small magazine – and work your way up. Now there aren't that many organisations which have large numbers of foreign correspondents so you also have to sort of work with that – er, that aim in mind.

Another way of doing it is to work abroad, erm, and work as a freelance. You er – What we call a stringer. That's somebody who, er sells stories, er, and gets paid by the piece, to newspapers and magazines and so on. And hoping to build up a reputation that way, and eventually to be offered, er, a full time job. And that does sometimes work. But I think, to be honest, most people just, er, drift into being, er, journalists and often drift into being foreign correspondents.

INT: What qualifications do you need? For example a degree?

BJ: I don't really know what qualifications as such. I

mean obviously a degree in modern languages or political science or economics would be very useful. But, in itself probably wouldn't be the key. It wouldn't be enough to get you the job. It wouldn't be enough to make an editor decide to send you abroad. Erm. So it's difficult to define the precise qualities. Erm. You're going to need stamina and the ability to assimilate information quickly and accurately and then produce stories which fit the style of the newspaper or radio or television station you work for. Erm. But, there's no list of qualifications that an editor is going to be looking for when he's trying to appoint, er, a new correspondent to a particular place. And so it often becomes a fairly personal – a fairly personal choice I think.

INT: Does a foreign correspondent, when he's actually working, specialise in one aspect of the country? In economics, for example, or politics, or foreign policy?

BJ: No. Not really. I think it's more a question of specialising in the country in which you work. So you have to become an expert on that particular country. Or more usually, er, the countries in the region, since it's er, nowadays very common for foreign correspondents to cover a complete region. Er. So for example you could be based in Cairo and cover the entire Middle East, or in Buenos Aires and cover the whole continent of South America, or in Singapore, and cover all of South East Asia. And within those very large geographical limits, er, you have to try to know, absolutely everything on every possible subject, which of course is impossible. And so, what you come back to is, if you like, the basic skill of journalism, which is you really just have to know how to find somebody who does know, er, about the subject you're trying to report, he does know the subject well, and then you elicit the information from him. And er, I think that that's – er, after a while, when you've worked in a region for, er, some period of time maybe a few years, er, you get to know the techniques, you get to know the tricks of finding out just who can be relied upon to provide you with – not just information as such – but a sort of cultural terms of reference to enable you to understand the country or the countries in which you're working.

141a *

BJ: I don't really know what qualifications as such. I mean obviously a degree in modern languages or political science or economics would be very useful. But, in itself probably wouldn't be the key. It wouldn't be enough to get you the job. It wouldn't be enough to make an editor decide to send you abroad. Erm. So it's difficult to define the precise qualities. Erm. You're going to need stamina and the ability to assimilate information quickly and accurately and then produce stories which fit the style of the newspaper or radio or television station you work for. Erm. But, there's no list of qualifications that an editor is going to be looking for when he's trying to appoint, er, a new correspondent to a particular place. And so it often becomes a fairly personal – a fairly personal choice I think.

143b *

INT: Bob, can you explain to us . . . how you find out what is happening?

BJ: News can be something the authorities want you to know, or something they would rather keep secret. An announcement of a government success, a denial of a failure, or, a secret scandal that nobody really wants you to talk about. If the authorities want to tell the world some good news, they issue statements, communiques, and call press conferences. Or, politicians make speeches. Local newspapers, radio and television help to alert foreign correspondents to what is going on. And by making contact with local officials, journalists can ask for more information or explanations to help them write their stories. Unless the correspondent is an eye-witness, it's rare to

trust any single source. Officials have a policy to defend, and opposition politicians want to attack it. Rumour and gossip can also confuse the situation. So, you have to check information as much as possible, using common sense and experience as final checks to help establish just what's likely to be the truth, or close to it.

143c *

BJ: Just getting the news is only half the job. A correspondent may be well-informed, but his job is to inform other people. The public. So, once the information is available it has to be written in an interesting way which is also easily understood. Particularly for radio, since, while a newspaper reader can turn back and re-read a sentence or two, the radio listener has only one chance. This also means that only a limited number of facts can be contained in a sentence. That there should be an element of repetition. And vital information necessary to understand the latest development should be presented at the start of a report – in case the producer of a news programme decides to shorten an item, by cutting for example the last sentence or two. Finally, the style of presentation much match the subject matter. A cheerful voice might be perfect for a royal wedding. But it would be sadly out of place for a report of a plane crash. And this would also confuse and distract the listener, probably making it difficult to understand just what had happened and to whom.

145

Song: **Lillibulero**

UNIT 15

---

149 *

BB: Okay. Mystery headlines. What could each of these news items be about? Suggest one or two things for each headline. Home Office urged to act on refugees. And erm –

RS: Well, I imagine erm, people – they're told to either stop them coming in to the country or putting out – or asking for visas. Or maybe to actually put them up in a camp.

BB: Yes, it could be either of those. It –

RS: Mm.

BB: Erm. Or people perhaps who are already here and er, you know, then you would need the camps for that wouldn't you? That's true. So it's either people who are here or people who are trying to come. Yeah. Women's guide on violence. Er –

RS: Well, I would imagine –

BB: Mm?

RS: How to protect themselves from violence.

BB: Yes. Do – You think this obviously refers to these recent cases that have been in the papers, doesn't it? Erm.

RS: Could be. Mm.

BB: Mm. Yeah. Cat's feat. Is that South America? Er.

RS: Cat's feet. I haven't got cat's feet.

BB: You haven't got that one? FEAT. Cat's feat.

RS: Cat's feat. I reckon it probably erm, jumped out of a tree or something and landed on all fours.

BB: Mm. Oh actually I think I read this one. It was – It was in one of the big cities in South America.

RS: Oh it's got South America at the end. Yeah.

BB: It jumped out of a tenth-storey window or something, and landed unharmed.

RS: Ah. That's amazing.

BB: It was something like that anyway.

RS: That's incredible . . . That's funny actually because I recently heard of a friend's cat who jumped out of the fourth storey.

BB: Mm. Oh, they're very good at that, yes. Mm. Mm. Yes.

RS: And er, it only erm, slightly cracked its palate. Didn't even hurt its jaw or anything.
BB: Yeah. Yes. It seems to happen quite regularly.
BB: CIA chief critical, New York.
RS: Well he's – Either critical of something, or he's ill. And I'm not sure which.
BB: Yes. It could be either, couldn't it?
RS: Yes, because look, there's – followed by kangaroo target. Er.
BB: Mm. Kangaroo target Sydney, yeah. That'll be the culling will it? Of kangaroos? Isn't that right? That they er – they shoot so many every year –
RS: Oh really?
BB: to er, prevent them er, becoming a menace.
RS: Ah, I hadn't thought of that. I was thinking maybe it was something to do again in the financial world, which I don't – I never read financial news –
BB: Mm.
RS: so I got very little idea of what erm –
BB: Mhm.
RS: have because of the Jaguar slump.
BB: Yeah. So you would read that into what? The erm, the fact that they can't sell Jaguar cars in America?
RS: Probably.
BB: Or possibly the wildlife population has decreased.
RS: I don't think so somehow.
BB: Could be either. Well, there are jaguars in America, aren't there? I think . . . .

 150a *

BB: Erm, let's see if we can find the – Here we are.
RS: Yes. You were right about the culling.
BB: Kangaroos. Ah. That's good, yeah. Mm. Exports of kangaroo products earn Australia more than twelve Australian, er, twelve million Australian dollars eh. Mm. So, one wonders whether it is to protect the farming and grazing or to er, earn their exports.
RS: Got my doubts actually. Definitely got my doubts.
BB: Yes. Erm. There's the cat. Twenty-second floor. British Columbia.
BB: Yeah. Sixteen-week-old kitten. Good Lord. I'm sure I read that as in South America but er – Rio, or somewhere like that.
RS: Yeah.
BB: But certainly it's fairly common. I know years and years ago I was staying with a friend in Paris and they had a beautiful er, grey Persian. They lived on the sixth floor. And it used to sleep on the window-sill.
RS: Mm.
BB: And we noticed at one stage it had disappeared. It had just fallen off in its sleep. So of course, mad panic on, was dashed down to – and then we met it on the way up. Nothing wrong with it at all. No.
RS: – at all. That's incredible. Yeah.
BB: Hadn't bothered it. No.
RS: I think it depends whether they fall onto concrete or earth, as well.
BB: Mm. This could be it, yes.
RS: Concrete's terrible.
BB: That's right. Now, CIA chief critical. That's er, your –
RS: Yeah, he's ill, isn't he?
BB: You were saying he was probably ill there, yeah. Mm. Age 74. Yeah.

RS: And the Jaguar slump. As you said, it's sales.
BB: Yes. Yes. It's always the money that gets reported isn't it?
RS: Yes.

RS: And erm . . . It's about the Vietnamese refugees.
BB: Ah yes. Mm.
RS: In Hong Kong.
BB: In Hong Kong. Yeah. That's right, still in the camps there. Yeah.
RS: Mm.
BB: That's a terrible business that, really. Have you met any of the people who've come here?

RS: Erm, no I haven't actually.
BB: No. We had some in the school I last worked in. Er, how they got sent up to us I don't know but we had two or three families.
RS: Yeah.
BB: Lovely people. They really were, really. Hard-working, pleasant. Erm. And they gave them a council house each, in the worst possible area of town.
RS: They always do that.
BB: Absolute disgrace it was.
RS: Mhm.
BB: But er. That's the way it goes, I suppose. But they were most impressive people, they really were.
RS: Mm.
BB: Terrific. And then they went and did that to them. Anyway, have we finished with that then? I think we've – Oh no, women's guide on violence. That was the other one wasn't it?
RS: Yes.
BB: The free booklet, yes, that's right.
RS: How to – yes – How to reduce the risk of falling victim to violent crime.
BB: Tips on jogging eh? Ah well. Right. Well. We move on.

 150b *

RS: That's funny actually because I recently heard of a friend's cat who jumped out of the fourth storey.
BB: Mm. Oh, they're very good at that, yes. Mm. Mm. Yes.
RS: And er, it only erm, slightly cracked its palate. Didn't even hurt its jaw or anything.
BB: Yeah. Yes. It seems to happen quite regularly.
BB: But certainly it's fairly common. I know years and years ago I was staying with a friend in Paris and they had a beautiful er, grey Persian. They lived on the sixth floor. And it used to sleep on the window-sill.
RS: Mm.
BB: And we noticed at one stage it had disappeared. It had just fallen off in its sleep. So of course, mad panic on, we dashed down to – and then we met it on the way up. Nothing wrong with it at all. No.
RS: – at all. That's incredible. Yeah.
BB: Hadn't bothered it. No.
RS: I think it depends whether they fall onto concrete or earth, as well.
BB: Mm. This could be it, yes.
RS: Concrete's terrible.
BB: That's right. . . . .

---

154 *

BB: Who, what, when, where, why. Write three questions that you would expect to find answered – answered in the rest of the seven to eight line news item.
A strike by Madrid underground workers. Erm . . . Mm . . . Er . . . Why were they striking? Erm. And – I suppose when would – you know, what time of day do you think? Or which day?
RS: Yes, I was going to say that.
BB: Mm.
RS: Time of day.
BB: And I suppose, erm, what was the response of the authority. Now. Kabul blast. A car bomb exploded, erm –
RS: Again, what time of day.
BB: Yes, what time of day.
RS: Was there anybody in the car?
BB: Yeah. Anyone in car. And erm – Mm. Who – claimed responsibility.
RS: Yes, yes.
BB: Who was responsible.
RS: And also who was in the car.
BB: I thought we'd said that.
RS: Oh no. – was anybody, I suppose. You know. Sometimes it's just anybody –
BB: Mm.

RS: sometimes it's a particular person.
BB: Yes. Anyone special, that's right, in the car. Yeah.
RS: Yeah.
BB: Who was responsible.
RS: Yes.
BB: Good. Woman wins million – dollars? Er.
RS: Must be, mustn't it?
BB: Yes. A woman aged sixty has won one million dollars. Erm . . . Where was this?
RS: How. Yes.
BB: And what she's going to do with her money.
BB: What's she going to do with it? Yes. Starvation fears. Three million Somalis face starvation. Er . . .
RS: Mm.
BB: Mm.
RS: It's such a big one, isn't it?
BB: It is, really, yes. Why are they facing starvation?
RS: Mm . . . Is there any chance of any getting aid? – getting aid there?
BB: Yes. Is there any chance of any aid? Is their own government doing anything about it? -
RS: Mm.
BB: or trying to do anything about it?
RS: Mm.
BB: Yeah. Right. So, let's see how we got on with that. Erm . . .

UNIT 16

161b

M1: Jack and Jill went up the hill
to fetch a pail of water.
Jack fell down and broke his crown
and Jill came tumbling after.

BJ: Jack and Jill went up the hill to fetch a pail of water, Jack fell down and broke his crown, and Jill came tumbling after.

161c

ANNOUNCER: A local man was badly injured today in an incident connected with the long running dispute over water supplies. Bob Jobbins reports:
BJ: The row over inadequate water supplies flared up again today with the announcement that a local man, identified only as Jack, received serious head injuries . . .

BJ: . . . received serious head injuries in an accident close to the main well. His female companion is not believed to have been seriously injured, although hospital sources say she has been admitted for medical checks.

Opposition party spokesmen, who have been calling for Government action to bring piped water into the centre of the town, now say they'll push for an official inquiry into the accident, and in particular into reports that Jack did not fall, but was pushed.

161d *

BJ: Different radio programmes require different styles of writing and broadcasting. Some programmes, for example on a pop-music channel, like short snappy reports. Others on more serious channels want more details and perhaps some analysis. So, let's look at a straight-forward official announcement, and then at some different ways of reporting it.

First the communiqué.

Jack and Jill went up the hill to fetch a pail of water, Jack fell down and broke his crown, and Jill came tumbling after.

So on a pop staton, er it might be something like this.

First of all, er, the announcer would cue in the piece, er, with, er, a summary of it, and then the correspondent would follow with his report.
ANNOUNCER: A local man was badly injured today in

an accident connected with the long running dispute over water supplies. Bob Jobbins reports:
BJ: The row over inadequate water supplies flared up again today with the announcement that a local man, identified only as Jack, received serious head injuries in an accident close to the main well. His female companion is not believed to have been seriously injured, although hospital sources say she has been admitted for medical checks.

Opposition party spokesmen, who have been calling for Government action to bring piped water into the centre of the town, now say they'll push for an official inquiry into the accident, and in particular into reports that Jack did not fall, but was pushed.

This brief report would be best understood by a listener who had heard earlier reports on the subject or who'd read about it in a newspaper.

163a *

BJ: In a long current affairs programme following the news, he or she might be asked a number of questions by the programme's presenter to try to explain even further just what is going on.

163b *

PRESENTER: Well Bob, I suppose the first question must be did he fall, or was he pushed?
BJ: Well, the official version definitely says that Jack fell, and implies that his companion Jill also slipped and tumbled down the hill, and I think that is probably just too much of a coincidence. Jill is conscious, but the press are being kept away. And I was able to speak briefly to a police official who says he believes that the couple fell after a scuffle at or near the summit of the hill with local farmers. Possibly members of the Protect Our Water group, known locally as POW.
PRESENTER: What is the basic complaint of the farmers?
BJ: Well they say that until recently they had exclusive use of the well, which most of the year had enough water for their crops and animals, but since the tremendous expansion of the nearby city area, they say there's no longer enough water, even for their minimum needs.

The POW group also accuse the Government of refusing to provide water as a deliberate policy. The farmers and their supporters say the Government wants to drive them off the land, to deprive them of water so they can't continue to farm, so they'll have to sell their land. And then the big property companies, the construction firms, will be able to build more houses and offices, which would solve the current land shortage in the city.
PRESENTER: But the Government only yesterday denied this, the Minister of Agriculture said in Parliament that no further permission would be given for building on farm land, and that the Government was committed to supporting the farmers in their drive to produce more food . . .
BJ: Yes. The Government is publicly commited to protecting farm-land. But the farmers themselves seem unconvinced. Unless the authorities do something to settle this fight over water, the farmers are going to believe those who say the Government is more interested in the future of the city than it is in farming and food production, and all the signs are that the militants in POW and other groups are prepared to fight. And as we've seen, the victims are likely to be the ordinary public who at the moment have no choice but to seek water where they can find it.
PRESENTER: Are there alternative sources of water?
BJ: Well. I think that must be the hope of everyone involved in this crisis. And earlier today I was speaking to an independent expert on water supply, and he made what I think was an interesting point. He said it's very unusual to find a well at the top of a hill. And if there's water up there, near the summit, then there's almost certainly even more water down in the valley.

163c *

BJ: So, using this formula of question and answer, in a slightly more casual style, even more information has been brought out. Perhaps a later programme will try to interview that water expert himself, and see just how sure he is about the possibility of other sources of water.

164

a Well, the official version definitely says that Jack fell . . .

b . . . and implies that his companion Jill also slipped . . .

c . . . and I think that's probably just too much of a coincidence.

d Jill is conscious, but the press are being kept away.

e . . . possibly members of the Protect Our Water group, known locally as POW.

f Until recently they had exclusive use of the well . . .

g . . . but since the tremendous expansion of the nearby city area . . .

h . . . they say there's no longer enough water even for their minimum needs.

i The POW group also accuse the government of refusing to provide water as a deliberate policy.

j They say the government wants to drive them off the land . . .

k . . . which would solve the current land shortage in the city.

166a *

BB: Decide which headline goes with each group of words. Erm, mm.

RS: Well I reckon the erm, first headline goes with the er –

BB: School blaze.

RS: One, two, three, Italian concert, et cetera.

BB: Italian concert. Wait a minute. That's – yes four hundred and forty a thousand dollar violin was the Italian one.

RS: Yeah.

BB: School blaze. Do you think that goes with the Paris one?

RS: Yes.

BB: Or not? Wait a minute.

RS: Oh. Ah. There was investigating fire damage. Oxford night.

BB: Ah yes. That's more like it isn't it? Oxford night. Births fall. Erm.

RS: Mm.

BB: Do you think that's the Italy one? Ten per cent? No?

RS: Oh.

BB: Do you think?

RS: Now that – Now that is er – That's pretty erm –

BB: Yes. I mean that's – Yeah. Seems a possible, doesn't it? Eight drowned. That'll be the Zambia river one.

RS: The Kafue river, yeah.

BB: Erm.

RS: Fire kills eight.

BB: Russian ship.

RS: Fire kills eight. It's another fire. Now that could either be erm – That – That must be the Oxford one, actually. Fire kills eight.

BB: Mm.

RS: And the school blaze must go with the Paris one.

BB: With the Paris one, yeah.

RS: I don't know, actually. They're both – They're both about fires, aren't they? Erm. The Russian ship. Yeah that must be the erm –

BB: Italian con . . . .

166b *

BB: Now. Erm. Try to reconstruct a possible version of the sentence. Mm. Erm . . . School blaze.

RS: Can you add words? Could add words.

BB: I suppose so.

RS: I suppose so, yeah.

BB: Yes. You can't really make a sentence up otherwise can you? Do you think?

RS: I would imagine the first one as something like erm, er Several people died and hundreds were injured as fires swept through . . . a hospital? early this morning in Paris?

BB: What happened to the school?

RS: Ah yes. That's right.

BB: Well how about –

RS: Ah. Yes of course, there could be a school and the children were taken to hospital.

RS: They were taken to hospital, yes.

RS: Yeah. But then –

BB: And so on.

RS: There'd be one sentence.

BB: Several children died and many were injured when fire swept through a school in Paris, erm, early, er, yesterday morning. The survivors were rushed to hospital. How about that?

RS: Yeah.

BB: Mm?

RS: It is two sentences but, doesn't really matter, as long as you get the message across.

BB: That's true, it is. It is a bit – it's a bit long-winded, isn't it? Mm. Let's try an easy one. Fire kills eight.

RS: Ah I would imagine for the erm –

BB: We decided that was the Oxford one, didn't we? Erm . . .

RS: Christies, erm – Ah. Yes. I see. I suddenly remembered Christies was an auctioneers.

BB: Oh very good. Right. Erm. So. Now the next one. Erm . . . How about the Italian concert one?

RS: Yes, I was looking at that before. I didn't really make sense of it actually. Erm . . . I think I'll try the Zambia's Kafue river.

BB: Mm.

RS: Erm. On Zambia's Kafue river — which flows by the southern town of Namwala – a hippopotamus sank a canoe – said police?

BB: Yes, fair enough.

RS: Said police – reported police.

BB: Yes, reported. Well, we've had reported once not – Yeah. Said police. Er . . . How about this. Erm, eight children died, and many were injured, as fire swept through a hospital in Paris early yesterday.

RS: Yes.

BB: Mm.

RS: Yes, that's good.

BB: That's three down. Er.

RS: Ah. Yes, the birth rates one.

BB: Mm. Now, the births.

RS: The number of births in Italy. Right.

BB: Oh yes, that's – Mhm.

RS: Fall. Oh yes.

RS: Trying to find another word for report.

BB: Erm. Stated?

RS: Yes. Stated in this study.

BB: Revealed.

RS: Revealed. That's the – That was it. Yes. So I've got erm, the number of – fall in the number of births in Italy, er was estimated at ten per cent in February? Because of radioactive fall-out, erm, due to the Chernobyl disaster, revealed a new study.

BB: Oh yes. Sounds good. Mm. Yes.

RS: Not sure about the erm, tense.

BB: Now what about this? Erm. Police are investigating fire damage in an Oxford school, last night.

RS: Mm.

BB: Okay?

166c *

BB: So we turn over do we? And see er –

RS: Mhm.

BB: Right. Mm. Have you got the violin one?

RS: Yes.
BB: Mm. Well if you read it out we'll see how it er, compares with er – with what you said. Er. Italian concert violinist Luigi Alberto Bianci paid a world record price of four hundred and forty thousand at Christies in London yesterday for the Stradivarius Colossus violin. It was made in seventeen-sixteen, Stradivarius' so-called Golden period, and was sold from the estate of the late American composer Doctor Simon Carfagno.

Police are investigating a fire which caused five hundred thousand pounds' worth of damage at Piers School, Littlemore, Oxford on Saturday night.

One building was destroyed and another badly damaged. Oh, we got that in a simplified version.
RS: Erm. Shall I read the birth fall one? The number of births in Italy fell by an estimated ten per cent last February, probably because of fears generated by radioactive fall-out after the Chernobyl accident, according to a new study. Well that's more or less the same.
BB: Mm. That's more or less what you had, isn't it? Yeah. Er. Eight people died and several were injured when fire swept through an annexe of a psychiatric hospital, south-east of Pari- – Paris early yesterday. Oh well, that's reasonable I suppose.
RS: Erm. Oh yes. Eight people drowned in Zambia's –
BB: Mm.
RS: Kafue river near the southern town of Namwala when a hippopotamus attacked and sank their canoe, police said yesterday.
BB: Yeah. Fair enough. Mm. Not too bad really, I suppose. Okay. Erm, now. Erm . . . .

UNIT 17

 *

BB: Divide these words into two categories, according to meaning.
CB: Explain how you are doing it.
BB: Erm . . . I'll do it on the basis of erm, intelligence I suppose.
RS: Yes.
BB: Bright, brainy, smart, intelligent, sharp, perhaps on one side.
RS: Then dumb, thick, stupid and dim.
BB: On the other. Mm. Yeah. Is there any other way of doing those? Er . . .
CB: I would think it was just how clever you are, whether you are clever or not so clever.
BB: Mhm. Mhm. You can divide them into pairs, can't you? With erm – on a different basis but er – like a light, bright light, dim light but – if you're taking the whole lot I can't see a different er, way of doing it.

 *

BB: True or false, yeah. How many are on average true?

The wife will get smarter if her husband is really smart. Well, that's one for you.
CB: The wife will get smarter if her husband is really smart. Now.
BB: I know what my wife would say about that.
CB: I think I'll er, read them through first.
BB: You're going to – Mm. If the husband is less bright than the wife, she will also get less smart as the years go by.
CB: The not-so-bright husband will get smarter if the wife is smart. During the course of a marriage, both the wife and husband change equally, as far as intelligence goes, and get more like each other.
BB: Your ability to do maths increases or decreases according to how good your spouse's maths is. The happiest time of a marriage is shortly after the wedding. The worst time is when the children have grown up and are leaving home. Well I don't care what the survey says I don't agree with that last one at all. That's – I would think that could be one of the best times.

CB: So. The wife will get smarter if her husband is really smart. True or false?
BB: I'd say true. If the husband – What do you think? You think it rubs off? You see – I suppose this is the idea isn't it?
CB: She'd have to compete, and get better.
BB: and get better that way.
CB: If the husband is less smart than the wife she will also get less smart as the years go by.
BB: I suppose on the – on the basis there that er, there's no sort of competition or –
CB: No motivation to –
BB: or stimulus. Yeah. Erm.
CB: True.
BB: Yeah, I think that's true. Mm.
CB: The not so bright husband will get smarter if the white is – wife is smart.
BB: Mm. It should be true. Probably isn't that one. Mm. Erm. Think. Do I know any? No. Now, go on, we'll say yes. Yeah.
CB: During the course of marriage both the husband and – wife and husband change equally. Whether that's true as far as intelligence goes and get more like each other. I would say that was quite true.
BB: Mm. It seems likely, I would think, yes. Your ability to do maths increases or decreases according to how good your spouse's maths is. I would say that's true.
CB: I would say that's false. The happiest time of a marriage is shortly after the wedding.
BB: No. I don't agree with that.
CB: And another one for you I think.
BB: Mm.
CB: The worst time is when the children have grown up and are leaving home.
BB: No I don't agree with that one either. No.
CB: Shall we read the report? . . . .

176b *

CB: Decide in what order the following paragraphs originally appeared.
BB: Yeah. Well that's the first one there obviously. Erm. I reckon it's the third one on the right that comes next. That, however was until –
CB: So –
BB: he found out –
CB: He found out his beloved was a mere seventeen-year-old.
BB: And then, the top one, trouble.
CB: Set on a career, they banned any prospect of marriage.
BB: And then, erm . . . Where are we?
CB: I think it was but trouble struck on the day.
BB: That's right. The – The fourth one on the right, isn't it? And then –
CB: And then undeterred.
BB: And then undeterred. Then Selina's parents. And finally career. I think that's probably the order.

176c *

CB: So what course of action would you have taken if you had been in the situation of Selina's parents? Being a parent.
BB: Mm. Being a parent, yes. Erm . . . Well I would certainly have contacted the police I think. Erm. It – Does it actually say – No I don't think it does say whether they left a note – or anything does it?
CB: They – No.
BB: No. So, on the basis that they didn't leave a note I would certainly contact the police if er, my daughter disappeared, to see what had happened. And one would presume you could do that on an international basis. Er, I'm not so sure about this ward of court business, erm.
CB: They hire detectives to track her down.
BB: Mm. Yeah . . . Erm. I was thinking, you know, you see people being made wards of court and I always

feel that this is perhaps something that should be kept within a family rather than being – bringing in the outside like that. So probably I wouldn't have done that.

CB: It depends. I mean she's almost eighteen. She's –
BB: Well quite.
CB: seventeen.
BB: Mm. A mere seventeen is a bit much isn't it really, the way things –
CB: I don't know what you can do in the situation.
BB: No. Quite. Try the – Decide on the best course of action. Mm. Try to come to an agreement and summarise exactly what you would have done. Yeah. Well I think, assuming there was no note, I would have – contact the police, to see if they had any news. Erm. Assuming that they managed to find out, erm, I would think then you would – I would er, make the best of a bad job perhaps. I mean they are married, aren't they? So that from that er point of view there are no arguments. Erm . . . It's perhaps not a very good er basis for friendship between parents and er son-in-law, but er I think I would try and make the best of a bad job there. Er. After all erm, they obviously have some feeling for each other.
CB: I think at that age she was old enough to –
BB: Yes. Yeah, quite.
CB: to know what she was doing.
BB: And he is, it would seem in a – in a position to er – to support her. You know, he's got er, a good salary and all the rest of it, so, there's no – shouldn't be any problem on that side. Erm. I hope I'm not that sort of parent who has a you know, a career planned for children like that without really asking them.

---

 *

CB: So what did they actually do then?
BB: Mm. Er, yeah. What did they do? Did they accept it? . . . Yes. Even Selina's parents have decided to forgive and forget. Mm. Yeah. Well, that's nice isn't it? A happy ending.
CB: So they understood.
BB: Yeah . . .

UNIT 18

ANNOUNCER: In the real world, a lot of news is bad news: disasters, wars, crashes and crises. These are the events which make the headlines, and which a foreign correspondent spends a lot of time covering – although we also, in specialist programmes, do also report positive developments.

---

 *

ANNOUNCER: For Bob Jobbins one of the most interesting news stories in recent years was a non-violent revolution.

BJ: The overthrow of a President, with tanks and troops on the street, sounds a recipe for disaster, particularly when the soldiers were facing unarmed civilians, including children and old people.

But the revolution in the Philippines, which led to the exile of President Marcos, and the take-over by Mrs Cory Aquino, was almost entirely . . . .

---

 *

The overthrow of a President, with tanks and troops on the street, sounds a recipe for disaster, particularly when the soldiers were facing unarmed civilians, including children and old people.

But the revolution in the Philippines, which led to the exile of President Marcos, and the take-over by Mrs Cory Aquino, was almost entirely non-violent. Although throughout the drama, there was always the risk of shooting, or of the situation getting out of control.

For several days my colleagues and I raced around Manila, a large and sprawling city, between the army camp where the rebels had their headquarters, to the Presidential Palace surrounded by loyalist guards, and back to our hotels to send our reports back to London.

Finally, after days and nights of tension, the defeated President left, and together with thousands of ordinary citizens, the world's press poured into the Presidential Palace to record the last minutes of a regime, which, against all the odds, had fallen because of popular protest, rather than military force.

BS: Here's a very short little song from Malaysia. Roughly translated it means 'I've got a parrot and my grandmother's got two teeth'. It's called 'Barong kakak tua'.

A song from Sarawak in praise of that country: 'Gelang si-paku gelang', saying 'let us return home, let us return home together'.

---

 *

EE: In my passage, erm, it's explaining that when we – we talk about – when we argue, that the words that we often use or the phrases that we use, are war – war-like, so –
EL: Oh.
EE: Which implies sort of in – agression – the agression of an argument.
EL: Mm. Yeah. That's interesting.
EE: That we use military, war-like words –
EL: Yes.
EE: in our arguments.
EL: Right. Yeah. Does he – Does he say that people do that the whole time? Or just er, when they're f– – trying to m– – er – win a particular point or –
EE: Well, it's to do with attack and defence.
EL: Oh I see.
EE: So – So the whole process of an argument –
EL: Yes.
EE: is very much that you attack, you defend, then you attack the other person.
EL: Yes.
EE: And that whole system of arguing is backed up by using, erm, phrases and words. Some examples are, your claims are indefensible.
EL: Mm.
EE: I've never won an argument with him.
EL: Mm.
EE: If you use that strategy, he'll wipe you out.
EL: Yeah. I see. Yeah well.
EE: Does that make sense?
EL: Yeah. No it does. Yes. No absolutely.
EE: Yes.
EL: Probably a lot clearer than my one was actually.
EE: Maybe I've over-simplified it.
EL: No, not at all.
EE: I don't know.

187b *

EL: Erm, what – Can you – Can we think of any, er, ideas of using words metaphorically, you know, which has just become part of the common language? Ourselves. Like I mean, here's the fight against famine.
EE: Yes.
EL: I mean literally of course it's not. You're not going out with a shield and a spear and taking on famine on a battlefield. But – And yet we've started to use that word, haven't we? as just part of the language.
EE: Yes. I do agree with that, but I think you could also say that there is a fight, but the tools for fighting are different.
EL: Mm. Mm. Yep. That's fair enough. Can you think of some er, other words that we use in the same way? Some other metaphors? I've got one here. The – That

story was lifted straight out of another book. Well er, you don't lift it. I mean –
EE: Yes.
EL: It — We know what it means, but if you actually stop and think of the word lift, that's used, it means usually literally something much more tangible. You know. You're actually picking something up, lifting it.
EE: Yes.
EL: Erm. I think we must use things like that the whole time without thinking about them.
EE: I'm sure we do. And now that I try to think of them, I can't think of one.
EL: I know, it's difficult, isn't it?
EE: Yes.

 188a *

BJ: The Government is under intense pressure from the main opposition parties to take urgent action following the third serious injury in less than a month at the main water-well on the outskirts of the capital.

In spite of repeated statements by the Ministry that there is no danger to the public, a young man, identified in an official statement as Jack, was seriously injured when he fell down the hill where the well is located. He was rushed to hospital, and is now in an intensive care unit after surgery for severe head injuries.

His female companion, Jill, was slightly hurt, but police sources say she has already been able to give them a description of what happened. The authorities have described Jack's injuries as the result of an accidental fall, although according to unconfirmed reports he may have been pushed. Requests for interviews with Jill have been rejected by the hospital on the grounds that she is still in shock.

But if Jack's injuries do turn out to be the result of a deliberate attack, it will not only increase the government's embarrassment, but could provoke a full-scale parliamentary crisis.

The Government has argued that current limits on spending make further developments in the water supply system impossible in the foreseeable future. While spokesmen for local farmers say the water available in the past for their crops is now being consumed rapidly by the growing number of people using the well – and that unless there is urgent action to find new sources of drinking water for the urban areas, they will take direct action to protect their own water supplies.

188b *

Now this gives much more of the political background to the incident, and makes it clear that there could be further developments. The correspondent has clearly spoken to a large number of people on all sides, involved in the dispute.

191a

[POP STATION STYLE NEWS]
M1: And finally a mystery!
It is rumoured that Lady Angela Fitzbrian, the daughter of the Duke of Birmingham and a distant cousin of the queen, has disappeared shortly before her marriage to the London businessman Lord Drinkwater. A good deal of mystery surrounds this disappearance. For example Miss Mary Bonnington, a close friend of the family, claims to have seen Lady Angela on the day of her disappearance riding in a gipsy caravan just beyond her father's estate. It is difficult to offer any explanation for this bizarre report. It is said that police suspect foul play.
[CLOSING JINGLE]

191b

Fragment of song: **The gypsy rover.**

 201b *

EL: Yeah well. What about these three stories? Mm.
EE: I think the reincarnation story. It's actually very straightforward. It's a story that I'm sure we've all read.
EL: Mm.
EE: Many times over.
EL: Yes.
EE: Erm. So I think that that is a genuine story.
EL: Right.
EE: I find the Spiderman to the rescue story very strange.
EL: Yes. It's pretty unlikely.
EE: I – I think that this is the hoax.
EL: Yeah.
EE: Erm.
EL: By the way, there could be more than one hoax.
EE: Yes. Well –
EL: So, I mean, they don't – none of them have to be true.
EE: Yes. I'm sure that that is a hoax.
EL: Mm.
EE: I mean the, sort of – How would you actually time jumping from the top of a building?
EL: Exactly.
EE: and the chance of catching somebody is –
EL: Yeah.
EE: I think that's much too –
EL: Yes.
EE: ridiculous to be true.
EL: I would have thought, to jump that far as well, even if you were s- – attached to a rope. You – I mean, think of the impact when he lands in the road. You know –
EE: Well, I mean –
EL: I mean it's something stopping him, isn't it?
EE: Well yes, I – I'm sure that he wouldn't actually fall to the ground, would he?
EL: No. I don't mean fall to the ground, but even if he fell to the – the end of the rope and the rope was fully extended, there'd be a hell of a jolt as he – as he –
EE: Yes.
EL: reached the –
EE: But, I mean people do do those type of stunts.
EL: Mm.
EE: Erm. So I mean I'm sure that that's possible. But I think the thing about it is the – being able to time when to jump.
EL: Yes.
EE: To – When to be able to catch the woman. And also, I mean, being able to control the direction in which you are going.
EL: Yeah.
EE: When you jump.
EL: Right. Er.
EE: I can't believe that.
EL: What about the erm, business –
EE: The photograph.
EL: The photograph, yes. Er, don't seem to have that.
EE: Ye- – Oh.
EL: Erm.
EE: I found this one quite intriguing.
EL: Mm.
EE: I can't see why it isn't possible. Erm. There were one or two things that –
EL: Mm.
EE: I was slightly suspicious about. Er. Namely being – Why contact Patrick Litchfield? I would have thought it would be far more likely that it would be sort of via a university.
EL: Yes. Yes.
EE: That the contact would be made.
EL: I think you're right. Yeah.
EE: And also this thing about . . . erm, due to scientific concern that exposure to the light could weaken the already faint image, it would be on display to the public for one day only.

EL: Mm. Mm.
EE: I can't believe that it would be displayed to the public for even one day if there was any chance of it being further damaged.
EL: Yes. Yes. No . . .

---

 *

EL: I think you've got the – Actually – funnily enough originally, when I read them yesterday, I thought that that one was, erm –
EE: The photograph?
EL: was the – possibly the only one that was genuine. And erm, that these two were both hoaxes, the reincarnation one, and the other one. But erm, in fact, I think hearing you talk about them, I think I probably agree with you. That erm, this one maybe is, you know, true.
EE: Yes.
EL: Er. But erm. Who knows? So are we – Shall we – We'll reach a conclusion that –
EE: Well I – yes, I mean that I think I would say that the Spiderman to the rescue story –
EL: We agreed on. Definite hoax. Yeah.
EE: is a complete hoax. And –
EL: And er –
EE: I could be tempted to believe in the photograph story.
EL: Right.
EE: Except that there are one or two elements that don't ring true.
EL: Yes. Whereas this one, the reincarnation one is, sort of, common enough for –
EE: Yes.
EL: it to be just – It's not that sort of unusual to find this sort of thing.
EE: No. No.
EL: Right.
EE: And there doesn't seem to be a – erm – it's not unusual enough.
EL: Right. Okay.
EE: Good.

UNIT 20

---

 *

CB: Are you a good sailor? Have you ever been sea-sick?
RS: Yeah I have been sea-sick, once. But I haven't sailed very much. Except in a –
CB: Was that on a long journey?
RS: Yeah. In fact I'm quite a good traveller normally. But this was erm- er- not on a long journey, no. It was about twenty miles. And erm, coming – on the way back, it was a very small boat, and it was very hot, and er me and the rest of my family were on this very – in the inside of the boat. And it was just like being in a – on a cork, carried by the water. And my brother started first and then it just sort of spread like the plague.
CB: Oh terrible.
RS: It was ghastly.
CB: I've been on a big boat coming back from France but, it's been rough but not that rough. But I've just sat in my chair and hoped it would pass, and it did.
RS: Yeah. You were lucky. Yeah, you did have to concentrate. On something.

BB: Er. I'm an average sailor I would think. Yes er – if it's not too tough I manage quite well but erm, if it gets really rough then I'm afraid I'm erm – I'm in agony usually.
EL: Yes I'm pretty bad. Erm. I don't like being on water really at all.
BB: No.
EL: I'm really er, an earth person I think.
BB: Mm.
EL: I went on one of the hovercrafts for the first time. Have you ever been on one of them?

BB: Yes I have. I quite enjoy that actually.
EL: Well it's okay if it's smooth, but this one, erm . . . it's supposed to take – It was just across the Channel – It was supposed to take erm, forty minutes, and it took an hour and forty-five minutes.
BB: Oh no.
EL: And we – But we all thought we were going to crash. – I mean, it was really bad.
BB: It was as bad as that was it?
EL: Yeah. And when we got to the other side they said right, that's the last one today, you know. They shouldn't have gone at all but, you know. They've got to make their money I suppose.
BB: So – Well quite. So that's put you off the hovercraft completely. Yes.
EL: Definitely. Yeah. I'll fly if ever I can now I think, rather than go by ship.
BB: No I've been on a hovercraft when it's been fairly rough, when the thing's sort of been hitting the waves and jumping but er – It was the noise angle I think that really got to me.
EL: Yeah. Yeah.
BB: I was sitting too near the engine I think. Erm. And er, my head was going boom boom all the time.
EL: Right. Right.
BB: Since then I've been lucky. Its been reasonably calm.
EL: Yes. Well.
BB: A big ship. I wonder what they mean by a big ship. I suppose an ocean liner. And I've not, so er, I can't say anything about that.
EL: I suppose the Sealinks are quite big, aren't they?
BB: Well, they're fairly big, yes, but er –
EL: Well maybe they mean something much bigger.
BB: In comparison to the thing that's in the story I suppose, no.
EL: Right. Oh I see. Yeah.
BB: Mm.

206

Dip in the pool
Chapter one: A change in the weather.

---

 *

CB: Why do you think the steward sprinkled water on the table?
RS: I don't know actually.
CB: I wondered about that.
RS: Let's have a look. Must be – it's – I would imagine it's some kind of superstition or something. I really don't know.
CB: I wondered whether it was to freshen the place up or –
RS: Possibly.
CB: I don't know. What do you think the – What do you think the last two sentences mean?
    What I want to know is will the captain already have made his estimate on the day's run. You know for the auction pool – I mean before it began to get rough like this.
RS: I'm not sure.
CB: I suppose it means how many miles, or how far they've gone in a day.
RS: Or how much –
CB: The distance that they covered.
RS: Do you think so? And not how much they've – money they've made during the day?
CB: In the auction pool.
RS: I ca- – I don't really see the relation between an auction and a ship really. Unless it's something to do with insurance.
CB: Have you every bought anything at an – at an auction or been at an auction sale? I haven't.
RS: No. I haven't either. I always thought if you move a finger you'd be in for spending a lot of money.

EL: Well er, why do you think the steward sprinkled

water on the table? I don't even remember him doing that.

BB: Yeah, er.

EL: Which point did he do that at?

BB: That was whe- – After it had become rough and erm, the erm, fellow's fish started to move, was it? Is it to stop the plates sliding do you think?

EL: Ah yes. Maybe that's it.

BB: That's a possibility, isn't it? Mm.

EL: Yeah. Yeah. That's probably right.

BB: Either that or to er – to cover up the thing that's been – the stuff that's been split on the table. I suppose it's possible.

EL: Yes. Yes.

BB: Yeah.

EL: Now – now this really confused me, this business about the auction pool, in the next question.

BB: Oh yes.

EL: Er. I noticed the title of the thing is A Dip in the Pool.

BB: Oh, I didn't notice that.

EL: So er, it must be something to do with that.

BB: Mm.

EL: But what – do you think they're auctioning er –

BB: This is something I have read about in lots of these sorts of travel books er – If you're on a long journey, erm, – these cruises particularly –

EL: Oh yeah?

BB: Erm, I think that they hold a, erm – I think auction's perhaps the wrong word, really – they hold a sort of competition where you guess the distance that the er – the boat has travelled.

EL: Oh I see. Aah.

BB: I think possibly it's referring to that.

EL: Yeah. Yeah. Like a sort of sweepstake, type of thing. Oh I see.

BB: Yes, that's right, yeah. Mm.

EL: Yep. Right. Erm.

BB: Erm. It seems a bit odd actually for the chap to er – I don't know, perhaps he wants to win it. I suppose the ship would slow down, wouldn't it?

EL: Yeah. When it gets rough. Exactly.

BB: Affect the mileage. Mhm.

RF: Yeah. Anyway it'll get creepy soon. They usually do. Erm.

BB: Well, do you want to summarise that or have we already done so do you think?

EL: Well, I think we have, yes.

BB: We've covered it pretty well. Yes.

EL: Yep.

Dip in the pool
Chapter one (continued)

Song: **Homeward bound**

Dip in the pool
Chapter two: If this gets any worse . . .

---

 *

CB: What do you think the purser means when he says they don't announce the range till the auction starts after dinner? I'm not sure about that.

RS: I'm not sure what the range is.

CB: Why is Mr Botibol so concerned about the weather?

RS: It's something to do with the estimate he's made. He's made his – made an estimate according to what the weather is. I think.

CB: So he wants it to go – to be related to what his estimate is.

RS: Mm.

CB: Why do you think he wants to go out on the

sundeck? To get a sun-tan?

RS: Possibly . . . I think it's probably again to do with the weather. Checking up on what's going on.

CB: Yes. Shall we go on to the next one?

BB: Well, what do you think the purser means when he says they don't announce the range till the auction starts after dinner?

EL: Well, presumably the range is just the range of, erm, you know, the kind of minimum estimated time of journey to the maximum, or something like that.

BB: Yes. I assume that's it.

EL: These numbers, it looks as if the low number corresponds to, erm, a long – the longest duration of journey.

BB: Er. Well I would have put it the other way round I think. Where was that erm? The – I would – I would take the, you know, the number of miles that they cover, in the time allowed, so that the low numbers would be a small mileage, and the higher number would mean they'd travelled further. So this would tie in with the rough weather reducing the number. So erm, he would be interested in the lower numbers rather than the higher ones.

EL: Ah.

BB: That's providing the captain has er, taken the weather into account, isn't it?

EL: Mm. There was something in it, I can't remember what, but there was something in it – that's right, if this gets any worse it might be worth buying some of the low numbers.

BB: That's right, yes. And it would slow the ship down.

EL: And slow the ship down.

BB: They would cover fewer miles.

EL: Oh I see. Yeah. Sorry. Yeah that's right.

BB: It seems likely, anyway.

EL: Yeah.

BB: Mm.

EL: Mm. Er. Why is he so concerned about the weather? And why do – why does he want to go out on the sundeck?

BB: Er. Well, I think we nearly covered that then, didn't we. The – If it's bad weather it will slow the ship down, it'll mean they've covered less mileage, so the lower numbers would be in with a better chance.

EL: Yes. Yes.

BB: And I assume he wants to go out on the sundeck so he can see what the weather's like.

EL: See if the sun's coming out.

BB: If it's improving or not, yes.

EL: Right.

BB: Okay.

211

Mystery recording

M2: This evening there are still showers running in across Britain on a westerly breeze but there are clear spells too and temperatures will be low enough tonight to give a frost and patchy ice in many areas. Cloud and rain to the south of Britain though is beginning to creep northwards. It's already raining in the Channel Islands and by the end of the night rain will have reached southern parts of England and Wales. Patchy rain will move north tomorrow morning turning to sleet in parts of North Wales, the Midlands and East Anglia and turning to snow over much of Northern Ireland and Northern England with some moderate falls of snow possible on the Pennines and the hills of Cumbria.

During Saturday, sleet and snow showers are likely in most parts though it should become brighter and drier from the west on Sunday. Well that's all from the weather centre for tonight, now back to Peter Evans.

M1: It's been confirmed . . . [FADE]

*

EE: I think the thing I've heard most from my parents and from other older people, about when I was young. All we had was the radio. And they always seem to be very conscious of not having television. That seems to be a very popular thing, and how we had to make our own amusements.
RS: Mm. Yeah, I f- – that's funny actually because I find erm, that I'm not very interested in television really an awful lot, but er, oh my parents are. Seems like they're making up for years of having to make their own amusements up.
EE: Mm.
RS: Yeah, I think sort of phrases like when I was young – erm, what's the other one?
EE: They usually seem to talk about things – you know, when I was young we didn't have – things that – I almost feel that they're always saying well, you know, it's not fair, I didn't have that when I was young. They think we've got a lot more advantages.
RS: Yes I think if only I'd had the advantages you've had. That's another one. If only.
EE: And education is – seems to be a very common thing that people bring up.

 *

INT: How does your family feel all – about the travelling that you do? Because I mean, some of your trips are fairly long, aren't they?
BS: They are. Erm. I think that – They get used to me breezing in and out all the time. Erm. Sometimes the most annoying pieces can be when you're actually just passing through. You know, if you stay for a day, well that's okay, but if you just come in late at night, get a night's sleep, and then you're off the next morning, that can be a bit annoying I think. The long trips – and the first one was seven weeks – erm, and my two boys were really quite small then.
INT: How old were they?
BS: Erm, well John was just five and Ben was three. And erm, I thought, this is going to be terrible. You know, that I really was going to miss them, and I did. And I thought that they would probably feel the same. And I – certainly when I got home, erm, you know, there was a tremendous party – well, a family party if you like. – We had a whale of a time. Erm. The next day, I got John in the car and took him off to school, and er, he saw his mates, piled into the playground, and didn't bother to say goodbye, and I thought, oh well. Fair enough then. Be like that. So I think, they've got used to it. And erm, really they get along. And I know my wife gets into a routine, er, when I'm away like that. And sometimes, coming home, you break that routine. So it can be er –
INT: Mm. Mm. Yeah. Because when our kids were little, one of the – one of the things they hated was when we were getting ready to go.
BS: Yes.
INT: Rather than when you actually went. So if there were suitcases around and so on, they didn't like that at all.
BS: Yes.
INT: When we'd gone, they probably weren't – weren't . . . .

 *

RS: What do you think the words or phrases that go in the blanks mean? Can you guess the actual words and phrases?
CB: Right. The first one. The wind caught him full in the face as he stepped out onto the deck.
RS: Yeah.
CB: He staggered and –
RS: I said and clung onto.

CB: Or clutched. Possibly.
RS: One of those isn't it, yeah.
CB: And then – Erm.
RS: I thought maybe it was terrible out there or fierce out there. Windy.
CB: Or awful out there.
RS: Yeah. Ghastly.
CB: Do you think that we've – at all – at all on account of the weather he asked. Erm . . . Number four.
RS: Something like er, slowed down.
CB: Or lost speed. Number five. Took a chair close to the auctioneer's table.
RS: Erm. I thought he's probably crossed his legs as he's folded his arms.
CB: Yeah. Settles himself into a chair. Yeah.

EL: Mhm.
BB: Okay?
EL: Next.
BB: Deck? do you think? for number one?
EL: Erm. Deck. Yes. Number one.
BB: He staggered and, grasped? or grabbed? or something like that, do you think? the rail?
EL: Well it's a bit of a longer – it's a longer gap.
BB: You're looking at the length. Took hold of.
EL: Yes. Something like that. Yep. Got hold of the rail or something.
BB: Mhm. Yes.
EL: Er. Then number three I should think, rough out there, or something like that.
BB: Yes. Or –
EL: Pretty rough.
BB: Or windy or something like – Yes. Pretty rough. Very windy. Yeah. Er. Do you think we've – slowed down I would have said anyway, but erm – just they've got slackened off and so on about four times haven't they?
EL: Yeah. Slacked. Yes. Yeah. And five he er – Hang on.
BB: I would have said sat down but on the basis of the spacing which you pointed out it might be a little bit longer than that.
EL: Mm.
BB: Erm he – found a seat? Or er, took a seat. Erm. Oh no it says took a chair doesn't it? Oh well he must have – what would you do when you sat down? Erm, Oh I know, he crossed his legs.
EL: Yeah. Yeah. Could be anything really.
BB: Yes . . . .

EL: Erm. How does he hope to get seven thousand dollars? Well. By winning the auction.
BB: Yeah, well obviously, yes. Everybody obviously buys a number and they – the money goes in.
EL: When it gets to the total, yeah.
BB: And you get the kitty. Yes.
EL: And er, if he's going to buy a Lincoln convertible with seven thousand dollars it must be quite a long time ago.
BB: It's certainly not this year is it? And I doubt it would be seventy-one either, really.
EL: Do they make Lincolns still, do you know?
BB: Er. No I couldn't really tell you. Never.
EL: Mm.
BB: I would have said about – would have said fifty-two, but I don't really know. But erm –
EL: Fifty-two. I think you're right. Because Ethel as well is quite an old name, isn't it?
BB: That's true, yes. Mhm. Yeah. Now I don't know whether the Lincoln convertibles were around in twenty-nine anyway. They may have been.
EL: Yeah. But then I think seven thousand dollars would be an awful lot of money.
BB: In twenty-nine, yes. That Wall Street crash business, wasn't it, twenty-nine, so –
EL: Right. Yes. Oh yeah.
EL: Shall we say fifty-two?

RF: Let's got for fifty-two.
BB: Right.
EL: Let's go for fifty-two. They don't give you the answer to that.
BB: Mhm. No. Bit of a let down, isn't it?

RS: How does he – Mr Botibol hope to get seven thousand dollars?
CB: He wants to – He hopes to win it. On the er – in the pool – from the pool. In the auction. . . . I'm not sure when the story was written. When do you think the story was written?
RS: I would guess 1952, but then I'm not really sure when the Lincoln convertible was around.
CB: Or 1929. Shall we say 1952?
RS: Okay.

Dip in the pool
Chapter three: Present for a wife?

BB: Erm. Well he's auctioning mileage I suppose basically, isn't he?
EL: Yes.
BB: Erm. And the person who gets the correct mile number presumably gets the kitty.
EL: Mm.
BB: Er. Don't know whether there's any – anything else you can say about that is there really?
EL: Well except that – I don't quite understand. If it's going to depend on the weather. I mean presumably the mile distance is the same no matter what. Oh except that they have to go out of their way to avoid heavy winds and things I suppose. If the wind's bad –
BB: It is affected by weather, wind particularly and er heavy seas, so –
EL: Yeah. Right. Yeah of course. It's like on a hovercraft we had to go all the way along the coast and up the other. Yeah.
BB: That's right, yes quite. Instead of forty minutes it's er – Instead of twenty miles you do forty miles or something like that. Yes.
EL: Mileage. And the high field and low field that's just a sort of a maximum and a minimum range outside of the –
BB: Outside the actual figures given, yes. Hm.
EL: The actual figures. Yeah. So they stop being specific about them once they get beyond –
BB: Perhaps a separate auction, do you think? Or a separate amount that er they have. Yes. Hm.
EL: Well he – they just make that into one category don't they? Whereas the others are just single numbers this is just a category.
BB: Yeah. Okay. How many more?
EL: Right.

RS: Do you know what the auctioneer is auctioning?
CB: What is the auctioneer auctioning? Erm. Well, they're betting on how far they've come. How many miles they've done in the day. So he's – erm – they're bidding on that.
RS: Yeah. Somehow doesn't seem quite fit. Er. I'm not sure. Maybe it's the meaning of the word auction that I'm confused about.
RS: I think auctioning's different to how we term it now.
RS: I think it's like betting, here. Yeah it's definitely been used as betting. I think that's where the confusion is.
CB: What do you think the high field and low field are? I suppose those are, erm, above and below, erm, the bet.
RS: Yeah.
CB: Erm. You know, a limit of so many above and so many below.
RS: Mm.

Dip in the pool
Chapter four: Last bid

UNIT 22

Dip in the pool
Chapter five: Twenty-one hundred-odd pounds (dramatisation)

BB: Could you now write a summary of the way the ship's run works?
EL: Well. I think we could couldn't we?
BB: Yeah I think so, yes. It's er – Doesn't seem particularly difficult, really. Erm. It's the – That was the only question really wasn't it, the – what they meant by this low field and high field, and that seems to be covered there.
EL: So the captain makes an estimate as to the miles of the journey, and then they take a range either side of that. Five is it? Five miles – ten miles outside of it?
BB: Ten miles, either side.
EL: And then outside of those two limits there's an additional low field and a high field.
BB: A high field.
EL: And then erm, people just bid for each number.
BB: Yes, they – and then the money is put together.
EL: Into a pool.
BB: Into a pool. Er, most of it going to the winner, and some to seamen's charity. That's it isn't it?
EL: Mm. Yeah.
BB: Yeah. But that doesn't really affect the auction though, does it?
EL: No. How much does he stand to win? Erm, two thousand something? Oh no.
BB: Er. Well, it's twenty-one hundred pounds, so, erm –
EL: It's five thousand four hundred dollars.
BB: Four hundred dollars and – How many did he say before? Erm. Five hundred did he say? For two hundred pounds?
EL: Yes he put in – He put in –
BB: Let's work this one out. Yes it's three dollars to the pound, isn't it? Twenty-one hundred pounds. Six thousand dollars. So that's about three dollars to the pound. Er. And he has paid two hundred pounds –
EL: So he's put in six hundred dollars.
BB: So he's put in six hundred.
EL: So he'll win four thousand eight hundred.
BB: Four thousand eight hundred. That's it. Mm. The Lincoln is cheaper than we thought.

EL: Let's move on to er more positive – Your three wishes. For the future.
RS: Erm. Well I'd like to teach violin. Erm. Which means I want to go to college and get some qualifications because that's necessary. Erm. And in a particular way –
EL: Is this erm, classical – classical violin or –
RS: No. Er – Well, I mean I could teach classical violin as well but I'm really interested in erm, improvising. For jazz. And would like to get into schools and somehow get that into the curriculum. Which is quite an ambition I must say.
BB: Mhm. Indeed yes.
EL: There's a course up at Leeds, isn't there? Jazz – Jazz course. At the university. Yeah.
BB: There is, that's true. That's right, yes. It's in the building just across from my – where my son is actually. The noise is absolutely incredible at times.

Mm. Mm.
RS: Sounds like my sort of place, yeah.
BB: Oh yes. It's a nice noise, I must admit, but er –
EL: Do you want to talk about your two other wishes?
RS: Oh I've got two other wishes. Ooh. Yes, I wish erm, that Labour would get in in the next election. Erm. Because I know it's getting – By that time all the damage has been done I should imagine but erm, you know still gives a little bit of hope at the end of the political tunnel. Erm. And I wish that er, the – something was done about starvation in the third world. Because I just think that it's horrendous and I go into a supermarket and I just see piles of food and I just think, well, you know, there's plenty of food around. Erm. So –
EL: Mm. Yeah.
BB: Yes, I understand that. Mm.
EL: Mhm. Erm. Liz.
EE: I find this very difficult. I wish for courage. Erm. All my three wishes I feel take a certain amount of courage. There's a lot of things that I'd like to learn. Erm. And I'd like to have the courage to learn new skills. Learn more about the world around me. And I'd like to go and work in a third world country, when my children are older. And I think having the courage to break out of the mould, and to be able to do that. It's asking quite a lot. And the fact that I shall be, huh, well over forty before I'm in the position to do those sorts of things.
EL: Any one in particular? Any country in particular?
EE: No, I mean, I can't anticipate where – where the work – I mean I'm sure there's countries all over the world where they need, erm, volunteer health workers. Wherever they'll have me.
BB: Mm. Yes. Of course.
EL: Is that erm, two wishes? Or three?
EE: Oh, let that be three.
EL: Let that be three. Okay. Bruce, what about you? . . . .

BB: Erm. Thirdly I suppose, connected with that, is this nuclear business. Erm. Being at the heart of it where we are in – in Barrow, erm, and having had people close who have died probably as a result of erm, leakages in the past, I feel that a stop should be put first to nuclear warfare, nuclear armaments, and secondly, er to the er, production even of er peaceful nuclear energy if there is such a thing. Erm. I've discovered over the last couple of years from my son who's taking a course in energy, erm, that erm, it's just not needed at all. The er – The production of er – of nuclear energy is a sort of totally redundant feature really. That erm there is ample natural energy if you like around without using up er, fossil resources to er – to get by without erm, you know building these ugly, dangerous er things all over the place. So that's the third wish.

Dip in the pool
Chapter 6A: Smooth as glass (dramatisation)

CB: What would you do if you were Mr Botibol? Think of two alternative strategies.
RS: Erm. Well he could jump off the boat but I think that might be a bit extreme.
CB: He could go and live in another country and not go back to his wife.
RS: Or he could just get in contact with her. Tell her what he's done.
CB: He could tell her what he's done, say he's sorry.
RS: Because he's going to get more debts. I'd imagine he wouldn't somehow. They never do in stories.
CB: I think he'd have to be honest here.

EL: Well. What would you do?
BB: I'm just trying to think. What would you do? I

suppose you – Could you telephone shore and cancel the cheque? Er –
EL: I suppose one of the things they want you to say is throw yourself off the –
BB: Yes. Quite.
EL: Erm.
BB: Cast around for something to sell? Erm. What else could you do? Mm. I suppose you could go along –
EL: Take a new job or something when you get ashore.
BB: Yeah. Go along to the purser and say er, you didn't mean it. Can you withdraw your offer?
EL: Mm. I shouldn't think he'd let you through.
BB: No. But er, I suppose it's – in that sort of situation you might try it.
EL: Mm.
BB: Otherwise you might – I suppose you could try robbing somebody on board.
EL: Mm. Yep.
BB: We're obviously not erm –
EL: – not very good at that . . . .

Dip in the pool
Chapter 6B: Smooth as glass

EL: Okay. Well.
BB: So he does decide to jump overboard, yes.
EL: Not to kill himself.
BB: Not to kill himself, no.
EL: Just to slow it up. What could go wrong? Er, somebody could not see him, is one thing.
BB: Yes.
EL: He could drown.
BB: Yes.
RF: Erm. They'd see him too soon. And wouldn't.
BB: Yes, that's true enough, yes. Or perhaps even see him too late I suppose. Erm. Mm. Yes.
EL: Yes. I didn't quite understand the bit about the time limit being mid-day, at the very end.
BB: No. I think the mileage runs from mid-day to mid-day. That's the impression I've got.
EL: Oh I see. Right. And what precautions will he need to take?
BB: Erm. Well he's dressing in light clothing isn't he? That'd be easy to swim in, rather than er, his ordinary clothes. Erm. I suppose he's leaving his watch behind to – so it doesn't get ruined but er. Erm. Now the main precaution is to make sure somebody sees him going.
EL: So he's – somebody sees him. Right.
BB: Mm. Mm.

CB: What did Mr Botibol decide to do? A drastic measure. He decided to –
RS: Ah. He decided to throw himself over so he'd delay the boat. They'll have to – because they'll have to save him, and so he'll win his auction or his bet.
CB: What could go wrong? He could drown.
RS: Certainly could. Erm –
CB: Do you think the plan will work? It could work if someone saw him.
RS: Mm. It's a bit risky.
CB: But then if they knew he had a bet, they may be a bit suspicious.
RS: Yeah. Thing is he could drown before he erm – he's saved. Even if he is seen.
CB: What precautions will he need to take?
RS: Make sure he's on the side with a lifebelt.
CB: He'd need a lifejacket.
RS: Yeah.

UNIT 23

INT: Erm. What sort of hopes do you have for the

future? I mean, how do you see the Yetties developing?

BS: What we're always trying to do is diversify. Erm. We started off as a group that just sang a few local folk-songs. And from there we've broadened out to doing things like pantomime. Er, we've written a book. Erm, we do er, things about Thomas Hardy and his connections with music. Erm. In fact, we're hoping to get a book – write a book about that soon, as well as doing a recording. Erm, we get er – we do quite a lot of radio work. Television. Erm. I can see – I would – What I would like to do is to be able to write songs for films and plays, and then Peter and Mac or Roger would write the music.

INT: Right.

BS: Er. There's all sorts of avenues down which we can go. Just generally broaden our horizons all the time.

232b

INT: What would you – What would you like to do? I mean what things would you really like to achieve? As an individual entertainer and as one of the Yetties? What do you look forward to?

PS: Erm. I don't know. It's very difficult because it's not the sort of business you can plan. I mean I remember sort of thinking years ago that, you know, that this is a – well it's a great fun thing to be in, but it is, erm, hard work at times. Erm. I always thought that er, you know, the age I am now, by this time you know I'd be rich. But that never happened. Erm. I would still like to be rich but er – I'm not sure that we will ever achieve that.

INT: I think everyone who goes into business for themselves, that's one possibility that they perhaps hope's going to turn up. Doesn't happen to very many though, does it?

PS: But we have a very interesting and varied life, so I suppose we have that to be thankful for. But it – you know when you get the er, bills coming for electricity and rates and erm, the mortgage and all that, it's er – it's not so good.

INT: Yeah if you could have the fun and make a lot of money as well that would be great.

PS: Yeah.

232c

INT: Erm. How do you see the next few years? Have you got any particular definite plans or ambitions or –?

MM: Erm not – Well that's difficult really. I mean, we tend to take the future day by day, and week by week. We're hoping to do a bit more foreign work again, you know, because we do enjoy the foreign travel. Although we've got Germany coming up, there's nothing exotic like the Far East or anything. But, I mean we don't know. It's possible.

INT: What about the family. How do they feel – You have a family, haven't you?

MM: I did have. Erm, I'm divorced now.

INT: But how did it work with family life, when you were travelling?

MM: Oh. I mean we were lucky I think, in as much as all of us got married after we turned professional. It wasn't the case that we were all bank managers or something and then suddenly decided to give up this secure job for the insecurity of singing. So, I mean in a way the wives married into the business, and knew what they were taking on in a way.

INT: Yeah. Right.

234a

Dip in the pool
Chapter seven: A cautious man (part A)

234b

EL: That was another thing we didn't think of, wasn't

it? That somebody might see him but still not bother to give the alarm.

BB: That's true, yes. Indeed. I hadn't thought of that one. Mm.

EL: I imagine he'll just go up and start talking to her, and see what kind of a person she is.

BB: Yes, that's one way of doing it. Er, perhaps see if she's wearing glasses or if she is capable of seeing, or even of er, making sufficient noise to attract attention.

EL: Right.

BB: Er. And obviously er, to make sure her collar's not turned up so that er, she can't see anything.

EL: Yes.

BB: Mm.

RS: He'll have to go and talk to her – to the old woman, to check up on her.

CB: Yeah. I said he should go and talk to her, erm, so that she's seen him and she knows that he's near. Just to make her aware of him.

RS: Mm.

234c

EL: How well did we guess?

BB: Not particularly really. I think we got the physical side of it. But er –

EL: We got the general areas, didn't we? We didn't quite get the detail. We didn't think of the fact that she might have a high number.

BB: No. No, that's true enough.

EL: But there again, he's under a lot of stress, so he'll be thinking about these things much more than we would.

BB: Yes, indeed. Mm.

234d

Dip in the pool
Chapter seven (part B)

239a

EL: Slowly?

BB: Yes. I would agree with that certainly.

EL: Er.

BB: Nice day?

EL: Erm. I really can't think what that is. Anyway. A bit floored on that one. Erm. Almost a –

BB: Beautiful, I would think.

EL: Right.

BB: Yeah. Though the face itself was very plain.

EL: Or ugly.

BB: Or ugly. Mm. That's cruel.

EL: He's a pretty cruel writer I think.

BB: Yes. Mm.

EL: Erm.

BB: She's neither deaf nor blind presumably.

EL: Yes, right. That's it. The – What do you think of the auction?

BB: Yes.

EL: You know that funny old thing in the lounge?

BB: Silly. Stupid perhaps. Yes. A word of that kind I think. I just wondered what you thought about it. Mhm.

EL: Yep. So nice to have dinner in bed. Or –

BB: Pleasant?

EL: Yeah. Something like that.

BB: Mm. Something like that. Yeah.

CB: What words do you think go in the blanks? Mr Botibol advanced slowly? –

RS: Yes. I thought that.

CB: towards the woman and took up a position beside her leaning on the rail. Hello he said.

RS: Politely?

CB: Mm. Yes.

RS: Or maybe –

CB: I'm not sure about that one. She turned and smiled at him, surprisingly lovely almost a –

RS: Beautiful smile.

CB: Beautiful smile. Although the face was very old?

The face itself was very –
RS: Plain, or old?
CB: She is neither blind or deaf.
RS: Mhm.
CB: What did you think of the auction last night? You know that silly? silly old thing?
RS: Yes. I think that would be it.
CB: Stupid. Silly. I just –
RS: Wondered.
CB: Wondered what you thought about it. I always go to bed early. I have my dinner in bed. It's so –
RS: Pleasant? to have dinner in bed?
CB: Mhm.
RS: Shall we check the . . . .

Dip in the pool
Chapter eight: Everything in order?

Dip in the pool
Chapter eight (continued)

CB: What do you think's going to happen? Well I think he's going to jump over and no-one will see him.
RS: Yes. I think that er, she's in fact got a very – is it a high bet?
CB: High field.
RS: Yeah. And that she knows that he's going to jump over.

BB: What do you think's going to happen?
EL: Oh sorry. I missed that one. Erm. Er. I really haven't a clue actually.
BB: Mm.
EL: I really don't know. That's the sign of a good story teller I suppose.
BB: Mm. Either he loses his nerve. Or perhaps one of the sailors er, grabs his arm as he's er, climbing over.
EL: Yes.
BB: Comes up behind him.
EL: Maybe.
BB: I don't know.
EL: Or perhaps he does jump and they see him – somebody sees him obviously jumping.
BB: Yeah. Mm, there's all sorts of possibilities anyway.
EL: Mm. Right, here we go. Poised for the kill.
BB: Oh yes, there he goes. Help, help.

UNIT 24

CB: Erm. The story so far. Er, well there's been an auction or a bet, on the boat, on the distance that they're going in one day. And, erm, Mr Botibol has, er, betted a lot of his savings away, so he's got to do, erm, something in order to be able to get his money, or win his money that he wants to win, and not lose his money.
RS: Mm. So he's decided to throw himself overboard to delay the – the boat.
CB: Yeah.

EL: Gosh. Now we've got to summarise the whole thing.
BB: Dear me.
EL: Would you like to start?
BB: Oh thanks. Erm.
  Er, well. We're on board ship, erm, shall we say crossing the Atlantic probably or – And erm, they're having their evening meal. Erm. Suddenly, the fine weather deteriorates, the ship begins to roll, people begin to be a little bit uneasy. Er, one of the er, passengers at the table has to get up and go away.

Presumably she's feeling sick. Er, the hero takes her place which happens to be near the purser and proceeds to erm – to grill him about how the weather might affect the er – er, the distance the ship will be travelling because he's interested in – obviously in winning this er daily pool that is held on the – erm – on the distance travelled by the ship. Er. After grilling the purser, he er – he comes to the conclusion that the lowest number possible is going to be the winning one, so he's literally going to put his shirt on it, and buy with the winnings his dream car, so that erm he can impress his wife when he gets home. Erm. He goes to bed, after the auction, and he's managed to get the number he wants, and in the morning, to his horror, finds that the – er – the weather has suddenly turned beautiful and the ship is steaming along at great speed so he's in a real panic then. What can he do? How can he face his wife having gambled all their savings? And then he hits on his crazy plan of er, jumping overboard, so that the ship will have to stop and erm – to pick him up.
EL: Right. And now he's found a woman who might be able to spot him doing it. Erm. But he's going to check on her, first of all, to see if she's the sort of person who would report it if he fell overboard and secondly just to make sure that she hasn't got a higher number so that she wouldn't be interested in erm, not stopping the ship.
BB: Okay.
EL: That's about it isn't it?
BB: I think so, yes.
EL: Right.

BB: Mhm. Well, has the woman seen him? Obviously I think she must have done, yes.
EL: Yes.
BB: She's not reported it.
EL: Not reported.
BB: Well not officially anyway, has she?
EL: No. Do you think he'll be rescued?
BB: Judging from that, no.
EL: No.
BB: And he'll probably win the pool? Of course.
EL: Yes. I think there's something a big fishy about this woman actually.
BB: Yep well, she – do you think she's a mental case of some sort who's being escorted or – ?
EL: Well, no, I think maybe she – she might be tied up with some conspiracy or – maybe – maybe one of them's – maybe the other one's his wife, or maybe his wife's trying to get rid of him or – you know may – I think there's something er – something funny going on. But actually with only one page to go there probably isn't time for all that, so –
BB: Mm.
RF: There's something er, about the way she reacted when he jumped over that was a bit –
BB: Yes. Well that's why I thought perhaps she had – she was disturbed in some way and was being escorted over the – over the Atlantic by this other one.
EL: Yeah.
BB: So that when she says he just dived overboard the other one will say oh no, you know, don't make up stories like that dear.
EL: Oh I see, yes. Yes. That would make sense. Er.

CB: Has the woman seen him? Yes, she's seen him.
RS: Yes.
CB: She hasn't reported what's happened.
RS: Er, by the end she has but she's taken a long time to do it. It suggests she's waited for somebody else to come along so it's almost –
CB: She's – because her friend's come.
RS: Yes, it's almost as if she's waiting for him to drown, perhaps, giving a bit more time.
CB: Do you think he will be rescued?
RS: He might have a chance.
CB: He may be eventually.

RS: But possibly he might be too late.
CB: Do you think he will win the pool?
RS: No
CB: No, I don't either.

Dip in the pool
Chapter nine: Help!

RS: Maggie presumably is mad and the bony woman is her nurse.
CB: Yes, or her travelling companion, or friends.
RS: So she's definitely – I definitely think that she's er, being looked after, because she's been led away by her hand and –
CB: And she's not allowed to go out on her own, or not supposed to.
RS: Mm. I don't think either that they'll really believe her.
CB: What will Maggie probably say?
RS: They may think she's just imagining things, telling stories.
CB: I don't think they'd believe her.
RS: Mm.
CB: From Maggie's point of view, he was just swimming, he'd dived overboard. And she didn't think that he was, erm, trying to drown himself. She just thought he was going out for a swim.
RS: Yes.
CB: She didn't understand.
RS: Yes. Yes because she was, erm, quite tense at first and then she was – she relaxed.
CB: So I don't think she actualy understood what he was doing.
RS: No.

BB: Now, when they found out he's missing the captain is bound to ask what happened. What will Maggie probably say?
EL: She – And presumably she's – she's the – the sort of nurse of this one with the fat ankles. Right?
BB: I would think so, yeah.
EL: Yeah. Erm. What will Maggie say?
BB: Mm.
EL: Well she'll say – Well she's got a choice really, hasn't she?
BB: Mm.
RF: She'll either have to pretend she knows nothing about it at all –
BB: That's right. Yes. Or –
RF: or she'll have to be honest and er –
BB: Tell the truth and er, reveal that this other woman is not erm, to be er – to be trusted. Yes.
RF: To be trusted. And that she therefore thought that there couldn't be any truth in it, because it was coming from her. When in fact there was.
BB: That's right. Yes.

BB: Well that's it from Maggie's point of view I suppose is it? erm. Either she says nothing at all, or she says she couldn't possibly believe the word of Miss X because erm, she is given obviously to making up tales because she is – has some sort of mental disturbance.
EL: Right.
BB: Mm. Not very clear but er, there we are.
EL: Yep.
BB: Mm.
EL: That ended a bit unhappily. He didn't get his money and he lost his life. Suppose the moral is, don't go for auctions on liners.
BB: Mm. Certainly don't dive overboard.

Grammar Book Key

a, an 1

1 (10ts ×2) *when I was nineteen, still* **a student**/*helped in a* **holiday camp** *for children*

2 (10ts) *I had* **a year** *in Vannes*

3 (10ts ×2) *went to Paris for* **a few days**/*lived there for* **a while**

as 3

1 (20c, 24) *their days* **as boy scouts**/*involved . . .* **as professional folk singers**/*Saturday job . . . working* **as a Sales assistant** *in Smith's shoe shop*

1.1 (29b ts ×2) *I've got that* **as my number one.**/*That's the job* **as we see it**

2 (24b ts) *Keep it* **(as) brief as possible.**

2.1 (17b ts end) *Since I joined the group, we haven't done any extensive tours* **as they have done** *in the past.*

3 (31) *if you can give him or her a smile* **as you leave the room**

4 (29b ts) *Yes, it looks* **as if you're interested**

5 (24) **As a career is important to me** *I have always felt that . . .*

6 (17b ts, 24a ts) *It erm –* **as I said,** *the bookings became more and more*/*He's not really,* **as you say,** *he's not giving them anything very specific.*

at 10

1 (24b ts) *Print your name* **at the bottom.**

1.1 (102 ×2, 14b) **at number 14**/*there was nobody* **at home**/**At football matches**

2 (65) *you nerve lets you down* **at the last minute.**

3 (59, 63ts) *thump the dog,* **glare at it** *each time it* **looks at you**/*I know,* **looking at my children**

4 (72a, 102 part 4) *travelling* **at up to 60 mph**/**at a 20% discount** *of £30*

5 (95 ×2, 100c ts) **At least** *6 of the 21 species*/**In at least one case**/*nothing like that* **at all.**

be (am, is, are, was, here, be, been) 9

1 (91, 95) *when he* **was** *a schoolboy.*/*Crocodiles* **are** *formidable enemies of man.*

2 (95, 94 ×2) *many of the others* **are large enough** *to . . .*/*the statements* **are true or false.**/*16 species* **are now extinct.**

3 (72c, 91ts) *Now discuss what* **might be** *in the last paragraph.*/*don't know if* **it's still there**/**He's been** *in Live and Let Die*

3.1 (94b ts, 95) *I'll go for the fact that* **there aren't** *any crocodiles in Europe.*/**There are** *many individual horror stories*

4 (80 ×2, 87a) *5000 gulls which* **were polluting** *the water*/*Seagulls* **were causing** *a potential health risk.*/*my brother, who* **had been playing** *outside*

5 (95 ×4) *Before they could* **be rescued** *42 people* **were attacked and eaten.**/**It is not reported** *. . .*/*This giant* **was seen** *one day sleeping . . .*/*This alligator* **was received** *by Dresden Zoo in 1880 and* **was recorded** *as still being alive in 1937.*

6 (68c ts, 94b ts) **The thing is,** *though, that sometimes being cautious . . .*/**This is where** *I get muddled between alligators and crocodiles.*

by 16

1 (150a, 163a) *issued* **by the Home Office**/*might be asked questions* **by the programme presenter**

2 (38, 113) *kept warm* **by jumping** *for 10 minutes at a time.*/*did the right thing* **by leaving the banda**

3 (133a ×2, 133e) **by the end of next week**/**by the beginning of February**/**by then** *I will need*

4 (21, 166b ts) *a castle fine,* **down by the River Plaidy**/*Kafue River which flows* **by the southern town of Namwala**

5 (154, 166c ts) *cut the number of trains* **by half**/*the number of births in Italy fell* **by an estimated 10%**

6 (94b ts) *it depends what you mean* **by refuse**

can, could 14

1 (140a ×2 143c ×2) *Or* **can be** *what we call a 'stringer'/a degree in political science or economics* **could be** *very useful./* **Can** *they always* **be/** *What if they* **can't get to**

1.1 (106a ts) *Well, maybe you* **could spend** *a month out there or something, one day.*

3 (133d ×2) **Could I please have** *details of starting times …?/* **Could I stress** *once more that all transport arrangements …*

4 (109, 116ts) **Can you remember** *if you closed the door of your banda?/I* **couldn't believe** *that we'd escaped.*

do, does, doing, done, did 6

1 (59a, 59b) **Does using** *the telephone* **worry you?/** *Which questions in this test* **did you think** *were inappropriate?*

2 (59a ts ×3) *No it* **doesn't worry** *me./I* **don't mind making**/*I'd buy something I* **didn't particularly want.**

2.1 (31 ×3) **Don't let** *your clothes be …/* **Don't put** *your handbag on …/* **Don't exaggerate …**

3 (25a, 45b) *Or type your letter if you can* **do it** *neatly./I said daddy look out of the window and* **he did.**

4 (56a ×2) *picture that my five-year-old son* **did for me**/*So he* **did this picture** *so I could keep it with me.*

5 (2ts, 64) **What do you do?** *I'm a pianist./I* **do** *what's required.*

6 (31, 27ts) **Do arrive** *in plenty of time/We* **do actually occasionally advertise.**

for 17

1 (172b ts, 176a) *that's one* **for you.**/*other, more independent plans* **for her**

2.1 (176 ts, 176) *studying* **for** *A levels/arrested Paul* **for driving** *while disqualified/*

2.2 (102, 176c ts ×2) *made* **arrangements for** *a neighbour to let them in/basis* **for friendship**/*some feelings* **for each other**

3.1 (137ts ×2, 172) **for** *that week/* **for** *20 minutes/levelled off* **for another seven years**

get, got 11

1 (104 ×2, 110b/c ts ×2) *a traffic warden* **got** *to his car first/when he* **got back** *to court/it was trying to* **get in**/*where we had to* **get out**

2 (45) *Daddy,* **you've got wings** *as well.*

3 (72b ts) *Once he's going* **they've got to stop** *him*

4 (110c ts ×2) *I asked my wife to* **get the key**/*she couldn't* **get it.**

5 (110c ts, 114ts ×2) *I began to* **get** *very panicky/If they are* **getting old**/*they* **get used to being** *near human habitation*

6 (95, 100c ts) *effect of* **getting the job done** *cheaply/go on to Nepal and* **get the British Council to sort** *the problem* **out.**

have, has, having, had 7

1.1 (56a ts) *It would be nice for me to* **have a picture.**

1.2 (63ts) *I* **had a brother** *and two sisters.*

2 (72a, 72c) *He* **had his hands handcuffed** *behind his back. All American cars* **have automatic gear change.**

3 (64) *Even if I* **had the time** *I feel too tired.*

4 (69c ts, 69b) *I* **had to start** *all over again. What do you* **have to do** *for a driving test in your country?*

5.1 (83c ts, 19) *… A lot of people* **have accidents** *on motorbikes./We always used* **have a campfire.**

5.2 (53) *she was* **having lunch** *one day*

5.3 (34ts, 47ts) *I always* **had this fear** *of falling downstairs/I used to* **have a lot of dreams.**

6.1 (20b, 56a ts) *much of the repertoire of the old singers* **has been preserved.**/*I've* **brought** *a picture*

7 (38b, 72) *Peter telephoned his parents, who* **has reported** *him missing./Claude Padilla, 28,* **had been handcuffed.**

8 (72b ts ×3) **Could have used** *his chin/ They must* **have left** *the car engine on/he couldn't* **have turned** *it on.*

if 12

1.1 (34, 121a ts) **If you win**, *you get where it's safe …/* **if** *you're actually out in it – I find that …*

1.2 (45c, 49ts) **If you were** *a teacher, what other alterations would you make?/I suppose you might,* **if you knew them** *well*

2 (71×2, 80c ts) *she asked me* **if she could borrow** *the car/ I asked* **if she knew** *how to …/what we've got to decide is* **whether** *these texts …*

3 (31, 59) *It looks* **as though** *you are withholding information …/Go in* **as if** *nothing had happened*

5 (68c ts, 72a) *What differences are there, **if any**, between …/Is it possible to drive a car with your hands tied tightly behind your back? **If so**, how?*

in 4

1 (36 × 3, 38 × 2) *in **New York**,/**crawled in** to safety,/**coming in** through a window/**trapped in** a butcher's cold store/**in Banbury Road**.*

1.1 (24) *in the **Bristol Evening Post***

2 (17a ts, 27ts) *in the **Scouts**/sat back **in the audience***

3 (17a ts, 34) *In **September**/as that room **in that moment** after …*

4 (24ts×2, 31 ×2) *spelt **in two different ways**/draft out what you want to say **in rough** first/arrive **in plenty of time**/ dress **in a business-like way***

5 (16, 24) *in a **printing firm**/in **full-time education***

it 2

1.1 (4ts ×5) *it's **grown** like mad/it's quite a **decent-sized bush** now./It's **not too bad**, is it? It's **lovely**. It's one of my **favourite photos**.*

1.2 (4, 17b ts) *it's **very exciting** (ie the experience of playing jazz)/sang a few songs, and **it really started from there**.*

2 (2) *It's **very hard work** getting established as a musician*

2.1 (10ts, 13ts) *It was a **German friend** of my wife's who took it./It must be the **accordion player** who's not there.*

3 (4ts end) *it was a **really hot day**, earlier*

must 15

1 (143c ts) *Finally the style of presentation **must match** the subject matter.*

2.1 (116ts, 94b ts) *It **must have taken** a good few days to recover./I **must have read** it in a newspaper.*

3 (48) *you **must come** and meet him.*

4 (10ts) *I **must admit** France is my favourite country.*

of 8

1.1 (87b ×2) *in a **fraction of a second**/a **couple of broken bones***

1.2 (87a) *a **slice of bread***

1.3 (87, 87b) *the **frame of the machine**/the **sticky side of** his bread*

2.1 (25b ×2, 36) *name and address **of firm**/name **of the person** you are writing to/the 85th floor **of the Empire State Building***

2.2 (47ts ×2) *the **secret of** how I can fly/reminded me **of** my flying dreams*

3.1 (45ts ×2, 76ts) ***Sort of**, I did, I said/in a **sort of** long flow of images/in terms **of** space and articles and objects and this **sort of thing**.*

3.2 (21, 43 ×2) *modern **version of** a traditional song/all **forms of** modern art/all **kinds of** materials*

4 (74) *a **man of 84***

5 (34ts) *I always had this **fear of falling** downstairs*

on 20

1.1 (150a ts ×2, 184b) *they lived **on the sixth floor**/on the **windowsill**/with tanks and troops **on the streets***

1.2 (110b ts, 210b) *throw the hurricane lamp **on the ground**./he wants to go out **on the sundeck**.*

2 (14b ×2, 24) *church service **on Sunday** to the village dance **on Saturday night**./the position of wages clerk which you advertised **on the 4th August**.*

3 (133e ×2, 201) *pointers **on the sort of programmes**/sum up our work **on the choice of material**/present a short report **on your decision***

4 (10ts, 204a ts) *I've also visited Greece and Spain **on holiday**./Was that **on a long journey**?*

5 (130b ts ×2, 27ts) *get them **on the radio stations**/He will play it **on the radio**./… a friendly chat **on the phone**.*

6.1 (184) *'I **fight on**' pledges Marcos.*

7 (133f) *considering the enormous fuss they made of the group **on departure** at Heathrow.*

that 19

1 (20lb ts ×3) *So I think that **that** is a genuine story./I'm sure that **that's** possible/I can't believe **that**.*

1.1 (176) ***That**, however, was until he found out that his beloved was a mere seventeen.*

2 (187a, 187b ts) *If you use **that strategy** he'll wipe you out./**That story** was lifted straight out of another book.*

3.1 (198a, 200) *She* **found that** *200 years ago it had been a workhouse./... leads experts to* **believe that** *the basic principles...*

3.2 (109, 201b ts) *I'm* **sorry that** *you were subjected to such a frightening time./I'm* **sure that** *that is a hoax*

3.3 (104, 133f ×2) *The clerk accepted the money on a* **promise that** *the remainder would be forthcoming./The fact that our Delhi office had two lots of* **assurance** *from the local XAL representatives* **that** *...*

5 (201c ts ×2) *I thought that* **that one** *was possibly the only one that was genuine./There are one or two* **elements that** *don't ring true.*

the 5

1.1 (36 × 6) *to* **the 86th floor** *of .../the safety fence around* **the observation floor/the specks of cars/the unsuccessful artist/the idea** *of committing suicide*

1.2 (34, 36, 43) *in* **the world/the Empire State Building/ against the sky**

1.3 (34ts × 6), *out in* **the street/the list/up all the stairs to the light-room** *and then* **the chap** *says/* **the door**

2 (43) *my father ... home from* **the office**

to 13

1 (135, 133a) *on the way* **to Kathmandu./I'm glad that you found the visit* **to Sherborne** *so useful.*

2 (135 ×2) *... Write a polite letter* **to XAL./a cheque made out* **to the Yetties.**

3 (124a, 137ts) **Listen to** *the grass blade growing. People would come up and try to* **speak to** *you.*

4 (131ts, 87) *They had an information desk there* **to tell people** *all about Birmingham./using both hands* **to turn the door knob**

5 (131ts, 133e) *problems with* **trying to get** *communciations from them/I would* **like to send** *out all the programme material in January.*

6 (110b ts, 114ts) *One of my plans which I never* **had to do** *was .../I was* **going to ask** *you what turns a normal leopard into a man-eater?*

7 (133a, 133e) *I'm sure it was* **useful to the Yetties./A list** *of the songs most* **likely to be included.**

8 (85 ×2) *His* **solution was to plaster** *the sticky side of the bread to the wall/... the obvious* **thing is to telephone** *the fire brigade*

9 (20a, 114ts) *every occasion, from the church service on Sunday* **to the village dance** *on Saturday night/one that they were moving from one area* **to another**

wh- words 22

1 (223a ×2) *a country* **where flowers grow** *beautifully is good to live in./The minds of the people* **who look at the flowers** *will become more beautiful.*

2 (226ts, 228b) *I'd like to go and work in a third world country* **when my children are older. When Mr. Botibol awoke** *next morning he lay quite still.*

3.1 (217b ts, 224a) *I'm not* **sure when** *the story was written./He did not want to go to bed before he* **knew how much** *there was in the pool.*

3.2 (228c, 229b ×2) **What would you do** *if you were Mr. Botibol./* **What could his idea be?/Why ever not?**

4.1 (226ts) *I'd like to teach violin,* **which means** *I want to go to college.*

4.2 (210a) *The purser,* **who had prepared himself** *to receive a personal confidence, smiled and leaned back ...*

5 (172b, 198b) **The worst time is when** *the children have grown up./* **That's where** *I used to be a nurse.*

will 18

1 (188a ts ×2) **It will not only increase** *the government's embarrassment but could provoke a full-scale parliamentary crisis./* **They will take** *direct action to protect their own water supply.*

2 (172b ×2) *I think* **I'll read them through** *first/Ah, go on.* **We'll say 'yes'.**

3 (95, 114ts) *At least six of the 23 species of crocodile* **will attack** *and eat human beings if they can./if they're getting old and they can't hunt easily* **they'll start-** *... they'll prey on easy meat.*

with 21

1 (200, 215) **Together with a team** *of Olympus experts, they flew ..../a father was discussing life* **with his 9 year-old son.**

2 (34ts ×2, 206 ×2) *sleep* **with the light on/narrow parapet* **with a rail .../the dining room was filled* **with people eating/with the assured and complacent air** *of ...*

3 (217 ×2, 217b ts) *held on tight* **with both hands/ combing his hair back into place* **with a small red comb./ gonna buy a Lincoln convertible* **with his £7000.**

4 (38, 206) *his face purple* **with cold/the passengers,* **with twelve hours of good weather behind them,** *were beginning to feel confident*

5 (207, 210c ts) *continued with their meal/probably something again to do with the weather*

would 23

1 (45a, 229b) *How would a six year old child write in your language?/He wouldn't have any trouble keeping afloat*

2 (210a) *"Suppose you were allowed to buy a number, which one would you choose today?"*

3 (32b ×2, 198) *I lived on a small farm in the farm cottages there and at weekends you would help./We'd get*

the cows in./On the way to the shops with her mother she would say "That's where I used to be a nurse."

4 (53, 243a ts) *Would you like some more dear?/Would you like to start?*

5 (232b ts × 3) *What would you like to do?/what would you really like to achieve?/I would still like to be rich.*

6 239a ts, 207b ts) *I would agree with that, certainly./I would imagine it's some kind of superstition*

Please return this questionnaire to:
Annette Capel, ELT Publishing Manager
Collins ELT, 8 Grafton Street, London W1X 3LA

QUESTIONNAIRE

Please help us to help you by commenting on this Collins ELT title.
Write your answers in the space provided or on additional sheets if necessary.
Thank you for giving us this invaluable feedback.

COLLINS COBUILD ENGLISH COURSE

YOUR CLASS	TIMETABLING
Number of students	Length of lessons
Age range	Number of lessons per week
Level	Total length of course
	Homework? Yes/No

1   Did you complete this Level of the Course?

2   Were the materials at the right language level?

3   Did your students make noticeable progress in

Fluency	☐	Listening	☐
Accuracy	☐	Reading	☐
Vocabulary acquisition	☐	Speaking	☐
Writing	☐		

4   Was there sufficient recycling in the Course?

5 Were the topics/themes suitable for your students?

6 Did your students enjoy doing the tasks?

7 Did you use the Practice Book?

8 Was the Teacher's Book clear and informative?

9 What did you/your students particularly like about this Level of the Course?

10 What did you/your students dislike?

Further Comments

Name
Institution
Address

Collins ELT
8 Grafton Street
London W1X 3LA

COBUILD is a trademark of William Collins Sons & Co. Ltd

© William Collins Sons & Co. Ltd 1989

10 9 8 7 6 5 4 3 2 1

First published in 1989

Printed in Hong Kong by Wing King Tong Co. Ltd.

ISBN 0 00 370236 7

Design: Caroline Archer (Student's Book), Gina Smart (Teacher's Book)
Cover design: Richard Morris
Photography: Chris Ridgers
Artwork: Terry Burton, David Eaton, Charles Fuge, Steve Gibson, Ricardo Guiraldes, Karen Hayles, David Holmes, Clare Melinsky, Mike Mosedale, Douglas Post, Laura Raine, Paul Shorrock.

This Teacher's Book is accompanied by a Student's Book ISBN 0 00 370234 0, a set of cassettes ISBN 0 00 370237 5, a Student's Cassette ISBN 0 00 370286 3, and a Practice Book ISBN 0 00 370235 9. A booklet containing transcripts of the unscripted recordings is included inside the back cover of the Student's Book.

COBUILD is the Collins Birmingham University International Language Database

Acknowledgements *(Figures in brackets refer to sections.)*

The syllabus of the Collins COBUILD English Course is based on the research findings of the COBUILD project at Birmingham University. Editor-in-Chief: Professor John Sinclair.

COBUILD and Collins computer support was provided by Tim Lane.

The authors would like to thank the COBUILD team, especially Stephen Bullon, Gwyneth Fox and Rosamund Moon for their detailed research. Michael Halliday and John Sinclair for guidance on the Grammar material, and Paul Meara and the many others for their advice on the teaching of lexis. The following teachers (and in some cases their students), as well as members of the COBUILD team helped us with the original selection of materials: Nick Davies, Caroline Egerton, Jan Gates, Matthew Hancock, Nici Hildebrandt, Elspeth Jones, Georgina Pearce, Debra Powell, Paula Walker. Possible short stories were vetted by Jane Bond, Barbara Mayor and Becky Willis. Special thanks are given to Martin Hewings for his work on intonation, and to Debra Powell for her lexical research and Review exercises (Units 13–24). Finally, the authors would like to thank their daughters, Jenny and Becky, for their patience and support throughout the course.

Many people read and commented on the manuscript and it is impossible to list them all here. The publishers and authors are especially grateful to the following: Stephen Bullon, Anthony Forrester, Kathy Gude, Georgina Pearce, Debra Powell, Paula Walker.

The following participated in the unscripted recordings, and provided supporting texts and information to ensure the contextualisation of the recordings was accurate: Chris Bates, Bruce Boyns, Elizabeth Egerton, Suzanne Juta, Edmund Lee, Rachel Sandon, Richard Webber. Special thanks must go to Bob Jobbins for sharing his expertise on radio broadcasting; to the members of the Yetties: Bonny Sartin, Mac McCulloch, Peter Shutler and Roger Trim; and to Alan Dury for acting as interviewer.

Most of those in the published recordings also gave time to be photographed, as did the following: Margaret Goodwin (1), Matthew Hancock (1), Ken Ruskin (1), Andrea Russo (173), Paul Stokes (2), David O'Sullivan (1), Douglas Williamson (188).

The publishers are grateful to the following for permission to use original material in the Student's Book: Maypole Music Ltd for their kind permission to reproduce *Come Stranger, Come Friend* © 1982 for all countries of the world by Maypole Music Ltd, London, England (9); Midland Bank plc for extracts from *Cheque In Magazine* (24, 25, 31); Octopus for extracts from *The World's Greatest Mistakes*, 1980 (35, 36, 104); the *Guardian* for extracts and headlines (38, 40, 45, 102, 200); © Quentin Blake 1974 for illustration from *Grimble and Grimble at Christmas*, reproduced by permission of Penguin Books Ltd (48); Mark Paterson on behalf of Clement Freud for permission to use extracts from *Grimble and Grimble at Christmas* (48); Sphere Books Ltd for extracts from *The Book of Texts* by Ben Hamilton, 1982 (59, 65); ITV Books/ Arrow Books for extracts from *It's Kidstuff* (68); © Exley Publications Ltd for 'Behind the Wheel' from *To Dad*, edited by Richard and Helen Exley (68), and for extracts from *Cry For Our Beautiful World*, edited by Helen Exley © 1985 (124, 223); The Reader's Digest for permission to reprint article from the 1978 *Reader's Digest*, © 1978 The Reader's Digest Association Ltd (71, 87); *The Straits Times* for permission to reprint articles (72, 83, 87); *Daily Express* for articles (74, 196); *Daily Mail* (10/5/87) for articles (74, 173, 176); Nigel Swabey and Partners Ltd for advertisements from New Horizons Catalogue 1987 (78); the *Observer* for article (80); *Adscene* (91); Piccolo Books, London for extracts from *The Guiness Book of Animal Marvels*, edited by Shirley Greenway (95, 97); Richard Webber (109), Bill Woodley (109, 113) and James Lloyd (133) for use of their letters; The British Council (100, 134) and Caroline Dacey at the British Council (133) for use of their letters and headed paper; Harold Matson Company, Inc. for permission to reprint 'Life In a Putty Factory', © 1943 by H. Allen Smith (118); BBC World Service for extracts from *London Calling* (139); Reuters Ltd for headlines and articles (149, 150, 152, 154, 158, 166); Associated Press for headlines and articles (149, 150, 152, 154, 158, 166); *Radio Times* for extracts (160, 184); *Mail on Sunday* for article (176, 178); *Titbits Magazine* and Robin Corry for article reprinted from November 1986 edition (198); Collett, Dickenson and Pearce Agency and Partners Ltd advertising and Olympus Cameras for kind permission to reproduce article (200); Roald Dahl for 'Dip in the Pool' from *Someone Like You*, Michael Joseph Ltd and Penguin Ltd (206, 207, 210, 217, 221, 224, 228, 229, 234, 239, 244, 250).

The publishers are grateful to the following for the use of photographs: Barnaby's (1, 121, 209); Robert Harding Picture Library (1, 32, 89, 95, 118, 171, 317); Chris Bates (2, 68); Bruce Boyns (4, 24); Rachel Sandon (4, 63); The Yetties (13, 100, 232); Scout Association (17); Brian Shuel (17); Cecil Sharp House (20); John Cornwell (24); Graham Cooper, Doug Sargeant and Phaidon Press Ltd (43); Suzanne Juta (43); National Gallery (51); Elizabeth Egerton (55); Reproduced by kind permission of Nigel Swabey and Partners Ltd (78); K Ghani (80); George Young (80); Ardea (89, 94, 204); The Martin Library (89); Adscene (90, 91); Ace Photo Agency (95, 109, 130, 137, 149, 150, 163, 166, 171, 173, 186, 223); John Cleare (100); Eastern Electricity (102); British Council (109); Tropix Photo Library (110); Natural History Picture Agency (113, 123); Tony Stone Worldwide (113, 130, 171); Bruce Coleman (116); Zefa (121); Dance Library (130); Allsport/ Vandystad (143); Metropolitan Police (143); Sally and Richard Greenhill (150, 186, 200, 223); Oxford Scientific Films (150, 166); Popperforo (150); Vilbert-Stokes (163); Magnum (184); Associated Press (187); Penny and John Hubley (188); Martyn Chillmaid (198, 215); Mary Evans Picture Library (198, 200, 232); Japanese Tourist Office (203); Becken of Cowes (204, 223); Lord Ambrose Greenway (204); Southeby's (213); Janet and Colin Bord (216); Barry Lewis/Network (226); Network Photographers (226); West Dorset Tourist Office (232); Adrian Boot (240). All other photographs by Nance Fyson.

Every effort has been made to contact the owners of copyright material. In some cases this has not been possible. The publishers apologise for any omissions, and will be glad to rectify these when the title is reprinted if details are sent.